China and Africa in Global Context

This book studies the relationship between China and Africa by reviewing this history and current state of interactions, offering a valuable addition to the often heated and contentious debate surrounding China's engagement in Africa from a Chinese angle.

Comprising four parts, the book covers a kaleidoscopic range of topics on China–Africa relations based on materials from different languages. Part I looks into early historical contact between China and Africa and the historiography of African Studies in China in recent decades. Part II probes the origins, dynamics, challenges and cultural heritage of China's policies towards Africa. Part III explores the issue of development cooperation from both a theoretical and a practical point of view, with a focus on the case of Chinese medical teams in Africa and China's technology transfer to the continent. Part IV illustrates bilateral migration, discussing the history and life of Chinese immigrants in Africa and African immigrants in China.

The insights in this book, as well as real-life case studies, make this work an indispensable reference for academics, students, policy-makers and general readers who are interested in international issues and area studies, especially China–Africa relations, China's rise and African development.

Li Anshan is Emeritus Professor in the School of International Studies at Peking University, Adjunct Professor at University of Electronic Science and Technology of China, President of the Chinese Society of African Historical Studies and Vice President of the International Scientific Committee of UNESCO General History of Africa (Vols IX–XI). He specialises in African history, overseas Chinese in Africa, African nationalism and China–Africa relations.

China Perspectives

The *China Perspectives* series focuses on translating and publishing works by leading Chinese scholars, writing about both global topics and China-related themes. It covers Humanities and Social Sciences, Education, Media and Psychology, as well as many interdisciplinary themes.

This is the first time any of these books have been published in English for international readers. The series aims to put forward a Chinese perspective, give insights into cutting-edge academic thinking in China and inspire researchers globally.

To submit proposals, please contact the Taylor & Francis Publisher for the China Publishing Programme, Lian Sun (Lian.Sun@informa.com).

Recent titles in politics partly include:

"The Belt and Road" International Migration of Asia
Research on Multilateral Population Security
Mi Hong, Li Yuan and Ma Qiyini

The Routledge Handbook of Chinese Citizenship
Edited by Zhonghua Guo

The Transformation of American Political Culture and the Impact on Foreign Strategy
Pan Yaling

China and Africa in Global Context
Encounters, Policy, Cooperation and Migration
Li Anshan

China and the Pursuit of Harmony in World Politics
Understanding Chinese International Relations Theory
Adam Grydehøj and Ping Su

For more information, please visit www.routledge.com/China-Perspectives/book-series/CPH

China and Africa in Global Context
Encounters, Policy, Cooperation and Migration

Li Anshan

LONDON AND NEW YORK

First published 2022
by Routledge
2 Park Square, Milton Park, Abingdon, Oxon OX14 4RN

and by Routledge
605 Third Avenue, New York, NY 10158

Routledge is an imprint of the Taylor & Francis Group, an informa business

© 2022 Li Anshan

The right of Li Anshan to be identified as author of this work has been asserted in accordance with sections 77 and 78 of the Copyright, Designs and Patents Act 1988.

All rights reserved. No part of this book may be reprinted or reproduced or utilised in any form or by any electronic, mechanical, or other means, now known or hereafter invented, including photocopying and recording, or in any information storage or retrieval system, without permission in writing from the publishers.

Trademark notice: Product or corporate names may be trademarks or registered trademarks, and are used only for identification and explanation without intent to infringe.

British Library Cataloguing-in-Publication Data
A catalogue record for this book is available from the British Library

Library of Congress Cataloging-in-Publication Data
Names: Li, Anshan, 1953– author.
Title: China and Africa in global context : encounters, policy, cooperation and migration / Anshan Li.
Description: Abingdon, Oxon ; New York, NY : Routledge, 2022. | Series: China perspectives. Politics |
Includes bibliographical references and index.
Identifiers: LCCN 2021038841 (print) | LCCN 2021038842 (ebook) | ISBN 9781032114996 (hardback) | ISBN 9781032115009 (paperback) | ISBN 9781003220152 (ebook)
Subjects: LCSH: Africans–China–History. | Chinese–Africa–History. | China–Relations–Africa–Case studies. | Africa–Relations–China–Case studies.
Classification: LCC DS740.5.A34 L5 2022 (print) | LCC DS740.5.A34 (ebook) | DDC 327.5106–dc23/eng/20211117
LC record available at https://lccn.loc.gov/2021038841
LC ebook record available at https://lccn.loc.gov/2021038842

ISBN: 978-1-032-11499-6 (hbk)
ISBN: 978-1-032-11500-9 (pbk)
ISBN: 978-1-003-22015-2 (ebk)

DOI: 10.4324/9781003220152

Typeset in Times New Roman
by Newgen Publishing UK

Contents

List of illustrations vii
Preface ix

PART I
Encounter and research 1

1 China–Africa contact before Vasco da Gama 3

2 African studies in China in the 20th century 29

3 African studies in China in the 21st century 55

4 Case study: The *Abirewa* movement in the Gold Coast 92

5 Case study: *Asafo* and destoolment in Southern Ghana 113

PART II
Policy and implementation 141

6 Origins of the Forum on China–Africa Cooperation 143

7 China's policy: Transition and discourse 170

8 China's policy: Continuity and challenge 203

9 Cultural heritage of China's policy 224

10 BRICS and Africa 246

PART III
Cooperation and dynamics 279

11 Bilateral cooperation and co-development 281

12 Chinese medical teams in Africa 302

13 China's technology transfer in Africa 333

14 People-to-people contact in China–Africa relations 356

15 Cultural similarities and mutual learning 381

PART IV
Migration and diaspora 401

16 Chinese indentured labour in South Africa 403

17 Early Chinese and Indians in South Africa 422

18 Chinese migration and China's African policy 441

19 African diaspora in China: History and present 459

20 African students in China: Trend, policy and roles 479

Postscript: China–Africa relations in globalisation 508
Appendix A 510
Appendix B 512
Index 514

Illustrations

Figure

20.1	African students in China (1996–2015)	488

Tables

2.1	Publications of African studies in China until 1994	36
3.1	Graduate theses on African countries, 1981–2005	58
3.2	Classification of articles on specific African countries, 1997–2005	60
6.1	Volume of trade between China and Africa, 1990–1999 (US$100 millions)	149
7.1	China–Africa trade statistics, 1980–1987 (US $ million)	174
7.2	China's medical teams and doctors in Africa, 1963–1983	174
10.1	Brazil's debt cancellation of African countries (US$10,000)	258
10.2	Amount and purpose of loan provided by the Export–Import Bank of India (part)	262
12.1	Chinese medical teams abroad, 1963–2008	308
12.2	China-supported anti-malaria centres in Africa	319
14.1	Chinese major articles related to the Ethiopian anti-Italian war	359
14.2	IPRCC international cooperation with Africa, October 2006–October 2013	370
14.3	CFPA foreign aid projects, 2007–2011	372
16.1	Mine workers' wages, 1901–1910	408
17.1	Indians and Africans in the canefields	426
17.2	Average numbers of Indians and Chinese in Transvaal prisons, 1902–1908	431
17.3	Chinese in South Africa, 1904–1995	432
17.4	Racial composition of Durban's population, 1904–1989	433
17.5	South African Chinese population, 1904–1911	434

20.1	African students in China, 1976–1995	486
20.2	African students in China, 1996–2015	487
20.3	Annual cost of a Shanghai Government scholarship – Class A	492
20.4	Comparison of CGS holders between Africa and Europe, 2003–2010	494

Preface

With its rapid rise to prominence on the world stage, China's engagement in Africa has become an event, a phenomenon, a trend and a discourse. This subject has also aroused a lot of interest and even tension in international academia and politics. Some common phases have emerged, such as "Beijing Consensus", "China model", "Looking East", "new colonialism" and "China's African empire", and various debates are raging regarding these terms. The subject is worth studying seriously.

As a Chinese who has studied Africa for more than 40 years and enjoyed it very much, I have been deeply engaged in various bilateral and multilateral activities in both academic research and policy-making. In other words, I am involved in China–Africa cooperation both as a researcher and a participant. I have attended many seminars, conferences and policy consultancies in Asia, Africa, Europe and America, and made a lot of friends around the world, especially African friends in various fields, including professors, students and academicians, reporters and media administrators, diplomats and government officials, social activists and local chiefs, entrepreneurs and ordinary people. Various opportunities to exchange ideas with African colleagues have made me feel more and more confident about the continent, its culture and history, its present and future.

When Mr Kofi Annan visited Peking University in 2015, the university sent him my book entitled *British Rule and Rural Protest in Southern Ghana* in both Chinese and English, published in China and the United States respectively. He was surprised to find a Chinese scholar studying his country, although I have taught courses on African history and China–Africa relations for many years both at home and abroad, supervised African graduate students and published articles in various international journals. I was invited to give lectures on African issues to the top leader of the Chinese government, high officials of the Communist Party of China (hereafter CPC) and different ministries related to African affairs. I have also been invited by foreign governments from both developing and developed countries – for example, South Africa, Tanzania, Mali, Mauritius, the United States, the United Kingdom, Spain, Germany, Japan, Sweden and Norway – to either to give a lecture or a talk, or participate in an event related to China–Africa relations.

Participation in various important events in China, such as the first FOCAC in 2000, the China–African Summit in 2006 is an honour but also a duty. I was commissioned by the Ministry of Foreign Affairs to lead a team to African countries to assess FOCAC follow-up actions. With a sense of responsibility, I have offered my opinions on African issues in various occasions, such as in the preparation of Chinese leader's speech or important documents related to international cooperation, or consultancies on African affairs in different ministries.

This book is part of my effort to try to understand and explain China–African relations in the global context. Featuring 20 chapters divided into four parts, the book deals with topics such as early historical contact and contemporary bilateral cooperation, a historiographical survey of African studies in China, a detailed case-study on the role of indigenous social forces (priests and commoners) in colonial Ghana, a probe into China's policy on Africa and a careful exploration of development cooperation in various fields, such as Chinese medical teams and China's technology transfer in Africa, and China–Africa bilateral migration.

Part I: Encounter and Research, contains five chapters on three subjects. Chapter 1 studies China–Africa relations before Vasco Da Gama. Da Gama's voyage around the Cape and further to East Africa and India in 1498 is considered a great event in history, yet China–Africa contact started as early as the Han Dynasty (206 BCE–220 CE). Du Huan of the Tang Dynasty (618–907 CE) left a note about his visit to Africa, and porcelain and other objects of the time were found in Africa. The chapter also includes Ibn Battuta's visit to China during the Yuan Dynasty (1271–1368 CE) and Zheng He's trip to Africa in the early 15th century. Chapters 2 and 3 are historiographical surveys of African studies in China in the 20th and 21st centuries respectively. Chapters 4 and 5 are two case studies on the role of indigenous priests and commoners in Ghana during the colonial period.

Part II: Policy and Implementation, has five chapters on China's policy on Africa and related important issues. There is a general presumption that the Forum on China–Africa Cooperation (FOCAC) is the result of a grand strategy of the Chinese government; however, Chapter 6 shows African's role in initiating the forum. Chapters 7 and 8 study important themes of China's policy on Africa, such as its continuity/change, history/discourse and principle/challenge. Chapter 9 explores the link between China's cultural heritage and the policies. Chapter 10 specifically deals with BRICS and Africa, with an emphasis on China's role. This part is intended to provide a broad and systematic survey of these issues and promote mutual understanding between China and Africa, thus giving a Chinese perspective on the bilateral relations in terms of China's policy on Africa.

There are five chapters in Part III: Cooperation and Dynamics. The cooperation between China and Africa has many aspects and development cooperation is the most important. Chapter 11 studies China's unique principle and perspective on the issue, based on its own historical experience. Mutual respect, non-conditionality in politics and non-interference in internal affairs, an emphasis on self-reliance and common development are among the essential features. Chapters 12 and 13 study Chinese medical teams and China's technology transfer respectively. The China–Africa relationship puts great emphasis on summit diplomacy. To counteract this lopsided focus, Chapter 14 deals with people-to-people relations. Great cultural similarities (philosophy, value systems, human behaviour, etc.) between China and Africa are examined in Chapter 15.

Part IV: Migration and Diaspora contains five chapters with two on Chinese immigrants in Africa and two on African immigrants in China. In addition, one chapter compares the early Chinese and Indian communities in South Africa. All the chapters tell us that there is a long history of bilateral migration between China and Africa. Chapter 16 studies the control of Chinese indentured laborers in South African mines and their resistance against this inhuman system in 1904–1910. Chapter 17 illustrates the similarities and dissimilarities of early Chinese and Indian immigrants in South Africa. Chapter 18 explores Chinese new immigrants in Africa and China's policy. Chapters 19 and 20 deal with the history and present of African diaspora in China and African students in China respectively.

The Appendices contain two tables presenting statistics of overseas Chinese in Africa and Confucius Institutes in Africa.

I would like to thank my colleagues and students in China who helped me in various ways to make the process smoother. Many African friends helped me through various ways. Mr Badoe picked me up at Kotoka International Airport when I set foot on Accra in 1992 and, with his charming wife, took good care of me at his home. Nana Brukum welcomed me into his house with his hospitable family (his wife and three daughters) during my field research in Ghana. Olabiyi Yai, a great Benin scholar with encylopaedic knowledge, always answered my questions patiently. Both gentlemen went to see their ancestors yet will live in my heart forever. Other African friends have helped me sincerely, including Femi Osofisan in Nigeria, I. Shivji and S. M. Rugumamu in Tanzania, I. Abdulla in Sierra Leone, Fantu Cheru of Ethiopia, A. Holl of Cameroon, J. Shikwati and H. Kiriama in Kenya, K.K. Prah and G. Shelton in South Africa, Aline Kwan of Institut Confucius de La Réunion, J. Tsang Mang Kin, M. Ngan Chai King and Kwang Poon in Mauritius, among others. My students Imen Belhadj (Tunisia), Erfiki Hicham (Morocco) and Antoine Roger Lokongo (D. R. Congo) and others helped me a great deal.

I appreciate warm support from my colleagues at home and abroad, especially Professors J. Gerson and my PhD supervisor M. Klein (University of Toronto), R. Roberts (Stanford University), Nakanyike Musisi (University of Toronto), P. Zachernuk (Dalhousie University), George Yu and P. Tiyambe Zeleza (University of Illinois at Urbana Champaign), R. Rotberg (Harvard University), W. van Binsbergen and T. Dietz (Leiden University), Deych Tatiana and Korendyasov Evgeiy (Russian Academy of Sciences), C. Alden (London School of Economics), A. Bodomo (University of Vienna), Funeka

Yazini April (Africa Institute of South Africa), Jing Men (European Institute at Bruges), H. Ronning and Li Shubo (University of Oslo), D. Brautigam (Johns Hopkins University), J. Monson (Michigan State University), Tan Chee Beng (Sun Yat-sen University), S. Schmid and U. Röschenthaler (Goethe-Universität, Frankfurt am Main) and others. Without their academic exchange, encouragement and support, the publication of this book would have been next to impossible. I would like to thank the copyright holders for their permission to include some chapters that have been published before. For various assistance of my colleagues and students, I showed my specific thanks in different chapters.

The ship of China–Africa cooperation is sailing in the Indian Ocean amid the turbulent waves of international politics and human development. There are difficulties ahead, yet we are moving slowly but steadily. May China and Africa continue the journey hand in hand towards the future.

Part I
Encounter and research

1 China–Africa contact before Vasco da Gama[1]

Introduction

W.H. Auden (1907–1973) is a well-known English-American poet. 'As I walked out one evening' is a poem about his feelings for his love. In order to show deep affection that will last until something impossible occurs, he uses metaphor to describe incredible scenes, and compares the meeting of China and Africa with the river jumping over the mountain, or the salmon singing in the street. He never considered that China and Africa may have had contact long before.

By examining the archaeological evidence, related documents and historiography in Chinese, this chapter is intended to show China–Africa contact in ancient times. It is divided into four parts: the pre-Tang Dynasty, the Tang Dynasty (618–907), the Song (960–1279) and Yuan (1271–1368) Dynasties, and finally the early period of the Ming Dynasty (1368–1644). It demonstrates that the bilateral relations probably started before the birth of Jesus Christ; Africans came to China in early times in different ways and the Chinese had sailed to Africa before Vasco da Gama.

Vasco da Gama's voyage around the Cape of Hope and further to India is considered a great event and marked an epoch in the history of geographical exploration. The most important data is in Vasco da Gama's journal (Jayne 1910; Hart 1950; Penrose 1955; Elton 1958; Ravenstein 2010). Fernand Braudel claimed that "Vasco da Gama's voyage (1498) did not destroy this ancient traffic between Europe and the Indian Ocean. It made a new route for it" (Braudel 1981: 402), and he termed it a "fantastic voyage" or "historical voyage" (Braudel 1984: 56, 139). However, there had been voyages around Africa and on the Asia–Africa sea routes for a long time (Hou Renzhi 1964). China and Africa had made contact long before Vasco da Gama, illustrated by archaeological discoveries, Chinese authentic histories[2] and classics by Du Huan (杜环, 8th century), Duan Chengshi (段成式, 803–863) and Jia Dan (贾耽, 730–805) of the Tang Dynasty, Zhou Qufei (周去非, 1135–1189) and Zhao Rukuo (赵汝适, 1170–1232) of the Song Dynasty, Wang Dayuan (汪大渊, 1311–1350) of the Yuan Dynasty and Fei Xin (费信, 1388–1433) of the Ming Dynasty. This evidence is supplemented by the contemporary research

DOI: 10.4324/9781003220152-2

of both Chinese and foreign scholars. Some have studied China–Africa contact in a general sense (Zhang Xinglang 1977 [1930]; Duyvendak 1949; Zhang Tiesheng 1963; Chen Gongyuan 1985; Snow 1988; Shen Fuwei 1990; Rashidi & Van Sertima 2007 [1995]; Ai Zhouchang & Mu Tao 1996). Others look at specific topics – either a period (Cen Zhongmian 1945; Filesi 1972; Sun Yutang 1979; Brunson 1985; Smidt 2001) or a subject (Zhang Xinglang 1928; Xia Nai 1963:71–97; Ma Wenkuan & Meng Fanren 1987; Li Anshan 2000, 2012, 2019, 2019a; Wyatt 2010; Wilensky 2002). However, more questions remain to be answered, such as when China–Africa relations began, what places in Africa the Chinese knew in ancient times and whether there were any Africans in ancient China.

When, where and who: Contacts before the 7th century

In studies on the early contact between China and Africa, three important questions are usually asked: when where and who? When did the bilateral contact begin? What places did the Chinese know in Africa? Were there any Africans in ancient China? Yet there are no definitive answers to these questions.

The two most interesting topics are the starting point of the contact and an examination of the places identified with African names (Wu Changchun 1991; Yongzhang 1993; Zhang Xiang 1993; Li Anshan 2019).

Archaeological and material evidence

In the Sudan National Museum in Khartoum, a Chinese-type *ding* (鼎) is exhibited, which was discovered near the sixth fall of the Nile in the ruins of Meroe, the ancient capital of the Kush Kingdom (1070 BCE–350 CE) (Zhang Junyan 1986). This is a three-legged cooking vessel made of bronze or ceramic as a symbol of dynastic and political power in ancient China. Whether it was made in China or is a copy of a Chinese model by a local smith, it indicates a kind of cultural contact. In 1993, Austrian archaeologists discovered silk fibre in the hair of a female corpse of the 21st Dynasty (1070–945 BCE) in Egypt. At the time, only China had the technology to produce silk (Lubec, et al., 1993). The product was probably made in China and taken to Egypt. This was long before the direct contact between the two countries and the start of trade in Ptolemaic Egypt in 30 BCE, when Egyptian merchants began trading with India (Herrmann 1913, quoted from Smidt 2001). The Greek classic *Periplus Maris Erythraei* (mid-1st century) mentions the Chinese metropolis Sinai or Thinai, a Sanskrit form from the Qin Dynasty (221–207 BCE). It is said that Cleopatra (69–30 BCE), the famous Egyptian queen, loved Chinese silk clothes (Charlesworth 1970). There was also contact between China and Ethiopia from ancient times through various channels (Selassie 1972:71, 84–85, 207).

Qilin (麒麟 also spelled *kilin/kylin*) is a lucky animal in Chinese tradition. The name appears first in *Shijin* (诗经) or *The Book of Songs,* an anthology of 305 poems covering more than 500 years from the beginning of the West Zhou Dynasty (1045–771 BCE) to the mid-Spring and Autumn Period (770–476 BCE). It is recorded that *qilin* was first found in the 14th year of Ai Gong (481 BCE). In 1979, several stone carvings of the Han Dynasty were discovered at Jiawang in Xuzhou, China. One carving depicts animals and three of them look very much like giraffes. As an explanation for the resemblance between giraffe and *qilin,* Ferrand suggests that *kilin* is a transliteration of *geri,* a Somali word for giraffe; the two words are similar, even though *kilin* has a nasal sound (n) at the end. The Somali word *geri* is equal to *giri*; the Chinese noted the similar pronunciation and connected *giri* with *kilin*.[3] This explanation is difficult to accept, since the Chinese term *qilin* appeared about 3000 years ago and the hypothetical animal has a changing form (Wu Qingzhou 1997). What's more, how could the Chinese have learned the Somali word?

Raymond Dart once found some interesting rock paintings by the San (so-called Bushmen) in southern Africa. There was a painting on a stone block at Eliweni, Kei River depicting a foreigner; Dart presumed the hat on the foreigner's head was a peaked Chinese hat (Dart 1925). The San are an indigenous people who settled in the region thousands of years ago. Whether the hat is really Chinese is not certain, but this kind of hat is very popular in southern China. It is called *dou li* (斗笠) and is used to protect the wearer from both rain and sunshine. Raymond Dart also found something resembling a Chinese character in a decorative motif in southern Africa (Dart 1939; Li Anshan 2019a).

There are cultural contacts in the opposite direction as well. Evidence has been found of the possible cultural impact of Africa on China. King Wu Ding (武丁，1250–1192 BCE) of the Shang Dynasty (17th–11th centuries BCE) was an excellent leader who enjoys a great reputation (Peng Bangjiong 1987). A report on an excavation in Anyang, the capital of the Shang Dynasty, shows similarities between a skull discovered there and that of Oceanic peoples and Black Africans (Chang Kwang Chih 1977 [1968]; Yang Ximei 1966). In Sati burial sites in ancient Nubia, Egypt and Mesopotamia, thousands of cowrie shells used as money and more than 500 jade objects were discovered in the tomb of Lady Fu Hao (妇好). She was the principal consort and general to Shang King Wu Ding and is described as evidence of African participation in royalty by Brunson, who concludes: "It can be safely estimated that an African presence existed in China from a most remote period and an evolution of this physical type is an indigenous phenomenon" (Brunson 1985: 130–133). His estimate is logical, though rather bold, and needs more evidence to verify it.

There is other indirect evidence. In Guangzhou, a city in southern China, more than 1000 tombs of the Han Dynasty have been excavated since the

1950s. Some 152 pottery figures were found, some of which look like Black people (Qin Jie 2010). It was suggested that Black people could have come from islands near Indochina, Indonesia and West Asia/East Africa (Institute of Archaeology of Chinese Academy of Social Sciences 1981: 78).

In 1975, a very big boat-building site of the Qin Dynasty (221–207 BCE) and Han Dynasty was found in Guangzhou, with three building berths where a boat as heavy as 50 tons could be built (Zhang Junyan 1986); this indicates advanced ship-building technology. It is not a coincidence that Panyu (番禺) was given its present name in 214 BCE. As an important coastal town for foreign trade, Panyu included Guangzhou and other places. This shows that China had the potential to carry out long-distance navigation.

Documentary evidence of African places

Documentary evidence also suggests a long history of contact between China and Africa. Places such as Lixian (黎轩 犁轩 also Li-kan Li-kien), Yichengbu State (已程不国), Daqing (大秦), Chisan and (迟散) Wuchisan (乌迟散 also Wu-ch'i-san), identical to African places, are mentioned in Chinese classics.

Shiji (史记 91 BCE) or *The records of the grand historian*, mentions a place called Lixian. When Chinese envoy Zhang Qian (张骞 164–114 BCE) returned from the West in 126 BCE, he reported to Han Emperor Wudi (汉武帝 156–87 BCE) that, besides the countries he visited, he had heard of five to six big countries surrounding them, including Lixian.[4] Many scholars suggest that this is the ancient Alexandria in Egypt – although there are, of course, differing opinions (Hirth 1909; Sun Yutang 1979; Xu Yongzhang 1984; Chen Lemin 1994). In *Han Shu* (汉书) or the *History of Han,* Yichengbu State in the sea was mentioned and there was contact between China and Yichengbu during 1–5 CE. Zhang Xinglang identifies it as Ethiopia after examining a South China dialect and Herrmann's presumption (Zhang Xinglang 1977). In *Hou Han Shu* (后汉书), or *History of the Post-Han*, Daqin State is mentioned. It is suggested that this is the eastern part of the Roman Empire, including Egypt, Syria and Asia Minor (Sun Yutang 1979).

A place called Dou-le (兜勒) appeared in *History of the Post-Han*. Shen suggests Dou-le as Adulis, a famous old port located in ancient Ethiopia – today's Eritrea. An important historical event occurred in 100 CE when a diplomatic mission from Dou-le arrived in Luoyang, the ancient capital of China, and the Chinese Emperor met the envoy and awarded the King of Aksum a gold seal and purple ribbon. The Aksum Kingdom of Ethiopia thus became the first African country to have diplomatic relations with China, thanks to its Adulis mission (Shen Fuwei 1990). This view is appealing, but needs more evidence.

The geography of the great astronomer-geographer Claudius Ptolemaeus of Alexandria had a vivid description of China and the Silk Road (Chou Yi Liang 1972). *Wei Lue* (魏略), or *Brief Accounts of the Wei Kingdom,* written by an official named Yu Huan (鱼豢), covers the history of the Wei Kingdom from Emperor Wei Wu (魏武帝 155–220 CE) to Emperor Wei Yuan (魏元帝 246–302 CE) who ruled from 260–265 CE. *Wei Lue* mentions Chisan and Wuchisan, which were regarded as Alexandria in Egypt.[5]

Africans in China in early times

Scholars have studied Black people in China since the 19th century, yet the Black people mentioned in their works seem to be Pygmy, Black people of Southeast Asia or Melanesian (De Lacouperie 1887; Li Chi 1928; Weidenreich 1939; Ling Shun-heng 1956; Chang 1977: 68, 76). It is also suggested that they were related to *Rouzhi* (月氏, also pronounced *Yuezhi* or *Yueshi*) (Chen Jianwen 1993) or Persian (Schafer 1963). Generally speaking, Black people were believed to have come to China during the Tang Dynasty (Zhang Xinglang 1930; Xu Yongzhang 1983; Ai Zhouchang 1987; Jing Zhaoxi 1998). However, this idea could be challenged by archaeological discoveries that indicate the possibility of contact between China and Africa in earlier times.

The earliest indication of Black people (黑色人 *hei-se-ren*) in China seems to be in *Juyan Han Jian* (居延汉简). Because height and skin colour are described in *Juyan Han Jian*, it is possible to understand the physical features of individuals at the time. Two studies are most interesting. Zhang argues that since the Black-skinned individuals were from different parts of the empire, they were ordinary Han Chinese (Zhang Chunshu 1977). Yang drew a different conclusion that those Black people might be foreigners most probably from the West Region, or from the Nile region (Yang Ximei: 1995: 974–975, 977).[6]

The above evidence indicates that direct or indirect commerce and cultural contacts existed between China and Africa from the Han Dynasty (Zhang Junyan 1986: 11; Yang Renpian 1984: 112; Chen Gongyuan 1985: 1). Sun studied the contact between China and Egypt specifically, and defined two silk routes on land and three maritime routes (Sun Yutang 1979). Some scholars even think the bilateral relations started earlier (Shen Fuwei 1990; Zhang Xiang 1987).

Molin, *Kunlun* and evidence in the Tang Dynasty

During the Tang Dynasty (618–907), there was a period of prosperity and active international engagement when China and Africa continued their contact. Classics, archeological evidence and studies concentrate mainly on two issues. One is geography, such as the location of Molin (摩邻), other African places and sea routes; the other is *Kunlun* (昆仑) or *Kunlun nu* (昆仑奴) and *Sengzhi* (僧祇 also as *Sengchi, or Zengqi*), the Black people of the time.

Molin *(摩邻) and early writings*

During the Tang Dynasty three works illustrated some aspects of Africa: Du Huan's *Jing Xing Ji* (经行记 762?), Duan Chengshi's *Youyang Zazu* (酉阳杂

俎 850–860) and Jia Dan's *Gujin Junguo Xiandao Siyi Shu* (古今郡国县道四夷述 8th century). Du Huan was captured in the battle of Talas by the Arabs in 751. He returned to Guangzhou in 762 and wrote *Jing Xing Ji* or *Record of My Travel*. Although the book itself has been lost, a paragraph of 1500 words about *Molin* was kept in the *Tong Dian* (通典 801) or *Encyclopedia* compiled by his uncle Du You (杜佑 Zhang Yichun 1963).

Where is Molin? There are different explanations, yet it is generally agreed that it is in Africa, with possible locations such as Mauritania or Libya, Morocco, the Maghreb region, the Egyptian coastal region near the Red Sea, Malindi or Mande in Kenya (near Lamu), Meroe in the Sudan or the Aksum Kingdom of Ethiopia. Some foreign historians have also offered their views, including Hirth, Dyvendak and Fileshi, and there are more than ten interpretations (Li Anshan 2012: 22–23; Smidt 2001). A Sudanese scholar thinks Du Huan visited his country (Ahmed 1999a, 1999b). Molin is also identified as the dry desert lowlands in the Sudan and Eritrea (Smidt 2001) or West Africa (Wang Ting 2001). Exactly where Molin is located is not so important here; rather, it is significant to indicate that Du Huan had direct contact with Africa as early as the 8th century.

Another name is *Laobosa* (老勃萨), mentioned together with *Molin* (Zhang Xinglang 1977; Xu Yongzhang 1992a). Although there are various interpretations, it is most reliably identified as al-Habasha, the ancient Arabic term used for the Ethiopian highlands and its kingdom (Smidt 2001).

Duan Chenshi mentions a place in Africa in his *Youyang Zazu,* or *Youyang Miscellaneous Writings* – special products and customs in *Bobali* State (拨拔力) – and the description is very vivid:

> *Bobali* State is located in the Southwestern Sea. [People] don't eat five grains but only meat. They usually prick a needle into the veins of their cattle and extract the blood, which they mix with milk and drink it raw. They wear no clothes but merely use sheepskin to cover the parts below their waists. The women are White and well-featured. People kidnap and sell them to foreign merchants and the price is several times more. The country only has ivory and ambergris … It has never been subject to any foreign power since the ancient time … It has 200 000 foot-soldiers. *Da Shi* (大食 the Arab Empire) is continually making raids on this country.
>
> (Duan Chengshi 1981)

Bobali has caused some discussion. It is generally thought to be located in Somalia, and the Director of the Tanzanian Museum supports this assumption (El Fasi 1993: 498). Duan Chenshi used 洁白端正 (*jiebai duanzheng*) to describe *Bobali* women, yet Hirth and Rockville translate the term as "clear-skinned and well-behaved" (Hirth & Rockhill 1911: 128). When describing a person, 洁白 (*jieba*) means pure white and 端正 (*duanzheng*) means well-featured or beautiful. The incorrect translation by Hirth and Rockhill obviously affected Freeman-Greenville, who seems to have been unable to understand Chinese, and thus translated it as "clean and well-behaved", and wrongly thought the *Bobali* people were Masai in present Tanzania and Kenya (Freeman-Greenville, 1962a, 1962b: 6–37). However, the Masai are Black people, while the *Bobali* women in *Youyang Zazu* are "White and well-featured". *Youyang Zazu* mentions other states supposed to be in Africa, such as *Xiaoyi* (孝亿), *Renjian* (仍建) and *Xida* (悉怛), with detailed descriptions. Zhang suggests that *Xiaoyi* refers to southern Egypt, *Renjian* to Tunisia and *Xida* to the Sudan (Zhang Xinglang 1977: 1–13), indicating Duan Chenshi's knowledge of African places at the time.

Jia Dan's work was preserved in *Xin Tang Shu* (新唐书), or *New History of the Tang Dynasty*, which illustrates a sea route between East Africa and China. The most interesting point is that the ports along the navigation route were listed from the East African coast through the Persian Gulf to Guangzhou and not the other way round. The work also mentions another place, *San Lan* State (三兰国). Where is *San Lan* located? Some suggest it is Sri Lanka or Aden, yet most think it is somewhere on the East Africa coast, according to the navigation time and the mention of Dar es Salaam (Cen Zhongmian 1945; Ai Zhouchang & Mu Tao 1996; Xu Yongzhang 1992b) and the port of Zeila in Somalia (Chen Gongyuan 1983).

There are several studies on mutual contacts of this period, such as the sea route between China and East Africa, the role played by Arabs as middleman, the indirect but prosperous sea trade and bilateral diplomatic relations (Cen Zhongmian 1945; Zhang Tiesheng 1963; Chen Xinxiong 1991; Shen Fuwei 1990: 88–240). Shen thought Somalia and Zanzibar sent envoys to China in 629 CE and 639 CE respectively, and China had diplomatic relations with Tunisia.

The issue of Kunlun

Kunlun is another issue of this period. Besides the three above-mentioned works, many contemporary works frequently mention *Kunlun* or *Sengzhi*, described as having curly hair and Black skin or Black skin with red lips and white teeth. As early as the Dong Jin Dynasty (东晋 317–420), *Kunlun* was used to described Black-skinned people, but there is no indication that Black slaves were known in China at this time. *Kunlun ren* (昆仑人 *Kunlun* people), not *Kunlun nu* (昆仑奴 *Kunlun* slave), appears in *Sui Shu* (隋书 636), or *History of the Sui Dynasty*. *Kunlun*, used as a name for mountain, water, place or state official position in ancient times, turns out to be an ethnic name meaning "Black people" (Goodrich 1931; Zhang Xinglang 1928; Ge Chengyong 2001). The Tang Dynasty was prosperous, with many merchants from the Arab world bringing Black or White slaves to China for different purposes – as commodity, gift or tribute to the royal court.

There are generally two views on the origin of *Kunlun* – in East Africa or Southeast Asia. In 1930 Zhang Xinglang (originally spelt Chang Hsing-lang) published a rich collection of materials about *Kunlun* in the literature of the

Tang Dynasty and concluded that *Kunlun nu* were not from *Zhenla* (真腊 present-day Cambodia) or Southeast Asia. The view of scholars in the Qing Dynasty (清朝 1616–1911) was that they were Black slaves from Africa (Zhang Xinglang 1930). Zhang's work provided useful material to academia and is supported by many scholars who quote his view directly or indirectly, indicating that Black people were from Africa and almost all of them were slaves (Hu Zhaochun & Zhang Weichi 1961; Zhang Tiesheng 1965; Xu Yongzhang 1983; Ai Zhouchang 1987; Jing Zhaoxi 1998; Cheng Guofu 2002). Yet there is a critique of the generalisation (Li Anshan 2015; Li Anshan 2019a).

In 2001, Ge Chengyong published an article to probe the origin of the Black people living in Chang-an (长安), the capital of the Tang Dynasty, and drew a different conclusion. He argued that the Black people were not from Africa, but Black people from Nan Hai (南海, present Southeast Asia). *Kunluns* were either tributes by foreigners to China or sold to China by foreign envoys or slaves. Another term in Chinese classics, *Sengzhi*, is generally regarded as identical to *Zanj* (and other forms such as *Zinj, Zenj, Zandj* and *Zanghi*), which is a word applied by the Arabs to the East African coast. It still survives in the name Zanzibar. The Arabs called the Africans who came from the East African coast the *Zanj* (Irwin 2007; Rashidi 1985). Ge considered *Sengzhi* an expression of Buddhism in Nanhai and that it is more appropriate to search for the origin of Black people in Southeast Asia rather than Africa (Ge Chengyong 2001).

Regarding the origin of the Black people in the Tang period, Zhang Xinglang points to Africa and Ge suggests Southeast Asia as a kind of singular origin. After examining their arguments, it is obvious that they both emphasised the data that fitted their view. Zhang stressed that Black people were brought by Arabs, yet ignored those from Zhenla or Keling (present-day Java). Ge Chengyong made the same error by focusing on the Black people from Nan Hai, yet lost sight of the Black people brought by the Arabs. My argument is as follows. First, multiple origin is a more reasonable answer to the question. Second, Black people in ancient China were not all slaves as usually suggested; they had various occupations and some became prominent figures. Third, since *Kunlun* has the connotation of race and colour, I wish to emphasize that the Chinese prejudice in ancient time was against all foreigners, not just Black people and Africans. Furthermore, ethnocentrism is a universal phenomenon – especially when mutual contact is rare (Dikotter 1992; Li Anshan 2015, 2019a).

Material evidence

The evidence of this period includes porcelain discovered in Africa, the currencies found on the East African coast and Black figures in China. A large quantity of porcelain is now stored in Fustat in the south of Cairo. In 642 CE, the Arabs invaded Egypt and established Fustat as a political and economic centre. It was destroyed during the second Crusade, in 1168. The study of the explorations in the city has a long history and many pieces of porcelain were excavated and stored in museums in Egypt, Sweden, Italy and Japan. The porcelain is characterised by large quantities, good quality, a long history and many kilns. Porcelain of the Tang Dynasty was found in, for example, north Sudan, Manda Island in Kenya and the Comoro Islands. There are four main types: Yue Kiln, white china in Xing Kiln, Changsha Kiln and *Tangshancai* (唐三彩) (Ma Wenkuan & Meng Fanren 1987: 37–55). Kenyan archaeologist Kiriama argues that the items were brought from China to Kenya in several waves, the first appearing in the 9th or 10th century. Exported shards of Yue ware, Changsha ware, Canton celadon and Northern white ware were found in the Lamu archipelago (Kiriama 2014).

Besides porcelain, a few coins of the Tang Dynasty have also been found in Africa. Four coins were found from Zanzibar and another in Mogadishu (Xia Nai 1963; Zhang Junyan 1986). There are other reports of discoveries in Kilwa and Mafia. In the Tang Dynasty tomb of Madame Pei in Xi-an, the former capital of the Tang, one Black pottery figure was discovered in 1954. It is 15 centimetres high with Black skin, curly hair, thick lips and other features typical of Black people (Du Baoren 1979). Black figures also appear in ancient pictures in China, but it is not certain whether they are Black African (Chen Xinxiong 1991). In the *Dunhuang* (敦煌) frescoes there are also figures with similar Black features (Yan Wenru & Chen Yulong 1986).

Writings, visits and diplomacy in Song–Yuan Dynasties

During the Song and Yuan Dynasties, contact between China and Africa increased in scale and depth and is expressed in various ways. There were works mentioning more African places, such as *Lingwai Daida* (岭外代答 1178), *Zhu Fan Zhi* (诸蕃志 1225) and *Dao Yi Zhilue* (岛夷志略 1349). Chinese porcelain of the period was discovered in Africa; maps showing African places were produced in China; and there were mutual visits and diplomacy.

Understanding of African places

Zhou Qufei is a geographer of the Song Dynasty. His *Lingwai Daida*, or *Notes on Lands Beyond Mountain* divides the sea into different areas and mentions several places in Africa, such as *Wusili* (勿斯离), *Molanpi* (木兰皮) and *Kunlun Cengqi* (昆仑层期). He gives more detailed descriptions of *Molanpi* and *Kunlun Cengqi*. According to *Lingwai Daida*, there were big ships in *Molanpi*, including one that could hold several thousand people. Zhang Xinglang thought *Molanpi* was a mispronunciation of Maghreb: it referred not only to Morocco but to the whole of North Africa (Zhang Xinglang 1977), a view supported by others. In the description of *Kunlun Cengqi*, several unique points stand out, such as a big bird with huge wings that can eat a wild camel. Ostriches, ivory and hippo horn, and wild men with Black skin were trapped and sold to the Arabs. *Cengqi* is the transliteration of the Persian word *zenj*, which means Black. *Bar* means coast and land, therefore Zanjibar is "the land of the Black people", referring to the coastal region of East Africa. For *Kunlun* or *Cengqi,* scholars generally agree that it refers to the East African coast (Zhang Xinglang 1977; Zhang Tiesheng 1963).

The names of African places in *Lingwai Daida* are used in *Zhu Fan Zhi* by Zhao Rukuo, a customs official in South China, who had opportunities to make contact with foreigners. There are 57 places mentioned in the book, including more than ten African places. The most valuable information is the description of East Africa. According to Zhao, *Cengba* State (层拔国) is an island and the population is mainly Arab and Muslim; there are a few special products such as ivory and gold. The place is identified as Zanzibar. *Lingwai Daida* and *Zhu Fan Zhi* both mention *Kunlun Cengqi*. Cengba seems to be a transliteration of Zenjibar (Zhang Tiesheng 1963, 1965). Zhongli State (中理国) is another place next to *Bibalo* (弼琶罗) or *Bobali*, meaning Berber. The description includes dress, houses, special products, customs and social classes. Here, 中 (*zhong*) is a miswriting of 申 (*shen*), thereafter *Shenli*, which is identical to the Somali word. Therefore *Zhongli* is generally considered to be present-day Somalia (Zhao Rukuo 1996).

In *Song Shi* (宋史 1343), or *History of the Song Dynasty,* another place is mentioned: Cengtan State (层檀国). Scholars have tried to locate the state and opinions differ. It has aroused interest because *Cengtan* State sent two diplomatic missions to China during the period of Song Emperor Shenzong (宋神宗 1048–1085). Some suggest a location outside Africa, such as the Jeddah port of Mecca (Zhang Junyan 1986:118), yet most think it is in Africa. Geographer Zou Daijun (邹代均 1854–1908) regards it as Zanzibar (Zou Daijun 1903). The view is supported by several historians (Zhang Tiesheng 1963; Hou Renzhi 1964; He Fangchuan 1984; Xu Yongzhang 1993b).

Porcelain and currency

Around 1887, the British Museum received a collection of ancient Chinese celadon porcelain from Sir John Kirk, former British Consul-General at Zanzibar. Dr W.S. Bushell wrote in 1888 about this occurrence in his review of a work by the sinologist F. Hirth (夏德):

> I may add that Sir John Kirk during his residence as Consul-General at Zanzibar made a collection of ancient Chinese celadon porcelain which he took to the British Museum last year. Some of it was dug up I believe from ruins mixed with Chinese cash of the Sung dynasty, a striking confirmation of the Chinese writer who was Inspector of Foreign Trade and Shipping in Fuhkien Province.
>
> (Hirth 1909: 56–57)

He mentions the porcelain and coins of the Song Dynasty, most probably discovered in Zanzibar, as a confirmation of Zhao Rukuo's work. The exquisite porcelain was a most precious item during the Song Dynasty and was described by a contemporary as "blue as the sky, shining as a mirror, thin as paper and sounds like music" (青如天 明如镜 薄如纸 声如磬). About 12,000 fragments of celadon were found in Fustat, some of Tang or Song Dynasty. More pieces of the Song Dynasty were found in the Sudan, Morocco, Ethiopia, Somalia, Kenya, Tanzania, Zimbabwe and Madagascar (Ma Wenkuan & Meng Fanren 1987).

In Egypt, the local people liked Chinese porcelain and some ware appeared to imitate Chinese models, made of local clay with the Arab potter's name on it (Xia Nai 1963; Chou Yi Liang 1972). In 2010, Chinese archeologists from Peking University and Kenyan colleagues explored ruins in Mumbrui in Magarini, located at the ancient mouth of Sabaki River, and found fragments of porcelain from Longquan Kiln (Qin Dashu et al 2013). In Great Zimbabwe, 43 pieces of china belonging to 13 distinct articles were found in one cave (Ma Wenkuan 1985: 31–36; Ma Wenkuan & Meng Fanren 1987). Ibn Battuta claims that porcelain in China was as cheap as in his country, or cheaper. The china that was transported to India or the Magreb was the best porcelain (Ibn Battuta 1929).

Kenyan archeologist Herman Kiriama termed the period from second half of the 13th century to the beginning of the 15th century as the second peak of Chinese porcelain imported into Africa. During this time, Longquan ware, Jingdezhen (景德镇) Qingbai ware, Fujian celadon, Qingbai ware and blue and white copper red ware from Jingdezhen were all found on coast of Kenya. Changsha ware and celadon shards produced in Guangdong were found in Shanga, and Fanchang ware made in the 10th century was discovered in Manda (Kiriama 2014).

Coins of the Song Dynasty made in the 1200s and 1300s were found in Mogadishu in 1898. In 1916, Chinese coins were discovered on the island of Mafia in Tanzania, including one of the Song Emperor Shenzong (宋神宗 1068–1085). *Qinyuan Tongbao* (庆元通宝) of the Song Emperor Ningzong (宋宁宗 1168–1224) and *Shaoding Tongbao* (绍定通宝) of the Song Emperor Lizong (宋理宗 1205–1264) were discovered in Gedi, Kenya. In Kilwa, six coins were found: one *Chunhua Tongbao* (淳化通宝), four *Xining Tongbao* (熙宁通宝) and one *Zhenghe Tongbao* (政和通宝). The most significant discovery was in Kazengwa, Zanzibar in 1945 when 176 coins were found. Among them, 108 are of the North-Song Dynasty, 56 of the South-Song Dynasty, four of the Tang Dynasty and eight are not identified (Xia Nai 1963; Zhang Tiesheng 1963; Li Ximi 1964; Tian Shumao 1982; Ma Wenkuan & Meng Fanren 1987; Shen Fuwei 1990; Xu Yongzhang 1993a, 2019). In 1991, coins of the Song Dynasty were discovered in Aihdab in the Sudan by a Japanese archeologist – the first discovery of this kind in the region (Ahmed 1999).

Sea routes and visits

During the Song and Yuan Dynasties, both non-official and official contacts increased. This is closely linked to the government's policy of encouraging foreign trade, which gave a big push to commercial activities. During the Yuan Dynasty, there were three sea routes between China and Africa:

1. from China to North Africa: China–India–Aden–Egypt
2. from China to East Africa: China–Maldives–East Africa
3. from China to Madagascar, divided into two sub-routes:
    a. China–Socotra Island–Madagascar
    b. China–Malabar Coast–Madagascar (Li 2012: 36).

Wang Dayuan's visit to Africa

Both Zhou Qufei and Zhao Rukuo wrote their books based on the materials taken from others, while Wang Dayuan twice travelled abroad by sea. He visited Zanzibar, Egypt, Morocco, Mombasa and Kilwa, and even Mozambique during his second voyage from 1334 to 1339 (Zhang Tiesheng 1963; Shen Fuwei 1983; Zhang Junyan 1986). His description of the Mamluk Sultanate of Egypt is a very detailed record. Jia-jiang-men-li (加将门里) in Mozambique is the first mention in Chinese literature. The gatherings of Muslims and trade in Black girls are also mentioned in his work (Wang Dayuan 1981).

It seems that during the Song Dynasty the Chinese were living and trading with Africans in Zanzibar. Arab geographer Al Idrisi (1100–1166) wrote that he had heard about the Chinese: they would transfer their trade to Zanzibar and neighbouring islands when there was a riot in China or something unjust happened in India. The Chinese traders did business with island residents and were content because the islanders were moral and just (Al Idrisi, quoted in Levathes 1994). Trading activities could have occurred earlier than Al Idrisi's time. Ahmed, a post-doctoral student at Peking University, did research on Sudan–China contact and found a long history of business between Sudan and China (Ahmed 1999a, 1999b). China's trade with Africa was rather active at the time, and was of four types: tributary exchange and trade, foreign trade by the government, civil trade and transferring trade (Xu Yongzhang 2011).

Ibn Battuta's visit to China

During the Yuan Dynasty, the great Moroccan traveller Ibn Battuta visited China in 1346 or 1347 (Li Ximi 1964: 3–47). One of few early foreigners who visited China, Ibn Battuta left notes about his impression of China (another visitor was Marco Polo). He visited Quanzhou and Guangzhou, stayed in China for one year and was greatly impressed by its prosperity. *Travel Notes of Ibn Battuta* records Chinese political and legal systems, local customs, construction style, local products, communication, economic life and the monetary system, and provides a very detailed description of the structure of Beijing city and the internal conflict within the royal court:[7]

China was using paper money as early as in the 14th century. The Chinese use neither [gold] dinars nor [silver] dirhams in their commerce. All the gold and silver that comes into their country is cast by them into ingots as we have described. Their buying and selling is carried on exclusively by means of pieces of paper, each of the size of the palm of the hand and stamped with the sultan's seal.

(Ibn Battuta 1929)

He admired and enjoyed the talent of Chinese artists:

The Chinese are of all peoples the most skillful in the arts and possessed of the greatest mastery of them. This characteristic of theirs is well known and has frequently been described at length in the works of various writers. In regard to portraiture, there is none whether Greek or any other who can match them in precision, for in this art they show a marvelous talent.

(Ibn Battuta 1929)

The Chinese hospitality industry at the time impressed him:

When a Muhammadan merchant enters any town in China, he is given the choice between staying with some specified merchant among the Muslims domiciled there or going to a hostelry. If he chooses to stay with the merchant, his money is taken into custody and put under the charge of the resident merchant. The latter then pays from it all his expenses with honesty and charity … If the visitor chooses to go to the hostelry his property is deposited under the charge of the keeper of the hostelry. The keeper buys for him whatever he desires and presents him with an account. China is the safest and best regulated of countries for a traveler. A man may go by himself a nine months' journey, carrying with him large sums of money, without any fear on that account.

(Ibn Battuta 1929)

He regarded Quanzhou as the biggest port in the world (Ibn Battuta 1929; Hamdun & King 1975). His knowledge of China greatly influenced the Arabs at the time, as well as the world in general.

Diplomatic contacts

In the Song and Yuan Dynasties, the official contacts also strengthened. *Dashi* (大食) is a loose geographical term to describe the Arab Empire. *Lingwai Daida* states that *Dashi* is a general name that covers more than 1000 countries, only few of which are known by name. The Al-Sulalah al-Fatimiyyah Dynasty (909–1171), with Cairo as its capital, was also referred to as *Dashi*. There was contact: *Dashi* sent envoys to the Song Dynasty 54 times in total, the earliest in 924 and the latest in 1207, recorded in *Liao Shi* (辽史 1344) or *History of the Liao Dynasty* and *Song Shi* (宋史 1346) or *History of the Song Dynasty*. Although *Dashi* covered a vast region including West Asia, Central Asia, North and East Africa, its envoys give a clear indication of African places, tributes or members of missions. For example, in 1073 CE *Yuluhedi* State (俞卢和地国), or Kilpwa-Gedi in Kenya, sent envoys to China. Official contacts existed between China and Egypt, Somalia, Kenya and countries on the East African coast. In 1008, China established diplomatic relations with the Fatima Dynasty and they exchanged envoys (Zhang Junyan 1986: 11–118; Shen Fuwei 1990: 52–258, 262–288).

The Yuan Dynasty is regarded as the heyday of East–West transportation in mid-ancient times. Besides the above-mentioned localities, the Sudan stood out as an important place in its contact with China. Ahmed draws two important conclusions in his study. First, ancient Aihdab was not an Egyptian port but a Sudanese port, where Chinese goods including porcelain were unearthed. Second, the famous Karimi family who carried out business with China during the Mamluk reign (1250–1517) was neither Jewish nor Egyptian, but Sudanese (Ahmed 1999). It is suggested that the Yuan Dynasty established relations with the Mamluk Dynasty of Egypt, set up diplomatic relations and exchanged envoys. Somalia (Mogadishu), Kenya (Pate Malindi) and Zanzibar sent delegations to China in 1285, 1286 and 1300 respectively. The Chinese emperor Kublai Khan sent envoys to Madagascar, Shen thought the Madagascar mentioned by Marco Polo was actually Mogadishu (Zhang Tiesheng 1963:26; Shen Fuwei 1990: 74–378, 380–81).

During the Song and Yuan Dynasties, China's understanding of Africa further improved and there was an increase in bilateral contact. More African places were mentioned and the description of African states and regions was more detailed and specific, indicating better understanding of their geographic position, local products, customs, mode of production and social systems. Marine communication between China and Africa was established and various trades grew. Furthermore, peaceful diplomatic relations developed and records show that both sides sent envoys or merchants to each other who acted as diplomatic envoys.

Zheng He, sea routes and porcelains: Early Ming

During the early Ming period, roughly up to the 1500s, contact and mutual understanding between China and Africa greatly increased. Zheng He's junk travelled across the Indian Ocean and reached East Africa. Several sea routes developed with this expanded geographic knowledge and more trading activities brought various Chinese goods to Africa – including porcelain.

Zheng He's voyage to the West

Zheng He (1371–1433) was brought to the royal palace as a child and later became a eunuch. His family name was originally Ma (马), and Zheng (郑) was granted to him as a family name by the Ming Emperor Chengzu (明成祖

1360–1424). Zheng He was a capable man and familiar with military affairs, thus he was chosen as the principal envoy for the voyages to the western ocean. From 1405 to 1433, Zheng He sailed westwards seven times to Southeast Asia, South Asia, the Persian Gulf, the Arabian Peninsula and Africa.

In an article published in 1903, the study of Zheng He is divided into four periods: the initiation (1903–1934); the first wave (1935–1949);[8] the second wave (1950–1984); and the third wave (1985–present) (Li Xinfeng 2012a: 5–88). There are different opinions about which voyage first brought Zheng He to Africa. The general view supports the fourth trip (1413–1415) theory (Zhang Tiesheng 1963; Zheng Yijun 1985). For a study of Zheng He, see Zheng He (1985, 2005). Yet the "third voyage" argument is based on two points: the sea route of the trip, with *Zhubu* (竹步) being recorded in *Shuyuan Zaji* (菽园杂记) by Lu Rong; and the fact that there is no mention of this place in the record of Zheng He's later voyages. Lu refers to Fei Xin's *Xingcha Shenglan* (星槎胜览 1436), or *Overall survey of the Star Raft* as his source materials (Shen Fuwei 1990:456–457). In 1412, Zheng He started his fourth voyage after preparing for more than a year, and he chose many talented people, including Ma Huan (late 14th century to early 15th century), the author of *Yingya Shenglan* (瀛涯胜览 1451) or *Overall Survey of the Ocean's Shores*, to accompany him. Zheng He visited *Mugu Dushu* (木骨都束 Mogadishu), *Malin* (麻林 Malindi) and *Bulawa* (布腊瓦 卜剌哇 Brava) in Africa.

On his fifth voyage (1417–1419), Zheng He visited various places including Mogadishu and Brava. Foreign envoys of 16 countries accompanied him with tributes on his trip back to China. According to *Nanshan Si Bei* (南山寺碑), or the *Tablet of Nanshan Temple*, Mogadishu sent zebras and lions, Brava camels and ostriches. For the sixth voyage (1421–1422), Zheng He's mission was to send foreign envoys back, including from several African countries. After a debate among court officials on the role of the voyages, his maritime activity stopped for a long time.[9] In 1431, Zheng He was ordered to start his seventh voyage to the West (1431–1433). This time the fleet visited more than 20 states, including Mogadishu and Brava.

Some important works were published on Zheng He's voyages, including *Xingcha Shenglan* by Fei Xin and *Yingya Shenglan* by Ma Huan. Since the two authors were part of Zheng He's fleet, their works are of great historical value. *Xingcha Shenglan* mentions *Zhubu*, *Mugu Dushu* and *Bolawa*. The description of *Zhubu* is worth citing.

> *Zhubu* is located adjacent to *Mugu Dushu*. There are few villages and cities houses are made by stones. The custom is simple and honest. Both men and women have curly hair. Men cover their skin with cloth, women use cloth to cover their body and hide their face. The land is yellow and barren. There is no rain for several years, thus no grass or wood.
>
> (Fei Xin 1954: 20)

He also mentions that people in *Zhubu* lived by fishing, and that there were lions, leopards and ostriches in the country. Local chiefs were moved by

Chinese gifts and sent back local products to show their friendship (Fei Xin 1954). *Zhubu* is identified as the mouth of the Juba River in Somalia. Ma Huan mentions *Mixi* (米息), Misr or Egypt (Ma Huan 1955). Another important work is *Zheng He Hang Hai Tu* (郑和航海图), or *Zheng He's Nautical Charts*, which refers to more than 15 places in Africa (Xiang Da 1961).[10]

In the context of world history of navigation, the scale of Zheng He's fleet is incredible. For the seventh voyage, the fleet consisted of 100 including 61 treasure ships, 27,550 officials, secretaries, interpreters, seamen, doctors, technicians and soldiers, recorded by Zhu Yunming (1460–1527), a scholar of the Ming Dynasty (Zhu Yunming 1938). The fleet of the seventh voyage was similar in scale to the first (27,800 members) and the third (more than 27,000) (Zhang Junyan 1986: 1–204).

Just think: Columbus's voyage across the Atlantic Ocean was 61 years later, with only three ships and 87 seamen, and Vasco da Gama's voyage to the East 66 years later took only four ships and 148 (or 170) seamen!

Maps and sea routes

China's understanding of African geography was improved during the Song-Yuan period. In maps by contemporary Arabs and Europeans, the southern part of Africa is drawn towards the east and this continued until the mid-15th century, according to sinologist Joseph Needham. Zhu Siben (朱思本, 1273–1333) drew a rather accurate map with Africa pointing to the south. The map has been lost, but can be traced in *Guangyu Tu* (广舆图 1541), or the *Broad World Atlas* drawn by Luo Hongxian (罗洪先 1504–1564) of the Ming Dynasty. Another map, *Shengjiao Guangbei Tu* (声教广被图 1330s), by geographer Li Zemin (李泽民), also includes Africa and Europe (Shen Fuwei 1990).

Based on their existing knowledge, the Chinese developed a better image of Africa during the Ming Dynasty. There is an impressive atlas made of colourful silk (3.86 x 4.75 metres) created in 1389, entitled *Da Ming Hun Yi Tu* (大明混一图), or *Amalgamated map of the Great Ming Dynasty*. It shows rivers (the Nile and the Orange) and mountains (the Drakensberg) in southern Africa (Huang Shengzhang et al. 1994: 54; Li Hongwei 2004: 33–136).

The map is currently kept in the First Historical Archive of China in Beijing, but a full-sized replica was made for the South African government in 2002. Its exhibition caused great excitement in South Africa:

> The oldest map of the African continent, dating back to 1389, has gone on display in Cape Town. It is part of an exhibition drawing attention to the history of South Africa and the way it is perceived around the world. The Chinese map, covering more than 17 square metres, was produced in silk.
>
> (Leithead 2002)

The achievements of Zheng He's expeditions in the western sea were the result of Ming policy. Ming Emperor Taizu (明太祖) put great emphasis on foreign communication even before he established the Ming Dynasty. After Ming Emperor Chengzu (明成祖) took the throne, he reopened the sea route and encouraged the development of foreign relations. In 1405, Ming Chengzu set up hotels in three coastal cities to welcome foreigners: *Laiyuan Yi* (来远驿 Fujian Hotel) *Anyuan Yi* (安远驿 Zhejiang Hotel) and *Huaiyuan Yi* (怀远驿 Guangdong Hotel). He also sent envoys to build harmonious relations with neighbouring states and other foreign countries.

Several routes to Africa from China developed from the ports of the Indian Ocean. There are generally three views on sea routes: two routes, three routes and five routes. Zhang Tiesheng thought that there were two sea routes from China to Africa, along the Arabian Sea coast to the northern coast of Somalia to Socotra and to the east Africa coast; and across the Indian Ocean to the Maldives islands (Male) or Kollam in India or Beligam in Sri Lanka to East Africa (Zhang Tiesheng 1963:6–97). Ai and Mu argue that there were three routes:

1. Maldives–Gulf of Aden–Egypt
2. Kollam–Mogadishu
3. India–Hormuz–Aden–Cape Guardafui–East African coast (Ai Zhouchang & Mu Tao 1996:75).

Shen Fuwei believes in five routes:

1. Sumatra–Maldives–Egypt
2. Sumatra–Maldives–Mogadishu–Kilwa
3. Kollam – Maldives–Mogadishu
4. Beligam – Maldives–Mogadishu
5. Beligam–Brava (Shen Fuwei 1990: 462).

In fact, the above classifications have some similarities. In general, there were at least three sea routes from China to the East Africa coast: (1) China–Kollam in India–Mogadishu; (2) China– Beligam in Sri Lanka–Male or Maldives–Mogadishu (or Brava); and (3) China–Male or Maldives–Mogadishu (Fei Xin 1954: 24; Xiang Da 1961: 7–58; Li Anshan 2012: 43). It was natural for Zheng He's fleet to sail from Mogadishu (or Brava) further south; the fleet could also sail from Aden (or Egyptian ports) and Cape Guardafui to the East African coast. It was a great historical event for Zheng He to cross the Indian Ocean and reach Africa about 600 years ago, although it offers us more puzzles than heritage (Li Anshan 2005: 90; Li Xinfeng 2012b, 2013).

Porcelain and special products

China–African trade also greatly increased during the Ming Dynasty. Chinaware was transported to Africa in large quantities. Blue-white porcelain, mainly made in Jingdezhen, was the main chinaware product at the time. This type of porcelain had made great strides in glaze, colour, shape and decoration. According to the statistics of Japanese scholar Koyama Fujio, there were 1656 pieces of blue-white porcelain in the ruins of Fustat in Egypt, fewer pieces of Longquan celadon ware and only seven pieces of colour porcelain (Ma Wenkuan & Meng Fanren 1987: 50). In addition, china ware of the Ming Dynasty was found in North Africa, East Africa and middle-southern Africa (Oliver 1977: 193), and porcelain of the period was found in the Sudan. From 1912 to 1991, many archaeologists in the Sudan and foreign countries explored Aihdab Badi and Suakin. Their primary but valuable research shows that the 1000 porcelain pieces dated from the 10th to 16th centuries (Ahmed 1999).

According to Kiriama, a Kenyan archaeologist, in the 14th and 15th centuries Chinese celadon was the most popular ware exported to Kenya, its plain glazes ranging through shades of green and grey to pure dark green. Celadon was more valued because of the belief that it could reveal the presence of poison by cracking. Recent work in Mambrui, Kenya by Chinese and Kenyan archaeologists headed by Qin Dashu and Herman Kiriama has unearthed large Longquan green-glazed stoneware dishes of a quality equal to those sent to the Chinese imperial court in the late 14th and early 15th centuries (Qin Dashu et al. 2013: 47–272).

Zheng He's voyage to the West certainly promoted trade. According to *Xingcha Shenglan,* the fleet exchanged Chinese goods such as gold, silver, coloured silk, porcelain, rice and beans for local products. China imported African products such as ivory, rhinoceros horn and red sandalwood (Fei Xin 1954: 1–25). Mastic, myrrh, ambergris and frankincense also attracted Chinese merchants, especially frankincense, a special product from Somalia. Furthermore, giraffes and zebras, two African animals, appeared in Chinese classics.

Did Zheng He arrive in the south of Tanzania? Opinions differ. Zheng Yijun argues that he did. During the sixth voyage, after arriving on the East African coast, Zheng He's sub-fleet went south and reached the South African coast. Based on a note and a Chinese boat shown next to Cap de Diab (most probably the Cape of Good Hope) on the world map by Fra Mauro in 1459 CE, Zheng Yijun believes that a ship from India that Fra Mauro described in about 1420 CE belonged to Zheng He's fleet. The sub-fleet navigated from Somalia and Kenya across the Mozambican Strait, around Cape Agulhas and the Cape of Good Hope, on to the Atlantic Ocean and along the south-west coast of Africa (Zheng Yijun 1985: 25–228; Shen Fuwei 2005: 19–134). Some historical writing seems to provide evidence for this. When Vasco da Gama arrived on the Mozambican coast in 1498 for the first time, his crews offered local Africans gifts, including clothes and food. To their surprise, local people were not surprised by their gifts and told them that some White people had arrived there before with the same kind of ships from the place where the sun rises. Later, when Vasco da Gama arrived in India, he realised that the people to whom the local African had referred were not Indians but most probably

Chinese (Snow 1988: 35). This indicates that Chinese people may have arrived in Mozambique much earlier than Vasco da Gama.

Conclusion

Zheng He's expedition to the western ocean was a significant event that signalled the coming of a great age of navigation in world history. Yes, Vasco da Gama finally reached Asia, thus finishing the last and most important passage of his voyage to realise the final purpose of searching for treasure in the Orient. Yet an Arab navigator, Shihab al-Din Ahmad B. Madjid, contributed a great deal to this success by guiding him all the way to India.[11] When McNeill praised Vasco da Gama's great efforts and attributed the fulfilment of the difficult voyage to a remarkable feat of navigation, he did not mention the help of Ibn Madjid (McNeill 1965: 625). This indicates bias in the writing of world history – or the importance of discourse.[12]

Unfortunately, the peaceful and friendly diplomatic relations between Asia and Africa did not continue. What did Vasco da Gama do in East Africa? R.R. Palmer disclosed:

> Cities were devastated, ships burned at their docks, prisoners butchered and their dismembered hands, noses and ears sent back as derisive trophies. One Brahmin mutilated in this way was left alive to bear them to his people. Such unfortunately was India's introduction to the West.
> (Palmer & Colton 1992: 109)

The scramble of African and colonialism followed. A Kenyan archeologist commented on the difference between Chinese and Portuguese contact with Africa in early times: one was equal and peaceful, the other arrogant and violent (Kiriama 2014).

Notes

1 This chapter was originally published in *World History* 2:1 (2015), entitled "Contact between China and Africa before Da Gama: Archeology, Document and Historiography". It is a revised version of my paper "Contact between China and Africa before Da Gama: Historiography and evidence", presented at the International Conference Rethinking Africa's Transcontinental Continuities in Pre-and Protohistory, African Studies Centre, Leiden University, 12–13 April 2012. My thanks go to Wim M.J. van Binsbergen, Wu Yugui (吴玉贵) of the Institute of the History of Chinese Academy of Social Sciences, and Wang Xiaofu (王小甫) of the Department of History of Peking University for their advice, and my graduate students Tian Xin (田欣), Xu Mingjie (许明杰) and Jia Ding (贾丁) for their help during my research.
2 In ancient times, the Chinese government had specific administration systems for writing dynastic history. There are 24 volumes (二十四史) covering Chinese history from early times to the Ming Dynasty. Reference to the dynastic histories is omitted here owing to limited space.

3 Ferand discusses the link between giraffe and *qilin* (or *ki-lin*) in the *Journal Asiatique* in 1918. Duyvendak even imagined it was the giraffe that caused the Chinese to sail to Africa (Duyvendak 1949). A story in Kenya offers an interpretation of the role played by this historical *qilin* (Li Xinfeng 2013).
4 Zhang Qian (张骞，164–114 BCE) was the first envoy sent by Han Emperor Wudi （汉武帝） to the West. His footprints reached Central and West Asia. Some argue that his mission visited Egypt.
5 For example, Hirth states there is little doubt that Wu-ch'i-san is Alexandria (Hirth 1909: 6). See also Sun Yutang (1979).
6 *Juyan Han Jian* are government archives discovered in Juyan, Northwestern China. This issue will be discussed in more detail in Chapter 19.
7 Ibn Battuta (1304–1377), full name Abū Abd allāh Muhammad ibn Abd allāh ibn Muhammad ibn Battuta al-Rawātī al-Tanjī, was born in Morocco. As a great traveller, he visited 44 countries, more than Marco Polo, and came to China in the Yuan Dynasty. In my class for international students, I usually ask whether they know about Marco Polo. The answer is always "yes", yet few of them know Ibn Battuta. This indicates a bias in the field of world history. There are several Chinese translations of the abridged version of his travel notes; the complete translation by Li Guangbin was published in 2008.
8 New data discovered continuously in 1935 by Zheng Hesheng, in 1936 by Wang Boqiu and Zheng Hesheng and in 1937 by Li Hongxiang greatly promoted the study of the time and place of the seven voyages. Sinologist J.J.L. Duyvendak published an article based on studies by Chinese scholars (Duyvendak 1938).
9 The official documents related to Zheng He's voyages, which had been kept in the War Office, were burned by Liu Daxia (刘大夏 1436–1516 CE), an official of the War Office strongly opposed to his voyages.
10 A nautical chart of the Ming Dynasty. The original name was "The chart of sailing from Bao shipyard to foreign countries from Longjiang Pass", later shortened to "Zheng He Nautical Chart". This picture is a record of Zheng He's voyage to the west, from the first year of Hongxi (洪熙元年 1425) to the fifth year of Xuande (顺德五年 1430). The original picture is a hand roll unfolding from right to left. Mao Yuanyi of late Ming Dynasty changed it to book style, with a total of 24 pages. Xiang Da of Peking University made the annotation.
11 For his life and relationship with Vasco da Gama, see Ibn Madjid 1934: 362–370. His works, including 32 manuscripts, are now stored in the Bibliotheque Nationale, Paris. It is interesting that Vasco da Gama's journal mentions that the pilot was born in Gujarat (Ravenstein 2010: 1–46).
12 For an unconventional view of Zheng He's contribution to the history of navigation, see Menzies (2003).

References

Ahmed, G.K. 1999a. China–Arab relations during the Tang Dynasty 618–907 CE. *Tang Studies*, 5: 323–366.
Ahmed, G.K. 1999b. Sudan–China relations during the Tang Dynasty to the end of Yuan Dynasty. In Qiu Shuseng, ed., *Collected essays on Yuan History No. 7*. Nanchang: Jiangxi Educational Press, 197–206.
Ai Zhouchang. 1987. A survey of the Black African coming to China. *West Asia and Africa*, 3: 49–55.

Ai Zhouchang & Mu Tao. 1996. *A history of Sino–African relations.* Shanghai: East China Normal University Press.

Braudel, F. 1981. *The structures of everyday life, the limits of possible: Civilization & capitalism 15th–18th century, Vol. 1*, trans. & rev. by Sian Reynolds. New York: Harper & Row.

Braudel, F. 1984. *The perspective of the world civilization & capitalism 15th–18th century, Vol. 3*, trans. by Sian Reynolds. New York: Harper & Row.

Brunson, J. 1985. African presence in early China. *Journal of African Civilizations* 1: 121–137.

Cen Zhongmian. 1945. Chinese sea routes in the Tang Dynasty: From the Persian Gulf to East Africa. *The Eastern Miscellany* 41(18): 46–51.

Chang Kwang Chih. 1977 [1968]. *The archaeology of ancient China.* New Haven, CT: Yale University Press.

Charlesworth, M.P. 1970. *Trade-routes and commerce of the Roman Empire.* New York: Cooper Square.

Chen Gongyuan. 1983. On China–Africa relations of the Tang Dynasty through Jia Dan's foreign sea route. *West Asia and Africa*, 3: 46–52.

Chen Gongyuan. 1985. *The friendly contact between China and Africa in ancient times.* Beijing: Commercial Press.

Chen Jianwen. 1993. The name and ethnicity of *Rouzhi* and the issue of Black people in border regions of Han Dynasty. In *Proceedings of International Society of Bamboo Slips' Studies*, Taibei: Lantai Press, 111–143.

Chen Lemin. 1994. Where is Lixian and Yichengbu State in the history of ancient China–Africa relations? *West Asia and Africa,* 1: 72.

Chen Xinxiong. 1991. China–Africa relations during the Tang Dynasty: Indirect but strong sea trade, in Wu Jianxiong, ed. *Collected essays on the history of China's marine development.* Taibei: Academia Sinica, 127–159.

Cheng Guofu. 2002. An examination on the phenomenon of the *Kunlun* slaves in the novel of the Tang Dynasty. *Journal of Jinan University: Philosophy & Social Science Edition*, 24(5): 79–84.

Chou Yi Liang. 1972. Early contacts between China and Africa. *Ghana Notes and Queries*, 12(6): 1–3.

Dart, R. 1925. Historical succession of cultural impacts upon South Africa. *Nature* 115(28): 425–429.

Dart, R. 1939. A Chinese character as a wall motif in Rhodesia. *South African Journal of Science*, 36: 474–476.

De Lacouperie, T. 1887. *The languages of China before the Chinese.* London: David Nutt.

Dikotter, F. 1992. *The discourse of race in modern China.* London: C. Hurst.

Du Baoren. 1979. Black African pottery figure in Tang tomb of Xi-an. *Cultural Relics*, 6: 88–90.

Duan Chengshi. 1981 [around 850]. *Miscellaneous writings (Youyang Zazu).* Beijing: Zhonghua Book Company.

Duyvendak, J.J.L. 1938. The true dates of the Chinese maritime expeditions in the early 15th century. *T'oung Pao*, 34: 341–413.

Duyvendak, J.J.L. 1949. *China's discovery of Africa.* London: A. Probsthain.

El Fasi, M., ed. 1993. *General history of Africa, Vol. 3.* Paris: UNESCO.

Elton, G.R., ed. 1958. *The new Cambridge modern history II. The Reformation 1520–59.* Cambridge: Cambridge University Press.

Fei Xin. 1954 [1436]. *Overall survey of the Star Raft, Vol. 2*. Beijing: Zhonghua Book Company.
Filesi, T. 1972. *China and Africa in the Middle Ages*, trans. D.L. Morison. London: Frank Cass.
Freeman-Greenville, G.S.P. 1962a. *The East African coast: Selected documents from the first to the earlier 19th century*. Oxford: Oxford University Press.
Freeman-Greenville, G.S.P. 1962b. *The medieval history of the coast of Tanganyika: With special reference to recent archaeological discoveries*. Berlin: Akademie-Verlag.
Ge Chengyong. 2001. On the origin of Black people of Chang-an in the Tang Dynasty. *Zhonghua Wenshi Luncong* 65: 1–27.
Goodrich, L.C. 1931. Negroes in China. *Bulletin of the Catholic University of Peking* 8: 37–39.
Hamdun S. & King, N. 1975. *Ibn Battuta in Black Africa*. London: Rex Collings.
Hart, H.H. 1950. *Sea road to the Indies*. New York: Macmillan.
He Fangchuan. 1984. An examination of Cengtan state. *Social Science Front* 1: 178–182.
Herrmann, A. 1913. Ein alter Seeverkehr zwischen Abessinien und Süd-China bis zum Beginnunserer Zeitrechnung. *Zeitschrift der Gesellschaft für Erdkunde*,10: 553–561.
Hirth, F. 1909. Early Chinese notices of East African territories. *Journal of the American Orient Society* 30(1): 46–57.
Hirth, F. & Rockhill, W.W. 1911. *Chau Ju-kua* St Petersburg: Imperial Academy of Sciences.
Hou Renzhi. 1964. Sea route contact between China and East Africa before the so-called discovery of new sea route. *Chinese Science Bulletin*, 11: 984–990.
Hu Zhaochun & Zhang Weichi. 1961. Han Dynasty Black slave figurines unearthed in Guangzhou. *Journal of Sun Yatsen University*, 2: 84–87.
Huang Shengzhang et al., eds. 1994. *China's ancient atlas: Ming Dynasty*. Beijing: Cultural Relics Press.
Ibn Battuta 1929. *Ibn Battuta travels in Asia and Africa 1325–1354*, trans. and selected by H.A.R. Gibb. London: George Routledge & Sons.
Ibn Madjid, S. al-D. A. 1934. *The encyclopedia of Islam, Vol. 4*. London: George Routledge & Sons.
Al Idrisi 1994. *Opus geographicum* Neapoli-Romai Instituto Universitario Orientale di Napoli 1970, in L. Levathes, ed., *When China rules the seas: The treasure fleet of the Dragon Throne 1405–1433*. Oxford: Oxford University Press.
Institute of Archaeology of Chinese Academy of Social Sciences et al. 1981. *Tombs of the Han in Guangzhou, Vol. 1*. Beijing: Relics.
Irwin, G.W. 2007. African bondage in Asian lands. In R. Rashidi & I. van Sertima, eds. *The African presence in early Asia*. New Brunswick, NJ: Transaction Press, 140–145.
Jayne, K.G. 1910. *Vasco da Gama and his successors, 1460–1580*. London: Methuen.
Jing Zhaoxi. 1998. On the coming of Black African to China during the Tang Dynasty. *Journal of the Second Northwest College for Nationalities* 4: 51–54.
Kiriama, Herman O. 2014. The Africa–China Exchange systems in the late first/early second millennium A.D. Lecture at the Centre for African Studies of Peking University, 28 October.
Leithead, A. 2002. Africa's oldest map unveiled. *BBC News,* 12 November. http://news.bbc.co.uk/2/hi/africa/2446907.stm. Accessed 28 November 2014.

Levathes, L. 1994. *When China rules the seas: The treasure fleet of the Dragon Throne 1405–1433*. Oxford: Oxford University Press.
Li Anshan 2000. *A history of overseas Chinese in Africa*. Beijing: The Chinese Overseas Publishing House.
Li Anshan 2005. On the significance of Zheng He's expedition in the history of China–Africa relations. *Southeast Asian Studies* 6: 85–92.
Li Anshan 2012. *A history of overseas Chinese in Africa till 1911*. New York: Diasporic Africa Press.
Li Anshan 2015. African diaspora in China: Research, reality and reflection. *Journal of Pan African Studies* 78: 1–41.
Li Anshan 2019. *The social and economic history of the Chinese overseas in Africa* (3 vols). Nanjing: Jiangsu People's Press.
Li Anshan. 2019a. The supplement and analysis of the historical materials of the communication between China and Africa in ancient times: On the origin of Black people in early China. *Historical Review* 2: 204–219.
Li Chi. 1928. *The formation of the Chinese people*. Cambridge, MA: Harvard University Press.
Li Hongwei. 2004. Silent for a hundred years and amazing the world with a single feat (Da Ming Hun Yi Tu). *Historical Archives* 1: 133–136.
Li Ximi. 1964. One of the earliest African visitors to China – Ibn Battuta. *Journal of Chinese Humanities* 2: 43–47.
Li Xinfeng, ed. 2012a. *Zheng He and Africa*. Beijing: China Social Sciences Press.
Li Xinfeng. 2012b. A voyage far away from China: Review of the study on the linkage between Zheng He and Africa. In Li Anshan & Pan Huaqiong, eds. *Annual Review of African Studies in China 2011*. Beijing: Peking University Press, 75–88.
Li Xinfeng. 2013. *Seek Zheng He's passage in Africa*. Beijing: China Social Sciences Press.
Ling Shun-heng. 1956. Negritoes in Chinese history. *Annals of Academia Sinica* 3: 251–267.
Lubec, G., et al. 1993. Use of silk in ancient Egypt. *Nature*, 362 (March 4 1993): 6415, p.25.
Ma Huan. 1955 [1451]. *Overall survey of the ocean's shores*. Beijing: Zhonghua Book Company.
Ma Wenkuan. 1985. Great Zimbabwe and Chinese porcelain. *Maritime History Studies* 2: 31–36.
Ma Wenkuan & Meng Fanren. 1987. *The discovery of Chinese ancient porcelain in Africa*. Beijing: Forbidden City Press.
McNeill, W.E. 1965. *The rise of the west: A history of the human community*. London: Mentor Books.
Menzies, G. 2003. *1421: The year China discovered the world*. New York: Bantam Books.
Oliver, R., ed. 1977. *Cambridge history of Africa, Vol. 3*. Cambridge: Cambridge University Press.
Palmer, R.R. & Colton, J.A. 1992. *History of the modern world*, 7th ed. New York: McGraw-Hill.
Peng Bangjiong. 1987. On Shang King Wu Ding. *Zhongzhou Academic Journal* 3: 101–105.

Penrose B. 1955. *Travel and discovery in the Renaissance 1420–1620*. Cambridge, MA: Harvard University Press.

Qin Dashu et al. 2013. Peking University's archeological expedition in Kenya and major achievements, in Li Anshan & Liu Haifang eds, *Annual review of African studies in China 2012*. Beijing: Peking University Press, 247–272.

Qin Jie. 2010. Discovery and research of pottery figurines in Han tombs in Guangzhou. MA dissertation, Jilin University.

Rashidi R. & Van Sertima I. eds. 2007. *The African presence in early Asia*. New Brunswick.NJ: Transaction Press.

Rashidi R. 1985. Commentaries. *Journal of African Civilizations* 1: 147–148.

Ravenstein E.G., ed. 2010. *A journal of the first voyage of Vasco Da Gama 1497–1499*. Cambridge: Cambridge University Press.

Schafer, E. (1963). *The golden peaches of Samarkand: A study of T'ang exotics*. Berkeley, CA: University of California Press.

Selassie, S.H. 1972. *Ancient and medieval Ethiopian history to 1270*. Addis Ababa: United Printers.

Shen Fuwei. 1983. The historical significance of Yuan navigator Wang Dayuan's voyage to Africa. *West Asia and Africa* 1: 33–40.

Shen Fuwei. 1990. *China and Africa: Relations of 2000 years*. Beijing: Zhonghua Book Company.

Shen Fuwei. 2005. Chinese junk voyages to Africa during the 14th & 15th centuries. *Historical Research* 6: 119–134.

Smidt, W.A. 2001. A Chinese in the Nubian and Abyssinian kingdoms, 8th century: The visit of Du Huan to Molin-guo and Laobosa. *Chroniques Yemenites* 9. http://cy.revues.org/document33.html. Accessed 20 May 2021.

Snow, P. 1988. *The Star Raft: China's encounter with Africa*. London: Weidenfeld & Nicolson.

Sun Yutang. 1979. China and Egypt in the Han Dynasty. *Journal of Chinese Historical Studies*, 2: 142–154.

Tian Shumao 1982. Chinese cultural relics discovered in East Africa. *Jinyang Academic Journal*, 6: 13–14.

Wang Dayuan. 1981 [1350]. *Records of island barbarians*. Beijing: Zhonghua Book Company.

Wang Ting. 2001. Molin: Chinese record on West Africa in Middle Ages. *Journal of Chinese Historical Studies* 1: 153–161.

Weidenreich, F. 1939. On the earliest representatives of modern mankind recovered on the soil of East Asia Peking. *Natural History Bulletin* 3(3): 161–174.

Wilensky, J. 2002. The magical *Kunlun* and 'devil Slaves': Chinese perceptions of dark-skinned people and Africa before 1500. *Sino–Platonic Papers*, 22 July. University of Pennsylvania http://sino-platonic.org/complete/spp122_chinese_africa.pdf. Accessed 1 December 2014.

Wu Changchun. 1991. Study on the forms, ways and related issues concerning the early sea communication between China and Africa. *West Asia and Africa* 6: 59–64.

Wu Qingzhou. 1997. A study on the evolution of Qilin from Spring–Autumn to Six Dynasties. *Journal of Ancient Gardens & Architecture* 3: 58–64.

Wyatt, D. 2010. *The Blacks of premodern China*. Philadelphia, PA: University of Pennsylvania Press.

Xia Nai. 1963. Porcelain as the evidence of the contact between ancient China and Africa. *Cultural Relics* 1: 17–19.

Xiang Da. 1961. *Zheng He Nautical Charts*. Beijing: Zhonghua Book Company.
Xu Yongzhang. 1983. Africans who visited China in ancient times. *History Monthly* 3: 96–97.
Xu Yongzhang. 1984. Africa recorded in twenty histories. *Journal of Henan University* 4: 95–101.
Xu Yongzhang. 1992a. An examination of Laobosa State. *Chinese Journal of Humanities* 2: 31–35.
Xu Yongzhang. 1992b. An examination of San Lan Guo. *West Asia and Africa* 1: 54–57.
Xu Yongzhang. 1993a. On several issues in ancient China–Africa relations. *West Asia and Africa* 5: 65–70.
Xu Yongzhang. 1993b. The discovery of the currency of the Song Dynasty in Africa and related issues. *Cultural Relics of Central China* 2: 80–84
Xu Yongzhang. 2011. A study on China's trade in Africa during the Song Dynasty. *Journal of Huanghe S&T University* 13(2): 66–69.
Xu Yongzhang, 2019. *Historical manuscripts of ancient China–African relations*. Shanghai: Shanghai Dictionary Press.
Yan Wenru & Chen Yulong, eds. 1986. *Festschrift of Mr Xiang Da*. Urumqi: Xinjiang People's Press.
Yang Renpian. 1984. *A concise history of Africa*. Beijing: Renmin Press.
Yang Ximei. 1966. A preliminary report of human crania excavated from Hou-chia-chuang and other Shang Dynasty sites at An-yang Honan, North China. *Annual Bulletin of the China Council for East Asian Studies* 5: 1–13.
Yang Ximei. 1995. *Collection on cultural history in pre-Qin period*. Beijing: China Social Sciences Press.
Zhang Chunshu. 1977. *Collected essays of history of frontier of the Han Dynasty*. Taibei: Shihuo Press.
Zhang Junyan 1986. *Contact at sea between China and West Asia and Africa during the ancient times*. Bejing: Haiyang Press.
Zhang Tiesheng 1963. China–Africa relations seen from the history of East Africa. *Historical Research* 2: 127–134.
Zhang Tiesheng. 1965. *History of Sino-African relations: A primary research*. Beijing: SDX Joint Publishing Company.
Zhang Xiang. 1987. Four high-tides of the contacts between Africa and China in ancient times. *History in Nankai University* 2: 118–131.
Zhang Xiang. 1993. Several issues in the study of China–African relations in ancient times. *West Asia and Africa* 5: 71–74.
Zhang Xinglang. 1930. The importation of African Negro slaves to China during the Tang. *Furen Xuezhi* 1: 101–119.
Zhang Xinglang. 1930. The importation of Negro slaves to China during the Tang Dynasty CE618–907. *Bulletin of the Catholic University of Peking,* 7: 37–59.
Zhang Xinglang, ed. 1977 [1930]. *Collected historical materials on Sino–Western contact, Vol. 2*. Annotated by Zhu Jieqing. Beijing: Zhonghua Book Company.
Zhang Yichun. 1963. *Jinxing Ji* (with annotation). Beijing: Zhonghua Book Company.
Zhao Rukuo. 1996 [1225]. *Records of foreign nations*. Annotated by Yang Bowen. Beijing: Zhonghua Book Company.
Zheng He. 1985. The 580th Anniversary of Zheng He's Voyage Preparing Committee for Memorial. *Collected essays on Zheng He's expeditions to the West Ocean, Vol. I*. Beijing: China Communication Press.

Zheng He. 2005. The 600th Anniversary of Zheng He's Voyage Preparing Committee for Memorial (1905–2005). *Selected essays on Zheng He's expeditions to the West Ocean 1905–2005.* Beijing: China Ocean Press.

Zheng Yijun. 1985. *On Zheng He's expedition to the West Ocean.* Beijing: China Ocean Press.

Zhu Yunming. 1938. *Record of previous news.* Shanghai: Commercial Press.

Zou Daijun. 1903. *Atlas of China and the world.* Shanghai: Yudi Association.

2 African studies in China in the 20th century[1]

African studies in China has been more or less a mystery to Africanists in other parts of the world. As a historiographical examination of African studies in China during the 20th century, this chapter is divided into four parts. "Sensing Africa" (1900–1949) illustrates Chinese contact with and sense about Africa. "Supporting Africa" (1949–1965) demonstrates the early start of African studies in China. "Understanding Africa" (1966–1976) explores how the Chinese tried to collect various materials and views about Africa. "Studying Africa" (1977–2000) gives a survey of Chinese studies during the period. From a Chinese perspective, the author tells how, when and why Chinese scholars have conducted their research on Africa according to paradigms that evolved during the last century. The conclusion offers the author's own thoughts and points out the achievements and the problems in African studies in China today.

Introduction

In 1981, George T. Yu, a Chinese American expert on China's policy on Africa, visited China and a delegation of American Africanists came to China in 1984. These visits were the start of a China–US African Studies Exchange Program.[2] However, Africanists outside China are still unfamiliar with African studies in China, owing to the language barrier and lack of involvement in international academia by Chinese scholars.[3] This chapter provides a general survey of African studies in China in the 20th century. Divided into four parts chronologically, it looks at the study of African history, politics, cultural studies and other related fields, with an analysis of the factors contributing to African studies in China.

Sensing Africa (1900–1949)

China has a long history of contact with Africa. There was cultural exchange between China and Egypt as early as the Han Dynasty (206 BCE–220 CE).[4] Du Huan, a Chinese in the Tang Dynasty (618–907 CE), visited Africa in the 8th century and is probably the first Chinese to have left a written record

DOI: 10.4324/9781003220152-3

about Africa (Du Huan 762 CE?).[5] The great African traveller of the Yuan Dynasty (1271–1368 CE), Ibn Battuta, visited China in the 14th century and left a vivid description of metropolitan life.[6] A Chinese fleet led by Zheng He visited the East African coast several times during the 15th century.[7] Interestingly enough, two African animals, the zebra and the giraffe, appear in Chinese classics of the Ming Dynasty (1368–1644 CE), and archaeological discoveries have also suggested early contact between China and Africa. Chinese archaeologists found a terracotta Black figure in the tomb of "Madame Pei" of the Tang Dynasty. Chinese porcelain produced from the Tang to the Ming Dynasties has been found in many parts of East Africa, and five pieces of Tang currency were discovered in Africa as well (Ma Wenkuan & Meng Fanren 1987).[8] From the 18th century on, there was more and more contact between China and Africa.[9]

Although the contact began long ago, the study of Africa in China did not start until modern times. With the coming of the Europeans, especially the missionaries who brought their knowledge of geography, Chinese intellectuals and court officials began to hear more about the outside world.[10] This contact increased during the Qing Dynasty (1616–1911), although on humiliating terms for the Chinese. While the partition of Africa was taking place in the late 19th century, there was also an effort on the part of the European powers to establish their "spheres of influence" in China. A wave of alarm swept across the land, especially among the intellectuals, the most prominent of whom was Lin Zexu, the official who led the opium burning in Canton that triggered the Opium War between China and Great Britain in 1840.

Lin Zexu collected whatever information he could about the West, and his efforts produced the important *Si Zhou Zhi* (Gazeteer of the Four Continents). Illustrating African geography and ethnology, the book mentions places, states, cities, leaders and ethnic groups in Africa (Lin Zexu 1841).[11] A scapegoat of the Qing government under pressure from the European invaders, he was exiled to the northwest region but left his materials to Wei Yuan, another reformer, who compiled the book and added new materials and his own comments.[12] Labelled "a landmark in China's relations with the West", this book "represent[ed] the first systematic attempt to provide educated men with a realistic picture of the outside world" (De Bary et al. 1960: 10). Wei Yuan also mentions Africa in his own book (Wei Yuan 1842), and another scholar of the time, Xu Jiyu, wrote in detail about North, West, Central, East and Southern Africa and the islands located in the West Indian Ocean (Ai Zhouchang 1989: 167–88).

In general, most early publications on Africa were of three sorts: translations or editions of world geography covering some parts of the continent, travel notes and books about Egypt (Zhang Qiwei 1904; Ren Baoluo 1907). It is understandable that books about Egypt were written or translated, since Chinese Muslims went there on pilgrimages every year and the Chinese were more familiar with Egypt than with other places in Africa. Chinese who travelled to Europe usually crossed Africa by land, or by sea after the opening of the Suez Canal. Aside from the translations of Egyptian works, the earliest translation on the African continent was probably *Feizhou Youji* (*Travel in Africa*) by a British writer, published by ZhongXi Publishing Company in 1900.

At the end of the Qing Dynasty, revolutionary leaders and intellectuals such as Chen Tianhua, Liang Qichao, Sun Yat-sen and others tried to mobilize the Chinese people using the African example.[13] Both Chen Tianhua and Liang Qichao praised the Boers for their bravery in their fight against the British. Chen called the Boers "hero[es] of indomitable spirit", asking, "Transvaal can do this, are we not as good as Transvaal?" Liang Qichao also stressed the connection between the Anglo-Boer War and the Chinese issue, and Sun Yat-sen used the example of the partition of Morocco, trying to show the rationale of "reform or perish" (Ai Zhouchang 1989: 192–195, 201–202). All the leaders attempted to alert the Chinese people by means of both positive and negative lessons from Africa. Several newspapers in China also played a role in transmitting information about Africa, such as *Waijiao Bao* (*Newspaper of Diplomacy*) and *Qing Yi Bao*.

After Sun Yat-sen established Republican China in 1911, very few works on Africa were published. *The Eastern Miscellany*, an important journal that was started in 1904 and lasted for more than 40 years, published various articles about Africa on subjects such as relations between Africa and European countries, the partition, and African peoples and customs. Scholars also analyzed the political situation there, especially important contemporary issues such as the Moroccan crisis and the Italian invasion of Ethiopia. Cen Zhongmian wrote an article in 1945 on the contact between China and Africa during the Tang Dynasty, illustrating the sea route between the Persian Gulf and East Africa (Cen Zhongmian 1945).

The first book on Africa written by Chinese scholars was a survey of the history, geography, ethnic groups, politics, economy, religion and culture of Ethiopia, published in 1936. Although the book was a general survey of Ethiopian history and culture, the authors' point of view was quite clear. At the very beginning, they list four similarities between China and Ethiopia: both were ancient civilizations, both had a political organization undergoing a transformation from a feudal to a modern system, both suffered from capitalist invasion and the decline of handicraft industries, and both were victims of imperialism. The authors showed great sympathy for the Ethiopian people in their struggle against the Italian invasion and realised that the cruel threat towards Ethiopians was an indirect threat to China (Wu Zuncun & Xie Defeng 1936). Another book on Ethiopia written by a Soviet scholar was translated into Chinese in 1935. In the early 1940s, two books on Egypt were published: a history of Egypt (Huang Zengyue 1940) and a book about the Suez Canal (Ren Mei'e & Yan Qinshang 1941). However, for the most part Africa was rarely studied during China's Republican period. Most of Africa was under colonial rule and it had no political status in international affairs. China itself was in chaos, with one war after another, and few people were interested in Africa. There were, however, occasional reports about overseas Chinese or labourers in Africa.

Supporting Africa (1949–1965)

The founding of the People's Republic of China (PRC) in 1949 has been regarded as an important part of the national liberation movements after World War II. Beginning in the late 1950s, African studies in China concentrated on nationalist independence movements, especially those in North Africa (Wu Xiu 1956; Luo Ke 1956; Fan Yong 1957; Yan Jin 1958; Chen Li 1959). Several academic journals published articles on the struggles against colonial rule in different countries (Na Zhong 1957; Zheng Daochuan 1957; Ma Tong 1959; Wang Junyi 1959; Wang Zhen 1959) or the nationalist movements in Africa as a whole. Two universities were pioneers in African studies: scholars at Nankai University in northern China focused particularly on North Africa, while the South China Normal University began to study Central Africa.[14]

Leaders of the Communist Party of China (CPC) encouraged African studies. On 27 April 1961, Chairman Mao Zedong admitted to a group of African and Asian friends visiting China that he did not have a clear understanding of Africa:

> An institute of Africa should be established, studying African history, geography and the socio-economic situation. We don't have a clear understanding of African history, geography and the present situation, so a concise book is badly needed. It doesn't need to be big, about one hundred to two hundred pages are enough. We can invite African friends to help and get it published in one or two years. It should include the content of how imperialism came, how it suppressed the people, how it met people's resistance, why the resistance failed and how it is now rising.
>
> (Mao Zedong 1994: 463, 465)[15]

On 4 July 1961, the Institute of Asian–African Studies was founded under the Central Party External Ministry and the Chinese Academy of Sciences. Zhang Tiesheng, an expert on China–African relations, was appointed as the first director.

On 30 December 1963, the Group of Foreign Affairs of the Central Committee of the CPC issued a report on strengthening the study of foreign countries. Accordingly, three institutes in three universities were set up specifically for this purpose. Peking University, with its solid foundation in the humanities and social sciences and its Department of Oriental Studies, which taught various languages spoken in Afro-Asian countries, was chosen as the site for the Institute of Afro-Asian Studies.[16] Ji Xianlin, a scholar who had received his PhD in Germany during the 1940s, was appointed as the director of the institute. Yang Ren-pian of the Department of History, who had received his degree in France, switched from French history to African history and began to train graduate students in this discipline.

Various institutions were also involved in African studies, the most prominent of which was the Institute of Asian–African Studies under the dual leadership of the International Liaison Department of the Central Committee of the CPC and the Chinese Academy of Sciences (which became an institute of the Chinese Academy of Social Sciences (CASS) in 1981). *African introduction* (1962), prepared especially for Premier Zhou Enlai's visit to Africa, was published by the institute and circulated internally among government cells. The institute also had two *Neibu Kanwu* (internal circulated journals): *Yafei Yicong* (*Translations on Asia and Africa*), beginning in 1959, and *Yafei Ziliao* (*Data on Asia–Africa*), beginning in 1963. All these developments introduced Chinese intellectuals to international scholarship in African studies, including publications and conferences, and gave Chinese scholars numerous opportunities to pursue African studies abroad.[17]

This time also saw the translation into Chinese of many books in the field of African studies. These were generally of four types: works by African nationalist leaders, academic works by Western or Russian scholars, government reports and popular works of non-fiction. The first type included works by Jamal Abd al Nasser (1954), Kwame Nkrumah (1957, 1965), Ahmed Ben Bella (Merle 1965) and the Senegalese political leader Majhemout Diop (1958). Works by academicians were also translated (Suret-Canale 1958; Woddis 1960, 1961; Fitzgerald 1955; Davidson 1955, 1961; McKay 1963). Some books were chosen specifically for their understanding of the contemporary situation, such as *The African awakening* (Davidson 1955) and *Les trusts au Congo* (Joye & Lewin 1961). Many books by Soviet scholars were translated, the best-known of which was *African nations* (Ольдерогге, Потехин 1954), a large volume on ethnic groups in Africa written by two leading Soviet Africanists. A work by the American scholar W.E.B. Du Bois, *Africa: An essay towards a history of the continent* (1961), was translated from Russian.[18] Government reports included *United States Foreign Policy: Africa* (Program of African Studies at Northwestern University 1959). Some popular books were also translated, such as John Gunther's *Inside Africa* (1955).

Two important books written by Chinese scholars at this time are worth mentioning: *A history of China–African relations: A primary research* (Zhang Tiesheng 1963); and *A concise history of modern Egypt* (Na Zhong 1963). Zhang Tiesheng's work is a compilation of five articles on China–Africa relations from the Han Dynasty to the Ming Dynasty, covering China's contact with East and North Africa and through the sea route. Na Zhong graduated from the University of Alazhar in Egypt in the 1940s. The first chapter of his book is on ancient history, while the rest deals with the period from Napoleon's invasion to the nationalist movement in Egypt after World War II. Besides these two works, a general introduction to the individual countries, colonies and areas of Africa was also published (Anonymous 1957).

Chinese African studies of this period were largely pragmatic and politically motivated rather than purely academic. China strongly supported the national liberation movements and wanted to win new friends in African nations.[19] History departments at universities took the lead primarily because both anthropology and political science were regarded as "capitalist" in China at the time. Studies were generally carried out collectively, and they concentrated on national independence movements or the anti-colonial struggle.[20]

Understanding Africa (1966–1976)

During the Cultural Revolution (1966–1976), China suffered a setback in intellectual life. Universities closed for several years and later enrolled students according to their "political performance". There were few studies of foreign issues. All cultural life, including drama, film and ballet, was motivated or controlled by political need and used for political purposes. Higher education was used "to consolidate the proletarian dictatorship". The study of the social sciences and humanities was almost stopped except for the indoctrination of Marxist-Leninist-Maoist thought.

Interestingly enough, however, African studies continued to be pursued in China. The International Liaison Department of the Central Committee of the CPC had its own section to study the situation in Africa and provide support to African liberation movements, and various studies of the Institute of Asian–African Studies contributed a great deal to decision-making at the central level. Nevertheless, the institute concentrated more on information collection or data analysis than on academic research.

The year 1971 witnessed two important events that indicated China was ending its political isolation and returning to the international community: the beginning of the normalisation of China–American relations marked by Henry Kissinger's secret mission to China, and the entry of the PRC to the United Nations. In view of its extended neglect of cultural issues, the Central Committee of the CPC realized the serious problems that existed in academic fields. A nationwide meeting of publishing companies was held in 1971, organized by the State Council, which decided to publish some important books of history, such as 24 classic histories and the history of Republican China.

In order for leaders at different levels to understand foreign affairs, histories, general surveys and works on the geography of different countries were chosen for translation. This huge project covered almost all the countries of the world and carried on right into the 1980s. Histories of different areas of Africa were translated, as well as histories of individual countries (including Ethiopia, Somalia, Sudan, Uganda, Tanzania, Central Africa, Nigeria, Niger, Sierra Leone, Ghana, Gambia, Dahomey, Togo, Congo, Liberia, Mauritania, Morocco, Tunisia, Mauritius and Malawi) and general surveys (of South-West Africa, Lesotho, Botswana, Swaziland, Zambia, Djibouti, Horn of

Africa, Republic of Central Africa, Rwanda, Burundi, Mali, Upper Volta, Angola, Zimbabwe, Libya, and Congo). Works by African scholars that were chosen for translation included *The independent Sudan: The history of a nation* (Shibeika 1959), *A history of Tanzania* (Kimambo & Temu 1969), *South-West Africa* (First 1963) and *Rhodesia: Background to conflict* (Mtshali 1967). Some are classics in African studies, such as *Old Africa rediscovered* (Davidson 1960) and *An introduction to the history of West Africa* (Fage 1969). Others were chosen for their documents and archival material, including *A history of Sierra Leone* (Fyfe 1962) and Cornevin's *Histoire du Togo* (1959), *Histoire du Dahomey* (1962) and *Histoire du Congo* (1970). Many works by Soviet scholars were also translated, including two important general histories of Africa compiled by the Institute of African Studies, and the Soviet Union Academy of Sciences, and a four-volume *History of Black Africa* (Sik 1966), written by a Hungarian historian.

Since the original purpose of the State Council project was not academic, the translations were originally intended for circulation within government cells only. With China's general opening up, however, it was inevitable that all the books would be sold publicly. As a carry-over from the Cultural Revolution, every translation had a preface written by the translator that was critical of the content from a political perspective, a measure that was intended not only to protect the translator but also to warn the reader. In addition, translations were generally done by a group rather than by an individual, so in case anything went wrong the responsibility would be taken collectively.[21] Most of the books were chosen neither for their content nor their academic quality, but rather for their titles. In every case, they were general histories rather than monographs, and their quality was uneven. Some had no academic value whatsoever because those who chose them had little knowledge of Africa or of African studies abroad, and libraries in China had few books on Africa that could serve as models.

Nevertheless, the importance of these translations should not be underestimated. According to the statistics, in the period 1967–1978, 117 books on Africa were published; 111 were translations, five were popular readers and one was a reference book. In other words, 95 per cent were translated from other languages (Zhang Yuxi 1997: 272–273). Although their quality varied, Chinese students at least began to acquire some knowledge about a continent far from China and to come across the names of some leading scholars in the field. They gradually became familiar with the topics, interests and trends in African studies, and this laid the foundation for later studies after the Cultural Revolution.

Studying Africa (1977–2000)

After the smashing of the Gang of Four, university teaching and research resumed in China.[22] The period from 1977 to 2000 was rather productive for African studies in universities, other academic institutions and institutions attached to ministries of government. Two nationwide organizations were also founded: the Chinese Association of African Studies (in 1979) and the Chinese Society of African Historical Studies (in 1980). While the former concentrates on the study of current issues, the latter focuses on African history; there is a lot of overlap between the two associations, with membership open to everyone interested in the fields. With the coordination of the two associations, African studies in China has made great progress. The Institute of West Asian and African Studies of CASS set up a Centre for South African Studies in 1996, and in 1998 the Institute of Afro-Asian Studies at Peking University established a Center for African Studies. Also in 1998, Xiangtan University in Hunan set up a Centre for African Law Studies (Hong Yonghong & Xia Xinghua 2000). The Department of Geography at Nanjing University has a research group that specializes in African economic geography; Yunnan University has a group specializing in African studies; and Zhejiang Normal University has established a Centre for the Study of African Education.

From the end of the 1970s, articles in academic journals generally have covered four topics: (1) the resistance movements during the colonial period, such as the Mahdi movement in Sudan, the Ethiopian war against Italian invasion, the Maji Maji Uprising in Tanganyika and the Mau Mau in Kenya (Pen Kunyuan et al. 1978; Jiang Xuecheng 1979; Mao Tianyou 1979; Luo Hongzhang 1979; Chen Gongyuan 1980; Lu Ting-en 1981b; Ding Bangying 1981); (2) African nationalist movements since World War I, such as the Pan-African movement; (3) nationalist movements in general (Li Qingyu 1979; Hu You'e 1980; Zhu Gang 1981; Tang Dadun 1981) or in particular countries (Tang Tongming & Xiang Qun 1979; Zhaojianping 1980; Wang Shaokui 1981; Tang Tongming 1981a, 1981b, 1983; Qin Xiaoying 1981); and (4) important figures, either the first generation of nationalists (Houphouet-Boigny, Nkrumah, Gnassingbe Eyadema, Robert Mugabe, Kenneth David Kaunda, Quett K.J. Masire, Leopold Sedar Senghor, Omar Mouammar Gaddafi, Ahmed Sukou Toure, Habbib Bourguiba) or influential figures who contributed to the liberation movement in Africa, such as Garvey, Du Bois, Padmore and Fanon. This list expanded in the 1980s and later.

In 1981, the first graduate student in African studies since the Cultural Revolution was enrolled in the graduate school of CASS, followed in later

Table 2.1 Publications of African studies in China until 1994

	Monograph	Translation	Popular Reader	Total
Before 1949		14	5	19
1949–1966	10	60	35	111
1967–1977		111	5	117
1979–1994	41	68	48	166

years by increased enrolment at Peking University.[23] During the 1980s, Chinese scholars began to turn their interests to specific topics. Lu Ting-en used archival data to show David Livingston's contradictory roles in the exploration of Africa, as a fighter against the slave trade and as a tool of colonial expansion (Lu Ting-en 1981a). Wu Bingzhen, Xu Jiming and others studied the slave trade, especially its links to the early capitalist development in Africa (Wu Bingzhen 1983a, 1984a, 1984b; Xu Jiming 1983a, 1983b; Lijidong 1983; Luojianguo 1984). Using Kenya as an example, Qin Xiaoying touched on the politically sensitive subject of the national bourgeoisie's positive role in the anticolonialism struggle, a topic also explored by Wang Chunliang in his study of the nationalist movement in Zaire (Qin Xiaoying 1980; Wang Chunliang 1981). There are studies on the formation, characteristics and role of modern intellectuals in West Africa (Li Anshan 1985, 1986).

In 1982, the Chinese Society of African Historical Studies published an important collection of papers (Chinese Society of African Historical Studies 1982). He Fangchuan's paper studied the politics, economy and culture of the ancient Aksum Kingdom. Zheng Jiaxing probed the early period of South Africa's socio-economic structure. Gu Zhangyi explored the origin and development of the African nations. Nin Sao discussed the issue of the "Hamitic hypothesis," argued that the African people were the creators of African civilization, and criticized the racist connotations of the hypothesis. Lu Ting-en probed the periodization of modern African history. Ai Zhouchang studied several important issues such as the origin of the Portuguese invasion of Africa, the slave trade, and the occupation of Africa. Qin Xiaoying studied the role of reform in the independence movements in Africa.

Several important books or monographs also were published in the 1980s, such as *A concise history of Africa* (Yang Renpian 1984), *A general history of Africa* (Chinese Society of African Historical Studies 1984), *Africa and imperialism* (Lu Ting-en 1986), *Study on the strategy of economic development in Africa south of Sahara* (Chen Zhongde & Wu Zhaoji 1987), *African socialism: History, theory and practice* (Tang Dadun 1988) and *Origin of the disturbance in Southern Africa* (Ge Jie 1989). Histories of individual countries were also published, such as *A modern history of Egypt* (Yang Haocheng 1985), *Concise history of Niger* (Xun Xingqiang 1983) and *Concise history of Zaire* (Zhao Shuhui 1981). Chen Gongyuan studied the history of the contact between China and Africa (Chen Gongyuan 1985). There were two important books on African geography (Su Shirong et al. 1984; Zeng Zungu et al. 1984), both published by scholars from the Department of Geography, Nanjing University. *Atlas of Africa* (Fei Zhi 1985), the largest of all the atlases printed in China, includes a comprehensive picture of Africa, its history, ethnic groups, economy and geography. Overall, Chinese scholars in the 1980s began to produce more systematic studies of the African anticolonial struggle as well as articles touching on related issues such as nationalist ideology, anticolonial religious movements, ethnic problems, economy and development, culture, and international relations. There was also an increased interest in African arts (Zhang Rongsheng 1986, 1988; Li Miao 1988), literature (Gao Changrong 1983; 1983a) and music (Nketia 1962).

In addition, the translation of important works continued. The authoritative work on African borders written by the former Secretary-General of the United Nations, Boutros-Ghali (1979), was translated, as was the important *Sundiata* (1983). Seligman's *Races of Africa* (1930) had been translated in 1966 by his student Fei Xiaotong, a famous Chinese sociologist. Owing to the Cultural Revolution, it was not published until 1982.[24] Among the translations were books on the slave trade, including one by a Soviet scholar, Abromova. Basil Davidson's book and biographies and autobiographies were also translated. Another large project was the translation of UNESCO's now completed eight-volume *General history of Africa*; in 1984, volumes 1 and 2 were published, with the rest appearing in the following years (UNESCO, 1979).

Overview of Africa, a comprehensive introduction to African countries, was published in 1981, covering topics in geography, history, ethnic groups, political systems, economic developments and China–African relations. Fang Jigen's work (1986) anthologises reports, articles and chapters of monographs about Chinese in Africa. *Contemporary African celebrities* (1987) profiles more than 1000 important figures. Several bibliographies were compiled and printed with the help of the Chinese Society of African Historical Studies (Chinese Society of African Historical Studies 1982; Zhang Yuxi 1990, 1997). During the period 1982–1989, 105 articles were published in China that were concerned with African studies in other parts of the world (Zhang Yuxi 1990:131–141) and several books on African nationalities were translated or compiled (Ge Gongshang & Chao Feng 1980, 1982, 1984; Ge Gongshang & Li Yifu 1981; Ge Gongshang & Song Limei 1987). Although the latter were not formally published, they contributed a great deal to African studies in China.

During the 1990s, the volume of publications on African studies in China increased enormously. East China Normal University Press published six monographs in its African Studies Series (Shu Yunguo 1996; Ai Zhouchang & Mu Tao 1996; Luo Jian-guo 1996; Xia Jisheng 1996; Lu Ting-en & Liu Jing 1997; Liu Hongwu 1997). Three compilations of historical materials (Ai Zhouchang 1989; Pan Guang & Zhu Weilie 1992; Tang Dadun 1995), including *Selection of materials on China–African relations* (Ai Zhouchang 1989), were the best, with travel notes, contemporary newspaper articles, letters and reminiscences. Other series included works relevant to African studies. For example, the *Study of British Commonwealth* series includes South Africa, Nigeria and Ghana (Chen Zhongdan 2000). In the *Series of the history of colonialism*, the volume on Africa deals with the origin, development and decline of colonialism in Africa (Zheng Jiaxing 2000).

A general history of Africa was published in 1995 as a collective work by the Chinese Society of African Historical Studies. Divided into three volumes, it covers the ancient, modern and contemporary history of Africa

(He Fangchuan & Nin Sao 1996; Ai Zhouchang & Zheng Jiaxing 1996; Lu Ting-en & Peng Kunyuan 1996) and summarizes recent scholarly work on Africa (Li Anshan 1996b). *A concise history of African national independence* (Wu Bingzheng & Gao Jinyuan 1993) was the first systematic study of the nationalist movements in Africa. Li Anshan's (2002) *British rule and rural protest in southern Ghana*, based on research carried out in the Public Records Office in London and the Ghanaian National Archives in Accra, argues that colonialism was a situation of paradox in which protest played an important role, and in most cases caused changes in colonial policy. Based on his PhD dissertation at the University of Toronto, the Chinese versions was published (Li Anshan 1998a).

During the 1990s, African studies in China focused on several subjects, such as socialism, ethnic issues, international relations, South Africa, cultural studies, economic studies and China–African relations. One of the most extensive debates, which continues to this day, concerned the process of African democratization and the future, if any, of African socialism. There are two major views on the wave of democracy in Africa. One considers the internal demand for a more democratic society as the major impetus for the process (Xu Jiming & Tan Shizhong 1999; Zhang Hongming 1999), with disturbances during or after democratization understood as either the natural consequence of longtime oppression and bad governance or as new conflicts generated by the process itself. The other perspective sees democratization in Africa as the result of both the decline of the Soviet bloc and pressure from Western countries. According to this view, most disturbances have come about because of a mismatch between Western systems of democracy and African reality (Cui Qinglian 1995; Lu Ting-en 1995). On the subject of African socialism, a collective project begun in 1989, *New analysis of African socialism* (Tang Dadung et al. 1994), has involved 16 scholars from different universities and institutions. The book discusses the origins, development and typology of African socialism, analyses different types of socialism and compares socialism and capitalism in Africa. The authors argue that African socialism contributed a great deal to the consolidation of national independence, the building of national culture and the control of national economies; and that it also raised the status of African countries in the world political arena. However, socialism in Africa has not been successful, with the decline of the movement attributable to several causes: internal factors (the forces of production, internal policies), the decline of the socialist bloc of Soviet and Eastern Europe, and pressure from Western countries. According to the authors, the rise of democratic socialism in Africa is inevitable.

Chinese Africanists have also been paying a great deal of attention to issues of ethnicity in Africa. One particularly heated debate among Chinese scholars involves the use of the terms "tribe" and "tribalism" (Wu Zengtian 1996; Li Anshan 1998b). Some think that "tribe" is an appropriate term and a useful concept (Nin Sao 1983; Ge Gongshang 1994; Zhang Hongming 1995), while others consider it derogatory and prefer to think in terms of "local nationalism" (Gu Zhangyi 1997; Yuan Xihu 1998; Li Anshan 1998b). Although opinions differ on this question, most Chinese scholars agree that ethnic conflict has been the greatest obstacle to nation-building in Africa. Li Jidong (1997), Zhang Hongming (1999) and Xu Jiming (Xu Jiming & Tan Shizhong 1999) argue that it has challenged the legitimacy of the nation-state and threatened its political stability and unity.

In the field of international relations, Liang Gencheng's work is perhaps the most impressive. Divided into eight chapters chronologically, his *United States and Africa* (Liang Gencheng 1991) explores American policy on Africa from World War II until the 1980s. From 1990 to 1996, more than a dozen articles were written by Chinese scholars on the subject of French policy on Africa. In recent years, the ongoing "African renaissance" has come to be of intense interest to Chinese scholars, as have developments in South Africa, especially after the normalization of China–South African diplomatic relations (see Yang Lihua et al. 1994; Ge Jie 1994; Chen Yifei 1994; Zhu Chonggui et al. 1994; Xia Jisheng 1996; Xia Jisheng et al. 1998; Zhang Xiang 1998; Ai Zhouchang et al. 2000). Even before the normalization of relations, both sides had set up research centres in the other's capital, which played semi-diplomatic roles but also promoted academic exchanges between China and South Africa.[25] Biographies and autobiographies of Nelson Mandela and Winnie Mandela have been written or translated by Chinese scholars (Yang Lihua 1995; Wen Xian 1995). In June 1996, the Institute of West Asian and African Studies of CASS held an international seminar, "Prospects of political and economic development in South Africa", sponsored by the Ford Foundation.

The last of a series of seminars organized by the China–US African Studies Exchange Program, this also served as a celebration and summary of the 15 years of Ford Foundation-sponsored cooperation between Chinese and American African studies research institutions. The seminar had a special significance since it was held after President Jiang Zemin's first visit to Africa and before the normalization of China–South African diplomatic relations. The papers focused on three topics: South Africa's political transition and its prospects; South Africa's reconstruction and development; and foreign affairs in the New South Africa. Another symposium titled "Africa Beyond 2000" was held in 1998 (Institute of West Asian and African Studies, CASS 1998).

Nin Sao is the first Chinese scholar to have written on African cultural life. His book is a study of social norms and festivals, worship and religion, technology and ideology, and the pursuit of beauty in art, literature and the performing arts (Nin Sao 1993). Li Baoping and Liu Hongwu have written works analyzing the links between tradition and modernity from a historical perspective (Li Baoping 1993, 1997; Liu Hongwu 1997). As a part of the Series of World Civilizations, Ai Zhouchang's work covers a wide range of topics. Part 1, "Formation of Black African civilization", studies different cultures such as the Upper Nile (Nubia, Rush, Aksum), iron culture in West Africa, Bantu migration, Islam, and Swahili and Hausa cultures. Part 2,

"Manifestations of Black African civilization", looks at different forms and expressions of African civilization, including arts and literature, religion and customs, and ideologies and technology. Part 3, "Black African civilization to the future", links Africa with the outside world and considers the connections and conflicts between tradition and modernity (Ai Zhouchang 1999).

Feng Jianwei's work is unique because the author, as a news reporter, went to the African interior for his study. He spent a half a year travelling to four West African countries and visited 150 towns, villages and schools. He explored social organization, economic patterns, class structure, political systems and historical stages. Opposing the negative view among Chinese scholars regarding the cash crop system, he argued that the system had some positive aspects (Feng Jianwei 1994).

The study of modernization has been popular in China since the late 1980s. Li Jidong's book analyzes the causes of the delayed modernisation in Africa and considers bad government and tribalism as significant negative factors (Li Jidong 1997). He Li-er's (1995). work on Zimbabwe was the first study of this newly independent country. Chinese scholars have also produced works on the African economy, including a book on the market economy (Yang Dezhen & Su Zeyu 1994; Chen Muo 1995) and one on the relationship between reform and economic or structural adjustment (Tan Shizhong 1998). For the Forum on China–Africa Cooperation Ministerial Conference held in Beijing in 2000, the Ministry of Agriculture organized scholars to compile the four-volume *Series of investment guides for the development of African agriculture* (Lu Ting-en 2000; Wen Yunchao 2000; He Xiurong, Wang Xiuqing & Li Ping 2000; Chen Zhongde, Yao Guimei & Fan Yushu 2000).

On the subject of China–Africa relations, one of the two collections published by the Centre for African Studies of Peking University (2000) considers the history of China–Africa relations from ancient times to the present. Until recently, most scholars believed that relations between China and Egypt had a long history but China's contact with sub-Saharan Africa started much later. This misconception is now being corrected by works such as the above and by the scholarship of Shen Fuwei, who argues that direct contact between China and sub-Saharan Africa actually began in the Han Dynasty (206 BCE–220 CE) when, in addition to various commercial activities between both sides, the first emissary from Black Africa to China was sent from Adulis, a port city in Ethiopia (in present-day Eritrea), arriving at Luoyang in 100 CE. Ethiopia thus became the first African country to establish diplomatic relations with China (Sheng Fuwei 1990). Ai Zhouchang and Mu Tao also argue that as early as 200 BCE–600 CE, China–Africa relations existed in the form of the Silk Road (Ai Zhouchang & Mu Tao 1996). Another commonly held notion is that China–African relations were cut off from the mid-1400s until the 1950s, and thus were interrupted for 500 years (Hutchison 1975:2). Ai Zhouchang criticises this view and shows that the relationship between China and Africa continued during this period, supported by data in Chinese (Ai Zhouchang 1989).

On the subject of the Chinese in Africa, three books have been published. As early as 1984, Chen Hansheng published data from government archives, documents, letters and various original materials concerning Chinese labourers in Africa, mainly in South Africa (*Chinese labor in Africa,* part of the *Compilation of data of Chinese labor abroad,* 1984). Fang Jigen also compiled material on the Chinese in Africa, most of it translations of secondary sources (Fang Jigen, 1986). Another work on the subject, *A history of Chinese overseas in Africa* (Li Anshan 2000) looks at the origin, adaptation and integration of the Chinese in Africa.

Three reference books are important, all compiled by the Institute of West Asian and Studies, CASS. The *Yellow Book of the international situation: The report of the development of the Middle East and Africa* (Zhao Guozhong et al. 1998–2001), published annually since 1998, provides regular updates on the political, economic, and diplomatic situation in Africa. The publication of the *Concise encyclopedia of Sub-Saharan Africa* (Ge Jie 2000) and that of the *Concise encyclopedia of West Asia and North Africa* (Zhao Guozhong 2000) were also important achievements in China. Most of the authors are experts on their subjects and the materials are relatively new. In addition, various introductions of foreign research institutions were published.

Conclusion

The achievements of African studies in China during the 20th century were quite impressive, and the contributions continue into the 21st century. The Chinese academy's attitude to Africa is more sympathetic than it is towards many other places, perhaps because of political and cultural similarities between the two (the experiences of colonialism and imperialism, the emphasis on collectivism and their status as the cradles of civilisation). The field of African studies in China has gradually moved away from its original political orientation to become a wide-ranging academic discipline, suggesting that Chinese scholars will make even more contributions in the future. The numbers of PhD theses have increased steadily since the late 1990s (Oh Il-hwan 1998; Wang Suolao 2000; Sun Hongqi 2000; Liu Naiya 2000; Liu Lan 2001), and both new and established scholars are working in the fields of history, geography, economics, literature, ethnic studies, cultural studies and others. At the same time, there continues to be a balance in Chinese academia between practical work and academic research, since the government needs information, analysis and assessment, while academia needs funding, stimulus and feedback.[26] Academic exchanges are going on between China and the world, gradually bringing China into international academia. With the opening up of China and increasing contact between Chinese individuals (or companies) and African people, Africa is no longer a mystery to the Chinese. In a globalized world, there is an increasing need to know about Africa, and this will certainly stimulate African studies in China.

Nevertheless, problems do exist. African studies are concentrated in big cities, especially Beijing and Shanghai. As this review of the literature indicates, few original studies have been done. Most of the books written by Chinese scholars are based on secondary materials from English sources. Few scholars have been to Africa to teach or conduct research. Not a single anthropologist has been to Africa specifically for study, and thus no serious ethnographic study of African people, or any study on the oral tradition, has been produced. Chinese archaeologists so far have been preoccupied with the ruins and relics in China, not with archaeological exploration or research in Africa. No African language is studied in China except for training purposes.[27] Neither the Chinese Association of African Studies nor the Chinese Society of African Historical Studies has its own journal, although *Xiya Feizhou* (*West Asia and Africa*) has made a great contribution to African studies.[28] There was an internally circulated journal of the Chinese Society of African Historical Studies, but it was irregular and short-lived. The studies are still too general, with few focusing on countries (although a series of country studies has recently started in CASS) or case studies. There are very few exchanges between China and the rest of the world, and while some progress is being made, it has not been enough. Moreover, Chinese scholars seldom have their research published in the English-speaking world.

African studies in China is a promising field, but there is room for more effort, hard work and collaboration.

Notes

1 The chapter was originally published in *African Studies Review*, 48(1): 9–78 (April 2005), entitled "African studies in China in the 20th century: A historiographical survey", and I am grateful for the journal's generous permission. I would like to thank Richard Robertson and Paul Tiyambe Zeleza respectively for inviting me to give a lecture on this subject at the Center for African Studies at Stanford University and the Center for African Studies at the University of Illinois at Urbana-Champaign respectively, which made me think about writing this survey. I also thank George Yu of the University of Illinois at Urbana-Champaign, George Brooks of Indiana University, Zhang Xiang of Nankai University in China, and Wu Yu-gui of the Chinese Academy of Social Sciences for providing me with information, and four anonymous reviewers who provided me with critical and valuable comments on an earlier version of this essay.
2 In 1983, the Ford Foundation provided funding for a Chinese delegation of Africanists to visit the United States. In 1985, it funded the US–China African Studies Exchange Committee, chaired by George Yu in the United States and Ge Jie in China. In 1986, at the suggestion of George Brooks in his report on African teaching and research in Asian countries, the African Studies Association invited Zhang Xiang of Nankai University in China, together with Hideo Yamada from Japan and Professor Har from South Korea, to attend the ASA annual meeting and visit African studies programs in the United States.

44 *Encounter and research*

3 So far, few Chinese Africanists have published formal articles or books in English in the West (Gao Jinyuan 1983; He Fanchuan 1987; Ge Jie 1997; Li Anshan 1994, 1995, 1996a, 2002). Zhang Hongming, a senior researcher at the Institute of West Asian and African Studies, CASS, has published articles in French journals. At Peking University, I met delegations from Great Britain (1996) and France (1997), and some American scholars. They all wanted to know about African studies in China.
4 In 1993, Austrian archaeologists found a piece of natural silk in a female mummy of the 21st Dynasty of Egypt (1070–945 BCE); only China could produce natural silk at that time. See previous chapter. For a detailed study of the contact between China and Egypt, see Sun Yutang (1979).
5 Du Huan was captured in the battle of Talas (751 CE) by the Arab army. He returned to China by sea after about ten years. In his work, he mentions a place in which Black people live called "Molin". Opinions differ as to the present location of Molin, with various scholars suggesting Maghrib, Malindi, Mendi, Meroe, Aksum and others (Li Anshan 2000: 49–50).
6 Ibn Battuta went to China in 1346 and made notes on various aspects of life there, such as its architecture, customs and habits, economic life and currency system, transportation, local products, legal system and politics, especially the political struggle within the court in Beijing (Ibn Battuta 1929: 282–300).
7 From 1405 to 1433, a Chinese eunuch-official named Zheng He led seven fleets across Southeast Asia and the Indian Ocean, and landed several times on the East African coast. Three people from the expeditions left accounts that mention places in East Africa (Li Anshan 2000: 65–75); two of them, Ma Huan (1955) and Fei Xin (1954 [1436]), describe places in detail.
8 See *Cultural Relics* (文物) 1979, 2:88. For the ancient records, see Du Huan (CE 762[?]); Duan Chengshi (850 CE); Ma Huan (1433); Fei Xin (1436); Ibn Battuta (1929). For studies of China–African relations in English, see Duyvendak (1947); Filesi (1972); Snow (1988). For studies by Chinese scholars, see Cen Zhongmian (1935); Zhang Xinglang (1940); Zhang Tiesheng (1963); Zhang Junyan (1986); Ma Wenkuan & Meng Fanren (1987); Shen Fuwei (1990); Ai Zhouchang & Mu Tao (1996); Li Anshan (2000).
9 Fan Shou-yi (1682–1753), a Chinese official who accompanied a missionary to Italy, passed the Cape coast and left some notes; he was probably the first free Chinese to visit Africa. Some Chinese in Southeast Asia were sent into exile in South Africa by Dutch colonists as early as the 1700s and early 1800s (Yap & Leong Man 1996; Li Anshan 2000).
10 It may be surprising to note that Zhu Siben, a Chinese scholar of the Yuan Dynasty, drew a map of Africa in 1311–1320 that showed a clearer understanding of the shape of the African continent than scholars in other parts of the world had (Needham 1959).
11 It mentioned places such as the Niger River, Lake Chad, Dahomey, Tukolor, Zaria, Sokoto, Accra, Lagos, Ouidah and Cabinda, and people such as Uthman dan Fodia, Ahmadu Bari and Mowlay Ahmad al-Mansur.
12 The first edition comprised 50 volumes, and the edition of 1852 increased to 100 volumes. Ironically, the Japanese government made great use of this book, but it was neglected by the Chinese imperial court.
13 Chen Tianhua (1875–1905), an early democratic revolutionary, went to Japan to study and organized anti-Qing activities there. He wrote several influential

African studies in China–20th century 45

books. In 1905 he founded *Tongmen Hui* (the United League of China) and later committed suicide in order to protest the Japanese policy on Chinese students. Liang Qichao (1873–1929), an early reformist, was exiled to Japan after the conservative coup of 1898. He used his writing to raise support for the reformers' cause among the overseas Chinese and foreign governments. Sun Yat-sen (1866–1925), the father of the Chinese republican revolution, led the anti-Qing activities and became the leader of *Tongmen Hui* and later *Guomindang* (the Nationalist Party).

14 In the late 1950s, the Department of History at Nankai University published several articles on the national independent movements in Tunisia, Morocco, Libya, and Algeria in *Lishi Jiaoxue (Teaching history)*. The Department of History at South China Normal University published articles on Congo and Cameroon in *Zhongxue Lishi Jiaoxue (Teaching history in middle school)*.

15 The group he was addressing included leaders of political parties and members of delegations from Guinea, Jordan, South Africa, Senegal, Northern Rhodesia, Uganda, and Kenya. Chairman Mao Zedong met them at Hangzhou. For the names of the participants, see Mao Zedong (1996: 478, n.1).

16 Renmin University of China in Beijing was chosen for the study of socialist countries, while Fudan University in Shanghai was chosen for the study of capitalist countries.

17 Their activities were recorded in the two journals mentioned above. See, for example, articles in *Yafei Yicong* on international Africanist conferences (1963, nos. 2, 3, & 4) and on Africanist conferences in the United States (1963, no. 3; 1965, no. 3; 1965, no. 5), Spain (1963, no. 7), Italy (1963, no. 8), India (1963, no. 9), Scotland (1964, no. 2), Japan (1964, no. 4), France (1964, no. 11), Holland (1964, no. 12), England (1965, no. 8), West Germany (1963, no. 4), and the Soviet Union (1963, no. 6).

18 About 60 books were translated during this period; 29 were from the Soviet Union and Eastern European countries. In other words, almost half were translated from Russian or related languages (Zhang Yuxi 1997: 260).

19 The relationship between China and Africa during the 1960s is a very important topic. Besides the works mentioned, former Minister of Foreign Affairs Qian Qichen has published a memoir that includes an entire chapter on Africa (Qian Qichen 2003: 243–287).

20 In 1965, the Institute of Asian-African Studies (later the Institute of West Asian and African Studies, CASS) decided that study should be concentrated in five fields: the development and characteristics of contemporary national liberation movements; the contemporary socio-economic situation, with a focus on the structure of social classes; the bourgeois ideology of nationalism; the revisionists' incorrect views on national liberation movements; and the policies of imperialist countries on national liberation movements.

21 Examples are the Shandong University Translation Group and the Shanghai Foreign Language School Translation Group.

22 The so-called "Gang of Four" was a political clique during the Cultural Revolution composed of Jiang Qing, Wang Hongwen, Zhang Chunqiao, and Yao Wenyuan. They were regarded as ultra-leftists and were very unpopular in China. Their downfall represented the end of the Cultural Revolution.

23 The author was the first graduate student in African history after the Cultural Revolution.

24 The translator Fei Xiaotong is a 1930s graduate of the London School of Economics and is now a famous sociologist at Peking University. He regarded this work as a "standard reader", which shows how poorly Chinese at the time understood international scholarship in African studies owing to their long academic isolation.
25 For example, Ken Smith, the chair of the Department of History at Unisa, visited Peking University at the invitation of Leslie Labuschagne, the Director of the South African Centre for Chinese Studies in Beijing at the time.
26 In October 1997, the Chinese Society of African Historical Studies held its conference in Beidaihe. Li Anshan and Liu Hongwu were asked by the society to draft a letter to President Jiang Zemin emphasizing the importance of African studies, which was signed by ten professors. President Jiang commented on the issue, "In recent years, I have stressed many times that the work on Africa should be taken very seriously. This issue should be paid great attention to, not only in politics, but also in the development of economic cooperation. The Central Committee and the related units of the State Council should all support this work" (Chen Gongyuan 2000: 244).
27 Hausa and Swahili are taught in two universities in Beijing, mainly for training personnel for the Xinhua News Agency and other media.
28 *West Asia and Africa* (*Xiya Feizhou*) is a journal run by the Institute of West Asian and African Studies, CASS. Started in 1980 and internally circulated, it was published openly in 1981 in China and became available to readers both at home and abroad in August 1982. *West Asia and Africa* has since served as the major academic journal for African studies in China.

References

Абрамова, С.Ю. 1978. Африка : четыре столетия работорговли, Москва: издательство <НАУКА>.
Ai Zhouchang, ed. 1989. *Selection of materials on China–African Relations*, Shanghai: East Normal University Press.
Ai Zhouchang, ed. 1999. *Black African civilizations*. Beijing: China Social Sciences Press.
Ai Zhouchang et al. 2000. *A study on modernization in South Africa*. Shanghai: East China Normal University Press.
Ai Zhouchang & Mu Tao. 1996. *A history of China–African Relations*. Shanghai: East China Normal University Press.
Ai Zhouchang & Zheng Jiaxing. 1996. *A history of Africa, volume of modern time*. Shanghai: East China Normal University Press.
Anonymous. 1957. *History of countries of Africa*. Beijing: World Affairs Press.
Boutros-Ghali, Boutros. 1972. *Les Conglits de Frontieres en Afrique*. Paris: Edition Technique et Economique.
Brose, M.C. 2002. Book review: *A History of Chinese overseas in Africa*. *Canadian Journal of African Studies* 36(1): 157–159.
Burns, Sir A. 1963. *History of Nigeria*, London: George Allen and Unwin.
Cen Zhongmian. 1945. Chinese sea route in Tang Dynasty: from Persian Gulf to East Africa. *The Eastern Miscellany* 41(18): 46–51
Center for African Studies of Peking University, ed. 2000. *China and Africa*. Beijing: Peking University Press.

Chen Gongyuan. 1980. Mahdi uprising in Sudanese history. *Bulletin for Teaching* 12: 9.
Chen Gongyuan. 1985. *Friendly contact between Africa and China in ancient times.* Beijing: Commercial Press.
Chen Gongyuan ed. 2000. *Strategic report for the development of China–African relations in the 21st Century: Special collection of the 20th anniversary of the Chinese Association of African Studies.* Beijing: Chinese Association of African Studies.
Chen Hansheng, ed. 1984. *Compilation of data of Chinese labor abroad. Vol. 9: Chinese labor in Africa.* Beijing: Zhonghua Book Company.
Chen Li, ed. 1959. *Cameroon people's Anti-colonialist struggle.* Shijiazhuang: Hebei People's Publishing House.
Chen Mo. 1995. *African market organization,* Beijing: Chinese Encyclopedia Publishing House.
Chen Yifei, ed. 1994. *Explore the market in South Africa: Environment and opportunity.* Beijing: China Social Sciences Press.
Chen Zhongdan. 2000. *Ghana: Looking for a base for modernization,* Chengdu: Sichuan People's Publishing House.
Chen Zhongde and Wu Zhaoji. 1987. *Study on the strategy of economic development in Africa south of Sahara.* Beijing: Peking University Press.
Chen Zhongde, Yao Guimei and Fan Zhishu, ed. 2000. *Generalization of agriculture development in African nations, Vol. 2.* Beijing: Chinese Financial Economic Press.
Chinese Society of African Historical Studies. 1982. *Collection of papers on African history.* Beijing: Joint Publishing.
Chinese Society of African Historical Studies. 1984. *A general history of Africa.* Beijing: Beijing Normal University Press.
Cornevin, R. 1959. *Histoire du Togo.* Paris: Edition Berger-Levrault.
Cornevin, R. 1962. *Histoire du Dahomey.* Paris: Editions Berger-Levrault.
Cornevin, R. 1970. *Histoire du Congo Leopoldville-Kinshassa,* Paris: Editions Berger-Levrault.
Cui Qinglian. 1995. Multi-party democratic model of the West does not fit the reality of Black Africa. *West Asia and Africa* 1: 44.
Davidson, B. 1955. *The African Awakening.* London: Jonathan Cape.
Davidson, B. 1960. *Old Africa Rediscovered.* London: Victor Gollancz.
Davidson, B. 1961. *Black mother: The years of the African slave trade.* London: Victor Gollancz.
De Bary, W.T., Chan Wing-Tsit & Tan, Chester, comp., 1960. *Sources of Chinese tradition, Vol. 2.* New York: Columbia University Press.
Diop, Majhemout. 1958. *Contribution à l'étude des Problèm Politiques en Afrique Noire.* Paris:Presence Africaine.
Ding Bangying. 1981. Maji Maji Uprising. *West Asia and Africa* 3: 60–61.
Du Bois, W.E.B. 1961. *Africa: An essay towards a history of the continent.* Moscow: n.p.
Du Huan. 762[?]. Record of My Travels, preserved in Du You, *Tong Dian* (Encyclopedia), A.D. 812.
Duan Chengshi. 850. *Assorted dishes from Yuyang,* A.D. 850.
Duyvendak, J.J.L. 1947. *China's discovery of Africa,* Hertford: Stephen Austin and Sons.
Fage J.D. 1969. *A history of West Africa: An introductory survey.* London: Cambridge University Press.
Fan Yong, ed. 1957. *The national independent movement in Morocco, Tunisia and Algeria.* Shanghai: Shanghai People's Publishing House.

Fang Jigen. 1986. *Selection of Data of the History of Overseas Chinese in Africa*. Beijing: Xinhua Press.
Fei Xin. 1954 [1436]. *Triumphant tour of the Star Raft*. Annotated by Feng Chengjun. Beijing: Zhonghua Book Company.
Fei Zhi. 1985. *Atlas of Africa*, Beijing: Atlas Press.
Feng Jianwei. 1994. *Notes on the exploration of River Niger Area*. Beijing: Beijing Language College Press.
Filesi, T. 1972. *China and Africa in the Middle Ages*. Trans. David L. Morison. London: Frank Cass.
First, Ruth. 1963. *South west Africa*. Harmondsworth: Penguin.
Fitzgerald, Walter. 1955. *Africa: A social, economic and political geography of its major regions*. London: Methuen.
Fyfe, Christopher. 1962. *A history of Sierra Leone*. London: Oxford University Press.
Gao Changrong. 1983. *Selection of dramas in Africa*. Beijing: Foreign Literature Publishing Company.
Gao Changrong. 1983a. *Selection of novels in contemporary Africa*. Beijing: Foreign Literature Publishing Company.
Gao, James. 2001. Book review: *A history of Chinese overseas in Africa*. *African Studies Review* 44(1): 164–165.
Gao Jinyuan. 1984. China and Africa: The development of relations over many centuries. *African Affairs* 83: 241–250.
Ge Gongshang. 1994. Nationalism and tribalism in Africa. *West Asia and Africa* 5: 30–35.
Ge Gongshang and Chao Feng. 1980. *Survey of African nationalities*. Beijing: Institute of Ethnic Studies, CASS.
Ge Gongshang and Li Yifu. 1981. *African nationalities: Population and distribution*. Beijing: Institute of Ethnic Studies, CASS.
Ge Gongshang and Chao Feng. 1982. *Hunting nationalities and nomadic nationalities in Africa*. Beijing: Institute of Ethnic Studies, CASS.
Ge Gongshang and Chao Feng. 1984. *Nationalities in West Africa*. Beijing: Institute of Ethnic Studies, CASS.
Ge Gongshang and Song Limei. 1987. *Nationalities in Central Africa*. Beijing: Institute of Ethnic Studies, CASS.
Ge Jie et al. 1989. *Origin of the disturbance in Southern Africa*. Bejing: World Affairs Press.
Ge Jie. 1994. *South Africa: A rich land with bitterness*. Beijing: World Affairs Press.
Ge Jie. 1997. China. In John Middleton, ed., *Encyclopedia of Africa, South of the Sahara, Vol. 4*. New York: Charles Scribner's Sons.
Ge Jie. 2000. *Concise encyclopaedia of Sub-Saharan Africa*. Beijing: China Social Sciences Press.
Gu Zhangyi. 1997. "Buzu" or "nation"? *World Ethno-national Studies* 2: 1–8.
Gunther, John. 1955. *Inside Africa*. London: Hamish Hamilton.
He Fangchuan. 1987. The relationship between China and African history. *UCLA African Studies Center Newsletter*, Fall.
He Fangchuan and Nin Sao. 1996. *A history of Africa: Volume of ancient time*. Shanghai: East Normal University Press.
He Li-er. 1995. *A pearl in Southern Africa – Zimbabwe*. Beijing: Contemporary World Press.

He Xiurong, Wang Xiuqing & Li Ping, eds. 2000. *African Afro-product market and trade*. Beijing: Chinese Financial Economic Press.

Hong Yonghong & Xia Xinghua. 2000. *An introduction to African law*. Changsha: Hunan People's Publishing House.

Hu You-e. 1980. African national independence movement after World War II. *West Asia and Africa* 3: 30–37.

Huang Zengyue. 1940. *A Study of Egypt*, Changsha: Commercial Press.

Hutchison, Alan. 1975. *China's African revolution*. London: Hutchinson.

Ibn Battuta. 1929. *Ibn Battuta travels in Asia and Africa 1325–1354*. Trans. and selected by H.A.R. Gibb, London: George Routledge & Sons.

Institute of West Asian and African Studies, CASS. 1981. *Overview of Africa*, Beijing: World Affairs Press.

Institute of West Asian and African Studies, CASS. 1998. *Africa Beyond 2000*, Beijing: Institute of West Asian and African Studies, Chinese Academy of Social Sciences.

Jiang Xuecheng. 1979. The anti-British struggle of the Matabele and Mashona in modern South Africa. *Journal of Jiangshu Normal College* 4: 46–50.

Jiang Zhongjin, ed. 2012. Graphical Records of African Agriculture. Nanjing: Nanjing University Press.

Joye, Pierre & Lewin, Posine 1961. *Les Trusts au Congo*. Bruxelles: Societe Populaire d'Edition.

Kimambo, I.N. & Temu, A.J., eds. 1969. *A history of Tanzania*. Nairobi: East African Publishing House.

Li Anshan. 1985. On the formation and development of West African intellectuals. *West Asia and Africa* 6: 40–53.

Li Anshan. 1986. The characteristics of West African intellectuals and their role in national independent movement. *World History* 3: 33–42.

Li Anshan. 1994. Book review of *African Eldorado: Gold Coast to Ghana*. *The Journal of Modern African Studies* 32:3, 539–541.

Li Anshan. 1995. *Asafo* and destoolment in colonial southern Ghana, *The International Journal of African Historical Studies*, 28(2): 327–357.

Li Anshan. 1996a. *Abirewa*: A religious movement in the Gold Coast. *Journal of Religious History*, 20(1): 32–52.

Li Anshan. 1996b. New glory, new beginning: Review of three volumes of *General history of Africa*. *West Asia and Africa* 1: 67–71.

Li Anshan. 1998a. *Colonial rule and rural protest in Ghana: A study of Eastern Province*. Changsha: Hunan Educational Press.

Li Anshan. 1998b. The issue of "tribe" in African studies in China. *West Asia and Africa* 3: 57–65.

Li Anshan. 2000. *A History of Chinese overseas in Africa*. Beijing: Overseas Chinese Publishing House.

Li Anshan. 2002. *British rule and rural protest in Southern Ghana*. New York: Peter Lang.

Li Baoping. 1993. The characteristics of traditional culture of Black Africa. *Journal of Peking University (Philosophy and Social Science Edition)* 6: 100–108.

Li Baoping. 1997. *Tradition and modernization in Africa*. Beijing: Peking University Press.

Li Jidong. 1997. *An analysis on delayed modernization in Africa*. Beijing: Chinese Economic Press.

Li Miao. 1988. *Sculpture in Black Africa*. Beijing: Workers Publishing Company.

Li Qingyu 1979. World War I and the national liberation movement in Africa. Nanjing: Nanjing University History Series.
Liang Gencheng. 1991. United States and Africa. Beijing: Peking University Press.
Lin Zexu. 1841. 四州志 Si-zhou zhi [Gazeteer of the Four Continents]. 20卷juan. In Wang Xi-qi 王錫祺, ed., 小方壺齋輿地叢鈔 *Xiao-fang-hu-zhai yu-di cong-chao* [Collected texts on geography from the Xiao-fang-hu Studio]. Shanghai: Xiao-fang-hu Studio.
Liu Hongwu. 1997. *A study on Black African culture*. Shanghai: East Normal University.
Liu Lan. 2001. A historical survey of the relationship between the White economy and Apartheid in South Africa. PhD dissertation, Peking University.
Liu Naiya. 2000. A study on migrant labour in the process of South African Industrilization, PhD dissertation, Peking University.
Lu Ting-en. 1981a. On David Livingston. *Journal of Peking University* 5: 89–96.
Lu Ting-en. 1981b. On the causes of Mau uprising. *History Monthly* 2: 92–97.
Lu Ting-en. 1986. *Africa and imperialism*. Beijing: Peking University Press.
Lu Ting-en & Peng Kunyuan. 1996. *A history of African: Volume of contemporary time*. Shanghai: East China Normal University Press.
Lu Ting-en & Liu Jing, 1997. *African Nationalist Parties and party system*. Shanghai: East China Normal University Press.
Lu Ting-en, ed. 2000. *Brief history of development of African agriculture*. Beijing: Chinese Financial Economic Press.
Luo Hongzhang. 1979. When did the Ethiopian anti-Italian war end? *Journal of Southwestern Normal College* 4: 45–47.
Luo Jianguo. 1984. A comprehensive review of the impact of the Atlantic slave trade on the development of capitalism. *Journal of Jiangxi University* 15(2): 1–6.
Luo Jianguo. 1996. A *study of African national bourgeoisie*. Shanghai: East China Normal University Press.
Luo Ke, ed. 1956. *Egypt, holding high the banner of anti-colonialism*. Changsha: Hunan People's Publishing House.
Ma Huan. 1955 [1451]. *Overall survey of the ocean's shores*. Beijing: Zhonghua Book Company.
Ma Tong. 1959. The national liberation struggle in Algeria, *Teaching History*, 1: 22–28.
Ma Wenkuan and Meng Fanren. 1987. *The discovery of Chinese ancient porcelains in Africa*. Beijing: Forbidden City Press.
McKay, Vernon. 1963. *Africa in World Politics*. New York: Harper and Row.
Mao Tianyou. 1979. The South African people's armed struggle against colonial invasion in the 17th–19th centuries. *Study of Asian African Issues* 1: 40–60.
Mao Zedong. 1994. *Selections of Mao Zedong's works on diplomacy*. Beijing: Central Documentation Publishing House and World Affairs Press.
Merle, Robert. 1965. *Ahmed Ben Bella*. Paris: Gallimard.
Mtshali, B. Vulindlela. 1967. *Rhodesia: Background to conflict*. New York: Howthorn Books.
Na Zhong. 1957. Egyptian people's struggle against Napoleon and the national wakening. *Humanities Science Journal* 1: n.p.
Na Zhong, 1963. *A concise history of modern Egypt*. Beijing: Joint Publishing.
Nasser, Gamal Abdul. 1954. *The philosophy of the revolution*. Cairo: Government Press.
Needham, Joseph. 1959. *Science and civilization in China, Vol. 3*. New York: Cambridge University Press.

Nin Sao. 1983. An analysis on the issue of "tribe" in contemporary Africa. *World History* 4: 40–48.
Nin Sao. 1993. *Black African Culture*. Hangzhou: Zhejiang People's Publishing House.
Nkrumah, Kwame. 1957. *The autobiography of Kwame Nkrumah*. Edinburgh: Thomas Nelson and Sons.
Nketia, Kwabena. 1962. *African Music in Ghana*. Accra: Longman.
Nkrumah, Kwame. 1965. *Neo-colonialism: The last stage of imperialism*. Edinburgh: Thomas Nelson and Sons.
Oh Il-kwan. 1998. On contemporary China's African policy and its practice. PhD dissertation, Peking University.
Ольдерогге, Д.А. & Потехин, И.И. 1954. Народы Африки. Москва: Издательство Академии Наук СССР.
Pan Guang and Zhu Weilie, eds. 1992. *Translated materials on Arabic Africa*. Shanghai: East China Normal University Press.
Parrinder, E.G. 1974. *African traditional religion*. London: Sheldon Press.
Peng Kunyuan et al. 1978. A glorious page in the Sudanese anti-colonialist struggle: the Mahdi uprising in 1881–1885. *Historical Research* 3: 75–84.
Program of African Studies at Northwestern University. 1959. *United States Foreign Policy: Africa*. Washington, DC: Northwestern University.
Qin Xiaoying. 1980. Whether national bourgeois can lead contemporary national liberation movement: An analysis of the characteristics of Kenyan proletariat and national bourgeois and their historical role. *Developments in World History Studies* 2: 25–32,45.
Qin Xiaoying. 1981. The rise of Nigerian modern nationalism and its characteristics. *World History* 2: 23–31.
Ren Baoluo, trans. 1907. *The political history of Egypt*. Shanghai: Commercial Press.
Ren Mei'e & Yan Qinshang. 1941. *Suez Canal*. Shanghai: Daozhong Press.
Seligman, C.G. 1930. *Races of Africa*. London: Thornton Butterworth.
Shen Fuwei. 1990. *China and Africa: Relations of 2000 years*. Beijing: Zhonghua Book Company.
Shibeika, Mekki. 1959. *The independent Sudan: The history of a nation*. New York: Robert Speller and Sons.
Shu Yunguo. 1996. *A study on African population increase and economic development*. Shanghai: East China Normal University Press.
Sik, Endre.1966. *The history of Black Africa* (4 vols). Budapest: Akadémiai Kiadó.
Snow, Philip. 1988. *The Star Raft: China's encounter with Africa*. London: Weidenfeld and Nicolson.
Su Shirong. 1984. *African natural geography*. Beijing: Commercial Press.
Sun Hongqi. 2000. Origin of land issue in South Africa: A study on the linkage between the land issue and Afrikaners' concept of land, their economy and class structure. PhD dissertation, Peking University.
Sun Yutang. 1979. China and Egypt in the Han Dynasty. *Journal of Chinese Historical Studies* 2: 142–154.
Suret-Canale. Jean. 1958. *Afrique Noire Occidentale et Centrale*. Paris: Éditions sociales.
Tan Shizhong, ed. 1998. *Reflection and development: African economic adjustment and sustainability*. Beijing: Social Science Academic Press.
Tang Dadun. 1981. The rise and development of Pan-Africanism and its historical role. *West Asia and Africa* 6: 21–27.

Tang Dadun. 1988. *African socialism: History, theory and practice*. Beijing: World Affairs Press.
Tang Dadun. 1995. *Documents of pan-Africanism and organization of African Unity*. Shanghai: East China Normal University Press.
Tang Dadun, Xu Jiming & Chen Gongyuan eds. 1994. *New analysis of African socialism*. Beijing: Educational Science Publishing House.
Tang Tongming. 1981a. On the Sudanese people's struggle for national independence. *Journal of Guiyang Normal College* 2: 63–73.
Tang Tongming. 1981b. National liberation movement in Sub-Sahara between the wars and its characteristics. *History Monthly* 2: 86–93.
Tang Tongming. 1983. On characteristics of national liberation struggle of Libyan people. *History Monthly* 4: 90–92.
Tang Tongming & Xiang Qun. 1979. On July revolution of 1952 in Egypt. *Journal of Guiyang Normal College* 3: 34–43.
UNESCO. 1979. *The African slave trade from the fifteenth to the nineteenth century*. Beijing: UNESCO.
Wang Cunliang. 1981. The struggle for independence in Zaire: With reference to the historical role of national bourgeois. *Journal of Shangdong Normal College* 4: 26–33.
Wang Junyi. 1959. South African people's fight against racial discrimination. *Study of International Affairs* 4: 60–61.
Wang Shaokui. 1981. Wafd and the national independent movement in Egypt, 1918–1922. *Teaching History* 1: 35–39.
Wang Suolao. 2000. A study on Egyptian nationalism. PhD dissertation, Peking University.
Wang Zhen. 1959. Imperialist invasion into Congo and the struggle of the Congo people. *Study of International Affairs* 8: 31–38.
Wei Yuan. 1842. *Illustrated gazeteer of the maritime countries*. Peking: Gu Wei Tang.
Wen Xian. 1995. *Mandela: Proud son of the Black people*. Beijing: Contemporary World Press.
Wen Yunchao. 2000. *Development and utilization of African agricultural resources*. Beijing: Chinese Financial Economic Press.
Woddis, Jack. 1960. *Africa: The roots of revolt*. London: Lawrence and Wishart.
Woddis, Jack. 1961. *Africa: The lion awakes*. London: Lawrence and Wishart.
Wu Bingzhen. 1983. A review of contemporary Western scholars' viewpoints of slave trade. *World History* 1:80–86.
Wu Bingzhen. 1984a The beginning and ending of African slave trade of 400 years. *World History*, 4: 83–88.
Wu Bingzhen. 1984b. A study on the impact of slave trade on Black Africa. *West Asia and Africa* 5: 1–10.
Wu Bingzheng & Gao Jinyuan. 1993. *A concise history of African national independence*. Beijing: World Affairs Press.
Wu Zuncun & Xie Defeng. 1936. *Ethiopia*. Shanghai: Zhengzhong Press.
Wu Xiu, ed. 1956. *The struggle of the Egyptian people to win independence and peace*. Beijing: Popular Readers Publishing House.
Wu Zengtian. 1996. A survey of the issue of tribe in the study of Black Africa in China. *West Asia and Africa* 5: 70–73.
Xia Jisheng. 1996. *Apartheid and ethnic relations in South Africa*. Shanghai: East China Normal University Press.

Xia Jisheng, et al. 1998. *Contemporary world political system: South Africa.* Lanzhou: Lanzhou University Press.

Xu Jiming. 1983a. Slave trade and the development of early capitalism. *World History* 1: 62–69.

Xu Jiming. 1983b. Slave trade as an important factor to cause African backwardness. *West Asia and Africa* 4: 26–33.

Xu Jiming & Tan Shizhong, eds. 1999. *Political transformation in contemporary Africa.* Beijing: Economic Science Press.

Xun Xingqiang. 1983. *Concise history of Niger.* Beijing: World Affairs Press.

Yan Jin. 1958. *The National Liberation Movement of Algerian People.* Beijing: World Affairs Press.

Yang Dezhen & Su Zeyu, ed. 1994. *African market economy system.* Lanzhou: Lanzhou University Press.

Yang Haocheng. 1985. *The modern history of Egypt.* Beijing: China Social Sciences Press.

Yang Lihua et al. 1994. *Political and economic development in South Africa.* Beijing: China Social Sciences Press.

Yang Lihua. 1995. *Mandela: Father of national unity.* Changchun: Changchun Press.

Yang Renpian. 1984. *A concise history of Africa.* Beijing: People's Publishing House.

Yap, Melanie and Dianne Leong Man. 1996. *Colour, confusion and concessions: The history of the Chinese in South Africa.* Hong Kong: Hong Kong University Press.

Yuan Xihu. 1998. About the term "Buzu". *World Ethno-national Studies* 4: 80.

Zeng Zungu et al. 1984. *Agricultural geography in Africa.* Beijing: Commercial Press.

Zhang Hongming. 1995. On the issue of "tribe" and tribalism in Black Africa. *West Asia and Africa* 5: 44–51.

Zhang Hongming. 1999. *African political development from a multiple perspective.* Beijing: Social Science Documentation Press.

Zhang Qiwei, trans. 1904. *Modern history of Egypt.* Shanghai: Commercial Press.

Zhang Junyan. 1986. *The contact between ancient China and West Asia and Africa.* Beijing: Ocean Publishing House.

Zhang Rongsheng. 1986. *Sculpture in Africa.* Shanghai: Shanghai People's Painting Publishing Company.

Zhang Rongsheng. 1988. *Black African arts.* Beijing: People's Painting Publishing Company.

Zhang Tiesheng. 1963. *History of China–African relations: A primary research.* Beijing: Joint Publishing.

Zhang Xiang, ed. 1998. *A rainbow country: New South Africa.* Beijing: Contemporary Press.

Zhang Xinglang. 1940. *Compilation of data of China–West contact.* Beiping: Furen University Press.

Zhang Yuxi, ed. 1990. *Bibliography of African studies in Chinese, 1982–1989.* Beijing: Institute of Afro-Asian Studies, Peking University, Chinese Society of African Historical Studies, Chinese Association of African Studies.

Zhang Yuxi, ed. 1997. *Bibliography of African studies in Chinese, 1990–1996.* Beijing: Institute of West Asia and Africa, CASS, Institute of Afro-Asian Studies, Peking University, Chinese Society of African Historical Studies.

Zhao Guozhong et al., eds. 1998–1921. *Yellow book of international situation: The report of the development of Middle East and Africa.* Beijing: Social Science Documentation Press.

Zhao Guozhong, ed. 2000. *Concise encyclopedia of West Asia and North Africa: Middle East*. Beijing: China Social Sciences Press.

Zhao Jianping 1980. The national independent issue of Namibia, *West Asia and Africa*, 4: 31–35.

Zhao Shuhui. 1981. *Concise history of Zaire*. Beijing: Commercial Press.

Zheng Daochuan. 1957. Nasser's ideology of anti-colonialism. *Academic Forum* 1: 26–35.

Zheng Jiaxing, ed. 2000. *History of colonialism: Africa*. Beijing: Peking University Press.

Zhu Chonggui et al., eds. 1994. *South African economy: Guide to trade and investment*. Beijing: Current Affairs Press.

Zhu Gang. 1981. A probe into the process of national democratic revolution in Africa. *West Asia and Africa* 3: 1–7.

3 African studies in China in the 21st century[1]

China's trade with Africa increased from US$10.5 billion in 2000 to US$200 billion in 2018. Chinese leaders have paid a lot of visits to Africa, and vice versa. There are about 500,000 Africans in China (Cissé 2021) and about 1.1 million Chinese live on the continent (Li Anshan 2019). Chinese companies have built a lot of roads, ports, railways and power stations in Africa – even the African Union Headquarters. China-Africa relations have made a big progress. It is usually said that academic study is a reflection of reality. Not Really. African study in China does not have the same fortune as the practical relations. However, the dramatic development of the bilateral relationship has provided Chinese scholars with new opportunities and challenges.

Introduction

With the rapid development of China–Africa relations, scholars, professionals, politicians and even ordinary people outside China are very interested in China–Africa academic engagement. The study of Africa in China before the year 2000 can be divided roughly into five phases: Contacting Africa (before 1900), Sensing Africa (1900–1949), Supporting Africa (1949–1965), Understanding Africa (1966–1976) and Studying Africa (1977–2000). This chapter tries to elaborate African study in China in the 21st century. What subjects are studied and what is the focus? The achievements and weaknesses? Are there any young scholars? Does African study in China have any impact internationally? The chapter is divided into five parts: focus and new interests; achievements; young scholars; engagement in international academia; and references and afterthoughts.

Focus and new interests

Over the past decade, the focus has been mainly on China–Africa relations and contemporary African affairs. The Forum on China–Africa Cooperation (FOCAC) has greatly promoted bilateral economic relations: with more Chinese companies in Africa, China needs to know more about the continent

DOI: 10.4324/9781003220152-4

and its people. A number of studies have been done on China–Africa relations and the current situation of African countries. According to statistics, in the period 2000–2005, 232 books on or about Africa were published (Chen Hong & Zhao Ping 2006). If we add books published in the period 2006–2015, the total number would be much more, covering a wide range of fields such as history, politics, foreign affairs, law, economy, culture, geography, ethnology and religion.

China–Africa relations

The subject of China–Africa relations is debated at home and abroad. A few books have been published. As early as 2000, the *Series of investment guides for development of African agriculture* in four volumes was published to celebrate the opening of FOCAC (Lu Ting-en 2000; Wen Yunchao 2000; He Xiurong, Wang Xiuqing & Li Ping 2000; Chen Zhongde, Yao Guimei & Fan Yushu 2000). (Li Zhibiao (2000) studied the links between the African Economic Zone and Chinese enterprises. A few investment guides were also published in various fields, such as mining, oil and gas, and emerging markets. Li Xinfeng, a journalist in Africa for eight years, travelled a great deal in African countries, experienced great occasions and wrote many reports. Exploring Zheng He's voyage to Africa, he published a work containing observations of his trip in African countries, especially Zanzibar (Li Xinfeng 2005). In another book, he gives us a fresh image of Africa and reports on important events (Li Xinfeng 2006). In 2012, his new work tried to link Zheng He and Africa through data about the maritime silk road and various records (Li Xinfeng et al. 2012). Some discoveries were made as a result of the cooperation between Kenyan and Chinese archaeologists that was headed by Qin Dashu of Peking University in his exploration of the Kenyan coast (Qin Dashi & Yuan Jian 2014).

Bilateral migration between China and Africa is another issue. In 2000, the first history of the overseas Chinese in Africa was published, with three sections: the early history of China–Africa relations and the origin of Chinese communities in Africa; the survival and adaptation of Chinese in Africa; and their transformation and integration. It states that there will be a boom in Chinese going to Africa in the 21st century (Li Anshan 2000). The book was reviewed in the *African Studies Review* (Gao 2001) and the *Canadian Journal of African Studies* (Brose 2002).[2] The first part of this book was translated into English in 2012 (Li Anshan 2012). A sister volume of data was published with records, reminiscences and articles in early journals and newspapers of the Chinese in Africa (Li Anshan 2006). A three-volume work was published in 2019 (Li Anshan 2019). Now increasing numbers of works are being written on this subject, some by young scholars (Zhao Jun 2013; Liu Shaonan 2019, 2020; Xu Liang 2020). Chinese scholars are also involved in the study of African communities in China (Li Anshan 2009a, 2012, 2015b; Bodomo & Ma 2010, 2012; Ma Enyu 2012; Xu Tao 2013). A new book on Africans in China explores a new field with descriptive language and vivid example (Zhang Yong 2021).

China–Africa relations are characterised by summit diplomacy, equality, co-development and the institutionalisation of cooperation. After the Beijing Summit in 2006, a Chinese–English bilingual appraisal was published (Li Weijian 2008). A collection in English by Chinese scholars was published to celebrate 50 years of China–African cooperation (Liu Hongwu & Yang Jiemian 2009). Another book analyses the theory, strategy and policies of China–Africa development cooperation (Liu Hongwu & Luo Jianbo 2011). A monograph on FOCAC deals with Africa's position in international arena, China's strategy on Africa, the funding of FOCAC and the pattern of China–Africa cooperation (Zhang Zhongxiang 2012). Qi Jianhua's book on new China–Africa partnerships deals with bilateral cooperation in various fields, including economic/financial, political/legal, security/military, cultural/social, and African regional integration. The contributors include scholars from African Francophone countries (Qi Jianhua 2014). A survey of African studies in various disciplines in China (1949–2010) was included in a collection of works celebrating the Institute of West Asia and Africa (IWAA 2011). Now there is a discussion on African studies as a discipline (Liu Hongwu 2019).

What are the implications of China–Africa economic diplomacy for the global value chain? Tang's works probes the issue from the angles of trade, infrastructure, mining, agriculture, economic zone, manufacturing and social transformation (Tang Xiaoyang 2014, 2014a, 2014b, 2014c, 2014d, 2014e, 2016, 2018, 2019). He described China–Africa economic cooperation as "coevolutionary pragmatism" (Tang Xiaoyang 2020). The development of China–African economic and trade relations is dealt with (Zhang Zhe 2014) and China–Africa cooperation in low-carbon development strategies is studied in terms of international law, international cooperation and an African low-carbon development strategy (Liang Yijian 2012; Zhang Yonghong et al. 2014). Another work deals with China–Africa economic and trade cooperation in the new situation (Shi Yongjie 2015). However, a different view argues that China lacks an African strategy and that "there is everything Chinese in Africa except a strategy" (Li Anshan 2011a). In addition, China's Achilles' heel is the shortage of strategic means and specific measures to realise its aim (He Liehui 2012).

Several important works have covered various aspects of China–Africa relations. Zhang's work deals with economic cooperation between Africa and big economies, including developed economies and new economies such as India, Russia, Brazil and China. It also compares economic cooperation between Africa and different powers (Zhang Hongming 2012). Covering a wide range of fields, Yang's work studies the comprehensive strategy of China–Africa economic cooperation in terms of historical heritage, trade, investment, project contracts, assistance, science and technology (Yang Lihua et al. 2013). There are studies comparing poverty and poverty reduction in China and Africa (Li Xiaoyun 2010a, 2010b).

58 *Encounter and research*

As for international development aid, several works have been published, including a study on different aspects of Chinese and Western aid to Africa (Zhang Yongpeng 2012) and Chinese medical cooperation with Africa, focusing on Chinese medical teams and a campaign against malaria (Li Anshan 2011a), or using the concept of "development-guided assistance" to describe China's model (Zhang Haibing 2013). Other studies partly deal with China–Africa development cooperation (Zhou Hong 2013; Liu Hongwu & Huang Meibo et al. 2013). Shen Xipeng has studied the Chinese assistance and the construction of TAZARA – for example, the Tanzania–Zambia Railway (Shen Xipeng 2018) – in detail. China–Africa relations are studied from various perspectives, such as African integration (Luo Jianbo 2006), African NGOs (Liu Hongwu & Shen Peili 2009) and African infrastructure (Hu Yongju & Qiu Xin 2014). "Entering into Africa to seek for development" is a theme of conferences held by CAAS and it publishes regular collections of papers.

Country study

Understanding all countries in the world is difficult, and a special committee was set up by the Chinese Academy of Social Sciences (CASS) in 2002 to be in charge of the series *Guide to the world states*, which deals with seven subjects: land and people; history; politics; economy; military; education (with cultural aspects); and foreign relations. A study of all African countries has been finished, with the exception of Nigeria, Sierra Leone, Zambia and Namibia. Several countries were written about by senior scholars, such as Niger (Peng Kunyuan 2006), Senegal and Gambia (Zhang Xiang et al. 2007), Ghana (Gu Zhangyi 2010), Libya (Pan Peiying 2007), Mauritania with West Sahara (Li Guangyi 2008) and South Africa (Yang Lihua, 2010).

In 2006, the Institute of West Asia and Africa (IWAA) of CASS, the Chinese Society of African Historical Studies (CSAHS) and the Centre for African Studies of Peking University, decided to assemble a bibliography of African studies in China during the period 1997–2005. Regarding graduate theses on individual countries, there are 152 titles on 29 countries. South Africa is at the top with 36 theses (Chen Hong & Zhao Ping 2006).

Table 3.1 Graduate theses on African countries, 1981–2005

Egypt 35	Kenya 2	Nigeria 18	Mali 3	South Africa 36
Sudan 5	Somali 1	Cameroon 1	Congo (B) 1	Lesotho 2
Libya 2	Tanzania 5	Benin 1	Congo (K) 4	Madagascar 3
Algeria 4	Uganda 2	Togo 1	Mozambique 7	Mauritius 2
Morocco 1	Burundi 1	Ghana 2	Botswana 2	Zimbabwe 2
Ethiopia 4	Niger 1	Côte d'Ivoire 1	Zambia 3	Total 152

As the statistics indicate, studies concentrate on big countries, with South Africa and Egypt the major focus. In more than 4000 articles published in more than 800 journals, five countries attract the most attention and articles on those countries make up more than one-quarter of the total. South Africa is at the top, with about half of all articles (620 out of 1256) (Chen Hong & Zhao Ping 2006).

The study of Portuguese-speaking African countries has been neglected for a long time owing to the language barrier, but the situation is now changing. The fourth volume of a series published by the Centre for African Studies at Peking University is a collection of articles on the development of these countries (Li Baoping et al. 2006). There are specific studies of individual countries as well, such as the history of Ghana (Chen Zhongdan 2000), Mali (Zhang Zhongxiang 2006), Nigeria (Liu Hongwu et al. 2014) and Egypt (Wang Tai 2014), as well as the development of Tanzania (Li Xiangyun 2014) and South Africa's politics and urbanisation (Qing Hui 2013).

Current situation

There have been quite a few studies of this type, on topics such as African transportation (Hu Yongju & Qiu Xin 2014), African tourism (Luo Gaoyuan 2010), African agriculture (Jiang Zhongjin 2012), industry and mining in Africa (Zhu Huayou et al. 2014), African education (Liu Yan 2014; Lou Shizhou 2014; Wan Siulan & Li Wei 2014), security in Africa (Mo Xiang 2014), resources and environment, and AIDS (Cai Gaojiang 2014).

The most important work is the *Oxford handbook of Africa and economics*, edited by two prominent economists, Célestin Monga and Justin Yifu Lin (Monga & Lin 2015). The book has two volumes: *Context and concept* and *Policies and practices*. Raising the issue of economics in Africa, the work reaches a couple of firm conclusions: that Africa as a region is still under-researched and the African contribution to economic knowledge has been neglected. Realising Africa is about to take off, the book attempts to provide useful knowledge to guide the continent's new phase of development and policy-makers in Africa (Monga & Lin 2015). The introduction to both volumes lays out the authors' rationale and general arguments (Monga & Lin 2015a, 2015b) and Lin's chapter indicates the links between China's rise and African economic structural transformation (Lin Yifu 2015).

According to the abovementioned 2006 statistics, most of the articles are on current issues. Among 1256 articles, there are 424 on economics, about one-third of the total, while 208 articles are on politics and law and 127 on foreign affairs.

It is noticeable that articles on the economy head the list for all five countries, reflecting China's focus today. There are more works on politics/law or foreign affairs for Ethiopia and Nigeria. History occupies the second place for articles on Egypt because Egyptology is included as a subject. The greater number of works on culture and society in South Africa indicate that more

Table 3.2 Classification of articles on specific African countries, 1997–2005

Subject/country	Egypt	Ethiopia	Kenya	Nigeria	South Africa	Total
Politics & law	42	2	15	31	118	208
Economy	107	31	41	44	201	424
Foreign affairs	61	14	3	6	43	127
Ethnicity		2			20	22
Religion	15				5	20
Military	5	1			33	39
History & archaeology	68	3		1	7	79
Culture	44	2	15	19	99	179
Society	10	6	25	10	67	118
Important figures	9	2	2		27	40
Total	361	63	101	111	620	1 256

Note: The classification is not very strict since ethnicity and religion or politics may be intertwined, as are culture and society. Geography is classified under either society or culture since it is usually linked to tourism, heritage or environment.

Chinese are familiar with the country. The numbers relating to graduate theses (1981–2005) have some implications. Of 238 MA and PhD theses, 73 titles are about Africa in general, 17 are on politics, 13 on the economy, 26 on foreign affairs, 12 on history and five on culture. There are four on East Africa, seven on West Africa and two on Southern Africa. More studies are interested in security, environment and climate change.

African integration is another field, with several works covering the issue (Luo Jianbo 2010). CSAHS held its annual conference on China–Africa cooperation and African integration in 2013. Papers covered Pan-Africanism and African unity, African integration, regional integration and China–Africa cooperation (Zhai Fengjie, et al. 2013). Xiao Hongyu (2014), emphasising the links between African regional integration and economic development. Taking West Africa as a case, she studied the interaction between integration and modernisation. Integration is an important phenomenon and Zhang Jin studied 30 years' development of SADC (Zhang Jin 2014).

Monographs and achievements

African history

Although contemporary Africa now attracts more attention from Chinese scholars, the historical study of Africa is still important in China. There are several works by scholars of the older generation: Ai Zhouchang wrote on modernization in South Africa (Ai Zhouchang et al. 2000); Lu Ting-en compiled his articles into a volume of four sections – African history in the colonial period, the history of African parties and politics, African economic history and the history of China–Africa relations (Lu Ting-en 2005). Zheng Jiaxing taught South African history at Peking University from the beginning of the 1980s. As a summary of his teaching, his book studies the history from the establishment of Cape Town until the formation of the New South Africa, with a chapter on literature in South Africa (Zheng Jiaxing 2010). His volume of colonialism in Africa forms part of the *Series on the history of colonialism* (Zheng Jiaxing 2000). Gao Jinyuan, a senior researcher at the Chinese Academy of Agricultural Sciences (CAAS), has published two works, one a collection of his studies of Africa in three sections – colonialism and liberation movements; area/country studies; and contemporary politics (Gao Jinyuan 2007); and the other on Britain–Africa relations from the slave trade to the present (Gao Jinyuan 2008). Xu Yongzhang compiled articles on the history of China–African relations and also published a comprehensive history of African countries (Xu Yongzhang 2004, 2014, 2019).

Shu Yunguo's work deals with structural adjustment in Africa, an important issue in African development. After an analysis of the interference of the international financial system and the response of African countries, he concludes that the World Bank's structural adjustment is a failure (Shu Yunguo, 2004). A history of African economies gives a survey from the 19th century to the 1990s, with additional chapters on South Africa and African economic relations with China and other countries (Shu Yunguo & Liu Weicai 2013). Another work is an introduction to African studies, which deals with data, historiography, topics and sources (Shu Yunguo 2012). A history of Pan-Africanism is another important work, which divides the movement into two parts. The first deals with its origin, ideology in the early period, the first phase (1900–1945) and the second phase (1945–1963). The second part (1963–2001) studies the movement during the period of the Organization of African Unity until the founding of the African Union (Shu Yunguo 2014).

A study on rural protest in Ghana during the colonial period is the first monograph in English by a Chinese scholar of African studies. Based on government documents and fieldwork, through the use of case studies he explores protests by the Ghanaian people: people against colonial government, commoners against chiefs, religious leaders against secular authority and lesser local leaders against paramount chiefs (Li Anshan 2002). This invited a review in foreign journal (Gocking 2003).[3] Another work introduces ancient kingdoms in African continent (Li Anshan 2012). As part of *World modernization series*, the volume of Africa covers the process from the different perspectives of history, politics, economy, nation-building and integration, with case studies of Ethiopia, South Africa, Nigeria, Ghana, Tanzania, Zambia, Angola and French-speaking countries (Li Anshan 2013a; Li Anshan et al. 2013).[4]

An excellent study of modern African intellectuals in modern times, Zhang Hongming's book deals with the ideological background of the slave trade through important figures of the 18th century, such as Antoin-Guillaune Amo, Olaudah Equiano and Ottobah Cugoano, then moves on to the three cultural trends of the 19th century – Westernization, Africanization and integration – with case studies of Samuel Ajayi Crowther, Alexander Crummell and Samuel Lewis. He ends with a study on Africanus Horton and Edward Blyden (Zhang Hongming 2008).

A study on De Gaulle and African decolonisation analyses the major factors, such as changes in the international situation, the struggle of the colonies, the demands of French-monopolised capitalism and the change in social configuration (Chen Xiaohong 2007). Sun Hongqi's study tries to analyse the role of colonialism in Africa (Sun Hongqi 2008).

Politics, international relations and law

At the beginning of the 21st century, the Chinese government called for a grand diplomacy that required effort, experiences and ideas from all walks of life: "It is recognizable that there should be more cooperation between practical work and academic research. The government needs information, analysis and assessment, while academia needs funding, stimulus and feedback" (Li Anshan 2005: 73). The situation is developing dramatically. Scholars were asked to give lectures to top leaders or opinions on the drafts of state leaders' speeches in FOCAC.[5] Africanists became involved in projects from various ministries to provide their thinking and ideas on how to carry out development cooperation with Africa. The Ministry of Education promoted the formation of think-tanks in universities. All this shows the adjustment of the government to a changing situation and its increasing interaction with academia.

Zhang Hongming's work discusses the internal and external factors of African politics. For the internal factors, he illustrates the relationship between politics and the state, tribalism, traditional culture and religion. The external factors cover Western, Eastern and Islamic political cultures and their links with political development (Zhang Hongming 1999). Xia Jisheng of Peking University explored the structure and function of the parliamentary systems of South Africa and Egypt (Xia Jisheng 2005). Li Baoping's book is on African culture and politics. It deals with traditional culture, political transformation and case studies of Tanzania and South Africa. He discusses President Nyerere's personality and contribution; democratization and its diplomatic philosophy; and the breakdown of apartheid in South Africa, the role of different ethnic groups during the transition and the country's political transformation (Li Baoping 2011).

Studying the origin and evolution of nationalism in Africa, Li Anshan approaches the subject through various facets, national, intellectual, religion, peasantry, nation-building, democratisation and international politics, and nationalism's different forms, such as Pan-Africanism, African nationalism, state nationalism and local nationalism. Using the term "local nationalism" to replace "tribalism", he argues that local nationalism has its origin in a pre-colonial social base and was strengthened by indirect rule. Since independence, ill-distribution of power, economic difficulties and external interference have strengthened ethnic conflicts (Li Anshan 2004).

With an increasing interest in democratisation in Africa, He Wenping's work on the subject enriches our understanding of the process. The author argues that different countries pursue democracy in different ways, using case studies of South Africa, Nigeria, Kenya and Uganda. She makes it clear that there is a common desire for democracy, yet no common way to realise it: people have to build a democratic society by themselves and any way of "transplanting" democracy forcefully by the "outside" is certain to be short-lived (He Wenping 2005).

To understand early communist leaders' views on Africa, a book was compiled of the sayings of Marx, Engels, Lenin and Stalin on the Middle East and Africa (Cui Jianmin 2010). There are studies of the early generation of African leaders (Lu Ting-en et al. 2005) and contemporary leaders such as President Museveni (Mu Tao & Yu Bin 2013); Nyerere's important works were translated (Nyerere 2015).

Another area of content comprises African diplomacy and foreign relations. The first diplomatic history of South Africa deals with its foreign policy during apartheid and the international reaction; South African's neighbouring policy; the adjustment of De Klerk's "new diplomacy"; and the foreign policy of the New South Africa (Mu Tao 2003). The relationship between modern Egypt and the United States, Russia, Israel, Saudi Arabia and China was studied (Chen Tiandu et al. 2010), and there are also studies on foreign relations in Nigeria (Yang Guangsheng 2014) and the New South Africa and its relations with China (Fang Wei 2014; Zhang Weijie 2015). There is a work on the political economy of South Africa's land issue (Sun Hongqi 2011).

The Darfur issue is probed in terms of its origin, its relationship with North and South Sudan, and with oil, geopolitics, the United Nations, the West, China and the Beijing Olympics, its process and impact (Jiang Hengkun 2014). Political systems are dealt with, such as Ethiopia's federalism and political transformation (Zhang Xiangdong 2012; Zhang Chun 2012; Xiao Yuhua 2014); the democratization and politics of Egypt (Wang Tai 2014); and Islamic socialism in Libya (Han Zibin et al. 2014). The role of the African Union is also studied in terms of the African economy, conflict management, common foreign policy, collective development and its contribution to world politics (Luo Jianbo 2010).

Despite the view questioning the existence of African law systems, Hong Yonghong has devoted more than ten years to the study of African law (Hong Yonghong 2005, 2014). In another work, the authors try to cover various law systems practised in the continent, such as ancient Egyptian law, the Islamisation of African law, African customary law, common law, civil law and mixed jurisdiction (He Qinhua & Hong Yonghong 2006). There is an important work on the International Criminal Tribunal for Rwanda (ICTR), of which Hong studied various aspects: its origin, institutional framework, jurisdiction, criminal elements under the ICTR's jurisdiction, the adjudication rule and the ICTR's contribution to international criminal tribunals (Mancuso & Hong Yonghong 2009), which helps the Chinese understand the work of the tribunal. Hong carried out a study of African law with his colleagues and continually published works, including translations (Hong Yonghong & Xia Xinhua 2010; Mancuso & Hong 2009; Dickerson 2009; Zhu Weidong 2011, 2013). *West Asia and Africa* ran a special column on the study of African law for more than ten years.

Geography

In the field of African geography, Chinese scholars have also made a contribution. Jiang's work offers a comprehensive survey of the position of agriculture in Africa, an assessment of agricultural natural resources, an analysis of socio-economic conditions in agriculture, the history of agricultural development, regional distribution and economic types of agriculture. It deals with agricultural natural resources, food crops, husbandry, forestry, fishery, agricultural food processing, consumption of agricultural products and nutrition security. This work probes the relationships between people, the culture of the agricultural economy and the environment (Jiang Zhongjin 2012).

As the research interest of the Centre for African Studies of Nanjing University, the *Series of security studies on China–Africa resource development and energy cooperation* covers various subjects, such as China–Africa energy cooperation and security (Jiang Zhongjin & Liu Litao, 2014), African agriculture and development (Jiang Zhongjin 2014), port economy and urban development (Zhen Feng 2014), land resource and food security (Huang Xianjin 2014), fishery and development strategy (Zhang Zhenke 2014), and modern African human geography (Jiang Zhongjin 2014). Cultural geography was also a subject of research (Chong Xiuquan 2014).

African art

African art is a rich source and various translations were published, yet few serious studies have been undertaken. Several works on African arts were published in 2000, yet their appeal is more visual than intellectual. Quite a few books on African art, especially Egyptian art and architecture, have been edited or translated. There are cultural studies, either general (Ai Zhouchang & Mu Tao 2001; Ai Zhouchang & Shu Yunguo 2008; Zheng Jiaxing 2011) or on specific countries (Yang Xuelun & Zheng Xizhen 2001; Jiang Dong 2005) and related subjects (Liu Hongwu & Li Shudi 2010). The most important work is a history of South African literature by Li Yongcai, a scholar long involved in the study of African literature (Li Yongcai 2009), and there are articles on African art, sculpture, film, literature, dance and drumming.

International engagement and young scholars

An increasing number of Chinese scholars are taking an active part in international academia. Some of them edit books related to China–African relations and some publish articles in journals, book chapters or online.

English publication

Engagement with international scholarship is another achievement. There are a few books in English, which are written or edited by Chinese scholars in international academia (Li Anshan 2002, 2011a, 2012, 2013a; Li Anshan et al. 2012; Li Anshan & April 2013; Berhe & Liu Hongwu 2013; Monga & Lin 2015; Sheldon et al. 2015). Chinese participation in international conferences is increasing and the Chinese viewpoint appears in international journals and magazines (Zhang Hongming, Liu Lide & Xu Jiming 2001; Zeng Qiang 2002; He Wenping 2002, 2006, 2007, 2008, 2008a, 2008b, 2008d, 2009, 2010c, 2011; Li Anshan 2005, 2007a, 2008a, 2009c, 2010a, 2013b, 2015b, 2015c; Li Baoping 2008; Liu Haifang 2006, 2008, 2015; Yang Lihua 2006; Luo Jianbo & Zhang Xiaoming 2011; Xia Xinhua & Xiao Yaiying 2011). More and more Chinese scholars have been involved in international cooperation, and their works are included in English books or conference paper collections (He Wenping 2005, 2007a, 2008e, 2009a, 2010, 2010a, 2010b, 2012, 2012a, 2012b; Li Baoping 2007; Hong Yonghong 2007, 2010; Zhang Yongpeng 2007; Li Zhibian 2007; An Chunying 2007; Li Anshan 2007c, 2008b, 2008c, 2009a, 2010b, 2011b, 2011c, 2011f, 2012b, 2013a, 2013c, 2013d, 2015a, 2021; Zeng Qiang 2010; Zhi Yingbiao & Bai Jie 2010; Zhang Xinghui 2011; Liu Hongwu 2012; Tang Xiao 2012; Zhang Chun 2012; Liang Yijian 2012; Pang Zhongying 2013; Wang Xuejun 2013; Lin Yifu 2015; Xu Liang 2015, 2015a) and Jiang Hui (2020, 2020a).[6]

After an international conference entitled *China–Africa relations: Past, present and future*, held in South Africa in November 2005, a collection of papers was edited by the prominent Ghanaian Africanist Kwesi Kwaa Prah, to which several Chinese scholars contributed their papers (Prah 2007). The China–African Civil Society Dialogue conference was held in Nairobi in April 2008, hosted by the Heinrich Böll Foundation, and ten Chinese scholars were invited. The proceedings were published and six articles by Chinese participants were included (Harneit-Sievers et al. 2010). A seminar was held in Nairobi by the Inter-Region Economic Network (IREN) as a concrete result of the China–Africa Joint Research and Exchange Program. The meeting was attended by a delegation from China whose speeches were included in a volume edited by James Shikwati (2012) (He Wenping, Tang Xiao, Liang Yijian, Zhang Chun, Li Anshan, Shi Lin, Liu Hongwu).

In October 2012, the China–Africa Think Tanks Forum (CATTF) held its meeting in Ethiopia, co-hosted by the Institute for Peace and Security Studies (IPSS) of Addis Ababa University and the Institute of African Studies (IAS) of Zhejiang Normal University, and a collection of writings was published, including those of Chinese scholars (Berhe & Liu Hongwu 2013). Some are actively involved in English networks, such as He Wenping, Liu Haifang, Sun Xiaomeng, Luo Jianbo and Zhang Xiaomin.

Academic monographs by young scholars

More young students than before are engaged in African studies, and they have better opportunities to go to Africa. Luo Jianbo has done work on African integration and China–Africa relations. A few PhD students in different disciplines finished their theses or did fieldwork, such as Chen Fenglan (2011) and Chen Xiaoying (2012) in sociology, Ding Yu in archaeology (2013, 2015), Yang Tingzhi (2015) and Shen Xiaolei in political science (2015). Chinese anthropologists and social scientists such as Si Lin and Xu Wei went to Africa through different channels or did fieldwork there (Si Lin 2012; Xu Wei 2011, 2014).

Scholars of a new generation have more opportunities for international contact, a more favourable academic environment and more time for African study. Most of their works are revised PhD dissertations. Bi Jiankang studied the links between Egyptian modernisation and political stability, covering a period from 1805 to the 1990s. He analyzed different political regimes, i.e. military and presidential, and related issues such as political participation, political parties, Islam, political violence, urbanization, and *Asyut*. He also analyzed the impact of the economy, unemployment and external factors on political stability (Bi Jiankang 2011).

The first Chinese master's graduate in the Hausa language at Ahmadu Bello University of Nigeria, Sun Xiaomeng, was awarded her PhD for a thesis on British educational policy in north Nigeria during the colonial period. In her research on original data in both Hausa and English, she studied the interaction between power and language. Analysing the language policy, the examination system, the development of Hausa and the educational policy, the author explains how the British colonial government used the Hausa language as a tool in its colonial administration (Sun Xiaomeng 2004, 2014).

Luo Jianbo has published two related books on China's responsibility in Africa. One analyzes the achievements, problems and perspectives of African integration and explores the links between China–African relations and the African integration process; the other looks at the African Union's relationship with its member states in terms of development, economic cooperation, conflict management and foreign policy, and its significance to the world (Luo Jianbo 2006, 2010).

The indigenous knowledge is a new subject, and Zhang Yonghong has made a detailed study of its role and relationship with development (Zhang Yonghong 2010). Li Weijian probed the history of Islam in West Africa and traced its historical origins to the *Jihad* movement in the 19th century, in Islam during the colonial period and in present day (Li Weijian 2011). Zhu Weidong excelled himself in the study of African law. Besides translations of related works, he has also published two books on legal systems in Africa (Zhu Weidong 2011, 2013). Jiang Hengkun has studied the Sudan for a long time and his work on the Darfur issue probed the cause, process, conditions for a peaceful solution and impact of the crisis (Jiang Hengkun 2014). Wang

Tao studied the Lord's Resistance Army in Uganda in terms of its origin, development, influence and links with international affairs (Wang Tao 2014). Based on his knowledge of Arabic and English, Huang Hui studied Berberism in Algeria from a different perspective (Huang Hui 2015).

The issue of African economy and investment has also been studied (Zou Hengfu & Hao Rui 2009). Several important works of African economies have been written by young scholars. An Chunying's (2010) study on African anti-poverty deals with origin and characteristics of poverty, anti-poverty policies and measures,, dynamics and international aid, etc. and her conclusion is that pro-poor growth is the proper way to poverty reduction (An Chunying 2010). Yang researched the links between liabilities and development in from a perspective of international relations, analyzing the theory, origin and development of debt in Africa as well as debt-relief programs and adjustments of policy with debt (Yang Baorong 2011). Comparative advantage is a different perspective on African economic development, and Liang Yijian (2014) argues that Africa can develop only on its own path, not by copying others The technology transfer and the development of African manufacture industry are also studied (Li Anshan 2016b; Wei Xiaohui & Huang Meibo 2018). In recent years, the complex situation in South Africa has also been examined (Jiang Hui 2020, 2020a).

Chinese engagement in international academia

Professor Na Zhong, Honorary President of the Chinese Society of African Historical Studies, was awarded the first International Prize of the Arabic Language Sharjah by UNESCO in Paris on 25 October 2001. In 2002, Yan Haiying was invited to attend the research database project of ancient Greek Olympic Games hosted by Willy Clarisse, academician of the Royal Academy of Sciences of Belgium and professor of Department of Classics of the KU Leuven. In 1998, Jin Shoufu, a PhD student in Egyptology at Heidelberg University, participated in the excavation of the Tomb of Thebes Amenhotep III by the archaeology team of Waseda University in Japan. In 2000, he also participated in the excavation of the official Tomb of Luxor in Egypt by Heidelberg University. On 24 May 2013, Yang Lihua and Li Anshan, at the invitation of the African Diplomatic Corps in China, gave keynote speeches at the Pan-Africanism and African Renaissance seminar held at Kempinski Hotel to celebrate the Golden Jubilee of the OAU/AU on 9 September 2013.[7] Zhu Weidong was appointed to the International Commercial Panel by the Arbitration Foundation of Southern Africa (AFSA).[8]

In order to satisfy the curiosity of the international community about African studies in China, several articles have been published in English (Li Anshan 2005, 2007c, 2010b, 2016a, 2017, 2018b). In addition, a few scholars have been involved in international academia. The Symposium to Celebrate the 15th Anniversary of the Establishment of Diplomatic Relations between China and South Africa was held on 19 September 2013 in the Ministry of

Foreign Affairs of South Africa. Li Anshan was invited to participate in the symposium and also delivered a speech at the new book launch for the volume edited by him and South African scholar F.Y. April in the building (Li Anshan & April 2013).[9] On 3 November 2013, Li Anshan was invited by the Director General of UNESCO, Irina Bokova, to join the International Scientific Committee of UNESCO *General History of Africa* (Vol. 9, later expanded to Vols. 9–11), and was elected Vice Chairman of the Committee at its first session held in Brazil.[10] The McMillan Center of Yale University invited Li Anshan and Ibrahim Gambari, former Foreign Minister of Nigeria and former Under Secretary General of the United Nations, to co-chair the international seminar on Africa China Relations: Balance, Growth and Sustainable Future, which was held in Nigeria from 15–18 March 2016, and the seminar held at Beijing Forum of Peking University in November 2017.[11] In 2018, Liu Haifang was appointed a member of the Executive Board of the CA/AC Research Network.

African studies in the School of Social and Anthropology of Xiamen University has been fruitful due to the invitation of Professor Augustin Holl (Chinese name Gao Chang) to join the team. As a Cameroonian-French scholar and a famous archaeologist, he once served as Professor/Curator of the Museum of Anthropology of the University of Michigan (2000–2008) and was Vice President of Université Paris X (2012–2014). At the invitation of Xiamen University, he resigned from the Centre National de la Recherche Scientifique (CNRS) in 2017 and went to the Department of Anthropology and Ethnology of Xiamen University for teaching. Later, he donated his archaeological and cultural collections to Xiamen University for teaching and research and established an archaeological anthropology laboratory. He led Chinese students to Senegal for archaeological excavation in the summer of 2018 and published a large number of papers and research reports in international academic journals (Holl 2017, 2018, 2019, 2019a, 2019b; Holl & Bocoum 2017; Santos et al. 2019).[12] In 2017, the University of Electronic Science and Technology of China established the Centre for West African Studies (CWAS) together with five universities in Ghana: the University of Ghana (UG), University of Cape Coast (UCC), Ghana Institute of Management and Public Administration (GIMPA), University of Education at Winneba (UEW) and University for Development Studies (UDS). The two sides jointly held a seminar to promote cooperation in education and scientific research. At present, CWAS regularly issues annual reports in Chinese and English. One of CWAS's innovative strategies is for African and Chinese scholars to publish articles together. This joint research has achieved good results (Ameyaw & Li Yao 2018; Asare & Shao Yunfei 2018; Larty & Li Yao 2018; Boadi et al. 2019; Asare-Kyire et al. 2019; Dumor & Li Yao 2019; Lartey & Li Yao 2019; Lartey, et al. 2019; Zhao Shurong et al. 2019, 2020; Li Anshan 2020; Mutiiri et al. 2020; Say et al. 2020; Yeboah & Feng Yi 2020; Appiah-Otoo 2021; Say 2021; Say & Sagoe 2021).

It is encouraging that some young scholars' capability has been recognised by international academia. For example, Cheng Ying's doctoral thesis won the Best Doctoral Thesis Award of the Lagos Studies Association, the first among Chinese scholars. Dr Liu Shaonan was the first Asian scholar to receive the Graduate Student Paper Prize at the 2018 annual meeting of the US African Studies Association (ASA),[13] followed by Xiao Gang, another Chinese PhD student, at the 2019 ASA meeting. Dr Zhou Yang's thesis on cross-cultural marriage between China and Africa was awarded the "sehr gut: 1.0 (excellent)" level. The Institute for International and Area Studies of Tsinghua University started to train young scholars in a multi-faceted way, covering different regions of Africa, several years ago. Now several PhD students have finished their study in China and developed countries, and have also done several years' fieldwork in African countries, such as Gao Liangmin (Tanzania and East Africa), Yang Chongsheng (South Africa) and Xiong Xinghan (Madagascar and West Indian Islands).[14]

Young scholars arriving back to China from abroad in recent years have published articles internationally. Wen Shuang (2014, 2015, 2016, 2016a, 2019) focuses on the history of China–Egypt relations and Asia–Africa exchanges. Zhang Qiaowen has noted the role of China Africa Development Fund (2015a, 2015b). Cheng Ying is specialized in Nigerian drama and the exchange of Chinese and African drama (2014, 2016, 2016a, 2018, 2018a, 2019). Xu Liang studies the economic development of South Africa and the role of Chinese (2015, 2015a, 2017, 2019). As mentioned, Tang Xiaoyang's articles on China–Africa relations have attracted attention among scholars. Lian Chaoqun's articles are on Arab politics and culture in English and Arabic (2016, 2016a, 2016b, 2018). Qiu Yu (2018) discusses social aspects of China-Africa contact, especially corporate ethics. Yuan Ding made an English proper noun, "Guoke" (过客), on the basis of his own study (Pang & Yuan Ding 2013; Yuan Ding & Pang 2019) and others' previous research, especially Niu Dong's (2015, 2016) study on Africans in Guangzhou, which took the Chinese concept of "过客" with the English equivalent "transient" in his English article (Niu Dong 2018). Liu Shaonan (2019) examined the contribution of overseas Chinese to Nigerian local society.

The *Journal of Ancient Civilizations*, a journal in English issued by the Institute for the History of Ancient Civilizations at Northeast Normal University, published relevant articles (Guo Dantong, 1995, 1998, 1999, 1999, 2002, 2003, 2004). *World History Studies*, an English journal of the Institute of World History, CASS, also published articles on Africa (Guo Dantong 2015, 2017; Li Anshan 2015c, 2017; Wang Haili 2017; Song Huicong & Guo Dantong, 2018; Guo Xiaorui & Guo Dantong 2019). Other English journals in China, such as *Contemporary International Relations* by the China Institute of Contemporary International Relations, *China International Studies* by the China Institute of international Studies, *Global Review* by the Shanghai Institutes of International Studies and *China International Strategy Review* by the Institute of International and Strategical Studies at Peking University, occasionally publish related articles. The *Journal of China–Africa Studies* (in Chinese, English and French), newly published by the China–Africa Institute, CASS, has provided a new platform for the international exchange of China's African studies.

Annual reports, memoirs and references

In China, associations and institutions of African studies hold academic events annually and usually publish their work in the form of collections of papers.

Annual reports and reviews

CAAS publishes a collection of papers almost annually, mostly on China–Africa relations (Chen Gongyuan 2006, 2007, 2009, 2010; Feng Zuoku & Chen Gongyuan 2008). CSAHS holds a conference annually and usually publishes a collection of papers. Different institutions of African studies publish annual reports or reviews regularly. The most important is the *Yellow Book of Middle East and Africa* by IWWA of CASS, which focuses on a different subject each year. For example, the 2001–2002 issue was titled *United and self-strengthening Africa* (Yang Guang & Wen Boyou 2002), while in 2004–2005 the title was *Special report on international experiences for the prevention of an oil crisis* (Chen Mo & Yang Guang 2005), and in 2006–2007 it was *History and reality of China–African relations* (Yang Guang & He Wenping 2007). Now a yellow book is published for each region, and the *Yellow Book of Africa* has a special emphasis each year. The 2011–2012 edition studied China–African relations, the 2012–2013 edition examined regional cooperation in Africa and the 2013–14 edition focused on new trends of the Great Powers' Africa policies (Zhang Hongming & Yao Guimei 2013; Zhang Hongming & An Chunying 2014).

The Centre for African Studies at Shanghai Normal University publishes *African Economic Review* and *African Economic Development Report* annually. The Institute of African Studies at Zhejiang Normal University has held several China–Africa Think Tank Forums and annually publishes the *African Studies, African Development Report* and several series of African studies. East China Normal University has concentrated its studies on East Africa and published a biography of Ugandan President Museveni and a translation of Julius Nyerere's writings. Traditionally focusing on Asian and African languages, the School of Asian and African Studies at Beijing Foreign Language University has sent graduate students to the UK School for Oriental and African Studies (SOAS) for area studies and publishes *Asian and African Studies* and two series of studies annually. Several new courses in African languages are included in the curriculum. The Centre for African Studies of Peking University has published four collections covering China–Africa relations, African transformation, African leaders and African Portuguese-speaking countries (CAS 2000, 2002; Lu Ting-en 2005; Li Baoping et al.

2006). It has published its *Annual Review of African Studies in China* since 2011 and its e-weekly *PKU African Tele-Info* is issued at home and abroad.[15]

Memoirs and references

With the opening up of China, this discipline gradually loosened up and officials started to write reminiscences or memoirs, especially after their retirement. Some diplomats with experience of working in Africa contributed articles to a volume subtitled *A glorious passage of China–African friendly relations* (Lu Miaogeng et al. 2006). Several diplomats' stories serve as supplementary data. *Witness the history: Republican ambassadors' narrations* is a series of ambassadors' life experiences. Wang Shu recounts his life as a reporter in Africa during the late 1950s and the early 1960s, including his experience during the Congo (Kinshasa) incident (Wang Shu 2007). Guo Jing-an and Wu Jun's work is included in the *Diplomats look at the world* series. As former ambassador in Ghana, Guo describes his experiences in African countries such as the severing of diplomatic relations with Liberia because of conflict with Taiwan, his mission as a special envoy in Somalia and his time as an ambassador in Ghana (Guo Jing-an & Wu Jun 2006). The *Chinese diplomats* series attracts students of international relations. *Chinese diplomats in Africa* includes 19 articles by diplomats who worked in African countries. The collection covers different topics: a sacred "mission impossible" (Botswana); their suffering (Zambia); witnessing important events in Ghana; the Tanzania–Zambia railway; events in Cameroon and South Africa; and reminiscences of their lives (Li Tongcheng & Jin Boxiong 2005). Former vice-premier and foreign minister Huang Hua, one of the early diplomats and Chinese Ambassador to Ghana and Egypt, has also published his memoir (Huang Hua 2008). Several ambassadors describe their life in African countries vividly (Zhou Boping 2004; Jiang Xiang 2007; Yuan Nansheng 2011; Cheng Tao & Lu Miaogeng 2013; Chinese Embassy in Rwanda 2013).

Former Vice-Premier Qian Qichen's memoir is by no means less important since he started his diplomatic career in Africa. In Qian's memoir we learn of things that do not appear in other writing, such as that President Jiang Zemin once wrote four letters to President Mandela to promote friendship and establish diplomatic relations between China and South Africa (Qian Qichen 2003: 245–87). A report of former President Jiang Zeming's visits abroad gives a vivid description of his time in African countries, especially two important visits and talks with several African leaders in 1996 and 2002 (Zhong Zhicheng 2006). Former Vice-Minister of Commerce Wei Jianguo devoted most of his career to Africa, and his book records many events and life experiences (Wei Jianguo 2012).

Dictionaries and encyclopedias have also been published during this period. Two important dictionaries of diplomacy are most useful for their Africa-related items. *Dictionary on China's diplomacy* mentions various diplomatic contacts between China and Africa in history (Tang Jiaxuan 2000). The

Dictionary on world diplomacy, published in 2005, contains important events, treaties and figures in African diplomacy (Qian Qichen 2005). The compilation of the *Encyclopedia of overseas Chinese*, with more than 15 million Chinese words, was finished in 2002. This monumental work has 12 volumes, and each contains some items on overseas Chinese in Africa (Zhou Nanjing 1999–2002). The *Dictionary of the world's educational events* covers schools and educational events in Africa (Gu Mingyuan 2000).

Some writing by news reporters or travellers also provides valuable material for African study. Their personal experiences have resulted in a unique understanding of Africa (Wang Dongmei & Wang Guotai 2000; Zhang Yun 2000; Liang Yu 2000; Guo Chaoren 2000). Gui Tao lived in Africa as reporter for the Xinhua News Agency for two years and visited many African countries. He tells his story and describes local customs, religion and food. Chen Xiaochen (2014) writes about his travel on the Tanzania–Zambia Railway and describes his experiences and thinking (Gui Tao 2012; Chen Xiaochen 2014; Chang Jiang & Yuan Qing 2013). Chinese or Chinese communities in Africa have also published books, records, magazines, newspapers and reminiscences (Anonymous 2014; Jian Hong 2003, 2007, 2010, 2010a).

Chinese scholars have always tried to introduce the best work in African studies to Chinese students. The translation of the UNESCO *General history of Africa* started rather early and has taken many years. Volume 5 (Ogot 2001) and Volume 8 (Mazrui 2003) of the series mark the completion of the translation of this monumental work. Different publishers have been involved in translating books related to African issues. Commercial Press, an old company with a long tradition of translation, started the World History Library project by organising an editorial committee. Now it has carefully selected more than 70 histories of countries, regions and continents, 11 of them being African, covering countries such as North Africa, Egypt, Libya, Tunisia, the Sudan, Ethiopia, Nigeria, Ghana, Zimbabwe and Somalia. They are written by African scholars such as Toyin Falola, Brian Raftopoulos (2009) and Alois Mlambo and Saheed A. Adejumobi (2007). Democracy and Construction Press published 20 books as a *Series of translations of Africa* in 2015, covering economy, law, history, China–Africa relations, politics, society, ethnicity/religion and culture/arts. The series introduces African scholars such as Nzongola-Ntalaja (2002), Terreblanche (2012) and Opoku (2010). One of the most impressive translations is Ibn Khaldun's *The Muqaddimah: An introduction to history.* Volumes 7–8 of the *Cambridge history of Africa* have been translated by Li Pengtao and Zhao Jun.

Conclusion

Several new features of African studies have emerged during the past years. First, with the increase of monographs, more academics now concentrate on the current situation in politics, the economy, culture and society, with the economy the most popular topic and South Africa the most studied state. Yet the proliferation of publications has underscored the importance of research quality, in which Chinese scholars have a long way to go. Second, various studies on African countries or related topics expand interdisciplinary study, which emphasises the significance of methodology, and solid long-term fieldwork with local language capability is very much needed. Third, more scholars are engaged in international academic exchanges and their views are gradually attracting attention from outside, yet this is concentrated on China–African relations. Young scholars are growing up with better opportunities to study Africa and some have displayed strong academic ability. Finally, there are many books by reporters and overseas Chinese that describe their adventures and personal experiences in Africa, which enriches Chinese understanding of Africa.

Chinese studies of Africa are promising, but they are in need of more effort and hard work.

Notes

1 This chapter is a revised and supplemented version of an article entitled African studies in China in 21st century: A historiographical survey, published in *Brazilian Journal of African Studies* in 2016. I thank the journal for permission to publish it in this book.
2 Professor Qi Shirong (齐世荣), the Vice-Chair of the Association of Chinese Historians, highly praised the work in his keynote speech at the conference "World History Study in China in the 20th Century" held at Peking University in April 2000, and the French international broadcaster reported publication of the book in its Chinese program.
3 Both English and Chinese versions of the published monograph were sent as a gift to Kofi Annan, the former General Secretary of UN, by Peking University during his visit in 2015. Kofi Annan was quite surprised to learn that a book on his country had been written by a Chinese scholar.
4 *World Modernization Process: Volume of Africa* was published in early March 2013 by the Jiangsu People's Publishing House. After President Xi Jinping raised the concept of an "African dream" during his visit to Africa from 24–30 March 2013. Jiangsu People's Publishing House decided to republish it under the alternative title *The African dream: In search of the road to modernization*, and held a book launch in Nanjing.
5 In May 2004, the author was invited to give two lectures about African history to former President Jiang Zemin and later a lecture on China–Africa relations to the General Office of the CPC Central Committee.
6 For example, on 8 November 2013 the author was invited by the Director-General of UNESCO, Irina Bokova, to become a member of the International Scientific Committee of UNESCO's *General History of Africa* (Vol. 9). He was elected Vice Chair of the Committee at its first session, held in Salvador of Brazil on 20–24 November 2013.
7 African Diplomatic Mission in China held the Golden Jubilee of the OAU/AU Seminar in Beijing, www.chinafrica.cn/chinese/zxxx/txt/2013-05/27/content_544893.htm

8 Zhu Weidong of Center for African Law was appointed to the International Commercial Panel by the Arbitration Foundation of Southern Africa, Xiangtan University Law School, 4 November 2013, http://law.xtu.edu.cn/infoshow-17-3869-0.html
9 China–South African held seminar to celebrate the 15th anniversary of establishment of diplomatic relations, Chinanet, 20 September 2013, https://caspu.pku.edu.cn/cn/zxlt/dwjl/230178.html
10 Report of the meeting: International Scientific Comsmittee for the drafting of Volume IX of the General History of Africa, Salvador, 20–24 November 2013; Chen Zhenyun, "Let the great African history tell the future: Interview with Li Anshan, Vice Chair of the International Scientific Committee of UNESCO General History of Africa (9–11 Vols.), *Peking University Gazette*, 10 January 2020. See also the net version in *The Paper* website, https://m.thepaper.cn/newsDetail_forward_6290328?from=singlemessage
11 Professor Li Anshan, Chair of the Chinese Society of African Historical Studies, was invited to co-chair the seminar on China-African Relations, World History Research of China Net, http://iwh.cssn.cn/yjdt/yjdt_xstt_gx_dfsk/201604/t20160413_2964555.shtml. In 2014, Li Anshan gave lectures/speeches as AFRASO Professor at Frankfurt University.
12 Featured Interview: Professor Augustin F. C. Holl, Office of International Cooperation and Exchange/Office of Taiwan, Hong Kong and Macao Affairs, 1 November 2019, https://ice.xmu.edu.cn/en/info/1015/1146.htm
13 Graduate Student Paper Prize Winners, https://africanstudies.org/awards-prizes/graduate-student-paper-prize/graduate-student-paper-prize-winners
14 The institute is very actively involved in international academic activities. On 5–7 July 2021, the Institute held 2021 Tsinghua Area Studies Forum "Areas of the World and the World in Areas" in Beijing with two panels on Africa: Sub-Saharan African Studies Panel and West Asian and North African Studies Panel.
15 Until the end of April of 2020, it has run 446 issues.

References

Adejumobi, Saheed, A. 2007. *The history of Ethiopia*. Santa Barbara: Greenwood Press.
Ai Zhouchang et al. 2000. *A study on modernization in South Africa*. Shanghai: East China Normal University Press.
Ai Zhouchang & Mu Tao. 2001. *Enter into Black Africa*. Shanghai: Shanghai Literature and Art Publishing House.
Ai Zhouchang & Shu Yunguo. 2008. *Black African Civilization*. Fuzhou: Fujian Educational Press.
Ameyaw, Bismark & Li Yao. 2018. Analyzing the impact of GDP on CO2 emissions and forecasting Africa's total CO2 emissions with non-assumption driven bidirectional long short-term memory. *Sustainability* 10(9): 1–23.
An Chunying. 2010. Mining industry cooperation between China and Africa: Challenges and prospects. In Kwesi Kwaa Prah, ed., *Afro-Chinese Relations: Past, Present and Future*, Beijing: CASAS, 309–330.
Anonymous. 2014. *Pursuing a dream: Shanghaiese in Africa*. Shanghai: Shanghai Business Association in Southern Africa.
Appiah-Otoo, Isaac. 2021. The impact of ICT on economic growth: Comparing rich and poor countries. *Telecommunications Policy* 45(2): 1–15.

Asare, Andy Ohemeng & Shao Yunfei. 2018. *Economy Ghana I: Information and communication technology (ICT) and growth for SMEs in Ghana*. Beijing: Social Sciences Academic Press.

Asare-Kyire, L. et al. 2019. An empirical examination of the influencers of pre-mature decline of African clusters: Evidence from the textile clusters in Ghana. *South African Journal of Business Management* 50(1): 318–330.

Berhe, Mulugeta Gebrehiwot & Liu Hongwu, eds. 2013. *China–Africa relations: Governance, peace and security*. Addis Ababa: Institute for Peace and Security Studies (Addis Ababa University) and Institute of African Studies (Zhejiang Normal University).

Bi Jiankang, 2011. *Modernization and political stability in Egypt*. Beijing: Social Sciences Academic Press.

Boadi, Evans Asante, He Zheng, Bosompem, Josephine, Say, Joy & Boadi, Eric Kofi. 2019. Let the talk count: Attributes of stakeholder engagement, trust, perceive environmental protection and CSR. *SAGE Open*, 9(1): 1–15.

Bodomo, A. & Ma, Grace. 2010. From Guangzhou to Yiwu: Emerging facets of the African diaspora in China. *International Journal of African Renaissance Studies* 5(2): 283–289.

Bodomo, A. & Ma, Grace. 2012. We are what we eat: Food in the process of community formation and identity shaping among African traders in Guangzhou and Yiwu. *African Diaspora* 5(1): 1–26.

Brose, Michael C. 2002. Book review: *A history of Chinese overseas in Africa*. *Canadian Journal of African Studies* 36(1): 157–159.

Bureau of International Cooperation, CASS, Institute of West Asia and Africa, CASS & DFID, UK. 2006. *The Symposium of China-Africa Shared Development*, Beijing, 2006.

Cai Gaojiang, 2014. *The Research on AIDS in Africa*, Hangzhou: Zhejiang People's Press.

Center for African Studies of Peking University (CAS), ed. 2000. *China and Africa*, Beijing: Peking University Press.

Center for African Studies of Peking University (CAS), ed. 2002. *Africa: Change and development*, Beijing: World Affairs Press.

Chang Jiang & Yuan Qing, 2013. *Babel caution: When China meets Africa*, Peking University Press.

Chen Fenglan, 2011. Cultural clash and the adaptive stratagem of the Transnational Group of Migration. *Huaqiao Huaren Historical Studies* 3: 41–49.

Chen Gongyuan, ed. 2006. *Development and perspective of China–Africa relations in the new period*. Beijing: CAAS, 2006.

Chen Gongyuan, ed. 2007. *China and Africa: A probe of new strategical partnership*. Beijing: CAAS.

Chen Gongyuan. 2009. *A probe to China–Africa relations and African issues*. Beijing: CAAS.

Chen Gongyuan. 2010. *A primary study on the history of China–Africa friendly contact*. Beijing: CAAS.

Chen Hong & Zhao Ping, eds. 2006. *Bibliography of Chinese writings on African issues, 1997–2006*. Beijing: Institute of West Asia and Africa of Chinese Academy of Social Sciences, Chinese Society of African Historical Studies and Center for African Studies, Peking University.

Chen Mo & Yang Guang, eds. 2005. *Middle East and Africa development report, 2004–2005*. Beijing: Social Sciences Academic Press.

Cheng Tao & Lu Miaogeng, eds. 2013. *Chinese ambassadors telling African stories*. Beijing: World Affairs Press.

Chen Tiandu et al. 2010. *Modern Egypt's relations with great powers*. Beijing: World Affairs Press.

Chen Xiaochen. 2014. *Finding the way in Africa: Chinese memory along the railway*. Hangzhou: Zhejiang University Press.

Chen Xiaohong. 2007. *A study on De Gaulle and African decolonization*. Beijing: China Social Sciences Press.

Chen Xiaoying. 2012. Chinese new immigrants' dilemma and causes in South Africa. *Huaqiao Huaren Historical Studies* 2: 28–35.

Chen Zhongdan. 2000. *Ghana: Looking for a base for modernization*. Chengdu: Sichuan People's Press.

Cheng Ying. 2014. Bàrígà boys' urban experience: Making manifest (im)mobility through "mobile" performances. *SOAS Journal of Postgraduate Research* 7: 48–62.

Cheng Ying. 2016. "Naija Halloween or wetin?": Naija superheroes and a time-traveling performance. *Journal of African Cultural Studies* 28(3): 275–282.

Cheng Ying. 2016a. China meets South Africa in the theatre: Some recent South African work about China & in China, & the Year of China in South Africa. In Martin Banham, James Gibbs & Femi Osofisan, eds, *African Theatre 15: China, India & the Eastern World*. Melton: James Currey.

Cheng Ying. 2018. The journey of the Orishas: An interview with Rotimi Babatunde. In Tiziana Morosetti, ed., *Africa on the contemporary London stage*. Palgrave Macmillan, 211–218.

Cheng Ying. 2018a. 'The bag is my home': Recycling China bags in contemporary African arts. *African Arts* 51(2): 18–31.

Cheng Ying. 2019. History, imperial eyes, and the "mutual gaze": Narratives of African–Chinese encounters in recent literary works. In Moradewun Adejunmobi and Carli Coetzee, eds, *Routledge handbook of African literature*. London: Routledge.

Chinese Embassy in Rwanda, ed. 2013. *Witness Rwanda*. Beijing: Party Building Books Publishing House.

Chong Xiuquan. 2014. *The cultural geography of contemporary African documentary photography*. Hangzhou: Zhejiang People's Press.

Cissé, Daouda. 2021. As migration and trade increase between China and Africa, traders at both ends often face precarity. *Migration Information Source*, 21 July.

Cui Jianmin, ed., 2010. *Marx, Engels, Lenin, Stalin on West Asia and Africa*. Beijing: China Social Sciences Press.

Dickerson, Claire Moore, 2009. *Unified business laws for Africa: Common law perspectives on OHADA*. London: IEDP Press.

Ding Yu (with Qin Dashu & Xie Rouxing). 2013. Peking University archaeological discovery in Kenya in 2010. In Li Anshan & Liu Haifang, eds, *Annual review of African studies in China 2012*. Beijing: Social Sciences Academic Press.

Ding Yu (with Qin Dashu). 2015. Archaeological discovery in Manburui of Kenya Coast. In Li Anshan & Pan Huaqiong, eds, *Annual review of African studies in China 2014*. Beijing: Social Sciences Academic Press.

Dumor, K. & Li Yao. 2019. Estimating China's trade with its partner countries within the Belt and Road Initiative using neural network analysis. Sustainability, 11(5): 1449.

Fang Wei, 2014. *A study on the foreign relations of the New South Africa.* Hangzhou: Zhejiang People's Press.
Feng Zuoku & Chen Gongyuan. 2008. *Strengthen economic and trade cooperation and open African market*, Beijing: n.p.
Gao, James. 2001. Book review: *A history of Chinese overseas in Africa. African Studies Review* 44(1): 164–165.
Gao Jinyuan, 2007. *Selection of Gao Jinyuan's works.* Beijing: China Social Sciences Press.
Gao Jinyuan. 2008. *Yingguo: A brief history of Britain–Africa relations.* Beijing: China Social Sciences Press.
Gocking, R. 2003. Rural protest in colonial Ghana. *The Journal of African History* 44(3): 531–532.
Gu Mingyuan, ed. 2000. *Dictionary of world's educational events.* Nanjing: Jiangsu Educational Press.
Gu Zhangyi. 2010. *Ghana.* Beijing: Social Sciences Academic Press.
Gui Tao. 2012. *Is Africa.* Beijing: China Encyclopedia Press.
Guo Chaoren. 2000. *Notes on Africa.* Beijing: Xinhua Press.
Guo Dantong. 1995. The Inscription of Khnumhotpe II: A new study. *Journal of Ancient Civilizations* 10: 54–64.
Guo Dantong. 1998. The relationships of Egypt and Western Asia during the Middle Kingdom reflected in the inscription of Amenemhet II from Memphis. *Journal of Ancient Civilizations* 13: 83–90.
Guo Dantong. 1999. The Inscription of Amenemhet II from Memphis: Transliteration, translation and commentary. *Journal of Ancient Civilizations* 14: 45–66.
Guo Dantong. 2002. The relationships of Egypt and Palestine during the Early Bronze Age (ca. 3400–2000B CE. *Journal of Ancient Civilizations* 17: 1–6.
Guo Dantong. 2003. The relationships of Egypt and Palestine during the Late Bronze Age (ca. 1550/1500–1200 BCE. *Journal of Ancient Civilizations* 18: 63–74.
Guo Dantong. 2004. The relationships of Egypt and Palestine during the Middle Bronze Age (ca. 2000–1550/1500BCE. *Journal of Ancient Civilizations* 19: 89–100.
Guo Dantong. 2015. A study of biographical inscription of Methen. *World History Studies*, 2(2): 12–23.
Guo Dantong. 2017. Relations between Egypt and Canaan in the Middle Kingdom: A re-examination. *World History Studies*, 2(4): 1–14.
Guo Xiaorui & Guo Dantong. 2019. The identity of nDs in Ancient Egypt. *World History Studies*, 6(1): 20–35.
Guo Jing-an & Wu Jun, 2006. *The years as diplomats in Africa.* Chengdu: Sichuan People's Press.
Han Zhibin et al. 2014. *The study of Libyan Islamic socialism.* Hangzhou: Zhejiang People's Press.
Harneit-Sievers, Axel et al., eds. 2010. *Chinese and African perspectives on China in Africa.* Nairobi: Pambazuka Press.
He Liehui. 2012. *China's Africa Strategy.* Beijing: China's Science and Culture Press.
He Qinhua & Hong Yonghong. 2006. *A history of development of African law.* Beijing: Law Press China.
He Wenping. 2002. China and Africa: Cooperation in 50 Years. *Asia and Africa Today (in Russian)* 12: n.p.
He Wenping. 2005. All weather friends: A vivid portrayal of contemporary political relations between China and Africa. In Kinfe Abraham, ed., *China comes to*

Africa: The political economy and diplomatic history of China's relation with Africa. Addis Ababa: Ethiopian International Institute for Peace and Development.

He Wenping. 2005a. *The study of the democratization process in African countries.* Beijing: Current Affairs Press.

He Wenping. 2006. China–Africa relations moving into an era of rapid development. *Inside AISA* 3&4: 3–6.

He Wenping. 2007. The balancing act of China's Africa policy. *China Security* 3(3): 23–40.

He Wenping. 2007a. "All Weather Friend": The Evolution of China's African Policy. In Kwesi Kwaa Prah, ed., *Afro-Chinese relations: Past, present and future.* Beijing: CASAS, 24–47.

He Wenping. 2008. How to promote "all-round cooperation" between China and Africa. African Executive, www.africanexecutive.com/modules/magazine/articles.php?article=3157

He Wenping. 2008a. Bottlenecks in China-Africa Relations. *African Executive,* www.africanexecutive.com/modules/magazine/articles.php?article=3129.

He Wenping. 2008b. China Africa Cooperation: What's in it for Africa? *African Executive,* www.africanexecutive.com/modules/magazine/articles.php?article=3120.

He Wenping. 2008c. Neocolonialisti? No. Aspenia 41: n.p.

He Wenping. 2008d. Promoting political development through democratic change in Africa. *Contemporary Chinese Thought* 40(1): 32–43.

He Wenping. 2008e. China's perspectives on contemporary China–Africa relations. In Chris Alden, Dan Large & Ricardo Soares de Oliveira, eds, *China returns to Africa: A superpower and a continent embrace.* London: C. Hurst.

He Wenping. 2009. China's African policy: Driving forces, features and global impact. *Africa Review* 1(1): 35–53.

He Wenping. 2009a. A Chinese perception of Africa. In Sharon T. Freeman, ed., *China, Africa, and the African diaspora: Perspectives.* Washington, DC: AASBEA.

He Wenping. 2010. Darfur issue and China's role. In Harneit-Sievers, Axel et al., eds. 2010. *Chinese and African perspectives on China in Africa.* Nairobi: Pambazuka Press, 176–193.

He Wenping. 2010a. The Darfur issue: A new test for China's Africa policy. In Fantu Cheru and Cyril Obi, eds, *The rise of China and India in Africa.* New York: Zed Books.

He Wenping. 2010b. *China's aid to Africa: Policy evolution, characteristics and its role,* in J. Stillhoff Sørensen, ed., *Challenging the aid paradigm: Western currents and Asian alternatives.* Houndmills: Palgrave Macmillan.

He Wenping. 2010c. Overturning the wall: Building soft power in Africa. *China Security* 6: 63–69.

He Wenping. 2011. From "aid effectiveness" to "development effectiveness": What China's experiences can contribute to the discourse evolution. *West Asia and Africa* 9: 120–135.

He Wenping. 2012. Infrastructure and development cooperation: Take China in Africa as an example, in Lim Wonhyuk, ed. *Emerging Asian approaches to development cooperation.* Seoul: Korea Development Institute.

He Wenping (with Sven Grimm), 2012a. Emerging partners and their impact on African development, in Erik Lundsgaarde, ed., *Africa toward 2030: Challenges for development policy.* Houndmills: Palgrave Macmillan.

He Wenping. 2012b. China–Africa economic relations: Current situation and future challenges, in James Shikwati, ed., *China–Africa partnership: The quest for a win-win relationship*. Nairobi: Inter Region Economic Network (IREN), 7–12.

He Wenping. 2013. *Development cooperation approaches to pro-poor growth: Strategies and lessons from China*. Seoul: Korea Development Institute (KDI).

Holl, A.F.C. (高畅). 2017. Beyond shamanism: Dissecting the paintings from Snake Rock, Namibia. *The Journal of Culture* 1: 27–35.

Holl, A.F.C. 2018. Senegambian megaliths as world heritage. *Arts and Humanities Open Access Journal* 2(3): 179–185.

Holl, A.F.C. 2019. The dynamics of mounds-clusters in the Mouhoun Bend (Burkina Faso). *Journal of Anthropological and Archaeological Science* 1(1): 1–12.

Holl, A.F.C. 2019a. The chalcolithization process: Dynamics of Shiqmim site-cluster (Northern Negev, Israel). *International Journal of Archaeology* 7(2): 30–46.

Holl, A.F.C. 2019b. Place, graves, and people: Archaeology of New York African burial ground (ca. 1650–1796). In V. Silva Santos, L.C.P. Symanski and A.F. C. Holl, eds, *Arqueologia e Historia da Cultura Material na Africa e na Diaspora Africana*. Rio de Janeiro: Brazil Publishing, 40–84.

Holl, A.F.C. & H. Bocoum. 2017. *Megaliths, cultural landscape and the production of ancestors*. Vienna: Sarrebruck Editions Universitaires Europeennes.

Hong Yonghong. 2005. *Review on Criminal Law in Africa*. Beijing: China Procuratorial Press.

Hong Yonghong. 2007. The African Charter and China's legislation: A comparative study of ideas of human rights, in Kwesi Kwaa Prah, ed., *Afro-Chinese relations: Past, present and future*. Beijing: CASAS, 88–100.

Hong Yonghong. 2009. International Criminal Tribunal in Rwanda ICTR. Beijing: China Social Sciences Press.

Hong Yonghong. 2010. Trade, investment and legal cooperation between China and Africa. In Axel Harneit-Sievers et al., eds. 2010. *Chinese and African perspectives on China in Africa*. Nairobi: Pambazuka Press, 82–90.

Hong Yonghong. 2014. *Contemporary African law*. Hangzhou: Zhejiang People's Press.

Hong Yonghong & Xia Xinhua. 2010. *African law and social development*. Xiangtan: Xiangtan University Press.

Hu Yongju & Qiu Xin. 2014. *The present situations and developing trend of African transportation infrastructure & China's participation strategies*. Hangzhou: Zhejiang People's Press.

Huang Hua. 2008. *My reminiscences*. Beijing: World Affairs Press.

Huang Hui. 2015. *A study on Berberism in Algeria*. Beijing: Social Sciences Academic Press.

Huang Xianjin et al., eds. 2014. *African land resource and food security*. Nanjing: Nanjing University Press.

IWAA CASS. 2011. *Middle East & African Studies in China (1949–2010)*. Beijing: Social Sciences Academic Press.

Jian Hong. 2003. *Chinese merchants in Africa*. Beijing: China Economy Press.

Jian Hong. 2007. *Last Gold Mines*. Beijing: China Times Economy Press.

Jian Hong. 2010. *Mozambique Guide Book*. Beijing: China Science Culture Audio-Video Press.

Jian Hong. 2010a. *Cross Southeast Africa*. Beijing: Beijing Press.

Jiang Dong, 2005. *Nigerian culture*, Beijing: Culture and Art Publishing House.

Jiang Hengkun, 2014. *The Darfur crisis: Causes, processes and impacts*. Hangzhou: Zhejiang People's Press.

Jiang Hui, 2020. A crisis of representation in the time of pandemic: The reconfiguration of the South African public sphere. *Inter-Asia Cultural Studies*, December.

Jiang Hui. 2020a. South Africa's wider divide in the disaster state. *Mediapolis: A Journal of Cities and Culture*, June.

Jiang Xiang. 2007. *My seventeen years in Africa*. Shanghai: Shanghai Lexicographical Publishing House.

Jiang Zhongjin, ed. 2012. *Graphical records of African agriculture*. Nanjing: Nanjing University Press.

Jiang Zhongjin, ed. 2014. *Modern African human geography*, 2 vols. Nanjing: Nanjing University Press.

Jiang Zhongjin & Liu Litao, eds. 2014. *A study on strategy of China–Africa energy cooperation and security*. Nanjing: Nanjing University Press.

Jiang Zhongjin, et al., eds. 2014. *African agriculture and rural development: Fieldwork research on nine countries*. Nanjing: Nanjing University Press.

Jing Men & Barton, Benjamin, eds. 2011. *China and the European Union in Africa: Partners or competitors?* Aldershot: Ashgate.

Lartey, Victor Curtis & Li Yao. 2018. Zero-coupon and forward yield curves for government of Ghana bonds. *SAGE Open* 8(3): 1–15.

Lartey, Victor & Li Yao. 2019. Daily frequency zero-coupon yield curve for government bonds traded on e-bond trading platform of the Ghana Fixed Income Market. *International Journal of e-Education, e-Business, e-Management and e-Learning* 9: 306–315.

Lartey, Victor Curtis, Li Yao, Lartey, Hannah Darkoa & Boad, Eric Kofi. 2019. Zero-coupon, forward and par yield curves for the Nigerian bond market. *SAGE Open* 9(4): 1–14.

Li Anshan. 2000. *A history of Chinese overseas in Africa*. Beijing: Overseas Chinese Publishing House.

Li Anshan. 2002. *British rule and rural protest in Southern Ghana*. New York: Peter Lang.

Li Anshan. 2004. *Study on African nationalism*. Beijing: China's International Broadcast Publisher.

Li Anshan. 2005. African studies in China in the twentieth century: A historiographical survey. *African Studies Review* 48(1): 59–87.

Li Anshan. 2006. *Social history of Chinese overseas in Africa: Selected documents 1800–2005*. Hong Kong: Hong Kong Press for Social Science.

Li Anshan. 2007. China and Africa: Policies and challenges. *China Security* 3(3): 69–93.

Li Anshan. 2007a. *Transformation of China's policy towards Africa*. CTR Working Paper. Hong Kong: Hong Kong University of Science and Technology, www.cctr.ust.hk/papers.htm.

Li Anshan. 2007b. African studies in China in the twentieth century. In Paul Tiyambe Zeleza, ed., *The study of Africa: Global and transnational engagements*. Dakar: CODESRIA.

Li Anshan. 2008. Gli studi africanistici in Cina agli inizi del XXI secolo. *Afriche e Orienti*, No. 2, as part of Cristiana Fiamingo, ed., *La Cina in Africa*, www.centrocabral.com/1797/La_Cina_in_Africa

Li Anshan. 2008a. China–Sudan relations: The past and present. *Symposium on Chinese-Sudanese Relations*. London: Center for Foreign Policy Analysis, 4–12.

Li Anshan. 2008b. China's New Policy towards Africa. In R. Rotberg, ed., *China into Africa: Trade, aid, and influence.* Washington, DC: Brookings Institution Press, 21–49.

Li Anshan. 2009. China's immigrants in Africa and China's Africa policy: Implications for China–African cooperation. In Sharon T. Freeman, ed., *China, Africa, and the African diaspora: Perspectives.* Washington, DC: AASBEA, 94–105.

Li Anshan. 2009a. The study of China–Africa relations in the past thirty years. *West Asia and Africa,* 4: 5–15.

Li Anshan. 2009b. What's to be done after the Fourth FOCAC. *China Monitor,* November, 7–9.

Li Anshan. 2010. Control and Combat: Chinese Indentured Labor in South Africa, 1904–1910. *Encounter* 3: 41–61.

Li Anshan. 2010a. African Studies in China: A historiographical survey. In Axel Harneit-Sievers et al., eds., *Chinese and African perspectives on China in Africa.* Nairobi: Pambazuka Press, 2–24.

Li Anshan. 2011. *Chinese medical cooperation with Africa: With a special emphasis on Chinese medical team and anti-malaria campaign.* Uppsala: Nordiska Afrikainstitutet.

Li Anshan. 2011a. La coopération médicale Sino-Africaine: une autre forme d'aide humanitaire. In Caroline Abu-Sada, ed., *Dans l'œil des Autre: Perception de l'action humanitaire et de MSF.* Geneva: Editions Antipodes.

Li Anshan. 2011b. From "how could" to "how should": The possibility of a pilot U.S.-China Project in Africa. In Charles W. Freeman III & Xiaoqing Lu Boynton, eds, *China's emerging global health and foreign aid engagement in Africa.* Washington, DC: Center for Strategic and International Studies, 37–46.

Li Anshan. 2011c. Cultural heritage and China's Africa policy. In Jing Men and Benjamin Barton, eds, *China and the European Union in Africa: Partners or competitors?* Aldershot: Ashgate, 41–59.

Li Anshan. 2012. *A History of Overseas Chinese in Africa till 1911,* New York: Diasporic Africa Press.

Li Anshan. 2012. China and Africa: Cultural similarity and mutual learning. In James Shikwati, ed., *China–Africa Partnership: The quest for a win–win relationship.* Nairobi: Inter Region Economic Network (IREN), 93–97.

Li Anshan. 2013. BRICS: Dynamics, resilience and role of China. *BRICS–Africa: Partnership and interaction.* Moscow: Institute for African Studies, Russian Academy of Sciences, 122–134.

Li Anshan. 2013a. Book review: *The dragon's gift: The real story of China in Africa. Pacific Affairs,* 86(1), 138–140.

Li Anshan. 2013b. China's African policy and the Chinese immigrants in Africa, in Tan Chee-Beng, ed., *Routledge Handbook of the Chinese Diaspora,* London: Routledge, 59–70.

Li Anshan. 2013c. Chinese medical cooperation in Africa from the pre-FOCAC era to the present. In Li Anshan & Funeka Yazini April, eds, *Forum,* 64–80.

Li Anshan. 2015. A long-time neglected subject: China–Africa people-to-people contact. In Shelton, Garth, April, Funeka Yazini & Li Anshan, eds, *FOCAC 2015: A new beginning of China–Africa Relations.* Pretoria: Africa Institute of South Africa, 446–475.

Li Anshan. 2015a. African diaspora in China: Reality, research and reflection, *The Journal of Pan African Studies* 7(10): 10–43.

Li Anshan. 2015b. Contact between China and Africa before Vasco da Gama: Archeology, document and historiography. *World History Studies* 2(1): 34–59.
Li Anshan. 2015c. 10 questions about migration between China and Africa. China Policy Institute, http://blogs.nottingham.ac.uk/chinapolicyinstitute/2015/03/04/10-questions-about-migration-between-china-and-africa
Li Anshan. 2016. African studies in China in the 21st century: A historiographical survey. *Brazilian Journal of African Studies*, 1(2): 48–88.
Li Anshan. 2016a. Technology transfer in China–Africa relations: Myth or reality. *Transnational Corporations Review* 8(3): 183–195.
Li Anshan. 2017. The study of China–Africa relations in China: A historiographical survey. *World History Studies* 4(2): 87–109.
Li Anshan. 2019. *The social and economic history of the Chinese overseas in Africa* (3 volumes), Nanjing: Jiangshu People's Press.
Li Anshan. 2020. *China and Africa in global context: Encounter, policy, cooperation & migration*. Cape Town: Africa Century Editions Press.
Li Anshan. 2021. African economic autonomy and international development cooperation. In Rahma Bourqia & Marcelo Sili, eds, *New paths of development: Perspective from the Global South*. Dordrecht: Springer, 43–53.
Li Anshan, An Chunying & Li Zhongren, eds. 2009. *China–Africa relations and the contemporary world*. Taiyuan: Chinese Society of African Historical Studies.
Li Anshan & Funeka Yazini April, eds. 2013. *Forum on China–Africa cooperation: The politics of human resource development*. Pretoria: Africa Institute of South Africa.
Li Anshan et al. 2012. *FOCAC twelve years later: Achievements, challenges and the way forward*. Uppsala: The Nordic Africa Institute.
Li Anshan et al. 2013. *African dream: Search for modernization*. Nanjing: Jiangsu People's Publishing House.
Li Baoping. 2007. Sino-Tanzanian relations and political development. in Kwesi Kwaa Prah, ed., *Afro-Chinese relations: Past, present and future*, Beijing: CASAS, 126–141.
Li Baoping. 2008. Sulla questione della cooperazione tra Africa e Cina nel settore dell'istruzione, *Afriche e Orienti*, No.2 (as part of the dossier, Cristiana Fiamingo, ed., *La Cina in Africa*).
Li Baoping. 2011. *Tradition and modern: African culture and political transformation*. Beijing: Peking University Press.
Li Baoping & Luo Jianbo. 2013. Dissecting soft power and Sino-Africa relations in education and exchanges cooperation, in Li Anshan & Funeka Yazini April, eds., *Forum on China-Africa Cooperation,* 28–42.
Li Baoping, et al., eds., 2006. *A study on the development of Portuguese-speaking countries in Asia and Africa.* Beijing: World Affairs Press, 2006.
Li Guangyi 2008. *Mauritania*. Beijing: Social Sciences Academic Press.
Li Tongcheng & Jin Boxiong. 2005. *Chinese diplomats in Africa*. Shanghai: Shanghai People's Publishing House.
Li Weijian, ed. 2008. *Beijing Summit & the Third Ministerial Conference of the Forum on China-Africa Cooperation: Appraisal and prospects*. Shanghai: Shanghai Institutes for International Studies.
Li Xiangyun. 2014. *Tanzania state-building and development*. Hangzhou: Zhejiang People's Press.
Li Xiaoyun, ed. 2010a. *Comparative perspectives in development and poverty Reduction in China and Africa*. Beijing: China Financial and Economic Publishing House.

Li Xiaoyun, ed. 2010b. *Development, poverty and poverty alleviation in China and Africa*. Beijing: China Financial and Economic Publishing House.

Li Xinfeng. 2005. *Following Zheng He's footprints through Africa*. Kunming: Chenguang Press.

Li Xinfeng. 2006. *An unusual journey across African continent*. Kunming: Chenguang Press.

Li Xinfeng. 2012. A quantitative study of Chinese overseas. *Chinese Overseas*, 1–2: 7–12.

Li Xinfeng et al. 2012. *Zheng He and Africa*. Beijing: China's Social Sciences Press.

Li Yongcai. 2009. *A history of South African literature*. Shanghai: Shanghai Foreign Language Education Press.

Li Zhibiao, ed. 2000. *African economic zone and Chinese enterprises*. Beijing: Beijing Press.

Li Zhibiao, ed. 2007. Contemporary economic and trade relations between China and Africa, in Kwesi Kwaa Prah, ed. *Afro-Chinese relations: Past, present and future*. Beijing: CASAS, 280–293.

Lian, Chaoqun. 2016. "١٣، «العربي الجديد» في " بديل لإيجاد والسعي .. المتوسط الأبيض البحر. مارس ٢٠١٦.

Lian, Chaoqun. 2016a."٨، «العربي الجديد» في " الشرق عن الغربية المعرفة استيراد .. الصين. مايو ٢٠١٦.

Lian, Chaoqun. 2016b. "٢٠١٦ يوليو ١٠، «العربي الجديد» في " الصين في اللغوية الثورة .

Lian, Chaoqun. 2018. "Metaphorical recurrence and language symbolism in Arabic metalanguage discourse. In Yonatan Mendel & Abeer Alnajjar, eds, *Language, politics and society in the Middle East*. Edinburgh: Edinburgh University Press.

Liang Yijian. 2012. Sustainable development and Sino-African low-carbon cooperation: China's role. In James Shikwati, ed., *China–Africa partnership: The quest for a win–win relationship*. Nairobi: Inter Region Economic Network (IREN), 40–45.

Liang Yijian. 2014. *The dynamics of comparative advantages and Africa's economic development*. Beijing: Social Sciences Academic Press.

Liang Yu. 2000. *Enter Black Africa*. Changchun: Jilin People's Press.

Lin, Justin Yifu. 2015. China's rise and structural transformation in Africa: Ideas and opportunities. In In Célestin Monga, & Justin Yifu Lin, eds., 2015. *The Oxford handbook of Africa and economics, vols 1–2*, Oxford: Oxford University Press, vol. 2, 815–829.

Liu Haifang. 2006. China and Africa: Transcending "threat or boon". *China Monitor*, March. Centre for China Studies, South Africa.

Liu Haifang. 2008. China–Africa relations through the prism of culture: The dynamics of China's African cultural diplomacy. *Journal of Current Chinese*

Liu Haifang. 2015. FOCAC VI: African initiatives toward a sustainable Chinese relationship, *China Monitor*. Centre for China Studies, South Africa.

Liu Hongwu. 2012. New impetus of African development and new path to sustainable development of China–Africa relations. In James Shikwati, ed., *China–Africa partnership: The quest for a win–win relationship*. Nairobi: Inter Region Economic Network (IREN), 177–181.

Liu Hongwu. 2019. *Introduction to African studies as a discipline*. Beijing: People's Publishing House.

Liu Hongwu & Luo Jianbo. 2011. *Sino-African development cooperation: Studies on the theories, strategies and policies*. Beijing: China's Social Sciences Press.

Liu Hongwu et al. 2014. *A century history of Nigeria since its foundation, 1914–2014*. Hangzhou: Zhejiang People's Press.

Liu Hongwu & Li Shudi, eds. 2010. *African art research*. Kunming: Yunnan People's Press.
Liu Hongwu & Shen Peili, eds. 2009. *The African NGOs and Sino-African relations*. Beijing: World Affairs Press.
Liu Hongwu & Yang Jiemian, eds. 2009. *Fifty years of Sino-African cooperation: Background, progress and significance. Chinese perspectives on Sino-African relations*. Kunming: Yunnan University Press.
Liu Hongwu & Huang Meibo et al. 2013. *A study on the strategy of Chinese foreign aid and international responsibility*. Beijing: China's Social Sciences Press.
Liu Shaonan. 2019. China Town in Lagos: Chinese migration and the Nigerian state since the 1990s. *Journal of Asian and African Studies* 54(6): 783–799.
Liu Shaonan. 2020. Symbol of wealth and prestige: A social history of Chinese-made enamelware in Northern Nigeria. *African Studies Review* 63(2): 212–237.
Liu Yan, 2014. *A study of African education reform modes in the postcolonial era*, Hangzhou: Zhejiang People's Press.
Lou Shizhou. 2014. *Studies on high education in Senegal*. Hangzhou: Zhejiang People's Press.
Lu Miaogeng, Huang Shejiao & Lin Ye, ed. 2006. *United hearts as gold: A glorious passage of China–African friendly relations*. Beijing: World Affairs Press.
Lu Ting-en, ed. 2000. *Brief history of development of African agriculture*. Beijing: Chinese Financial Economic Press.
Lu Ting-en. 2005. *Treatises on Africa*. Beijing: World Affairs Publishers.
Lu Ting-en et al., eds. 2005. *African leaders who effect historical passage*. Beijing: World Affairs Press.
Luo Gaoyuan. 2010. *Contemporary tourism in Africa*. Beijing: World Affairs Press.
Luo Jianbo. 2006. *African integration and Sino-African relations*. Beijing: Social Sciences Academic Press.
Luo Jianbo, 2010. *The road to renaissance: Studies on the African union and the African integration*, Beijing: Chinese Social Sciences Press.
Luo Jianbo & Zhang Xiaoming. 2011. Multilateral cooperation in Africa between China and Western countries – from differences to consensus. *Review of International Studies* 37(4): 1793–1813.
Ma Enyu 2012. Yiwu mode and Sino-African relations. *Journal of Cambridge Studies* 7(3): 93–108.
Mancuso, S. & Hong Yonghong. 2009. *Research on legal environment for Chinese investments in Africa*. Xiangtan: Xiangtan University Press.
Mazrui, Ali A. 1993. General history of Africa VIII: Africa since 1935. Assistant editor C. Wondji. Paris: UNESCO.
Mo Xiang. 2014. *The research on security of contemporary Africa*. Hangzhou: Zhejiang People's Press.
Monga, Célestin & Lin, Justin Yifu, eds. 2015. *The Oxford handbook of Africa and economics, vols 1–2*. Oxford: Oxford University Press.
Monga, Célestin & Lin, Justin Yifu. 2015a. "Introduction: Africa, the next intellectual frontier", in In Célestin Monga, & Justin Yifu Lin, eds., 2015. *The Oxford handbook of Africa and economics, vols 1–2*, Oxford: Oxford University Press, vol. 1, 1–26.
Monga, Célestin & Lin, Justin Yifu. 2015b. Introduction: Africa's evolving economic policy frameworks", In Célestin Monga, & Justin Yifu Lin, eds., 2015. *The Oxford handbook of Africa and economics, vols 1–2*. Oxford: Oxford University Press, vol. 2, 1–20.

Mu Tao. 2003. *A study on South African external relations*. Shanghai: East China Normal University Press.
Mu Tao & Yu Bin. 2013. *Y.K. Museveni: President of the Permanent Snow on the Equator and the Pearl of Africa-Uganda*. Shanghai: Shanghai Dictionary Press.
Mutiiri, Onesmus Mbaabu et al. 2020. Infrastructure and inclusive growth in sub-Saharan Africa: An empirical analysis. *Progress in Development Studies* 20(3): 187–207.
Niu Dong. 2015. Transient association: African's social organizations in Guangzhou. *Sociological Studies* 2: 124–148.
Niu Dong. 2016. "Transient household": Kinship and residence patterns of Africans in Guangzhou. *Open Times* 4: 108–124.
Niu Dong 2018. Transient: A descriptive concept for understanding Africans in Guangzhou. *African Studies Quarterly* 17(4): 85–100.
Nzongola-Ntalaja, G. 2002. *The Congo from Leopold to Kabila: A people's history*. New York: Zed Books.
Nyerere, Julius Kambarage. 2015. *Selected works of Julius Kambarage Nyerere*, 4 vols. Shanghai: East China Normal University.
Ogot, B.A. 1992. *General history of Africa V: Africa from the sixteenth to the eighteenth century*. Paris: UNESCO.
Opoku, D.K. 2010. *The politics of government–business relations in Ghana, 1986–2008*. Basingstoke: Palgrave Macmillan.
Pan Peiying. 2007. *Libya*. Beijing: Social Sciences Academic Press.
Pang Zhongying. 2013. The non-interference dilemma: Adapting China's approach to the new context of African and international realities. In Mulugeta Gebrehiwot Berhe & Liu Hongwu, eds, *China–Africa relations: Governance, peace and security*. Addis Ababa: Institute for Peace and Security Studies (Addis Ababa University) and Institute of African Studies (Zhejiang Normal University)., 46–54.
Peng Kunyuan. 2006. *Niger*. Beijing: Social Sciences Academic Press.
Prah, Kwesi Kwaa, ed. 2007. *Afro-Chinese relations: Past, present and future*. Beijing: CASAS.
Qi Jianhua. 2014. *Developing China–Africa partnership of new and comprehensive cooperation*, Beijing: World Affairs Press.
Qian Qichen. 2003. *Ten stories of a diplomat*. Beijing: World Affairs Press.
Qian Qichen, ed. 2005. *Dictionary on world's diplomacy*, 2 vols. Beijing: World Affairs Press.
Qin Dashu & Yuan Jian, eds. 2014. *Ancient silk trade road*. Singapore: World Scientific.
Qin Hui. 2013. *South Africa's revelation*. Nanjing: Jiangsu Literature and Art Publishing House.
Qiu Yu. 2018. The Chinese are coming: Social dependence and entrepreneurial ethics in postcolonial Nigeria. In Franck Billé & Sören Urbansky, eds, *Yellow perils: China narratives in the contemporary world*. Honolulu: University of Hawai'i Press.
Raftopoulos, Brian & Alois, Mlambo. 2009. *Becoming Zimbabwe: A history from the pre-colonial period to 2008*. Harare: Weaver Press.
Santos, V. Silva, Symanski, L.C.P. & Holl, A.F.C., eds. 2019. *Arqueologia e Historia da Cultura Material na Africa e na Diaspora Africana*. Rio de Janeiro: Brazil Publishing.
Say, Joy. 2021. Sources of economic growth: Bankerteers or marketeers or both? An auto regressive distributed lag (ARDL): Evidence from Ghana. *International Journal of Finance and Economics*, 15 February, 1–17.

Say, Joy & Sagoe, Frank Ebo. 2021. Intention to use high speed rail (HSR) in Ghana: A comparative study. *Journal of Psychology in Africa* 31(1): 76–81.

Say, Joy, Zhao Hongjiang, Agbenyegah, Francisca Sena, Abena Nusenu, Angela, Asante Boadi, Evans & Egbadewoe, Samuel Morkporkpor. 2020. Regional efficiency disparities in rural and community banks in Ghana: A data envelopment analysis. *Journal of Psychology in Africa* 30(3): 249–256.

Shelton, Garth, April, Funeka Yazini & Li Anshan, eds. 2015. *FOCAC 2015: A New Beginning of China-Africa Relations*. Pretoria: Africa Institute of South Africa.

Shen Xipeng. 2018. *A study on China aided construction of Tanzania Zambia Railway*. Beijing: Huangshan Publishing House.

Shen Xiaolei. 2015. Dilemma of Chinese new immigrants' integration in Zimbabwe. *International Politics Quarterly* 5: 129–152.

Shi Lin. 2012. The ethnographic study of the contemporary Africa from the perspective of China. In James Shikwati, ed., *China–Africa partnership: The quest for a win–win relationship*. Nairobi: Inter Region Economic Network (IREN), 104–109.

Shi Yongjie. 2015. *Strengthening the nation through breaking the siege: A study on China–Africa economic and trade cooperation in the new situation*. Beijing: China Commerce and Trade Press.

Shikwati, James, ed. 2012. *China–Africa partnership: The quest for a win–win relationship*. Nairobi: Inter Region Economic Network (IREN).

Shu Yunguo. 2012. *An introduction to African history*. Beijing: Peking University Press.

Shu Yunguo. 2014. *History of pan-Africanism 1900–2002*. Beijing: The Commercial Press.

Shu Yunguo & Liu Weicai, eds. 2013. *The economic history of Africa in 20th century*. Hangzhou: Zhejiang People's Press.

Sun Hongqi. 2008. *On colonialism and Africa*. Beijing: China University of Mining and Technology Press.

Sun Hongqi. 2011. *Land Problem and the Political Economy of South Africa*, Beijing: Central Compilation and Translation Press.

Sun Xiaomeng. 2004. A study on written Hausa drama. MA thesis, Ahmadu Bello University.

Sun Xiaomeng. 2014. *Language and power: The application of Hausa in Northern Nigeria during the British administration*. Beijing: Social Sciences Academic Press.

Tang Jiaxuan, ed. 2000. *Dictionary on China's diplomacy*. Beijing: World Affairs Press.

Tang Xiao. 2012. Africa's regional integration and Sino-Africa cooperation: Opportunities and challenges. In James Shikwati, ed., *China–Africa partnership: The quest for a win–win relationship*. Nairobi: Inter Region Economic Network (IREN), 13–19.

Tang Xiaoyang (with Deborah Brautigam). 2009. China's engagement in African agriculture. *The China Quarterly* 199: 686–706.

Tang Xiaoyang. 2010. Bulldozer or locomotive – the impact of Chinese enterprises on the local employment market in Angola. *Journal of Asian and African Studies* 45(3): 350–368.

Tang Xiaoyang (with Deborah Brautigam). 2011. African Shenzhen: China's special economic zones in Africa. *The Journal of Modern African Studies*, 49(1): 27–54.

Tang Xiaoyang (with Deborah Brautigam). 2012. Economic statecraft in China's new overseas special economic zones: soft power, business or resource security? *International Affairs* 88(4): 799–816.

Tang Xiaoyang. 2014. *China–Africa economic diplomacy and its implications for the global value chain*. Beijing: World Affairs Press.

Tang Xiaoyang (with Deborah Brautigam). 2014a. Going global in groups: China's Special Economic Zones overseas. *World Development* 63: 78–91.

Tang Xiaoyang. 2014b. Models of Chinese engagement in Africa's extractive sectors and their implications. *Environment: Science and Policy for Sustainable Development* 56(2): 27–30.

Tang Xiaoyang. 2014c. *The Impact of Asian Investment on Africa's Textile Industries*. Carnegie-Tsinghua Center for Global Policy. http://carnegietsinghua.org/publications/?fa=56320

Tang Xiaoyang. 2014d. Investissements chinois dans l'industrie textile tanzanienne et zambienne. *Afrique Contemporaine* 250: 119–136.

Tang Xiaoyang (with Jean-Jacques Gabas). 2014e. Coopération agricole chinoise en Afrique subsaharienne. *Perspective: Stratégies de Dévelopment*, 26.

Tang Xiaoyang. 2016. Does Chinese employment benefit Africans? Investigating Chinese enterprises and their operations in Africa. *African Studies Quarterly* 16(3–4): 107–128.

Tang Xiaoyang. 2018. Geese flying to Ghana? A case study of the impact of Chinese investments on Africa's manufacturing sector. *Journal of Contemporary China* 27(114): 924–941.

Tang Xiaoyang. 2019. Chinese economic and trade cooperation zones in Africa. In Arkebe Oqubay & Justin Lifu Lin, eds, *The Oxford handbook of industrial hubs and economic development*, Oxford: Oxford University Press.

Tang Xiaoyang. 2020. *Coevolutionary pragmatism: Approaches and impacts of China–Africa economic cooperation*. Cambridge: Cambridge University Press.

Tang Xiaoyang & Janet Eom. 2018. Time perception and industrialization: Divergence and convergence of work ethics in Chinese enterprises in Africa. *The China Quarterly* 238 : 1–21.

Terreblanche, S.J.S. 2012. *Lost in transformation: South Africa's search for a new future since 1986*. Johannesburg: KMM Review Publishing Company.

Wan Siulan, Li Wei et al. 2014. *Studies on higher education in Botswana*. Hangzhou: Zhejiang People's Press.

Wang Dongmei & Wang Guotai. 2000. *Enter Africa*. Beijing: China International Radio Press.

Wang Haili. 2017. Liu Wenpeng's contributions to the study of ancient world history in China. *World History Studies* 4(2): 65–71.

Wang Shu. 2007. *Stories of five continents*. Shanghai: Shanghai Dictionary Publications.

Wang Tai. 2014. *A study on the political development and democratization process in Egypt*. Beijing: People's Press.

Wang Tao. 2014. *The Lord's Resistance Army in Uganda*. Hangzhou: Zhejiang People's Press.

Wang Xuejun. 2013. The corporate social responsibility of Chinese oil companies in Nigeria: Implications for the governance of oil resources. In Mulugeta Gebrehiwot Berhe & Liu Hongwu, eds, *China–Africa relations: Governance, peace and security*. Addis Ababa: Institute for Peace and Security Studies (Addis Ababa University) and Institute of African Studies (Zhejiang Normal University, 128–145.

Wei Jianguo. 2012. *My life and Africa*. Beijing: World Affairs Press.

Wei Xiaohui & Huang Meibo. 2018. *The international industrial transfer and the development of manufacture industry in Africa*. Beijing: Renmin Press.

Wen Shuang. 2014. Muslim activist encounters in Meiji Japan. *Middle East Report*, 44: 270.
Wen Shuang. 2015. Two sides of the story: How historians and journalists can work together. *Perspectives on History* 53(7): 33–34.
Wen Shuang. 2016. China's increasing engagements and moderate ambitions in the Middle East. *Middle East Insights* 137: 1–3.
Wen Shuang. 2019. From Manchuria to Egypt: Soybean's global migration and transformation in the twentieth century. *Asian Journal of Middle Eastern and Islamic Studies* 13(2): 176–194.
Xia Jisheng. 2005. *Two African parliaments*. Beijing: China's Financial and Economic Press.
Xia Xinhua & Xiao Yaiying. 2011. On Sino-Africa relations and legal cooperation. *Botswana University Law Journal* 4:173.
Xiao Hongyu. 2014. *Interactive nature of modernization and integration in Africa: The case of regional integration in West Africa*. Beijing: Social Sciences Academic Press.
Xiao Yuhua. 2014. *From monarchy to federalism: A study on Ethiopia's political modernization*. Hangzhou: Zhejiang People's Press.
Xu Liang (co-authored with Akyeampong, Emmanuel). 2015. The three phases/faces of China in independent Africa: Re-conceptualizing China–Africa engagement. In Célestin Monga, & Justin Yifu Lin, eds., 2015. *The Oxford handbook of Africa and economics, vols 1–2*. Oxford: Oxford University Press, vol. 2, 762–779.
Xu Liang. 2015a. Historical lessons, common challenges and mutual learning: Assessing China–Africa cooperation in environmental protection. In Shelton, Garth, April, Funeka Yazini & Li Anshan, eds, *FOCAC 2015: A new beginning of China–Africa Relations*. Pretoria: Africa Institute of South Africa, 425–445.
Xu Liang. 2017. Cyrildene Chinatown, suburban settlement and ethnic economy in post-Apartheid Johannesburg. In Young-Chan Kim, ed., *China and Africa: A new paradigm of global business*. London: Palgrave Macmillan.
Xu Liang. 2020. The comforts of home: A historical study of family well-being among Chinese migrants in South Africa. *Asian Ethnicity* 21(4): 507–525.
Xu Tao. 2013. *The social adaptions of African merchants in China*. Hangzhou: Zhejiang People's Press.
Xu Wei. 2011. Field work on the Wayeyi of Botswana and thought on state-building. *African Studies* 1: 61–80.
Xu Wei. 2014. *Ethnicity, everyday life and social change in Botswana*. Hangzhou: Zhejiang People's Press.
Xu Yongzhang. 2004. *Research on the history of relations between China and Asia-African countries*. Hong Kong: Hong Kong Press for Social Sciences.
Xu Yongzhang. 2014. *A brief history of fifty-four African countries*. Hangzhou: Zhejiang People's Press.
Xu Yongzhang. 2019. *Historical manuscripts of ancient Sino-African relations*. Shanghai: Shanghai Dictionaries Press.
Yang Guang & Wen Boyou. 2002. *Middle East and Africa development report, 2001–2002*. Beijing: Social Sciences Academic Press.
Yang Guang & He Wenping, eds. 2007. *Annual report on development in the Middle East and Africa 2006–2007: History and realities of Sino-African relations*. Beijing: Social Sciences Academic Press.
Yang Guangsheng. 2014. *A study on the foreign relations of Nigeria*. Hangzhou: Zhejiang People's Press.

Yang Lihua. 2006. Africa: A view from China. *South African Journal of International Affairs* 13(1): 23–32.
Yang Lihua. 2010. *South Africa*. Beijing: Social Sciences Academic Press.
Yang Lihua et al. 2013. *A comprehensive strategic study on development of China–Africa economic cooperation*. Beijing: China's Social Sciences Press.
Yang Tingzhi. 2015. *On the historical evolution of Zambian chieftaincy*. Beijing: China Social Sciences Press.
Yang Xuelun & Zheng Xizhen. 2001. *The culture of Tunisia*. Beijing: Culture and Arts Press.
Yeboah, Nyamah Edmond & Feng Yi. 2020. *Agricultural supply chain in Ghana: Risks, mitigation strategies and performance*. Beijing: Social Sciences Academic Press.
Yuan Nansheng. 2011. *Enter into Africa*. Beijing: China Social Sciences Press.
Zeng Qiang. 2002. Some reflections on expanding Sino-African trade and economic cooperative relations in the new century (the viewpoint of a Chinese scholar). *TINABANTU: Journal of African National Affairs* 4(1): 3–25.
Zeng Qiang. 2010. China's strategic relations with Africa. In Axel Harneit-Sievers et al., eds, *Chinese and African perspectives on China in Africa*. Nairobi: Pambazuka Press, 56–69.
Zhai Fengjie et al. 2013. *China–Africa cooperation in the integration of Africa*. Beijing: World Affairs Press.
Zhang Chun. 2012. China's engagement in African post-conflict reconstruction: Achievements and future developments. In James Shikwati, ed., *China–Africa partnership: The quest for a win–win relationship*. Nairobi: Inter Region Economic Network (IREN), 55–62.
Zhang Jin. 2014. *Regional economic integration in Africa: Thirty years of the Southern African Development Community*. Hangzhou: Zhejiang People's Press.
Zhang Jin. 2015. China and Africa regional economic cooperation: History and prospects. *PULA: Botswana Journal of African Studies* 29(1): 13–26.
Zhang Haibing. 2013. *Development-guided assistance: A study on the model of Chinese aid to Africa*. Shanghai: Shanghai People's Press.
Zhang Hongming. 1999. *African political development in multiple perspective*. Beijing: Social Sciences Academic Press.
Zhang Hongming. 2008. *A study on the thoughts of African scholars: 18th and 19th centuries*. Beijing: Social Sciences Academic Press.
Zhang Hongming, ed. 2012. *China and world major economies' economic and trade cooperation with Africa*. Beijing: World Affairs Press.
Zhang Hongming & Yao Guimei, eds, 2013. *Yellow book of Africa no. 15 2012–2013*. Beijing: Social Sciences Academic Press.
Zhang Hongming & An Chunying, eds. 2014. *Yellow book of Africa no. 16, 2013–2014*. Beijing: Social Sciences Academic Press.
Zhang Hongming, Liu Lide & Xu Jiming, 2001. Focus: Sino-African relations. *Africa Insight* 31(2): 33–42.
Zhang Qiaowen. 2015a. China Africa Development Fund: Beyond a foreign policy instrument. *CCS Commentary*, 13 January, www.strathink.net/ethiopia/from-the-center-for-chinese-studies-china-africa-development-fund
Zhang Qiaowen. 2015b. Responsible investing in Africa: Building China's competitiveness. *CCS Commentary*, 18 February.
Zhang Weijie. 2015. South Africa, China and the African Union. In Garth Shelton, Funeka Yazini April & Li Anshan, eds, *FOCAC 2015: A new beginning of China–Africa Relations*. Pretoria: Africa Institute of South Africa, 64–79.

Zhang Xiang et al. 2007. *Senegal and Gambia*. Beijing: Social Sciences Academic Press.
Zhang Xiangdong. 2012. *A study on Ethiopia's federalism: 1950–2010*. Beijing: China Economic Publishing House.
Zhang Xinghui. 2011. China's aid to Africa: A challenge to the EU? In Jing Men & Benjamin Barton, eds, *China and European Union: Partners or competitors?* Aldershot: Ashgate, 209–224.
Zhang Yong. 2021. *Africans in China: Stories of intercultural communication*. Wuhan: Changjiang Publishing & Media/Hubei Science & Technology Press.
Zhang Yonghong, 2010. *Indigenous knowledge in Africa's development*. Beijing: China's Social Sciences Press.
Zhang Yonghong, Liang Yijian, Wang Tao & Yang Guangsheng. 2014. *A study on the background of China–Africa low-carbon development cooperative strategy*. Beijing: World Affairs Press.
Zhang Yongpeng. 2007. Reality and strategic construction: Globalisation and Sino-African relations. In Kwesi Kwaa Prah, ed., *Afro-Chinese relations: Past, present and future*. Beijing: CASAS, 268–279.
Zhang Yongpeng. 2012. *International development cooperation and Africa: A comparative study on Chinese and Western aid to Africa*. Beijing: Social Sciences Academic Press.
Zhang Yun. 2000. *Personal experience in Black Africa*. Beijing: People's Daily Press.
Zhang Zhe. 2014. *The development of China–Africa economic and trade relations*. Hangzhou: Zhejiang People's Press.
Zhang Zhenke. 2014. *A study on the strategy of African fishery and development*. Nanjing: Nanjing University Press.
Zhang Zhongxiang. 2006. *Mali*. Beijing: Social Sciences Academic Press.
Zhang Zhongxiang. 2012. *The study on Forum on China-Africa Cooperation*. Beijing: World Affairs Press.
Zhao Jun. 2013. On overseas Chinese in Africa and China's public diplomacy towards Africa. *African Studies* 4(1): 206–218.
Zhao Shurong, Fan Wenxue, Dong Yufei & Du Ying, 2019. On the risk analysis and countermeasures concerning the Chinese enterprises' international industrial capacity cooperation with Africa: A case study for Sichuan and Ghana. In *Public Administration I: Governance in Anglophone West Africa: Challenges and Responses*. Beijing: Social Sciences Academic Press.
Zhao Shurong, Xie Jihua, Tong Fei, Yang Enhua, Duan Peijun, Xu Jirui, Guillaume Moumouni, 2020. *The National Think Tank reports: Research reports on the elimination of poverty in China – Cenggong County, Guizhou Province, China*. Beijing: Social Sciences Academic Press.
Zhen Feng. 2014. *African port economy and urban development*. Nanjing: Nanjing University Press.
Zheng Jiaxing, ed. 2000. *History of colonialism: Africa*. Beijing: Peking University Press.
Zheng Jiaxing. 2010. *A history of South Africa*. Beijing: Peking University Press.
Zheng Jiaxing. 2011. *The path of African civilization*. Beijing: People's Press.
Zhi Yingbiao & Bai Jie. 2010. The Global Environmental Institute: Regulating the ecological impact of Chinese overseas enterprises. In Axel Harneit-Sievers et al., eds, *Chinese and African perspectives on China in Africa*. Nairobi: Pambazuka Press, 247–254.
Zhong Zhicheng. 2006. *For a more beautiful world: Record of Jiang Zemin's visit abroad*. Beijing: World Affairs Publishers.

Zhou Boping. 2004. *Diplomatic days in an unusual period*. Beijing: World Affairs Press.
Zhou Hong, ed. 2013. *China's foreign aid 60 years in retrospect*. Beijing: Social Sciences Academic Press.
Zhou Nanjing, ed. 1999–2002. *Encyclopedia of Chinese overseas*, 12 vols. Beijing: Chinese Overseas Publishing House.
Zhu Huayou et al. 2014. *Contemporary industry and mining in Africa*. Hangzhou: Zhejiang People's Press.
Zhu Weidong. 2011. *A specific study on the legal system of international trade in South Africa*. Xiangtan: Xiangtan University.
Zhu Weidong. 2013. *Multiple settlement mechanism of civil and commercial disputes in African countries*. Xiangtan: Xiangtan University Press.
Zou Hengfu & Hao Rui, eds. 2009. *A study on African economy and investment*. Beijing: People's Daily Press.

4 Case study

The *Abirewa* movement in the Gold Coast[1]

Introduction

There are two general interpretations regarding the anti-witchcraft phenomenon among the Akan in the Gold Coast. One school argues that anti-witchcraft cults are the creation of the 20th century and have arisen to meet the challenges and strains of colonial rule (Ward 1956; Field 1960; Debrunner 1961). The other rejects this view of causative linkage, suggesting that anti-witchcraft cults first appeared far back in the precolonial period and colonial rule actually brought about an increased personal security in the Gold Coast (Goody 1957, 1975). These two views both hold some truth, but neither is fully convincing. This article studies a religious movement that occurred in the early colonial period in the southern Gold Coast and offers a synthetic interpretation of the historical development of this phenomenon.[2] From 1906 to August 1908, a religious movement spread first throughout Asante, then to the Gold Coast colony. At first the colonial government regarded it as helpful for law and order, and did not pay much attention to it. Later, the movement gained such popularity that many chiefs began to complain about its subversion of their power. Having realised the political implications of the movement, the government finally put an end to it in 1908.

Origin and principles

In 1906, a new "fetish"[3] by the name of *Abirewa* appeared in Asante. The place of its origin is still a mystery. Some suggested it had come from the Northern Territories. Others believed it had been brought from the Ivory Coast, or Gyaman country (Ffoulkes 1909; McCaskie 1981).[4] All information indicates that it came from the hinterland to the north, but the government believed it had been introduced from the French colony (McLeod 1975).[5] There are several versions regarding the origin of *Abirewa*. According to one legend, an old woman in the interior fell sick and died. Upon entering the "world of spirits", a great man standing at the door said to her, "Your time to die has not yet come. Witchcraft has killed you, return to the earth!" Offering her a charm

DOI: 10.4324/9781003220152-5

to protect her against any kind of evil magic or witchcraft, he sent her back to life, telling her, "You will die natural death in old age." The news spread very quickly and the religion became famous throughout the hinterland and was called *Abirewa* (old woman). Other versions had the same features. First, *Abirewa* was sent by God, implying the power of the religion. Second, it came to serve the people "by destroying the evil". Third, it appeared particularly as anti-witchcraft.[6]

Abirewa was made of some black substance wrapped in string and laid on the top of a small mound. *Abirewa* was accompanied by a male god, *Manguro*, made of fibres and cowry shells bound together. Together they were called *Borgya*. The medicine that the worshippers of *Abirewa* had to drink was made of the root of a certain tree, ground into powder and diluted with water. Its preparation was a great secret known only to the priests. *Abirewa* had its own temple, or shrine, which had been prepared before the high priest's introduction of it. *Manguro* had a long horn, giving forth a terrifying sound, which was said to collect all the evil spirits or witches. When someone died, the priests would decide whether the person was killed by *Abirewa*. If so, the property of the dead would be confiscated and usually divided between the priest and the chief.[7]

Unlike some other religious movements, *Abirewa* lacked institutional leadership and systematic organization. The high priest was said to be in Bunduku, and there were three kinds of people involved in the introduction of *Abirewa*. Some were strangers, who benefited from selling the medicine said to be able to kill witchcraft. Some converted to it and became priests. Most were already priests, or were elected by villagers.[8] Membership in *Abirewa* was open to both men and women without having to serve any probation. After a ceremony, the applicant was admitted or rejected according to the priest's judgment. Members were initiated by taking an oath to observe certain rules. The rules seemed so beneficial to the people that even a colonial officer admitted, "It is difficult to find fault with the principles of this new religion for it inculcates speaking the truth and living a good life as essential."[9] According to a missionary, the principles of *Abirewa* included 20 commandments:

1. You shall not covet your neighbor's property or else you will die.
2. Don't envy rich men and wealthy persons, or else you will soon stiffen in death!
3. If you plan evil against your neighbor, you are a child of death!
4. Never walk past a neighbor's farm without weeding a little or doing any necessary repairs to the fence, or death will soon catch you.
5. If during a meal you become angry and leave the food, you must wipe the mouth with a cola nut and then ask *Abirewa* for pardon – otherwise *Abirewa* will kill you!
6. Disobedience against chiefs means death!
7. Selling of stolen things: Death!

8. Slandering your neighbor: Death!
9. Using magic against your neighbor: Death!
10. Adultery with your neighbor's wife: Death!
11. Refusing a request for help: Death!
12. Bringing others into debt by litigation: Death!
13. Having community with the witches: Death!
14. Cursing your neighbor: Death!
15. Carrying firewood in bundles into town: Death!
16. You must clean away the remainders of food after eating at once, or else you will die!
17. Neglecting to further the interests of *Abirewa* brings death!
18. Coming to the shrine in an unclean state: Death!
19. Forgetting about *Abirewa* when traveling: Death!
20. If you neglect to pay your debts: Death!

Akan society was generally organized in groupings of kin or small states where face-to-face relations were of paramount importance. A close look at the code reveals that the principles really stress those relations in three aspects: to obey and respect authorities, whether that of the elders, the chief, the government, the souls of ancestors or the new religion; to be kind and cooperative with others, especially neighbours; and to behave properly according to social norms. All these laws seemed to be very constructive and even the colonial officials believed that *Abirewa* would "work for law and order".[10]

Debrunner suggests that the intention of all these laws with their terrible threats was obvious: "to reknit society by the imposition of new moral and legal sanctions. In this way, they hoped to overcome the various stresses and frictions in society which were brought about by the culture contact" (Debrunner 1961: 113) This observation is true in the sense that the cultural contact and economic expansion brought about rapid social changes, and the people wanted to hold the dissolving society together by adjusting themselves to the new situation. But the "imposition of new moral and legal sanctions" was not necessarily guaranteed. To achieve this, the priests had to hold on to their power if it still remained in their hands, or to regain the power if it had been lost. Since the latter was the case in the southern part of the Gold Coast. *Abirewa* offered an excellent opportunity for the priests to recover their power. As a result, all the rules ordered respect for *Abirewa* (Reindorf 1966: 109; Field 1960: 74–81; Maier 1983: 37–60, 120–133). Besides numbers 17, 18 and 19 in the above-mentioned code, there were other versions of the principles: "You must obey your Fetish and Chief." Here the authority of the religious leader obviously came before the chief's. "To respect the departed souls of your Ancestors and family Fetishes." "To bewail no person whom the fetish kills." All precepts stressed the indisputable authority of the religion in terms of its legitimacy and judgement.

Reaction and suppression

Since *Abirewa* became a challenge to chief's authority and a threat to Christianity, the reaction from missionaries and chiefs was not at all favorable. Missionaries complained about the "barbarous" character of local religions. Their criticism was due to both their attitude of cultural superiority and their devotion to the mission of converting "pagans" to Christianity. This deep-rooted prejudice prevented them from seeing the real value of traditional religion and those practices "which to the unscientific mind seem barbarous, but which, when critically examined, cover a mine of truth and inspiration" (Hayford 1970 [1903]: 101).

When *Abirewa* was spreading in the south, the Basel missionaries urged the government to suppress it. They called *Abirewa* a "dangerous religion" and laid several charges against it. First, it was a practice of human sacrifices and threatened people with terror. "It is a messenger of death and has done more harm than all the witches and sorcerers together." Second, the property of the person killed by *Abirewa* all went to the priest, which withdrew wealth from the region and made people poor. Third, the ill-treatment of the body of the person killed by *Abirewa* was harmful for public sanitation. The missionaries also warned the people were becoming completely spellbound: "It is binding the whole nation into a league as strong as that of any Dervish Band, a league of men and women convinced that no shot can harm them, no sickness can attack them, no untimely death can come upon them, nothing can touch them as long as they obey implicitly and unquestioningly every law and demand of the priest."[11]

Unlike missionaries, who stressed "uncivilised" and "inhuman" aspects of *Abirewa*, chiefs generally worried about its effect in reducing their power and privileges to the priests' advantage. Chiefs either opposed it because of its political implications or supported it if they could benefit from it. On 3 August 1907, F.C. Fuller, the Chief Commissioner of Asante, held an inquiry concerning the spread of *Abirewa*. Participants were chiefs and priests. Among the 21 participants, ten supported, ten opposed and one made no comment. Supporters either were informed of its introduction or got one-third of the property of the dead. Their power was acknowledged and legitimized by their villagers. In contrast, chiefs opposed *Abirewa* not because of its principles or practice, but because of its introduction without their knowledge. Typical of the opposing group, a chief named Frimpon accused the *Abirewa* of body-mutilating and sending away the property of the dead, but his real concern was that: "My people did not inform me before introducing the fetish into my village so that proves that the Fetish is held higher than myself ... The Fetish should be introduced with the knowledge of the chiefs." The majority of chiefs complained that their people were being taken away by the new religion. One chief found that "those of my people who have accepted the fetish no longer visit or salute me".[12] From this testimony, it is evident that what caused the chiefs' discontent was not *Abirewa* itself, but the appropriation of their own power by priests.

Common people, by contrast, seemed to have welcomed the new religion. Once it was brought to Asante, it spread "with astonishing rapidity" and attracted a lot of people. A priest named Yaw Wua, who had served the government for 37 years, was initiated into *Abirewa*. Soon he had 6000 followers, some of whom were other chiefs' subjects. *Abirewa* was also found in the Central Province, especially in the Aguna District. It involved so many people that almost all the chiefs were frightened. According to a missionary's report, "People believe in it, love it and become devoted to it more and more by [*sic*] every day." The gathering of the ceremony became so big that, "Every time the dance stops, the people indulge in feasting and drinking; the noise of these orgies can be heard far away." In the Eastern Province, the more the chiefs tried to prohibit it, the more people converted to it. In less than a year, worshippers of *Abirewa* were found in all towns in New Dwaben and Kwahu, in almost every town in Eastern Akyem and in Akuapem.[13]

The government's reaction was different. When *Abirewa* appeared in Asante, the colonial officials reported it immediately. Western District Commissioner T.E. Fell held a meeting with the chiefs and people of Sunyani, together with Sei Kwahu, who had introduced *Abirewa* to the region. After the meeting, he concluded that, "Personally I don't object to its existence in Sunyani where the Chief and people honestly appear to think it a safeguard against quarrels, bad Fetish and bad medicines." Five days later, he suggested that government should not forbid *Abirewa* because "it is of no political importance whatever, that it tends rather to settle than unsettle the people".[14] As Chief Commissioner of Asante, F.C. Fuller followed the same course of action. After he received various complaints about the new religion, he called a meeting with chiefs and priests. After the meeting, he decided that the worship of *Abirewa* would be allowed with the approval of head chiefs. Chiefs and priests should be responsible for breach of the law occasioned by the worship. No part of a deceased man's property should be sent out of the country. *Abirewa* should not show hostility to Christians or missions.[15]

Without a general policy, the government left it to the chiefs to decide who could either support *Abirewa* or leave it alone. In either case, they helped its spread. Even if the chiefs wanted to suppress it, they could do nothing without the government's backing. As a result, *Abirewa* spread so rapidly that it caused still more complaints from chiefs and also alarmed district commissioners. On 6 June 1908, Commissioner C.N. Curling of the Eastern Province received a letter from the *Omanhene* of Eastern Akyem, complaining that "certain fetishism called '*Abirewa*' had been brought to Akim from Ashanti and that most of my people had received and were worshiping same", and requesting that "steps may be promptly taken with a view to the entire abolition of this fetishism in my country".[16]

Chiefs in the Central Province had the same fear. According to Provincial Commissioner Eliot, chiefs regarded *Abirewa* with fear, and "those Chiefs who have not already come under the influence of the priests would view with satisfaction any action on the part of the government to suppress this heathen worship". He also enclosed in his letter a report by a Basel missionary in the Winneba District, who claimed that the "*Abirewa* is creating a 'reign of terror'".[17] Here Eliot expressed his opposition and began to talk about the possibility of suppression. A month later, Curling again reported that *Abirewa* had spread to Akuapem, New Dwaben, Eastern Akyem and Kwahu. The chiefs of these districts were all afraid of the subversion of their authority by the new religion. Since they could not stop it without assistance, Curling took action, "suppressing the fetish from New Juabin upwards". He hoped the Governor would support his action.[18]

From all these steps, we can sense a kind of emergency in the Central and Eastern Provinces. However, the final decision was made after the Acting Colonial Secretary submitted a report on *Abirewa* on 29 June 1908. He pointed out the possible political significance of this new religious movement. On 17 July the Executive Council decided to abolish *Abirewa*. Since "it appears to the Government that the celebration of the rite, ceremony and worship of the fetish known as *ABIREWA* tends towards the commission of crime", the Order was issued to have it suppressed and "whosoever continues this order shall be liable to a fine not exceeding twenty-five pounds".[19]

The most interesting point relates to Asante Chief Commissioner Fuller's attitude. At first, he was quite optimistic about the new movement, saying, "I am inclined to believe that the '*Abirewa*' worship will work for law and order." He criticised the Basel missionaries who "have assumed such an extremely hostile attitude towards it" and suggested that *Abirewa* was "in fashion" and "the Christian Missionaries find that they are unable to attract congregation when on 'preaching tour' so they have only too readily ... accepted and utilized a vague rumor of mutilation of dead bodies, to counteract the proselytizing success of the *Abirewa*' propaganda".[20]

After a meeting with some chiefs and priests, Fuller decided that *Abirewa* should be allowed if the chiefs approved of it. Ten months later, C.H. Armitage, Acting Chief Commissioner of Asante, expressed the same view and explained the attitude of missionaries: "The Missionaries naturally object to '*Abirewa*', as the dancing and singing associated with it attract the people and militate against their efforts to proselytize the Ashantis." But the Acting Colonial Secretary at Accra took the matter more seriously, pointing out that the movement's potential political importance might have been neglected by the Ashanti authorities.[21]

This opinion, together with the news that the colony had taken action to suppress *Abirewa*, seemed to have changed Fuller's mind. Since "the Detractors failed hopelessly to establish, or prove, a case against '*Abirewa*' as an institution likely to promote crime", Fuller decided to "fight the new worship by ridicule". In a circular addressed to all the Paramount Chiefs of Asante, he enclosed a letter from Commissioner Fell on this subject. Fell said that the priests of *Abirewa* who lived in the neighbourhood of Bontuku were becoming "inordinately rich" and that the large presents of money they received were from Ashanti: "Over these payments the natives of the French side are laughing in their sleeve and ... they clap their hands and say, 'By these tricks of Fetishes we are getting back from Ashanti all the moneys and tributes they took from us in the old days'".[22]

But after 15 days, Fuller decided that he had found enough excuses for the suppression and resolved to strike a "crushing blow" to this worship, "owing to a sudden eruption of *Abirewa* fanaticism". This was an astonishing turn-around. The charges he laid against *Abirewa* included ill-treatment of corpses, subversion of chiefly power and wholesale collections for the benefit of the high priests living in the French colony. He quickly convened a meeting of all the chiefs of the Central Province in Asante "together with all their *Abirewa* Priests (whom I inveigled into Coomassie by guaranteeing them their personal safety)".[23] Four to five thousand people attended the meeting. The Chief Commissioner made a thoughtful speech: "I have waited to see the working of this Religion for a whole year and I tell you the net result is that crime is encouraged by it; that the land is being impoverished by it; and that the land has become unsettled by it."

He attacked *Abirewa* severely, despite the fact that only half a month earlier he had said he could not "discover any political or criminal danger in the cult". In order to justify his action, the Chief Commissioner piled up a series of charges. He ridiculed the Asante as cowards, and scolded them for being credulous, thus permitting them to be laughed at by their neighbours for sending back "part of the wealth that the Ashanti had taken from them in former times". He accused the priests of cheating the rich and undermining the chiefly power. He also blamed the chiefs for supporting the worship.[24]

Debrunner argues that the main reason for the suppression was the priests' direct involvement in witch-hunting (Debrunner 1961:123). Fuller expressed the same view (Fuller 1921: 221–222). Yet a study of the evidence reveals a quite different picture. It was the missionaries who first called the attention of the government to the political implications of this new religious movement. This new religion threatened to become "a greater danger" to Christianity, as well as the trade, peace and prosperity of the country, "than any other superstition yet known"; "Let us not forget that this *Abirewa* has spread from Dweso and it is in this district the last insurrection originated. This is rather significant!"

The Acting Colonial Secretary noticed "its organization and constitution emanate from a mind of a caliber out of the common". He suggested that "the injunction of obedience to the government and the power and material prosperity of the priesthood are secured" must be "an attempt to avert official disfavor". Provincial Commissioners Curling and Eliot strongly supported the suppression, especially because of the subversion of chiefly power by the priests. Curling also worried about the underlying doctrine of *Abirewa*, that "those who have drunk the medicine need fear nothing, need obey no one, for no one can harm them. They are immune from danger of all kind [*sic*] whether from man or beast and spiritual as well as temporal".[25] A doctrine defying everything could not be allowed.

By August 1908, most colonial officials and chiefs realized that *Abirewa* was a threat to their authority and *Abirewa* was suppressed. John P. Rodger, the Governor, showed his concern about the danger of *Abirewa* and was greatly relieved when it was suppressed.[26] Although the charges against it focused on criminal acts, the real reasons for its suppression were more political than humanitarian: namely to prevent the weakening of chiefly power and to kill the potential for disturbances. However, two questions remain to be answered. Why did so many people believe in *Abirewa*? Why did the priests try so hard to spread *Abirewa*?

Causes: A tentative explanation

The colonial government was obviously more concerned about the effects of *Abirewa*, so it never analysed the causes of this religious movement. A missionary explained why people welcomed *Abirewa*, "because it fosters and encourages just these things which they delight in, drumming, obscene dances, feasting and drinking etc. Then the doing away of people, who are not wanted and that seems to satisfy the old love for manslaughter and cruelties, which seem to be a part of their very nature".[27] Full of cultural bias, this explanation shows no intention even to try to understand the movement. The missionaries cared much more about the actions of the followers than anything else. However, the most important factor seems not to be the nature of *Abirewa* itself, but its social significance.

There are two more thoughtful interpretations regarding the *Abirewa* movement in the Asante area. Malcolm McLeod suggests that the breakdown of political control and the suppression of older anti-witchcraft cults gave young men the chance to import and profit from *Abirewa*, and some chiefs seemed "to have ineffectually tried to combat the movement which further reduced their power" (McLeod 1975). T.C. MaCaskie refutes this explanation and argues that this was the case only in some areas, while in others chiefs were able to make use of *Abirewa* to strengthen their own decreasing power (McCaskie 1981). But neither has mentioned the possibility that a change in the status of the priest may have resulted in the rise of the movement. In order to understand fully *Abirewa* as a protest, we have to study its historical origin and the favourable conditions for its spread. The previous status and authority of priests shaped its non-institutional leadership, and the grievances of the people played an important role in the advance of the movement.

Cultural heritage

G. Parrinder suggests that in West Africa, religious belief resembles a triangular structure. At the apex is God, the supreme and creator spirit. The two sides of the triangle are the lesser deities and ancestors, and the base comprises those beliefs and practices called magic. P. Sarpon agrees that this summary would "apply to Ghanaian religious thought" (Parrinder 1969:12; Sarpong 1974: 44). In Akan religion, *Nyame* (or *Nyankopong*) is God, the Creator and the Supreme Being, who keeps a loving but watchful eye on people. The world is full of spirits, the minor gods or lesser deities (*abosom*), who are worshipped by people. They believe that ancestors keep a close contact with the living members of the lineage and try their best to protect them (Danquah 1968; Fynn 1976; Ellis 1964 [1883]). This structure shows that while the priest acted as a representative of the deities, the chief as secular leader also played a sacred role as intermediary with the ancestors.

People in the Gold Coast also believed in witches (*abayifo*, sing. *obayifo*) and witchcraft. The belief acted as a sanction against antisocial behaviour: witches were wicked people and their ill-feeling, hatred or envy caused harm. Besides supporting the moral order of the community, the belief also explained why a particular person at a particular time and place suffered particular misfortunes. People believed all the tragedy and misfortune were due to such evil works as witchcraft, curses or bad medicines. But the distinguishing feature of witchcraft was that the killing or harming was wrought by the silent, invisible projection of influence from witches. Their attack on the individual took various forms, such as sickness, barrenness, sorrow or death.[28] It was believed that the misfortunes caused by witches could be protected against or cured by medicine or traditional religion.

There has been a long tradition of use of medicine for special purposes. Among the Akan, the word "medicine" has a much more comprehensive meaning than the term usually indicates. It is common to use it to describe magic, religious object and the related ritual. The Akan believe that there is some medicine for every kind of illness or misfortune. M. Field once stated that there is no activity in life that cannot be assisted by medicine. A hunter can "medicine his gun and his bullets to make them unerring"; a blacksmith can "medicine his tools"; a fisherman or a lorry-driver can medicine their canoe or lorry. Even a suitor could "medicine himself to make his charms irresistible"(Field 1960: 40).

Generally speaking, there are three kinds of medicine: common remedies used by everybody without ritual; family secrets handed down through generations; and medicines known only to professional priests. Medicine is so closely linked with religion that it is suggested that the Akan or the Ga made no or little distinction between medicine and religion, or "fetish" (Appiah-Kubi 1981: 2, 37; Field 1937: 110–134; Field 1960).

For the Akan, *asuman* means certain particular articles – for example, charms and amulets. They are supposed to be inhabited by *abosom*, or the lesser deities, and are all supplied by priests. There are also natural phenomena, such as rivers, hills and forests, which are abodes of *abosom*. Different people have different classifications of these minor gods. People consider it good to have a minor god living among them. Early Europeans mentioned articles worn by people or hung in the house or a tree at the entrance of a village (De

Marees 1987 [1602]; Ellis 1964 [1883]; Hodgson 1901). They were put there for a protective purpose.[29] In fact, *Abirewa* was so closely linked with *Sakrabudi*, an old religious object, that one priest was carrying *Sakrabudi* on his back and *Abirewa* in front. The practice of *Abirewa* was "also in close resemblance to the *Katawere* and other fetishes".[30]

The belief in God or minor gods and related rituals, the fear of witchcraft and the use of medicine were essential elements of the traditional religion in the Gold Coast. These factors were all conditions favourable to the spread of *Abirewa*. This cultural heritage explains the people's willingness to convert to the new religion. But why should the movement spread at this particular time? To answer this question, we have to understand the dramatic change that occurred at the beginning of this century and its impact upon the people.

Situation of crisis

At the end of the nineteenth century, the spread of Christianity, the introduction of cash crops and the establishment of colonial rule significantly altered Gold Coast society. As a result of the penetration of Christianity, traditional religion began to lose its believers. For example, at Late, a "fetish town," priests were reported in 1880 as having withdrawn from the vicinity of a new chapel. The mission hoped "may they soon creep into the holes of moles and bats." According to a report, "the belief in fetishes had weakened, especially among the younger generation who no longer believe in them" (Brokensha 1966: 10–15; Ansah 1955).

A colonial officer also noticed the difference in attitudes between the old and the young. In 1886, he attended a religious ceremony, where he noted the old people, "particularly the old women, appeared most impressed by what they saw; and they apparently had the most implicit faith in the genuineness of the whole proceeding", while the younger people appeared sceptical and some "openly laughed" (Ellis 1964 [1883]:136–137).

A rapid change of daily life resulted in wealth, anger and jealousy, but most importantly a crisis in faith. Epidemics brought about high rates of child death and infertility. More and more people got into debt as a result of being involved in litigation over land rights. A chief expressed his sorrow and despair when he talked about the dramatic change after 1900: "If our tribe is degenerating, our fame declining and the former splendor of our kingdom vanishing, whence does it come, if not from the wrath of the tutelar spirits and the anger of the ancestors!" Then he named all the changes: "the thunder of the big guns ... the noise of the church bells ... the wires of the telephone": all these made their spirit unhappy(Debrunner 1961: 66).

This disastrous impact on Gold Coast society created a sense of insecurity and fear.[31] Human relations became tenser than ever, and more and more witches were suspected or accused. In spiritual or temporal crisis, people resorted to old ways, relying on the vitality of traditional belief and the strength of the priests, who were believed to be able to remove stress as well as to seek out and cure social disturbances. As a result, the fear of witchcraft became widespread, and powerful religion was sought for protection; thus various kinds of anti-witchcraft cults arose.

There are two interpretations regarding anti-witchcraft phenomenon among the Akan. One school argues that anti-witchcraft cults are the creation of the twentieth century and have emerged to meet the challenge and strain brought about by the colonial situation (Ward 1956: 47–61). Jack Goody rejects this view, suggesting that anti-witchcraft cults first appear far back in the precolonial period (Goody 1957; Goody 1975: 91–106). These two views both hold some truth, but neither is convincing enough. A synthesis is needed in order to make sense of this historical phenomenon.

On the one hand, although very few early sources mentioned this matter, no doubt the anti-witchcraft cults did exist in the Gold Coast before colonial rule. Joseph Dupuis described the struggle for the throne between the Asante King and a usurper during 1818–1819, an event that resembled the way witchcraft and anti-witchcraft are understood today (Dupuis 1966 [1824]: 114–117; McCaskie 1981: 128–129). Some early Europeans also recorded the methods of witch-finding that they came across in the Gold Coast (Bosman 1967 [1705]: 124; Bowdich 1966 [1819]: 163; Hutton 1971 [1821]: 88; Hutchinson 1858: 70). It seems that chewing or drinking a decoction of certain poisonous bark and corpse-carrying, two major methods used in early witch-finding, were both adopted in the *Abirewa* ceremony.

On the other hand, the frequency of this phenomenon indicates colonial rule did bring about such a severe change that there was a marked increase in uncertainty and strain among people. Goody argued that the British occupation in many ways brought about "an increased rather than a decreased personal security" (Goody 1957: 362). He is certainly right if by "personal security" he only meant life security. But economic anxieties caused by more opportunities, political oppression caused by colonial rule and chiefs' abuse of power and social disorientation caused by the declining of traditional institutions all resulted in increased insecurity and uncertainty. Fear, envy, accusations and confessions provided a favourable climate for increasing witchcraft and anti-witchcraft.

Priests' change of status

In order to understand the significance of *Abirewa* as a new religious movement, we also have to analyse the change of the social status of the priests after the arrival of Europeans, especially after the establishment of colonial rule.

According to Casely Hayford, in the Akan traditional system the king (or chief) was the spiritual head, but the actual working of the system was in the hands of priests (Hayford 1970 [1903]: 101).[32] Danquah suggests that the priest was the first and highest person in the Ga-Adangbe state, while in the Akan institutions a priest was "the maker of a country, but not the governor of it" (Danquah 1928a: 23).[33] The Guans were ruled by priests. The system was later introduced into the Akan by Guan Priest Okomfo Anokye, a man of Awukugua in Akuapem who helped Osei Tutu win the fight against Denkyira and form the Asante Kingdom (Williamson 1965: 23). The Ga form of government was an "absolute fetishocracy", where "foretelling fetish-priests" controlled the supreme power (Cruickshank 1966 [1853]), Vol. II: 124–190). No matter how the priests were described, there is no doubt they played a crucial role in the traditional state system.

Priests generally performed three functions: ritual performance, daily protection and war preparation. During the annual festival, the priests offered sacrifices to God or ancestors, purification of the nation for the past year and prayer for direction and protection for the coming year (Bowdich 1966: 274–280; Rattray 1927: 121–143). They performed sacrifices to *abosom* and also acted as their mouthpiece. This oracular function of the *abosom* was very important because people had to consult them about their fate. In daily life, priests were supposed to protect people by foretelling and curing. In case of illness or misfortune, people always went to them to seek advice or cures. Priests were good healers and doctors. Their knowledge of herbs and plants greatly contributed to the mystery of their calling (Appiah-Kubi 1981: 39–80; Beecham 1968 [1841]: 192; Fink 1990). During wartime, the king and elders would consult oracles from their own religion, or even the shrine in other places (Maier 1983: 38–40). The priests were supposed to help prepare for the battle and be able to prophesy the result of the war. "Eat fetish" or "drink fetish" was also a way of swearing the oath of allegiance by which a whole army was bound together (Cruickshank 1966 [1853]),Vol. II: 172–176; Beecham 1968 [1841]: 193–222).

In the traditional system, priests had also enjoyed economic benefits. T.J. Hutchinson, a colonial officer, once described his impression of priests in the interior country at Akyem: "The fetish house is ornamented with swords and axes having golden handles; the drums are ornamented with gold also. The fetish man or high priest is always rich" (Hutchinson 1858: 70). The priests' fortunes generally came from three sources: service charges, punishment and duties. They served deities by holding various ritual ceremonies. They had the right to make a prophecy or judgment on grand occasions, such as royal succession and funeral, or in cases of crisis. They received handsome presents and payment for service(Maier 1983: 59; Beecham 1968: 189–190).[34] In the nineteenth century, they earned a good living and received handsome payment for service. They afforded protection for runaway slaves and received presents from "influential and rich people who washed themselves with holy water or made vows in sickness". The denial of protection to slaves was also a way to make money. In Asante, priests would deliver fugitive slaves to their master on receiving two ounces of gold and four sheep (Reindorf 1966 [1895]: 107–108).

Priests could also inflict a punishment by confiscating the property of the dead. According to Hutchinson, a priest was so powerful that if a person died without having conciliated him, he had the power of ordering the corpse to be placed in an upright position inside the house. "Should the body retain its perpendicularity all the property it possessed when living is claimed by the family; if it fall, which the fetish man has knowledge enough of the peculiarity of gravity in a dead body always to secure, the effects of the defunct must of course be at once handed over to the Moloch of superstition" (Hutchinson 1858: 70).

Another way to obtain wealth was through the imposition of a customs tariff. Some priests imposed "heavy dues" on traders and secured law and order in return. In Krachi, the priest dominated the king and "gets hold of the custom money which is on all articles transported to the interior especially on salt". In Accra, the priests of *Nai* (sea) could claim a duty of $16 and rum from every captain anchoring in the roads at Accra, besides annual presents from the merchants. In addition, they had other sources of income. The ferrying of Sakumo was a large source of revenue to traditional rulers. The rate of ferrying was 25 strings: "The amount collected on Monday and Tuesday belongs to the priests" (Maier 1983: 55; Reindorf 1966 [1895]: 108).

In the 18th century, European traders fully recognised the great influence of local priests and sought their help on several occasions. When the French tried to establish themselves on the Fante coast in the early 1750s, both the British and the French tried to win support from the priests of *Nananom Pow* by offering goods worth 20 ounces and 60 ounces of gold respectively. Later in 1765, when the war broke out between the Asante and the Fante, both Dutch and British traders sent messengers with gifts to the Fante priests asking them to urge on chiefs to settle the dispute with the Asante (Fynn 1971: 103).[35]

All these practices began to change after the arrival of Christian missionaries. In 1835, the Wesleyan Methodists began their work at Cape Coast and the Basel Mission moved to the Akuapem Ridge. Since the missionaries' success directly depended upon their undermining traditional religion, it became their primary task to destroy it and its related structures. "Fetishism" became the immediate target of this general assault.

In 1851, the Mankessim Case put the local religion on trial. In order to retaliate against the Christians who insulted the worshipers of the local religion, a group of priests and priestesses attempted to murder four prominent African Christians by poison. The plot was discovered and they were charged with conspiracy. Nineteen were convicted. The priests were sentenced to be publicly flogged and imprisoned with hard labour for five years, and the priestesses were given two years' imprisonment. The trial shocked the community and some people were crying, "What can we now do in sickness or distress? Whither can we fly for succor? Our gods have been proved to be no gods. Our priests have deceived us" (Reindorf 1966 [1895]: 234). Christianity gradually gained the upper hand in the Gold Coast. Missionaries produced the New Testament in local languages, which became a convenient help in converting Africans. Some priests "renounced their paganism" while more and more people abandoned local religion and converted to Christianity (Kemp 1898: 182–184).[36]

But the fatal attack on traditional religion came from the colonial government. Early Europeans described African religion as "fetish", or "fetishism", and painted an uncivilised picture of priests. The same attitude prevented colonial officers from understanding local religion, much less the status and function of priests. For them, the traditional ruler simply meant a single chief, or monarch, and the important thing was the position of traditional rulers under the colonial administrative and judicial set-up (Metcalfe 1964: 390–393). Although the government tried to make use of the local authority, it failed to see the role of priests in the traditional power structure. The fate of the *Dente Bosomfo* is a typical example.

The Krachi people were Guans. *Dente* was a powerful local god who had been worshipped not only by the Krachi, but also by the neighbouring people, including the Asante. During the nineteenth century, it seems the *Dente Bosomfo* (the priest) was superior to the *Krachiwura* (the king), not only in religious matters, but also in political, economic and military authority. But the fact was ignored by the German and British colonial governments. The *Dente Bosomfo* was executed in 1894, followed by the decline of religious power (Maier 1983: 37–60). Reindorf wrote in 1895 that the power of the priest over lands and revenue was gradually falling into the hands of the Kings (Reindorf 1966 [1895]: 109). The same thing happened in Ga towns, where Europeans only recognised the power of the secular ruler, the *Mantse*, causing the change of the power structure and disturbances among the Ga people (Field 1960: 77).

Although Christianity weakened the local religions, it by no means replaced them. In crises of life such as birth, marriage, misfortune, illness or death, traditional religion played a greater role than Christianity. Since priests had lost their political influence, economic benefits and social privileges, and could hardly contest their rivals politically, the best way for them to regain their lost power was to revive traditional religion. As noted by a contemporary, this aim was achieved more or less by the new religion. The chiefs who had allowed *Aberewa*'s service in their villages at last repented of doing so, because their subjects no longer came for cases as before: "they have to decide all their cases before the priest of *aberewa* in the villages, even the oath matters; the chiefs consequently see that they have put themselves in a strait"(McCaskie 1981: 140).

However, this analysis by no means suggests that the deterioration of priests' status was the only element involved in the *Abirewa* movement. As well as the priests' attempts to regain their lost power, another important factor was people's grievances towards their chiefs.

People's voice of grievances

Since the chiefs were generally appointed or approved by the government, their authority was not well accepted, nor did it go unchallenged. It is interesting to compare what happened in Asante before and after 1901. Before the Asante uprising, the government did not have any title to rule Asante by conquest. Governor Maxwell once told Captain D. Stewart, Resident of Kumasi, that, "You should interfere as little as possible in the ordinary administration carried on by the Kings and Chiefs of a tribe. They should be encouraged to manage their own affairs, and they are entitled to hold their own courts of justice" (Newbury 1971: 296). Therefore, kings and chiefs generally retained their power.

At the same time, two legal systems existed, English Courts and Native Courts, but very few local cases went to the former. There were complaints about this "unsatisfactory" situation, especially inland, where local courts dealt with all other cases except those of murder and the most important land disputes. Although Kwahu was part of a district under the Supreme Court Ordinance, it was reported that "there has not been for the last six months a single case brought from there either to the District Commissioner's Court or to the Divisional Court; there having been no Resident District Commissioner, the native courts have dealt with all the cases that have arisen".[37] It is quite clear that people still trusted their own rulers in matters of justice.

Things changed dramatically after 1901. The traditional leaders who had been involved in the uprising were severely punished. About 60 Asante chiefs were sent down either to the coast or to join their Paramount Chief Prempeh in exile in the Seychelles. Governor M. Nathan suggested all the vacant stools be filled "with men duly elected and recommended to me by Resident in Coomassie" (Newbury 1971: 333).[38] New chiefs were picked up not because they were entitled to offices according to local law or custom, but based on their loyalty to the government during the uprising. As a result, the people's reaction towards these new chiefs was non-cooperative. In 1906, the Chief Commissioner reported on the new conditions in the Southern District. The people there began "to recognize that government is the chief guardian of their interests, judging by the way they have sought advice on every matter, however small, that concerned them, and they have displayed a trusting and friendly spirit towards the Commissioner of their district that is most pleasing to record".[39]

This indicated the decreasing power of the chief over his people, not only because of the change of his status to a "subordinate authority", as Busia suggested, but also because of his lack of both legitimacy and accountability (Busia 1951: 110). People began to turn to the government – the real boss – for protection. This contemptuous attitude partly explained the conversion to *Abirewa* and religious leaders.

The problem of legitimacy became more serious owing to the improper behavior of those newly elected chiefs, who now enjoyed the government support and neglected checks and balances in the traditional law, and showed very little concern for the interests of the people. There were various complaints about the abuse of chiefly power.[40] As a result, a movement developed at the beginning of the 20th century to destool the appointed chiefs, an interesting phenomenon that will be discussed later.

In 1905, the people at Agona refused to serve their chief, Kwame Boakye. The government interfered but the rebellion burst out again in September 1906. The government supported the chief and the rebellious leaders were punished. Rebellions against chiefs appointed by the government occurred in the same year at Ejisu, Akropong, Ahinkuro and Nsuatre. In some areas, even the Queen Mother and elders were punished for their opposition to their chiefs (Busia 1951: 105–106). Disturbances also occurred in the Eastern Province. According to official reports, between 1906 and 1908 two chiefs were murdered and three chiefs deposed. Other religious movements emerged in the region at the same time. In 1906, a religious practice called "*Yi Abeyi*" or "witch-finding" caused a serious riot at Abetifi. The origin of *Yi Abeyi* is not quite clear, but a group of young men were involved. *Yi Abeyi* was also responsible for an attempt made by the people of Wenchi to destool their chief, Kobina Akyere, who was one of the principal chiefs of Akyem Abuakwa. He was, however, reinstated by the government (Simensen 1975: 68–70).[41] The suppressed religious movement *Katawere* was revived in Akyem Abuakwa, *Otutu* and *Ati* also caught the government's attention and were suppressed.[42] There were other sabotages. In Asante, a great deal of unrest occurred among the young men.[43] In Adda District, a series of cases of alleged poisoning gave rise to intervention by the Provincial Commissioner. The ensuing trial disclosed that secret poisoning societies existed in the district.[44] All these instances show that tension did exist between the chiefs and their subjects.

Conclusion

In summary, although not many early sources mentioned this matter, there is an indication that anti-witchcraft movements did exist in the Gold Coast before colonial rule. On the other hand, the frequency of this phenomenon indicates that colonial rule brought about such a severe change that there was a marked increase in uncertainty and strain among people, which resulted in an increase of witchcraft and anti-witchcraft. The *Abirewa* movement reflects the colonial impact on the traditional system and varied responses from different social groups.

The traditional power structure in the Gold Coast had its own characteristics, one of which was the function of the priests. The establishment of colonial rule began with its encroachment on the traditional power structure. Poor understanding of African society and cultural imperialism based on technological superiority made it impossible for the colonial government to make optimum use of traditional power. The intervention by European authorities and the abuse of power by the chiefs created tensions that inevitably resulted in protests from those who were hurt by the newly established system. *Abirewa* provided an example of this kind of protest.[45]

As a religious movement, *Abirewa* was surely a success. It not only attracted many people in a short time, becoming a great threat to both the secular authority and the missionaries; it was also revived time and again despite the government's suppression.[46] But, as a political protest, the *Abirewa* movement was a failure. Lacking institutional leadership, a unique doctrine and a sound organization, it could cause disturbances within the system but it could not overthrow or even change the system. Moreover, it met a joint counter-attack from the government, the chiefs and the missionaries. With this kind of opposition, failure was inevitable. Later, in the 1930s and 1940s, fetishes with the same content but different names occurred in Asante and the Gold Coast. Among them, *Tigare*, which bore the resemblance of *Abirewa*, was the best known and most widespread (Appiah-Kubi 1981: 41–58; Debrunner 1961: 128–130).[47] All these religious movements became part of anti-colonial factors that contributed more or less to the coming national liberation movement.

Notes

1. This chapter is a revised version of an article published as "Abirewa: A Religious Movement in the Gold Coast, 1906–08" in *Journal of Religious History* (University of Sydney) 20(1) (1996). The article was originally presented to the 1991 CAAS conference at York University, Canada. I would like to thank the journal for the permission and many Ghanaian friends for their help during my fieldwork in Ghana. I also thank Professor M. Klein, G. Mikell and Gareth Austin for their critical comments.
2. Although it mainly concentrates on the Akan, this article occasionally refers to other ethnic groups as well. CO represents Colonial Office archives found in Public Records Office in London and ADM indicates the archives stored in the Ghana Archives in Accra.
3. From the Portuguese *feitico*, meaning "charm, amulet". The word was first used by early Europeans to describe everything related to African local religion. *Abirewa* was referred to as "religion" or "fetish" by contemporaries, Africans and Europeans. Owing to its derogatory denotation, the term will not be used in this work except in quotes.
4. CO96/471. Extract from the Annual Report on Ashanti for 1907. Encl. (5) in (Confidential) Sir John P. Rodger to Crewe, 17 August 1908; F.C. Fuller, "Meeting held on the 6th August 1908 outside the fort at Coomassie" Encl. (2) in (Confidential), Rodger to Crewe, 25 August 1908.
5. CO98/17. Report on the Native Affairs Department for the year 1908. It is believed in Asante that, "Northern societies are almost totally free from witchcraft."
6. CO96/471. *Abirewa* a new dangerous religion; C. N. Curling (Commissioner of East Province) to the Secretary for Native Affairs, 1 July 1908. Sub-encl. to Encl. (7)(8) in (Confidential) Rodger to Crewe, 17 August 1908.
7. In some places, one-third of the property of the dead went to their family. The most detailed description is found in (Ffoulkes 1909). But the meaning of *Borgya* in his article is different from this version.
8. CO96/471. "Palaver held on the 3rd Aug. 1907 in connection with certain allegations brought about against the '*Abirewa* Fetish' worship", Encl. (1) in (Confidential) Rodger to Crewe, 17 August 1908.
9. CO96/471. Curling to the Secretary for Native Affairs, 1 July 1908.

Abirewa *movement in the Gold Coast* 109

10 CO96/471. Fuller to the Colonial Secretary at Accra, 8 August 1907. Encl. (1) in (Confidential) Rodger to Crewe, 17 August 1908.
11 CO96/471. *Abirewa* a new dangerous religion.
12 CO96/471. Palaver held on the 3rd Aug. 1907.
13 CO96/471. *Abirewa* a dangerous religion; CO96/471. Curling to the Secretary for Native Affairs, 1 July 1908.
14 CO96/471. T.E. Fell (Western District Commissioner) to Fuller, 26 May and 1 June 1907, Sub-encl. (1) and (2) to Encl. (1) in Rodger to Crewe, 17 August 1908.
15 CO96/471. Palaver held on the 3rd Aug. 1907.
16 CO96/471. Amoaku Atta to the Commissioner of Eastern Province, 6 June 1908. Sub-encl. to Sub-encl to Encl.(8) in Rodger to Crewe, 17 August 1908.
17 CO96/471. E. C. Eliot (Commissioner of Central Province) to the Secretary for Native Affairs, 8 June 1908. Sub-encl. to Encl. (7) in Rodger to Crewe, 17 August 1908.
18 CO96/471. Curling to the Secretary for Native Affairs, 1 July 1908.
19 CO96/471. Account of the *"Abirewa"* Fetish by the Acting Colonial Secretary. Encl.(6) and Encl.(9) in Rodger to Crewe, 17 August 1908.
20 CO96/471. Fuller to the Colonial Secretary at Accra, 8 August 1907. Encl. (1) in Rodger to Crewe, 17 August 1908.
21 CO96/471. C. H. Armitage (Acting Chief Commissioner of Asante) to Acting Colonial Secretary, 1 June 1908. Encl. (5) in Rodger to Crewe, 17 August 1908. CO96/471. Account of the *"Abirewa"* Fetish by the Acting Colonial Secretary.
22 CO96/471. Fuller to Acting Colonial Secretary, 22 July 1908; Fell to Fuller, 5 July 1908. Encl to Sub-encl. (1) to Encl. (10) in Rodger to Crewe, 17 August 1908.
23 CO96/471. Fuller to the Acting Colonial Secretary, 15 August 1908. Fuller swallowed his words by detaining two of the priests as hostages after the meeting.
24 CO96/471. Fuller to the Acting Colonial Secretary, 22 July 1908; Meeting held on the 6th August 1908.
25 CO96/471. *Abirewa* a new dangerous religion; *CO96/471*. Account of the *"Abirewa"* fetish by the Acting Colonial Secretary; CO96/471. Curling to the Secretary for Native Affairs, 1 July 1908.
26 CO96/471. (Confidential) Rodger to Crewe, 17, 25 and 29 August 1908.
27 CO96/471. *Abirewa* a new dangerous religion.
28 Debrunner's book is the most comprehensive research on this subject. See also (Manoukian 1950: 55, 60–61, 103–104; Gluckman 1970: 81–108). For an early general study of African witchcraft, see a special issue of *Africa*, 8(4) (1935).
29 As late as 1953, during research in Late, a man gave the names of nearly 40 fetishes in one quarter alone. See Ansah (1955: xiii).
30 CO96/471. Fell to Fuller, 26 May 1907. Encl. (1) in Rodger to Crewe, 17 August 1908; CO98/17. Report on the Native Affairs Department for the Year 1908.
31 M. Field's *Search for Security* is a detailed study of the psychotherapy practised by the priests at various shrines in rural Ghana. Although the time is different, the study shows how people became increasingly preoccupied with a sense of insecurity and troubled by desire, depression and fear (Field 1960).
32 His view is challenged by Ghanaian historian J.K. Fynn, who acknowledges the important function of the priests in the religious life of the Akan people, but argues that in all Akan states, "priests and priestesses were subservient to the political establishment" (Fynn, 1976).

33 He did not agree with Casely Hayford's view that fetishism was a national institution, but admitted that the fetish system no doubt existed among all the people in Akanland. See (Danquah 1928b: 83–84).
34 In Krachi, gifts and payments were also sent to *Dente* for permission to establish branch shrines; a king gave no less than £100 to the *Dente Bosomfo* for a consecrated stone for establishing a branch. CO879/30. African (West) No. 384. Sunter to Colonial Office, Burnham, Somerset 25 October 1890.
35 *Nananom Pow* was an important shrine situated at the outskirts of Mankessim. According to J.K. Fynn, it was made the abode of gods deliberately by the Borbor Fante for political consideration.
36 The New Testament in Fanti was produced in 1895, and by 1900 it had been translated into all the major languages of southern Ghana. Ga was the fifth and Twi the seventh African language into which the entire Bible was translated. (Groves 1958, Vol. IV: 358–359).
37 CO96/342. W. Brandford Griffith, Memorandum: Jurisdiction in Ashanti, 9 August 1899.
38 CO879/67. No. 649. William Low (Colonial Secretary) to Joseph Chamberlain, 8 March 1901.
39 *Colonial Reports: Ashanti, 1906.*
40 CO98/11. The Governor's Address to the Legislative Council, 26 September 1904. Minutes of the Legislative Council, 1904.
41 CO98/16. Report on Native Affairs Department, 1906–1907.
42 CO98/16. Report on Native Affairs Department 1906–1907. CO99/20. Native Affairs Department Annual Report for 1907. CO98/17. Report on Native Affairs Department for the year 1908.
43 CO96/471. Fuller to the Acting Colonial Secretary, 22 July 1908. Encl. in Rodger to Crewe, 17 August 1908.
44 CO98/16. Report on Native Affairs Department 1906–1907.
45 There is no intention to claim that this is the only valid interpretation. McLeod suggests that there is a close linkage between commoners and the Abirewu movement, while McCaskie argues that even some office-holders made use of the religion (McLeod 1975: 109; McCaskie 1981: 139).
46 Clifford to Harcourt, 24 March 1914, CO96/543, PRO. The *Gold Coast Nation*, 26 March, 2 April, 7 May, 26 November 1914. The latest evidence of Abirewu was in 1921. See Acting Commissioner of Central Province to District Commissioner of Nsuaem, 5 September, 26 September 1921, ADM36/1/8.
47 ADM11/1/1679. Native custom and fetish (1 August 1908 to 2 November, 1948); ADM36/1/8. Fetish 1920–46. Acting Commissioner of Central Province to District Commissioner of Nsuaem, 5 September, 26 September, 1921.

References

Ansah, J.K. 1955. *The Centenary History of the Larteh Presbyterian Church 1853–1953*. Larteh: Larteh Presbyterian Church.
Appiah-Kubi, K. 1981. *Man cures, God heals: Religion and medical practice among the Akans of Ghana*. Montclair, NJ: Allanheld, Osmun & Co.
Beecham, J. 1968 [1841]. *Ashantee and the Gold Coast*. London: Dawsons of Pall Mall.
Bosman, W. A. 1967 [1705]. *New and Accurate Description of the Coast of Guinea*. London: Frank Cass.

Bowdich, T.E. 1966 [1819]. *Mission from Cape Coast Castle to Ashantee*. London: Frank Cass.
Brokensha, D. *Social change at Larteh*. Oxford: Clarendon Press.
Busia, K.A. 1951. *The position of the chief in the modern political system of Ashanti*. London: Oxford University Press.
Cruikshank, B. 1966[1853]. *Eighteen years on the Gold Coast of Africa*. Vol. II. London: Frank Cass.
Danquah, J.B. 1928a. *Gold Coast Akim laws and customs and the Akim Abuakwa Constitution*. London: George Routledge.
Danquah, J.B. 1928b. *The Akim Abuakwa handbook*. London: Froster Groom.
Danquah, J.B. 1968[1944]. *The Akan doctrine of God*. London: Frank Cass.
De Marees, P. 1987. *Description and historical account of the Gold Kingdom of Guinea 1602*, trans. Albert van Dantzig & Adam Jones. London: Oxford University Press.
Debrunner, H. 1961. *Witchcraft in Ghana*. Accra: Presbyterian Book Depot.
Dupuis, J. 1966. *Journal of a residence in Ashantee*. London: Frank Cass.
Ellis, A.B. 1964 [1883]. *The land of fetish*. London: Chapman and Hall.
Ffoulkes, A. 1909. Borgya and Abirwa; or, the latest fetish on the Gold Coast. *Journal of the Royal African Society* 8(32): 387–397.
Field, M.J. 1937. *Religion and medicine of the Ga*. Oxford: Oxford University Press.
Field, M.J.1960. *Search for security*. London: Faber & Faber.
Fink, H. 1990. *Religion, disease and healing in Ghana*, trans. Volker Englisch. München: Trickster Wissenschaft.
Fuller, F. 1921. *A vanished dynasty: Ashanti*. London: John Murray.
Fynn, J.K. 1976. The Nananom Pow of the Fante: Myth and reality. *Sankofa Legon Journal of Archaeological and Historical Studies* 2: 54–59.
Fynn, J.K. 1971. *Asante and its neighbours 1700–1807*. London: Longman.
Gluckman, M. 1970. *Custom and conflict in Africa*. Oxford: Basil Blackwell.
Goody, J., ed. 1975. *Changing social structure in Ghana: Essays in the comparative sociology of a new state and an old tradition*. London: International African Institute.
Goody, J. 1957. Anomie in Ashanti? *Africa* 27: 356–363.
Groves, C.P. 1958. *The planting of Christianity in Africa 1914–54*. London: Lutherworth Press.
Hayford, C. 1903. *Gold Coast native institutions*. London: Sweet & Maxwell.
Hodgson, Lady. 1901. *The siege of Kumassi*. London: C. Arthur Pearson.
Hutchinson, T.J. 1858. *Impressions of Western Africa*. London: Longman.
Hutton, W. A. 1971 [1821]. *Voyage to Africa*. London: Frank Cass.
Kemp, D. 1898. *Nine years at the Gold Coast*. London: Macmillan.
Maier, D.J.E. 1983. *Priests and power: The case of the Dente shrine in 19th-century Ghana*. Bloomington, IN: Indiana University Press.
Manoukian, M. 1950. *Akan and Ga-Adangme peoples*. Oxford: Oxford University Press.
McCaskie, T.C. 1981. Anti-witchcraft cults in Asante: An essay in the social history of an African people. *History in Africa* 8: 125–154.
McLeod, M. 1975. On the spread of anti-witchcraft cults in modern Asante. In J. Goody (ed.), *Changing social structure in Ghana: Essays in the comparative sociology of a new state and an old tradition*. London: Routledge, 107–117.
Metcalfe, G.E. ed. 1964. *Great Britain and Ghana: Documents of Ghana history, 1807–1957*. Accra: University of Ghana.
Newbury, C.W. 1971. *British policy towards West Africa: Selected documents 1875–1914*. Oxford: Clarendon Press.

Parrinder, G. 1969. *West African religion*. London: Epworth Press.
Rattray, R.S. 1927. *Religion and art in Ashanti*. Oxford: Oxford University Press.
Reindorf, C.C. 1966 [1895]. *The history of the Gold Coast and Asante*. Accra: Ghana University Press.
Sarpong, P. 1974. *Ghana in retrospect*. Tema: Ghana Publishing.
Simensen, J. 1975. Commoners, chiefs and colonial government, British policy and local politics in Akim Abuakwa, Ghana, under colonial rule. PhD thesis, University of Trondheim.
Ward, B. 1956. Some observations on religious cults in Ashanti. *Africa*, 26:47–61.
Williamson, S.G. 1965. *Akan religion and the Christian Faith*. Accra: Ghana Universities Press.

5 Case study
Asafo and destoolment in Southern Ghana[1]

Introduction

The study of the political history of colonial Ghana has generally focused on two indigenous political forces: the chiefs' involvement in the struggle against or the collaboration with the government, and the role of Western-educated Africans in the emergence of the nationalist movement.[2] This interpretation, however, seems to be only part of the story. Stories on the chiefs or on educated Africans cannot explain a widespread political phenomenon: under colonial rule, chiefs were frequently deposed by commoners, or "young men", organized as *Asafo* companies. There were some significant studies on local politics and the role of the commoners, especially in some PhD dissertations (Twumasi 1971; Simensen 1975a; Addo-Fening 1980). Yet there are still issues to be explored and to fit into both the history of the nationalist movement and the wider frame of Ghanaian history.

Destoolment was widespread in colonial southern Ghana between 1900 and the early 1950s, as a traditional means to check a chief's violation of the oath of office.[3] Considering the changes in the position of traditional leaders and the policy of indirect rule, it is not surprising that the destoolments were mainly launched by the *Asafo* company, an indigenous organization that represented the interests of the common people. In this article, the phenomenon will be studied comprehensively, with emphasis on the mechanism of *Asafo* and its linkage with destoolment. I will argue that the colonial government destroyed democratic features of traditional chieftaincy and made it less possible for the commoners to participate in local politics. The *Asafo* company therefore took on the responsibility of guarding their interests and became the main instrument for mass political action in southern Ghana.

Asafo and its features

Among the Akan people, the warrior organization known as *Asafo* (*osa,* war, *fo,* people) is found in almost every town or village. This system has also been introduced to the Ga, the Krobo, the Guan and some other ethnic groups. J.D.

DOI: 10.4324/9781003220152-6

De Graft Johnson, a colonial officer who was a Fante himself, once described the system:

> *Asafu* is primarily a warrior organization and is the name given to all male adults banded together for any purpose, particularly war. In its wider sense it is a socio-politico-military organization embracing both men and women, including stool-holders or persons holding positions ... In its narrower sense the *Asafu* connotes the third estate, or common people, which socially goes by the nomenclature of *Kwasafu*, sometimes also described or referred to, politically, as *mbrantsie*, or "young men" to distinguish them from the *mpanyinfu*, chiefs and elders.
>
> (Johnson 1932: 308)

Here Johnson distinguishes two kinds of *Asafo*, one in general and one in particular. Our interest here is in the second, the *Asafo* in its narrow sense. So far, the studies on the *Asafo* company system suggest that historians have been more concerned with its origins or its changing impact on local politics, while sociologists and anthropologists have treated it as a social institution, stressing its patrilineal character complementary to the matrilineage (Field 1948: 27–34; Busia 1951: 9–10; Datta & Porter 1971; Johnson 1972; Stone 1974; Simensen 1974, 1975b; Chukwukere 1980). Since there are both published and unpublished case studies, we seem to have enough information about the system as a whole to be able to describe its main features.[4]

Originally a military organization, the *Asafo* company had its own flag, song, drums, horns, caps, emblems and post, the rallying place of the company, where all its paraphernalia was kept. It also had its own fetish, medicines, and priests (Ffoulkes 1908). All able-bodied males, except the chief and the elders, were members of the *Asafo*. Each *Asafo* had its own leader. In Fante, the commander of all the *Asafo* companies was called *tufuhene* (captain-general). The titles of *Asafo* leaders vary in different areas. The equivalents of the Fanti *tufuhene* are *nkwankwaahene* in Asante, *akwasontse* in Ga and *Asafoakye* in Akyem. His appointment was originally by popular choice. Other *Asafo* leaders – like captains, as they were usually called – were also chosen or approved by the members of the company. According to J.C. De Graft Johnson, the appointment of the *tufuhene* "was originally by popular choice ... but the office now tends to become hereditary and in one state, at least, the post is held by a hereditary *Ohin* of a division" (Johnson 1927). But in Akyem Abuakwa, the *Asafoakye*, as an appointee of the chief and his elders, was liable to dismissal by them. "From the last quarter of the nineteenth century, however, there is evidence of Asafo asserting the right to choose their own leaders and merely presenting them to the Chief and his Councilors for confirmation"(Addo-Fening 1980: 22, 449). Each *Asafo* held an annual custom, where there were company performances. All affairs in the *Asafo* were managed along patrilineal lines. A father trained his sons in all possible skills of war, providing them with war medicines and weapons.

Captaincies descended from father to eldest son (Christensen 1954: 107–126). Occasionally there were women captains, who usually took charge of cooking and domestic arrangements. It is recorded that a woman was once elected as *tufuhene* (Johnson 1932: 217–218). The role of women is described by contemporary scholars (Christensen 1954: 111–112; Arhin 1983: 91–98).

There are various interpretations of the origin of the *Asafo*. Two main schools have offered their explanations. One view holds that the *Asafo* is indigenous to Fante society, while the other attributes its origin to the presence of early Europeans. Wartemberg, a native of Elmina, thought the *Asafo* originated during the Fanti-Ashanti wars with the help of the Dutch (Wartemberg 1950: 53). E.J.P. Brown, another Gold Coast scholar, suggested that *Asafo* was indigenous (Brown 1929: 197–217). But Kwame Arhin argues that the *Asafo* companies had their origin in the slave trade. *Asafo* leaders might have been local wealthy merchants (Arhin 1966). Porter and Datta maintain that the *Asafo* is indigenous to various Akan peoples, but the character and development of the system have been much influenced by the situations created through contact with Europeans. Their view seems to be more convincing (Porter & Datta 1971: 279–297). A lack of evidence prevents us from reaching a definite conclusion; however, several generalisations can be made from the available evidence. First, although the contact with Europeans might have influenced its formation or adaptation, the *Asafo* company's fundamental characteristics were indigenous. Second, the history of its introduction and spread is not clear. In addition, chiefs were reluctant to accept the *Asafo* as an indigenous organization and everyone claimed to have borrowed the *Asafo* from someone else. The reason might be that the *Asafo* was claiming political rights that would challenge their authority. However, it seems to have appeared among the Fante first. Meyerowitz suggests that the Fante borrowed the *Asafo* system from the Effutu, but others hold different views (Meyerowitz 1974; Akyempo n.d.; Wyllie 1967).

Third, since the word "*Asafo*" has multiple meanings, it is necessary to distinguish different kinds of *Asafo* to avoid any confusion.[5] Moreover, the *Asafo* in various areas might have different origins, and its organization varies from locality to locality. Most importantly, the *Asafo* must have undergone some changes through different periods, so it would be better to interpret its origin from the perspective of a process of adaptation to social change rather than a stagnant traditional form. Although certain basic features are universal in Akan areas, *Asafo* companies assumed a wide variety of institutional forms. Since most accounts are about Fante *Asafo*, which seems to be the best known and fully developed, differences between *Asafo* companies in Fante and those in other areas should be noted.[6]

In the Eastern Province, for example, the *Asafo* seems to have been introduced from the coastal Fante, since it was less elaborated and developed.[7] Moreover, the *Asafo* of the Eastern Province and Eastern Asante was by definition a movement among people of low status (Jenkins 1971).[8] There were also different forms of *Asafo* organization. For example, in Akyem Abuakwa, the *Asafo* on the central level consisted of the Amantoomiensa (the Council of Three Counties) lying within a 7 mile radius of the capital town. It had the right to criticise all acts of the executive and was regarded as representative of the common people (Danquah 1928: 16–20).

All these features had political implications. First, fewer inter-company conflicts occurred in the Eastern Province compared with the Fante, who had a reputation for fierce fighting between rival *Asafo* companies.[9] Second, the unified character provided a favourable condition for the involvement of *Asafo* in destoolment. Third, it was easier for them to adapt to the changing political force that began to challenge the chiefs' authority. To explain this transformation, we have to compare its main functions before and after the establishment of colonial rule.

Asafo and its functions

The *Asafo* among the Akan used to be a military force. In the precolonial period, wars between states were frequent. To obtain greater mobilization and to provide for an effective supervision in wartime, all the male members in the state, town or village were organised into fighting groups.[10] J.M. Sarbah and Casely Hayford described the military spirit of the *Asafo* and its operation during early times. The *Asafo* either fought against other states or were responsible for the peace of their own state. The commander of *Asafo* companies had to be brave and able to provide some ammunition. Although the Pax Britannica rendered the military function redundant, the military origin of the *Asafo* was always stressed.

During annual festivals, the *Asafo* performed before the chief in order to show their strength and loyalty (Hayford 1970 [1903]: 85–92). The *Asafo* played an important role in the rituals associated with installation or deposition of a chief. After a new chief was elected, members of the *Asafo* went to fetch him from his house. As a farewell to him as a commoner, they gave him a last ceremonial flogging and smeared him with white clay, then brought him before the assembly. They also performed the same duty when a chief was destooled (Field 1948: 22; Brokensha 1966: 114). They were involved in other religious activities too. The *Asafo* was important on account of its religious power to affect people's status in the next world by honouring them at the funeral. Being responsible for fetching the dead body and carrying it to the town, the *Asafo* also performed at the funeral, drinking and dancing, accompanied by *Asafo* songs. People believe the "play that you are given here is the play that you will be received with in the next world" (Field 1948: 145–146; Brokensha 1966: 195). They were also involved in witch-hunting (Debrunner 1961). In Agona, north of the Winneba district, people believed in the "great *Aku* (river god) of the Akora River, he who drowns only 'strangers'". It was accepted that only members of the *Asafo* companies could save a drowning stranger or retrieve a drowned person (Owusu 1970). The *Asafo* also filled a wide range of social functions, ranging from cooperative groups providing labour for public works to local units called upon in cases of emergency, which formed part of their routine duties. They formed hunting teams, a fire brigade or a search party to find missing persons. They also worked as communal labourers when needed, such as in the building of markets, the maintenance of routes, grave digging and so on, and they were responsible for the sanitation of the town (Field 1948: 27–33). The *Asafo* also acted as guardians over the morals of their members' wives.[11]

But the most interesting function of the *Asafo* was their role in the traditional political structure. Having a recognised and effective way to express their opinion, *Asafo* members had a say not only in the election of the chief, but also in all matters affecting the state. Without their approval, a candidate could not be elected as chief. The *Asafo* leader was officially recognised as representative of the commoners; elders would consider any representations he had made to them (Busia 1951: 9–10). Commoners could oppose any unpopular measures issued by the chief, while the elders could not, for fear of being accused of disloyalty, as they were responsible for any decision along with the chief.

Asafo leaders had different responsibilities in different areas. In Fante, the *tufuhene* was the next authoritative person after the *ohene*, or chief. The *tufuhene* could become a regent, or even a chief himself (Christensen 1954: 109). The Ga *Asafoakye* (the captain-general) had a constitutional role in the Akyem Abuakwa political structure and was recognized as a member of the councils. In Ga state, when a Ga *Mantse* (chief) died, the *akwasontse* was the first person to be told by the elders that a new chief was needed (Manoukian 1950; Field 1973: 138–139).[12] In Asante, the *nkwankwaahene* represented the interest of commoners or young men (*mmerante*), but he was not a member of the chiefs' council (Busia 1951: 10–11; Tordoff 1965: 373–74, 383).

No matter how its functions varied, it was universal that through the political role of the *Asafo* an individual could make his opinion heard concerning state affairs, and commoners could offer or withhold their support to the chief. Under colonial rule, the functions of the *Asafo* underwent a great change, especially in the field of local politics. Although the *Asafo* represented the commoners' interests, its role received no recognition from the colonial government. Because of ignorance, the British government at first did not interfere with the *Asafo* company as a political force, while they checked the chief's authority at will. A colonial official pointed out in 1887 that, "The Colonial Government, while destroying the chiefs' power, left the company organization intact; and the captains of the companies now arrogate to themselves an independence and freedom from restraint which formed no part of the original scheme" (Ellis 1964 [1883]: 280).

Since colonial rule put an end to inter-state wars, the *Asafo* transformed its main function from a military one to a "public works department" and acted as a task force in particular situations. Although the duties were always important, they now gradually became the major role of the *Asafo*. Resistance did exist, especially against public work. Agbodeka points out that the refusal of the Gold Coast people to permit alien interference in their affairs caused the British one particular difficulty, among others, that of obtaining labour, even paid labour, for public works (Agbodeka 1971: 134). To solve this problem, the government issued several ordinances. A Public Labour Ordinance was passed in 1883, under which paid labor could be recruited. Under the Trade Roads Ordinance of 1894, chiefs were given power to call on people for six days' labour in each quarter. Then the Compulsory Labour Ordinance was enacted in 1895, requiring chiefs to provide workers for the government.

Compulsory labour became a heavy burden on commoners under colonial rule for several reasons. First, the demand for service now came from the government or the chief, not from the community. Some recruitment had nothing to do with communal interests, such as the service needed for the battle against the Asante, which met some resistance.[13] Second, almost all these public works were performed on a compulsory basis with little or no payment. In addition, labourers suffered severe penalties under the Ordinance.[14] Third, it was not uncommon for chiefs to require some extra service for their own benefit. As a result, communal labour recruitment became a major source of grievances later (Mikell 1989: 89–90). J. Simensen has argued that the main reasons for both the 1915–1918 rising in Akyem Abuakwa and the 1932 attempted deposition of Paramount Chief Ofori Atta were the use of communal labor for public purposes on government directive and dissatisfaction with payment for the labour (Simensen 1975b: 150–152).

Another change in the function of the *Asafo* is that commoners in different companies were now more united and usually acted with one voice. For example, in Kwahu the *Asafo* of each town and village organised themselves in 1905 by uniting all companies into a new and wider organisation, the *Asafo Kyenku* – that is, the united *Asafo* (Twumasi 1971: 39–40)[15] – which became very active from the 1910s to the 1930s and was a threat to the *Omanhene* (the major chief). An official commented on this *Asafo* in 1931:

> In order to induce the *Omanhene* and State Council to redress certain grievances the *Asafo* have combined under one *Asafoakye*. The movement is well organized and is a visible expression of the desire of the younger generation to take a hand in the control of affairs. Unfortunately the *Omanhene* and many of the subchiefs regard the movement with the greatest disfavour and have decided to ignore it as much as possible ... the *Asafo* were prepared to bring about the destoolment of the *Omanhene* if their demands which are undoubtedly reasonable are not met.[16]

This shows that there were different opinions regarding the *Asafo*'s activities among the colonial officials, which may throw some light on the fact that the government never adopted a strong measure to prohibit its existence. In 1920, a provincial commissioner noticed that, "*Asafos* (who are known as the 'young men' of Kwahu) have formed themselves into an organized body and have members in nearly every town in this district. Its policy seems to be a consistent opposition to established authority."[17] The "opposition to established authority" was characterized by an increasing number of destoolments. The *Asafo* risings in Akyem Abuakwa in 1915–1918 shared the same feature. Simensen suggests that the risings were not only spontaneous protest reactions against various forms of exploitation, but a general expression of the political level of increasing socio-economic differentiation in Akyem Abuakwa (Simensen,1975b).

The Native Jurisdiction Ordinance passed in 1878 and enacted in 1883 remained the basis for the administration until 1927. In the Ordinance, nothing was mentioned about the position of other political forces except the chiefs. The amended Ordinance in 1910 gave traditional tribunals exclusive jurisdiction without either effective control from above or practical checks from below. The chiefs took advantage of the situation, and cases of oppression and exploitation greatly increased. Consequently, commoners organized as *Asafo* began to fight back. Destoolment became the most frequently used means of retaliation. During the three decades before 1920, more than 70 attempted destoolments occurred in Akyem and Kwahu.[18] The *Asafo*'s influence spread so rapidly that Governor Slater was surprised to discover in 1927 that in Akyem rural areas the real power did not belong to the chief, but rather to the *Asafo* leader: "An extraordinary fact has come to light ... in the majority of villages, the person who has power today is the *asafuakye*, not the *odikro* (chief). In some villages, the *odikro* is not informed what his young men have done or intend to do. This metamorphosis has taken place in the last year or so."[19]

The *Asafo* company faced greater challenges with the introduction of the Native Administration Ordinance in 1927, which strengthened the paramount chief s power. In 1928, a protest against the application of Native Administration Ordinance led to the actual running the Kwahu State by the *Asafo*. The Omanhene, who was finally destooled in 1932 by the *Asafo*, described the condition in Kwahu when he asked Ofori Atta I, the paramount chief of Akyem Abuakwa, for help in his political difficulties:

> Kwahu *Asafo* is something entirely different from all other *Asafo*s in all Akan, Twi and Fanti States of the Gold Coast ... The *Asafo* in Kwahu is a thing quite different from the old constitutional *Asafos*, It is a Kyenku of no *Asafo*, It comprises the rabble of Kwahu, Commoners of the town and villages headed by desperados known as *Asafoakyes* the word itself gave [sic] you an idea of their origin – Akan and Ga instead of Stool Captains. They are quite independent of the natural rulers, have their own oaths ... and their object is mainly to make laws for their Chiefs and oppose the Native Jurisdiction Ordinance of 1883 and the new Native Administration Ordinance of 1927.[20]
>
> (Twumasi 1971: 41–42)

120 *Encounter and research*

This description outlined almost all the important features of the modem *Asafo* system. First, it was new in organization, in terms of both its members and leaders. Although epithets such as "rabble of Kwahu" and "desperados known as *Asafoakyes*" were unpleasant, they did indicate that the members of *Asafo* included the people of the lower class in the traditional sense. Second, being "independent of the natural rulers", the *Asafo*'s main function seemed to be to balance the chief's authority, and they were thus feared by the chief. Third, the *Asofo*'s aim was to make laws for the chiefs and oppose the Native Administration Ordinance. The *Asafo* became such a challenge to the established order that chiefs desperately looked for help from outside.

Asafo and destoolment: A historical perspective

As the chief's position, the stool symbolises the pride and stability of the state. Therefore, destoolment – the formal removal of a chief from his position – is a politically significant matter. As Danquah points out:

> The founders of the Akan State Constitution in their wisdom instituted a mode of procedure whereby an unwanted and oppressive Chief, an insufficient or incapable Chief, an unmoral or easy-going Chief, could be deprived of his position permanently at any time the governed felt that there were good reasons for deposing and replacing him by a better man. governed felt that there were good reasons for deposing and replacing him by a better man.
>
> (Danquah 1928: 68)

Among the Akan people, there is a long tradition of destoolment. "Destoolment, for all that, is not a new thing to the Akan peoples. It has been a part of their constitution since the earliest times"(Danquah 1928a: 115). Destoolment, however, was usually the last resort as a constitutional means to keep the political power in balance. Only the ruler who committed grave offences was subject to such punishment.

According to customary law, the specific offences generally included: (1) notorious and habitual adultery; for the second and third offences, the chief was generally made to give the injured husband sufficient money for compensation; (2) habitual drunkenness and the resulting disorderly conduct, which degraded him; (3) habitually opposing the councillors and disregarding their advice without just cause; (4) theft; (5) perverting justice when hearing cases, and inflicting extortionate fines and penalties as well as failing to protect his subjects; (6) cowardice in war; (7) circumcision;[21] (8) unwarranted disposal of stool property, extravagance and persistently involving his people in debt, and other liabilities improperly contracted or incurred; (9) defiling his stool – inability to uphold the dignity and good reputation of the stool; (10) insufficient provision for the members of the stool family; and (11) general misconduct unworthy of his position, such as constantly provoking strife by acts and words, or referring contemptuously to the genealogy or pedigree of his subjects and elders, who might have come from a low status (Sarbah 1968 [1906]: 22–24; Danquah 1928: 115–117).

Owing to the scarcity of evidence, it is very difficult to discern a general pattern of destoolment in pre-colonial period. However, some interesting material does exist on the subject (Dupuis 1966 [1824]: 245; Bowdich 1966 [1819]: 238–240; Busia 1951: 99; Arhin 1981, 1989). Take the Asante area, for example.[22] Asantehene (Asante King) Osei Kwame ruled from 1777 to the end of the century, during which time he tried to establish Islam as the official religion. This change was rejected by both chiefs and commoners. The powerful chiefs feared that the king would use Islam to strengthen his individual power, which would threaten their own prestige and interests. According to oral tradition, the chiefs worried

> that the Moslem religion, which they well know levels all ranks and orders of men, and places them at the arbitrary discretion of the sovereign, might be introduced, whereby they would lose that ascendancy they now enjoy. To anticipate the calamity they dreaded, a conspiracy was entered into.
>
> (Dupuis 1966: 245)

Commoners realised that the acceptance of Islam would weaken the very basis of their religious beliefs, and political and social institutions as well. As a result they deposed the king (Bowdich 1966: 238–240).

In 1874, Asantehene Kofi Kakari took some gold trinkets and other valuable treasures from the royal mausoleum at Bantama without the consent of his councillors in Kumasi or the chiefs. People were angered when the case was discovered. The chiefs of four districts, together with Kumasi councillors, denounced this action as unconstitutional and sacrilegious. Consequently, the king was destooled (Busia 1951: 99).[23] In the 1880s, the young men of Asante openly took the lead in the movement that eventually overthrew Asantehene Mensa Bonsu. In 1882, the Bonsu regime introduced new rates of taxation on the southern gold-mining industries and imposed heavy fines for violations. This measure caused protest from *nkwankwaa* elements in the southern districts of Asante. The Kumasi *nkwankwaa* led the campaign against the Asantehene by uniting both the *ahiafo* (the "poor") and the *asikafo* ("men of gold", or "rich men"). They carried out a successful coup and Mensa Bonsu was destooled in early March 1883 (Wilks 1975: 534–43; Lewin 1978: 74–75,115–116).

Under colonial rule, several changes occurred regarding grounds for destoolment. Abuse of power became a frequent cause of deposition, which included a chief's exploitation of his people by means of the native tribunal or a chief's action beyond the limit of his authority, such as collaborating with the government in the application of certain ordinances without consulting his people. In addition, since bribery was increasing, both in legal cases and in the election of chiefs, acceptance of bribery also became a ground for destoolment. Many chiefs were also destooled because of their involvement in land dealing or financial misappropriation, which included extortion, collecting unlawful tribute and cheating in order to get some money (Li Anshan, 2002).

General mismanagement could also lead to destoolment. A ruler could be questioned for improper conduct that caused discontent among his subjects, elders or commoners. For example, if a chief absented himself continuously from his traditional duties in order to attend to his private interests, he would be asked to explain his conduct. In 1903, the chief of Tumentu in Gwira was destooled on the ground that for several years he had neglected his district by residing permanently at Axim, spent the rents and monies paid for concessions for his own use, and wasted the stool revenue (Sarbah 1968 [1906]: 47). If a chief constantly made use of his subjects for his own benefit, or ignored the *Asafo*'s warning, he faced destoolment. A chief's actions could also bring about discontent or even unrest among his people.[24] Such cases usually happened when a chief's engagement in expensive litigation resulted in increasing taxes, or when he collaborated with the government at the sacrifice of his people.

From the turn of the century, there was an increase in the number of destoolments.[25] There were about 119 destoolments during the period 1904–1925.[26] As early as 1908, the Secretary for Native Affairs warned that "the chiefs have been losing influence of late owing to the growth of the 'Companies'".[27] When a destoolment occurred in Begoro in 1908, the provincial commissioner said, "Destoolments are very rare still, but much more frequent than they were." He suggested that the inland people were probably "taking over the customs of the coastal towns, where destoolments were much more frequent".[28] The colonial report of 1918 disclosed that there had been "an unusual number of depositions" when the destoolment of no fewer than 16 chiefs was confirmed in that year.[29] The governor complained in 1922 that, "Elections and destoolments were unfortunately frequent among the Omanhin [paramount chiefs] and Ohin [chiefs]".[30]

During the first quarter of the 20th century, the *Asafo* company had pursued its political activities without much interference. According to a 1924 colonial report, the *nkwankwaa* in Asante had enjoyed a "feeling of independence and safety which gives vent to criticism of their elders, and a desire when dissatisfied to take the law into their own hands" (Tordoff 1965: 204)[31] In 1926–1927, the situation seemed to stabilise and a provincial commissioner used a very optimistic tone in his report: "There has been an almost complete absence of destoolments during the year ... the relations between the Chiefs and their people are better than I have ever known them to be." He suggested that the reason for this was that people were beginning to show more respect to their chiefs, who were taking their responsibility more seriously.[32]

The Native Administration Ordinance, enacted on 21 April 1927, increased the authority of chiefs, especially the paramount chief. Together with the governor's power to withhold recognition of destoolment, this generated some protest. A local newspaper predicted that, "The time is coming when a chief once installed will sit firmly on the neck of the people, like the old man of the sea, and rule them in his own way without any lawful means of getting rid of him."[33] Did this Ordinance check the tendency of destoolment? The effect seemed to vary. According to G. Mikell, there was a decrease in destoolments after 1927 in the Brong-Ahafo area. She suggests the reason for this decrease was that the application of the Ordinance "increased the powers of chiefs and their ability to control native courts and treasuries" (Mikell 1989: 142). The situation in the Eastern Province differed. There were three destoolments in the province in 1926–1927. But in 1927–1928 and 1928–1929, there were nine and seven respectively.[34]

Throughout the 1930s, the *Asafo*'s involvement in local politics assumed an aggressive aspect. In 1930, the *nkwankwaa* in Asante were outraged by the news that *Kumasihene* Nana Prempe I and his chiefs were considering a law requiring that a percentage of a deceased person's property be given to the *Kumasihene* and his chiefs. In a letter to the chief commissioner, the *nkwankwaa* reminded him of the case of Mensa Bonsu in 1883, whose overthrow was caused by a similar measure. Following the chief commissioner's advice, Nana Prempe I dropped the issue (Tordoff 1965: 375–82; Allman 1990: 269).

The propaganda for the Native Administration Revenue Measure and the launch of Income Tax Ordinance in 1931–1932 caused great confusion and protest, followed by a wave of destoolments. For example, in Akyem Abuakwa, all the main divisional chiefs were destooled and Paramount Chief Ofori Atta was facing a political crisis (Shaloff 1974; Simensen 1975b: 31–57, 90–104).[35] The chiefs took advantage of the power granted to them by the Ordinance to either seek their own benefits or keep opposition under control, usually with the support of the government police.[36] A district commissioner commented that "the chiefs with their autocratic methods have been sowing the seed of unrest ever since the introduction of the Native Administration Ordinance" (Simensen 1975b: 255).[37]

On the other hand, neither colonial officials nor chiefs were comfortable with the *Asafo*'s involvement in destoolment. After Kwahu *Asafo* destooled their paramount chief in 1932, the official in charge of the investigation strongly suggested the abolition of the office of senior *Asafoakye* and the repeal of *Asafo* laws.[38] In 1935, some of the Kumasi young men failed in an attempt to remove Asantehene Prempe II from the Golden Stool (Tordoff 1965: 365–69). In response to the *nkwankwaa*'s challenge to chiefly power, the Asante Confederacy Council voted unanimously in 1936 that, "The position of *Nkwankwaahene* and *Asafoakye*, also *Asafo* should be abolished from the whole of Ashanti in view of the fact that they are the cause of political unrest in Asante."[39] But it is not so easy to "legislate away the historically entrenched *nkwankwaa*", as Allman (1990: 270) points out.[40]

During the 1930s, destoolment was widespread. In the period between 1932 and 1942, no fewer than 22 paramount chiefs were destooled. In the case of subordinate chiefs, the situation was "as bad or worse".[41] By 1942, the *Asafo* organisations were so actively involved in local politics that it caught the acting governor's attention. G.E. London noted with deep concern "the number of riots and disturbances which have been caused by members of the Company (*Asafu*) Organization existing in different forms in various parts of the colony and Ashanti". He had to consider seriously "the question of disbanding these companies throughout the colony and Ashanti".[42]

Sir Alan C. Bums, the new governor, was "struck with dismay" by this gloomy picture. Although he warned that the disorder caused by destoolment "will not be permitted and will be put down with a strong hand",[43] the situation did not change for the better. In 1943 and 1944, 17 chiefs were deposed.[44] Then there came a big wave of deposition from 1945 to 1949, when more than 93 chiefs were destooled.[45] At the same time, a great number of chiefs abdicated, in most cases in order to forestall deposition.[46]

There are three possible reasons for this boom in destoolment. First, the growth of nationalist feeling after World War II contributed to the increase in destoolments. The local political situation was tense, with various protests against chiefs' wrongdoing, taxation schemes and high living standards. The 1948 Accra riots brought great attention from Westminster, spread elsewhere and finally became a national protest.[47] In Yilo Krobo, there was a movement in 1948 to break down the Native Authority and refuse to pay the annual rate. It was believed that one *Asafo* leader named Kwadjo Dei was "the leader and instigator of the abortive attempt to break into the Yilo Krobo prison and rescue prisoners" in 1949.[48] Simensen's study on Akyem Abuakwa indicates at least two removals were caused by the commoners' dissatisfaction with the chiefs' lukewarm reaction towards the arrest of nationalist leaders after the Accra riot (Simensen 1974: 38).

Second, the enactment of the Native Authorities Ordinance in 1944 greatly increased the governor's power in both the election and deposition of native authorities,[49] yet made no mention of the problem of popular representation. This not only upset the already tenuous balance of power, but also raised mass resentment against both the chiefs and the governor. Simensen called this the "administrative tie-up between the chiefs and Government effected by the Ordinances of 1944" (Simensen 1975b: 46). Third, Sir Alan Burns, who occupied the governorship for most of this period (1941–1947), seemed fully occupied with the Kyebi murder trial (1945–1949) in respect of native affairs. He seemed to lack the time or energy, or the tactical reasons, to review cases of destoolment even though he had been granted the power to do so.[50]

Destoolment continued to be a conspicuous phenomenon in the early 1950s. In some cases, even the Convention People's Party (CPP) members joined the *Asafo* company in the deposition of unwanted chiefs. Nana Sir Tsibu Darku, OBE was enstooled as paramount chief of the Assin Attandasu State in 1930. A very influential chief, he was a member of the executive council until February 1952 and a knighthood was conferred upon him in 1948. As a staunch supporter of the colonial government, he became the object of "increasingly violent political attacks" from the CPP in 1950. Because of his unpopularity, he even failed in his own rural electoral district against a CPP candidate in the general elections. Soon after the election, 66 charges were laid against him. He was "properly destooled", according to a commissioner's words, by the chiefs, elders and *Asafo* leaders.[51] From 1950 to 1953, no fewer than 36 chiefs were destooled, while 43 abdicated.[52]

The rise of nationalism gave birth to various political organisations, which gradually took over the role the *Asafo* used to play. The educated gradually gained an influential position in the arena of local politics and the young men's protests began to assume different forms. As a result, the influence of the *Asafo* company gradually declined, but it by no means disappeared.[53] They are still present in local affairs even today.[54]

Irregularity and legitimacy

All these examples show that destoolment was a very popular practice from about 1900 to the early 1950s. Almost every colonial officer noticed the frequency of destoolment. They either complained of the disobedience of the young men, who they believed were the "rabble" or the "lazy and discontented part of the population", or they attributed destoolment to the "weakness of the native institution". The *Asafo* enjoyed such popularity that in some places they became the real "bosses" in local politics.

For example, in the early 1900s, owing to complaints about the heavy oath fines, an agreement was reached between the *Asafo* and chiefs in Kwahu State, which was reaffirmed in 1913. In 1917, the *Asafo* passed a system of by-laws, which was later referred to as the Magna Carta of Kwahu. The Omanhene and his divisional chiefs agreed to observe these *Asafo* laws, which imposed extensive price controls, forbade any stool heir to offer a bribe to any party with power to elect and install a chief, forbade chiefs to apply for gunpowder unless with the permission of the *Asafo* leader, and laid down that any chief who cohabited with the wife of a commoner would be deposed.[55] This agreement shows the *Asafo* became a real challenge to both the chief and the government.

Regarding the *Asafo*'s attempted destoolment of the Ga *mantse* in Accra in 1924, the governor explained why the government should stand firm in dealing with the *Asafo*:

> it is clearly the duty of the administration not to confirm a deposition which has been conducted irregularly and without justifiable cause. To act otherwise would be to encourage the wholesale destoolment of head chiefs, an evil which is already sufficiently great to be serious.[56]

To analyse this accusation of irregularity, several factors have to be considered. First, the British officials did not quite understand precolonial political institutions in the Gold Coast, as they considered the young men, or the *Asafo*, insignificant in local politics. Early in 1913, Governor Clifford observed that:

> Under the curiously democratic native constitution, a Chief who abuses his powers to an extent sufficient to arouse popular indignation against him, is liable to be destooled, and that destoolment is now-a-days by no means an uncommon practice.[57]

The word "curiously" reflected the governor's understanding. He also noted the threat of the *Asafo* to the chiefly power: "if the *Asafo* is allowed to exert … its authority in opposition to that of the chiefs, it will be impossible for the latter to carry out the administration of the tribe".[58] He noticed the rise of the "'young men' – who are the third estate" in traditional kingdoms and thought "in the actual management of the little kingdom they hitherto have had no real voice". He insisted that the effective administration "can only be carried on by us through the agency of the native system of tribal government".[59]

In 1919, a report was sent to the governor claiming that there was "a marked tendency on the part of the *Asafo* to usurp powers it was never intended they should possess", and that the young men were trying to "destroy the existing form of power".[60] Later, it was said that the *Asafo* "has endeavored from time to time both in the Kwahu and other Akan Divisions to arrogate to itself powers which it was never intended that it should possess".[61] All these assumptions are dubious, since the young men had to be consulted in enstoolment or destoolment, or in any important matter concerning state affairs.

Second, the government did not understand "what an important and sacred thing" the stool was. Speaking of the Golden Stool, Ward correctly pointed out that "the Government did not understand at that time what an important and sacred thing the Golden Stool was. The British thought that it was an ordinary stool to sit on, important because it was a seat of the Asantehene" (Ward 1935: 209). That is why the governor, seeking to strengthen British claim to authority in Asante, made his infamous and inflammatory demand on March 28, 1900, for the Asante people to hand in their Golden Stool (Lewin 1978: 136). Nor did they understand the symbolic meaning of the stool. After the establishment of British rule, the process of enstoolment or destoolment became less regular because of interference from the government. The governor or the provincial commissioner, who knew very little about the indigenous system, began to destool disloyal chiefs or punish rebellious elders at will. For instance, Yaw Dakwa, chief of Pankesi, was removed from his position because he refused to accept the governor's ruling regarding a land dispute.[62] From 1917 to 1921, several divisional chiefs and elders in Peki were either fined or suspended from office by the governor for their protest against a newly elected chief who was not entitled to the position. In addition, some new practices were introduced, such as the suspension of a chief from his office, a notion totally strange to the traditional system.

Third, the so-called "irregularity" can also be seen as the result of the decreasing participation by the elders in state affairs. According to an annual report, "those Elders who should assist and advise the natural rulers of the inhabitants of the capital of the country are, by their acts, shown to be indifferent to the well-being of their state, regardless of their national welfare and quite obviously antagonistic towards native institution".[63] This "indifferent" and "antagonistic" attitude is understandable considering the changing situation. The economic opportunities affected everybody, and individuals now became less concerned about the state's affairs than ever before. The elders were no exception.

But more importantly, the colonial government destroyed the democratic features of traditional institutions. Now the elders had less say since the chief, backed by the government, was less concerned about their advice. No initiative was left for them, only the choice between supporting the chief, and thus the government's decision, or being indifferent. The elders were antagonistic not towards the "well-being of their state", as the report suggested, but towards the chief, "a government creature, a quasi-official". It was really their passive resistance against the colonial establishment, which left a political vacuum, making it possible for the *Asafo* to play a more active political role.

Fourth, for those areas where there was no tradition of destoolment, the people had to resort to this measure to protect themselves. As a new tactic in a new situation, this might be regarded as irregular. A 1924 colonial report stated:

> The custom of destoolment which was known only among certain tribes is becoming general throughout the Province, the result being that chiefs of today are faced with the possibility of being destooled for the smallest indiscretion on their part.[64]

For example, the Ga people had no custom of destoolment. A *mantse* (paramount chief) was granted his position by a magical process that could not be undone. He could not be destooled and replaced by another *mantse*. He could be removed by killing or desertion, according to the degree of his misconduct.[65] In the Krobo state, destoolment was also a new phenomenon. The paramount chief of Manya Krobo once stated: "We do not recognize destoolment in Krobo as there are no cases in our history. No Konor (paramount chief) has ever had the misfortune of being destooled." In the 1930s, however, Manya Krobo, Yilo Krobo, Shaim and Osudoku all decided to adopt the practice of destoolment of the Akan states.[66] By the 1940s, the *Asafo* company had become very active in the Krobo state.

At the end of 1948, the *Asafo* company's involvement in local politics in Yilo Krobo caused alarm from the government. Eight *Asafoiatsemei* and nine *sipim* (*Asafo* captains), together with other elders, sent a petition to the governor, protesting the payment of levy. They complained that the native authorities collected taxes for five years from herbalists, fetish priests and girls who had reached the age of puberty, and there was a "double system of taxation on palm oil and palm wine and also on timber", yet "the condition of affairs in the state of Yilo Krobo has grown progressively worse" and "the Authority have done nothing whatsoever to improve the standard of life of the people". They therefore requested "an immediate investigation into Yilo Krobo Native Authorities account and financial affairs".[67]

The criticism of the *Asafo*'s irregularity and the frequency of destoolment calls into question the legitimacy of destoolment. How could the *Asafo* companies arrogate their powers? What is the justification for the *Asafo* company's constant challenge to the established authority? These questions lead to another issue: the legitimacy of the *Asafo*'s activities. Not only does an authority need legitimacy, as is usually argued, but the process of offering power or depriving power also needs legitimacy.

According to customary law, it is the right of those who elect the chief to destool him when they find him no longer suitable for the position. Danquah analysed the function as well as the legitimacy of destoolment:

> This, as a formidable weapon in the hands of the people when properly manipulated, is a certain and sure safeguard of the democratic element in Akan State Constitution in that the knowledge of the existence of the right and of the people's readiness to exercise it on any necessary occasion acts as a check on the ruling princes reminding them perpetually that first and last the supreme interest or political ideal before them is the good and welfare of the governed and of the State as a whole.
>
> (Danquah 1928:68)

Once incorporated into the framework of colonial government, the chief's status underwent several changes. Now loyalty to and cooperation with the government became the essential requirement for newly elected chiefs. For example, it was a common practice for the government to appoint the chief for important areas in Asante, especially after the 1900 Uprising. According to the Chiefs Ordinance issued in 1904, when the election or deposition of a chief was questioned, the governor had the final say, which was not subject to challenge in the courts.[68] Yet this power threw some doubt on the legitimacy of the chief's position. Regarding a destoolment that occurred at Bekwai, the commissioner in charge of the investigation reported:

> In the case of Bekwai, for instance, the "youngmen," that is to say the lower classes, those who were not Elders, complained that they were not consulted in the choice of the Headchief, that they did not respect him in Bekwai itself, or when he visited the villages, and to a man they refused to serve him. The Elders remarked that "One cannot be a chief without subjects. If we support the Headchief we shall be alone. The whole of the youngmen refuse to serve the Headchief and we support them.[69]

Although the government claimed many times that the content and operation of the traditional political system should remain intact, there was an inherent dilemma in their intention and practice. By promoting certain chiefs and punishing others, the government had already breached the mechanism of the very structure they wanted to keep. The sacred notion of chiefly power was weakened and a chief was regarded as a mere mouthpiece of the governor or a local administrator, rather than as a paramount leader of his people. The image problem was worsened by the abuse of chiefly power. A more important change occurred in the chiefly power and the institutional channels through which the authority was exercised. Except for the loss of power to wage war or to inflict capital punishment, chiefs now enjoyed a more secure authority within the colonial administration. A chief's authority over his people increased, while at the same time it became less legitimate and less acceptable. This seemingly contradictory situation resulted from two circumstances: the weakening of the traditional checks from his people and elders; and the military backing by the government. A chief now cared much more about the favour of the government than the support of his people.

If the elders' indifference could be regarded as a passive resistance, the *Asafo*'s posture was more active and initiative. The *Asafo* leaders seemed to take it as their responsibility to represent the commoners and to guard their interests. Also, they were quite confident of their legitimate right. In an interview with the secretary for native affairs, one of the *Asafo* leaders in Accra stated the following theory of the constitution:

> The Stool of Accra belongs to the *Asafoatsemei* and *Manbii* (townspeople). The *Mantse* is merely a caretaker. A *Mantse* reigns, but never rules. A *Mantse* is not responsible for the actions of his people. If his people ask him to do a thing, he has only to do it.[70]

This theory seems to be true, for the chief can only decide matters on which his people have agreed, as is clearly shown in the oath and ceremony in his election. The limitation of the power of a king or a chief has also been described by other scholars (Busia 1951: 11; Christensen 1954: 117).

In those areas where the *Asafo* company gained power, their function in local politics was no longer questioned. In Akyem Abuakwa, the *Asafo*'s constitutional role was no longer a subject of debate in 1932. It was settled during the earlier risings against the chiefs when Paramount Chief Ofori Atta and the state council failed to deny the young men the right to organise for independent political action. Finally, the *Asafo* leaders gained the right to sit on the councils of the divisional chiefs as representatives of the commoners. They even learned how to use modern legal means in destoolment (Simensen 1975a: 255–256). In Kwahu, the paramount chief had to compromise to some extent by encouraging the wing chiefs to bring their *Asafo* leaders to the state council meetings, where they had the opportunities of advising them in matters before the council. These *Asafo* leaders even refused to sit with their chiefs and tried to speak for themselves and to vote as though they were equal with the council members.[71]

Causes within and without

There have been various interpretations of destoolments bought about by *Asafo* companies. Governor Clifford suggested that chiefs were destooled because they were "more enlightened and progressive than their subjects".[72] Governor Guggisberg thought it showed the weakness of the native system (Guggisberg 1927). Others considered it the result of the younger generation's demand for a share of power. According to Martin Wight, the cause of destoolment was "the struggles to control stool wealth and to enjoy the perquisites of office"(Wight 1946: 36). Macmillan held the same view by comparing the stool in the Gold Coast with the office in 18th century England: "an office is not so much an opportunity of service as a 'place of profit'"(Macmillan 1940). This issue was dealt with more systematically by F. Crowther, the Secretary for Native Affairs, who attributed the increase of destoolments to the spread of education, the increase in wealth, the change of the demand for a chief's duty and the lack of mutual respect and cooperation.[73] All these interpretations ignore the impact of colonial policy on local politics.

By establishing the chiefs as administrative agents, the colonial government could back them up with warrants, orders or police.[74] Whenever there was a conflict between the chief and the people, the government would try to support the chief if it was possible. Governor Clifford stated this policy in 1914:

> The democratic institutions of the people cannot be safely tampered with, but I none-the-less consider that some means should, if possible, be devised whereby Government can afford a greater measure of support than is today available to Native Chiefs whose unpopularity is due, not to excesses or extravagance, but to the fact that they are more enlightened and progressive than their subjects.[75]

He stated very clearly that "it has been the endeavor of the government to strengthen the position of the chiefs and to support their authority over their subjects".[76] Colonial Secretary R. Slater once said that if a chief was deposed in attempting to carry out a government order, this deposition would not automatically be recognised.[77] The chiefs, however, knew how to take advantage of this condition. A district commissioner complained of the difficult situation in 1934:

> Whenever the Chief hears any rumor that his opponents intend to do anything to which he can take the slightest objection he rushes to the D.C., often grossly exaggerates the importance of the intended action,

and asks that Government police will stop its occurrence ... If strong contingents of police are rushed to the spot and actually do cause the opposition to postpone or even abandon their intentions, then it is said that the Chief has the full support of Government in anything he may do, and is, in fact, little more than a Government servant. It is obvious that if this happens many abuses will creep in to his administration and the opinion of the people will be set at naught. He becomes a complete autocrat. On the other hand Government is bound to assist the Chiefs in upholding their position to a certain extent and the difficulty comes in deciding to what extent.[78]

These words disclosed the real problem of colonial rule. First, the chief became "little more than a government servant" in his people's eyes. Second, he could now count on the government support whenever he met a challenge from his opponent, even if the challenge was reasonable. Abusing his power, he became "a complete autocrat". Third, the government was bound to assist the chief even if it knew the chief was wrong. This policy was adjusted consistently to strengthen the chiefly power, frequently bringing about a direct confrontation between the government and the common people.

Besides consolidating chiefly power, the government was also trying to incorporate the chiefs into local administration by increasing central control. This attempt, however, was less successful for three major reasons. First, the Bond of 1844 had its impact on the government. The Bond was the first treaty signed by eight Fanti chiefs under which they acknowledged the power and jurisdiction of the Crown. Later, both the chiefs and the educated Africans always reminded the government that its rule rested not on conquest but on free agreement.[79] Therefore the government – often reluctantly or unwillingly – tried to leave some room for traditional authorities.

Second, the Native Jurisdiction Ordinance in 1878 did not mention the appointment of chiefs, which implied that the right was not vested in the government, but in native institutions. The amending Native Jurisdiction Ordinance in 1910 further strengthened the chiefly power by giving the traditional tribunals exclusive jurisdiction. Third, the elimination of educated Africans from high government positions since the last quarter of the 19th century created an educated group who became increasingly critical of the colonial rulers (Kimble 1963: 98–105). Ironically, this constant pressure from educated Africans put the chiefs in an advantageous bargaining position while dealing with the government to preserve their power. Colonial rule eroded the checks and balances within the indigenous power structure. As Simensen correctly points out, "a reduction of the democratic element in the traditional constitution was a necessary precondition for establishing the chiefs as effective administrative agents" (Simensen 1975a: 48). This breakdown of traditional political mechanisms resulted in serious abuse of chiefly power, and misconduct in financial matters, such as the expropriation of stool land and money or extortion in native tribunals, became very serious. During the 1920s, there were 13 destoolments of chiefs whose charges were detailed in *Government Gazette*. Among the 13 deposed chiefs, 12 were charged for economic offences. On average, each chief was charged with nearly four financial misdeeds.[80]

This problem was worsened by two other factors. First, there was no distinction between the chiefs' personal income and the stool revenue, nor any system of control to ensure their expenditures should be on public purposes. In the 1930s, various reports revealed that many disturbances resulted from the dissatisfaction the *Asafo* felt at not being consulted before any expenditure. It was they who were ultimately to be responsible for the payment.[81] Second, owing to the lack of normal incomes and adequate funds to maintain their prestige, chiefs continued to depend on fines from native courts and revenue from stool lands, which resulted in destoolment (Busia 1951: 208).

In addition to the legitimacy problem and abuse of chiefly power, another cause for frequent destoolment was the commercialisation of stools. When stool debt became a serious problem owing to the constant involvement in land litigation, it was not uncommon for stools to be offered to those who promised to pay the stool debt. In 1920, a candidate in Asante was offered the Kumawu stool on his undertaking to pay the stool debt. He accepted the offer, but persuaded the elders to sign a document making them responsible for reimbursing him in case he was destooled. When he became a chief, he tried every means to get as much profit as possible by levying fines and fees. As a result, the people refused to serve him and brought him before the chief commissioner.[82] Frequent use of bribery in elections also showed the tendency to commercialise the stool. This greatly alarmed the chiefs in Asante, who decided to make some regulations to address the problem (Busia 1951: 212).

Conclusion

This study shows that, owing to its ignorance of the traditional system, the colonial government accepted the chief as an autocrat who enjoyed absolute power, taking no notice of the democratic features of indigenous system. The role of the *Asafo* company in the power structure was disregarded and its normal participation in state affairs became less and less possible. Later, when the government noticed the clash between the *Asafo* and the chief, it consciously supported the chief in order to follow the principles of indirect rule and to strengthen local administration. This new condition caused by the colonial rule had a psychological impact on both common people and the chief.

To meet this challenge, the *Asafo*, with its traditional tendency to balance political power, took the lead to protect commoners' interests. During the period we have discussed, it was common for the *Asafo* to destool unpopular chiefs. Thus the situation became paradoxical. On the one hand, chiefs felt quite secure under the protection of British rule. On the other hand, since destoolment was unpredictable and meant total loss of power, the chiefs also had a sense of insecure possession of authority. A vicious circle thus developed: fear of losing privileges led to an excessive use of power at hand; and more abuse of power usually meant more destoolments.

Notes

1 Originally presented at the 21st annual conference of the Canadian Association of African Studies in 1992, this chapter is a revised version of an article published in *The International Journal of African Historical Studies* 28(2) 1995. My thanks to the journal for the permission and Professors M. Klein, J. Barker, G. Mikell, and J. Addo-Fening and others for their suggestions.
2 For example, Martin Wight argued that there were two indigenous political forces in the colony: the native rulers and the educated class (Wight 1946: 181). D. Kimble has mentioned the commoners' role in local politics in his classic work. Yet by arguing that the indigenous chieftaincy was threatened by the educated young men, "who felt that the old apparatus of government was out of date", he treats both chiefs and the educated much more systematically (Kimble 1963: 458). In his Danquah lecture, Robert K.A. Gardiner used such a title for one section: "Reactions to British Rule-The Chiefs and Intelligentsia" (Gardiner 1970: 20). There is a similar tendency in African historiography. This "elite history" has been criticised by some African historians (Ayandele 1979).
3 Colonial Ghana had four parts: the Gold Coast colony, Asante, the Northern Territories and the British Mandated Togoland. The area covered by this article includes the Gold Coast colony and Asante (unless otherwise indicated), where mainly the Akan live. In Akan political culture, the stool represents the soul or spirit of the community. Every state has a stool. In abstract sense, the stool is the symbol of authority of a chief, thus "enstoolment", the installation of a chief, and "destoolment", the deposition of a chief. Chiefs in the northern part of Ghana sit on leather puffs (skins), the symbol of chiefly authority. So they are "skinned" and "deskinned".
4 For original documents, see Ghana National Archives, ADM11/1/738, Case no. 11/1919, "*Asafo*: Origin and the Powers of"; ADM11/1136, "Kwahu *Asafo*"; ADM11/1311, Case no. ANA9/1920, Banbata Native Affairs. (This file contains materials of the *Asafo* in Asante Akym.) ADM11/1/1393, Case no. 88/1913, "Destoolment"; ADM11/1/712, Case no. 56/1918, "Kwahu-Agogo Land Dispute".
5 For example, the Christian congregation and dancing and playing clubs formed by youngsters are all called *Asafo* (Danquah 1928a, 1928b; Nkrumah 1957).
6 For Fanti *Asafo*, see Sarbah (1968 [1906]: 231–232); Ffoulkes (1908: 261–277); Johnson (1932: 307–322); Datta (1972). For Asante, see Busia (1951: 9–13); Tordoff (1965: 373–83); Wilks (1975: 535–543). For *Asafo* in Akyem Abuakwa, see Danquah (1928a); Addo-Fening (1980: 447–459); Simensen (1974: 25–41). For Kwahu, see Twumasi (1971: 39–44); Simensen (1975a: 383–406). For Winneba, see Owusu (1970: 40–44). For the Effutus, see Akyempo (n.d.). For Accra, see Fortescue (1990).
7 The earliest mention of young men and the company system of the Eastern Province in the colonial documents was by Traveling Commissioner H.M. Hull in his report dated 12 September 1898. ADM11/738, Case no. 11/1919, *Asafo*: Origin and Powers of, enclosed in Secretary for Native Affairs to Acting Commissioner, Eastern Province, Confidential, 4 December 1905.

8 I should thank Jenkins for sending me this unpublished article. In Accra, not only was the organisation of *Asafo* copied from the Fante, but the terms and songs were all Fante. Then other towns copied from Accra (Field 1973: 168).
9 The letter written by the Mayor of Cape Coast to the Chief Justice, 29 November 1859 (Sarbah 1968 [1897]: 12–13).
10 For its early activities, see Kea (1986).
11 A member notified the company of his marriage by presenting his wife to the assembled company, who offered the protection of his conjugal rights. When he died, the scouts of his company would take the widow to the company post and question her to see whether she was responsible for his death. It was to show to the spirit of the dead man that the *Asafo* was concerned about his affairs (Christensen 1954: 120).
12 *Asafoatsemei* in origin were hunters. After warfare ceased and population increased, they took over the management of secular affairs.
13 CO96/363, Gold Coast 403, Low (Governor) to Chamberlain, 6 October 1900. The district commissioner of Axim complained about "the difficulty of obtaining carriers to take service under the Government in connection with the expedition".
14 These complaints were very common among those carriers recruited by the government (Agbodeka 1971: 135–136).
15 The Omanhene once cursed this *Asafo* company by saying, "'*Asafo* Kyenku' of Kwahu is in all but in name a Bolshevic [sic] or Communist society seeking to pull down the native administration." GNA, CSO, 1174/31, "Kwahu *Asafo* Company Papers".
16 CO98/58, Report on the Eastern Province for the year 1930–31, Birim District (Kwahu).
17 ADM11/738, Case no. 11/1919, Colin Hardings to the Governor, April 1920.
18 For *Asafo* in Akyem Abuakwa and Kwahu (Simensen 1974, 1975c; Johnson 1972; Stone 1974).
19 ADM11/1332, SS Conf. 2, Slater to Avery, 7 November 1927.
20 GNA, CSO 1174/31, "Akuamoa Boateng II to Ofori Atta 1, 30 December 1927" included in "Kwahu *Asafo* Company Papers".
21 The Akan custom used to look upon circumcision as an attribute of inferior foreign people. No stool in Akan tolerated it (Danquah 1928a: 116). But it is no longer regarded as a bar to the office (Agyeman-Duah 1965).
22 Busia once collected some informative cases in the traditional histories of the divisions of the Asante area. Chiefs Kwabena Aboagye of Asumegya, Kwabena Bruku and Kwai Ten of Nsuta were destooled for drunkenness; Kwame Asonane of Bekwai for being a glutton; Kwame Asona, also of Bekwai, for dealing in charms and noxious medicines; and Akuamoa Panyin of Dwaben for his abusive tongue, and for not following the advice of his elders. In Kokofu, Osei Yaw was destooled for disclosing the origin of his subjects (i.e. reproaching them with their slave ancestry), and Mensa Bonsu for excessive cruelty (Busia 1951: 21–22).
23 It seems the reason for the destoolment was much more complicated than Busia described. Kofi Karikari's militant policy was thought to have brought the British invasion of Asante in 1874, when the Asante army was badly beaten: "Remembrance of these horrors influenced all future decisions with British officials and made dissident Asante politicians very eager to have British assistance in their opposition to authorities in Kumasi" (Lewin 1978: 44–48). It was not clear whether the young men played a crucial role in this destoolment. But, as Wilks points out, the

Asafo and destoolment in Southern Ghana 135

nkwankwaa acquired "their first experience of political action in the anti-war and anti-conscription movements" of the late 1860s and early 1870s (Wilks 1975: 535).

24 Rattray noted that, "A Chief who was always ordering his subjects to be flogged would, however, soon be destooled" (Rattray 1929: 377).
25 Addo-Fening points out that, "Cases of destoolment in the 19th century were few and far between." Then he mentions three cases of destoolment in the 20th century: "By contrast no fewer than thirteen cases of destoolment or attempted destoolment were reported in the period 1900–1912." (Addo-Fening, 1980: 404, n. 37).
26 CO96/663, Memorandum by Secretary for Native Affairs for the visit of Ormsby-Gore in 1926. There is a register of deposed chiefs from 1904 to 1929 in ADM11/2/14. After 1929, the depositions were recorded in the *Gold Coast Gazette* only. Some case studies also indicate that the number of destoolments was increasing during the first decades of colonial rule (Simensen 1975a: 64, 141–60).
27 CO96/473, Ellis memo (n.d.) enclosure in Governor Rodger to Secretary of State, 8 November 1908.
28 ADM1/457, Commissioner of Eastern Province to Secretary for Native Affairs, 5 November 1908.
29 CO96/601, Gold Coast 530, Native Affairs Department Report for 1918, enclosure in Acting Governor Slater to Viscount Miller, 27 June 1919.
30 CO98/45, "A Review of the Events of 1921–22 and the Prospects of 1922–23", Governor Guggisberg's Address to Legislative Council, 27 February 1922.
31 Colonial Reports: Ashanti, 1923–24.
32 CO98/48, Annual Report of the Eastern Province for the Financial Year, 1926–27. There were seven destoolments in the whole colony during the year.
33 *The Gold Coast Times*, 19 March 1927.
34 CO98/50, Report on the Eastern Province for the Year 1927–28. Among the nine chiefs, six were from Akyem Abuakwa. CO98/53, Report on the Eastern Province for the Year 1928–29. In addition, three paramount chiefs in the province were destooled by their subjects. However, the deposition of the Ga *Mantse* was confirmed in 1930; the *Omanhene* of Kwahu was later allowed to abdicate and the *Omanhene* of New Dwaben was reinstated by the governor on 12 February 1929. See CO99/45–50, *Government Gazette*, 1927–29.
35 CO96/699/7050A, Income Tax and Protest, Minute. CO96/704/7260, G.C., Confidential, Governor to Lister, 31 March 1932; Acting Governor to Lister, 20 August 1932.
36 A chief in Begoro insisted that "he ruled the people and not they him", and made a list of 12 persons whom he wanted to have arrested by the government police. MP22/32, Acting Commissioner of Eastern Province to Secretary for Native Affairs, 17 October 1932.
37 MP1163/31, Quarterly Reports, September 1932.
38 GNA, CSO 1174/31, "Review of Evidence and Recommendations", in "Kwahu *Asafo* Company Papers" (Twumasi 1971: 43).
39 *Ashanti Confederacy Council Minutes*, January 1936.
40 She also quoted M. Fortes' observation in the mid-1940s when he was in Asante completing his "Ashanti Social Survey". It was found that youngmen's association and self-help groups (modelled on the *nkwankwaa* organizations) continued to give expression of the opinions of commoners.
41 Legislative Council Debates, 29 September 1942, pp.3–4.

42 ADM11/1679, Case no. 18/1910, no. 82, Confidential, 26 February 1942, "The Company (Asafu) System."
43 Legislative Council Debates, 29 September 1942, 3–4.
44 CO99/71–72, *Government Gazette*, 1943–44.
45 Among them three were in the British Mandated Togoland; the rest were in the Gold Coast Colony and Asante, CO99/73–77, *Government Gazette*, 1945–49.
46 The figures are 26 for 1947, 23 for 1948 and 16 for 1949. See CO99/75–77, *Government Gazette*, 1947–49.
47 For the Accra riots, see *Report of the Commission on Enquiry into Disturbance in the Gold Coast, 1948*. (Colonial no. 231, Watson Report.) for the postwar situation (Austin 1964: 92).
48 ADM11/1797, Case no. 1501, Chief Commissioner to Colonial Secretary, 18 February 1949.
49 The most different part from the Native Administration Ordinance of 1927 is that the governor, if he thought the chief and council unfit for the job, could appoint other temporary or permanent executive authority in their place. Thus "native authority" was no longer automatically synonymous with "traditional authority". See Native Authority (Colony) Ordinance, 1944, Sections 3–6, Supplement to the *Gold Coast Gazette*, no. 43, dated 22 June 1944.
50 In February 1944, the *odikro* of Apedwa, one of the three leading *amantoommiensa* villages in Akyem Abuakwa, was reported missing (he was later said to have been ritually murdered) in connection with the Paramount Chief Ofori Atta's funeral. When Governor Burns refused to exercise his prerogative of mercy, a series of appeals was started. The case was brought four times before the Privy Council in London and kept the matter before the courts through 1945 and 1946. A settlement was finally reached in 1949, and the guilt men executed. The case itself was a reflection of the conflict between the local *Asafo* company and the paramount chief in Kyebi (Simensen 1975a: 330–335). For an analysis of this story, see Rathbone (1993).
51 CO554/702, Destoolment of Chiefs in the Gold Coast, no. 3, Governor of the Gold Coast to Secretary of State, 14 December 1951.
52 CO99/78-79; CO99/81-82; CO99186, *Government Gazette*, 1950–1953. After 1954, there is no destoolment recorded in *Government Gazette*. For the period 1948–1951, see also CO554/702. Destoolment of Chiefs in the Gold Coast, no. 1, Governor of the Gold Coast to Secretary of State, 6 December 1951. The figure he quoted did not include the destoolment of subchiefs. From 1954 on, there is no record of destoolment in *Government Gazette*.
53 As late as 1955, some *Asafo* company members were among those protesting against the imposition of new property rates (Owusu 1970: 217). For his publications on the role of the *Asafo* in postcolonial Ghanaian politicism see Owusu (1979, 1986, 1989). For the Asante youngmen's involvement in local politics in the 1950s, see Allman (1990).
54 When I was doing the research in Ghana in 1992, it was reported that an *Asafo* company was involved in a blood feud in Akyem-Chia. See *People's Daily Graphic*, 27 June 1992.
55 ADM11/1/738, Case no. 11/1919, "New Orders and Regulations Inaugurated by the Whole Kwahu *Asafos* at Abetifi on the 6th November 1917 and which will be always adhered to." See also ADM11/1/712, Case no. 56/1918; ADM11/1393 (Confidential), Ofori Atta to the Secretary for Native Affairs, 3 August 1915.

56 CO96/654, Gold Coast Secret, CO18836, G17152/T19212, Guggisberg to L.S. Amery (MP), 4 April 1925.
57 CO96/528, Gold Coast (Confidential), Governor Clifford to Secretary of State, 3 March 1913.
58 CO99/33, "Governor's Address to the Legislative Council, 28 October 1918", *Government Gazette*, 1918, no. 82 (Extraordinary). But the government seemed at a loss facing this "curiously democratic constitution" and nothing effective had been done before 1927, when the Native Administration Ordinance was enacted.
59 CO96/567, Gold Coast Confidential, Governor Clifford to A. Bonar Law, 26 May 1916.
60 ADM11/1/738, Case no. 11/1919, "Report on the Akim *Asafo* by the District Commissioner, Kwahu 1919". For documents of the *Asafo* in Akyem Abuakwa, see ADM11/ 1/1311, A.N.A9/1920, "Bompata Native Affairs."
61 CO98/48, Annual Report of the Eastern Province for the Financial Year 1926–27.
62 CO96/380, "A Land Dispute Between the Chief of Pankesi under the King of West Akim and the Chiefs of Obo and Obomeng under the King of Kwahu", Gold Coast (Confidential), 13 May 1901.
63 CO96/55, Report on the Eastern Province 1929–30.
64 CO98/42, Report on the Eastern Province for the period April 1924–March 1925.
65 It is told that the usurper Queen Dode Akabi (1610–1635) was trapped inside a well and buried alive by angry subjects for her cruelty. Her tyrannical successor, Okaikoi, held power until 1660 when he was deserted by his warriors. His last question was, "My people, do you wish me to commit suicide?" The answer was, "Yes, we won't have any king to govern us." (Reindorf 1966 [1895]: 29–30; Field 1973: 76–77).
66 ADM11/1393, Resolutions, Enclosure in Acting Commissioner of Eastern Province to Acting Secretary for Native Affairs, 13 August 1930.
67 ADM11/1797, Cast no. 1501, "Yilo Krobo Native Affairs", Petition by *Asafoiatsemei* of Yilo Krobo about the payment of levy, 22 December 1948. Their petition, however, was not warmly received by the government. In a letter to the colonial secretary, the chief commissioner indicated that the leader was a troublemaker and a charge of inciting persons not to pay the annual rate was already pending against him. He therefore recommended that the governor should not agree to the petitioners' withholding payment of annual rate to the Native Authorities. ADM11/1797, Case no. 1501, Chief Commissioner to Colonial Secretary, 18 February 1949.
68 Chiefs Ordinance, 1904, Sec. 29.
69 Colonial Report: Ashanti, 1920.
70 CO98/44, "Ga Mantse Incident", p. 14.
71 CO96/718/21755/A, Annual report on the Eastern Province 1933–34, enclosure in Gold Coast, no. 457, 12 September 1934. But the senior *Asafo* leader's demand to become a member of the council and equal in rank to the wing chiefs was refused.
72 CO96/543, Gold Coast Confidential (A), Clifford to Harcourt, 24 March 1914.
73 CO96/543, Gold Coast, Confidential (A), enclosure in Clifford to Harcourt, 24 March 1914. CO96/577, Gold Coast, Confidential (A), "Native Affairs Report submitted by Mr. Crowther, enclosed in Acting Governor Slater to Walter Long, 25 January 1917".
74 This was confirmed in the Peace Conservation Ordinance (1897).

75 CO96/33, Gold Coast, Confidential (A), Clifford to Secretary of State, 24 March 1914. See also CO96/567, Gold Coast, Confidential, Clifford to Secretary of State, 26 May 1916.
76 CO99/33, "Governor's Address to the Legislative Council, 28 October 1918". *Government Gazette*, no. 82, 1918 (Extraordinary).
77 CO96/614, Note on Conference on Native Jurisdiction Bill with the Legislative Council Chiefs, 24 February 1920, enclosure in Confidential to Secretary of State, 7 July 1920.
78 CO96/718/21755A, Annual Report on the Eastern Province 1933–34, enclosure in Gold Coast, no. 457, 14 September 1934.
79 For its significance, see Danquah (1957).
80 The sources limit my choice of this particular period, which was the only period offering some cases with detailed charges. In most cases, charges did not appear in the *Government Gazette*. CO99/42–50, *Government Gazette*, 1925–29.
81 CO96/711, Gold Coast, no. 468, S. Thomas to P. Cunliffe Lister, 19 August 1933. A specific case was described in CO96/706, Northcote to P.C. Lister, 18 August 1932.
82 *Colonial Reports: Ashanti, 1920*.

References

Addo-Fening, R. 1980. Akyem Abuakwa c. 1874–1943: A study of the impact of missionary activities and colonial rule on a traditional society. PhD thesis, University of Ghana.
Agbodeka, F. 1971. *African politics and British policy in the Gold Coast 1868–1900*. London: Longman.
Agyeman-Duah, J. 1965. The ceremony of enstoolment of the Asantehene. *Ghana Notes and Queries* 7: 8–11.
Akyempo, K. n.d. *Deer Hunt Festival of the Effutus*. Accra: Anowou Educational.
Allman, J. 1990. The young men and the porcupine: Class nationalism and Asante's struggle for self-determination 1954–57. *The Journal of African History* 31(2): 263–279.
Arhin, K. 1966. Diffuse authority among the coastal Fanti. *Ghana Notes and Queries* 9: 66–70.
Arhin, K. 1981. *Traditional rule in Ghana: Past and present*. Accra: Sedco.
Arhin, K. 1983. The political and military roles of Akan women, in Oppong C. *Female and Male in West Africa*. London: George Allen & Unwin, 91–98.
Arhin, K. 1989. Sanction against abuse of authority in pre-colonial Africa. Unpublished conference paper, Wurzburg.
Ashanti Confederacy. Council Minutes January 1936.
Austin, D. 1964. *Politics in Ghana 1946–1960*. Oxford: Oxford University Press.
Ayandele, E. 1979. *African historical studies*. London: Frank Cass
Bowdich, T.E. 1966 [1819]. *Mission from Cape Coast Castle to Ashantee*. London: Frank Cass.
Brokensha, D.W. 1966. *Social change at Larteh*. Oxford: Clarendon Press.
Brown, E.J.P. 1929. *Gold Coast and Ashanti reader book I*. London: Crown Agents for the Colonies.
Busia, K.A. 1951. *The position of the chief in the modern political system of Ashanti*. Oxford: Oxford University Press.

Christensen, B. 1954. *Double descent among the Fanti*. New Haven, CT: Ethnographic Arts Publications.
Chukwukere, I. 1980. Perspective on the Asafo institution in Southern Ghana. *The Journal of African Studies* 7(1): 39–47.
Danquah, J.B. 1928. *Gold Coast Akan laws and customs and the Akim Abuakwa Constitution*. London: George Routledge.
Danquah, J.B. 1928a. *The Akim Abuakwa Handbook*. London: Forster Groom.
Danquah, J.B. 1957. The historical significance of the bond of 1844. *Transactions of the Historical Societies of Ghana* 3(1): 3–29.
Datta, A. & Porter R. 1971. The Asafo system in historical perspective. *The Journal of African History* 12(2): 279–297.
Datta, A. 1972. The Fante Asafo: A re-examination. *Africa* 42(4): 305–314.
De Graft Johnson, J.D. 1932. The Fante Asafu. *Africa* 5(3): 307–322.
De Graft Johnson, J.D. 1927. The significance of some Akan titles. *Gold Coast Review* 2(2): 17–18.
Debrunner, H. 1961. *Witchcraft in Ghana*. Accra: Presbyterian Book Depot.
Dupuis, J. 1966 [1824]. *Journal of a residence in Ashantee*. London: Frank Cass.
Ellis, A.B. 1964 [1887]. *The Tshi-speaking peoples of the Gold Coast of West Africa*. Chicago, IL: Benin Press.
Ffoulkes, A. 1908. The company system in the Cape Coast Castle. *Journal of the Royal African Society* 7(27): 261–277.
Field, M. 1948. *Akim-Kotoku: An Oman of the Gold Coast*. London: Crown Agents for the Colonies.
Field, M.J. 1973. *Social organization of the Ga People*. London: Crown Agents for the Colonies.
Fortescue, D. 1990. The Accra crowd: The Asafo and the opposition to the Municipal Corporations Ordinance 1924–25. *Canadian Journal of African Studies* 24(3): 348–375.
Gardiner, R.K.A. 1970. *The role of educated persons in Ghana society*. Accra: The J.B. Danquah Memorial Lectures.
Guggisberg, Sir G. 1927. *Gold Coast: A review of the events of 1920–1926 and prospects of 1927–28*. Accra: Government Printer.
Hayford, C. 1970 [1903]. *Gold Coast Native Institution*. London: Frank Cass.
Jenkins, 1971. Towards a definition of social tension in rural Akan communities of the high colonial period: The Asafo movement in the Eastern Province and Eastern Asante. Seminar paper, University of Ghana Legon, 9 February.
Johnson, T. 1972. Protest, tradition and change: An analysis of Southern Gold Coast riots 1890–1920. *Economy and Society* 1(2): 164–193.
Kea, R. 1986. 'I am here to plunder on the general road': Bandits and banditry in the pre-19th-century Gold Coast. In D. Crummey, ed., *Banditry, rebellion and social protest in Africa*. London: James Currey, 109–132.
Kimble, D. 1963. *A political history of Ghana 1850–1928*. Oxford: James Currey.
Lewin, T. 1978. *Asante before the British: The Prempean years 1875–1900*. Lawrence, KS: Regents Press.
Li Anshan. 2002. *British rule and rural protest in Southern Ghana*. New York: Peter Lang.
Macmillan, W.M. 1940. Political and social reconstruction: The peculiar case of the Gold Coast. In M. Manoukian, ed., *Akan and Ga-Adangme peoples of the Gold Coast*. London: Oxford University Press.
Manoukian, M. 1950. *Akan and Ga-Adangme peoples*. Oxford: Oxford University Press.

Meyerowitz, E. 1974. *Early history of the Akan State of Ghana*. London: Red Candle Press.
Mikell, G. 1989. *Cocoa and chaos in Ghana*. New York: Paragon House.
Native Authority (Colony) Ordinance 1944.
Nkrumah, K. 1957. *Ghana: The autobiography of Kwame Nkrumah*. London: Thomas Nelson and Sons.
Owusu, M. 1970. *Uses and abuses of political power*. Chicago: University of Chicago Press.
Owusu, M. 1979. Politics without parties: Reflections on the Union Government proposals in Ghana. *African Studies Review* 22(1): 89–108.
Owusu, M. 1986. Custom and coups: A juridical interpretation of civil order and disorder in Ghana. *Journal of Modern African Studies* 24(1): 69–99.
Owusu, M. 1989. Rebellion, revolution and tradition: Reinterpreting coups in Ghana. *Comparative Studies in Society and History* 31(2): 372–397.
Peace Conservation Ordinance. 1897.
Rathbone, R. 1993. *Murder and politics in colonial Ghana*. New Haven, CT: Yale University Press.
Rattray, R.S. 1929. *Ashanti law and constitution*. London: Oxford University Press.
Reindorf, C.C. 1966. *History of the Gold Coast and Asante* [1895]. Accra: Ghana University Press.
Sarbah, J.M 1968 [1906]. *Fanti national constitution*. London: Frank Cass.
Sarbah, J.M. 1968 [1897]. *Fanti customary laws*. London: Frank Cass.
Shaloff, S. 1974. The income tax indirect rule and the depression: The Gold Coast riots of 1931. *Cahier d'Etudes Africaines* 14(2): 59–75.
Simensen, J. 1974. Rural mass action in the context of anticolonial protest: The *Asafo* movement of Akim Abuakwa, Ghana. *Canadian Journal of African Studies* 8(1): 25–41.
Simensen, J. 1975a. The *Asafo* of Kwahu, Ghana: A mass movement for local reform under colonial rule. *The International Journal of African Historical Studies* 8(3): 383–406.
Simensen, J. 1975b. Commoners, chiefs and colonial government: British policy and local politics in Akim Abuakwa, Ghana, under colonial rule. PhD thesis, University of Trondheim.
Stone, R. 1974. Protest: Tradition and change – a critique. *Economy and Society* 3(1): 84–95.
Tordoff, W. 1965. *Ashanti under the Prempehs 1888–1935*. London: Oxford University Press.
Twumasi, E.Y. 1971. Aspects of politics in Ghana 1923–39: A study of the relationship between discontent and development of nationalism. DPhil dissertation, Oxford University.
Ward, W.E. 1935. *A short history of the Gold Coast*. London: Longmans, Green and Co.
Wartemberg, J.S 1950. *Sao Jorge d'El Mina Premier West African Settlement*, Ilfracombe: Stockwell.
Wight, M. 1946. *The Gold Coast Legislative Council*. London: Faber & Faber.
Wilks, I. 1975. *Asante in the 19th century*. London: Cambridge University Press.
Wyllie, R.W. 1967. The Aboakyer of the Effutu: A critique of Meyerowitz's account. *Africa* 37(1): 81–85.

Part II
Policy and implementation

6 Origins of the Forum on China–Africa Cooperation

Introduction

In 1997, Benin Minister Albert Tevoedjre proposed the establishment of a China–Africa cooperation mechanism while in Hong Kong. In early 1998, a Mauritian director specifically advised setting up a one-to-one multi-partnership, such as a China–Africa dialogue platform. Other diplomats from Madagascar, Ethiopia and Benin did the same, yet China still did not provide a positive response. In January 1999, a senior Egyptian diplomat, Mr Ahmed Haggad, who also served as Egyptian Ambassador to Kenya and the former Assistant General Secretary of the Organisation of African Unity (OAU), suggested the formation of a multiparty mechanism between Africa and China. No action was forthcoming from China. In the spring of 1999, Ms Lila Ratsifandrihama, the Foreign Minister of Madagascar, raised the issue again and asked Chinese Foreign Minister Tang Jiaxuan to consider establishing a multilateral forum, since China and African countries maintained a good relationship. On 10–12 October 2000, the Forum on China-Africa Forum Ministerial Conference was held in Beijing.

With the change in the international situation, economic globalisation provided an incentive for China to adopt a comprehensive approach to engaging the African continent. Senior African officials realised the importance of a China–Africa cooperation mechanism and proposed the establishment of the Forum on China–Africa Cooperation (FOCAC). Chinese academics and political professionals advised on upgrading and institutionalising China–Africa relations, and these ideas were finally put into practice.

Many years have passed since the establishment of FOCAC in 2000. Its creation is an important event in the history of China–Africa relations and has caught the world's attention since then. FOCAC has now become an important mechanism that influences contemporary history in several ways. It created a model for South–South cooperation and provided new thinking and a fresh new paradigm for solving global poverty. Based on equality and mutual benefit, FOCAC is linked directly to the legitimacy of the present politico-economic world order. The basis of FOCAC is mutual respect and a pragmatic and realistic win–win principle; this approach has achieved great success, and has been followed by other similar forums. At the same time, from a relatively uniform organisation the forum has gradually developed into a flexible and fixed mechanism with an auxiliary body.

However, the world still finds FOCAC somewhat mysterious, with limited news being released. The natural result of this lack of information is doubt, questions, speculation and rumours. Why was FOCAC established and who is operating behind the scenes? Did China set up this forum for its own benefit (Asche 2007)? There is a view that FOCAC was proposed and created by China alone, with some even considering that FOCAC formed part of China's African geopolitical strategy (Alves 2008; Alden et al. 2008). By using the existing literature and data from first-hand interviews, the author presents a different view: that many factors contributed to the founding of the forum. Long-standing cooperation and coordination in international affairs between China and Africa had laid a solid foundation for this new China–Africa strategic partnership.

The 1990s witnessed a fast, comprehensive and stable development of relations between China and Africa, which naturally required them to upgrade their cooperation mechanism; this contributed to the birth of FOCAC. In China, many professionals in both the academic and political fields offered suggestions for upgrading and institutionalising China–Africa cooperation and finally were able to put them into practice.

Solid foundation

The history of China–African relations indicates a type of continuity within a framework of partnership following the principles of equality, non-interference in political affairs, mutual respect of sovereignty and common development. It can be divided into three periods: normal development (1956–78); transformation (1978–94); and rapid rising (from 1995). Before FOCAC, China–African relations fluctuated, yet both sides have always cooperated and supported each other on the international stage.

There are significant aspects of Africa's support for China. In October 1971, with the support of other countries, China resumed its legal seat in the United Nations. Of the 76 countries that voted for China, 26 were African. Chairman Mao described this vividly and expressed his appreciation of African's support to China (Weng Ming 1995: 9).

After the "Tiananmen Square incident" of 1989, the first head of state, the first prime minister and the first foreign minister who visited China were all from African countries. Former Foreign Minister Qian Qichen pointed out that:

> What they did indicated the reason why they visited China at that very moment. It was exactly to show that Africa was a real friend of China, even though China was going through its toughest situation. They

remembered that China used to help them in the past, and therefore they should try their best to support China.

(Qian Qichen 2003: 255–257; Taylor 1998)

In the 1980s, 51 African heads of state visited China, up from 33 such visits in the 1970s. From 1990 to April 1998, 53 African heads of state, 15 African prime ministers and many African senior officials visited China (Chen Gongyuan 2007l; Chen Gongyuan 2009: 132). These visits indicated the mutual trust between China and Africa, and also promoted China–Africa relations. For many years, Africa has supported China over issues such as Taiwan, human rights, Tibet, China's candidacy for the position of Director General of the WHO and China's bid to host the 2008 Olympic Games.

From 1990, Western countries (with the United States at the forefront) often interfered in China's internal affairs by using human rights as a pretext. They quoted the so-called "situation of human rights in China" resolution of the Human Rights Commission seven consecutive times, criticising the Chinese government. However, at the 53rd Conference of the UN Human Rights Commission in 1997, African and other developing countries proposed a "no-action taken" motion to fight against the Western anti-China resolution. During the final vote, the anti-China resolution was defeated by 22 votes to 17. Among the 22 votes, 14 were from African countries. In 1998, the West had to declare that it would no longer raise an anti-China resolution on the issue of human rights.

The following embodies China's support for Africa (among other actions). China has always supported the African anti-colonial struggle. In 1950, the South African government issued the Group Area Act, an Apartheid act. Chairman Mao Zedong was asked by the South African Indian leader for support. In his reply, Chairman Mao severely condemned the Apartheid policy in South Africa and expressed his firm support for the South African people. The Chinese government, represented by Mrs He Xiangning, also showed strong support for the South African people in their struggle against Apartheid (*People's Daily*, 15 September 1950).

In 1951, a protest movement against British colonial aggression took place in Egypt, receiving a warm response from the Chinese people. The newspapers carried letters stating that people from all walks of life had expressed their belief that the Chinese and Egyptian people would win the final victory in the struggle against imperialists. Professor Ma Jian, an expert on Egyptian studies at Peking University, also wrote an article on Egypt's struggle against British colonial rule. The China Democratic Youth Federation sent a telegram to the Egyptian students, expressing that the Chinese youth would unite with them to oppose imperialism and defend world peace. China also supported the Ethiopian, Tanzanian and other peoples in their struggle for national independence.

In April 1960, the China African Peoples' Friendship Association (CFPA), initiated by 17 national people's organizations in China and attended by 20 people's organizations as member groups and social celebrities from all walks of life who were enthusiastic about Africa, was established in Beijing.

When the Algerian people won independence in 1962, they called for support owing to a serious shortage of doctors and medication after the immediate withdrawal of French doctors. China soon sent its medical teams, which provided regular assistance to other African countries (Li Anshan 2009). After becoming a permanent member of the UN Security Council (UNSC), China continued to uphold justice for African countries, fighting external forces that attempted to interfere with the internal affairs of these countries.

Even when China was still a very poor country and was going through difficult times, it offered several different kinds of aid to Africa. Besides the industrial and agricultural projects, the Chinese government also helped to build some large projects, which can be seen as a milestone in the early period of independence in African countries. This aid played an important role in the process of nation-building in these African countries.[1]

China always offers assistance to African countries without any political conditions attached, which dates back to the Eight Principles of foreign aid put forward by Premier Zhou Enlai in 1964 (*People's Daily*, 18 January 1964).[2] From 1956 to 1996, China completed nearly 800 projects throughout Africa, involving farming, fishery, textiles, energy, transportation, broadcasting and communications, hydro-electric power dams, machinery, public and civil construction, education, health, technology and handicrafts, and food processing (Huang Zequan 2000: 45). In 1970, China began to build the Tanzania–Zambia Railway (TAZARA), which the West had refused to do after making many excuses about the cost and other logistically impractical conditions. The Chinese government took on the enormous job and finished it in 1976 (Yu 1975; Monson 2009; Shen Xipeng, 2018).

China supported the endeavours of African countries to strengthen the unity of the international community, to solve problems through peaceful means and to build a new and just international economic and political order. In 1996, when the new UN Secretary General was chosen, China supported the African candidate and Kofi Annan was elected (Wang Qinmei 1999; Li Anshan 2006).

Urgent need

The development of China–African relations since the 1990s required a more systematic way to maintain the momentum. Africa went through tough times as it suffered drastic economic decline in the 1980s, which is often described as "the lost decade". From 1980 to 1990, foreign investment either diminished or vanished completely. For instance, 43 out of a total 139 British companies left Africa. Being pessimistic about the African economy, Japanese companies in Kenya dropped from 15 to only two. Another problem was debt. The debt of Sub-Saharan Africa reached US$6 billion in 1970 and increased to US$84.3

billion in 1980 (Harbeson & Rothschild 1995: 44–45). Africa experienced the pain of strict measures and structural adjustment programs followed by marginalisation of the world's economy.

The end of the Cold War brought three serious consequences to Africa. First, its strategic importance decreased sharply, and so did its strategic status. Second, national and religious struggles that were covered up by the US–Soviet rivalry in the Cold War era were exposed. Internal conflicts within and between many African countries stimulated regional conflicts relating to territorial issues. Third, the West was pushing the wave of democratisation with no constraints. Affected by all these factors, Africa became entangled in the economic recession. As a result, Africa's debt increased, reaching US$200.4 billion in 1993 and US$210.7 billion in 1994. These debts equalled 82.4 per cent of its GNP and 254.5 per cent of its gross exports. According to the 1995 World Bank report, at the end of 1994, the ratio of debt to export in 28 African countries was higher than 200:1 (Gordon & Gordon 1996: 116). In 1992, one-third of the African countries were fighting politically motivated wars; the African economy faltered and experienced negative growth. In the early 1990s, because of Africa's decreasing strategic importance, the West lessened its emphasis on Africa until the mid-1990s, when the United States started to change its African policy.

China's African policy was also adjusted. In the early 1980s, a reassessment of the international situation (with an emphasis on peace and development) and a great change in strategic thought (with an emphasis on internal economy) resulted in the strategic transformation of China. In 1982, the 12th CPC Congress made two strategic decisions: from that time onward, emphasis would be put on the domestic economy internally and also on an independent and peaceful foreign policy externally. In order to emphasise the importance that Beijing attached to China–Africa relations, Premier Zhao Ziyang made a visit to Africa just three months after this conference. During the visit, he announced the four principles underlying China's economic and technological cooperation with Africa.[3]

The mid-1980s was regarded as "the golden era of China–Africa relations since 1949". From 1982 to 1985, 29 African heads of state visited China, and Chairman Li Xiannian visited three African countries in 1986. China–Africa economic and trade cooperation was greatly strengthened. From the 1970s to the end of the 20th century, China signed more than 6000 labor contracts with African countries, amounting nearly to US$10 billion (Huang Zequan 2000: 50).

China started to reform its foreign trade and foreign assistance institutions in 1991. The Chinese government cancelled financial subsidies for foreign trade exports. The foreign trade enterprises began to take responsibility for their own profits and had to repay debts by themselves, which created conditions for an increase in trade with Africa. The reform included the improvement of assistance projects as well as the separation of the foreign assistance agency and enterprises, and the takeover of Chinese medical teams by the Ministry of Health. In order to train in technological and management skills for Africa, forms of foreign assistance were diversified. The Chinese government began providing preferential loans as a measure of aid to Africa (Li Anshan 2006a).

These adjustments and reforms laid the basis for the fast development of China–Africa relations. The "going abroad" and the "two resources and two markets" strategies pushed Chinese enterprises to enter and to invest in Africa. In 1995, China–Africa relations developed rapidly. Apart from the reforms mentioned above, Chinese leaders visited 23 African countries. An oil project was carried out in the Sudan and African oil subsequently became the top commodity on the list of imports to China, increasing trade between China and Africa by 48.3 per cent (Almanac of China's Foreign Economic Relations and Trade (1996–1997) 1996: 554–555). Three Vice- Premiers, Zhu Rongji, Qian Qichen and Li Lanqing, visited 18 African countries, publicizing Chinese governmental preferential loans and other forms of foreign assistance and investments. Mutual trade grew and the Chinese enterprises increased their investment in Africa. On the other hand, more African businesspeople were gradually taking part in Chinese trade fairs. The African economy started picking up in 1994 (Xia Jisheng1997: 295–296).

After 1995, China–Africa cooperation experienced a meteoric rise. First, there was an increase in mutual visits and a higher level of mutual trust in the political arena. Jiang Zemin, Hu Jintao, Chinese Premiers and Foreign Ministers visited African frequently, substantially progressing China–Africa mutual relations. In 1996, Chairman Jiang Zemin visited six African countries and delivered his "Build a new historical monument for China–African friendship" speech at the headquarters of the Organization of African Unity (OAU), now the African Union (AU). He put forward the five principles for building a long, stable, comprehensive and cooperative China–Africa relationship for the 21st century: sincere friendship; equality and mutual respect; common development and mutual benefit; consultation and cooperation in international affairs; and looking into the future to create a better world. These became the guiding principles for China–Africa cooperation.

Second, there were mutual benefits in the economic arena. Chinese investments in Africa and the volume of trade were accelerated. Preferential government loans were continued in 1995 after a three-year experiment. Vice Premier Zhu Rongji visited seven African countries in eastern and southern Africa from July to August 1995, and Vice Premier Li Lanqing also visited six western African countries from October to November of the same year. One of the important purposes of the visits was to publicise China's new form of foreign assistance. At the end of 1996, China had signed a framework agreement on preferential loans with 16 African countries, which gradually took them up (China's Foreign Economic and Trade Yearbook Editorial Board 1996). By the end of 2000, the number of countries that had signed the framework agreement of preferential loans had increased by 22 (Huang Zequan 2000: 75).

Chinese enterprises contributed a great deal to China–Africa cooperation. During the mid-1990s, China's need for oil was increasing on the one hand, and the price in the international market was rising on the other. China was anxious to obtain its own oil bloc abroad. However, Canada and Australia did not want to see this happen, and nor did Russia want to cooperate with China in the energy field. The oil in the Middle East was almost all taken by the United States and Europe, and Latin America was America's backyard. Africa was an exception, but even there the big oil companies in the West had had exploited the oil-rich countries (such as Nigeria) for decades. The retreat of the West from the Sudan offered an excellent opportunity for China's entry into the oil-fields in Africa.

The exchange of development experience is another form of China–Africa cooperation. In order to "improve the understanding of China, introduce their own nations and strengthen friendship and long-term cooperation between China and African countries", the first "seminar of China–Africa economic management officials" was held on 3 August 1998, with 22 members from 12 African countries. Proposed by the former Chinese President Jiang Zemin, such seminars would be held twice a year (*People's Daily* 4 August 1998).

The Chinese developed various forms of communication and exchanges on culture, education and health with the Africans (Thompson 2005: 4). The fast development of China–Africa relations requires further institutionalization of China–Africa cooperation.

Table 6.1 Volume of trade between China and Africa, 1990–1999 (US$100 millions)

Year	Volume of trade	Africa's exports to China	China's exports to Africa
1990	9.35	2.75	6.60
1994	26.43	8.94	17.49
1995	39.21	14.27	24.94
1996	40.31	14.64	25.67
1997	56.71	24.64	32.07
1998	55.36	14.77	40.59
1999	64.84	23.75	41.08

Note: The Ministry of Foreign Trade and Economic Cooperation of the People's Republic of China is the former Department of the State Council of the People's Republic of China in charge of foreign trade and economic cooperation. It was established in March 1993. In March 2003, the Ministry of Foreign Trade and Economic Cooperation was no longer retained in accordance with the institutional reform plan of the State Council adopted at the first session of the Tenth National People's Congress. From 2004, *China Commerce Yearbook* started to replace *Almanac of China's Foreign Economic Relations and Trade*.

Source: *Almanac of China's Foreign Economic Relations and Trade*, 1991–2000.

New opportunity and challenge

Economic globalization has provided both opportunities and challenges for China–Africa cooperation. After the mid-1990s, the impact of the wave of multi-party democracies pushed by the West subsided and Africa's situation improved. It began to stabilise, with many countries emerging from wars and turmoil. In addition, the African economy started to recover and achieved 2.4 per cent growth in 1995. The number of African countries with negative economic growth indicators decreased from 14 in 1994 to three in 1995, while those with a growth rate above 6 per cent increased from two in 1994 to eight in 1995. According to the statistics of the African Development Bank, Africa's economic growth rate rose to 4.8 per cent, exceeding population growth for the first time and reversing the situation of decreasing income in the continent (Xia Jisheng 1997: 296–299).

With the promising signs emerging in Africa, new consolidation measures were taken internationally. Starting with the United Nations, the "United Nations' new agenda for the development of Africa in the 1990s", initiated in 1991, was considered to have yielded specific and substantial accomplishments by the mid-term review in 1996. In 1996, UN Secretary-General Boutros Boutros-Ghali proposed another ten-year development program for Africa, which would grant Africa US$25 billion in financial aid consolidate its development in 14 fields, including education, health, peace, good governance, food security and water. As for the major powers of the West, especially the United States, Japan and France, there was a change to their policy towards Africa. This phenomenon was noticed by China (Liu Yueming & Zhu Chonggui 1996; Fei Yan 1999).

In 1997, the United States sent a high-level delegation led by Finance Minister Slater to the Sullivan Conference, intending to strengthen its engagement in African economic affairs.[4] Some American congressmen proposed the "African Growth and Opportunity Act", contending that the United States should increase the opportunities for sub-Saharan African countries to be export textiles and clothing to America. The Bill was passed in both houses in 1999 after several rounds of discussions and revisions.

In 1998, President Bill Clinton undertook an 11-day visit to Ghana, Uganda, Rwanda, South Africa, Botswana and Senegal. This trip signified an important change in US–Africa policy. In Cape Town City Hall, Clinton said he wished his trip to Africa could help Americans see the continent from a new perspective, and adopt a new policy in accordance with the changed situations of Africa. From 15 to 18 March 1999, the US government held the first America–Africa 21st Century Partnership Ministerial Conference. Both the size and accomplishments of the conference were unprecedented. Eight cabinet ministers including the secretary of state, the finance minister and four senior officials from the Agency for International Development, Export–Import Bank and Overseas Private Investment Corporations took part in the conference. Africa was represented by 83 ministers of foreign affairs, finance, economy and trade from 46 sub-Saharan African countries, and ambassadors from four North African countries to the United States participated in the conference. The UN's Economic Commission of Africa, the World Bank, the IMF, the African Development Bank, the Common Market for Eastern and Southern Africa and the Economic Community of West African States also sent official representatives to the conference. President Clinton, UN Secretary-General Kofi Annan and OAU Secretary Salim attended the and delivered speeches. The main discussions were prospects for new US–Africa cooperation in trade, investment, aid, debt relief, and political and economic reforms. The meeting issued a Joint Statement, and the US Department of State issued a meeting summary entitled "Blueprint for the partnership between the US and Africa in the 21st century". It declared that a forum on US–SADC (Southern Africa Development Community) would launch a new America–Africa economic forum. These actions showed that the United States was trying harder to improve its relationship with Africa (Xia Jisheng 1998; Yao Guimei 1998; Du Xiaolin 2006).

France's actions were also noticeable. Three months after Clinton's first visit to Africa, French President Jacques Chirac visited Namibia, South Africa, Mozambique and Angola, accompanied by a huge delegation. This signified that France had given up its tradition of limiting itself to French-speaking countries – known as "Françafrique", referring to France's special relationship with its former African colonies – and was trying to expand its influence to the whole of Africa.

From 26 to 28 November 1998, a Franco-African Summit Conference was held in Paris. President Chirac and 49 African state leaders came together to confer about the security of African countries and districts, peacekeeping, and economic development. Before 1998, France had divided countries that enjoyed its aid-assistance into two groups: the "bloc countries" and the "non-bloc countries". The former were 37 African countries, either formerly French colonies or others that had joined the group; all other countries that received French aid constituted the non-bloc countries. Since 1998, France has adjusted its policy from this binary division to that of "prior solidarity regions". These are not only the least-developed French-speaking African countries but also non-French-speaking countries, which guaranteed France better coordination in its regional actions. Countries in "prior solidarity regions" (La Zone de Solidaritée Prioritaire, or ZSP) were able to obtain more extensive forms of cooperation and the most favourable aid funds. In early 1999, the French Inter-divisional Commission of International Cooperation and Development confirmed the existence of prior solidarity regions for the first time. Apart from the 37 old bloc countries, many sub-Saharan English-speaking African countries in Central and Southern Africa were added to the list. In May 2005, the French government decided to expand the prior solidarity regions to 55 countries in total, which can enjoy the Prior Solidarity Fund. Among them, 43 were African.

In 1993, the Japanese government, the United Nations and the Global African Union held the Tokyo International Conference on African

Development (TICAD). At the conference, Japan stated that it would play an important role in aiding Africa to carry out economic reform and to ensure a sustainable development. It also announced its African policy of providing support to political reform, economic reforms, training of talented people, environmental protection, and the effects and the efficiency of aid. From 1993 to 1995, Japan provided 37 billion Japanese yen in "non-project assistance gratis" to 20 African countries. In respect of personnel training, Japan boosted it by organizing a forum or a symposium (Zhong Weiyun 2001).

Regarding environmental protection, Japan offered economic aid in projects such as tapping underground water, preventing water pollution, protecting forests and controlling deserts. In terms of improving the effects and efficiency of aid, Japan strengthened bilateral official communication and policy conversation to make a better plan and to oversee the projects (Jin Xide 2000: 243–245). When Europe and America showed signs of "aid tiredness", Japan stepped up its aid to Africa by holding international conferences, followed by relevant measures, thereby giving rise to a new international awareness on aiding Africa. In 1998, Japan and the United Nations jointly organized the TICAD II. The size of the conference was unprecedented, with representatives from 51 African countries, 11 Asian countries and 18 European and American countries. Representatives from 44 international organizations were also invited to the meeting. Based on the first TICAD, the conference put forward the "Tokyo Action Plan". The theme of the conference was "Eliminate poverty and blend into global economic integration, emphasizing the importance of South–South cooperation and the necessity to push democratization and conflict resolution" (Luo Jianbo 2003; Li Anshan 2008).

Pushed by economic globalization, the pace of "going outside" (going abroad) by Chinese enterprises was accelerated, a move directed and supported by the country's foreign policy. Vice Premier Zhu Rongji said in 1995 when he visited Africa that "to support the joint ventures by Chinese enterprises and African enterprises and to provide the starting fund, China is willing to provide preferential governmental loans". When Premier Li Peng visited Africa in 1995 and 1997, he said "the Chinese government encourages Chinese enterprises to have a direct cooperation with African enterprises, and supports Chinese companies to invest in Africa and to enlarge the fields of cooperation". Chairman Jiang Zemin stated in 1996 when he visited Africa that "the Chinese government encourages mutual cooperation in different sizes, extensive fields and various forms. It will hold on to the principle of keeping promises and ensuring quality in cooperation, broadening the methods of trade, increasing the imports from Africa, and finally promoting the balanced and fast development of China–Africa trade" (Huang Zequan 2000: 49).

The improvement of Africa's political and economic situation, the West's adjustment of its Africa policy and the opportunities and challenges of economic globalization have all contributed to the establishment of the FOCAC.

African countries' initiative

The most important push that contributed to the establishment of the FOCAC was exerted by the Africans. The proposal for the setting up of a China–Africa cooperation mechanism was first put forward by Albert Tevoedjre, Benin's Minister of Planning, Economic Adjustment and Employment Promotion. In September 1997, Minister Tevoedjre attended the 56th Annual Meeting of the International Monetary Fund (IMF) and World Bank in Hong Kong. He was invited by the Ministry of Foreign Affairs to visit China after the meeting and met Vice-Premier Zhu Rongji. During the meeting, he proposed that China and Africa should establish a cooperation mechanism such as TICAD. Zhu Rongji asked the present person in charge of the Ministry of Economic and Trade to study the applicability of the matter, but their report considered that this was not applicable.

From 1996 to 2004, the Chinese Foreign Ministry authorised China's Foreign Affairs University to hold workshops for African diplomats to give them a better understanding of China. During this period, nine workshops were conducted in both English and French. In 1997, some African leaders and envoys to China (including those of Ethiopia and Mauritius) proposed to establish a "one to one multi-partnership", but China did not take it seriously considering its maneouvrability. Diplomats attending the workshops, such as those from Mauritius, Benin and Madagascar, had already advised on some mechanism between China and African countries, but this was not put into practice. Mr Ahmed Haggad, the former Assistant General Secretary of the OAU, former Egyptian Ambassador to Kenya and a senior Egyptian diplomat, once offered a similar suggestion when he was representing the OAU to attend the opening ceremony of an African Art Exhibition held in Beijing Art Museum on 25 January 1999. That afternoon, Vice-Premier Li Lanqing met him. The Assistant to the Minister of Foreign Affairs met him the following day, and Ambassador Liu Guijin was present at both meetings. Mr Haggag proposed establishing a multi-party mechanism between Africa and China. The suggestion was considered, but China did not adopt it owing to the difficulty of managing it.

New situations required new measures and new institutions. With the progress made by Western countries in high-level communication mechanisms, an increasing number of African countries proposed the establishment of a new kind of partnership with China. "How do we face challenges and protect our own legitimate interests?" was the common question being asked by both China and African countries at the turn of the century, as Yao Guimei points out. Some African nations argued that the China–African relationship should adjust itself to the new situation, building similar mechanisms for large-scale high-level contacts in the manner of the US–Africa Business Forum, the British Commonwealth Conference, the Franco–African Summit, The Tokyo International Conference of African Development and the Euro-African Summit, they should also strengthening mutual communication on about concerned issues such as peace and development (Yao Gumei 1998: 263).

In February 1998, Ambassador Liu Guijin came back home from Zimbabwe and was appointed the Head of the Department of African Affairs in the Ministry of Foreign Affairs. In March 1998, Tang Jiaxuan assumed the position of Foreign Minister. He not only took over from Minister Qian Qichen, but also inherited his custom that the first destination of his diplomatic visit was Africa. Taking Liu Guijin's advice, Tang Jiaxuan visited five western African countries: Guinea, Côte d'Ivoire, Ghana, Togo and Benin. This visit led to him realising the importance of Africa on the international political and economic stage, and the urgency of reinforcing China–African cooperation.

In 1999, Lila Ratsifandrihama, the first woman in Madagascar to hold the position of Foreign Minister since the country gained independence from France, visited China: "The talented female foreign minister comes from a famous literary family, and her vision has always been wide enough to comprehend the possibilities. She was very friendly to China, and China and laid a great emphasis on China–African relations" (Tang Jiaxuan 2009: 433). In her talks with Minister Tang Jiaxuan, she mentioned many forums for cooperation mechanisms between African countries and developed countries, such as the Franco-African Summit Conference, the Commonwealth Heads of Government Meeting, TICAD and the American–African Ministerial Conference. Furthermore, she asked Minister Tang Jiaxuan whether China would consider establishing a multilateral forum, since the bilateral relations between China and African countries were strong and were considered to be in such good condition as both sides continued to cooperate in many areas (Tang Jiaxuan 2009: 433).

Ambassador Liu Guijin recalled an interesting episode during his speech at the United Nations in 2007. As the Chinese government's Representative of African Affairs, he visited the United States to discuss the issue of Sudan. He made a public speech in the hall of the UN Economic and Social Council and the atmosphere was hot, with a large audience, including UN Deputy Secretary-General Sha Zukang and UN officials in charge of African affairs. Coincidentally, the African observer into the United Nations sitting on the platform was Madame Lila Ratsifandrihama. When Ambassador Liu Guijin mentioned that Madagascar's Foreign Minister was the person who put forward the suggestion to set up a China–Africa cooperation mechanism to the Chinese government, Madame Lila Ratsifandrihama spoke out very excitedly, "That's me! That's me!" (Shu Zhan & Wang Feng 1999). In short, African diplomats raised the issue of the establishment of a mechanism of China-Africa cooperation on many occasions. As mentioned, the United States, France and Japan were all adjusting their African policy. Shu Zhan, who was then an official at the Department of African Affairs (later Chinese Ambassador to Eritrea and then Rwanda), pointed out in an article:

> High-level US government officials are visiting Africa frequently, trying to develop new relations with African countries in both diplomatic and

legislative ways and simultaneously endeavoring to establish normal mechanisms to push the American–African economic and trade relations forward ... The US is now imitating Britain, France and Japan by establishing fixed mechanisms such as the American–African Ministerial Conference, the American–African Economic Forum and the America–Southern Africa Bilateral Commission in order to be fully involved in the scramble and then to control Africa's resources.

(Shu Zhan & Wang Feng 1999: 14–18)

As mentioned before, France intensified its competition with the United States, relying on its long-term traditional relations with Africa (Zhao Huijie 1999; Ma Shengli 2000: 259–308). Japan intended to strengthen its role in the international community through its foreign aid and TICAD is a strategic move towards this aim.

There was no time to wait. Tang Jiaxuan realised that China–Africa cooperation should be improved and taken to a higher level at the beginning of the new millennium, with its new challenges and opportunities. Thus Lila Ratsifandrihama and Tang Jiaxuan happened to sing from the same hymn sheet. Tang Jiaxuan conferred with Vice-Foreign Minister Ji Peiding, then the Africa Department Director Liu Guijin and other relevant personnel about Lila Ratsifandrihama's proposal, and advised Ambassador Liu to summon the Department of African Affairs to study the plan. Ambassador Liu convened two meetings above the vice-section level, but the attendees at the meetings failed to reach a consensus on this issue. The proponents believed that the proposal even represented an opportunity that could be used to solve some outstanding bilateral issues. Eventually, after several rounds of discussion, the proponents prevailed and the proposal was submitted to the State Council. Then Chairman Jiang Zemin and then Premier Zhu Rongji immediately ratified it.

China's own sensitivity over the Western powers' competition in Africa and the urgency of building a permanent cooperation mechanism led the Chinese government to accept the suggestion by African countries to establish the FOCAC.

China's action

The China–Africa cooperation experienced a developed fast development after the 1990s. Scholars engaged in African studies paid greater attention to China–Africa cooperation. Chinese scholars, especially those with both strategic vision and practical experience, put forward their views and recommendations for China's Africa policy. In the early 1990s, attention was mainly directed to specific areas of cooperation, such as assistance to Africa, technological cooperation, agricultural development, educational and health assistance. However, from the late 1990s scholars started to consider China–Africa cooperation at the level of long-term strategic planning, and some scholars clearly raised the idea that the China–Africa cooperation mechanism needed to be developed further.

In October 1997, the Chinese Society of African Historical Studies (CSAHS) held a conference at Beidaihe in Qinhuangdao, Hebei province. Scholars who attended the conference came to the realisation that the fast development of China–Africa cooperation required new responses from the academic community. The conference decided to report the need to strengthen African studies and reflect the relevant analytical research works conducted in Africa to the central government. It also entrusted Li Anshan and Liu Hongwu to write a draft of the proposal. In addition to strengthening China's African studies, the proposal pointed out that

> there are obvious deficiencies existing in the work of government related to Africa. There is no unified leadership and enough communication between ministries and commissions involved in African affairs. There are also little formal study and coordination about how to combine the mutual cooperation with Africa in economy, education, military, health and culture. We raise two pieces of advice as reference to the central government: first, the central government should make an overall plan about China's cooperation with Africa which provides a whole set of comprehensive and specific resolutions for the developmental goals, practical methods, expected difficulties and apposite measures about the future China–African relations. It is recommended that the central government set up a leading institution or agency (such as a working group of the central government on Africa) which includes relevant ministries and commissions, thus coordinating their jobs and strengthening the working efficiency. In the meantime, it is advised to hold regular meetings into which relevant specialists and officials who involved in African affairs are invited.

After being reviewed and revised by the Council of the Chinese Society of African Historical Study, the CSAHS proposal was delivered to Jiang Zemin under the names of 17 professors and researchers headed by Lu Ting'en. Chairman Jiang Zemin issued a response to the proposal. In his reply, President Jiang Zemin wrote:

> Comrade Qichen: Please read the letter. In recent years, I have put emphasis on African works in many speeches, which indicates that we need to pay enough attention to both politics and economic cooperation, and State Council and related departments should support.[5]

Although the proposal did not mention FOCAC explicitly, the issue of institutionalisation of African affairs was put on the table. At that time, an article pointed out that

the current African situation tends to be more stable while the economy is getting better. More than ten years of reform and opening up has resulted in the substantial progress of China's economy. These have offered good conditions for China–African cooperation. It is sure that under the new circumstances, a new level of China–African cooperation will be realized, in the near future with endeavor from both sides.
(Gao Fei 1998: 1–3)

Another article put forward a much more lucid view, that required China–Africa cooperation to

perfect its mechanism, improve measures, and achieve greater progress ... Africa has finished the historical mission of decolonization and has stepped into the new historical period of stability, reform and development. At the time, China and Africa share extensive common interests and goals in maintaining world peace, opposing hegemony, and establishing a fair and rational new international political and economic order. The two sides hold a common view regarding major international issues. They depend on each other, endeavor to push the world structure to multi-polarity, support peaceful methods to solve international conflicts, oppose military force to solve conflicts, and object to any forms of interference into other countries' internal affairs. In order to develop their economies together, they should perfect their cooperation mechanism, improve measures, and achieve greater progress through mutual cooperation in various levels, directions and approaches.
(Ren Weidong 1998: 37)

The advice on "perfecting the mechanism" raised new requirements for China–Africa cooperation. Some scholars who had long been engaged in the study of China–Africa relations now raised their views on the international situation. He Wenping pointed out that:

Western countries' policies of confrontation and their indifferent attitudes toward socialist countries and developing countries were actually objective propulsions to the South–South communication and cooperation. The multi-faceted diplomacy strategy that China and Africa have carried out, the common requirements of opposing international power politics and hegemonism and the establishment of a fair and rational new international political and economic order, have provided internal driving forces for the amicable relationship between China and Africa.
(He Wenping 1999: 29; He Wenping 2008)

Fei Yan raised the view that China should build and perfect a consultation mechanism with African countries:

158 *Policy and implementation*

It is indicated that in the aspect of politics, China is supposed to realize the necessity, urgency, and far-reaching significance of strengthening its works about African affairs, based on the traditional China–African friendship and the emphasis of African countries on our status as a big power. It has to choose appropriate regions or specific countries to establish consultation mechanisms with, and make use of multiple channels including official and non-official, thus consolidating the China–African cooperation.

(Fei Yan 1999: 58)

The proposal "to establish consultation mechanisms and make use of multiple channels" had provided fresh thinking about establishing a new mechanism for China–Africa cooperation. Zhao Changhui, a strategy and investment risk analyst at the Export–Import Bank of China, worked in Africa for a long time. He came up with his own idea about China's African strategy while working in West Africa in 1997. He put forward a highly original viewpoint in an unpublished report entitled "China's African Strategy" (Zhao Changhui 1997). First, Zhao Changhui believed there was "serious and fierce competition in African markets". The United States, France, the European Union, Canada, Australia, Japan, Korea and Malaysia all had their own traditional, regional or newly developed regional ties with Africa. There were few opportunities left for China, and "these opportunities will slip away from China's fingers forever if China is negligent and careless". China therefore had to seize these opportunities. Second, Zhao thought China–Africa cooperation should be promoted at the level of the overall situation, strategy and history. China–Africa cooperation should be closely related to the accomplishment of China's strategic objectives. China therefore must expand its international economic space and formulate its development strategy for the 21st century, especially regarding the enlargement of China's role in African economy. It was the "century choice", as Zhao Changhui termed it. Third, he proposed some specific measures, including the establishment of an authoritative national leading agency on African works, or the African Affairs Office of the State Council. The office would be responsible for making an overall plan for China's African strategy and policy, leading the African works in every department, every area, offering guidance and coordinating relevant relations. As a formal executive team, the office should act as a substantial inter-ministerial or inter-departmental commission and take part in the Council of Ministers. The constituent units should reflect Africa's real situation and the clear intentions of China. Major governmental departments should all be part of, or be represented in, the office. When it came across some important issues involving other departments, regions and industries, representatives from these fields should also attend such meetings.

As far as the government was concerned, the practical situation also promoted China–Africa cooperation. In 1995, when the reform of foreign assistance was carried out, Li Lanqing visited six African countries, including Senegal. On his trip back to Beijing, Senegal declared the establishment of diplomatic relations with Taiwan, which had a great impact on the Chinese government. The State Council instructed the Export–Import Bank to establish agencies in Africa within a three-month period. It can be deduced that the Export–Import Bank carried out the government policy and played an important role in supporting Chinese enterprises' global economic cooperation.

The requirements of African countries were another factor. In 1998, ambassadors from Cameroon, Gabon and Zimbabwe requested bilateral cooperation, and the Chinese State Council instructed the Export–Import Bank to start financing African projects. Such perspicuous instructions made the Chinese banks pay attention to African projects. For example, the Export–Import Bank's leaders gradually realised the important role of Africa in the Chinese economy and decided not to reject projects proposed by any African country, even if the country did not have diplomatic relations with China. Within a period of three to five years, the Export–Import Bank's achievements in Africa became obvious. In the past, the former Ministry of Foreign Trade and Economic Cooperation had held meetings to discuss the issues related to specific regions (such as southeastern and northern Africa). However, it later found out that these regions were having similar problems. They were different only in size. China started to think about how to integrate all of them into a structure or platform big enough to hold all the issues together, thus facilitating the management of African countries' business. These were the internal factors that contributed to the birth of the FOCAC mechanism and that were the driving force of behind the deepening, opening up and mechanisation of China–Africa cooperation. The Export–Import Bank was probably one of the earliest institutions to think systematically about China's strategy towards Africa.

It is undeniable that Chinese enterprises made a great contribution to the process of establishing such a China–Africa cooperation mechanism. Despite the meteoric rise in oil prices, Chinese companies had intended to obtain as many oil fields as possible, but geopolitical and strategic factors and mistrust made it difficult for China to obtain oil fields from other regions of the world. Therefore, Africa – one of the few remaining undeveloped oil regions of the world – became the only place left for Chinese enterprises to enlarge their shares by securing new oil fields on the continent. Even in Africa, the oil fields of good quality were already occupied by companies from Europe and the United States (Carbone 2011).

In 1999, at an academic symposium organized to commemorate the 20th anniversary of the establishment of the Chinese Association of African Studies (CAAS), Liu Guijin, the Director of the Department of African Affairs in the Ministry of Foreign Affairs, mentioned in a speech that "China should set up various forms of consultation mechanisms with Africa and enlarge mutual communication in international affairs". He pointed out that the establishment of new consultation mechanisms was prevalent in the international community. Many developed countries depended on such mechanisms to increase their influence in Africa. At the same time, he announced that China would hold a FOCAC conference in 2000:

> China has started to act positively to utilize the common practice and to meet the needs of African countries. China so far has set up consultation mechanisms with the foreign ministries of South Africa, Kenya and Guinea, and is going to hold the FOCAC – the First Ministerial Conference – in Beijing in October 2000. During the conference, China will discuss a number of issues with African countries such as building a new international political and economic order that is beneficial to developing countries and the China–African cooperation in economy and trade.
>
> (Chen Gongyuan 2000).

In October 1999, Chinese President Jiang Zemin personally wrote a letter to all heads of state of African countries and the Secretary-General of the Organization of African Unity (OAU), now the African Union (AU), to formally propose the convening of the first FOCAC Ministerial Conference. He introduced the background, objectives and subjects of the conference and invited them to send their ministers to attend the conference. Special guests on President Jiang Zemin's list included the current Algerian President Bouteflika, the former chairman of the OAU, the late Togolese President Eyadema, who was then acting as chairman of the OAU, the former Zambian President Chiluba, who would be the next chairman of the OAU, and Dr Ahmed Salim, then the Secretary-General of the OAU. They all later attended both the opening and closing ceremonies and delivered speeches (Tang Jiaxuan 2009). The FOCAC was formally established in October 2000.

China's Africa strategy

As mentioned, it was exactly the composite force of various factors that led to the establishment of FOCAC. The long-term and friendly China–Africa cooperation laid a solid foundation for the establishment of FOCAC; the fast development of China–Africa relations in the 1990s made it more urgent to establish such a mechanism; the new economic globalization offered better opportunities and greater challenges for China–Africa cooperation; and the African side's active promotion and cooperation played a decisive role in setting up the forum. Therefore, the combined efforts of African diplomats, Chinese scholars, enterprises and the government turned the establishment of FOCAC into a reality.

Undoubtedly, China's Africa strategy has achieved a great deal in Africa since the reform and opening up; otherwise, it is difficult to explain why China–Africa cooperation caused such a big shock in the world. However,

Chia and Africa are now very different countries from those they were in previous eras, and international politics has witnessed a great change. Facing the new situation, does China's Africa strategy need to adjust? The answer is yes. On 6 September 2011, the White Paper on China's peaceful development was issued for the first time and the key interests of China were clearly defined: national sovereignty, national security, territorial integrity, national unity, national political and social stability established by China's constitution, together with a basic guarantee of sustainable economic and social development. The national strategy of China is to realise and protect national interests. One of the most important characteristics of the so-called "strategy" is its foresight; however, forward-looking thinking and conscious awareness of the whole are lacking in the formulation of African policy.

"China lacks nothing in Africa except strategy" (Li Anshan 2011a). This view was not expressed without reason. China–Africa cooperation is a long-term cause, and it needs a long-term strategy. If Western powers continue to coordinate with each other against China's national interests, China must have a strategy to deal with them, and should not cope with a changing situation by sticking to old policies.

China's lack of strategic thinking and design could be seen in three aspects.

1. *"Responsive diplomacy"*. This means denying whatever others criticise. This modus operandi is neither convincing nor objective, but the situation has continued for many years. Being short of initiative, China's diplomacy was conducted in a rather passive way. China has never really been involved in colonialism, but has now on various occasions stated to the old colonial powers that China did not practise colonialism. This reaction is both ridiculous and passive.
2. *Lack of long-term planning.* China's African strategy is based mainly on a FOCAC Ministerial Conference once every three years. However, FOCAC is only a bilateral cooperation framework. China's African strategy should have its own plan and focus. Now, in order to run the three-year forum, all the departments involved must deal with various meetings (senior officials meetings, foreign ministers' meeting of regular dialogue). The Ministry of Foreign Affairs and the Ministry of Commerce are especially busy with preparation, coordination and summary, and they do not have enough human or material resources and time to consider the strategic layout and strategic planning.
3. *Separate action without unified planning.* Three major ministries are in charge of FOCAC: the Ministry of Foreign Affairs, the Ministry of Commerce and the Ministry of Finance. Although their duties are respectively defined, there are various difficulties in the unified coordination. The individuals or departments of the relevant 27 units are either temporary or part-time, and it is difficult for them to implement the responsibility. It is a good thing that all units want to participate in China–Africa

cooperation, but in most cases the FOCAC Follow-up Committee has no authority to coordinate and intervene in those activities. Therefore, it is necessary to make a long-term strategic plan from overall perspective.

At present, from the view of sustainable development and the overall situation, China's Africa strategy should pay attention to the following aspects.

Emphasis on both economy and politics

For the past few years, China and Africa have cooperated mainly in the economic field. The previous four forums have concentrated on economic cooperation. The "old eight measures" proposed by President Hu Jintao in the China–Africa Summit in 2006 and the "new eight measures" proposed by Premier Wen Jiabao in 2009 all emphasise economic cooperation. In the public's opinion, China has often said that Western countries should not politicize China–Africa economic cooperation. On a practical level, the China–Africa relationship is claimed as all-round cooperation, but many fields are form rather than content; only economic cooperation has had significant achievements. Although China–Africa relations are centred on economic cooperation, the West has tried to check their cooperation by political means.

A few examples illustrate my point. The Western countries are opposed to China's cooperation with Africa in economic fields, and thus have set up various obstacles. Either the international financial organisations threatened to stop aid to related countries (such as the Democratic Republic of Congo) or the international NGOs attacked China for its construction of infrastructure building in Africa (such as Merowe Dam in the Sudan), politicising every aspect of China's economic behaviour. During her visit to Africa in 2011, US Secretary of State Hillary Clinton slandered China's investment in Africa and aid to its countries, and warned of a "new colonialism" in Africa, alluding to China's increasing influence over African the continent. British Prime Minister David Cameron attacked the Chinese political system and criticised the Chinese invasion in Africa: "What is this, economy or politics?" It is obvious that politics interacts with economy all the time. To emphasise economic cooperation while ignoring political cooperation will bring great trouble. The transformation in Libya is a good lesson.

Strengthen China–Africa strategic cooperation by supporting Africa's integration actively and steadily

China–Africa strategic cooperation can be strengthened in three aspects. The first is by actively supporting African countries to become permanent members of the UNSC. China should offer its wholehearted support for African countries to apply for permanent membership of the UN Security Council, without worrying about its own gains and losses. Diplomacy embodies practical benefit and morality. From the perspective of human development, it is against nature for a continent with 54 countries not to have a single seat as a permanent member of the UNSC. China should take the moral high ground and support Africa. This is a matter of principle. China can itself put forward the proposal, or it can support Africa's proposal. If African countries become permanent members of the UNSC, it will strengthen the power of developing countries and promote the trend of multi-polarisation.

Second, China should promote the integration process in Africa. China can make plans with Africa in terms of consultation, training, practice and infrastructure construction. In the international arena, if empowered with integration, Africa could offer more political support to China. In the economic field, a unified African market could expand economic and trade cooperation. In the cultural field, Africa and China have a common language regarding cultural diversity. In aid and investment, China should take Africa's integration as an important factor to consider, especially in engineering projects such as transportation, water power, electricity and telecommunications, which can play a connecting role in integration.

Third, there is a need to strengthen economic and strategic cooperation in Africa. At present, Chinese investments in Africa is mainly in the fields of mining, oil and gas, which are non-renewable resources; this could easily create resentment among the local people. In fact, there are many other strategic fields that need investment. Agriculture is a potential area; investment can help address the problem of food security in Africa by using Chinese advanced technology in agriculture. Agricultural investment should try to increase the added value of local agricultural products, but also make full use of favourable conditions to develop organic food production.

The manufacturing industry is a bottleneck for development in Africa. The Chinese government should encourage enterprises to invest in manufacturing in order to enhance Africa's industrial level and increase employment of more local workers. Renewable energy is another example. These fields could have a far-reaching influence on Africa's development by solving the problems of unemployment and poverty, thus bringing peace and stability. With a great demand for investment, those fields are closely related to livelihoods and have unlimited potential. Africa's population is growing rapidly and the market is expanding. Because of superior natural conditions, the development prospects of these fields are immeasurable. Moreover, these investments are sustainable. In the areas of investment, construction and assistance, land issues must be properly handled (contracting instead of purchasing land should be encouraged). Otherwise, there will be endless trouble in the future.

Cherish our own advantages.

China is experiencing the same process that any great powers have experienced, and thus becomes the target of many groups with vested interests. The Chinese government needn't worry too much about these "growing pains". Allowing criticism is necessary: to be too nervous or to ignore are both expressions of the mentality of the weak. In the past, when China was enduring an extremely difficult time, it dared to contend with the West in order to safeguard its own interests. Now, China's comprehensive power is strengthening day by day, and China–Africa cooperation is moving in the right direction, China should move ahead with nothing to fear. As for China–Africa cooperation, China should cherish a strong belief in its desire to make a contribution to the common development of humankind, which is a moral high ground and spirit that nobody could challenge.

However, the criticism from African society should be taken seriously. Although the criticisms are mainly from NGOs, their influence cannot be ignored. China should work with Africa to rectify the undesirable phenomenon or behaviour (Ampiah & Naidu 2008). China's huge fiscal reserves have become a powerful leverage in the world economy. The equal cooperative relationship and mutual respect between China and Africa represent a new trend in international politics. The unique mode of Chinese assistance with mutual respect and non-political conditions is independent of the international aid regime. China's successful experience is attracting more and more African countries to "Look East", thus shaking the Western model of development. Westerners are interested in those phenomena and are studying them earnestly. China should have self-confidence.

Take a broad perspective on various factors

The relationship with big powers is important, but it is not everything. It seems that in the formulation of policies, we attach too much importance to the relations with big powers and ignore other factors, especially the interests of developing countries. When casting a vote in the United Nations, China clearly shows its own position, but also expresses its morality in international politics. Caring too much the about relations between China and the major powers causes China to lose some true friends, one by one. While emphasising the relations with big powers, China should not neglect the big powers' African policy. How and in what hidden way does the United Kingdom maintain the "framework of the British Empire"? What are the strategic intentions and deployments of the US Africa Command? Why do the French strive to promote the Mediterranean Union Plan? A lack of research of the important subjects leads to China's failure to make strategic counter-moves of some important events. As in the handling of the situation in Libya, China lacked an understanding of the overall strategy of NATO countries, so it did not argue firmly against the UN proposal to establish a no-fly zone in Libya and was not psychologically prepared for NATO's bombing. China's voting choice damaged not only the interests of developing countries, but also their own interests, thus a precedent was set up for the use of UN resolutions to obtain the legal rights to carry out a military attack on a small country. China also lacked awareness of France's strategic move to influence the situation in Ivory Coast through the regional organisations in Africa, and did not understand Hillary Clinton's activities in Zambia, which were designed to influence the upcoming election; these things led to a power transfer in favour of the Western vested interest groups through either obvious or hidden foreign intervention.

The proper way to create alliances

Alliances are necessary in international politics. In certain circumstances, 30 years ago, China adopted a policy of non-alignment. However, regional alliances such as the European Union, the African Union, the Arab League and the Association of Southeast Asian Nations (ASEAN) are all growing. A new Latin American alliance is taking shape. The United States is drawing together Japan, South Korea and Australia to form a new alliance, and is also calling for the establishment of international union against China's currency policy. Of course, China is also strengthening its alliance in the Shanghai Cooperation Organization (SCO), BRICS countries and neighbouring countries. Obviously, national action on the world stage usually succeeds by way of alliances. Of course, this kind of alliance could be just for short-term expedience or long-term strategy, as a makeshift measure or as a strategic alliance. Consider why people are accustomed to the use of the expression "the West" to describe certain countries in analysing the world situation. It is because these countries can cooperate with each other in most international political affairs. At present, the emerging powers' positions in many international affairs are very similar and consistent. They are very unhappy about the unfair international economic order and outraged about the hegemony that exists in international politics. They are opposed to the conditions attached to the international aid regime and loathe the West's frequent use of sanctions, embargoes and military intervention to achieve its objectives. The emerging countries are quite critical of Western practices in Iraq and Afghanistan, and they are clearly opposed to both the Western action in Libya and the proposed sanctions against Syria. In the new situation, China's alliance with emerging countries will be conducive to playing a greater role in the international arena.

National interests are the top consideration

With the changes occurring in China, the institutions must also be changed. The same applies to work on Africa. We should be innovative instead of cherishing an outmoded system. Take aid mechanisms as an example. China's aid mechanism still follows that created a few decades ago, with the Department of Aid to Foreign Countries within the Ministry of Commerce in charge of the aid to foreign countries. China's national strength is growing, and her international responsibility is becoming more and more significant; the scope is broader and the volume is bigger.

Correspondingly, the thinking and concepts should also change. The aid issue is no longer positioned in purely diplomatic terms, and is now linked to the interests of the recipients with regard to the development and the Millennium Development Goals. It is surely inappropriate for such an important job to be managed by a ministry that takes charge of economy and trade. Moreover, the focus of the Ministry of Commerce is on the fields of commerce and trade; using money properly to make profit is a kind of occupational requirement, so it is difficult for the ministry to bear the responsibility for international development aid, which needs broad vision and overall planning. Assistance requires specialty and professional training. It also needs talent and experience, and cooperation with various departments. If the aid work is in the charge of the Department of Aid to Foreign Countries (援外司), it is unable to cope with the coordination of various ministries involved due to a lack of authority. The result won't be ideal.[6]

To disseminate the idea and experience of "self-reliance-first, foreign-aid-second" while strengthening assistance to Africa

The development of China shows that dependence on aid alone cannot solve the problem of development. In the past 50 years, developed countries have provided US$2 trillion in aid to developing countries, mostly in Africa, but Africa has not changed for the better. During the decades from the 1970s to the 1990s, the population living in poverty greatly increased in Africa while the biggest amount of aid was coming in. Therefore, aid will not bring about a fundamental change to development in Africa. In view of this, Chinese leaders should reconsider self-reliance in China–Africa cooperation. It is not proper to constantly raise the volume of aid. This is unsustainable, and African countries would easily develop a mentality of dependency. In terms of aid projects, it is indispensable to "teach a man to fish" and seek sustainable development, with a particular emphasis on small projects and those closely related to livelihoods. The aid projects must be carried out hand in hand with training to help African people master the technology; this will thus avoid both the accusation that "China does not transfer technology" and the Chinese management of the project after the end of construction. The aid for big projects must be carefully selected, since such projects involve various factors, including large amounts of money, and do not necessarily brings about only positive effects. Large projects usually involve many factors. Once any problems (such as ecological, environmental, immigration, disputes with villagers, relations with the local authorities) occur, the local people can only blame the aid-provider, resulting in an untenable situation.

Conclusion

There is no doubt that FOCAC has made great achievements. However, it also has defects and problems due to lack of experience in the initial phase. The forum is not perfect and is still in the process of constant learning, change and adjustment. I once termed the imperfections the "mechanism plight", which prevents the forum from maximising its role, and this mechanism plight expressed in three aspects: China, Africa and the bilateral interaction (Li Anshan 2011). Only by overcoming these defects can the cooperation mechanism be improved. FOCAC should be put into the context of China's Africa strategy, and the Africa strategy in the context of China's state strategy against the background of globalisation; then every part can play its proper role.

Notes

1 It is inappropriate to over-emphasise the economic cost of these buildings. Instead, their political and cultural significance should be noticed. They can be regarded as the accomplishments of state leaders, and the symbol of a nation-state. More importantly, they embody cultural decolonisation. Regarding China's aid to big projects in Africa, see Huang Zequan (2000); Li Anshan (2004: 285–318).
2 The principles are: (1) Assistance should not be considered as a unilateral grant but as mutual help. (2) Neither conditions nor privileges should be attached to the assistance. (3) To reduce the burden of the countries to which China provides assistance, no-interest or low-interest loans can be extended if necessary. (4) The purpose of the assistance is to help those countries develop independently. (5) To increase the income of those countries, the program should produce quicker results with less investment. (6) China will provide the best equipment and materials to the recipient countries, and promises to change them if the quality is not as good as the agreement permits. (7) China guarantees the recipient countries will master the relevant technology when technical assistance is provided. (8) Experts from China should never enjoy any privileges and should receive the same treatment as the local experts in recipient countries.
3 Equality and mutual benefit, stress on practical results, various forms and common development. *People's Daily*, 15 January 1983.
4 The Sullivan Conference, also called the African-American and African Friendship Conference, was initiated by Reverend Leon Sullivan.
5 "Proposals on Further African Work and Training of Talents", a letter written to President Jiang Zemin from 17 professors in Chinese Society of African Historical Studies, 19 December 1997. See the records of Chinese Society of African Historical Studies.
6 In March 2018, the first session of the 13th National People's Congress voted and adopted the decision on the institutional reform plan of the State Council to China International Development Cooperation Agency.

References

Alden, C., Daniel Large & Ricardo Soares de Oliveira, eds. 2008. *China returns to Africa: A rising power and a continent embrace.* London: Hurst.
Almanac of China's Foreign Economic Relations and Trade Editorial Board. 1996. *China's foreign economic relations and trade 1996–1997.* Beijing: China Economics Press.
Alves, Ann Cristina. 2008. Chinese economic diplomacy in Africa: The Lusophone strategy. In Chris Alden, Daniel Large & Ricardo Soares de Oliveira, eds, *China returns to Africa: A rising power and a continent embrace.* London: Hurst, 69–81.

Ampiah, K. & Naidu, S., eds. 2008. *Crouching tiger, hidden dragon? Africa and China.* Durban: University of KwaZulu-Natal Press.

Asche, H. 2007. China's engagement in Africa: A survey. Paper presented at the International Conference China in Africa: Who benefits? Interdisciplinary perspectives on China's involvement in Africa. Frankfurt am Main: Johann Wolfgang Goethe University, 14–15 December.

Carbone, M. 2011. The European Union and China's rise in Africa: Competing visions, external coherence and trilateral cooperation. *Journal of Contemporary African Studies* 29(2): 203–221.

Chen Gongyuan, ed. 2000. *Strategic report on the development of China–African relations in the 21st century.* Beijing: Chinese Association of African Studies.

Chen Gongyuan, ed. 2007. *A probe into the new strategic partnership between China and Africa.* Beijing: Chinese Association of African Studies.

Chen Gongyuan. 2009. *China–Africa relations and the quest of African issues.* Beijing: Chinese Association of African Studies.

Du Xiaolin. 2006. The evolution, features and trends of the United States policy towards Africa after the Cold War. *Contemporary International Relations* 3: 11–15.

Fei Yan. 1999. A new round of contending among the Western powers in Africa. *West Asia and Africa* 4: 56–58.

Gao Fei. 1998. Current African situation and China–African relations. *West Asia and Africa* 1: 1–3.

Gordon, A.A. & Gordon, D., eds. 1996. *Understanding contemporary Africa.* Boulder, CO: Lynne Reiner.

Harbeson, J.W. & Rothschild, R., eds. 1995. *Africa in world politics.* Boulder, CO: Westview Press, pp. 4–45.

He Wenping. 1999. China–Africa relations facing the 21st century. *West Asia and Africa* 1: 25–30.

He Wenping. 2008. China's perspective on contemporary China–Africa relations. In Chris Alden, Daniel Large & Ricardo Soares de Oliveira, eds, *China returns to Africa: A rising power and a continent embrace.* London: Hurst, 143–165.

Huang Zequan. 2000. Fifty Years of China–African friendly cooperation. In Center for African Studies of Peking University, ed., *China and Africa.* Beijing: Peking University Press.

Jin Xide. 2000. *Development aid of Japanese government.* Beijing: Social Sciences Academic Press, 43–245.

Li Anshan 2004. *A study of African nationalism.* Beijing: China International Broadcasting Press.

Li Anshan. 2006. China–Africa relations in the discourse on China's rise. *World Economics and Politics* 11: 7–14.

Li Anshan. 2006a. On the adjustment and transformation of China's African policy. *West Asia and Africa* 8 : 1–20.

Li Anshan. 2008. TICAD and Japan's aid policy to Africa. *West Asia and Africa* 5: 5–13.

Li Anshan. 2009. Chinese medical teams abroad: History, scale and impact. *Foreign Affairs Review* 1 : 9–40.

Li Anshan. 2011. Principles and dilemmas of China–African Cooperation. *Journal of Shanghai Normal University* (Philosophy and Social Sciences Edition) 6: 111–121.

Li Anshan. 2011a. Reality and truth of China's entry into Africa. *Social Observer* 8: 27–29.

Liu Yueming & Zhu Chonggui. 1996. The African policy of the US and France and their conflict. *Contemporary International Relations* 1: 43–45

Luo Jianbo. 2003. Japan's foreign policy after the Cold War. *International Survey* 1: 69–74.

Ma Shengli. 2000. France: Foreign aid policy and diplomatic strategy. In Zhou Hong, ed., *Foreign aid and international relations*. Beijing: China Social Sciences Press, 259–308.

Ministry of Education, PRC. n.d. Educational exchange and cooperation between China and Africa. Unpublished.

Monson, J. 2009. *Africa's freedom railway: How a Chinese development project changed lives and livelihoods in Tanzania*. Bloomington, IN: Indiana University Press.

Qian Qichen. 2003. *Ten episodes in China's diplomacy*. Beijing: World Affairs Press.

Ren Weidong. 1998. African situation and its strategic status. *Contemporary International Relations* 8: 34–37.

Shen Xipeng, 2018. *A study on China aided construction of Tanzania Zambia railway*. Heifei: Huangshan Publishing House.

Shu Zhan & Wang Feng. 1999. A survey of Clinton government's strategy to sub-Saharan Africa from the perspective of America-Africa Ministerial Conference. *West Asia and Africa* 3: 14–18.

Tang Jiaxuan. 2009. *Strong rain and warm wind*. Beijing: World Affairs Press.

Taylor, I. 1998. China's foreign policy towards Africa in the 1990s. *Journal of Modern African Studies* 36(3): 46–449.

Thompson, D. 2005. China's soft power in Africa: From the Beijing Consensus to health diplomacy. *China Brief* 5(21): 1–5.

Wang Qinmei. 1999. Twenty years of great development of China–African relations. *Journal of Foreign Affairs College*, 1:48–54.

Weng Ming. 1995. Appointing just before leaving: "Milord Qiao" led delegation to General Assembly of UN for the first time. In Fu Hao & Li Tongcheng, eds, *Great talents and their great achievement – diplomats in UN*. Beijing: Overseas Chinese Publishing House, 7–13.

Xia Jisheng. 1997. Reviews of African economic development in the 1990s. *Asian and African Studies* 7: 296–299.

Xia Jisheng. 1998. Clinton government's African policy. *West Asia and Africa* 1: 16–22.

Yao Guimei. 1998. The background and influence of the shift of the US African policy. *West Asia and Africa* 3: 5–10.

Yu, George T. 1975. *China's African policy: A study of Tanzania*. New York: Praeger.

Zhao Huijie. 1999. France's adjustments of policy and its strategic thought. *West Asia and Africa* 1: 31–36.

Zhong Weiyun. 2001. Strategic scheme of Japan's aid to Africa. *West Asia and Africa*, 6: 14–19.

7 China's policy

Transition and discourse[1]

Introduction

International affairs expert Gerald Segal said in 1992 that, "There may be grounds for believing that as China grows strong, it will grow somewhat more important for Africans. But from the Chinese perspective, it seems that while Africa will attract attention from the writers of official policy statements, the continent will remain the least important area for Chinese foreign policy, whether of an expanding or a withdrawing kind" (Segal 1992: 126). We understand that political prophecy usually goes wrong, and what is happening today obviously challenges Segal's prophecy. As a dynamic part of China's foreign policy, its Africa policy shows both continuity and change. With the establishment of FOCAC, the strategic partnership between China and Africa has become both more important and stronger.

With China's rapid economic growth and impressive role in the international arena, there have been constant concerns about whether China's peaceful rise is negative or positive. The negative is expressed by two views: collapse theory and threat theory. The collapse theory holds that the Chinese government would fall pretty soon (Chang 2001), or draws a gloomy picture of China's reform, which has stalled with problems such as corruption, declining state power and credibility, and increasing inequality, and would end nowhere (Pei 2006). The threat theory regards US dominance as being challenged by China's rise, a threat to the big powers and world peace (Swaine & Tellis 2000; Gertz 2000; Brzezinski and Mearsheimer 2005; Mearsheimer 2006). The positive is expressed in two views as well: gradualism (Friedman 1996) and optimism (Gilley 2004; Zheng Bijian 2005). Among those opinions, one fact is striking: China's rapid economic growth and impressive role in the international arena have sparked concerns about China's engagement in Africa.[2] The concern started in a serious tone when two influential articles were published in 2004 (Giry 2004; Muekalia 2004). *China's African Policy*, issued by the Chinese government in January 2006, may be considered an active diplomatic manoeuvre and attracted further international attention.

China and Africa's mutual dependence is evident in the FOCAC held every three years since 2000. In 2006, the FOCAC Beijing Summit included the heads of state, government officials and representatives from 48 African countries. Former Chinese President Jiang Zemin visited Africa four times, while, as of 2007, President Hu Jintao had paid five visits to the continent (twice as vice-president and three times as president). The intention of China's involvement in Africa, though, has been questioned extensively, especially by Western powers. China's policy on Africa is clearly set out, but how did it come into being? And how does it fit into China's grand strategy?

By analysing three transformations in China's Africa policy, this chapter draws a conclusion different from most analysts' claim that China's policy has changed in recent years owing to its thirst for Africa's oil and other natural resources (CSIS Prospectus 2003; Eisenman & Kurlantzick 2006: 219–224.) It is argued that changes in China's Africa policy are closely linked to China's transformation of its grand strategy of economic reform. Emphasising transition of the China's policy in three aspects, various misunderstandings and accusations are addressed and new challenges related to China–Africa relations and possibilities for bilateral and multilateral cooperation are pointed out and discussed.

Ideology: From emphasis to diversified approach

China's Africa policy can be divided into three periods: a period of normal development (1949–1978); a transitional period (1978–1994); and a period of fast development (1995 to the present). With the end of the Cultural Revolution and the change of Chinese leadership, there was a gradual shift in China's policy on economic development. The relationship between diplomacy and economy was reversed; "economy serving diplomacy" became "diplomacy serving economy" (Qu Xing 2000: 440–441). This shift was followed by a new foreign policy of independence, peace and development.

The first change in China's Africa policy lies in its move from a posture of forming an alliance in international politics for the purpose of fighting against the superpowers to strengthening exchange and dialogue with Africa, on the basis of seeking common ground while also reserving differences.

After the founding of the People's Republic of China (PRC), China's foreign policy was greatly circumscribed by international politics. In the 1950s, China first adopted a pro-Soviet Union and anti-United States policy, which was termed *yi-bian-dao* (one-sided policy). In the 1960s, China adopted the policy of anti-imperialism and anti-revisionism. The 1970s witnessed China's policy of reconciliation with the United States and opposition to the Soviet Union (Qu Xing 2000: 375–376; Ross 1993: 11–61). The focus of China's policy on Africa was anti-colonialism, anti-imperialism and anti-revisionism (Mao Zedong 1994: 403–413, 416–420, 463–467, 490–492, 497–502, 526–528, 587–588, 600–601), derived from the unfavourable international situation after the founding of the PRC. The hostile policy of Western countries and later of the Soviet Union forced China to seek more "diplomatic room" to survive as a sovereign state.

The link between China's foreign policy and its ideology hindered diplomacy between China and Africa. The CPC had contact with communist parties only in South Africa and Reunion. Later, due to the conflict between China and the Soviet Union, the CPC discontinued its friendly relations with those two African parties. Early in the Cultural Revolution, China's ultra-leftist policy affected its foreign policy, and Chinese diplomats began to "export revolution" to Africa (Ogunsanwo 1974).

In 1967–1969, the CPC discontinued its contact with Partido Africano da Independência da Guiné e Cabo Verde-PAIGC because of its pro-USSR policy. The *Parti Congolais du Travail* wanted to establish inter-party relations to promote cooperation with the CPC, yet its offer was refused because it was not a communist party. The *Partido Frelimo* had been in contact with the CPC, yet the proposal to establish formal relations between the two parties was refused as well. Later, *Partido Frelimo* invited the CPC to attend its third National Congress, without success. The two parties did not establish formal relations until 1981. The radical policy was once rectified under the leadership of Premier Zhou Enlai. Starting in May 1969, China began to send its ambassadors to all countries with which it had diplomatic relations; in October all the new Chinese ambassadors were sent to their positions in African countries. However, the real change in China's policy did not come until the late 1970s (Barnouin & Yu 1998: 75–78; Long Xiangyang 2000).

The CPC's 12th Congress in 1982 defined the new principles of its party relations – "independence, complete equality, mutual respect, non-interference in others' internal affairs" – and proposed to establish relations with progressive parties and organizations (*People's Daily*, 8 September 1982). China's contacts with parties in developing countries have greatly increased since the 1982 Congress of the CPC.[3] From 1978 to 1990, more than 230 delegations from parties in sub-Saharan countries visited China. At the same time, the CPC sent out 56 delegations to visit ruling parties of 39 sub-Saharan countries (Jiang Guanghua 1997: 670–671).[4]

As of 2002, the CPC had established relations with more than 60 political parties in more than 40 sub-Saharan countries. More than 30 were ruling parties (Li Liqing 2006; Zhong Weiyun 2000). According to the news reports of *People's Daily* and *Observer*, 16 African parties visited China while 17 CPC delegations visited Africa. In 2003–2005, the African parties' visits to the CPC numbered 13, 16 and 24 while CPC to African parties numbered 8, 20 and 19 respectively. In 2006, 21 African parties sent their delegations to China, while 14 CPC delegations visited Africa. During these visits, a wide range of topics were discussed, such as politics, the economy, culture and military relations. In addition to the contact between parties, China and Africa also increased exchanges between their congresses and parliaments (Zeng Jianhui 2006: 101–103, 184–186).

The CPC no longer uses ideology as a standard of practice. The *principle* of contact is no longer ideological. The CPC cooperates not only with socialist or communist parties, but also with other parties that adhere to different ideologies. *Partnership* is not confined to ruling parties, but includes also non-ruling parties. The *content* of this contact is not limited to party politics but extends to economic cooperation and cultural exchange. For example, in 2000 Jia Qinglin, then secretary of CPC Beijing, visited Uganda and promoted cooperation in the coffee trade. Former CPC Secretary of Shandong Province Wu Guanzheng, CPC Secretary of Guangdong Province Zhang Dejiang and CPC Secretary of Hubei Province Yu Zhengsheng visited Africa in 2001, 2004 and 2005, respectively, and their large economic and trade delegations signed cooperation agreements with African countries (Li Liqing 2006: 18.)

Due to China's transition, the political relationship between China and Africa has deepened. High-level visits have been frequent, especially since the 1990s. Vice-Premier Zhu Rongji paid his first visit to Africa in 1995, which kicked off the new "African boom" in China. President Jiang visited Africa four times, and in 1996 put forward five suggestions for strengthening China–Africa relations. President Hu Jintao visited Africa five times, and in 2004 he noted that China and Africa should help each other economically and support each other in international and regional affairs (*People's Daily* 2004). The opening up of political relations with various African parties indicated that there was no longer any political criterion attached to relationships with Africa. The CPC could exchange ideas with various African parties or political organisations of different ideologies, and discuss subjects such as politics, governance, ethnicity, the economy and education. The change has greatly promoted China–Africa cooperation and has become an important component of China's Africa policy. China has just one political demand for Africa: no political relations with Taiwan (Smith 2006).

Bilateral exchange: From unilateral to multilateral

The second change in China's Africa policy was a switch from an emphasis on political contact to exchanges through multiple channels.

From 1949 to 1978, China's Africa policy concentrated on three aspects: supporting African people in their drive for national independence; uniting African countries in the struggle against colonialism, imperialism and hegemony; and helping African countries with economic development. In the political arena, China tried its best to assist African independence movements; it also offered military assistance, such as training military and political personnel (Weinstein & Henriksen 1980: 102–111; Jiang Guanghua 1997: 130, 303–305, 442–443, 621–622). After Africa's nations achieved independence, China began to seek out Africa as an ally in its fight against imperialism and hegemonism. Despite internal pressure as China's economy suffered, its assistance to Africa continued.

China–Africa economic cooperation comprised bilateral trade and economic assistance. The total sum of bilateral trade in 1977 only reached US$720 million (Almanac of China's Foreign Economic Relations and

174 *Policy and implementation*

Trade Editorial Board 1984: 5–30). Between 1956 and 1977, China provided US$2.476 billion in economic assistance to 36 African countries, about 58 per cent of China's total foreign aid (US$4.276 billion), according to an external source (Weinstein & Henriksen 1980: 117, 121). During the 1970s, although the Soviet Union was the biggest arms trader in Africa, its economic aid to Africa lagged far behind China's aid, which totalled US$1.8 billion – double the amount of Soviet aid (Chazan et al. 1992: 410).

The end of the Cultural Revolution witnessed a short period of shrinkage in China–Africa relations. First, the assistance to Africa decreased: China's assistance to Africa during 1976–1980 was estimated at $94 million (Chazan et al. 1992: 410). The bulk of this assistance was given between 1976 and 1978.[5] Second, the trade between China and Africa dropped. Trade volume decreased after 1980 (1982 was an exception) and did not pick up until 1986 (Table 7.1). Third, the number of Chinese medical teams and doctors sent to Africa also decreased. China did not send doctors to Africa in 1979 or 1980, and between 1978 and 1983 the number of doctors and medical teams sent to Africa was at its lowest (Table 7.2).

Table 7.1 China–Africa trade statistics, 1980–1987 (US $ million)

Year	1980	1981	1982	1983	1984	1985	1986	1987
Export	747	798	978	675	623	418	638	854
Import	384	299	212	244	252	207	216	154
Total	1131	1097	1190	920	876	626	854	1008

Note: Sums may not tally due to rounding.

Source: *Almanac of China's Foreign Economic Relations and Trade*, 1980–1988.

Table 7.2 China's medical teams and doctors in Africa, 1963–1983

Time range	Countries with Chinese medical teams	Numbers	Doctors
1963–1967	Algeria, Tanzania, Somali, Congo	17	326
1968–1972	Mali, Tanzania, Mauritania, Guinea-Bissau, Sudan, Equatorial Guinea	18	197
1973–1977	Sierra Leone, Tunisia, Zaire, Togo, Senegal, Madagascar, Morocco, Niger, Saõ Tomé and Príncipe, Upper Volta, Guinea-Bissau, Gabon, Gambia	23	300
1978–1983[a]	Benin, Zambia, Central Africa, Botswana, Djibouti, Mozambique, Rwanda, Uganda, Libya	13	173
Total		71	996

Note: During 1979–1980, no new medical teams were sent to Africa.

Source: Almanac of China's Foreign Economic Relations and Trade Editorial Board (1985).

The shrinkage in China–Africa relations was due to several factors. First, China's economy struggled during the Cultural Revolution, and even when the revolution ended there was little money to be spent on foreign aid. Second, in order to recover, China's economy needed funding and technology. With the cooling of relations with the West, the Chinese government's attention naturally turned to developing countries. Third, relations with Albania and Vietnam – two major Chinese aid recipients – deteriorated, suggesting the limitations of China's foreign aid. Of course, the change in China's leadership also had some impact on continuity in foreign aid policy.[6] New thinking was needed to establish better relations between China and Africa.

International development cooperation

Three months after the 12th CPC Party Congress held in September 1982, Premier Zhao Ziyang set his first footprint in Africa. Before his departure, Zhao declared that his visit showed China's diplomatic focus on Africa, as well on other developing countries; it was intended to establish mutual understanding and friendship and strengthen the two sides' cooperation. During his visit to 11 African countries, Zhao announced the "Four Principles on China-African economic and technical cooperation": equality and mutual benefit; variety of forms; emphasis on effectiveness; and co-development (*People's Daily* 15 January 1983). Zhao's "Four Principles" were a supplement to Zhou Enlai's Eight Principles of foreign aid put forward in 1964 (*People's Daily* 18 January 1964).

While the Eight Principles were concerned with China's assistance to Africa, Zhao's Four Principles stressed mutual economic and technological cooperation. The former policy guaranteed that China would provide the most favoured assistance to Africa, with additional restraints on Chinese aid personnel. The latter stressed bilateral cooperation and co-development. The newer policy was noticed by the international community (Harris & Worden 1986: 100–119).

The international community's popular perception is that the fast development in China–African relationship arose after a long-dormant period, revealing new and potentially unsettling Chinese ambitions in Africa. For example, a Center for Strategic and International Studies (CSIS) report stated: "After remaining dormant for thirty years, China's contemporary engagement in Africa reflects the emergence of a new and ambitious vision" (Muekalia 2004: 8). This view does not hold water. During the transitional period (1978–1995), China continued to promote cooperation with Africa in various fields. African presidents or heads of state paid 33 visits to China in the 1970s and 51 visits in the 1980s (Wang Taiping 1999: 699; Ai Ping 2000). Chinese leaders such as Chen Muhua, Geng Biao, Ulanfu, Ji Pengfei and Li Xianlian visited 33 African countries from 1978 to 1980. Premier Zhao Ziyang visited 11 African countries after the 12th Congress of the CPC and visited Tunisia in 1986. Other high-ranking officials – Li Xianlian (1986), Li

Peng (1986, 1991), Wu Xueqian (1987, 1990) and Qian Qichen (1989) – also visited many African countries to promote bilateral relations.

Studying Chinese projects from the 1980s and 1990s, Brautigam notes that China continued its aid to Africa after the Cultural Revolution, although the emphasis differed from that of earlier periods: "Chinese projects in the 1980s and [19]90s stress[ed] economic results, efficiency, and profits, and they were deeply affected by China's domestic political contexts, values, and ideologies" (Brautigam 1994: 340). She drew a different conclusion from most Western scholars: "Although marginalized in the foreign policy calculations of current and former superpowers, sub-Saharan Africa does still figure in Chinese global geopolitics" (Brautigam 1998: 43).

After the "Tiananmen Square incident" in 1989, Western countries enforced sanctions against China, while African countries helped China. Foreign Minister Qian visited eight African countries (Lesotho, Botswana, Zimbabwe, Angola, Zambia, Mozambique, Egypt and Tunisia) that year. The next year he visited Morocco, Algeria and Egypt. Beginning in 1991, he visited a group of African countries each January, and this has become a tradition for Chinese foreign ministers (Qian Qichen 2003: 256–257). Although Chinese diplomacy has increased in Africa, educational exchange and economic cooperation between the two sides have developed even more rapidly.

Educational exchange

Between 1949 and 1978, China sent volunteer teachers to nine African countries – Algeria, Egypt, Togo, Congo (Brazzaville), Guinea-Bissau, Mali, Somali, Tanzania and Tunisia – with the first group going to Egypt in 1954. The period 1978–1995 witnessed an increase, with teachers sent to 21 countries (China-African Countries' Educational Cooperation and Exchange Compilation Group (Hereafter CACECE) 2005: 24–25; Gillespie 2001). In 2003 there were 238 teachers in more than 30 African countries. Since the late 1980s, China has tried various means to help African countries build their own educational systems. From the beginning of the 21st century, Chinese teachers in Africa started to teach African students from undergraduate through to PhD levels.[7] In June 2005, the first Confucius Institute in Africa opened at the University of Nairobi.[8] Since then, Confucius Institutes have been founded in Kenya, Nigeria, Zimbabwe and South Africa. As of 2007, 15 Chinese volunteers were in Zimbabwe, four of them Chinese language teachers, and two were at the Confucius Institute at the University of Zimbabwe. In South Africa, a Confucius Institute has been established at the University of Stellenbosch (Zhao Zuojun et al. 2007).

Likewise, the number of African students in China has increased greatly since the 1950s, when there were only 24 students. In the 1960s and 1970s, the figure increased from 164 to 648, and reached 2245 in the 1980s. There were 5569 Africans studying in China during the 1990s (CACECE 2005: 12–22). In 2000, at the time of the first FOCAC in Beijing, there were 1388 African students in China; in 2005, the number was 2757. Aside from the enrolment of African university students, China has held seminars, training courses, and symposia on fields such as management capabilities, engineering skills, and school administration. By the end of 2003, China had established 43 educational and research programs in areas such as agriculture, Chinese medicine, long-distance education and computer technology, in addition to setting up 21 research laboratories (CACECE 2005: 3–5; Zhang Xiuqin 2004).

China's Ministry of Education (MOE) has supported courses at local universities for African teachers, engineers and professionals. From 2002 to 2006, Jilin University trained 225 Africans in long-distance education. Northeastern Normal University also set up a base for training Africans. Since 2002, it has run nine seminars for over 200 administrators from more than 30 African countries. China Agricultural University also managed ten seminars from 2001 to 2006, training 206 experts, scholars and officials from Africa (Chengdu 2007). Zhejiang Normal University started cooperation with Cameroon in 1996 by setting up a Chinese Language Training Centre there.

With the help of the MOE, in 2003 Zhejiang Normal University set up the first Centre for African Education Studies in China. Since 2002, the university has run 13 seminars for African educational administrators. Although the seminars have paid attention to higher education and have included African university presidents and high-level administrators, they have also covered the administration of middle school and elementary education. The university cooperates with more than 20 universities in 12 African countries. In October 2006, Zhejiang Normal University held the first China–Africa University President Forum, with a focus on "capacity building of higher education institutions in developing countries", "reform of management system in higher education institutions" and "international cooperation and partnership". Participants included more than 30 presidents and education officials from 14 African countries (Li Xu 2004: 11).

In 2003, Tianjin University of Technology and Education was designated as another MOE assistance base for vocational education training programs. In answer to the call from the Forum on China–Africa Cooperation's Addis Ababa Action Plan, in 2005 the university set up the Centre for African Vocational Education Studies to train mid-range engineering professionals from Africa. It has trained more than 200 students and sent out 84 teachers in the past few years to facilitate vocational education in African countries (Wang Yuhua 2005: 20).

In 2005, the MOE entrusted 11 universities to run 12 seminars and training courses on higher education management, long-distance education and vocational technical education. Participants were from 41 countries, most of them African. In November 2005, the first China–African Ministers of Education Forum was held in Beijing, with State Councillor Chen promising cooperation regarding educational assistance and exchange (Chen Zhili 2005).

Every year, the MOE holds a workshop on educational assistance in developing countries, with an emphasis on Africa. In March 2006, together

178 *Policy and implementation*

with the Ministry of Commerce and the Ministry of Foreign Affairs, the MOE held the fourth Seminar on the Exchange of Experience on the Training of Educational Personnel from Developing Countries, attended by more than 70 participants from different universities (Yunnan University 2006). In December 2006, the Centre for African Studies at Peking University held a National Universities' Workshop on Africa: Teaching, Study and Assistance. Officials from the Ministries of Education, Commerce and Foreign Affairs attended, along with participants from universities. All contributed their opinions on teaching and research in Africa, assistance to African education and how the ministries could make the best use of their resources in universities. In May 2007, the fifth workshop was held in Chengdu, with more than 50 participants from the Ministries of Education, Commerce, and Foreign Affairs, as well as participants from more than 20 Chinese universities.

Economic and trade cooperation

New developments in economic cooperation are the engagement of state-run companies and private companies in funding (some are funded by foreign investment). Such private companies are developing quickly. Statistics for January to October 2005 indicate that the export of state-run, private and funded enterprises (China–foreign joint ventures, China–foreign cooperative enterprises and foreign-invested enterprises) to Africa reached US$559 million, US$511 million and US$286 million respectively, with corresponding increases of 23, 59.6 and 52.7 per cent (Zhou Jianqing 2006: 16).

Trade commodities also reflect the cooperation between Africa and China. In 2004, the top four commodities exported from China to Africa were electrical equipment and machinery (41 per cent), textiles (18 per cent), garments (11 per cent) and new technology (8 per cent), such as electronic and information facilities, software, and aviation and aerospace equipment. These numbers demonstrate that production machinery, everyday goods (instead of luxury goods) and high-tech commodities constituted a large percentage of China's exports. The top commodities imported to China from Africa were crude oil (64 per cent), iron ore (5 per cent), cotton (4 per cent), iron or steel (3 per cent), diamonds (3 per cent) and timber (3 per cent) (The Editorial Board of China Commerce Yearbook 2005: 182–183).

Economic cooperation can be seen not only in trade but also in areas such as investments, contract business, labour services and consultant services, all of which have shown rapid progress. By the end of 2004, approximately 715 non-financial projects in Africa were approved by the PRC's Ministry of Commerce (The Editorial Board of China Commerce Yearbook 2005: 183). By the end of 2005, the number of Chinese firms reached 813, and they had invested US$18 billion in Africa in areas such as infrastructure, natural resources, transportation and agriculture. Chinese-contracted construction projects have greatly increased as well. In 2005, the contracted projects of

China's policy: Transition and discourse 179

labor service totalled $8.61 billion. China would also provide US$3 billion in preferential loans and US$2 billion of export credits over the next three years, and establish a special fund of US$5 billion to encourage Chinese investment in Africa (The Editorial Board of China Commerce Yearbook 2006: 725). China set up 11 centres for the promotion of investment in Africa and for regularised bilateral trade (Zhou Jianqing 2006: 16). In addition, timely information was issued on the trade policies of African countries, shortages of commodities and reports of the market situation.

In summary, there have been changes in China–Africa economic cooperation. Unitary state-managed trade has split into two parts (state-owned and private companies). Trade volumes have greatly increased, and aid-type cooperation has become cooperative: "Gone are the days when cooperation between China and Africa concentrated mainly on state-to-state cooperation, political support in international affairs, and economic assistance" (Adam 2006). A China–Africa multilateral cooperation system is gradually emerging, and the forms of cooperation have become multifactorial (Zong He 2005: 59). China has likewise established a diplomatic consultative system in African countries. The exchange covers economy and trade, culture and education, medicine and sanitation, military and civil administration (Thompson 2005; Department of Health of Hubei Province 1993; Xu Chunfu 2003; Zhan Shiming 2004).

Field of cooperation: From aid to co-development

This is the third change. After the adjustment of China's Africa policy, the emphasis was put on cooperation, bilateralism and a win–win strategy, followed by a change in China's aid pattern, from unitary aid to multiple forms of aid, such as government deducted-interest loans, aid combined with co-investment, and grants. Naturally, China's Africa policy has its own strategic aim, yet one of its starting points was to help African countries eliminate poverty and consolidate their independence. In other words, co-development was the most important principle, and China–Africa cooperation clearly follows this principle.

From the early 1980s to the mid-1990s, Africa experienced a process of marginalisation, expressed as a decrease in investment and an increase in debts. From 1980 to 1990, although Africa was undergoing structural adjustments due to Western pressure, 43 out of 139 British companies withdrew from Africa (*Financial Times* 1990). Japan also held a pessimistic view of Africa, and its companies in Kenya dropped from 15 to two in the 1980s. The total debt of sub-Saharan Africa was US$6 billion in 1970; that figure grew to US$84.3 billion in 1980. After the Cold War and the disintegration of the Soviet Union, the importance of Africa's strategic position greatly decreased, contributing to its further marginalization. African debt reached US$200.4 billion in 1993 and US$210.7 billion in 1994, equal to 82.8 per cent of its GNP in 1994, as well as 254.5 per cent of its export earnings. According to a 1995 World Bank report, the debt-to-export ratio of 28 African countries was over 20:1 at the end of 1994 (Gordon & Gordon 1996: 116; Lawrence 1986).

Change in aid

At the Tokyo International Conference on African Development held in 1993, African countries suggested that foreign investment based on development and production was more effective than traditional aid (Almanac of China's Foreign Economic Relations and Trade Editorial Board 1995: 62). China's early grant assistance accrued a significant return from its African counterparts: China became a member of the United Nations (Weng Ming 1995: 9). Yet grants hardly changed the reality of poverty. As Hu Yaobang pointed out in 1982, "As for economic assistance, the method of sheer gift is disadvantageous to both sides, judging from historical experience" (Documentation Office of CPC Central Committee 1982: 1127–1128). Therefore, during the late 1980s and early 1990s, China underwent foreign trade and aid reform.

In 1987, a Togo sugar plant assisted by the Chinese had a shortage of technicians and management experience. Chinese experts took over and the plant began to run effectively. The Togolese government praised the remarkable increase in enterprise (Yan Yiwu 1990: 55). This combination of China's assistance and joint-investment cooperation gradually spread to other China-aided enterprises. In 1991, the Malian government decided to privatise the Segu Textile Plant, a Chinese aid project. After negotiation, however, the Malian government transferred 80 per cent of its shares to a Chinese company on the condition that the company paid its debts. Since then, the company has been running smoothly, valued in 1996 at 7.6 billion African francs (He Xiaowei 1997: 75). In 2003, China cancelled Mali's debt of 37 billion African francs (Zhang Zhongxiang 2006: 215).

In late 1995, after three years of experimentation, the Chinese government put into effect its interest-deducted loan scheme.[9] Vice-Premier Zhu and Vice-Premier Li visited 13 African countries during that year to explain China's new foreign aid policy. A year later, China signed agreements giving low-interest loans to 16 African countries (He Xiaowei 1997: 75). The new form of aid was gradually accepted. In 2000, FOCAC implemented a new stage of bilateral relations; in response, China promised to relieve African debt. In 2002, China signed agreements with 31 African countries to relieve 156 debts, the sum reaching RMB5 billion (US$145 million) (Qiu Deya 2003: 91). As of the end of 2007, the figure had increased to RMB10.9 billion (Xinhua Newsnet 2007). According to the PRC's Ministry of Commerce, China was due to have signed debt relief agreements with 33 African countries by the end of 2007, honouring pledges made at the FOCAC Beijing Summit in 2006.

Exchange of development experience

Providing different seminars is another way to help African countries in terms of training various professionals. For example, a seminar on economic reform and development strategies was held in 2003; participants included 22 administrators from different economic or financial units in 16 African countries, together with seven officials from the African Development Bank. Both sides exchanged ideas on development, and African participants learned more about China's ongoing reform. Nigerian historian Femi Akomolafe recognises that "China's rapid economic transformation holds special lessons for those in Africa ... the Chinese opted for an indigenous solution to their economic backwardness" (Akomolafe 2006: 48–50).

The Chinese government has also frequently invited African diplomats to visit China to help them understand the country. The Understanding China symposium was first designed in 1996 specifically for young African diplomats. The China Foreign Affairs University ran the symposium for nine years (1996–2004) for participants from more than 130 countries and nine international organizations. A total of 161 diplomats from African countries having diplomatic relations with China attended nine symposia; ten African regional organizations also participated. The symposium included lectures on Chinese history, culture and arts, and a tour of both rich and poor regions. From 2001 on, Peking University also ran various seminars and training courses for African diplomats and economic administrators. The School of Government at Peking University has run several symposia for African diplomats from English-, French- and Arabic-speaking countries, as for the one held from August to October 2007, with 35 participants from 14 French-speaking countries. The Chinese government holds seminars to train African professionals. In the first half of 2007, it held 93 such training seminars, with 2241 trainees from 49 African countries. According to its action plan, China will train 15 000 Africans between 2007 and 2009.

This approach has been praised by African governments such as Nigeria, Mozambique, Uganda, Madagascar, Ethiopia, South Africa and Zambia. For example, in 2005, Sudanese officials expressed their thanks for China's training program in economic management, which was attended by senior officials from the Sudanese Ministry of Foreign Affairs and the Ministry of Finance and International Cooperation. About 40 Sudanese went to China for training related to their respective fields.[10]

Co-development and bilateralism

The most impressive demonstrations of China–Africa economic cooperation have been China's tariff relief for African exports, leading to increased trade between China and Africa. Vice-Minister of Commerce Wei Jianguo said in November 2007:

182 *Policy and implementation*

From January to September 2007, China–Africa trade volume was $52.3 billion and the figure for the whole year is expected to reach $70 billion. Under the zero-tariff category, by the first half of 2007, China had imported commodities worth $440 million from Africa. (Ministry of Commerce 2007)

These increases indicate the positive impact of the Chinese policy of promoting African exports to China. The original 199 zero-tariff African goods have increased to 454 types of goods from 26 of the least developed countries in Africa. In 2005, about 12,400 African businessmen came to the 97th Guangzhou Trade Fair, where the volume of business transactions totalled US$7 billion. From January to September 2005, 30 African countries' trade with China totalled more than $100 million, while nine other countries' trade with China reached more than US$1 billion (Zhou Jianqing 2006: 15–18).

In 2000, China–African trade volumes were US$10.598 billion and China's imports from Africa surpassed its exports to Africa (US$5.5 billion versus US$5.04 billion) (Almanac of China's Foreign Economic Relations and Trade Editorial Board 2001: 503). China–African trade reached about US$30 billion in 2004, and China's imports from Africa were again more than its exports to the continent (US$15.6 billion versus US$13.8 billion) (Editorial Board of China Commerce Yearbook 2005: 182). This trade reached US$39.75 billion in 2005, with imports again exceeding exports (The Editorial Board of China Commerce Yearbook 2006: 724). In 2006, China–African trade reached a value of US$55.5 billion, with African exports to China making up over half of that at $28.8 billion (*China Daily*, 30 January 2007).

According to Ministry of Commerce (2006, 2007) statistics, it took 20 years for China–Africa trade to increase from US$100 million to US$1 billion, and another 20 years to reach US$10 billion, but only six years to reach US$55.5 billion. From January to September 2007, the China–Africa trade volume was US$52.3 billion and the figure for the whole year was expected to reach US$70 billion.

With such trade increases, Chinese export goods have become better suited to Africa. Sales of machines, electronics and new high-tech goods grew rapidly, totalling more than half of the value of China's exports to Africa. China's aid emphasizes a combination of technical and economic support and the transfer of technology with commodities. For example, China has provided much of the technology necessary for satellite launch and on-orbit services, and has even trained Nigerian command and control operators. While Nigeria acquired satellite technology, China also gained from the collaboration by burnishing its credentials as a reliable player in the international commercial satellite market (Xinhua News Agency 2007). China also sent oil expert and engineer Wang Qiming of Daqin to the Sudan to provide African engineers with new technology that would assist with the best-use practices of seemingly exhausted oil fields (*China Petroleum Daily* 2007; Li Anshan 2007). This framework for China's aid – based on the principles of sustainability and mutual benefit rather than charity – has proven beneficial to African development.[11]

Discourse, criticism and explanation

China's Africa policy has become a point of interest among the international community. The discourse on China–Africa relations can generally be divided into three phases (Li Anshan 2014): before 2000, 2000–2008 and 2008 onwards. The first witnessed few specialised studies (Duyvendak 1947; Larkin 1971; Filesi 1972; Ogunsanwo 1974; Yu 1975; Hutchison 1975; Snow 1988). Although the 1990s was the time when Chinese enterprises laid their base in Africa, neither China's world status nor China–Africa relations in global politics were important, so it attracted little attention from international academia. Few scholars engaged in research on China–Africa relations at this stage and concentrated mainly on international relations or aid issues (Brautigam 1998; Taylor 1997,1998; Sautman 1994; Sullivan 1994). The competition between the PRC and Taiwan for Africa is also touched upon (Yu & Longenecker 1994; Brautigam 1994,1994a; Taylor 1998). Research in this phase is vividly coloured by politic inclination.

FOCAC, set up in 2000, attracted international attention and Western governments were surprised by the rapid growth of China's influence in Africa, thus a sense of threat arose spontaneously. This phase is characterised by strong anxiety, Western dominance and the limited involvement of a small number of Chinese and African academics. With a sharp increase in research on the subject, many projects were funded by Western foundations, especially those on China's infrastructure and aid programs in Africa.[12] Second, the ideological tendency of Western scholarship is prominent, with arbitrariness, accusation and a lack of academic rigor features of the discourse.[13] Yet a few studies are comparatively objective or based on field research (Brautigam 2003, 2009; Alden 2005, 2005a, 2007; Monson 2004, 2006, 2008; Davies 2007; Mwanawina 2007) and works with different attitudes and themes.[14] However, conference proceedings or special issues of journals contain multiple voices.[15] Third, Africans and Chinese academics started to voice their opinions – albeit rather weakly (Gaye 2006; Ajakaiye 2006; Prah 2007; Owusu & Carmody 2007; Ankomah 2008; Li Anshan 2005,2007; Yang Lihua 2006; He Wenping 2006, 2007; Liu Haifang 2006, 2008) – which affected the discourse. Fourth, various reports were issued by the government institutions, international organisations and NGOs with different tones (Kaplinsky, McCormick & Morris 2006; Broadman 2007; RAID 2007; Foster et al. 2008; Wang 2007; Zafar 2007).

A signal came in 2008 that both the European Union and United States wanted to cooperate with China in Africa.[16] The study of the phase has following features. First, all the studies are concentrated on China–African economic activities except a few, either in general (Shinn & Eisenman 2012; Mohan 2012; Thoburn 2013) or in specific fields, such as trade, investment and foreign aid.[17] Second, African academia – especially overseas Africans – joined the debate and African think-tanks started to show their international influence.[18] Their participation multiplied the discourse.[19] Third, the research has changed from general theory to specific issues and more case studies appeared with rational and objective voices (Brautigam 2009; Monson 2009; Jansson, Burke & Jiang 2009; Jansson & Kiala 2009; Centre for Chinese Studies 2010; Esteban 2010; Men & Barton 2011; Berger, Brautigam & Baumgartner 2011; Taylor 2011; Power & Alves 2012; Glennie 2012).

However, Western countries still regard Africa as being in their "sphere of influence" and China, with other developing countries, is usually considered an "external player" in Africa (Berger 2006: 115–127; Lyman 2006: 129–13). Chinese engagement was taken as a threat to their interests in Africa, and thus they voice various criticisms and suspicions. Some of the criticisms are caused by misunderstanding, some by bias or groundless fear.

"New colonialism"

In February 2006, the United Kingdom's foreign secretary Jack Straw said during a trip to Nigeria that what China is now doing in Africa is the same as what the British did 150 years ago, and this sparked a discussion about China's "new colonialism". On 11 June 2011, US Secretary of State Hillary Clinton warned in Zambia that Africa must beware of "new colonialism" as China expands ties there. The accusation goes on that China develops its relations with Africa solely to secure natural resources and China is engaging in "new colonialism" or acting as "new economic imperialists" in Africa (Games 2005; Hilsum 2006: 23–24; Jones 2011; Johannes 2011; Keating 2012). This view has become very popular in the Western media. However, in its dealings with African states, China views them as equals, respecting their sovereignty.[20] In addition, China's trade with Africa, especially its imports of oil and other natural resources, has turned Africa's potential wealth into real wealth. China's involvement has contributed to Africa's economic development for the past years. China's engagement has brought hope to Africa, and its positive impact is demonstrated by economic development and technology transfer. For example, the Sudan has changed from being an oil importer to an oil exporter. With China's help, Nigeria launched its first communication satellite. As a Nigerian journalist points out, "The Chinese have effectively ended the Western dominance of one of Africa's most powerful countries, and their presence has resulted in a change in Nigeria's global relations" (Mbachu 2006: 82).

As previously mentioned, China–Africa relations were established long before China's need for raw materials in the mid-1990s. At present, while China imports oil from Africa, it exports electronic, mechanical and high-tech products that satisfy critical needs in Africa, creating a rough equilibrium in the economic and trade relations between the two countries. The oil drilling and exploration rights that China has obtained have been secured through international bidding mechanisms in accordance with international market practices, posing no "threat" to any country. Rights to oil fields in the Sudan and Nigeria were purchased by Chinese companies after the withdrawal of competitors (Agence France-Presse 19 May 2006).

Human rights issue

The limits and norms of the international system only allow China to deal with sovereign states through their governments. The European Union constantly criticises China's human rights record, yet Britain, France and Germany are trying to promote trade with China. The United States and China have issued human rights reports criticising each other for several years, yet such criticism by no means hinders the exchange of goods and ideas. Human Rights Watch (HRW) conducted a survey on eight copper mining areas in Zambia and Lusaka to investigate the labour situation of Chinese state-owned copper mining enterprises in Zambia and concluded that there were three major problems: health and safety problems; human rights issues; and working hours (Human Rights Watch 2011), yet another article criticised the HRW's biased view and offered a different opinion on the issue (Yan & Sautman 2013).[21] When there is an accusation of the Sudanese government's violation of human rights, China used its ties to the Sudan to persuade the Sudanese government to cooperate with the United Nations (*Chutian Metropolis Daily* 8 July 2007). Since there is mutual respect and trust, China can work with the Sudanese government to find a solution that is agreeable to all parties to alleviate the suffering of the Sudanese people. Finally, the Sudanese government has accepted a "hybrid peacekeeping force" in Darfur (Xinhua News Agency 2007). That is the best way to solve the human rights problem.

Zimbabwe and Darfur

Zimbabwe and Darfur were picked out as two important cases among the accusations levelled against China's engagement in Africa (Eisenman 2005: 9–11). China's position of non-interference with regard to Zimbabwe is in accord with that of the African Union (AU). In 2005, when Robert Mugabe demolished urban dwellings in an attempt to crack down on illegal shantytowns in Harare, Britain and the United States called on the AU to act. However, the AU felt it was not its role to start running the internal affairs of member states and gave Mugabe its blessing to resist sanctions imposed by the West (*Guardian* 25 January 2005). In March 2007, Britain and the United States criticised Mugabe for taking strong measures against Zimbabwe's political opposition. However, the leaders of southern African governments held a special meeting on Zimbabwe; all supported Mugabe unanimously and asked Western countries to give up their sanctions against the country.

The Darfur issue is a very complicated case, with historical origins, national integration, religious conflict, refugee migration and poverty all playing a role.

First, the crisis in Darfur is mainly caused by environmental degradation, as pointed out by the United Nations Environment Program report issued in 2007: "Environmental degradation, as well as regional climate instability and change, are major underlying causes of food insecurity and conflict in Darfur – and potential catalysts for future conflict throughout central and eastern Sudan and other countries in the Sahel belt."[22]

Second, Darfur is a regional tragedy that affects many people and disastrously impacts the region. However, except for the United States, neither the United Nations nor regional organisations – nor, indeed, other countries – use "genocide" to describe the situation in Darfur.[23] Third, the crisis in Darfur is related to development and can only be solved through development. Fourth, the Darfur crisis is expressed as a conflict between different Sudanese peoples. Nation-building is a difficult process for all countries. Consider the Civil War in the United States: after more than 80 years of independence, the United States undertook a war to prevent part of the country from seceding, resulting in 620,000 deaths. The international community should give the Sudanese people time to solve this problem.

There is an accusation from the media that "China [has taken] Sudan under its wing" (Blair 2005). Some scholars echo this view (Shichor 2005). In refutation, one could look at China's reaction after the Canadian oil firm Talisman decided to sell its interest in a Sudan consortium that also involved Chinese and Malaysian firms. The China National Petroleum Corporation wanted to purchase the interest, but Khartoum turned down the Chinese offer and awarded the shares to an Indian firm instead (Sautman & Yan Hairong 2007).[24] This shows that China and the Sudan are equal partners, and they each make decisions to guard their national interests independently. China has constantly supported the Sudanese people with humanitarian aid. Besides offering help to Sudan to build its oil industry and infrastructure, China also sent its fourth shipment of humanitarian aid, including tents, blankets, and medical and agricultural equipment. At the time of writing, the Chinese government had sent humanitarian aid valued at RMB80 million.[25]

Observation of the current international situation indicates that foreign intervention – especially by force – brings no solution but rather more trouble, as demonstrated by events in Afghanistan and Iraq, for example. Peaceful settlement is the best solution for all parties. Furthermore, the situation in Darfur currently is moving in a better direction.

Transparency in China's aid to Africa

There is a suspicion that China hides the amount of its aid to Africa. It is true that there are no accurate official figures available from Chinese sources. This lack may be due to China's sensitivity about the aid figure, domestic politics or Chinese culture. First, although China has been providing support to Africa for more than half a century and there is a strong belief that the sums are large, the amount of Chinese aid to Africa is still rather small compared with that of Western countries.[26] Second, China is a developing country, with more than 20 million people living below the poverty line. With a large number of poor people, it is not wise for the Chinese leadership to publicise the amount of China's aid to Africa. Third, according to Chinese tradition, it is improper and even immoral to reveal one's assistance to others. A Chinese saying goes, "Do not forget how others have helped you, and do forget how you have helped others." It is not only a matter of saving face, but also a matter of sovereignty.

Characteristics of bilateral relations

China–Africa relations are characterised by summit diplomacy, equality, co-development and cooperation (Li Anshan 2007). Such summit diplomacy cannot be seen in Africa's relations with any other country, or in the relationship between China and other continents. Although the principle of equality has been advocated among individuals in modern times, there is no mention of it in international relations. The equality in China–Africa relations is a model for international relations. Equality means respect for sovereignty, mutual benefit, discussion and coordination. A unique feature of China's foreign policy is the principle of non-interference in the internal affairs of other countries. Mutual benefit and co-development are likewise features of China–Africa relations, their purpose being to improve Africa's ability to self-develop. The most impressive characteristic of the China–Africa relationship is the standardized mechanism of cooperation – for example, FOCAC and its follow-up actions.

Opportunity, suspicion and cooperation

There is a plenty of room for multiple cooperation in Africa. It is not surprising that China's engagement in Africa has benefited African countries and the world as a whole. The roads, railways and ports built by the Chinese company benefited not only Africans, but Chinese and all the investors. China's demand for raw materials and energy enables the rich resources of Africa to be used effectively, benefiting both Chinese purchasers and African suppliers. Chinese demand has stimulated raw material prices, increasing the income of resource-rich countries in Africa, and has accelerated African development, turning potential wealth into real wealth. For example, Nigeria has paid off its outstanding loans, and Sudan has gone from being a net oil importer to an oil exporter. The investment of Chinese enterprises has promoted African industries and is breaking the long-standing hold that the West has had over trade in commodities between Africa and the rest of the world (Naidu & Davies 2006).

China, together with other new emerging countries, has entered Africa as an investor, promoted African industries and "fueled the revival of a global interest in Africa because of high commodity prices" (Vines 2006: 153–156).

Such investment is also enhancing the autonomy of African countries in production, sales and investment. China–Africa trade has the potential to help Africa win greater and truer independence. China's engagement also provides African countries with more choices for business partnerships, markets for their exports and opportunities for pricing their commodities.

China's investment flow is usually accompanied by infrastructural construction, which can enable Africa to attract more investment. South African scholars have acknowledged China's role in helping African economies to achieve long-term growth through the principle of mutual benefit (Davies & Corkin 2006). One particularly poignant analysis explains that, "Unlike Belgium, which built roads solely for the extraction of resources in the Democratic Republic of Congo, China is constructing or improving roads that are suitable not only for the transport of resources but which citizens can also use to travel" (Marks 2007). Frankly speaking, the infrastructure that China built also provided better conditions for other international investors.

China's involvement in Africa faces various major problems or challenges. There are incongruities between China's interests and Africa's interests in market and labour; conflicts between China's national interests and Chinese as well as African enterprises' interests; disagreements between China's interests and the Western powers' vested interests; challenges regarding China's need for natural resources and Africa's need for sustainable development; and conflict between temporary interests and long-term interests – an issue not only for China but also for other countries as African partners (Li Anshan 2007a).

Vines points out that China's engagement in Africa "has worried Western and Japanese governments and businesses" (Vines 2007: 215). Berger says that "the emergence of external players such as China and India poses a challenge to the European strategy" (Berger 2006: 124–125). Why? It is probably because they take Africa as their own sphere, yet Africa is an independent continent and all countries involved must pursue confidence-building measures with African countries. Through mutual confidence, a win–win strategy could be achieved, with other partners' interests considered, thus guaranteeing the vitality of the cooperation and strengthening African partners' capacity for both self-reliance and equal cooperation with the international community. With mutual confidence, cooperation in Africa can address areas such as research on the treatment of diseases (such as malaria, AIDS and COVID-19), research and development of new resources (such as solar and nuclear energy, and biofuels) and various kinds of assistance.

Conclusion

China's African policy has retained its principles while adapting to changing domestic and international conditions. This approach is closely linked to the transformation of China's grand strategy, as well as its outlook on world development. China's engagement in Africa is changing Africa and the world, providing more opportunities and creating more challenges. Despite such challenges, China–Africa cooperation demonstrates what equality and co-development in international relations can produce. The world needs peace and cooperation. The promise of bilateral and multilateral cooperation in Africa will be realised only if we act equally on the opportunities.

Notes

1 The paper on which this chapter is based was first presented at the "LSE-PKU China's Foreign Policy and Global International Affairs" seminar, London, May 2006; at the international workshop "China–Africa Links" at Hong Kong University of Science and Technology, 11–12 November 2006; and at the off-the-record meeting "China in Africa: Geopolitical and Geoeconomic Considerations" at the John F. Kennedy School of Government, Harvard University, 31 May–2 June 2007. I am grateful for the conference organisers, LSE colleagues David Zweig and Robert Rotberg, and would like to thank the participants and Niu Jun, Zhao Changhui, Li Wengang, Zhang Chongfang for their comments.
2 Since the end of 2005, there have been international conferences, seminars, workshops and expert roundtable meetings on Chinese–African relations in Johannesburg, Beijing, London, Cambridge, Hong Kong, Tokyo, Berlin and Shanghai, and special journal issues such as *China Brief* V (2005); *Southern African Journal of International Affairs*, XIII (2006); *International Politics Quarterly*, 4 (2006); and *West Asia and Africa*, 8 (2006).
3 China hosted the Third Asian Parties International Conference in 2004. See also Huang Wendeng 1998.
4 As the Vice-Minister of the International Department of the CPC, Jiang recorded his 11 visits to sub-Saharan African countries in the book.
5 After the PRC returned to the United Nations in 1971, China's foreign aid increased rapidly (Yan Yiwu 1990: 55).
6 However, China established 181 foreign aid programmes from 1979 to 1983, 90 per cent of which were carried out in Africa. China's foreign aid programmes accomplished from 1979 to 1983, in Ministry of Foreign Trade Almanac 1984 IV: 217–218.
7 Deputy Minister Zhang Xinsheng's speech at the Fifth Workshop on the exchange of experience on the training of educational personnel from developing countries, Beijing, 24 May 2007.
8 In March 2004, Cao Guoxing, director of the Department of International Cooperation and Exchanges in the Ministry of Education (MOE), led an Africa assistance working group to Kenya. Guo Chongli, Chinese ambassador to Kenya, proposed to establish a Confucius Institute at the University of Nairobi. In June 1994, Minister of Education Zhou Ji visited Kenya and signed a Memorandum of Understanding with George Saitoti, Kenyan Minister of Education, Science and Technology, to establish a Confucius Institute in Nairobi (MOE 2006).
9 This low-interest loan is provided by Chinese banks, which are encouraged to do so by favourable government policies that offer subsidies to cover the difference between the low-interest and the standard loan rates. The low-interest loans are mainly used in programmes that benefit the economic development of developing countries, as well as improving their infrastructures.

190 *Policy and implementation*

10 Speaking at the symposium, a representative of the Sudanese Ministry of International Cooperation expressed his thanks to the Chinese Embassy for arranging the training program. Xinhua News Agency, 27 July 2005.
11 Premier Wen Jiabao pointed out three focuses during his visit to Africa. China is going to try every means to increase imports from Africa; to closely combine technological export and economic cooperation, with a special emphasis on strengthening the African capacity for self-development; and to help African countries train African technicians and management personnel. *People's Daily* 2006; He Wenping 2007: 23–40.
12 For example, Stellenbosch University Centre for Chinese Studies under the leadership of Martyn Davies published several important reports on the subject (Corkin & Burke 2006; Rocha 2008; Davies 2008). There are other reports on the subject by different organization.
13 The accusation is mainly concentrated on China's thirst for oil and energy (Jaff & Lewis 2002; Lyman 2005, 2006; Zweig and Bi Jianhai 2005; Berger 2006; Taylor 2006; Jiang 2006; Eisenman & Kurlantzick 2006; Large 2007; Meyers, et al. 2008; Oliveira 2008). However, the view is questioned (Downs 2004, 2007) and some also take China's engagement as an attempt to broaden South–South cooperation (Alves 2005).
14 There are different attitudes (Sorbara 2006; Looy 2006; Akaki 2007; Edinger 2008; Sautman & Yan Hairong 2006, 2007, 2007a, 2008; Asche 2008; Asche & Schuller 2008; Collender 2008). Different subjects were also studied (Gu 2006, 2009; Tull 2006; Gill & Reilly 2007; Henley et al. 2008; McCormick 2008; Jenkins & Edwards 2005, 2006; Kaplinsky & Morris 2008; Morris & Einhorn 2008; Kragelund 2007).
15 Various conferences on China–Africa relations were held in different countries and collections of papers or special issues of journals were published (Zeleza 2007; Alden, Large & Oliveira 2008; Rotberg 2008; Strauss & Saavedra 2009; Guerrero & Manji 2008; Fiamingo 2008).
16 In March 2008, the European Commission issued a document formally proposing EU–Africa–China trilateral dialogue and cooperation. During her visit to Beijing to attend the Third China–US Consultation on African Affairs, US Assistant Secretary of State for African Affairs Ms Fraser emphasised the willingness of the United States to cooperate with China on African affairs in her speech at the Centre for African Studies in Peking University on 15 October 2008. US attitude today seems to be less positive towards trilateral cooperation (Rolland 2021).
17 For trade, the focus is on the analysis of the bilateral trade relations, the balance sheet and the multiple impacts of trade on Africa, especially agricultural products. For example, the *European Journal of Development Research* published a special issue to discuss various aspects especially the impact of the rapid development of Sino-African trade (Ademola, Bankole & Adewuyi 2009; Giovannetti & Sanfilippo 2009; Villoria 2009). On other topics, see (Montinari & Prodi 2011; Grauwe, Houssa & Piccillo 2012; Villoria 2012). China's investment is another hot topic (Kaplinsky & Morris 2009; Peh & Eyal 2010; Vicente 2011; Kaplinsky, Terheggen & Tijaja 2011; Farooki & Kaplinsky 2012; Vliet & Magrin 2012). China's aid to Africa also attracted attention (Nam 2007; Davies 2008; Chaponnière 2009; Mohan, Tan-Mullins & Power 2010; Dreher & Fuchs 2011; Grimm 2011; King 2013.).
18 For example, the AU Commission issued a report on strategic relationship (AU 2010), and the African Development Bank issued one on China's trade and

investment in Africa (Renard 2011). The African Economic Research Consortium actively promoted the research on China–Africa relations (Obwona et al. 2007; Odada & Matundu 2008; Onjala 2008; Corkin 2008; Mwanawina 2008; Tsikata, Fenny & Aryeetey 2008). The African Center for Economic Transformation (ACET) has made great achievements in the field of China–Africa relations. Its research series "Looking East: China Africa Contact" covered various cases, such as Ghana, Rwanda and Liberia to provide a guide to the exchange and cooperation between African policy-makers and China (ACET 2009). The African Forum and Network for Debt and Development (AFRODAD) is committed to promote the relations between governments and citizen organizations. In 2011, It held a symposium on China's development assistance in southern Africa to discuss the effect of China's loans from different perspectives. The participants not only criticised the so-called "colonialism" of China against Africa, but also pointed out some mistakes of Chinese engagement in Africa.

19 There are different opinions (Guerrero & Manji 2008; Munyoro 2008; Freeman 2009; Aidoo 2012; Lokongo 2009; Renard 2011; Odada & Matundu 2008; Onjala 2008; Mwanawina 2008; Cheru and Obi 2011; Mbayem 2011; Morais 2011; Mukanga 2012; Hwede 2012) and various debates, such as the AU Headquarters issue (Ezeanya 2012; Lokongo 2012) and the free press issue (Keita 2012; Li Anshan 2012).

20 As the Nigerian general consul in Hong Kong claimed, "We Nigerians just want to do business with China, because we respect each other, can sit there and talk to each other equally." Speech at the China–Africa Links Workshop in Hong Kong University of Science and Technology, 12 November 2006.

21 The author believes that the starting point of this report is not the research on the human rights situation of copper mining enterprises in Africa or Zambia, but rather the accusation specifically aimed at China. The article also confirms from the aspects of wages, working hours, unionization and job stability that the topic selection angle of the HRW's report is biased, the data is rough, there are many loopholes, and many conclusions are inconsistent with the facts. More importantly, almost all mining companies in the world have some common problems. Human Rights Watch has an ulterior motive in picking out Chinese companies for analysis (Yan Hairong & Sautman 2013).

22 United Nations Environment Program, Sudan Post-Conflict Environmental Assessment (2007: 329). See also the program's Post-Conflict and Disaster Management Branch website at http://postconflict.unep.ch. This view on the role of environmental degradation is not new, but it has been neglected by the outside world. For a similar perspective, see Mohammed (2004: 230–240). The Sudanese ambassador to the United States provided the same explanation in his speech at the National Press Club in Washington, DC on 30 May 2007 when addressing the Bush administration's new sanctions on the Sudan.

23 It is noteworthy that a much more serious disaster in the neighbouring Democratic Republic of the Congo did not elicit as much attention from the US. See Autesserre (2006).

24 For an analysis of India's entry into the oil enterprise in the Sudan and its impact, see Mohan (2002).

25 Since 2004, China has sent five shipments of material for humanitarian aid to Darfur. The fourth shipment, worth RMB20 million (US$2.6 million), left for Sudan on 16 August 2007, and included pumps, tents and blankets to help

residents in the Darfur region improve their living conditions (FOCAC 2007). The fifth batch of aid material, valued at RMB40 million, was shipped on 25 August 2007 and included boarding houses for at least 120 schools, generators, vehicles and pumps. See http://news.enorth.com.cn/system/2007/08/24/001839261.shtml

26 According to a Chinese source, over the past 50 years China has provided a total of RMB44.4 billion in aid to Africa and assisted with about 900 infrastructure and social welfare projects (Zhang Hongming 2006).

References

ACET. 2009. Volume II: Key Dimensions of Chinese Engagements in African Countries, in ACET's report *Looking East: A guide to engaging China for Africa's policy-makers*, November.

Adam, Mahamat. 2006. Africa starting to rise in partnership with China. China Daily (North American Edition), 13 January.

Ademola, Oyejide Titiloye, Bankole, Abiodun S. & Adewuyi, Adeolu O. 2009. China–Africa trade relations: Insights from AERC scoping studies. *European Journal of Development Research* 24(4): 485–505.

Agence France-Presse. 2006. Nigeria gives China oil exploration licences after auction, 19 May.

Ai Ping. 2000. Communist Party of China's contacts with African political parties. In Chen Gongyuan, ed., *Strategic reports on the development of China–African relationship in the 21st century*. Beijing: n.p., 12–17.

Aidoo, Richard. 2012. China's "image" problem in Africa. *The Diplomat*, 25 October.

Ajakaiye, Olu. 2006. China and Africa: Opportunities and challenges. Paper presented at African Union Task Force on Strategic Partnership between Africa and the emerging countries of the south, Addis Ababa, September.

Akaki, Sam. 2007. Uganda: Would we prefer a Chinese "Commonwealth" today? allAfrica.com, 29 October.

Akomolafe, F. 2006. No one is laughing at the Asians anymore. *New African* 1552: 48–50.

Alden, C. 2005. China in Africa. *Survival* 47(3): 153–156.

Alden, C. 2005a. China's Africa relations: The end of the beginning. In Peter Draper & Garth le Pere, eds, *Enter the dragon: Towards a free trade agreement between China and the Southern African Customs Union*. Midrand: Institute for Global Dialogue/South African Institute for International Affairs, 137–153.

Alden, C. 2007. *China in Africa*. London: Zed Books.

Alden, C., Large, D. & de Oliveira, R. Soares, eds. 2008. *China returns to Africa: A rising power and a continent embrace*. London: C. Hurst.

Almanac of China's Foreign Economic Relations and Trade Editorial Board. 1984. *Almanac of China's Foreign Economic Relations and Trade 1984*. Beijing: China Foreign Economic and Trade Press.

Almanac of China's Foreign Economic Relations and Trade Editorial Board. 1995. *Almanac of China's Foreign Economic Relations and Trade 1995*. Beijing: China Foreign Economic and Trade Press.

Almanac of China's Foreign Economic Relations and Trade Editorial Board. 1996. *Almanac of China's Foreign Economic Relations and Trade 1994–1995*. Beijing: China Foreign Economic and Trade Press.

Almanac of China's Foreign Economic Relations and Trade Editorial Board. 1997. *Almanac of China's Foreign Economic Relations and Trade 1997/98*. Beijing: China Economics Press/China Economic Herald Press.
Almanac of China's Foreign Economic Relations and Trade Editorial Board. 2001. *Almanac of China's Foreign Economic Relations and Trade2001*. Beijing: China Foreign Economic and Trade Press.
Alves, Ana. 2005. The growing relevance of Africa in Chinese foreign policy: The case of Portuguese speaking countries. *Daxiyangguo: Revista Portuguesa de Estudos Asiticos* 7: 93–108.
Ankomah, Baffour. 2008. China in Africa: Why the West is worried. *New African* 471: n.p.
Asche, Helmut 2008. Contours of China's "Africa mode" and who may benefit. *Journal of Current Chinese Affairs* 37(3): 165–180.
Asche, H. & Schuller, Margot. 2008. *China's engagement in Africa: Opportunities and risks for development*. Eschborn: GTZ.
AU Commission. 2010. *AU Commission on Africa's Strategic Relationships*, EX. CL/ 544(XVI), January.
Autesserre, S. 2006. Local violence, international indifference? Post-conflict "settlement" in the eastern DR Congo (2003–2005). PhD dissertation, New York University.
Barnouin, B. & Yu Changgen. 1998. *Chinese foreign policy during the Cultural Revolution*. London: Kegan Paul.
Berger, Alex, Brautigam, Deborah & Baumgartner, Philipp. 2011. *Why are we so critical about China's engagement in Africa?* Bonn: German Development Institute, August 15.
Berger, B. 2006. China's engagement in Africa: Can the EU sit back? *South African Journal of International Affairs* 8(1): 115–127.
Blair, D. 2005. Oil-hungry China takes Sudan under its wing. *Telegraph*, 23 April.
Brautigam, D. 1994. What can Africa learn from Taiwan? Political economy, industrial policy and adjustment. *Journal of Modern African Studies* 32(1): 111–138.
Brautigam, D. 1994a. Foreign assistance and the export of ideas: Chinese development aid in the Gambia and Sierra Leone. *Journal of Commonwealth and Comparative Politics* 32(3): 325–349.
Brautigam, D. 1998. *Chinese aid and African development: Exporting green revolution*. London: Macmillan.
Brautigam, D. 2003. Close encounters: Chinese business networks as industrial catalysts in Sub-Saharan Africa. *African Affairs* 102(408): 447–467.
Brautigam, D. 2009. *The dragon's gift: The real story of China in Africa*. Oxford: Oxford University Press.
Broadman, H. 2007. *Africa's silk road: China and India's new economic frontier*. Washington, DC:World Bank.
Brzezinski, Z. & Mearsheimer, J.J. 2005. Clash of the titans. *Foreign Policy* 146: 46–50.
Center for African Studies of Peking University, ed. 2000. *China and Africa*. Beijing: Peking University Press.
Chang, Gordon. 2001. *The coming collapse of China*. New York: Random House.
Chaponnière, Jean-Raphal. 2009. Chinese aid to Africa: Origins, forms and issues. In Meine Pieter Van Dijk, ed., *The new presence of China in Africa*. Amsterdam: Amsterdam University Press.

Chazan, N. et al. 1992. *Politics and society in contemporary Africa*. Boulder, CO: Westview Press.
Chen Zhili. 2005. Speech at the China–Africa Education Ministers Forum. Unpublished.
Chengdu, 2007. Collection of Materials of Fifth Workshop on the Exchange of Experience on the Training of Educational Personnel from Developing Countries. Unpublished, Chengdu.
Cheru, Fantu & Obi, Cyril. 2011. De-coding China–Africa relations: Partnership for development or "(neo) colonialism by invitation"? *The World Financial Review*, January: 72–75.
China Daily. 2007.China Africa trade exceeded 50 billion US dollars for the first time in 2006, 30 January.
China Petroleum Daily. 2007. Wang Qimin is welcomed by Sudanese, 26 June.
China-African Countries' Educational Cooperation and Exchange Compilation Group (CACECE). 2005. *China and African countries' educational cooperation and exchange*. Beijing: Peking University Press.
Chutian Metropolis Daily. 2007. What kind of issue is Darfur: A special interview with the special representative of the Chinese Government, 8 July.
Collender, G. 2008. *Challenging the perception of Chinese Business in Africa*. London: UK Institute of Development Studies, 17 December.
Corkin, L. 2008. *AERC scoping exercise on China–Africa relations: The case of Angola*. Nairobi: Draft report submitted to AERC.
Corkin, L. & Burke, C. 2006. *China's Interest and activity in Africa's construction and Infrastructure Sectors*. Stellenbosch: Centre for Chinese Studies, Stellenbosch University.
CSIS Prospectus. 2003. *Opening a Sino-US dialogue on Africa*. Washington, DC: Center for Strategic and International Studies.
Davies, M. 2008. *How China delivers development assistance to Africa*. Stellenbosch: Centre for Chinese Studies, Stellenbosch University.
Davies, M. & Corkin, L. 2006. China's market entry into Africa's construction sector: The case of Angola. Paper presented at the international symposium on China–Africa shared development, Beijing, 19 December.
Davies, P. 2007. *China and the end of poverty in Africa: Towards mutual benefit?* Brussels: Diakonia and Eurodad Report.
Department of Health of Hubei Province, ed. 1993. *Famous doctors in North Africa*. Beijing: Xinhua Press.
Documentation Office of CPC Central Committee, ed. 1982. *Collection of important documents since the Third Plenary Session of the 11th Central Committee of the CPC*. Beijing: CPC Central Committee.
Downs, E.S. 2004. The Chinese energy security debate. *The China Quarterly* 177: 21–41.
Downs, E.S. 2007. The fact and fiction of Sino-African energy relations. *China Security* 3(3): 42–68.
Dreher, A. & Fuchs, A. 2011. *Rogue aid? The determinants of China's aid allocation*. CESifo Working Paper No. 3581. https://onlinelibrary.wiley.com/doi/full/10.1111/caje.12166.
Duyvendak, J.J.L. 1947. *China's discovery of Africa*. Hertford: Stephen Austin and Sons.
Edinger, H. 2008. How China delivers rural development assistance to Africa. Presentation at the 6th Brussels Development Briefing, 2 July.

Editorial Board of China Commerce Yearbook. 2005. *China Commerce Yearbook 2005*. Beijing: China Commerce and Trade Press.
Editorial Board of China Commerce Yearbook. 2006. *China Commerce Yearbook 2006*. Beijing: China Commerce and Trade Press.
Eisenman, J. 2005. Zimbabwe: China's African ally. *China Brief* 5: 9–11.
Eisenman, J. & Kurlantzick, J. 2006. China's African strategy. *Current History* 105: 219–224.
Esteban, M. 2010. Silent invasion? African views on the growing Chinese presence in Africa: The case of Equatorial Guinea. *African and Asian Studies* 9(3): 232–251.
Ezeanya, C. 2012. The AU and the tragedy of a new headquarters. http://chikafo rafrica.com/2012/01/24/the-au-and-the-tragedy-of-a-new-headquarters/hunHail emikael.
Farooki, M. & Kaplinsky, R. 2012. *The impact of China on global commodity prices: The global reshaping of the resource sector*. London: Routledge.
Fiamingo, C. 2008. La Cina in Africa. *Afriche e Orienti*, Vol. 2.
Filesi, T. 1972. *China and Africa in the Middle Ages*. London: Frank Cass.
Financial Times. 1990. UK companies sell African investments. 28 June.
FOCAC. 2007. Humanitarian aid from China leaves for Sudan's Darfur. 20 August.
Foster, V., Butterfield, W. Chuan Chen & Pushak, N. 2008. *Building bridges: China's growing role as infrastructure financier for Sub-Saharan Africa*. Washington, DC: World Bank.
Freeman, S.T., ed. 2009. *China, Africa, and the African diaspora: Perspectives*. Washington, DC: AASBEA.
Friedman, E. 1996. Why China matters. *Journal of International Affairs* 56: 302–308.
Games, D. 2005. Chinese: The new economic imperialists in Africa. *Business Day*, February.
Gaye, A. 2006. *Chine-Afrique, le dragon et l'autruche*. Paris: L'Harmattan.
Gertz, B. 2000. *The China threat: How the People's Republic targets America*. Washington, DC: Regnery.
Gill, B. & Reilly, J. 2007. The tenuous hold of China Inc. in Africa. *The Washington Quarterly* 30(3): 37–52.
Gillespie, S. 2001. *South–South transfer: A study of Sino–African exchanges*. New York: Routledge.
Gilley, B. 2004. *China's democratic future*. New York: Columbia University Press.
Giovannetti, G. & Sanfilippo, M. 2009. Do Chinese exports crowd-out African goods? An econometric analysis by country and sector. *European Journal of Development Research* 21(4): 506–530.
Giry, S. 2004. China's Africa strategy, *The New Republic* 231(20): 19–23.
Glennie, J. 2012. The West has no right to criticise the China–Africa relationship. *The Guardian*, 8 February.
Gordon, A.A. & Gordon, D.L., eds. 1996. *Understanding contemporary Africa*. Boulder, CO: Lynne Rienner.
The Guardian. 2005. African Union defends Mugabe, 25 January.
Grauwe, P. de, Houssa, R. & Piccillo, G. 2012. African trade dynamics: Is China a different trading partner? *Journal of Chinese Economic and Business Studies* 10(1): 15–45.
Grimm, S. et al. 2011. *Transparency of Chinese aid: An analysis of the published information on Chinese external financial flows*. Stellenbosch: Centre for Chinese Studies, Stellenbosch University.

Gu Jing. 2006. The impact of Africa on China. www.africaportal.org/dspace/articles/impact-africa-china

Gu Jing 2009. China's private enterprises in Africa and the implications for African development. *European Journal of Development Research*, 21(4): 570–587.

Guerrero, Dorothy-Grace & Firoze, Manji, eds. 2008. *China's new role in Africa and the South: A search for a new perspective.* Nairobi: Fahamu.

Harris, L.C. & Worden, R.L. eds. 1986. *China and the Third World: Champion or challenger?* Dover, MA: Croom Helm.

He Wenping, 2006. China–Africa relations moving into an era of rapid development. *Inside AISA*, 3&4: 2–6.

He Wenping. 2007. The balancing act of China's Africa policy. *China Security* 3: 23–40.

He Xiaowei. 2006. Continue to carry out the reform of foreign aid methods and strictly implement foreign aid agreements. In *Almanac of China's foreign economic relations and trade yearbook 1997–98*. Beijing: China Economics Press/China Economic Herald Press, 75.

Henley, John, Kratzsch, Stefan, Kulur, Mithat & Tandogan, Tamer. 2008. *Foreign direct investment from China, India and South Africa in Sub-Saharan Africa: A new or old phenomenon?* UNUWIDER Research Paper no. 24.

Hilsum, L. 2006. China's offer to Africa: Pure capitalism. *New Statesman*, 3 July: 23–24.

Huang Wendeng. 1998. Deng Xiaoping theory and China–Latin American party relations. *Latin American Studies* 6: 1–7.

Human Rights Watch. 2011. "You'll be fired if you refuse": Labor abuses in Zambia's Chinese state-owned copper mines, 3 November.

Hutchison, A. 1975. *China's African revolution.* London: Hutchinson.

Hwede, B. & Osei, Z. 2012. The dynamics of China–Africa cooperation. *Afro Asian Journal of Social Sciences* 3(1): 1–25.

Jaff, A.M. & Lewis, S.W. 2002. Beijing's oil diplomacy. *Survival* 44(1): 115–133.

Jansson, J., Burke, C. & Jiang Wenran. 2009. *Chinese companies in the extractive industries of Gabon & the DRC: Perceptions of transparency.* Stellenbosch: Centre for Chinese Studies, University of Stellenbosch.

Jansson, H. & Kiala, C. 2009. *Patterns of Chinese investment, aid and trade in Mozambique.* A briefing paper by CCS prepared for World Wide Fund for Nature, October.

Jenkins, R. & Edwards, C. 2005. *The effect of China and India's growth and trade liberalization on poverty in Africa.* Norwich: Overseas Development Group.

Jenkins, R. & Edwards, C. 2006. The economic impacts of China and India on Sub-Saharan Africa: Trends and prospects. *Journal of Asian Economies* 17(2): 207–226.

Jiang Guanghua 1997. *Records on visits to foreign parties.* Beijing: World Affairs Press.

Jiang Wenran. 2006. China's booming energy ties with Africa. *Geopolitics of Energy* 28(7). https://jamestown.org/program/chinas-booming-energy-relations-with-africa

Johannes, E.M. 2011. Colonialism redux. *Proceedings Magazine*, April: 298.

Jones, M.T. 2011. China and Africa: Colonialism without responsibility. *Somalilandpress*, 20 March.

Kaplinsky, R., McCormick, D. & Morris, M. 2006. *The impact of China on Sub-Saharan Africa.* London: DFID China Office.

Kaplinsky, R. & Morris, M. 2008. Do Asian drivers undermine export-oriented industrialization in SSA? *World Development* 36(2): 254–273.

Kaplinsky, R. & Morris, M. 2009. Chinese FDI in Sub-Saharan Africa: Engaging with large dragons. *European Journal of Development Research* 21(4): 551–569.

Kaplinsky, R., Terheggen, A. & Tijaja, J. 2011. China as a final market: The Gabon timber and Thai cassava value chains. *World Development* 39(7): 1177–1190.

Keating, J. 2012. Africa: Made in China. *Foreign Policy Webzine*.

Keita, Mohamed. 2012. Africa's free press problem. *The New York Times*, 15 April.

King, K. 2013. *China's aid and soft power in Africa: The case of education and training*. Rochester, NY: James Currey.

Kragelund, P. 2007. Chinese drivers for African development? The effects of Chinese investments in Zambia. In Marcel Kitissou, ed., *Africa in China's global strategy*. London: Adonis and Abbey, 162–181.

Large, D. 2007. *China's Involvement in Armed Conflict and Post-War Reconstruction in Africa: Sudan in Comparative Context*. Copenhagen: Danish Institute for International Studies.

Larkin, B.D. 1971. *China and Africa 1949–1970*, Berkeley, CA: University of California Press.

Lawrence, P., ed. 1986. *World recession and the food crisis in Africa*. Boulder, CO: Westview Press.

Li Anshan. 2005. African studies in China the twentieth century: A historiographical survey. *African Studies Review* 48(1): 59–87.

Li Anshan. 2007. Africa in the perspective of globalization: Development, assistance and cooperation. *West Asia and Africa* 7 : 5–14.

Li Anshan. 2007a. China and Africa: Policy and challenges. *China Security* 3(3): 69–93.

Li Anshan. 2012. Neither devil nor angel: The role of media in Sino-Africa relations. allafrica, 17 May. http://allafrica.com/stories/201205180551.html

Li Anshan. 2014. Changing discourse on China–Africa relations since the 1990s. *World Economy and Politics* 2: 19–47.

Li Liqing. 2006. Communist Party of China's contacts with African political parties: History and present. *West Asia and Africa* 3: 16–19.

Li Xu. 2004. Zhejiang Normal University holds seminars for university presidents of African English-speaking countries. *West Asia and Africa* 6: 11.

Liu Haifang. 2006. China and Africa: Transcending "threat or boon". *China Monitor*, March.

Liu Haifang. 2008. China–Africa relations through the prism of culture: The dynamics of China's African cultural diplomacy. *Journal of Current Chinese Affairs* 37(3): 10–45.

Lokongo, Antoine Roger. 2009. Sino-DRC contracts to thwart the return of Western patronage. *Pambazuka News*, 11 March.

Lokongo, Antoine Roger. 2012. New AU headquarters: A tribute to China–Africa relations – a response to Chika Ezeanya, Pambazuka, 1 February. www.pambazuka.org/en/category/features/79584.

Long Xiangyang. 2000. The preliminary probe to the China–Africa relations from 1966 to 1969. In Center for African Studies of Peking University, ed. *China and Africa*. Beijing: Peking University Press: 72–86.

Looy, J. van de, 2006. *Africa and China: A strategic partnership?* Leiden: ASC.

Lyman, P.N. 2005. *China's rising role in Africa*. Boston, MA: Council on Foreign Relations.

Lyman, P.N. 2006. China's involvement in Africa: A view from the US. *South Africa Journal of International Affairs* 13(1): 129–138.

Mao Zedong. 1994. *Selections of Mao Zedong's works on diplomacy*. Beijing: Central Documentation Publishing House and World Affairs Press.

Marks, T. 2007. What's China's investment in Africa? *Black Enterprise*, 1 March.
Mbachu, D. 2006. Nigerian resources: Changing the playing field. *South African Journal of International Affairs* 13(1): 77–82.
Mbayem, S. 2011. Africa will not put up with a colonialist China. *The Guardian*, 7 February.
McCormick, D. 2008. China and India as Africa's new donors: The impact of aid on development. *Review of African Political Economy* 35(115): 73–92.
McCormick, D. 2009. African perceptions of Afro-Chinese relations. Paper presented at ERD Workshop on Financial Markets, Adverse Shocks and Coping Strategies in Fragile Countries, Accra, 21–23 May.
Mearsheimer, J.J. 2006. China's unpeaceful rise. *Current History* 105: 160–162.
Men, Jing & Barton, B., eds. 2011. *China and the European Union in Africa: Partners or competitors?* Aldershot: Ashgate.
Ministry of Commerce. 2006. China–Africa trade expected to top USD100 billion by 2010. Beijing: Ministry of Commerce.
Ministry of Commerce. 2007. Speech at the progress briefing on the implementation of the 8 Africa-Targeting Measures of the Beijing Summit of the Forum on China–Africa Cooperation. Beijing: Ministry of Commerce.
Mohammed, A. 2004. The Rezaigat camel nomads of the Darfur region of Western Sudan: From cooperation to confrontation. *Nomadic Peoples* 8 : 230–240.
Mohan, G. 2012. *China in Africa: Impacts and prospects for accountable development*. Manchester: Effective States and Inclusive Development Research Centre, University of Manchester.
Mohan, G., Tan-Mullins, M. & Power, M. 2010. Redefining "aid" in the China–Africa context. *Development and Change* 41(5): 857–881.
Mohan, R. 2002. Sakhalin to Sudan: India's energy diplomacy. *The Hindu*, 24 June.
Monson, J. 2004. Freedom railway: The unexpected successes of a Cold War development project. *Boston Review* 29(6). https://scholar.google.com/citations?view_op=view_citation&hl=en&user=uIj21aEAAAAJ&citation_for_view=uIj21aEAAAAJ:kNdYIx-mwKoC
Monson, J. 2006. Defending the people's railway in the era of liberalization. *Africa* 76(1): 113–130.
Monson, J. 2008. Liberating labour? Constructing anti-hegemony on the TAZARA Railway in Tanzania, 1965–1976. In Chris Alden, Danniel Large & Richardo Soares de Oliveira, eds, *China returns to Africa: A rising power and a continent embrace*. London: Hurst & Company, 197–219.
Monson, J. 2009. *Africa's freedom railway: How a Chinese development project changed lives and livelihoods in Tanzania*. Bloomington, IN: Indiana University Press.
Montinari, L. & Prodi, G. 2011. China's impact on intra-African trade. *The Chinese Economy* 44(4): 75–91.
Morais, R.M. de. 2011. The new imperialism: China in Angola. *World Affairs*, March/April. www.worldaffairsjournal.org/article/new-imperialism-china-angola.
Morris, M. & Einhorn, G. 2008. Globalisation, welfare and competitiveness: The impacts of Chinese imports on the South African clothing and textile industry. *Competition and Change* 12(4): 355–376.
Muekalia, J.D. 2004. Africa and China's strategic partnership. *African Security Review* 13(1): 1–11.
Mukanga, C. 2012. China's new colonialism in Africa. *Zambian Economist*, 17 May.

China's policy: Transition and discourse 199

Munyoro, F. 2008. Africa: Journalists urged to strengthen China–Africa relations. *The Herald*, 4 June.

Mwanawina, I. 2007. *An assessment of Chinese development assistance in Africa: Zambia.* Zimbabwe: African Forum and Network on Debt and Development.

Mwanawina, I. 2008. *China–Africa economic relations: The case of Zambia.* Draft scoping study. Nairobi: AERC.

Naidu, S. & Davies, M. 2006. China fuels its future with Africa's riches. *South African Journal of International Affairs* 13(2): 69–83.

Nam, Moiss. 2007. Rogue aid. *Foreign Policy* 159: 95–96.

Obwona, M. et al. 2007. *China-Africa economic relations: The case of Uganda.* Draft scoping study. Nairobi: AERC.

Odada, John E. & Matundu, Omu Kakujaha. 2008. *China-Africa economic relations: The case of Namibia.* Draft scoping study. Nairobi: AERC.

Ogunkola, E. Olawale, Bankole, Abiodun S. & Adewuyi, Adeolu. 2007. *China–Nigeria economic relations: AERC Scoping Studies on China–Africa Relations.* Revised report. Nairobi: AERC.

Ogunsanwo, Alaba. 1974. *China's policy in Africa.* Cambridge: Cambridge University Press.

Oliveira, Ricardo Soares de. 2008. Making sense of Chinese oil investment in Africa. In Chris Alden, Daniel Large & Ricardo Soares de Oliveira, eds, *China returns to Africa: A rising power and a continent embrace.* London: Hurst, 83–109.

Onjala, Joseph. 2008. *A scoping study on China–Africa economic relations: The case of Kenya.* Revised report. Nairobi: AERC.

Owusu, Francis & Carmody, Padraig R. 2007. Competing hegemons? Chinese versus American geo-economic strategies in Africa. *Political Geography* 26(5): 504–524.

Peh, Kelvin H.S. & Eyal, Jonathan. 2010. Unveiling China's impact on African environment. *Energy Policy* 38(8): 4729–4730.

Pei, Minxin. 2006. *China's trapped transition.* Cambridge, MA: Harvard University Press.

Power, Marcus & Alves, Ana Cristina, eds. 2012. *China and Angola: A marriage of convenience?* Cape Town: Pambazuka Press.

People's Daily. 1982. CPC's relations with Asian and Latin American parties are strengthened, 8 September.

People's Daily. 1983. Equality and mutual benefit, variety of forms, emphasis on effectiveness and co-development, 15 January.

Prah, Kwesi Kwaa. 2007. *Afro-Chinese relations: Past, present and future.* Cape Town: CASAS.

Qian Qichen. 2003. *Ten notes on diplomacy.* Beijing: World Affairs Press.

Qiu Deya. 2003. China's foreign aid in 2002. In Ministry of Foreign Trade and Economic Cooperation, ed., *Almanac of China's Foreign Economic Relations and Trade 2003.* Beijing: China Commerce and Trade Press.

Qu Xing. 2000. *The forty years of China's diplomacy.* Nanjing: Jiangsu People's Publishing House.

RAID. 2007. *Advice to Chinese companies operating in the mining sector in Africa.* Briefing Paper.

Renard, Mary-Françoise. 2011. China's trade and FDI in Africa. African Development Bank Working Paper No. 126.

Rocha, John. 2008. China and African natural resources: Developmental opportunity or deepening the resource curse? in Hannah Edinger, Hayley Herman & Johanna Jansson, eds., *New impulses from the South: China's engagement of Africa*. Stellenbosch: Centre for China Studies, Stellenbosch University.

Rolland, Nadège. 2021. *A new great game? Situating Africa in China's strategic thinking*. Washington, DC: National Bureau of Asian Research.

Ross, R., ed. 1993. *China, the United States, and the Soviet Union: Tripolarity and policy making in the Cold War*. New York: Sharpe.

Rotberg, R., ed. 2008. *China into Africa: Trade, aid, and influence*. Washington, DC: Brookings Institution Press.

Sautman, B. 1994. Anti-Black racism in post-Mao China. *The China Quarterly* 138: 413–437.

Sautman, B. & Yan Hairong. 2006. *East Mountain Tiger, West Mountain Tiger: China, the West, and "colonialism" in Africa*. Baltimore, MD: University of Maryland School of Law.

Sautman, B. & Yan Hairong. 2007. Wind from the East: China and Africa's development. Paper presented at the conference China's New Role in Africa and the South, Shanghai, 16–17 May.

Sautman, B. & Yan Hairong. 2007a. Friends and interests: China's distinctive links with Africa. *African Studies Review* 30(3): 75–114.

Sautman, B. & Yan Hairong, 2008. Africa perspective on China–Africa links. *The China Quarterly* 199: 728–759.

Segal, Gerald. 1992. China and Africa. *Annals of the American Academy of Political and Social Science* 519(1): 115–126.

Shichor, Y. 2005. Sudan: China's outpost in Africa. *China Brief* 5: 9–11.

Shinn, David H. & Eisenman, Joshua. 2012. *China and Africa: A century of engagement*. Philadelphia, PA: University of Pennsylvania Press.

Smith, B. 2006. Western concern at China's growing involvement in Africa. *Asian Tribune*, 10 April. www.asiantribune.com/showarticle.php?id=3102

Snow, Philip. 1988. *The Star Raft: China's encounter with Africa*. London: Weidenfeld and Nicolson.

Sorbara, Mark. 2006. With China calling, is it time to say goodbye to US and Europe? *The Nation* (Nairobi), 14 April.

Strauss, J.C. & Saavedra, M. 2009. *China and Africa: Emerging patterns in globalization and development*. Cambridge: Cambridge University Press.

Sullivan, Michael J. 1994. The 1988–89 Nanjing anti-African protests: Racial nationalism or national racism? *The China Quarterly* 138: 438–457.

Swaine, M.D. & Tellis, A.J. 2000. *Interpreting China's grand strategy*. Santa Monica, CA: Rand Corporation.

Taylor, Ian. 1997. The "captive state" of Southern Africa and China: The PRC and Botswana, Lesotho and Swaziland. *Journal of Commonwealth and Comparative Politics* 35(2): 75–95.

Taylor, Ian. 1998. Africa's place in the diplomatic competition between Beijing and Taipei. *Issues and Studies* 34(3): 126–143.

Taylor, Ian. 2011. *The Forum on China–Africa Cooperation*. London: Routledge.

Taylor, Ian. 2006. China's oil diplomacy in Africa. *International Affairs* 82(5): 937–959.

Thompson, D. 2005. China's soft power in Africa: From the "Beijing Consensus" to health diplomacy. *China Brief* 5(21): 1–5.

Thoburn, John. 2013. *China's development lessons for low income Africa: A scoping study*. Norwich: International Development UEA.
Tsikata, Dela, Fenny, Ama Pokuaa & Aryeetey, Ernest. 2008. *China–Africa relations: A case study of Ghana*. Draft scoping study. Nairobi: AERC.
Tull, Denis M. 2006. China's engagement in Africa: Scope, significance and consequences. *Journal of Modern African Studies* 44(3): 459–479.
United Nations Environment Program. 2007. Sudan Post-Conflict Environmental Assessment, June 2007. UNEP. http://postconflict.unep.ch/publications/UNEP_Sudan.pdf
Vicente, Ruben Gonzalez. 2011. China's engagement in South America and Africa's extractive sectors: New perspectives for resource curse theories. *The Pacific Review* 24(1): 65–87.
Vines, A. 2006. The scramble for resources: African case studies. *South African Journal of International Affairs* 13(1): 63–75.
Vines, A. 2007. China in Africa: A mixed blessing? *Current History* 106(700): 213–219.
Vliet, Geert van & Magrin, Geraud, eds. 2012. *The environmental challenges facing a Chinese oil company in Chad*. Paris: Agence Francaise Development.
Villoria, Nelson. 2009. China's growth and the agricultural exports of Sub-Saharan Africa. *European Journal of Development Research* 21(4): 531–550.
Villoria, Nelson. 2012. The effects of China's growth on the food prices and the food exports of other developing countries. *Agricultural Economics* 43(5): 499–514.
Wang, Jian-Ye. 2007. *What drives China's growing role in Africa?* IMF Working Paper WP/07/211.
Wang Taiping, ed. 1999. *Fifty years' diplomacy of new China*. Beijing: Beijing Press.
Wang Yuhua. 2005. Center for African Vocational Education Studies established in Tianjin University of Technology and Education. *West Asia and Africa* 4: 20.
Weinstein, W. & Henriksen T.H., eds. 1980. *Soviet and Chinese aid to African nations*. New York: Praeger.
Weng Ming. 1995. Appointing just before leaving: "Milord Qiao" led delegation to General Assembly of UN for the first time. In Fu Hao & Li Tongcheng (eds), *Great talents and their great achievement – diplomats in UN*. Beijing: Overseas Chinese Publishing House, 7–13.
Xinhua News Agency. 2007. China launched satellite for Nigeria, 14 May.
Xinhua News Agency. 2007. Sudan government deals with Darfur issue with a light pack. http://news.xinhuanet.com/world/2007-07/15/content_6377969.htm
Xinhua Newsnet. 2007. Relief of debt of RMB10.9 billion of 31 African countries. http://news.163.com/06/1029/12/2UJOAR4D.html
Xu Chunfu. 2003. Chinese medical workers building bridges of friendship with Africa. *West Asia and Africa* 5: 73–75.
Yan Hairong & Sautman, B. 2013. "The beginning of a world empire"? Contesting the discourse of Chinese copper mining in Zambia. *Modern China* 39(2): 131–164.
Yan Yiwu. 1990. The work of China's foreign aid in 1989. In Ministry of Foreign Trade and Economic Cooperation (ed.), *Almanac of China's Foreign Economic Relations and Trade*. Beijing: Ministry of Foreign Trade and Economic Cooperation, 55.
Yang Lihua. 2006. Africa: A view from China. *South African Journal of International Affairs* 13(1): 2–6.
Yu, George T. 1975. *China's African policy: A study of Tanzania*. New York: Praeger.
Yu, George T. & Longenecker, D.J. 1994. The Beijing–Taipei struggle for international recognition: From the Niger Affair to the UN. *Asian Studies* 34(5): 475–488.

Yunnan University. 2006. Working materials of the fourth seminar on the exchange of experience on the training of educational personnel from developing countries (conference papers).

Zafar, Ali. 2007. The growing relationship between China and Sub-Saharan Africa: Macroeconomic, trade, investment and aid links. *The World Bank Research Observer* 22(1): 103–130.

Zeleza, Paul Tiyambe, ed. 2007. *The study of Africa, Volume II: Global and transnational engagements.* Dakar: DODESRIA.

Zeng Jianhui. 2006. *Parliamentarian diplomacy: Communication and contention – dialogues with foreign congressmen and politicos.* Beijing: Chinese Intercontinental Press.

Zhan Shiming. 2004. African students from the University of National Defense have informal discussion at IWAAS. *West Asia and Africa* 3: 23.

Zhang Hongming. 2006. China policy of assistance enjoys popular support. *People's Daily*, 23 June. http://english.people.com.cn/200606/23/eng20060623_276714.html

Zhang Xiuqin. 2004. Educational exchanges and cooperation between China and African countries. *West Asia and Africa* 3 : 24–28.

Zhang Zhongxiang. 2006. *Mali.* Beijing: Social Sciences Academic Press.

Zhao Zuojun, Yuan Ye & Liang Shanggang. 2007. Chinese teachers entered African continent with Confucian School. *Reference News,* 7 June.

Zheng Bijian. 2005. *China's peaceful rise: Speeches of Zheng Bijian, 1997–2005.* Washington, DC: Brookings Institution Press.

Zhong Weiyun. 2000. The contemporary situation of parties in Sub-Saharan Africa and China–African parties' relationship. In Centre for African Studies of Peking University, ed., *China and Africa.* Beijing: Peking University Press, 129–142.

Zhou Jianqing. 2006. China–African economic and trade cooperation develops steadily: Survey of 2005 and prospects for 2006. *West Asia and Africa* 1: 15–18.

Zong He. 2005. China–African friendship, cooperation and common development. *West Asia and Africa* 2: 55–59.

Zweig, David and Bi Jianhai. 2005. China's global hunts for energy. *Foreign Affairs* 64(5): 25–38.

8 China's policy

Continuity and challenge

In *China's second continent: How a million migrants are building a new empire in Africa,* Howard French proposed President Jiang Zemin's visit to Africa in 1996 as a turning point in China's Africa policy:

> The most definitive commencement date was perhaps the state visit to six African countries by the then head of state, Jiang Zemin, in 1996. In a speech at the African Union headquarters in Addis Ababa, Ethiopia, Jiang proposed the creation of the Forum on China–Africa Cooperation (FOCAC). This turned out to be an important first move in a momentous two-step. Upon his return to China, Jiang gave another speech in the city of Tangshan, in which he explicitly directed the country's firms to "go out", meaning go overseas in search of business. No Chinese leader had ever said anything like that before, and from the very start Africa was clearly a principal target. Six years later, I was working in China when Jiang's Forum convened triumphantly for the first time, gathering fifty-three African leaders in Beijing. Among China's many pledges, Jiang promised to double development assistance to the continent, create a $5 billion African development fund, cancel outstanding debt, build a new African Union headquarters in Ethiopia, create three to five 'trade and cooperation' zones around the continent, build thirty hospitals and a hundred rural schools, and train fifteen thousand African professionals.
> (French 2014: 16)

Introduction

From the perspective of a historian, I found many errors just in this short paragraph: (1) In 1996, there was no African Union. (2) Jiang Zemin did not mention the setting up of FOCAC in his speech in 1996. Instead, it was the former Prime Minister of Madagascar, Lila Ratsifandrihama, who made this proposal in 1999, as indicated previously. (3) The first FOCAC was held on 10–12 October 2000, not six years after 1996. (4) More than 80 ministers from 44 African countries and representatives from 17 international regional organizations attended the first FOCAC, not "fifty-three African leaders".

DOI: 10.4324/9781003220152-10

(5) The China-Africa Development Fund was created at the China-Africa Summit (third FOCAC) in 2006, not at the first FOCAC. (6) All the measures he mentioned were issued at the China-Africa Summit in 2006, not the first FOCAC. (7) President Hu, not President Jiang, chaired the China-Africa Summit in 2006.

Interestingly, despite having so many errors in a short paragraph, this was nevertheless recommended by both *The New York Times* and *Financial Times* as one of the 100 best books of the year!

As indicated in the previous chapters, Africa is very important to China in various aspects. In January 2006, *China's African Policy*, the white paper promulgated by the Chinese government, was the first of its kind in China's diplomatic history. This document embodies a comprehensive and long-term plan for enhanced cooperation in China–Africa relations, and it marks a milestone in the progress that China and Africa have made together.

In recent years, China–Africa relations has become a fashionable subject in academia. Brautigam's work makes a great contribution to the literature. Many Western scholars opine that China neglected Africa in practice in the past 30 years, and that its comprehensive engagement with the continent not only reflects a set of ambitious and unsettling goals for the continent, but that a competitive quest for energy, trade and geopolitical interests will underscore that agenda (Muekalia 2004: 8). There are two flaws in this view. First, it ignores the historical fact. Deborah Brautigam has been engaged for a long time in the study of China–Africa relations and her doctoral dissertation on China's agricultural aid in Africa was formally published (Brautigam 1998).[1] In *The dragon's gift: The real story of China in Africa*, she describes China–Africa cooperation from the 1960s to the 1980s and reveals that even in 1978, China had aid programs in more African countries than the United States (Brautigam 2009: 42). Many Western authors ignored the fact that China–Africa cooperation is long term and consistent, not just a result of China's need for raw materials: "When no one was really looking, the groundwork for China's current engagement in Africa was being laid" (Brautigam 2009: 60). The second issue is that the view is conventional, following the old logic that the West's policies and actions in Africa are the rule and China is "rogue donor". Brautigam explains that China's mode of assistance and China–Africa cooperation under state control are a common developmental pattern rather than a communist pattern. "Rogue donor" is a Western designation for China because China has not followed the established rules. That is why Brautigam claimed that "all kinds of terror about China's aid and involvement resulted from false information" (Brautigam 2009: 210).

In addition, biased viewpoints stress practical aspects of China's policy on Africa, but fail to convey the most important element in China–African relations: the development of the relationship over the past 50 years has been based on equal treatment, respect for sovereignty and co-development. Despite many shifts in the interactions between China and Africa, certain principles have remained constant, underpinning the relationship. To accurately judge China's strategic considerations in the China–Africa relationship, it is important to understand the relation of transition and continuity in China's policy on Africa. The transition and change indicate that there is no pattern or model in China–Africa economic cooperation, or "a 'model' with no model", as Tang Xiaoyang (2020) describes it. Every step of the cooperation is carried out according to the changing situation.

Reform and continuity

The China–African relationship is not new: it dates back to ancient times and has progressed gradually based on common historical experiences (Duyvendad 1949; Filesi 1972; Snow 1988; Ma Wenkuan & Meng Fanren 1987; Shen Fuwei 1990; Ai Zhouchang & Mu Tao 1996; Li Anshan 2019). However, it was not until 1956, when Egypt became the first African nation to establish diplomatic relations with the People's Republic of China (PRC) that inter-governmental relations between the PRC and African countries were inaugurated. Over the subsequent half-century, the trajectory of China–Africa relations has undergone several fundamental shifts.

From the establishment of the PRC to its economic opening up (1949–1978), China's Africa policy was heavily influenced by ideology. During this period, China's foreign policy was deeply impacted by the unique international environment of the time (Ross 1993: 1–16). China placed itself on the front line of the struggle against colonialism, imperialism and revisionism in the Third World (Mao Zedong 1994). By linking its ideological stand with its foreign policy, China's diplomacy in Africa was initially circumscribed by Beijing's ideological position (Qu Xing 2000: 375–376). In the wake of the China–Soviet split in the 1960s, China accused the pro-Soviet communist parties in various African countries of "revisionism", regarding them as ideological rivals. Based on this political bias, China refused requests by some African parties to establish diplomatic relations. All ties between CPC and pro-Soviet political parties in Africa were severed. This situation was changed only during Chairman Hua Guofeng's government in 1977 (Jiang Guanghua 1997: 191, 451, 667).[2]

From 1949 to 1978, China's policy on Africa stressed politics, fully supporting the independence movements in Africa and going beyond mere moral support to the provision of weapons and human assistance for the movement (Jiang Guanghua 1997:130, 303–305, 442–443, 621–622). China trained and educated 2675 military intellectuals for Africa between 1955 and 1977 (Weinstein & Henriksen 1980: 102–111). Following the wave of national independence throughout most parts of Africa, China sought Africa as an ally in its struggles against imperialism and hegemony.[3] During these times of political orientation, economic assistance was provided to Africa gratis, even though China's own domestic economic circumstances were far from optimal. Despite the Soviet Union supplying more arms than other nations to Africa during the 1970s, its economic aid to the continent was far behind that of China (Chazan et al. 1992: 410). In short, relations were narrow in scope and without a practical or sustainable basis.

During this period, China aided Africa with billions of dollars despite China's own economic situation being precarious. Yet the financial assistance alone is unlikely to significantly transform the reality of the poverty in the continent.[4] Although the political atmosphere changed dramatically in China during the mid-1960s, a dogmatic approach was maintained in relations with Africa. At the beginning of the Cultural Revolution, China's diplomacy was affected by an ultra-leftist mentality. Some scholars have described China's aims in Africa at that time as promoting Maoism (Cornelissen & Taylor 2000: 616; Brautigam 1998: 175–195). The so-called "exporting revolution" became the primary objective for Africa, something that was challenged by the African countries on the receiving end. This campaign threatened the power and position of many African governments and deviated from the principle of "non-interference in internal affairs". Thus, only a handful of groups in Africa (for example, the Ethiopian People's Revolutionary Party) sustained contact with the CPC.

Using aid as the basis to build bilateral relations was an approach largely formulated in 1963–1964, when Premier Zhou Enlai proposed the "Five Principles governing the development of relations with Arab and African countries" and the "Eight Principles of economic assistance" during his visit to Africa (Huang Zhen 1987; Li Jiasong 2001: 310–311). In this period, China supported the political struggles for African independence and provided free aid to Africa. It was a time when China also helped African countries build a number of landmark structures (e. g. stadiums, hospitals, conference centres) – projects that were more than just bricks and mortar. They were national symbols of independence and embodied the spirit of cultural decolonisation (Huang Zequan 2000). At the end of the 1960s, China ended its policy of "exporting revolution" and started to provide more aid to Africa that was "free and unconditional". As a result, the broad-based relationship between China and Africa gradually recovered (Ogunsanwo 1974; Barnouin & Yu Changgen 1998; Wang Qinmei 1999; Long Xiangyang 2000). Despite high economic costs, these projects provided important assistance to African countries in need of moral support in forming a national consciousness (Li Anshan 2004: 291–300) and resulted in a positive impression of China in the minds of the African people, laying a solid foundation for the path ahead in China–Africa relations. By 1978, China had established diplomatic relations with 43 African countries.

The end of the Cultural Revolution marked a shift in China's policy on Africa from one based almost exclusively on ideological alliance to one with a far more pragmatic and diversified approach. With a new political direction and the uncertainty of economic development in China, the period from 1979 to 1982 saw a temporary fluctuation in China–Africa relations: economic assistance was reduced, accompanied by a decline in bilateral trade and a drop in the number of medical teams (Almanac of China's Foreign Economic Relations and Trade Editorial Board, 1994: 62). The 12th CPC National Congress in 1982 officially marked a shift from a policy that emphasised "war and revolution" to one focused on "peace and development". Likewise, China shifted from policies emphasising that "economy serves diplomacy" to those based on "diplomacy serves the economy". In the same year, the Chinese premier visited Africa and announced the "Four Principles".[5] This shifted the stress to practical effectiveness in assistance and in relations more generally, as well as to a spirit of "developing together".

The 12th National Congress of the CPC in 1982 decided on two strategic elements that had implication for China's policy on Africa. First, the country would emphasise Chinese domestic economic development. Second, China would pursue a peaceful and independent foreign policy.[6] The implication was that China sought to bring the relationship down to earth and base it on very practical goals applicable within its means. The 12th CPC Congress established principles for a new type of political relationship based on "independence, complete equality, mutual respect, and non-interference in others' internal affairs" (*People's Daily* 1983). Thus, in the 1980s, China attuned its economic assistance to Africa by attempting to make Africa help itself. China also began to explore reforming its foreign trade system and its approaches to foreign assistance. Economic assistance began to include other forms of support, such as preferential and discounted loans, cooperatives and joint ventures for projects in Africa (Li Anshan 2006a). Cooperatives and joint ventures helped to bring new technology and management practices to projects in Africa, while preferential loans obliged African nations to use money more effectively (Lin Mei 1997). Sixteen African countries benefited from such initiatives during the first two years of China's new aid policy (Almanac of China's Foreign Economic Relations and Trade Editorial Board, 1997: 75). Such shifts were not a retreat by China from its commitment to relations with Africa; on the contrary, they sped up and expanded economic cooperation in various fields.

Such shifts led to party-to-party relations between the CPC and numerous African countries, representing a breakthrough in the diplomatic history of China–Africa inter-party relations, thus giving great impetus to the development of China–Africa relations. It tried to ensure that the two sides maintained a steady course despite political transitions of African governments. By 2002, the CPC had established relations with more than 60 political parties in 40 sub-Saharan countries, which included both ruling and non-ruling parties (Jiang Guanghua 1997: 191, 451, 667, 670–671; Li Liqing 2006; Zhong Weiyun 2000: 129–142). Relations based on these principles have convinced many Africans of China's sincerity in respecting African political choices and helping to promote economic and trade cooperation.[7] This new direction also shifted China's focus to "economic co-development" in its relations with Africa. Therefore, more extensive cooperation took place on far more diverse levels than previously.

China's new approach expanded its relations with Africa in many ways, including enhanced economic and trade cooperation, cultural and educational exchange, medical and public health, military exchange and non-governmental communications (Mahamat 2006: 4). Another noteworthy shift in China's African policy was the change from providing free aid to assistance intended to benefit both sides economically.

However, a reorientation of China's policy on Africa has given priority to economic cooperation. The rich natural resources of Africa help satisfy China's increasing demand for raw materials and energy. Conversely, Chinese energy investment in Africa is often accompanied by aid for infrastructure, which helps to attract more foreign investment in Africa. In Sudan, Chinese companies have been involved in the oil production industry for roughly a decade. Not only does China now import a great percentage of Sudan's total oil exports,[8] but these companies also help Sudan to establish a complete and viable oil export industry from exploration, production and refining to sales of crude oil, gasoline and petrochemical products (Oilnews Online 2002). China also shares the benefits of trade and commerce with Africa. In 2006, trade volume between China and Africa reached a value of US$55.5 billion, with African exports to China making up over half of that at US$28.8 billion (*China Daily* 30 January 2007).

China's African policy has thus shifted from an unsustainable and ideologically motivated approach to political pragmatism and on to the present relationship based on economic pragmatism. While these shifts have markedly changed China–Africa relations over the past 50 years, another look reveals the persistence of core principles that continue to underpin the relationship.

Change in policy, not principle

Equality

Equality is a principle that indicates equal treatment and respect for sovereignty for both sides, and extends to the principles of non-interference, mutual benefit and co-development. China is highly sensitised to notions of sovereignty and equality among nations. This is largely because violations of China's sovereignty by other major powers and the intervention of outside powers in China's internal affairs have been salient diplomatic threats since the foundation of the PRC (Qu Xing 2000: 375–376). Past experience has led China's foreign policy to embrace a principle of "non-interference" in the internal affairs of other sovereign countries. This principle emphasises sovereignty as the common denominator among all nations, regardless of other factors, and fundamentally holds that all countries should be equal and no country has the right to dictate the sovereign affairs of others.

The principle of equality in China's dealings with other countries is more than a slogan. Although today the concept is largely the norm between individuals, it has never been applied effectively to the realm of international relations. Powerful nations have always made the rules in the global community. Perhaps China's practice in Africa challenges this reality and offers an alternative model for interstate behaviour.

Non-interference

The principle of non-interference has served to safeguard China's own sovereign rights. Take human rights as an example. The West is inclined to believe that human rights arose historically from a need to protect citizens from abuse by the state, which might suggest that all nations have a duty to intervene and protect people wherever they are. But the developing countries, including China and most African nations, argue that state sovereignty is paramount, not least because the human rights-protection regime is a state-based mechanism. A non-interference principle holds that human rights should not be a reason for one country to interfere in others' internal affairs (*People's Daily* 3 April 2006). By holding to this principle, China can both ensure its own sovereignty and gain the trust of African nations. Over the past decade, proposals against China's human rights were defeated 11 times at the United Nations. Without the support of African nations, China could not have defeated those proposals.

Both China and Africa have suffered the ill-effects of the colonial era. This shared experience underlies the ideas of equality and respect for sovereignty that both highlight in their approach to international relations. For example, China shares with the African Union (AU) the policy of non-interference on the Zimbabwean issue. In 2005, when Robert Mugabe demolished countless urban dwellings in an attempt to crack down on illegal shanty towns in Harare, Britain and the United States called on the AU to act. However, the AU felt it wasn't appropriate for the AU Commission to start running the internal affairs of member-states and gave Mugabe its blessing to resist sanctions imposed by the West (*The Guardian* 25 January 2005).

In the context of Darfur, there is debate in the international community over whether the situation there should be described as "genocide", which would invoke a responsibility on the part of the international community to protect the people there. The United States was the only major player to describe the conflict as "genocide"; neither the United Nations nor regional organizations use this term to describe that complex issue.[9] While the situation in Darfur is complicated, China and Africa share the view that different countries are in different stages of development and it is neither fair nor effective to use the standard of developed countries to judge the situation of developing countries. This foreign policy approach has remained unchanged since the beginning of China–African relations.

But the principle of non-interference is not fixed in the AU. When joining the AU, all members agree on the aim of bringing an end to intra-African conflict. In Sierra Leone and Liberia, the AU has stepped in to halt humanitarian disasters. In Togo and Mauritania, the AU intervened in support of democracy. China respects the AU's principles and the goal to end conflict on the continent, but as an outsider considers it has no right to intervene in the domestic affairs of African countries even though there are many critics of China's policy. Even in the face of human rights violations and political corruption in African countries (Eisenman 2005; Shichor 2005: 9–11; Eisenman & Kurlantzick 2006: 223), China does not consider itself qualified to make judgements on the domestic affairs of African countries and considers the AU more qualified to do so. In diplomatic discussions with African nations, China does make suggestions on issues of governance and intra-state affairs. What distinguishes Chinese suggestions from Western intervention is that they are provided in a friendly rather than a coercive manner.

On the Darfur issue, China consistently opposed the economic sanctions on Sudan (Reuters 31 May 2007). China believes the Darfur issue is related to development, where sanctions would only bring more trouble to the region, especially in light of a UN Environment Program (UNEP 2007) report that states: "Environmental degradation, as well as regional climate instability and change, are major underlying causes of food insecurity and conflict in Darfur" (Reuters 31 May 2007). Since the Darfur issue is a conflict between different Sudanese peoples, and nation-building is a difficult process for any country, the international community has to give Sudan some time to solve the problem. China's aid targets the root cause of conflict: poverty. China has aided infrastructure development such as schools, hospitals and water projects for Sudan, given $10 million in humanitarian aid and promised to offer more (*China Daily* 27 July 2007).

China also insists on using influence without interference. It views respect as vital to finding solutions. China has used its ties with the Sudan to persuade the Sudanese government to cooperate with the UN (*Chutian Metropolis Daily* 8 July 2007). Since China had sought to alleviate the suffering of the Sudanese people with a solution agreeable to all parties, the Sudanese government trusted China and had finally accepted the "hybrid peacekeeping force" in Darfur (Xinhua News Agency 2007b). The turning point for the political process resulted from negotiations with the Sudanese government based on equality – not coercion or the threat of sanctions. In fact, over the past 50 years China has never used its aid commitments to intervene in African countries' internal affairs. However, this principle of non-interference reflects China's respect for the economic and political choices that African nations make – a position, it should be noted, that does not always play to China's advantage. A good example is the failed purchase of the interests sold by a Canadian oil firm in the Sudan, as indicated in the previous chapter (Sautman & Yan Hairong 2007: 3).

Mutual benefit and co-development

China and Africa have always supported the common development of politics, economics and other areas. Prior to the 1980s, China backed the anti-colonial struggles and independence movements in Africa. During this period, numerous African nations returned the favour and gave political support to China. In 1971, China regained its seat at the United Nations with the help of 26 votes from African countries (out of 76 affirmative votes). The Chinese people acknowledge that the developing countries helped with this (Weng Ming 1995: 9). China has supported African candidates for the position of UN Secretary-General as well as reform of the Security Council in favour of greater representation of African nations, while the African countries have supported China on the issues of human rights and Taiwan (Qian Qichen 2003: 55).

Some African scholars reaffirm China's role in helping African economies to achieve long-term growth through the principle of mutual benefit (Davies & Corkin 2006: 10). One particularly poignant analysis explains that, "Unlike Belgium, which built roads solely for the extraction of resources in the Democratic Republic of Congo, China is constructing or improving roads that are suitable not only for the transport of resources but which citizens can also use to travel" (Marks 2007: 34). Mutual benefit is also reflected in such areas as fair trade and debt reduction. China will further open its market to Africa by lifting tariffs on the number of items (from 190 to over 440 before the end of 2009) exported by countries in Africa that are least developed and have diplomatic relations with China (Xinhua News Agency, 2007a). In addition, when China benefits economically from Africa's emerging markets, it reduces and relieves African countries' debts. At the Beijing Summit of the Forum on China–Africa Cooperation (FOCAC) in 2006, China waived all debt from governmental interest-free loans due at the end of 2005 for 31 heavily indebted African countries.[10]

Technical assistance and cooperation in science and technology with Africa are an area that has largely been ignored by Western countries but is now a rapidly expanding part of China–Africa relations.[11] The collaboration between China and Nigeria to launch a communications satellite, Nig-Sat I, is a groundbreaking project in which China has provided much of the technology necessary for launch, on-orbit service and even the training of Nigerian command and control operators (Xinhua News Agency 2007a). Additionally, China sent oil expert and engineer Wang Qiming of Daqin to Sudan to provide African engineers with new technology that assists with the best-use practices of seemingly exhausted oil fields (*China Petroleum Daily* 26 June 2007).

Summit diplomacy

China's core Africa policy principles have been elucidated by China's leaders. Chairman Mao, meeting Asian and African visitors for the first time in 1964, declared them close friends (Li Jiasong 2001: 32–33). Despite changes in leadership and a transformation of political outlooks, in reinforcing China's position in 2006 President Hu Jintao stated that, "China and Africa are good friends, good partners and good brothers" (*People's Daily* 22 June 2006).

212 *Policy and implementation*

Major meetings or "summit diplomacy" between Chinese and African heads of state also clearly reveal China's core policy principles (Lu Ting'en 2000). Since the 1960s, these meetings have been a key way to establish direct communication at the highest levels of government and set the tone of relations and bilateral policies. They have created mutual trust between heads of state and demonstrated mutual respect between China and African countries. As early as 1963–64, Premier Zhou's visits to Africa impacted the structure of international relations as China won the friendship of many African nations, expanding its diplomatic reach.[12]

Throughout China's policy shifts in Africa in the 1980s, the Chinese premier initiated more visits to Africa, designed to reassure Africa of China's committed friendship despite China's burgeoning growth and new business partnerships with previous ideological competitors. China stated publicly, "We will not forget old friends when making new friends, or forget poor friends when making rich friends" (Almanac of China's Foreign Economic Relations and Trade Editorial Board, 1986: 47).

Importantly, summit diplomacy has sought to instil confidence in the consistent application of these principles to China–Africa relations. Reinforcing China–Africa cooperation on the basis of equality has become a tradition in Chinese diplomacy. While the West largely neglected Africa after the Cold War, China's foreign minister made his visits to African nations the first official stop abroad in every year from 1991 to 2007. These visits have been both symbolic and real gestures of China's respect for Africa. Since the turn of the 21st century, two-way visits have increased dramatically.[13] FOCAC has also been established, which in addition to its ambitious plans for China–African cooperation provides a mechanism for routine meetings between Chinese and African heads of state.

Challenges and risks

While Africa has been transformed by China's growing presence on the continent, conflict has also surfaced with expanding interaction, particularly with labour practices and market strategies, competing commercial and national interests, competition from Western players already established on the continent and striking a sustainable balance between industry and the environment. China has recognised these challenges and is searching for the most tenable solutions.

Labour practices and market strategies

With Chinese businesses and manufactured goods flowing into Africa, conflict over differing labour practices and market strategies has arisen between Chinese and African enterprises. Chinese entrepreneurs rarely employ local workers in Africa (CNTextile.com 7 November 2006). Instead, they are accustomed to bringing in labourers from China and most management positions are filled by Chinese nationals. From an economic perspective, it is more efficient and convenient for Chinese entrepreneurs to recruit skilled workers in China than to train local workers. The former are often more familiar with the technologies and face fewer language and cultural obstacles in communication with management. Chinese labourers abroad are also more compliant with the demanding labour practices Chinese managers insist upon, and are accustomed to working longer hours, working during local holidays and working overtime on weekends (*Southern Weekly* 26 July 2007). Employing African workers entangles Chinese enterprises in local laws to a greater degree than employing Chinese nationals. There is no doubt that these factors have a dramatic effect on efficiency.

Chinese company practices also lead to discontent among the communities in which these enterprises operate, which perceive that Chinese companies are not contributing enough to local economies and employment (Brookes 2007). However, China's participation in African markets does help to improve the situation of African communities, judging from the newly built roads and railways, schools and hospitals, residential areas and supermarkets, dams and power states, oil refineries and exports. Furthermore, as the role of Chinese enterprises shifts in Africa, the opportunity to contribute more to African society will emerge. In the past, Chinese enterprises were engaged in finite, short-term infrastructural "aid projects". However, profit-driven Chinese businesses are increasingly establishing themselves in African countries, with longer-term prospects. While for the moment such enterprises hire Chinese workers due to the short-term benefits they provide, as Chinese business continues to expand in Africa, it will shift towards greater localisation of its practices. This change has the potential to eventually lower production costs and build a virtuous cycle of increased investment by Chinese companies and benefits to the local community.[14]

Another source of conflict arises from the success of Chinese goods in African markets, which are often of better quality and cheaper than local products. While African consumers are happy, parallel domestic industries (especially textile industries) suffer as a result. This conflict is evidenced through two mass demonstrations in Dakar: one in support of Chinese merchants, the other in opposition.[15] Similar protests have occurred in South Africa. However, tensions dissipated when China–South African government discussions on the issue led China to unilaterally impose quotas upon its textile exports in order to allow South African producers time to make their products competitive. Solving these situations has been difficult, but involves, in the first place, consultation between the two governments. It is interesting to look at the issue from another perspective. Owing to the South Africans' complaints about Chinese goods, the Chinese government once decided to reduce Chinese textile exports to South Africa. In the seminar China–Africa Link held by the Hong Kong University of Science and Technology on 11–12 November 2006, a South African scholar stated that it was certain South Africa could benefit from the Chinese government's decision to reduce its textile exports to South Africa, but it still had to deal with the challenges posed by textiles from Malaysia, Vietnam and other developing countries. The key to the textile problem for South Africa is not to cut imports of Chinese textiles, but to strengthen the competitive edge of South African textiles. In this regard, routine multilateral talks between China and Africa have the potential to play an important role, as the two sides can rapidly facilitate communication between the conflicting parties, reach an understanding and diffuse trade frictions before they escalate any further. In addition, China's willingness to export technologies to Africa will also help local industries to gradually raise the quantity and quality of production.

Chinese national vs corporate interests

The reality is that the interests of Chinese corporations operating in Africa lie in maximising short-term economic gains, while Chinese national interests are more long term and centred on the overall relationship between China and Africa.

Take the oil industry as an example. The main purpose of Chinese transnational oil enterprises in Africa is to make profits, which in this case often means selling processed oil back to the country of origin or another country wishing to purchase it, rather than back to China. In 1999, the Sudan project undertaken by CNPC began producing oil with an annual crude production figure over two million tons. However, only 266,000 tons were imported to China (Zha Daojiong 2006: 56). Although CNPC is a state holding company, its pursuit of profit does not necessarily coincide with China's pursuit of national interests.

The view that state-owned enterprises (SOEs) can be equated with the state is largely outdated (Huang Sujian & Yu Jing 2006). Government and SOEs must compromise in order to maximise benefits for their increasingly divergent interests. China's inability to control the actions of its SOEs in Africa has been the subject of intense criticism by the West, and is a significant cause of Western concerns about China's rising influence in Africa. This censure is unreasonable when the diverging interests and increasingly distant relationship between the government and these companies are taken into account.

Some Western analysts have criticised China's developing relations with Africa as based purely on securing oil supplies and other natural resources (Giry 2005: 9–23; Lyman 2005), which has led to claims that China supports authoritarian regimes at the expense of "democracy" and "human rights" (Eisenman 2005). China–Africa relations were established long before China's demand for raw materials caused it to shift from being a net oil exporter to importer in 1993. Also, while China imports oil from Africa, it exports electromechanical and high-tech products that satisfy critical needs in Africa, creating a rough equilibrium in economic and trade relations between China and Africa. The oil drilling and exploration rights China has obtained in Africa were obtained through international bidding mechanisms in accordance with international market practices, posing no "threat" to any particular country. Rights to oilfields in Sudan and Nigeria were purchased by Chinese companies after the withdrawal of competitors (Agence France-Presse 19 May 2006).

Western suspicion and criticism

The presence of Western powers has been felt in Africa – from the colonial legacy and their geo-strategic influence during the Cold War to the current advantage that their transnational corporations hold on the continent. Western countries still consider Africa in terms of their "spheres of influence" and China is usually considered an "external player" in the region (Berger 2006; Lyman 2006). As the Chinese presence in Africa spreads and deepens, it is likely that conflicts between Chinese and Western interests will emerge, particularly in the competition to secure energy supplies.

As for the criticism that China is dealing with corrupt African regimes, a number of issues are at stake. First, the limits and norms of the international system only allow China to deal with sovereign states through their governments. Second, China has its own problems of human rights and corruption, and therefore feels it does not have the right to criticise others. All governments – the West included – as well as international financial institutions also have corrupt elements. Rather than preaching good governance to others, they would gain far more credibility and avoid the label of hypocrisy if they first tackled their own corrupt practices (Bossard 2007). Third, each nation may have a different judgement and opinion of "corruption". China does not necessarily accept naming and shaming certain African regimes as corrupt by Western standards.

In its relations with Western powers in Africa, China needs both courage and wisdom: the courage to withstand Western criticism of its African policy, and the wisdom to fully engage with Africa while at the same time reassuring Western powers that such acts will not contradict their interests. The West and China have common interests in Africa regarding economic development and environmental protection. For example, China, Africa and Western countries must discuss effective methods for increasing cooperation on the continent. Creating mechanisms of mutual trust and improving dialogue are the best ways to prevent potential conflicts between China and the West over Africa.

Sustainable development

China has now realised the importance of comprehensive development, not just GDP growth. While China's past 30 years of rapid economic growth have led to unprecedented achievements, its negative effects are also becoming apparent. They include poor workplace safety, a deteriorating environment and a deficient social safety system, all of which must be balanced against sustainable economic growth. Worse, some harmful and damaging Chinese practices are making their way into Africa. If China transplants these problems to Africa, they will not only impact the healthy development of China–Africa relations, but also the future wellbeing of African people.

Because a culture of corporate responsibility has yet to mature in China, some of its unsafe production methods have appeared in Africa.[16] Unsafe working conditions in China lead to the deaths of 320 Chinese people each day (Cheng Siwei 2007). In 2005, a blast at an explosives factory on the premises of a copper mine in Zambia killed 47 people; both the mine and the explosives factory were owned by Chinese enterprises (*New Zealand Herald* 21 April 2005). The Vice-Chairman of the Standing Committee of the National Congress of China, Cheng Siwei, has harshly criticised Chinese enterprises, warning that a lack of social responsibility toward the communities in which they are working will threaten their reputation and even their viability in African markets (Cheng Siwei 2007).

Another issue – perhaps the most pressing in China now – is the environmental implications of China's rapid economic development. Some progress is being made as the Chinese government works to standardise the behaviour of Chinese enterprises overseas through the development of environmental and corporate laws.[17] Through these regulations, companies working overseas must factor social responsibility into their business plans and the Chinese government will have a closer supervisory role over them and an approval system for project applications. Successful implementation of these regulations will require government-to-government cooperation between China and African nations. The action plan agreed upon at the China–Africa Summit stresses the critical need for both sides to enhance communication and cooperation on environmental protection.

Coevolutionary pragmatism: A "model" without a model

Tang Xiaoyang represents China–Africa economic cooperation as "coevolutionary pragmatism" (Tang Xiaoyang 2020). This term describes the effect of co-development of both sides, a process that has occurred during the last decades. For China, the interests of Chinese corporations operating in Africa have tried to gain what they need in the continent while African interests are practically realised, as indicated in the example of Ethiopia, Sudan, Angola, Kenya, Ghana, Algeria and so on. On the whole, FOCAC has promoted overall cooperation in economic, political and social fields between China and Africa. As Tang Xiaoyang illustrates in his book, "the China–Africa interaction gradually move structural transformation forward and spread the impact of this transformation to various aspects of African society" (Tang Xiaoyang 2020: 44).

The view that state-owned enterprises (SOEs) can be equated with the state is largely outdated (Huang Sujian & Yu Jing 2006). The government and SOEs must compromise in order to maximise benefits for their increasingly divergent interests. China's weak control of the actions of its SOEs in Africa has been the subject of intense criticism by the West and is a significant cause of Western concerns about China's rising influence in Africa. This censure is unreasonable when the diverging interests and increasingly distant relationship between the government and these companies are taken into account.

China's need for raw materials and energy enables the rich resources of Africa to be fully utilised, benefiting both Chinese purchasers and African suppliers. Chinese demand has stimulated raw material prices, increasing the income of resource-rich African countries and accelerating African development. For example, Nigeria has paid off its outstanding loans (Li Anshan 2006); Sudan has gone from being a net oil importer to an exporter. The investment of over 800 Chinese enterprises has promoted African industries and is breaking the longstanding hold that the West has had over trade in commodities between Africa and the rest of the world (Naidu & Davies 2006). Such investment is also enhancing the autonomy of African countries in production, sales and investment, which offers Africa more opportunities in terms of market options, investment partners and product prices. In addition, in order to carry out the trade, China has helped African countries to build the roads, railways and ports, as well as with the production of finished goods. Moreover, China–African cooperation in trade in resources and other fields has gradually made an impact on the industrialisation of Africa, thus it has the potential to help Africa win greater and truer independence, especially in the economic field.

After case studies in different fields, such as trade, infrastructure, agriculture, manufacturing, Special Economic Zones, employment and training, and social and environmental responsibility, Tang Xiaoyang has realised that what effectively drives China's quick growth and China's great impact on Africa is not specific incidents, development model or political or economic patterns, since the impact of incidents is temporary. China's long-lasting and comprehensive ties with Africa is "attributed mainly to the adoption of pragmatism in the collaboration", which consists of three interrelated elements: "(1) the unwavering target to promote sustainable economic development, (2) corresponding transformation toward market economy and industrialization, and (3) flexible approaches to coordinate multiple aspects and interact with partners during the transformation." He has therefore reached the conclusion that, "The key to China's success is, paradoxically, the lack of a defined model, as it allows diverse practices and flexible adjustments" (Tang Xiaoyang 2020: 259, 265). The coevolution pragmatism testifies that it is only by taking care of the interests of the local society and considering the establishment of good relations with African people that the mutual benefit of both Chinese enterprises and local communities can be guaranteed.

Conclusion

China can enhance bilateral and multilateral cooperation by continuing to use its unique multilateral channels with Africa and international mechanisms, such as UN peacekeeping operations, to secure Africa's future. China can also use such routes to minimise and prevent conflict both today and in the future. China should exchange information and promote full and flexible consultations with other groups affected by its relations with Africa.

In order to manage the growing tensions resulting from the closer economic relationship between China and Africa, China must increase the frequency and depth of consultations with both African nations and other nations with interests in Africa. These tensions are most acute in the context of energy. China can help to reduce tensions resulting from competition for energy resources in Africa by building mutual trust in relations with other emerging countries (India and Brazil, for example), the European Union nations, the Group of Seven powers and international organisations. China should also initiate dialogue with a view to establishing an energy security mechanism on the basis of enhancing joint research and development of alternative energy sources.

China's programme of assistance will also require cooperation with other donors so that resources are used in the most effective way possible and the maximum benefit for Africa is obtained. The international effort of research and development related to AIDS and malaria control also provides broad prospects for medical cooperation and coordination between China and the United States or European countries in Africa (Stith 2006; Li Anshan 2007, 2007a). In order to achieve this, reliable mechanisms for collaboration based on mutual trust should be made a priority to help Africa.[18]

China–Africa cooperation has played a positive and multifaceted role in Africa. However, China's expanded presence in Africa brings new challenges for China's policies on the continent. From a perspective of dialectics, it is a promising sign of more challenges between China and Africa relations. If there is no contact, there is no challenge. More challenges indicate more contacts. The important thing is for both China and Africa to face the problems and make an effort to find a solution. When one problem is solved, the relations get better. It is natural that China's policies will lag behind the rapidly evolving economic, social and security environment in Africa and so it will need to adjust accordingly. Although committed to meeting these fluid challenges, China will never waver in its principles of treating Africa with equality, respect and mutual development.

Notes

1 Professor Brautigam maintains good relations with many Chinese scholars and once visited the Centre for African Studies in Peking University and exchanged ideas with my colleagues and me. She sent me her book *The dragon's gift* in Bamako in 2011 when the China-DAC Project invited her to a conference on China-Africa Experience Sharing in Agriculture in Mali.
2 In 1977, under the leadership of Chairman Hua Guofeng, the Political Bureau of the CPC made a positive decision and the International Department of the CPC began to receive African party delegations in 1978 (Ai Ping 2000). This was a breakthrough in the CPC's history of foreign affairs. Since then, the CPC's relations with African parties have been greatly promoted.

3 For Africa's different response to the ideologies of the Soviet Union and China, see Ottaway 1978: 77–487.
4 Hu Yaobang, former General Secretary of the CPC, pointed out in 1982 that, "According to historical experience and economic situation, the form of 'giving as a gift' in foreign economic aid is harmful to both sides" (Documentation Office of CPC Central Committee 1982: 1127–1128).
5 Namely, the principles of equality and mutual benefit, variety of forms, emphasis on effectiveness and co-development (*People's Daily* 1983).
6 For a description of the 12th CPC Congress, see www.people.com.cn/GB/shizheng/252/5089/5104/5276/20010429/467489.html
7 The former Party Secretary of Beijing, Jia Qinglin, visited Uganda and promoted coffee trade cooperation in 2000; the former Party Secretary of Shandong Province, Wu Guanzheng, and the Party Secretary of Guangdong Province visited in 2001; Zhang Dejiang and the Party Secretary of Hubei Province visited in 2005; and Yu Zhengsheng visited Africa and the economic and trade delegation signed many cooperation agreements with African countries.
8 In 2006, China took 64 per cent of Sudan's oil exports (Pan 2006).
9 US Department of State 2007. For more information on the list of declarations of genocide in Darfur, see http://en.wikipedia.org/wiki/International_response_to_the_Darfur_conflict Declarations_of_genocide
10 China has remitted a total debt of US$10.9 billion owed by 21 African countries. Xinhua News Agency, 17 October 2006.
11 At the international conference on China's New Role in Africa and Global South (17 May, Shanghai), a Kenyan student pointed out that the United States has been doing business with Nigeria for decades, but it has never thought about launching the satellite for Nigeria. China did it; although partly for the Chinese government's benefit, it will definitely benefit Nigerians as well.
12 Brian Horton, chief diplomatic correspondent of Reuters, believes that Zhou Enlai's visit is "a big move for China to expand China's presence and influence in Africa" and "a significant development in Asian-African political relations and the relations between the East and the West". *The Christian Science Monitor* published an article, "Beijing focuses on Africa", on 9 December 1963, stating that this visit "has long-term significance" and "helps to confirm the remote but mutual-beneficial relations between Beijing and burgeoning Africa", and "this relation may reposition the diplomacy of countries in the international community in the coming ten years". AFP and other European media also said that Zhou Enlai's visit to Africa was the start of China's important diplomatic offensive to Africa (Lu Ting'en 2000: 5).
13 In 2000, five national leaders of African countries visited China, and five Chinese counterparts visited Africa; between 2002 and 2004, 30 national leaders of African countries visited China.
14 For example, a Chinese oil company is improving its practice in Sudan, which was praised by both the Sudanese government and people (*Economic Daily*, 13 July 2007).
15 From a discussion with American scholar D.Z. Osborn and a conversation with Togo journalist Adama Gaye at the seminar China in Africa: Geopolitical and Geo-economic Considerations, Harvard University, 31 May–2 June.
16 African investment came under supervision from 8 October 2006: http://news2.eastmoney.com/061008,490464.html

17 The Chinese government has put into effect a series of laws and regulations to enhance the management of foreign aid and foreign labour service cooperation projects, such as the "Measures for the Accreditation of Qualifications of Enterprises Undertaking the Construction of the Complete Foreign-aid Projects" (2004), "Measures for the Accreditation of Qualifications of Projects for Foreign-aid Materials" (2004) and "Administrative Regulations on Operation Qualifications of Foreign Cooperation of Labor Service". At the time of writing, the government was working on the "Provisions of the Management of Foreign Contracted Projects" and the "Provisions of the Management of foreign Cooperation of Labor Service".

18 China and Europe, as well as China and the United States, are trying to build this mutual trust system. The Center for Strategic and International Studies report on the relations between China and Africa in 2007 also addressed the possibility and necessity for China and Africa to build bilateral and multilateral cooperation as well as cooperation between governments, enterprises and non-governmental organizations. See Gill et al. (2007). This report was released after its delegations returned from the mission of exchanging opinions with China on the relations between China, Africa and the United States.

References

Agence France-Presse. 2006. Nigeria gives China oil exploration licences after auction, 9 May.

Ai Ping. 2000. Communist Party of China's contacts with African political parties. In Chen Gongyuan, ed., *Strategic reports on the development of China–African relationship in the 21st century*. Beijing: Chinese Association of African Studies, 12–17.

Ai Zhouchang & Mu Tao. 1996. *The history of relations between China and Africa*. Shanghai: East China Normal University Press.

Almanac of China's Foreign Economic Relations and Trade Editorial Board. 1986. *Almanac of China's foreign economic relations and trade 1986*. Beijing: China Foreign Economic and Trade Press.

Almanac of China's Foreign Economic Relations and Trade Editorial Board. 1994. *Almanac of China's foreign economic relations and trade 1994*. Beijing: China Social Press.

Almanac of China's Foreign Economic and Trade Yearbook Editorial Board. 1997. *Almanac of China's foreign economic relations and trade yearbook 1997–98*. Beijing: China Economics Press/China Economic Herald Press.

Barnouin, B. & Yu Changgen. 1998. *Chinese foreign policy during the Cultural Revolution*. Boulder, CO: Westview Press.

Berger, B. 2006. China's engagement in Africa: Can the EU sit back? *South African Journal of International Affairs* 13(1): 115–127.

Bossard, P. 2007. China's role in financing African infrastructure. Paper presented at China's New Role in Africa and the Global South conference, Shanghai, 15–17 May.

Brautigam, D. 1998. *Chinese aid and African development*. New York: Macmillan.

Brautigam, D. 2009. *The dragon's gift: The real story of China in Africa*. Oxford: Oxford University Press.

Brookes, P. 2007. Into Africa: China's grab for influence and oil. Washington, DC: Institute for International Studies at The Heritage Foundation, 9 February. www.heritage.org/Research/Africa/hl1006.cfm

Chazan, N., et al. 1992. *Politics and society in contemporary Africa*. Boulder, CO: Lynne Rienner.

Cheng Siwei. 2007. China cannot accept the theory of capitalism without morality concerns. *China Economics Weekly* 5: 13.

China Daily. 2007. China Africa trade exceeded 50 billion US dollars for the first time in 2006, 30 January. www.chinadaily.com.cn/jjzg/2007-01/30/content_796427.htm

China Daily. 2007. Confrontation over Darfur "will lead us nowhere", 27 July. www.chinadaily.com.cn/2008/2007-07/27/content_5445062.htm

China Petroleum Daily. 2007. Wang Qimin is welcomed by the Sudanese, 26 June

Chutian Metropolis Daily. 2007. What kind of issue is Darfur? A special interview with the special representative of the Chinese government, 8 July.

CNTextile.com. 2006. The opportunities and risks for textile enterprises to invest in Africa. http://news.ctei.gov.cn/show.asp?xx=79750

Cornelissen, S. & Taylor, I. 2000. The political economy of China and Japan's relationship with Africa: A comparative perspective. *The Pacific Review* 13(4): 615–633.

Davies, M. & Corkin, L. 2006. China's market entry into Africa's construction sector: The case of Angola. Paper presented to the international symposium on China–Africa shared development, Beijing, 19 December.

Documentation Office of CPC Central Committee, ed. 1982. *Collection of important documents since the Third Plenary Session of the 11th Central Committee of the CPC*. Beijing: People's Publishing House.

Duyvendad, J.J.L. 1949. *China's discovery of Africa*. London: A. Probsthain.

Economic Daily. 2007. CNPC is on the internationalized road with win–win, 13 July.

Eisenman J. 2005. Zimbabwe: China's African ally. *China Brief* 5(15): 11.

Eisenman, J. & Kurlantzick, J. 2006. China's Africa strategy. *Current History* 105(691): 219–224.

Filesi T. 1972. *China and Africa in the Middle Ages*. Trans. David L. Morison. London: Frank Cass.

French, Howard W. 2014. *China's second continent: How a million migrants are building a new empire in Africa*. New York: Knopf.

Gill, B., Huang, C. & Morrison, J.S. 2007. *China's expanding role in Africa: Implications for the United States*. A report of the CSIS Delegation to China on China–Africa–US relations.

Giry, S. 2005. China's Africa strategy. *The New Republic* 231(20): 19–23.

The Guardian 2005. African Union defends Mugabe, 25 January.

Huang Zequan. 2000. Fifty years of China–African friendly cooperation. In Center for African Studies of Peking University, ed., *China and Africa*. Beijing: Peking University Press.

Huang Zhen. 1987. Paving the road of friendship to the awakening Africa. In Anonymous, ed., *Endless Missing*, Beijing: CPC Literature Press, 364–373.

Huang Sujian & Yu Jing. 2006. The nature, objectives and social responsibility of state-owned enterprises. *China Industrial Economy* 2: 68–76.

Jiang Guanghua. 1997. *Records on visits to foreign parties*. Beijing: World Affairs Press.

Li Anshan. 2004. *Study on African nationalism*. Beijing: China's International Broadcast Publisher.

Li Anshan. 2006. China–African relations in the discourse on China's rise. *World Economics and Politics* 11: 7–14.
Li Anshan. 2006a. On the adjustments and changes of China's foreign policy to Africa. *West Asia and Africa* 8: 11–20.
Li Anshan. 2007. Africa in the perspective of globalization: Development, aid and cooperation. *West Asia and Africa* 7: 5–14.
Li Anshan. 2007a. China's engagement in Africa: Singular interest or mutual benefit? Paper presented at the Expert Round Table Meeting, Resource Governance in Africa in the 21st Century. Berlin, 26–28 March.
Li Anshan. 2019. *The social and economic history of the Chinese overseas in Africa*. Nanjing: Jiangsu People's Publishing House.
Li Jiasong, ed. 2001. *Big events in the history of foreign affairs of the People's Republic of China, Vol. 2*. Beijing: World Affairs Press.
Li Liqing. 2006. The history and current situation of China-African Party Communications. *West Asia and Africa* 3: 16–19.
Lin Mei. 1997. The reform and practice of foreign economic aid: Conference of exchanging experience on promoting the discount government loans in foreign economic aid. *International Economic Cooperation* 11: 4–7.
Long Xiangyang. 2000. The preliminary probe to the China–Africa relations from 1966 to 1969. In Center for African Studies of Peking University, ed., *China and Africa*. Beijing: Peking University Press.
Lu Ting'en. 2000. The example of summit diplomacy between China and Africa – Premier Zhou Enlai's first visit to Africa, In Center for Africa Studies of Peking University, ed. *China and Africa*. Beijing: Beijing University Press.
Lyman, P. 2005. China's rising role in Africa. www.cfr.org/publication/8436/chinas_rising_role_in_africa.html
Lyman, P. 2006. China's involvement in Africa: A view from the US. *South African Journal of International Affairs* 8(1): 129–138.
Ma Wenkuan & Meng Fanren. 1987. *The discovery of Chinese ancient porcelains in Africa*. Beijing: Forbidden City Press.
Mahamat, A. 2006. Africa starting to rise in partnership with China. *China Daily* (North American Edition), 13 January.
Mao Zedong. 1994. *Selections of Mao Zedong's works on diplomacy*. Beijing: Central Documentation Publishing House and World Affairs Press.
Marks, T. 2007. What's China's investment in Africa? *Business Enterprise*, March.
Muekalia, J.D. 2004. Africa and China's strategic partnership. *African Security Review* 13(1): 1–11.
Naidu, S. & Davies, M. 2006. China fuels its future with Africa's riches. *South African Journal of International Affairs* 13(2): 69–83.
New Zealand Herald. 2005. Blast at Zambia copper mine kills 47, 21 April.
Ogunsanwo, A. 1974. *China's policy in Africa*. Cambridge: Cambridge University Press.
Oilnews Online. 2002. Revelations on China Oil project in Sudan. www.oilnews.com.cn/gb/misc/2002-08/01/content_115986.htm
Ottaway, M. 1978. Soviet Marxism and African socialism. *Journal of Modern African Studies,* September: 477–487.
Pan, Esther. 2006. *Q&A: China, Africa, and oil*. US Council for Foreign Relations, 18 January, 63–75.
People's Daily. 1983. Equality and mutual benefit, variety of forms, emphasis on effectiveness and co-development, 15 January.

People's Daily. 2006. Good friends, good partners and good brothers, 22 June.
Qian Qichen. 2003. *Ten episodes in China's diplomacy*. Beijing: World Affairs Press.
Qu Xing. 2000. *The forty years of China's diplomacy*. Nanjing: Jiangsu People's Publishing House.
Reuters. 2007. China urges patience on Sudan, opposes sanctions, 31 May.
Ross, R. (ed.) 1993. *China, the United States, and the Soviet Union: Tripolarity and policy making in the Cold War*. New York: Sharpe.
Sautman, B. & Yan Hairong. 2007. Wind from the East: China and Africa's development. Paper presented at China's New Role in Africa and the Global South, Shanghai, 15–17 May.
Shen Fuwei. 1990. *China and Africa: Relations of 2000 years*. Beijing: Zhonghua Book Company.
Shichor, Y. 2005. Sudan: China's outpost in Africa. *China Brief* 5(21): 9–11.
Snow, P. 1988. *The Star Raft: China's encounter with Africa*. London: Weidenfeld & Nicolson.
Southern Weekly. 2007. Chinese in Africa, 26 July.
Stith, C. 2006. Africa–Sino relations: A summary assessment from an American perspective. *International Politics Quarterly* 102(4): 21–31.
Tang Xiaoyang 2020. *Coevolutionary pragmatism: Approaches and impacts of China–Africa economic cooperation*. Cambridge: Cambridge University Press.
United Nations Environment Program. 2007. *Sudan post-conflict environmental assessment, June 2007*. New York: UNEP. http://postconflict.unep.ch/publications/UNEP_Sudan.pdf
Wang Qinmei. 1999. Twenty years of great development of China–African relations. *Journal of Foreign Affairs College* 1: 48–54.
Weinstein, W. & Henriksen, T.H., eds. 1980. *Soviet and Chinese aid to African nations*. New York: Praeger.
Weng Ming. 1995. Appointing just before leaving – "Milord Qiao" led delegation to General Assembly of UN for the first time. In Fu Hao and Li Tongcheng, eds, *Great talents and their great achievement–diplomats in UN*. Beijing: Overseas Chinese Publishing House, 7–13.
Xinhua News Agency. 2007a. Eight steps to boost China–Africa partnership, 30 January.
Xinhua News Agency. 2007b. China launched satellite for Nigeria, 14 May.
Zha Daojiong. 2006. China's oil interests in Africa– An international political question. *Studies of International Politics* 4: 53–67.
Zhong Weiyun. 2000. Current situation of African parties and the communication between CPC and African parties. In Center for African Studies of Peking University, ed., *China and Africa*. Beijing: Peking University Press.

9 Cultural heritage of China's policy[1]

Introduction

At the end of 2014, Bob Wekesa, a Kenyan student who had met me several years ago in Peking University and earned his PhD of the Communication University of China, told me that he and others were planning to study Chinese media history in Africa and asked me to serve as their reviewer for the project. He told me that he would be "going through archives in Kenya on Xinhua, Chinese Radio International and *Beijing Review*-the National Museums of Kenya, the Kenyan parliament and the Kenya Broadcasting Corporation". I had mixed feelings. On one hand, the more studies there were on China–Africa relations, the more mutual understanding would result. On the other hand, why China? I replied uncertainly, "Good, yet it is strange. Did you or anybody else ever think of studying the history of British media in Africa or British cultural influence in Kenya? Or the BBC or CNN? They are in Africa for such a long time and worth studying. That's bizarre."

However, cultural influences and cultural factors need to be explored. It is generally acknowledged that China's success in Africa is expressed in the economic field. Why? Is there any secret? This chapter tries to use Africa as a case study to analyse the cultural factors behind China's foreign policy.

China's engagement in Africa is attracting much international attention. Whether this is criticism or praise, two facts have been noticed. First, China's increasing engagement in Africa has made a great impact on international politics. Piles of literature are produced because this is a fashionable topic and an easy way to receive funding (Large 2008: 45–61). Second, many have noticed that China's African policy has characteristics quite different from those of the West (Berger 2006). This uniqueness has been analysed, criticised, extolled and questioned (Strauss & Saavedra 2009). Chinese scholars generally consider China's African policy positive, but whether it is effective is another question (Li Anshan 2008). Except for a few scholars, Westerners take a negative view of China's role in Africa, yet there seems to have been a shift to a milder tone lately (Eisenman & Kurlantzick 2006: 223). African leaders and others usually consider China's involvement in Africa constructive

DOI: 10.4324/9781003220152-11

and have highly praised China's contributions to African development (Wade 2008), and China's reputation is durable in Africa (Olander 2020; Ray 2019),[2] although African academics and NGOs differ regarding China's engagement in Africa (Manji & Marks 2007; Guerrero & Manji 2008; Ampiah & Naidu 2008; Harneit-Sievers et al. 2010; Soudien & Houston 2021; Sall 2021).

Deborah Brautigam has studied Chinese aid to Africa since the 1990s and challenged many stereotypes and clichés in the Western literature on China–Africa relations, leading to serious debate among academics and policy-makers. She clearly states the differences of approach between China and the West in terms of aid distribution:

> Where the West has regularly changed its development advice, programs and approach to Africa, such as integrated rural development in the 1970s, policy reform in the 1980s, governance in the 1990s, and so on), China does not claim to know what Africa must do to develop. China has argued that it was wrong to impose political and economic conditions in exchange for aid, and that countries should be free to find their own pathway out of poverty. Mainstream economists in the West today also question the value of many of the conditions imposed on aid over the past few decades.
>
> (Brautigam 2009:308)

Her observation is accurate and the reasonable comment deserves consideration.

What factors have shaped China's African policy? The making of foreign policy is surely a result of a combination of reactions to external challenges and reflections on diplomatic affairs. It is, however, also influenced by internal affairs, such as the political system, ideological orientation, policy choices, public media, think-tanks and different interest groups such as the business sector (Hao & Lin 2007). Moreover, culture has impacted on its development and some believe that it can play a decisive role in this process. We can trace this view to de Tocqueville (1835) and Max Weber (1905). De Tocqueville argued that democracy could exist in the United States because of its cultural heritage, while Weber believed capitalism in essence a phenomenon of religious culture.

Although there are various studies on China–Africa relations, little research has explored the links between culture (or civilisation) and China's African policy. This is undoubtedly a very interesting yet difficult subject. It is interesting because all foreign policy embodies the historical traditions, social values and political ideology of the nation-state concerned, and therefore has direct links with the culture of that country. It is also difficult because "culture" is a rich and ambiguous term and has countless interpretations. There is a wide use of the term almost in all fields and disciplines; even such a term as "cultural merchant" has appeared. Owing to the disjuncture between its popular and academic connotations, we have to clarify the understanding first. Moreover, culture is closely connected with another notion: civilization. China has a long history of being considered a great culture or civilisation, yet is there any link between Chinese culture and China's policy on Africa? There is no systematic study on this subject so far. In this chapter, the intention is to analyse the connotation of "culture", challenge the Eurocentric definition of "civilization" and explore the links between China's African policy and its cultural traditions.

Culture: Different connotations

The term "culture", as well as "civilisation", embodies rich and ambiguous connotations. Probably first used by Marcus Tullius Cicero (106–43 BCE), a Roman statesman and scholar, "culture" did not become popular until the mid-18th century, while the term "civilisation" appeared in print in 1766 (Braudel 1980: 180). There are hundreds of definitions of "culture", some complex – culture includes utensil culture, spiritual culture, institutional culture and so on – and some simple – culture is anything that makes your life worth living. In the 1950s, anthropologists Kroeber and Kluckhohn analysed almost all the important definitions of "culture" proposed by anthropologists, sociologists and social psychologists in the West since the publication of anthropologist Edward Burnett Taylor's masterpiece *Primitive Culture* in 1871. They analysed 169 definitions exemplifying a dozen distinct conceptual approaches from 1871 to 1951 and classified them into six types. It was believed that it would be better to understand "culture" as a behaviour system, the core element of which was composed of traditional ideas, especially the value system, and they pointed out the integrity and historicity of "culture" (Kroeber & Kluckhohn 1952).

Various disciplines define "culture" in different terms. Anthropologists believe that the value level is a more important and universal factor of culture, and that it is of universal significance to explore culture from the value level (Kuper 1999). R.A. Shweder, Professor of Cultural Anthropology of the University of Chicago and President of the Society of Psychological Anthropology, emphasizes more about values in his understanding of culture – for example, "community-specific ideas about what is true, good, beautiful and efficient" (Shweder 2000:163). Bagby defined "culture" as "regularities in the behaviour, internal and external, of the members of a society, excluding those regularities which are clearly hereditary in origin". In addition, he stated by virtue of being "the patterned or repetitive element in history", culture is "history's intelligible aspect" (Bagby 1958: 84, 95, 124). As a political scientist, Samuel Huntington considered that language and religion were two major factors of any culture or civilisation. In his view, "The central elements of any culture and civilization are language and religion" (Huntington 1996: 59).

If the specific items such as language and religion are listed as "central elements" of culture or civilisation, who is entitled to decide, for example, which belief system is considered religion?[3] Historian Qian Mu pointed out that:

> When we say culture, we mean human life. When all aspects of human life come together, we call it culture. But the so-called various aspects of life, not specifically refer to the temporary flat surface, will be a long time to add continuity, The various aspects of life of a country and a nation, coupled with the continuous evolution of time and history, become the so-called culture. So culture is the life of this country and this nation. If a nation has no culture, it has no life. Therefore, every so-called culture must have a lasting spirit for a period of time. In other words, every culture must have its traditional historical significance. So we say that culture is not plane, but three-dimensional. In this large plane space, all kinds of life, and then experienced the continuity of time, that is the whole life of a nation, that is, the culture of that nation.
>
> (Qian Mu 2001: 346–347)

Therefore culture can be understood as the whole life of a community. It has four characteristics: collectivism, totality, historicity and vitality. Culture does not belong to individuals, but to human groups; it is not a certain aspect, but the sum of all aspects of life; it is not temporary and has historical dimensions. It carries the history of the community and is the life of that community.

Civilisation: Bias, paradox and redefinition

There are two understandings of the concept of civilisation, both carrying a biased view. One holds there are obvious differences between civilisation and culture. The former includes skills, technology and material factors, while the latter includes values and ideas as well as higher ideological, artistic and moral qualities of a society (Kroeber & Kluckhohn 1952: 15–29). This view of distinguishing civilisation from culture was strengthened by colonialist ideology, which divided the world into two categories: "civilised" and "barbaric". European nations became "cultured" and "civilised" while all the colonised peoples are classified as "barbaric" and "uncivilised".[4] Another understanding is that civilisation is regarded as a cultural entity, and civilisation and culture constitute a nation's way of life. Huntington believes that civilisation and culture are related to a nation's comprehensive way of life. Civilisation is a culture writ large, and civilisation is the most extensive cultural entity (Huntington 1996).

In historical studies, Toynbee (1966) regards "civilization" as the smallest research unit of history, which is equivalent to cultural body. There are 21 kinds of "similar civilisations" such as "Egyptian civilisation", "Western civilisation", "Indian civilisation" and "Chinese civilization". Toynbee has never given an accurate definition of civilisation, which was ridiculed by Fernand Braudel. Braudel believes that civilisation is the focus of cultural characteristics and cultural phenomena (Braudel 1980: 179–203). Chinese historian Qian Mu points out that:

> Civilization is characteristic of being external and belongs to material aspect, while culture being internal and belongs to spiritual aspect. Therefore, civilization can be spread and accepted to the outside world, and culture must be generated by the spiritual accumulation within the group ... Culture can produce civilization, but civilization does not necessarily produce culture.
>
> (Qian Mu 1994: 1)

This statement tries to clarify the relationship and characteristics between civilization and culture.

However, under the influence of various prejudices (mostly expressed in the form of race bias) in modern times, the exploration of civilisation has coincided with colonialism. Ethnocentrism as both an "epistemological filiation" and an "ideological connection" (Mudimbe 1988:19) becomes the top guideline for colonial expansion and the control of international discourse, meaning the objectivity of the study of civilisation is greatly reduced. Most works about other regions, nations or continents are based on ethnocentrism, specifically Eurocentrism, and there are many biased ideas about the concept of civilisation and culture (Li Jianming 2016; Li Anshan 2018).[5] For the practical reason of colonial dominance, European nations self-claimed as "cultured" and "civilised" while all the colonised nations were classified as "barbaric" and "uncivilised". Arnold Toynbee's viewpoint is quite representative. In his early published *A Study of History*, he never thought of including Sub-Saharan Africa in the scope of civilisations. In 1966, he still regarded only the entry of "Western Man" into Africa as an indicator of civilization (Toynbee 1966: 94–95). However, in 1972, he included tropical Africa in the ranks of civilisation in the new edition of *A Study of History*; the reason is that he now realised that tropical Africa had a history comparable to that of Western Europe in agriculture and metallurgy (Toynbee 1972: 13).

In other words, the concept of "civilization" has been greatly politicised in modern times, especially by the colonial powers: "Other civilizations are now in contact with Europe and as a result of colonization have been subjected to an involuntary process of Westernization" (Hountondji 1996: 163). This "involuntary process" always goes with Christianity, which is why Ghanaian philosopher Kwasi Wiredu, while acknowledging that colonial mentality is a reality, fervently calls for the "need for conceptual decolonization in African philosophy" (Wiredu 1996: 4, 136–144). Another African scholar, Abiola Irele, points out in the "Introduction" of Hountondji's book:

> The intellectual presuppositions of colonialism represented a formulation in negative terms of African identity; its racism was a large statement about the nature of the African which called for a refutation. In the

intellectual reconfrontation with imperialism, it was necessary to enforce this refutation by elaborating a new set of valuations which reversed the terms of the colonial ideology.

(Hountondji 1996:17).[6]

From another perspective, human development is affected by the local environment and climate conditions, so the achievements of civilization cannot be measured by the same standard – for example, the plough, the wheel, domestication, architecture, city, language, weapons, smelting and so on. In order to seek a rational basis for colonial expansion and domination, the European colonial powers politicised the concept of "civilisation" for a long time, and the concept became an important part of the Western discourse and a convenient tool to oppress and exploit other nations. As a result, the nations of the world are artificially divided into "civilised (Europeans)" and "barbaric (other regions or nations)". The myth of Africa was created by a strange yet convenient combination of "beastly savages" or "White man's grave" with "tropical treasure house", or "the ivory-sugar-cotton Negro complex" and "nothing civilized is Negroid" and "The very vocabulary of civilization expressed this idea" (Du Bois 1992: 34) Christianising and civilising Africans not only became a necessary job, but was also viewed as a mission (Mudimbe 1988: 49, 51, 53; Mudimbe 1988; Hammond & Jablow 1977). This approach offers a perfect pretext for European colonialism.

Nigerian philosopher Mudimbe has analysed the links between civilisation and Christianity in the African context under colonial rule, which he described as an "Ideological Model of Conversion". After studying three models of the missionary behaviour in Africa, he described them as: Pagan (evil) through Christianity converted to Christian (good); the Naked (child) through education converted to Civilised (adult); Cannibals (beast) through evolution converted to *"Evolué"* (human being). After the process, "Primitiveness" converted to "Civilization". In the process, we see a connection as well as an equal position between civilisation and Christianity:

> We can perceive in them an expression of a common ideology. They are, all of them, people for whom commitment to God is central. Concretely, they believe that they are the ones in charge of saving Africa. This, for them, means the promotion of the ideals of Christian civilization. Finally, they are secure in their knowledge of the correct means for Africa's conversion.
>
> (Mudimbe 1988: 50–51)

In other words, Christianity is believed to be of superior and universal character, equated with civilization. Africans can only become civilised by conversion to Christianity.

However, it is worth noting that there is a triple paradox in the connotation of the "civilization" or "civilized nation". First, in the relationship between human being and natural environment, the civilised nations have more advanced means of destroying the environment, thus creating many natural disasters.[7] Second, the civilised nations have obtained more sophisticated means of killing each other or destroying human civilisation, with World Wars I and World War II the best examples.[8] Third, in the so called "civilised nations", such as the United States, France, Germany, Austria, Switzerland, Australia, New Zealand and the Nordic countries, there is a relatively high suicide rate (Laverty & Kelly 2019; WHO 2021).[9] Therefore, it becomes vital to redefine "civilisation". This work can be carried out from the perspective of humanity and its history. A tentative definition is offered as follows. Civilisation refers to the systematic strategy of human survival and development, including three aspects: first, the method to better manage the relations between human beings and nature – that is, to live in harmony with nature while using nature appropriately to serve humankind; second, the capability to manage relations among human societies – that is, to coexist with others in a harmonious way; and third, the skill to mediate the individual problems of human beings, thus achieving a happy life without physical or mental troubles. In addition, civilisation has the characteristics of pluralism, integrity, continuity and transmutation, including accumulation and revision. Civilisation is the sum of value system and social life with a historical dimension. It is the result of the historical development of human beings and affects human life from all aspects (Li Anshan 2021: 11–12).[10]

After the analysis of concept of "culture" and the attempt to redefine the term "civilisation", it is proper to consider the theme of the chapter: the linkage between culture and China's Africa policy. In order to provide a thorough answer, I will concentrate on four notions of Chinese values, which represent the principles or rules regarding human relations: *ren*, (benevolence 仁); *xin* (trustfulness 信); *shu* (forbearance 恕); and *pingdeng* (equality 平等). By illustrating the links between the four traditional notions and China's contemporary foreign policy, we may discover the origins of the cultural implications of China's external relations.

Essence of *ren* (仁 virtue, benevolence or humanity)

Ren signifies, to a certain extent, benevolence or humanity in English. As the Chinese character indicates, *ren* presents two people. Confucius once said, "A benevolent person loves people (*ren zhe ai ren*)", which really shows the humanitarian nature of *ren*. As the key notion of Confucianism, *ren* has caused a lot of debate in Chinese academia. However, the criticism mostly targets the fact that the ruling class exercised this notion rather than criticising the notion itself. This section analyses the application of *ren* in China's policy on developing countries, particularly Africa.

The typical example of *ren* indicated in foreign policy is Chinese medical cooperation with developing countries, especially concerning the dispatch since 1963 of Chinese medical teams (CMT) to the world, and more specifically

African countries (Li Anshan 2011). In July 1962, after the victory of the liberation movement and the withdrawal of French medical staff, the Algerian government called on the international community for medical assistance. The Chinese government received the message through two channels, the Red Cross and the Algerian Minister for Health. In January 1963, China was the first to express its willingness to provide medical assistance to Algeria, marking the beginning of CMTs abroad (*People's Daily* 7 April 1963). By 2009, 45 CMTs had worked in 44 different African countries.[11]

About 900 members are now working in about 100 hospitals or health centres in Africa. The total figure for CMT person/time is 16,000 and they have served about 26 million Africans. It is not unusual for Chinese doctors to donate blood to save African patients. On 26 January 1965, an Algerian woman lost a lot of blood while giving birth and was in a very critical condition. Dr Shen Xingzhi and Dr Xu Zexian immediately transfused their blood to the woman and saved her life (Health Department of Hubei Province 1993: 33). In another incident, when a Tanzanian woman was very weak after a serious operation and needed a blood transfusion, Dr Liu Fangyi donated 250 cc of blood to the woman. Dr Liu, who had been to Africa three times, eventually died in Tanzania and was praised by President Julius Nyerere as "Doctor-Ambassador of friendship and kindness" (Liu Jirui 1998: 62–63). By the mid-2000s, 45 CMT members had died in Africa (Bo 2007). Their humanitarian service brought them much merit and many honours: more than 600 CMT members received different top awards from different countries where they worked for more than 40 years (Department of International Cooperation of the Ministry of Health 2003: 16). Furthermore, their service was extended to diplomats and others in the country where they were working. For example, CMTs in Algeria served not only Algerians, but also diplomats and other people from more than 60 countries (Health Department of Hubei Province 1993: 12). The same applied to CMTs in Tunisia, Mali and other countries.

Ren is expressed in other fields besides CMT. China's humanitarian assistance to Africa includes anti-malaria campaigns, humanitarian efforts, and the building of hospitals, schools and community centres for the elderly. For example, in Liberia, through a series of bilateral cooperation agreements with China, the latter has expanded teaching facilities at the University of Liberia's Fendell Campus, established an anti-malaria treatment center at the JFK Hospital in Monrovia, set up a modern hospital in Tappita (Nimba county) and built primary and secondary schools across Liberia. Chinese goodwill was also expressed in the construction of roads and streets across Liberia (allAfrica.com 2009).

Tropical diseases and epidemics represent a major threat to the health and lives of African people. A United Nations of International Children's Emergency Fund (UNICEF) report disclosed that five million children under the age of five died in Africa in 2006. Malaria is the number one killer and about one million children die of it annually in Africa (Thompson 2005: 1–4; Shinn 2006: 14–16; Siringi 2003: 456). To fight malaria in Africa, the Chinese

232 *Policy and implementation*

government adopted several measures simultaneously, namely CMT, training programs, anti-malaria projects, donation of facilities and drugs, and building anti-malaria centres. In 2006, during the China–Africa summit, President Hu promised to continue China–African medical cooperation and offered to help build 30 anti-malaria centres in Africa. In the run-up to the fourth FOCAC meeting, the work was progressing smoothly. A very effective anti-malaria medicine, Côtecxin, is now the most widely used medication in Africa and has become one of the most welcome gifts presented by Chinese leaders on official visits to African countries (Lu Chunming 2006).

China has also constantly supported the Sudanese people with humanitarian aid. China's aid helps to target the root of the country's conflicts – poverty – and has provided infrastructure such as schools, hospitals and water projects. Apart from offering help to Sudan to develop its oil industry and infrastructure, China has sent several shipments of humanitarian aid, including tents, blankets, and medical and agricultural equipment. Since 2004, China has sent five shipments of material for humanitarian aid to Darfur. The fourth shipment, worth RMB20 million (US$2.6 million), left for Sudan on 16 August 2007 and included pumps, tents and blankets to help people in the Darfur region improve their living conditions (FOCAC 2007). The fifth batch of aid material, valued at RMB40 million, was shipped on 25 August 2007 and included boarding-houses for at least 120 schools, generators, vehicles and pumps (Enorth.com.cn 2007; Humanitarian Aid 2007).[12] Up to July 2007, China had already provided US$10 million in humanitarian aid and promised more.[13] China also provided humanitarian aid by sending peacekeeping forces to four African countries, all of which are involved in engineering or medical assistance.

Belief in *sin* (信 trust, good faith)

Confucianism always employs *xin* as one of the most important principles for human beings, either in terms of governance or in one's personal life. Meaning trust or good faith, *xin* is mentioned 24 times in Confucius's *Analects*, indicating how seriously he and his followers regarded this principle. Confucius once put good faith first in governance when he discussed how to administer a state. In order to govern a state, the leader should work earnestly and live up to their words. Confucius once said, "I do not know how a man without truthfulness is to get on" (*Ren er wu xin, buzhi qi ke ye*). His student Zi Gong also illustrated his idea as "to be true to one's words" or "to live up to one's words" (*Yan er you xin*) (Yang Bojun 1960). All these sayings indicate that once a person has promised something, they have to live up it and be a trustworthy person – especially towards friends.

China has followed this principle in its cooperation with African countries. During his visit to Africa, Premier Zhou Enlai heard the news of an unsuccessful coup d'état against President Nkrumah of Ghana on 2 January 1964 – the next destination of his tour. Chairman Liu Shaoqi and Premier Zhou

Enlai both immediately sent a telegram of comfort to Nkrumah. The Chinese delegation hesitated about whether to push ahead with the visit and there was heated debate among the members of the delegation. Some suggested that the visit should be cancelled owing to the political instability and the dangerous situation in Ghana. Yet Premier Zhou thought the delegation should go ahead as planned since President Nkrumah needed moral support more than ever at this critical moment. Premier Zhou thus sent Mr Huang Zhen and Mr Huang Hua to pay an official visit, first, to convey his sincere solicitude to President Nkrumah, who was injured during the coup (Huang Hua 2007).

Considering Nkrumah's situation, Premier Zhou also suggested that all the official arrangements be cancelled and Nkrumah should not hold a welcome ceremony at the airport or an outdoor banquet. Nkrumah did not expect the Chinese premier would continue the visit as planned. He was moved by the two telegrams, yet showed a desire to receive a letter from Chairman Mao Zedong. When Zhou arrived in Accra he presented the letter from Chairman Mao and enjoyed a very successful visit to Ghana. It was here that he put forward the Eight Principles of foreign aid (*People's Daily* 18 January 1964; Huang 2007: 122–126).

Confucius once emphasised that a good person is "to be trustworthy in word and resolute in deed" (*Yan bi xin, xing bi guo*). TAZARA is a good example of the practice of *xin*. This is one of the biggest aid projects that China has ever undertaken in terms of development aid. After both Tanzanian President Nyerere and Zambian President Kaunda failed to receive financial support from the West and the Soviet Union, they turned to China for assistance, and China decided to help the two countries build the railway (Zhang 1999; Yu 1975). The 1860 kilometre railroad begins in Dar es Salaam (Tanzania) in the east and ends in Kapri Mposhi (Zambia) in the west. Chinese experts and engineering technicians did all the exploration work, surveying and designing. They also assisted the Tanzanian and Zambian governments to organise the construction. During the Cultural Revolution, China's economic relations greatly suffered, yet Chinese leaders continued to support their African friends via the "poor helps poor" model.

During the period of the TAZARA construction, China was experiencing very difficult times. The economy was strongly impacted by the political chaos and people were suffering from food shortages and the rationing of daily goods. There were also unimaginable difficulties in the building of TAZARA: besides the mountainous regions and the tropical diseases, building bridges and tunnels in swampy mud and quicksand was a huge challenge. Many Chinese experts and technicians were injured and 65 Chinese died during the construction (Zhang Tieshan 1999: 386–387). Running through mountains, valleys, torrential rivers, and dense and primitive forests, this railway required about US$400 million in long-term interest-free loans from China, employed 30,000–50,000 Chinese railway experts and took about ten years to accomplish. Notwithstanding the motives, living up to one's words and helping one's friends were the most important drivers behind this operation. In order to fulfil its promise, China even bought 98 Japanese bulldozers (worth about US$1.7 million) from Komatsu Manufacturing in Japan and transported them directly to Dar es Salam. They eventually arrived in early 1970 and were used in the construction of the railway (Yu 1975: 140–141; Monson 2009).

During the early 1990s, the West largely neglected Africa after the Cold War. China's Foreign Minister has made visits to African countries the first official stop every year since 1991 (Qian Qichen 2003: 255–257). China also insists on using its influence without interference, viewing respect for others as vital to finding solutions in international politics.

The financial crisis testified to China's determination to fulfil its promise while many Western countries failed to realise their official development aid (ODA) pledges to Africa. Although China suffered immensely during the Wen-chuan earthquake – as its economy was severely hit, especially in the export field – China kept its word and tried every means to finish the projects President Hu had put forward during the China–Africa summit. After great effort and close cooperation from both sides, China's promise was fulfilled before the fourth FOCAC.[14]

Sense of *shu* (恕 forbearance)

When his student, Zi Gong, asked him about the most important doctrine in life, Confucius answered, "That should be 'forbearance'; for example, what you do not want done to yourself, you should not do to others." As an important principle of social relations in the daily life of Chinese people, this doctrine of forbearance has also left its mark on China's foreign policy. The most criticised policy in China's relationship with African countries is the no-strings-attached principle, or the absence of political conditions. This is because China follows its own principle of non-interference. However, certain countries criticise others through the lens of their own interests, be they economic, political or cultural. The criticism is usually carried out under the guise of "universal values" or "international standards", implying that Western doctrines or principles are universal. This practice has been applied in developing countries for a long time but is not questioned.

The idea of *Shu*, or forbearance, affects China's foreign policy. China learnt hard lessons when receiving conditional assistance from other countries. In 1958, when the Soviet Union provided aid to China, it also proposed that China should agree to the establishment of a long-wave transceiver by the Soviet Union and its allied fleet. Chairman Mao Zedong realised that the two issues belonged to the realm of China's internal affairs, and that any concession would jeopardise Chinese national defence, so he resolutely refused the proposal. This explains why China has always set self-reliance as the first principle of development, with foreign aid as a subsidiary; China thus never allows itself as an aid provider to interfere with the recipient country's internal affairs.

When China offers assistance to African countries or other developing countries, it does not attach political conditions, while Western countries usually do so, regardless of the process or the stage of development. A typical example is the criticism of the Chinese government for its role in the Darfur crisis. The Darfur issue is a very complicated case, with historical origins, national integration, religious conflict, refugee migration and poverty all playing a role.

As mentioned in a previous chapter, the crisis is chiefly a result of environmental degradation (United Nations Environmental Program 2007: 329; Mohammed 2004).[15] In addition, it is a regional tragedy and few described it as "genocide" except the U.S. (Autesserre 2006; Apps 2007).[16] What is more, as a development related problem, the Darfur crisis can only be solved through development. It is clear that the crisis is a conflict between different groups inside the Sudan. Nation-building is not an easy process and has to undergo a long period, as in the United States, which caused the death of 620,000 to prevent secession (Faust 2008). Yet this seemed to escape most people's attention while the Sudanese government was blamed for the crisis. The international community should give the Sudanese people time to solve this problem. Interference from outside can only worsen the fragile political situation, as in Iraq and Afghanistan.

China's policy of non-interference does not equate to ignoring humanitarian disasters; rather, China respects the sovereignty of nations and acknowledges its limits in solving such crises. In diplomatic discussions with African nations, China does make suggestions on issues of governance and intra-state affairs. What distinguishes Chinese suggestions from Western interventions is that they are provided in a friendly rather than a coercive manner. China has used its ties with Sudan to persuade the Sudanese government to cooperate with the United Nations (*Chutian Metropolis Daily* 2007). Since there is mutual respect and trust, China can work with the Sudanese government to find a solution agreeable to all parties to alleviate the suffering of the Sudanese people. The Sudanese government accepted a "hybrid peacekeeping force" in Darfur (Xinhua News Agency 2007).

Another good example to illustrate *shu* is the forbearance shown by a recipient towards others' decisions or choices that may not be beneficial to the recipient. In 2003, a Canadian oil firm decided to sell its interest in a Sudanese consortium that also involved Chinese and Malaysian firms. The Chinese company wanted to buy the Canadian share but was refused permission by the Sudanese government. Instead, Sudan awarded the share to an Indian firm with a higher bid in order to multiply the investors (Mohan 2002). This shows two things: China and Sudan are equal partners, and they can make decisions on their own without the need to be complimentary or complicit.

With China's investment and support, Sudan has transformed itself from an oil-importing country to an exporting one, and has built a complete infrastructure for exploration, production, refining, transport and sales of crude oil, gasoline and petrochemical products.

Principle of *pingdeng* (平等 equality)

Pingdeng or "equality" is a modern concept, and one of the most important concerns in social movement and human history. In world history, the realisation of the principle of equality was not only one of the major aims of the revolutions in Great Britain, France and the United States (among others); it is a term that is highly praised in the West. However, in international politics, it seems that the "might is right" approach reigns supreme and that equality is never mentioned.

The principle of equality has been understood as equivalent to that of socialism, and is also claimed as the guiding principle of the Communist Party of China (CPC). However, the concept was always embodied in ancient Chinese philosophy, expressed in various ways and becoming a heritage embodied in China's diplomacy. Zi Xia, one of Confucius's students, once said, "All men under Heaven are brothers" (*Sihai zhi nei, jie xiongdi ye*) and there is a strong sense of equality throughout Confucianism. Confucius himself claimed this principle as his educational philosophy: "education for all" or "teach everybody without prejudice" (*You jiao wu lei*). In another case, he even treated teacher and student as equals by stating that "teaching and learning improve each other" (*Jiao xue xiang zhang*). As another Confucian thinker and a typical equalitarian, Mencius was famous for his ideology of a *min beng* (people-oriented) community. He once described his ideal society by saying, "Treat your elders as elders, and extend it to the elders of others; treat your young ones as young ones, and extend it to the young ones of others" (*Lao wu lao yiji ren zhi lao, you wu you yiji ren zhi you*) (Yang Bojun 1960). It is noticeable that in this scenario every elder is equal, so is every youngster. In this philosophical approach, human beings must care for each other and treat others as equals, as their own family, which represents the incarnation of an ideal world.

This idea seems to be utopian but has a real meaning in China's foreign policy-making. For example, the four following characteristics are often used to describe China–African relations: summit diplomacy; a sense of equality; mutual benefits; and mechanism of cooperation (Li Anshan 2006: 11–13). China and Africa have a similar history as they have both suffered from the ill-effects of the colonial era, and this shared experience underpins the ideas of equality and respect for sovereignty that each highlights in their approach to international relations. The Eight Principles of foreign aid make it clear that China will guarantee that technicians of recipient countries will be able to master the relevant technology when assistance is provided by Chinese experts. Despite working on specific missions abroad, these experts are restricted from enjoying any privileges, so they receive the same treatment as the local experts (*People's Daily* 18 January 1964; Li Anshan 2007: 10).

Since the 1960s, meetings between top leaders in China and Africa have become a key mechanism for establishing direct communication at the highest level of government and have set the tone for relations and bilateral politics. This "summit diplomacy" has created mutual trust between heads of state and demonstrated mutual respect between China and African countries. Premier Zhou Enlai's visit to Africa during the early 1960s left a rich legacy in the framework of China–Africa relations. It was during this visit that he put forward the Four Principles that emphasize mutual benefits.

In the same light, Chairman Mao Zedong always emphasised the equal status of Chinese and African people. China's help to Africa was not entirely altruistic and both sides helped one another. When meeting African friends in 1959, Mao Zedong pointed out, "You need support, we also need support, and all socialist countries need support." In 1961, he said to African guests, "Africa is the front line of struggle. You support our struggle and we support your struggle." Chairman Mao once told African leaders that their struggle against colonialism and imperialism distracted the imperialists' attention and thus helped China in another way. Furthermore, China was rather isolated by the West so political allies such as African countries provided much leverage to battle against the strategic enemy. He once mentioned that Chinese and African people are both coloured, have the same historical experiences and are also despised by the West and bullied by imperialists. China and African countries are thus considered equal: "The mutual relationship between us is that of brotherhood, not father–son" (Mao Zedong 1994: 270, 467, 490–492).

Deng Xiaoping held the same attitude to African leaders. In 1989, he met the Burundian president at the age of 85 and called him his "young friend". He met Ugandan President Museveni in the same year and they exchanged experiences (Deng Xiaoping 1993: 289–290). Jiang Zemin visited Africa four times and made an important speech at the OAU on the consolidation of an equal partnership. President Hu Jintao visited many African countries and expressed Chinese willingness to entertain friendly relations with Africa. The principle of equality in China's dealings with other countries is more than just a slogan. It is noticeable that although the concept is largely the norm between individuals, it has never been effectively applied to the realm of international relations. Powerful nations have always made the rules in the global community. China's practice in Africa challenges this reality and may offer an alternative model for interstate behavior.

This attitude of equality also exists among ordinary people. Jamie Monson, an American historian and TAZARA expert, described the situation:

> During TAZARA's construction, the Chinese railway technicians did indeed labor 'side by side" with African workers, camping out with them in some of the most remote and rugged areas of the East African interior.

They did not stand aside shouting out instructions, but taught the African recruits by example. They did not confine themselves to handling complex engineering technology, but were willing to pitch in on the most basic tasks. Chinese technicians remember assisting their young African friends with fatherly advice on matters ranging from saving their wages to repairing their shoes.

(Monson 2009: 7)

It is worth noting that China has never adopted a patronising attitude as a "donor", since a "donor–recipient" relationship implies an unequal relation, both semantically and factually – for example, rich and poor, top and bottom, superior and inferior or arrogant and humble. The unequal relations leads to a series of consequences. For example, the former is always condescending, and their requirements become necessary preconditions for aid to the latter; the latter is subject to these conditions totally, or risks losing the aid. That is why Western aid to Africa has failed most of the time. The Chinese government stresses that China pursues a philosophy different from that of the West; it does not view aid as an instrument of political conditionality and understands assistance as a relationship based on mutuality. As early as 1964, Premier Zhou Enlai put forward the Eight Principles of foreign aid, which are impressive in several aspects. First, they are self-disciplined rules rather than regulations on bilateral relations. Second, the first principle directly outlines that Chinese aid should not be considered a unilateral aim, but rather mutual help. Third, several principles can be considered as lessons learned by a recipient country from its dealings with previous donors; more specifically, it highlights the lessons that China learnt from the aid formerly provided by the Soviet Union. Finally, the eighth principle concerning Chinese experts is a reflection of China's experience with Russian experts, who asked for many privileges when working on projects in China; this caused a great deal of trouble and dissatisfaction from many Chinese citizens.

With Premier Zhao's visit to Africa in 1982, China's new policy was issued. Zhao announced the "Four principles on China–African economic and technical cooperation": equality, bilateralism, effectiveness and co-development – which emphasize mutual benefits and co-development (*People's Daily*, 15 January 1983). Zhao's Four Principles were a supplement to Zhou's Eight Principles; both follow the principle of equality. While the Eight Principles guarantee that China will provide the most favourable assistance to Africa, with additional restraints on Chinese aid personnel, the Four Principles stress bilateral cooperation and co-development.

In the field of aid and economic cooperation between China and Africa, we can also trace the influence of cultural heritage. "Transparency" is a hot issue that has caused much criticism from the West, yet we can also find the cultural origin of this policy. According to Chinese values, people should cherish others' help, but should not talk of their assistance to others. A classic *Policy of Warring States* contains a Moral maxim, "If others have helped me, I should never forget; if I have helped others, I should forget" (Zhu Zudi 1985).[17] It is common sense that those helped do not like others to remind them of the help they have received. The same logic applies to China's assistance to Africa – even if there may be practical reasons as well (Li Anshan 2008: 21–49). China's assistance to Africa also emphasizes the traditional philosophy that "teaching others to fish is better than giving them fish". That could explain why the Chinese are so busy building infrastructure on the African continent.

However, three points must be stressed here. First, by no means do I intend to indicate that culture is the only factor to make its mark on foreign policy; on the contrary, culture influences diplomatic affairs in combination with various alternative factors. Second, it is obvious that Chinese culture has had different impacts on China's foreign policy, both in a positive and negative sense. Third, China's policy is not necessarily always consistent. Take, for example, its non-interference policy. During the Cultural Revolution, some revolutionary measures were exported, which happened to interfere with the receiving countries' political affairs, as demonstrated by the works of certain Chinese scholars who have explored China's interference during the Cultural Revolution (Wang Qinmei 2000; Long Xiangyang 2000). This topic has also been extensively covered by Western scholars (Taylor 2006).

Conclusion

There is a link between Chinese culture and China's policy on Africa. In order to understand China's Africa policy, we should try to appreciate Chinese culture. The European Union and China have different cultural traditions, yet they both want to develop good relations with Africa. Mutual criticism will not lead to this ideal, but the exchange of ideas and lessons from their own process of development would increase their mutual understanding.

China's engagement in Africa may be considered an experiment – one taken from China's culture and China's own development – which still remains unimaginable for many in the West, who need time to fully understand this process. In concluding *Dragon's gift*, Deborah Brautigam states:

> At the end of the day, we should remember this: China's own experiments have raised hundreds of millions of Chinese out of poverty, largely without foreign aid. They believe in investment, trade, and technology as levers for development, and they are applying these same tools in their African engagement, not out of altruism but because of what they learned at home ... These lessons emphasize not aid, but experiments; not paternalism, but the "creative destruction" of competition and the green shoots of new opportunities. This may be the dragon's ultimate, ambiguous gift.
>
> (Brautigam 2009: 312)

This statement is true. It is possible to reach a win–win situation, even for different partners engaged in a fight against poverty and in the fulfilment of humankind's destiny; yet, in order to achieve such an end, it is essential for both partners to attempt to forge greater cooperation.

Notes

1 This was a combination of papers prepared for four international workshops in 2010: "The EU and China: Partners or Competitors in Africa?" at the College of Europe on 4–5 February 2010 by the European Institute in Bruges in Belgium; "Working Days on Perception of Medical Humanitarian Action" at Geneva on 30 September–1 October by Medecins Sans Frontieres (MSF); "China-Africa Civil Society Dialogue Development Challenges in Africa and the Chinese Development Experience" at Beijing on 18–19 October 2010 by the Institute of West-Asian and African Studies (IWAAS) of the Chinese Academy of Social Science and Heinrich Böll Stiftung; and "Asian Studies in Africa" on 3 December 2010 by the International Institute of Asian Studies at Leiden, SEPHIS at Amsterdam and African Studies Centre of Leiden University. I would like to thank Men Jing (European Institute), Christian Captier (MSF), Marina de Regt (SEPHIS), Ton Dietz (African Studies Centre of Leiden University), Yang Guang (IWAAS) and Axel-Harneit Sievers (Böll Foundation) for inviting me to attend those workshops. A different version was published in Jing Men and Benjamin Barton, eds, *China and the European Union in Africa: Partners or Competitors?* (Aldershot: Ashgate, 2011).
2 This attitude is indicated in the Pew Research Center's annual poll and Afrobarometer's annual survey. See also "President Sirleaf hails China–Africa partnership, says it increases continent's chances", 10 November 2009. http://allafrica.com/stories/200911091586.html
3 Colonial officials and missionaries used to think Christianity was the only orthodox religion and it equalled civilisation, as the people who believed in Christianity were civilised (Mudimbe 1988: 49, 53). The Europeans often describe the indigenous religions in Africa as "at best 'folk' or 'tribal' religion", or even as "fetish" (Mazrui 1980: 51; Li Anshan 2002: 23–46).
4 German ethnologist Leo Frobenius recorded his own impression of Africa in *Histoire de la Civilization Africaine* (translated from the German by Back and Ermont (Paris: Gallimard, 1936, p. 56): "What was revealed by the navigators of the fifteenth to the seventeenth centuries furnishes an absolute proof that Negro Africa, which extended south of the desert zone of the Sahara, was in full efflorescence, in all the splendour of harmonious and well-formed civilizations ... The idea of the 'barbarous Negro' is a European invention that has consequently prevailed in Europe until the beginning of this century" (Du Bois 1992: 79).
5 "A gracious culture was built up ... The race that produced the ugly features of a Darwin or a Winston Churchill was always 'beautiful,' while a Toussaint and a Menelik were ugly because they were Black" (Du Bois 1992: 22–23).
6 That is why Ghanaian philosopher Kwasi Wiredu, while acknowledging that the colonial mentality is a reality, fervently calls for the "need for conceptual decolonization in African philosophy" (Wiredu 1996: 4, 136–144).
7 According to the statistics of the World Bank, the developed countries account for only 16 per cent of the world's population, but they produce 34 per cent of the world's garbage.

8 According to the British Encyclopedia, 8.5 million soldiers and 13 million civilians died in World War I. The World War II website indicates that the number of casualties in that war reached about 130 million.
9 In East Asia, South Korea, Japan and Singapore have the highest rate of suicide (WHO 2021: 14–28).
10 Benin philosopher Paulin J. Hountondji considers that when civilisation is mentioned as singular, it should refer to "the real empirical unity of a specific geographical area" (Hountondji 1996: 160). Du Bois described various cultures in Africa – for example, Arab culture, East African culture, Ethiopian culture, Egyptian culture, Nigerian culture, Sudanese culture (Du Bois 1992).
11 Refer to Chapter 18 of this book, on Chinese medical teams in Africa.
12 The fifth batch of Chinese humanitarian aid to Sudan's Darfur left from Tianjin on 24 August 2007. http://news.enorth.com.cn/system/2007/08/24/001839261.shtml; "Humanitarian aid from China leaves for Sudan's Darfur" www.focac.org/eng/zxxx/t353371.htm
13 "Confrontation over Darfur 'will lead us nowhere'", *China Daily*, 27 July 2007. www.chinadaily.com.cn/2008/2007-07/27/content_5445062.htm
14 "Chinese Foreign Minister Yang reviewed FOCAC achievements in the past three years". Xinhua News Agency, 2010. www.focac.org/chn/zxxx/t625612.htm.
15 The programme's report provided the following explanation: "Environmental degradation, as well as regional climate instability and change, are major underlying causes of food insecurity and conflict in Darfur – and potential catalysts for future conflict throughout central and Eastern Sudan and other countries in the Sahel belt." See also the programme's Post-Conflict and Disaster Management Branch website at http://postconflict.unep.ch. This view on the role of environmental degradation is not new, but has been neglected by the outside world.
16 It is noteworthy that a much more serious disaster in the neighbouring Democratic Republic of the Congo did not elicit as much attention from the United States.
17 *Policy of Warring States* or *Intrigues of Warring States* (战国策) consists of 33 volumes of various states at different times, mainly describing the political opinions and strategies of political strategists (lobbyists) in the Warring States period (490–221 BCE). The author is anonymous, yet there have been various commentators since Liu Xiang of the Western Han Dynasty (202 BCE–8 CE). Indicating the historical characteristics and social features of the Warring States period, it is an important historiographical classic for the study of that time.

References

allAfrica.com 2009. "President Sirleaf hails Sino-Africa partnership, says it increases continent's chances", 10 November. http://allafrica.com/stories/200911091586.html

Ampiah, K. & Naidu, S. 2008. *Crouching tiger, hidden dragon? Africa and China*. Cape Town: University of KwaZulu-Natal Press.

Apps, P. 2007. Watch your facts, UK ad watchdog warns campaigners. www.alertnet.org/thenews/newsdesk/L14822855.htm

Autesserre, Séverine. 2006. Local violence, international indifference? Post-conflict 'settlement' in the eastern D. R. Congo (2003–2005). PhD thesis, New York University.

Bagby, Philip. 1958. *Culture and history*. London: Longmans.

Berger, B. 2006. China's engagement in Africa: Can the EU sit back? *South African Journal of International Affairs* 8(1): 115–127.

Bo, Z. 2007. The life of foreign aid of doctors from Hubei. www. africawindows. com/bbs/thread-9931-1-1. html

Braudel, Fernand. 1980. *On history.* Trans. Sarah Matthews. Chicago: University of Chicago Press.

Brautigam, D. 2009. *The dragon's gift: The real story of China in Africa.* Oxford: Oxford University Press.

China Daily. 2007. Confrontation over Darfur "will lead us nowhere", 27 July. www.chinadaily.com.cn/2008/2007-07/27/content_5445062.htm

Chutian Metropolis Daily. 2007. What kind of issue is Darfur? A special interview with the special representative of the Chinese government, 8 July.

De Tocqueville, A. 1835. *Democracy in America.* London: Saunders and Otley.

Deng Xiaoping. 1993. *Selected works of Deng Xiaoping, Vol. 2.* Beijing: People's 6 Press.

Department of International Cooperation of the Ministry of Health. 2003. Strengthening the implementation of the new strategic reform and assisting African medical work: On the 40th anniversary of the dispatch of Chinese medical team for foreign aid. *West Asia and Africa* 5: 15–18.

Du Bois, W.E. Burghardt. 1992. *The world and Africa: An inquiry into the part Africa has played in world history.* New York: International Publishers.

Eisenman, J. & Kurlantzick, J. 2006. China's Africa strategy. *Current History* 105(691): 216–224.

Enorth.com.cn 2007. The fifth batch of Chinese humanitarian aid to Sudan's Darfur leaves from Tianjin, 24 August. http://news.enorth.com.cn/system/2007/08/24/001839261.shtml.

FOCAC 2007. Humanitarian aid from China leaves for Sudan's Darfur. www.focac.org/eng/zxxx/t353371.htm

Faust, Drew Gilpin. 2008. *This republic of suffering: Death and the American Civil War.* New York: Alfred A. Knopf.

Guerrero, Dorothy-Grace & Manji, Firoze, eds. 2008. *China's new role in Africa and the South: A search for a new perspective.* Nairobi: Fahamu and Pambazuka.

Hao, Y. & Lin, S. 2007. *Chinese foreign policy making: An analysis of societal factors.* Beijing: Social Sciences Academic Press.

Hammond, D. & Jablow, A. 1977. *The myth of Africa.* New York: Library of Social Science.

Harneit-Sievers, A. et al., eds. 2010. *Chinese and African perspectives on China in Africa.* Nairobi: Pambazuka Press.

Health Department of Hubei Province. 1993. *Famous doctors in North Africa.* Beijing: Xinhua Press.

Hountondji, Paulin J. 1996 [1983]. *African philosophy: Myth and reality.* Bloomington, IN: Indiana University Press.

Huang Hua. 2007. *My reminiscences.* Beijing: World Affairs Press.

Huntington, S.P. 1996. *The clash of civilizations and remaking of world order.* New York: Simon and Schuster.

Kroeber, A. & Kluckhohn, C. 1952. *Culture: A critical review of concepts and definitions.* Cambridge, MA: Harvard University Press.

Kuper, Adam. 1999. *Culture: The anthropologist's account.* Cambridge, MA: Harvard University Press.

Large, D. 2008: Beyond "dragon in the bush": The study of China–African relations. *African Affairs* 107(426): 45–61.
Laverty, William Henry & Kelly, Ivan William. 2019. Yearly suicides across Canada, Great Britain and the United States from 1960 to 2015: A search for underlying long-term trends. *Open Journal of Social Sciences* 7(6): 107–115.
Li Anshan 2002. *British rule and rural protest in Southern Ghana*. New York: Peter Lang.
Li Anshan 2006. On the adjustment and transformation of China's African policy. *West Asia and Africa* 8: 11–20.
Li Anshan 2007. Africa in the perspective of globalization: Development, assistance and cooperation. *West Asia and Africa* 7: 5–14.
Li Anshan 2008. China's new policy towards Africa. In R. Rotberg, ed., *China into Africa: Trade, aid, and influence*, Washington, DC: Brookings Institution Press.
Li Anshan. 2011. *Chinese medical cooperation in Africa: With special emphasis on the medical teams and anti-malaria campaign*. Uppsala: Nordic African Institute. http://nai.diva-portal.org/smash/get/diva2:399727/FULLTEXT02.pdf.
Li Anshan 2018. Studies on mutual learning among civilizations. *Journal of Northwestern Polytechnical University (Social Sciences)* 4: 42–50.
Li Anshan 2021. *A history of modern Africa*. Shanghai: East China Normal University Press.
Li Jianming 2016. Research on the concept and history of civilization. *Journal of Central China Normal University (Humanities and Social Sciences Edition)* 1: 108–116.
Liu Jirui, ed. 1998. *Chinese medical teams in Tanzania*. Jinan: Health Department of Shandong Province.
Long Xiangyang. 2000. The preliminary probe to the China-Africa relations from 1966 to 1969. In Center for African Studies of Peking University, ed., *China and Africa*. Beijing: Peking University Press, 72–86.
Lu Chunming 2006. Côtecxin—Tie of China–African Friendship, Voice of Friendship. http://qkzz.net/magazine/1003-5303B/2006/06/1849404.htm
Manji, F. & Marks, S. 2007. *African perspective on China in Africa*. Nairobi: Fahamu and Pambazuka.
Mao Zedong. 1994. *Selections of Mao Zedong's works on diplomacy*. Beijing: Central Documentation Publishing House and World Affairs Press.
Mazrui, Ali A. 1980. *The African condition: A political diagnosis*. Cambridge: Cambridge University Press.
Mohammed, A. 2004. The Rezaigat camel nomads of the Darfur region of Western Sudan: From cooperation to confrontation. *Nomadic Peoples* 8: 230–240.
Mohan, R. 2002. Sakhalin to Sudan: India's energy diplomacy. The Hindu, 24 June.
Monson, J. 2009. *Africa's freedom railway: How a Chinese development project changed lives and livelihoods in Tanzania*. Bloomington, IN: Indiana University Press.
Mudimbe, V.Y. 1988. *The invention of Africa: Gnosis, philosophy and the order of knowledge*. Bloomington, IN: Indiana University Press.
Olander, Eric. 2020. China's surprisingly durable reputation in Africa. *The Africa Report*, 11 September. www.theafricareport.com/41380/chinas-surprisingly-durable-reputation-in-africa
People's Daily. 1963. Chinese medical team went to Algeria, 7 April.
People's Daily. 1964. Premier Zhou answered the questions of the news reporter of the Ghana news agency, stating a new independent powerful Africa will appear in the

world and China will support the newly rising countries in developing their independent national economy strictly according to the eight principles, 18 January.
People's Daily. 1983. Premier Zhao talked his visits to ten African countries had reached the expected purpose at the Dar Salaam press conference, 15 January.
Qian Qichen. 2003. *Ten episodes in China's diplomacy.* Beijing: World Affairs Press.
Qian Mu. 1994. *Introduction to the history of Chinese culture.* Beijing: Commercial Press.
Qian Mu. 2001. *New theory of national history.* Beijing: SDX Joint Publishing Company.
Ray, Julie. 2019. Image of US leadership now poorer than China's, 28 February, Gallup.com.
Sall, Alioune. 2021. What can be the position of Africa in contemporary globalisation? A few thoughts on the matter. In Rahma Bourqia & Marcelo Sili, eds, *New paths of development: Perspective from the Global South.* New York: Springer, 69–75.
Shinn, D.H. 2006. Africa, China and health care. *Inside Asia* 3&4: 14–16.
Shweder, Richard A. 2000. Moral maps, "First World" conceits, and the new evangelists. In Lawrence E. Harrison & Samuel P. Huntington, eds, *Culture matters: How values shape human progress.* New York: Basic Books, 158–176.
Siringi, S. 2003. Africa and China join forces to combat malaria. *The Lancet* 362: 456.
Soudien, Crain & Houston, Gregory. 2021. African perspectives on development in the context of a changing international system. In Rahma Bourqia & Marcelo Sili, eds, *New paths of development: Perspective from the Global South.* New York: Springer, 25–41.
Strauss, J.C. & Saavedra, M. 2009. *China and Africa: Emerging patterns in globalization and development.* Cambridge: Cambridge University Press.
Taylor, I. 2006. *China and Africa: Engagement and compromise.* London: Routledge.
Thompson, D. 2005. China's soft power in Africa: From the Beijing Consensus to health diplomacy. *China Brief* 5(21): 1–5.
Toynbee, Arnold. 1966. *Change and habit: The challenge of our time.* Oxford: Oxford University Press.
Toynbee, Arnold & Caplan, Jane. 1972. *A study of history.* Oxford: Oxford University Press.
United Nations Environmental Program. 2007. *Sudan post-conflict environmental assessment.* http://postconflict.unep.ch/publications/UNEP_Sudan.pdf.
Wade, A. 2008. Time for the West to practise what it preaches. *Financial Times*, 29 February.
Wang Qinmei. 2000. A setback of China-African relations. In Centre for African Studies of Peking University, ed., *China and Africa.* Beijing: Peking University Press, 59–71.
Weber, M. 1905. The Protestant ethic and the spirit of capitalism. London: Routledge.
WHO. 2021. *Suicide worldwide in 2019: Global Health Estimates.* Geneva: World Health Organization.
Wiredu, Kwasi. 1996. *Cultural universals and particulars: An African perspective.* Bloomington, IN: Indiana University Press.
Xinhua News Agency. 2007. Sudan government deals with Darfur issue with a light pack. http://news.xinhuanet.com/world/2007-07/15/content_6377969.htm
Yang Bojun. 1960. *Mencius with annotation.* Beijing: Zhonghua Book Company.

Yu, Gorge. 1975. *China's African policy: A Study of Tanzania*. New York: Praeger.
Zhang Tieshan 1999. *A road of friendship: Record of building TAZARA railway*. Beijing: China Foreign Trade Press.
Zhu Zudi. 1985. *A study on policy of Warring States*. Nanjing: Jiangsu Classics Press.

10 BRICS and Africa[1]

Introduction

In 1992, Professor Lester Thurow, a famous US economist from MIT, published a book entitled *Head to head: The coming economic battle among Japan, Europe, and America*, to analyse and judge the coming competition between economic powers and economic development in the 21st century (Thurow 1992). The author seems very confident in the future economic giants Japan, Europe and the United States and believes that in the 20th century, the rich club accepted only one country – Japan. It would not be surprising if no country entered the rich club in the 21st century. Once published, the book had a huge reaction in Japan, Europe and the United States and became a bestseller. Yet no matter how famous Mr Thurow is, his prediction has not been fulfilled. Neither BRICS nor any country among the BRICS even entered his vision. He never thought China would become the second world economy in 2010.

At the close of the Fifth BRICS Summit on 27 March 2013 in Durban at South Africa, the leaders reached a broad consensus on "jointly dealing with major global and regional issues, reforming the international monetary and financial systems, and promoting the cause of global development". China reaffirmed its commitment to the promotion of international law, multilateralism and the central role of the United Nations. The equal discussions reflected the growing intra-BRICS solidarity and a shared goal to contribute positively to global peace, stability, development and cooperation. "We also considered our role in the international system to be based on an inclusive approach of shared solidarity and cooperation with all nations and peoples" (BRICS 2013). Several agreements were signed to strengthen cooperation within the group and enhance engagement with other emerging and developing economies. BRICS leaders agreed to set up a BRICS Development Bank, a Contingent Reserve Arrangement (CRA), a business council and a think-tank council. This event may be a watershed moment in the reform of the international system set up after World War II.

DOI: 10.4324/9781003220152-12

BRICS and "looking East"

After World War II, the international financial system established according to the Bretton Woods Agreement had three major tasks: to work for European reconstruction; to monitor international financial changes; and to provide assistance for development. The first task was completed, the second has been undertaken by regional banks or national banks, and the aid issue has become the task of international financial organisations. However, this has not made it easy for developing countries to apply for financial aid from international financial institutions, while excessive intervention (such as the structural adjustment imposed by international financial organisations on Africa and the political conditions imposed by Western countries in aid) has caused suffering rather than benefiting developing countries. Various African countries have been receiving aid since independence and Western aid to Africa has not been a small amount, yet the effect seems to be poor – a fact recognized by Western academia and governments (Easterly 2006; Calderisi 2006; Collier 2006). Some scholars call this debt "immoral", "illegal" and "usury" because it has been repaid many times by African countries in the form of interest.

In fact, African countries have paid much higher interest than their principal to repay their debts. In this way, capital sometimes flows not from North to South, but rather from South to North. French scholar Gabas points out that if we consider just the interest paid by the countries benefiting from the aid, we find it accounts for US$100–120 billion between 1995 and 2000 (Gabas 2002: 28). Therefore, the international aid system is facing a crisis of trust, and the world is undergoing unprecedented changes. The establishment of the BRICS Development Bank on 15 July 2014 was a historic event, which fundamentally changed the international financial system and international political pattern established after World War II.[2]

It is under such international background that "looking East" has become a new trend of African countries and emerging countries becoming increasingly close partners. According to the data of *Africa and its Emerging Partners* in 2011, due to the economic crisis in 2008–2009, the centre of world economic development has rapidly shifted from OECD countries to Eastern or Southern countries and the ties between Africa and emerging economies have expanded rapidly in both depth and breadth. First, the volume of trade has increased rapidly. The proportion of emerging countries in Africa's total foreign trade is rising. Second, the attractiveness and development potential of African countries promote the increase in foreign investment, especially in emerging countries. Research shows that the number of foreign direct investments in Africa increased from 339 projects in 2003 to 857 projects in 2011. The proportion of emerging market countries' investment in Africa has increased significantly, from 99 in 2003 to 538 in 2011, far more than the 319 in developed countries (African Development Bank 2011). Third, China, India and Brazil have greatly strengthened their economic and trade relations with Africa.

BRICS has now become an interest-point of world academia, which prefers to use the term to describe a global economic trend. This chapter studies the relationship between BRICS and Africa. It begins with the wrong prediction, followed by the different names and similarity of emerging economies, the dynamics of BRICS, BRICS' relations with Africa and China's role.

Famous professor, wrong prediction

BRICs, an acronym coined by Goldman Sachs' chief economist Jim O'Neill in 2001 for the four developing economies and emerging markets – Brazil, Russia, India and China – has taken the world's breath away with its rapid growth and future economic prospects. Only eight years after publishing the research report that introduced the term, Jim O'Neill forecast in 2009 that BRICs would overtake the combined GDP of the G7 nations by 2027, nearly a decade sooner than predicted. In 2010, South Africa became a new member of the group, thus bringing BRICS into being. South Africa had three objectives in mind in joining the group: to advance national interests; to promote regional integration programs and related continental infrastructure programmes; and to partner with key players of the Southern Hemisphere on issues related to global governance and reform. South Africa's membership obviously expanded BRICS' geographic and intercontinental reach, which was more balanced with the African continent represented. Africa has enormous human and natural resources and rich culture, although O'Neill disagreed somewhat with its inclusion. Now BRICS is substantial in terms of population, land mass and economy. Together, the five countries comprise 40 per cent of the world's population, 25 per cent of the world's land mass and about 20 per cent of global GDP. They already control some 43 per cent of global foreign exchange reserves, and their share keeps rising.

The 21st century witnesses the important phenomenon of BRICS in global geopolitics and economy. It is almost like a shock on the stage of world affairs. As a prominent economist in the United States, Professor Lester Thurow was a member of President Johnson's economic consultant team, one of the original founders of the Economic Policy Institute in 1986 and former dean of the MIT Sloan School of Management. In a book published in 1992, he analysed the economic powers and made predictions for the coming century. He was quite confident in naming the coming economic powers: Japan, Europe and the United States. The argument was that in the 20th century, the "rich country" club admitted only one member, Japan, and it would not be at all strange if no country were admitted in the 21st century. Analysing the economic development of world powers in the next century, the book became a bestseller in Japan, Europe and United States. The author seemed to be quite sure of the future of economic giants and believed that things would remain the same in the 21st century (Thurow 1992).

Yet, no matter how brilliant his academic achievements are, the situation in the 21st century was very different from what he had expected. His prediction was off base, largely because none of the BRICS or other emerging economies entered his vision. Nor did he foresee the financial crisis experienced by Europe and United States at the beginning of the new century. Furthermore, he never though that China, one of the BRICS, would become the second largest economy in 2010 and the world's largest trading country in goods in 2013. China surpassed the United States in the recognition of the leadership in the world. On 18 January 2019, the well-known Gallup Global Leadership Approval Center issued its annual survey, Rating World Leaders, reporting that people in 134 countries and regions around the world recognised China's leadership by 34 per cent, higher than 31 per cent in the United States (Ray, 2019). Since 2005, this Center has been tracking the entire world's perceptions of the performance of the leadership of some of the biggest players on the global stage, such as the United States, Germany, China and Russia, rating the result of the poll indicating the rise and fall of the world's leading powers in more than 130 countries and areas, where the biggest gains and losses came from and how each country stacks up in different parts of the globe. This is the second time since 2008 that China's global recognition of leadership has surpassed that of the United States, setting a record for China in ten years (Ray 2019).

Obviously, Thurow ignored the emerging economies. Why? It seems reasonable from a historical viewpoint.

> Until the beginning of the 1990s, Russia was still behind the Iron Curtain, China was recovering from the Cultural Revolution and the Tiananmen Square unrest, India remained a bureaucratic nightmare, and Brazil experienced bouts of hyperinflation combined with a decade of lost growth. These countries had largely muddled along outside the global market economy; their economic policies had often been nothing short of disastrous; and their stock markets were nonexistent, bureaucratic, or super volatile. Each needed to experience deep, life-threatening crises that would catapult them onto a different road of development.
> (Van Agtmael 2012)

This was the situation when Thurow wrote his book, yet things changed dramatically. The prediction itself indicates one thing: Thurow was confident about the global order established by the West after World War II and believed that in the 21st century it would be still dominated by Europe and United States, with some competition from Japan. He never thought that the situation would change so much, and certainly didn't consider the extraordinary speed of the change.

Emerging economies: Different names and similar characters

In the international field, it is customary to use names or titles to describe countries with similar characteristics in the present, regardless of their different histories or cultures. Acronyms have long been a favorite of economic experts and policy-makers as a convenient tool to illustrate the world as it stands or the changes taking place. In this century, various terms or acronyms have appeared to describe groups of countries with impressive performances in the global economy.

VISTA 5

In 2005, BRICs Economic Research Institute of Japan put forward a new acronym, VISTA (Vietnam, Indonesia, South Africa, Turkey and Argentina), to indicate emerging countries that have an emerging market, rich natural resources, increasing numbers of young workers, stable political and economic situations, active attraction of foreign investment and an expanding consumer base.

Next Eleven (N11)

On 1 December 2005 "Next Eleven" was coined by Goldman Sachs to refer to 11 developing countries with a large population and fast economic development: Mexico, Indonesia, South Korea, Turkey, Vietnam, the Philippines, Pakistan, Nigeria, Egypt, Iran and Bangladesh. A bright future was predicted for the 11 countries (O'Neill et al. 2005).

Group of Five (Outreach Five)

In 2007, the term "Group of Five" was used by the G8 in the so-called "Heiligendamm Process" created by German Prime Minister Angela Merkel to indicate five promising countries – Brazil, China, India, Mexico, and South Africa – that the G8 wanted to include in discussions of global issues.

B(R)ICSAM constellation

Owing to Russia's entry to the G8, the country was removed by some from BRICS, which prompted the aforementioned Group of Five. However, the Centre for International Governance Innovation (CIGI) in Waterloo, Canada includes Russia in the group, thus creating the B(R)ICSAM constellation: Brazil, Russia, India, China, South Africa, and Mexico (Cooper 2007).

Emerging 7 (E7)

In 2009, the name "Emerging Seven" was put forward by PricewaterhouseCoopers to include China, India, Brazil, Russia, Indonesia, Mexico and

Turkey. It was predicted that in 2020 the economic aggregate of E7 would reach 70 per cent of the G7, and in 2032 it would surpass the present G7 in all fields.

CIVETS (CIVITS)

In 2009, the acronym CIVETS was created by *The Economist* to include Colombia, Indonesia, Vietnam, Egypt, Turkey and South Africa. All possess the characteristics of a significant young population and vigorously diversified economy, and are thus optimal places for international investment. Later, Colombia was exchanged for China, and Egypt for Indonesia. Since the pronunciation is the same, the term remained the original one: "CIVETS" (*The Wall Street Journal* 2010).

Emerging 11

On 9 April 2010, the Boao Forum for Asia held in Hainan, China put forward a new concept, Emerging 11, which includes Argentina, Brazil, China, India, Indonesia, South Korea, Mexico, Russia, Saudi Arabia, South Africa and Turkey. Those countries are also members of the G20. It was based on the premise that these emerging countries should be studied as a unit.

MIST

In 2011, Jim O'Neill created another acronym indicating ideal countries for foreign investment. MIST includes four countries out of the N11 – Mexico, Indonesia, South Korea, and Turkey – which compared with Bangladesh, Egypt, Nigeria, Pakistan, the Philippines, Vietnam and Iran. The original N11 performed much better than BRICs. "MIST is probably another Goldman market edict" (Gupta 2011).

Growing economies

In February 2011, Jim O'Neill also put forward the idea of "growing economies", which include both BRICs and Next 11: Brazil, Russia, India, China, Mexico, Indonesia, South Korea, Turkey, Vietnam, the Philippines, Pakistan, Nigeria, Egypt, Iran, and Bangladesh. These countries have formed an emerging market and comprise the newest and biggest driving force in the world economy. BRICS and N11 are the top hotspots for investment, since each nation has a large population, rich natural resources and a large consumer base.

There are also other terms to describe the new economies, such as Asian Drivers of Global Change, Anchor Countries, Emerging Economies, Emerged Markets, Emerging Countries, Emerging Marketing Countries, Future 7, and Emerging Market Economies (EMEs).[3]

Although some of the acronyms were coined by financial or investment companies, different think-tanks, fora and even journals are also involved in this name-coining boom, which indicates that the phenomenon is not only economic but has rich connotations. What else does it indicate? It is not an exaggeration that an unexpected or even seismic change is occurring in the international arena, be it economic, political or social.

It is meaningless to name a group of countries just to catch the eyes of the world. There must be some unique characteristics binding those countries. What does it mean to coin new acronyms, names and titles? Generally speaking, emerging countries possess the following characteristics: they are developing countries, not developed countries in the traditional sense; they have experienced steady economic development for a period of time, with a ratio of growth above the average of the global level; they have shown resilience during a period of difficulty and proved to be a more dynamic and vigorous force than other countries; they usually have a large population, which serves as a significant consumer market for economic growth; they have a reasonable economic aggregate demand, which can bring about a greater impact on the world economy; they usually have a large, young labour force, driving sustainable and vigorous development; and they have a reasonably stable political and social situation, which lays the foundation for the healthy development of the economy.

The emerging economy has similar characteristics. Furthermore, favourable policies and macro-economic conditions offer a better environment for economic development, thus attracting more foreign investment than other countries.

Indicators of change

The advent of emerging economies or emerging countries is clearly a challenge to the present international system. The formation of BRICS is one of the indicators of a defiance of the current order. The G7, established in 1975, has represented the strongest, biggest and most prosperous economies in the world for decades. Yet the economic situation has changed in the traditional big powers. Since the financial crisis occurred on Wall Street, not only have the developed countries deteriorated but the damage has spread to the global economy. While the old balance is being shaken up, a new status quo is emerging.

The Concept Paper for the 3rd International Solidarity Conference says, "Who would have thought that one day Europe or the US would be on its knees, begging for money from China?" (ANC 2012: 3). Although the statement is obviously an exaggeration, it voices an opinion never before heard in the world. We also see some unexpected phenomena, such as the role reversal between the former colonial masters and the colonised – a good example is Angola, a former colony of Portugal, which is now offering financial support to its former colonial metropolitan state (*The Economist* 2011;

The Guardian 2011). Developing countries are tired of unequal relations with the West; however, the present international system was set up and based on the interests of the big powers, so it will not disappear at once but linger on for some time.

Striving for equality and a better world

The appearance of emerging countries also indicates a new hope for a better and more equal world order. The ideal of equality is embodied in the constitution of almost every country, and is also a major theme in the history of social movements and human development. The established international socio-politico-economic order does not really recognize the principle of equality; the principle of "might is right" or "power matters most" plays the major tune. History has witnessed various unequal incidents or situations, and under-development was created not only by colonialism, but also by the current unequal political and economic order. For example, Niger has an enormous deposit of uranium that could provide an excellent foundation for its normal development. However, the deposit has been monopolised by the French company AREVA for more than half a century and Niger is still one of the least developed countries on the UN list. When the US economic situation deteriorates, it just turns on the machine to print more money so the world has to pay for its debt. Inequality does not only exist in the economic field: the West can use its power to interfere with other countries under the pretext of democracy or human rights – extreme cases include the situation in Afghanistan, Iraq and Libya.

Undoubtedly, people are longing for a just world order and a better future. Who is going to bring this bright future? The goal has to be realised with the joint efforts of the people of the world. The hope is now projected onto the emerging economies. This may take a long time, but it represents a vision.

BRICS: Dynamics, resilience and weakness

The BRICS initiative has gradually evolved into a regular forum for cooperation and coordination on different issues concerning emerging economies and the world, indicating the group's unique dynamics and resilience.

The BRICS share similar views on the issues of development, face many challenges in world politics and hold a promising vision for the future. BRICS have achieved a great deal in various fields, with an emphasis on economy (Lin Yueqin 2012). According to *World Economic Outlook 2013* issued by the IMF in 2013, the BRICS took the lead in world economic growth. In 2013, Brazil's economy was expected to grow by 2.5 per cent. Russia's growth was projected to average 1.5 per cent but would increase to 3 per cent in 2014. Economic growth was expected to be around 3.7 per cent in India and 7.5 per cent in China. South Africa's growth slowed further yet was forecast to improve gradually in 2014 and beyond (IMF 2013: 62–63, 66, 69, 76–77).

In international trade, the BRICS have consistently strengthened economic ties among themselves. Between 2001 and 2010, the trade volume among the five countries increased 15 fold. In 2011, trade continued to increase rapidly. Between China and Russia, the trade volume was US$79.3 billion; trade between China and Brazil reached US$84.2 billion; that of China and India was U$73.9 billion; and that of China with South Africa was US$45.4 billion (IMF 2012: 10). Since mutual complementarity does exist, trade between other members is also growing rapidly. With more and more economic cooperation, the trade volume among BRICS countries has greatly increased (Xue Rongjiu 2012: 4–8).

The BRICS countries have also played a very important role in trade with the African continent. Over the past decade, an intensified strategic engagement between BRICS and Africa has developed. In South African Ambassador Dr Bheki Langa's words:

> In terms of economic links, BRIC–Africa trade has increased nearly eightfold between 2000 and 2008, and the BRIC countries share of African trade increased from 4.6 per cent to almost 20 per cent in 2008. Today, China, India, and Brazil rank as Africa's second, sixth and 10th largest trading partners respectively.
>
> (Lin Yueqin 2011: 18)

Traditionally, the United States and European Union have been the significant partners of low-income countries (LIC), yet their share of exports fell from 60 per cent in 1980 to less than 45 per cent in 2009. Moreover, LIC–BRIC bilateral trade relations are growing stronger. On average, from 2005 to 2008, the share of BRIC countries in LICs' total exports was about 70 per cent more than that of BRIC countries in world exports. Moreover, over the last decade all four BRIC member-states have established themselves as increasingly influential players across Africa (Biswas 2012). The BRIC countries' role in world investment is also impressive. In 2010, the sum of overseas mergers and acquisitions in BRIC countries was US$402 billion, with an increase of 74 per cent from the previous year, and made up 22 per cent of the global aggregate of US$2230 billion. In 2010, China's overseas non-finance investment reached more than US$60 billion, making it one of the top three countries that invested most internationally (Lin Yueqin 2012: 11).

The BRICS countries cooperate in other fields as well. They created a forum for regular meetings to discuss international issues and exchange ideas. First, they are trying to fight protectionism and improve liberalisation of international trade. Second, they are endeavouring to promote reform of the international financial order, such as a diversified international monetary system, stricter supervision of international financial institutions and more prominent positioning of developing countries in the international financial system. Third, they have strengthened their efforts in protection and cooperation in terms of climate change policy and other global issues. During the

Fifth BRICS Summit held in South Africa in 2013, the group agreed upon additional economic mechanisms to safeguard its shared interests and provide more support for developing countries.

As for establishing a dynamic and vigorous system, there is a long way to go for BRICS. Owing to different political systems and cultural variations among the group, mutual trust and consensus are needed. Until now, cooperation and coordination have been concentrated mainly on economic issues; the political influence of the BRICS countries is not as great as their economic strength. The field of international politics and economy requires concrete cooperation, and the group is still in the stage of "discussion", "dialogue" and "exchange of ideas". The Fifth Summit paved the way for some concrete action.

Since the five countries are regional powers, their individual interests and concerns are different. On issues such as value systems, UN Security Council membership, prices of natural resources and tariffs, consensus is yet to be reached. There is even a border conflict between China and India. In order to gain momentum, a greater effort is required to unite in concern for the direct interests of member countries.

In the economic field, there have been many disputes about natural resources, investment and trade. Take China for example: China and Russia pursue cooperation, but also demonstrate friction in the acquisition of natural resources. Relations between China and Brazil are similar. Between China and India, there are tariff frictions and obstacles to investment or trade, while a trade imbalance also exists between China and South Africa. The most observable obstacle is the friction in trade between member countries. Again taking China as an example, its trade with three WTO members of the BRICS group causes various tensions, and China has more trade disputes than India, Brazil and South Africa. From 1995 to 2010, India initiated 637 anti-dumping case investigations with 58 countries, with China receiving the most complaints. The cases concerning China totalled 142, or about 22.3 per cent of the cases opened for investigation. During the same period, Brazil initiated 216 anti-dumping investigations concerning 53 countries, and China was again at the top with 44 cases, or about 20.4 per cent. Among South Africa's 212 anti-dumping investigations with 43 nations during this period, China made up 33 cases or 15.6 per cent of the total, again ranked first (Xue Rongjiu 2012: 7). The reasons for these disputes are varied, such as competition in trade, similarity in types of commodity and the natural expression of protection for national goods and industries.

BRICS and Africa: Linkage and interaction

Since 1995, Africa's economic growth continued at about 4–5 per cent annually. The sustained growth of Africa's economies depends on many factors, one of which is economic cooperation with emerging countries. Some Asian countries (such as China and India) and Latin American countries (such as Brazil) have promoted the development of African countries in one way or another, creating a strong link between African economies and emerging countries, including the BRICS countries.

According to data in *African Economic Outlook: Africa and the New Partnership* (African Development Bank 2011), the economic crisis of 2008–2009 facilitated the transfer of development of the world economy from the centre of OECD states to Eastern and Southern countries. The newly issued *World Investment Report 2013* indicates that, although the world economy was down, Africa attracted much more investment than the global average. Foreign direct investment (FDI) flows to African countries increased by 5 per cent to US$50 billion in 2012, even as global FDI fell by 18 per cent (UNECA 2013). The ties between Africa and emerging economies have developed rapidly in both depth and breadth. First, trade increased rapidly; in 2011, trade volume reached US$673. 4 billion and the figure is increasing (African Development Bank 2012). Trade between China and Africa also maintains reasonable momentum despite the financial crisis. Trade volumes with emerging countries are growing quickly and reached 20 per cent of the total foreign trade in Africa.

Second, the development potential of African countries has attracted foreign investment, with that by emerging countries the most impressive. It shows that South–South investment comprised the largest share of announced greenfield investment to Africa for the second year in a row:

> India, followed by the United Arab Emirates (UAE) and Qatar, contributed up to 60% of total south-south greenfield investment to Africa in 2012. The UAE made the largest total greenfield investment to Africa over the past decade (2003–2012), some $133 billion, about 30 per cent of total south–south investment for the period. The UAE announced its investment peaked in 2007–08 which mainly focuses on ports, tourism infrastructure and telecoms. India and China followed with $52 billion and $45 billion respectively.
>
> (African Development Bank 2013: 47)

Third, China, India and Brazil greatly strengthened their economic and trade relations with countries in Africa, and this cooperation will promote economic development in Africa. Russia is catching up, especially in the field of energy cooperation. Furthermore, their development assistance to African countries is much more advantageous than the aid from the West. The general principles followed by the BRICS countries are equality between partners, mutual assistance, no political conditions, and common development and exchange of development experience, and African countries prefer to have relations with them (Shikwati 2015; Li Anshan 2021).

Brazil

Brazilian and Africans are described as "Brothers separated by the Atlantic", which is regarded as the natural connection between Africa and Brazil. This connection is directly set up during the Atlantic slave trade (Lovejoy 1983; Miers & Roberts 1988; Manning 1990). As early as 1820, the total number of Black Africans transported to Brazil reached 2.942 million (Inikori & Engerman 1992: 208). Such an important blood relationship and historical heritage have undoubtedly become important factors in the cooperation between Brazil and Africa. Statistics show that there are 76 million people of African descent in Brazil (Cao Shengsheng 2013). The Brazilian population statistics of 2011 indicate that more than half of the total population of 200 million are of African descent or have African origins, and Brazil has the largest number of Black people except Nigeria (Wu Jing 2013; Zhou Zhiwei 2014). President Lula's 2009 speech at the African Union Summit held in Sirte has three implications. First, he expressed Brazil's new understanding of the African continent. Second, Brazilians have acknowledged their long-standing blood relationship with Africans, and this kind of gene permeated in Brazilians' blood is the essence of Brazilian culture. Third, Brazil has decided to take Africa as its brother. This relationship has laid a foundation for future Brazil Africa cooperation because of this continuous blood relationship (Stolte 2015: 83–84).

Since President Luiz Inácio Lula da Silva took office in 2003, Brazil has been trying to consolidate its relations with Africa in the political, economic, cultural and social fields, and to expand its influence on the international arena. During Lula's second term, Brazil not only enhanced its relations with South Africa and important oil-producing countries in Africa, but also strengthened cooperation with African regional organisations, such as providing funding to African integration programs. In 2008 and 2009, it provided more than US$600 million to the African integration plan. The rapid growth of Brazilian investment in Africa was accompanied by top official visits. Former President Lula visited 29 African states and President Rousseff visited three African countries in her first year in office. In addition, Brazil has also strengthened the influence of African history on national education.[4] During Lula's eight years in office, Brazil not only restored its former embassies in Africa, but also opened new ones, with a total of 37 embassies meaning Brazil has even more embassies in Africa than the United Kingdom (33) and Germany (34) (Stolte 2015: 93). In international development cooperation, both Lula and Rousseff contributed a great deal to Africa's debt relief (Table 10.1).

Agriculture, energy and health have also become important areas of bilateral economic and trade cooperation between Brazil and Africa. For example, since 2002 Brazil and 18 African countries have signed more than 50 agricultural cooperation agreements. In terms of technical cooperation, Brazil has carried out about 150 technical cooperation projects in Africa, involving 40 countries, covering tropical agriculture, tropical medicine, vocational and technical education, energy and social management development. In July 2011, Brazil began exporting rice to South Africa. Brazil's trade with Africa has grown by 16 per cent annually since 1990, reaching US$4.2

Table 10.1 Brazil's debt cancellation of African countries (US$10,000)

Country	Amount	Country	Amount
Mozambique*	31,500	Mauritania	4,950
Nigeria*	8,310	DR Congo	580
Cabo Verde*	400	Republic of Congo	3.52
Gabon*	3,600	Sao Tome and Principe	420
Cote d'Ivoire	940	Senegal	650
Gabon	2,700	The Sudan	4,320
Guinea	1,170	Tanzania	23,700
Guinea-Bissau	3,800	Zambia	11,340

* Lula government debt relief. The rest are debts canceled by the Rousseff government.

Source: Zhou Zhiwei (2014). Brazil's African policy since the new century: Objectives, means and effects. *West Asia and Africa* 1: 125–139.

billion in 2001 and US$28.5 billion in 2013. This makes Brazil the third-largest BRICS trading partner with Africa after China and India. Brazil's most important trading partners in Africa are Nigeria, Angola, Algeria and South Africa, which account for 32 per cent, 16 per cent, 12 per cent and 7 per cent respectively of Brazil's total trade with Africa (Liu Haifang et al. 2018: 75). Agriculture is an important area of bilateral economic and trade cooperation between Brazil and Africa. Brazil's agricultural cooperation with Africa is mainly manifested in the construction of agricultural cooperation institutions and mechanisms, focus on cooperation in agricultural development capacity-building, and financial support for agricultural development cooperation. The Lula Institute, the Food and Agriculture Organization and the AU are committed to cooperation projects to solve food-related problems in Africa (Xu Guoqing 2014; Alves 2013).

Brazil and Africa are prominent in energy cooperation. Angola is regarded as an important partner by Petrobras, which has become Brazil's fourth largest international investment target. The oil cooperation between Brazil and Nigeria is also growing. Brazil plays an increasingly important role in Africa's energy development, especially in helping Africa to expand its power generation capacity. In May 2012, Brazil signed an agreement with Mozambique to help the latter realise the "Bright Plan" and provided technical cooperation programs to help people in remote areas use electricity and to promote the development of clean energy. In 2013, a survey on the involvement of Brazilian enterprises in the international market showed that 30.16 per cent of the companies had operations in Africa. Over the past decade, Brazil's technical cooperation with African countries and its principle of not being involved in the internal affairs of African countries have both won its reputation and opened up a market for its goods. Tunisia, Morocco, Cape Verde and Ghana have attracted many Brazilian companies (Xu Guoqing 2012; Cao Shengsheng 2013).

As for the cooperation mechanism between Africa and Brazil, there are three main mechanisms: the India–Brazil–South Africa Dialogue Forum (IBSA), the South America Africa Summit and the Community of Portuguese Speaking Countries. From 2003, the Brazilian Foreign Ministry began to organise the Brazil–Africa Political Cooperation and Trade Forum to symbolise this historic new stage of Brazil–Africa relations. As a result, the forum, with India at the end, was officially launched in 2003 as the India–Brazil–South Africa (IBSA) Dialogue Forum. Brazil donates $1 million annually to the IBSA Dialogue for poverty reduction. This cooperation forum is based on three aspects of concrete cooperation. The first is the common aspiration for the reform of the United Nations. As major regional powers, Brazil, India and South Africa are all dissatisfied with the unreasonable structure of the existing UN system, especially the UN Security Council. They have become important forces to promote the reform of the United Nations. They all hope that the United Nations can expand the seats in Asia, Africa and Latin America to represent the interests of developing countries more widely, and strive for them to be appointed to the position of permanent members of the United Nations. Second, the role of the three regional powers in the WTO, the promotion of South–South cooperation and self-strengthening of developing countries highlight the importance of the three regional powers. As Brazilian Foreign Minister Amorim said, "without India, Brazil and South Africa, there would be no G20". Lula also made it clear that "the coordination among India, Brazil and South Africa has increased our political weight in the World Trade Organization". Third, the three countries also want to promote the realization of the Millennium Goals within the UN framework and strengthen cooperation in poverty reduction and sustainable development in Africa (Jiang Shixue 2007; Jiang Tianjiao 2015).[5]

The South America–Africa Summit was proposed by Brazilian President Lula in April 2005. The first South America–Africa Summit was held in Nigeria in November 2006. A total of 54 African countries and 12 American countries attended the summit. The meeting signed the Abuja Declaration and Action Plan, and reached agreement on the following topics: (1) coordinating the positions of Latin America and Africa to promote the interests of developing countries; (2) Africa inviting Latin American countries to invest in energy and mining in Africa, and establish a two-continent Energy Commission; and (3) opening up direct shipping between two continents to rationalise the shipping route across the Atlantic Ocean. The South American–African Summit is held every three years. In September 2009, the second South America–Africa Summit was held in Venezuela. More than 20 African leaders and eight Latin American heads of state attended the summit and signed the Magrita Declaration and Action Plan. The meeting made clear that there was a consensus on in-depth exchange of experiences of regional organizations and regional cooperation in order to promote sustainable economic growth and carry out cooperation in the field of energy. On specific measures, it decided to establish a regional development bank between the two continents, the Southern Bank. Seven South American countries jointly invested US$20 billion as the start-up fund to provide new international financing channels and set up the Southern Radio Station to strengthen information exchange and communication between the two continents (Wang Tao & Yi Xianglong 2010). In February 2013, the third South America–Africa Summit was held in Malabo, Equatorial Guinea. In order to promote cooperation between the two sides more effectively, the Permanent Secretariat and the Presidential Committee were established at the meeting. As a core member of this mechanism, Brazil has played an important role in promoting bilateral relations (Stolte 2015: 96).

Due to historical, linguistic and cultural ties, Portuguese-speaking countries in Africa, such as Angola and Mozambique, are Brazil's main partners in Africa, and Mozambique has become an important destination for Brazilian enterprises to internationalize. The Community of Portuguese Speaking Countries (CPLP) and the South America–Arab Summit have also played a role in promoting cooperation between Brazil and African countries. The bilateral or multilateral "strategic partnership" or "strategic dialogue mechanism" between Brazil and African regional organizations, as well as the African Union, have provided strong momentum to their development cooperation. The three-party cooperation projects in Brazil, Germany and recipient countries – especially the fight against AIDS – have been extended to African countries (Li Xiaoyun, Xu Xiuli and Wang Yihuan 2013: 28).

It is believed that the development and cooperation between Brazil and Africa are a strategic decision taken by the rising power in order to seek its international status. In 2008, an opinion poll conducted by Brazil's foreign policy agency showed that more than 90 per cent of Brazilian respondents believe their country will play a more important role in the future (Stolte 2015: 44). Development cooperation becomes an important means of implementing Brazil's African policy and the core content of its South–South cooperation with Africa.

India

With convenient geographical advantages of the sea route, Africa and India have a long history of exchanges. In ancient times, Africans immigrated continuously to India, and Black people once established a Black dynasty in India (Rashidi & Sertima 2007). The development of the Arabian route made the communication between the Indian subcontinent and the East African coast more convenient, and the Arab slave trade led to a large number of Black Africans being trafficked to India and even the Asian continent (Lovejoy 1983: 59–60, 76–77, 150–151; Manning 1990: 79–81, 136–140). It is believed that the trade relationship between East Africa and India has existed for a long time. In a series of long papers, Sakarai discussed the relationship among Indian businessmen, British colonialists and East Africa, as well as the status of the slave trade in the East Africa–Persian Gulf–India triangle, some of which came from Indian historical records (Sakarai 1980, 1981). Until now, India still retains the mark of Black culture in race and historical tradition.

Since its independence in 1947, India has firmly opposed the racial discrimination policy in southern Africa. The Nehru government's foreign policy towards Africa has three basic principles: to support the South African people's struggle against racial discrimination; to support African countries in their struggle against colonialism and for national liberation; and to support the unity of the people of Asian and African countries to jointly safeguard national independence and sovereignty. In 1954, India announced the severance of diplomatic relations with South Africa, and became the first country to challenge the racist regime in South Africa (Zhu Mingzhong 2005). More importantly, the "Pancasila Principle" (the five principles of peaceful coexistence in Hindi – mutual respect for sovereignty and integrity of trust, mutual non-aggression, non-interference in each other's internal affairs, equality and mutual benefit, and peaceful coexistence) has been the cornerstone of India's foreign policy since the 1950s, and became the principle for Asian and African countries to deal with the state relations at the Bandung Conference.

A large number of Indian diaspora exist in Africa, especially in East and South Africa (Biswas 1992; Dubey 1989, 2009, 2010). According to a research, there are 1.1 million Indians/Asians in South Africa (Burger 2005/2006: 2), this group has also made a big contribution to economic development in the continent. Since the beginning of the 21st century, bilateral cooperation has been greatly accelerated. The Pan African e-network Project, proposed by India in 2004, aimed to help African countries realise online education, medicine, trade, management, entertainment, resource map and meteorological services through computer networks. The Techno-Economic Approach for Africa-India Movement is an aid-project with US$500 million of technology and equipment provided by India in 2004 to eight African countries – Burkinabe, Chad, Cote d'Ivoire, Equatorial Guinea, Ghana, Guinea, Mali and Senegal – to help them develop. From 2002 to 2007, the Focus Africa Program was another important measure taken by India to promote trade relations with African countries. India's aid to Africa is concentrated on two aspects: provision of loans and debt relief (Table 10.2). For example, in 2003 India's finance minister announced the implementation of India's development plan, under which Ghana, Mozambique, Uganda, Tanzania and Zambia benefited to the tune of US$24 million (UNCTAD 2010). India has strongly supported the regional integration of Africa and provided $200 million to NEPAD.[6]

Since the beginning of the 21st century, bilateral cooperation has achieved remarkable results. India's total investment in Africa has been growing. In the automotive industry, Mahinda and Tata have invested in South Africa. The first wave of India's investment in Africa mainly came from large enterprises, and the second wave comprised small and medium-sized enterprises. India not only promotes relations with South Africa, but also advocates strengthening economic and trade cooperation in a multilateral framework (Shen Dechang

Table 10.2 Amount and purpose of loan provided by the Export–Import Bank of India (part)

Recipient	Amount (US$10,00)	Purpose
Zambia	1000	Buy Indian equipment
Djibouti	1000	Buy Indian equipment
Mozambique	2000	Subsidies for equipment imported from India
Ghana	1500	Buy Indian product
The Sudan	5000	Buy Indian equipment
Lesotho	500	Buy Indian product
Kenya	2000	Railway project
Senegal	1500	Rural power grid and purchase of agricultural equipment
Angola	4000	Railway Resettlement Project
Senegal	1790	Purchase 350 buses from Tata

Source: ODI (2005. Quoted from Li Xiaoyun, Xu Xiuli & Wang Yihuan (2013: 39).

2008). It is true that Indian trade with Africa was less than that with China (Vidyarthee 2008), yet it has its own advantages.

In 2009, investment in Africa accounted for 33 per cent of India's total investment. In 2012, during the India Africa Trade Ministerial Conference, the two sides agreed to set up the India Africa Commerce and Trade Commission to ensure a substantial increase in trade and investment. According to statistics, India ranks sixth in the source countries of investment projects in Africa from 2003 to 2009, with a total of 130 investment projects and an annual growth rate of 42.7 per cent, far stronger than China. In May 2012, when Indian President Patil visited South Africa, there were extensive exchanges on how to promote economic and trade cooperation. The economic relationship between India and Africa has greatly strengthened, and Africa has become one of India's oil import diversification regions. The African Development Bank stated that Africa had become one of the most diversified regions for oil imports in India. India has established a close relationship with oil-producing countries such as Nigeria and the oil from these countries accounts for about 20 per cent of India's total oil imports. India has also pledged to help Africa establish five research institutions to study agriculture and food security issues. The 2012 India Africa dialogue of trade ministers fully discussed the current trade situation and the prospects of promoting bilateral trade, with both agreeing to establish the India Africa Enterprise Council to ensure that trade and investment would increase dramatically in the future (Ochieng & Musyoka 2017). India has also decided to set up ten cooperative research institutions in Africa, including in the textile industry and civil aviation (Qiu Changqing & Liu Erwei 2012; Biswas 2013).

In order to promote India–Africa cooperation, the India–Africa Summit was established in 2008 . The mechanism of the forum is quite similar to that of the Forum on China–Africa Cooperation; it is held once every three years, alternately in India and African countries. The first India–Africa Summit invited the heads of 14 African countries, including Algeria, the Democratic Republic of Burkinabe, the Democratic Republic of the Congo, Egypt, Ethiopia, Ghana, Kenya, Libya, Nigeria, Senegal, South Africa, Tanzania, Uganda and Zambia. The India–Africa Summit also invited the leaders of NEPAD, ECOWAS, SADC, COMESA, EAC, the Economic Community of Central African States (ECCAS), the Maghreb Union and other important regional organisations, which shows that India attaches importance to the development of multilateral cooperation with Africa and ways to solve development problems through multilateral cooperation. At the end of the India–Africa Summit, two documents, the Delhi Declaration and the India Africa Cooperation Framework, were issued (Yu Zhongjian 2009; Du Ying 2011). India's policy of promoting international development cooperation with African countries is highly valued by Western countries. The German International Development Research Institute believes India has made rapid progress in strengthening bilateral trade, promoting inter-regional cooperation in Africa, direct investment, technology transfer, actively participating in peacekeeping and providing various educational opportunities for African countries, thus posing challenges to the international development cooperation led by the West (Sheth 2008; Naidu & Hayley 2009).[7] The institutionalization of the summit has greatly promoted economic and trade cooperation between India and Africa (Tang Lixia & Liu Xinmiao 2016).

In 2012, South–South investment accounted for the largest share of the announced green space investment for the second year in a row. India ranked first in South–South green space investment in Africa in 2012, with a total investment of US$52 billion, accounting for 60 per cent of the total investment (African Development Bank 2013: 47). Economic cooperation between India and Africa in other areas is also expanding. In 2013, in a dialogue with senior officials from 42 African countries, Indian government officials said that India–Africa cooperation was carried out on the basis of bilateral consultations, and India's assistance was stressed on capacity-building. The Indian government is establishing 80 capacity-building centres in African countries, and six institutions within the framework of the second India–Africa Summit to help Africa's economic and social development, conducting vocational training for young people at the regional level. For example, India's civil society set up another 10 vocational training centres in African countries. In 2012, 53 per cent of South Africa's coal and 6 per cent of its iron ore were exported to India. Indian cars are popular in Africa. Other commodities exported to Africa include telecommunications equipment, agricultural machinery, electronic machinery, plastic products, steel and cement. The bilateral trade is also developing rapidly, reaching $74 billion in 2014, an increase of 80 per cent over 2008. In 2008, India's trade with Africa was only a quarter of that between Africa and the United States and half that between Africa and France. In 2014, India's trade with Africa exceeded that between the United States and France (Freemantle 2015).

Russia

Russia's role in cooperation with Africa started when it was part of the Soviet Union. Soviet aid to Africa began after African countries' independence and it spent a lot of effort to compete with the United States in Africa. The evolution of the Soviet Union's policy towards Africa, the strengthening of national strength and the challenge of the international situation are the main reasons for the change in Africa's position in the Soviet Union's diplomatic strategy. From Stalin to Gorbachev, the Soviet Union's African policy mainly experienced four phases: limited contact, deepening cooperation, strong intervention and pragmatic cooperation. Its strategic or military sites once spread all over the continent, and Africa became an important part of the Soviet Union's global strategic expansion (Tarabrin 1977; Donaldson 1981; Xu Guoqing 2017).

During this period, Soviet experts participated in the construction of more than 600 enterprises and infrastructure projects in 35 African countries, including power stations, ferrous metallurgy, light and food industries, and refineries. With the participation of Soviet professionals, about 130,000 African workers received vocational training, and 12,000 Africans received higher and secondary education in the Soviet Union. The Soviet Union signed agreements with many African countries on the establishment of 130 teaching institutions at all levels, including 17 institutions of higher learning and 20 secondary technical schools (Weinstein & Henriksen 1980; Donaldson 1981; Xu Guoqing 2017; Russian Satellite News Agency 2019). The economic cooperation of both side is characterised by strong complementarity covering many fields for a long time, yet it started to decline seriously from the 1990s, owing to the change of Russia's diplomatic policies towards Africa after the Cold War. Russia switched its emphasis to the development of economic relations with Western powers while withdrawing from Africa.

Since the 21st century, in the face of the enhancement of Africa's international political and economic influence, Russia has gradually adjusted its policy towards Africa to meet the needs of restoring its status as a great power and integrating into the global economic system. It has begun to deepen its cooperation mechanism with Africa, making use of its advantages in energy, armaments and other fields to promote Russia's African politics. Both sides can cooperate in various fields. In the context of globalisation and diversification of the world economy, strengthening Russia's Africa economic cooperation has gradually become the consensus. There is potential for further cooperation between Russia and Africa in resource development, investment and markets. Putin visited Africa twice in 2016, which helped to strengthen Russia's economic and trade relations with Africa (Zhang Laiyi 2007). Yet Russian aid seemed to be implemented through multilateral organizations rather than bilaterally, and the country is also reluctant to work with non-governmental organizations. It is understandable that the Russian aid budget has only recently begun to increase (Brezhneva & Ukhova 2013).

In terms of development cooperation, development assistance from Russia to Africa is focused on debt relief, energy, health, agriculture, food and education, aiming to help African countries reduce poverty and achieve the Millennium Development Goals, as well as establishing close ties with African regional organizations, such as the African Union, SADC and ECOWAS. The recipients are mainly Sub-Saharan African countries, especially Ethiopia, Namibia and Mozambique (Li Xiaoyun, Xu Xiuli & Wang Yihuan 2013: 60–78). Economic cooperation covers various fields, especially in energy cooperation. With the soaring energy prices, Russia's economy has recovered and thus paid great attention to encouraging its energy enterprises to explore the African energy market. Besides promoting the bilateral cooperation with specific African countries in the energy field, Russia supported South Africa's entry to the BRICS cooperation mechanism and attached importance to energy cooperation within the BRICS framework. Signing the agreement of Sanya Declaration in 2011 and Delhi Declaration in 2012 respectively, Russia agreed to strengthen the exchange of knowledge and skills in energy efficiency, energy conservation and environmental protection among member states, and supported member states in the peaceful use of nuclear energy. At the 2013 BRICS Summit in Durban, together with other member states, Russia promised to support Africa's industrialisation and integration process, finance African infrastructure construction and fully support South Africa's construction of nuclear power plants. In 2014, Russia proposed to establish an energy alliance within BRICS, including an energy reserve bank, an energy policy and fuel reserve bank, and a nuclear power plant. It is recognised that:

> Russia hopes to integrate into the world economic trend and seize the opportunity of Africa's economic development. Russia's energy cooperation with Africa will leverage Russia-Africa economic cooperation and enhance Russia's position in the international energy and international system. The energy company is an entity of energy cooperation between Russia and Africa. With the support of the Russian government, Russian oil companies expand their business in Africa and become a tool to achieve Russian foreign policy objectives. Russia's energy diplomacy towards Africa is of pragmatism and its in-depth energy cooperation in Africa in recent years has benefited from the recovery of Russia's comprehensive national strength and the linkage between the government and enterprises.
>
> (Xu Guoqing 2015)[8]

There has been a boom in promoting Russia–Africa relations since 2014; this covers various fields, including top bilateral visits, mechanism construction, economic and trade cooperation, development assistance to Africa, financial cooperation, legal protection and educational training, etc. Take top visits, for example. In 2018, the exchange of visits between Russian and African heads of state and senior officials reached the peak in recent years, and the number of meetings between the two parties exceeded 20 times. The promotion resulted in the decision to open a Russia-Africa Summit (Qiang Xiaoyun 2019). The Russia–Africa Summit and Economic Forum was held in Sochi from 23–24 October 2019. Leaders of 54 African countries were invited to attend the meeting. At the plenary session of the summit, Russian President Vladimir Putin declared the cancellation of more than US$20 billion in debt on the first day of the opening, and stated that Russia has always supported the African national liberation movement and has made significant contributions to setting up young African countries, economic development and the establishment of armed forces with combat effectiveness. "Our cooperation is strategic and long-term." Within the framework of this summit, a series of important agreements were signed, including economic agreements in the fields of oil, rare earth and diamonds.

As a permanent member of the UN Security Council, Russia intends to continue to participate actively in the formulation of strategic lines and specific measures of the international community to strengthen peace and stability in Africa and ensure regional security. Russia has signed military technical cooperation agreements with many African countries, and has provided Africa with a wide range of weapons and technical equipment, as well as training African military personnel. During the 2018 BRICS Summit, President Putin proposed for the first time that the ties with African countries should be restored to the previous level. The idea of Russia's return to Africa has been moving forward since 2018, and the 2019 Summit shows that Russian Foreign Ministry has seriously started to work towards implementing the idea (Qiang Xiaoyun 2019; Russian Satellite News Agency 2019).

South Africa

As a regional power in Africa and the leading country of southern Africa, South Africa has increased its engagement with the continent, including cooperation with Nigeria, investment in telecommunications in the Democratic Republic of the Congo, and the construction of the Lamu traffic corridor in East Africa. Most importantly, South Africa is pushing for the formation of a free trade zone in southern Africa, which would greatly reduce the economic cost of integration to member states and promote trade between members through various measures such as exemption from customs duties, implementation of standardised customs clearance procedures and uniform clearance documents, and the reduction of pass-through procedures, in order to realise a southern African common market. As the African Union decided to establish an African free trade area in 2017, the practice of foreign trade agreements in the SADC is a good example of economic integration with other parts of Africa. At present, the SADC is planning a traffic blueprint, including connecting Namibia and the South African railway line through the Kalahari Desert in Botswana. Another contribution of South Africa is that the rand serves several countries in southern Africa (Lesotho, South Africa,

Swaziland and Namibia) as the currency in circulation; Zimbabwe is also considering whether to join the rand monetary union.[9]

South Africa has also contributed to Africa–Asia–Latin American relations. In January 2003, after Lula's government came to power, the Brazilian foreign ministry began to organise the Brazil–Africa Political Cooperation and Trade Forum to symbolise the historic new stage of Brazil–Africa relations. The forum aims to bring together scholars, government officials and civil society from Brazil and Africa to enhance mutual understanding. At that time, Brazil was also strengthening its strategic cooperation with South Africa. Economic and trade cooperation between South Africa and India is going smoothly, with a large population of Indian diaspora. Take Durban, for example. In 1949, there were 123,165 migrant Indians in the city, and the Indian population increased to 624,000 in 1989 (University of Natal 1952: 35; Vahed 1995: 5, 72). In 2005/2006, there were 1.1 million Indians/Asians in South Africa (Burger 2005/2006: 2). As a result of the Indian government's encouragement policy, overseas Indian investment in Africa also increased greatly. By 2009, it had reached US$105 billion.[10]

The sustained development of the African economy has demonstrably benefited from cooperation with other emerging economies – particularly with BRICS nations – and vice versa.

The role of China

China and Africa have always maintained close relations. With the transformation of China's economic structure, Chinese enterprises are now increasing their investment in Africa. Huajian in Ethiopia is a good example. A leather shoe factory, Huajian Group, which based its business at Dongguan, Guangdong province in southern China, moved its operations to the Oriental Industrial Park located in Addis Ababa in Ethiopia at the end of 2011. It began production in January 2012, exporting shoes to the United States and Europe in March. In October the same year, Huajian began to make a profit, and it now employs 2300 local workers (Yifu Lin 2013; Zhao Yanrong & Chen Yingqun 2012). This is a trend of economic globalisation and the integration of Chinese and African economies into the world economy.

Owing to the financial crisis, the European and US debt crisis continued to worsen. Although the Chinese economy was affected, it has maintained a certain growth rate overall. In Africa, apart from a few countries, the economy of the continent has not been seriously hit and still maintains a strong growth rate. The Fifth Ministerial Conference of the Forum on China–Africa Cooperation held in July 2012 resulted in three measures of cooperation. These were directly related to the aim of promoting economic cooperation, which will provide greater vitality to Africa's development. It is particularly worth noting that China's intention was to provide Africa with US$20 billion in loans in order to meet the special needs of African countries. Focusing on the fields of infrastructure, agriculture, manufacturing and small and medium-sized enterprises, these loans were intended to promote industrialization and employment in the continent.[11]

The BRICS countries share many views on issues within the framework of various international organisations and forums, such as the reforms of the Bretton Woods Institutions; the Doha Development Round; the UN Millennium Development Goals; support for an equitable and democratic world order; principles of equal cooperation and mutual respect in the international arena; the gradual transition to new multipolarity; trade protectionism; and international terrorism. All these have laid a foundation for the unity of BRICS.

At present, the five countries see BRICS as a forum of increasing importance for dialogue and coordination. They are also prepared to work towards strengthening the group's mechanism. BRICS countries should keep a forward-looking and open attitude to engaging in dialogue and cooperation not only among themselves, but also with other international or regional groups and countries. China has made a great contribution to the initiation and formation of BRICS, so what role could the country play in consolidating BRICS in the future?

First, China could promote mutual understanding and mutual learning in various areas, especially in the fields of history, culture and development, in order to build mutual trust – a key factor in deepening multilateral cooperation. Only through mutual learning can BRICS improve essential mutual understanding, which can gradually transform into confidence-building and finally establish mutual trust.

Since the inception of BRICS, the focus has always been on the economy. However, humans are not only creatures of economics; social evolution also depends on cultural achievements. The BRICS group comprises five nations with different cultural traditions covering four continents; they boast a rich history and civilisation, which can diversify and enhance humankind when shared. Yet it is also a fact that the populations of the BRICS countries are not familiar with one another's histories and cultures. Therefore, the BRICS nations should gradually build up a mutual understanding and mutual learning process by organising various activities, such as visits by artists, students and scholars, conferences to discuss cultural themes and different types of civilisation, exhibitions of history and art, the development of related courses, and an exchange of ideas in international affairs.

The impetus for the coinage of BRICS was that the five countries had developed rather rapidly, thus catching the eye of investors. Yet different countries have different development strategies. Thus far, the BRICS countries have gradually developed mechanisms at the government level for economic cooperation, with an emphasis on trade and investment. Besides the prodigious cultures of its group partners, China can learn a great deal from the development experiences of the other four countries. Russia is traditionally a leading force in science and technology. Furthermore, it has a comprehensive system combining theory and practice, from which China can learn and benefit. Brazil's concept of environmental protection is far more advanced than that of China, which has embraced the idea of "development first and environment second", resulting in many problems. Financial institutes in India have built up an effective system to support small businesses, a pursuit that their Chinese counterparts have more or less ignored. Furthermore, India has established a solid legal system in the financial field, from which China should learn. By solving ethnic conflicts in a peaceful way after the apartheid system, South Africa has provided a good example for resolving ethnic issues in China, a country with 56 ethnic groups and similarly complicated situations.

Moreover, China should take the lead in pushing the cooperation agenda, for bilateral and multilateral cooperation can be broadened in various ways. Since BRICS came into being, cooperation has been concentrated on trade and investment, as well as a few issues of climate change and the environment in the international arena. Obviously, there are more fields for cooperation. BRICS should have a stronger voice in the establishment of global norms and rules, such as international development cooperation and financial systems. For international development cooperation, it is clear that developing countries have a common language and can offer practical assistance to the least developed countries. I attended an off-record workshop on South–South Aid Policy organised by the South African Institute of International Affairs in 2007, where the participants included scholars from Brazil, India, China, South Africa and other development institutions from Europe. It was found that the aid policy of Southern countries followed similar rules that were quite different from those of Western countries, which put conditionality first – a stance that spurred several complaints and grievances from developing countries. The Millennium Challenge Account (MCA) set up by the Bush administration in 2004 is a good example.[12] According to the statement, the Millennium Challenge Corporation (MCC) is an "independent US Government agency with the mission to reduce poverty in developing countries through sustainable economic growth". However, the MCC worked out various strict yet changeable indexes or indicators of three categories (ruling justly, investing in people and encouraging economic freedom), which are used to measure whether a candidate country is qualified. The indicators in the year 2021 are *ruling justly*, including political rights, civil liberties, control of corruption, government effectiveness, rule of law and freedom of information; *investing in people*, including immunization rates, public expenditure on health, public expenditure on primary education, girls' primary education completion rate, girls' secondary education enrolment rate, child health and natural resource protection; and *encouraging economic freedom*, including regulatory quality, land rights and access, access to credit, business start-up, trade policy, inflation, fiscal policy and gender in the economy.[13]

Obviously, it is not easy for African countries to fit these criteria. Ironically, if any African country does meet the requirements of the 21 indicators, it no longer needs foreign aid. In fact, the role of the MCC indicator is triple. The primary goal is to use it as *a condition to force developing countries to follow the Western model politically, socially and economically*. Since no country could meet the indicators, the US can *choose the candidate country at will*. Thus the process with the result becomes a measure to *control and beat the candidate country*.[14] Indian scholar Aparajita Biswas noticed that that both India and China practised the same principles, which were quite different from the US type in international aid to Africa (Biswas 2012). Therefore, it is necessary that BRICS countries should set up their own international development cooperation agenda.

After the global financial crisis began, the catastrophe of the US policy of quantitative easing was prevalent and obvious. The special status of the US dollar in the international monetary system makes its domestic monetary policy affect the global economic situation through international trade and other ways. Today, the world is facing the similar situation. In July 2021, a Chinese report predicts that quantitative easing will magnify the real status of the dollar. Under the condition of quantitative easing, the US monetary policy will cause the global financial cycle, and the change will affect the financial stability of developing countries. Yet the tools for developing countries to control financial stability are not sufficient, resulting in the global financial shock due to the fluctuation of US monetary policy.[15] It would be most beneficial for BRICS countries to carry out their trade in the most convenient way to avoid a disastrous impact of the US currency policy. It is important for the Chinese *renminbi* to become convertible. As one entrepreneur pointed out, as China is the largest economy among the BRICS countries, it is imperative for China to ensure that its currency is fully convertible with restrictions on moving money into and out of the country lifted, as this would make it more effective in using the *renminbi* in intra-BRICS and international trade (Sule 2011). Vice President and Chief Financial Officer of the BRICS New Development Bank (NDB) Leslie Maasdorp suggests that multilateral banks should reconsider their positioning, increase the scope of their activities, raise funds from places with relatively low cost, then lend them to emerging market countries. In the face of a huge crisis such as COVID-19, multilateral banks can play a more important role and broaden their influence. The New Development Bank has provided about US$1 billion of credit to the countries and regions that suffered serious disasters: "We have not only approved the funds quickly, but also put the funds in the worst affected areas in a very short time" (Maasdorp 2021).[16] Therefore, BRICS should unite to make the currency system more beneficial for members, rather than being passive victims of the US-controlled monetary system.

Finally, to facilitate the solidarity of the BRICS members, including a review of previous policies and the establishment of an information exchange network and conflict-resolution system, China should take the lead in reviewing previous policies relating to other member countries. The BRICS countries established bilateral relations long before the acronym came into being, signing various agreements and developed cooperation policies. Are these agreements still effective or a stimulus of bilateral relations, or are they out of date, and thus obstacles to cooperation? There may be different cases and it is important to re-examine the effectiveness of these agreements and discuss the possibility of signing new ones.

Furthermore, information has become more and more important in issues of international politics and economies. BRICS should gradually set up an exchange network to share various kinds of information, especially regarding important issues in the international arena such as the adoption of certain measures for sanctions, interference or even war. The five countries usually have similar standards for those issues, but they need more consultation, a freer exchange of ideas and information-sharing in order to coordinate their actions. Cohesive action is vital for issues such as non-traditional security, terrorist threats, drug trafficking and illegal cross-border activities. Information-sharing can also include immigration and trade issues. Establishing conflict-resolution mechanisms is also essential. Since China, Russia and India share borders, and the five countries overlap in the production or trade in certain goods, it is more than necessary to build mechanisms to avoid conflicts.

Ona Akemu is a Kenyan doctoral student studying in northern Europe. When he returned to Kenya to do a field interview for his thesis, a Kenyan professor answered his question about the difference between China and the West. The assistance from the West often ends up in the Hilton Hotel in Nairobi, where expensive Western consultants hold capacity-building seminars and spend little or no money locally. The Chinese do not work in that way, but follow that local needs. They build a road if you need one. African government officials and ordinary Africans want to see development in their own country and they like the Chinese way (Akemu 2013). Africa sees hope in the resurgence of emerging countries, especially in Asia. Nigerian scholar Fermi Akomolafe believes that as long as people have confidence, determination and vision, anything is possible. The Westerners are not born to be superior and Africans should abandon the mentality of relying on the West and find the road suitable for themselves (Akomolafe 2006).

Conclusion

African countries have developed rather close relations with the BRICS. The trade has been growing between Africa and emerging countries – especially China, India and South Africa, which are among the top ten trading partners in Africa. In 2014, half of Africa's top 20 trading partners' total trade of $940 billion was with emerging countries (Freemantle, 2015) However, African scholars expect that cooperation with emerging countries is not limited to economic and trade exchanges, but a new type of partnership:

> This partnership should be based on a new type of bilateral obligation and unity and cooperation, so as to benefit from the cooperation together,

thus completely abandoning the unique system of exploitation, slavery and dependence in the historical relationship with the West.

(Iye 2017)

Realizing such cooperation should avoid the privatisation of cooperation that leads to corruption and dereliction of duty. Thus, rather than being confined to high-level dialogue, the cooperation should be extended to all areas: "It would be naive to think that these emerging countries would also be concerned about Africa's interests without the supervision of African cooperative countries" (Iye 2017). Emerging countries must uphold the principle of equality and mutual benefit in their cooperation with African countries.

As part of the world's emerging economies, BRICS countries have gained momentum because of their coordination and cooperation. Russia is a traditional leader in science and technology. India has been named the "world's office". Brazil not only has rich natural resources, but also a reputation for renewable energy. South Africa possesses a fairly advanced system in both politics and economy, with vast natural resources. China is regarded as a "world workshop" for economic success. With all these special characteristics, the BRICS countries boast a significant competitive advantage. Academics sometimes ask whether BRICS should choose to be integrated into the existing system or challenge it. Instead of taking a zero-sum attitude to the present system, BRICS should be more open-minded and work within the present framework, but gradually transform the system. The first step is to establish mutual trust, thus paving the way forward. There have been various predictions about the 21st century: that it will be the "century of India", "century of China" or "century of Africa". There is no way to tell which prediction is accurate, yet one thing is certain: the 21st century will be one of emerging countries, including BRICS.

Notes

1 This is a revised paper first presented at an international workshop on South-South Cooperation and New Forms of Southern Multilateralism: BRICS/IBSA-Africa Relations: Turning Threats to Opportunity, held 13–14 June 2011 by Nordic Africa Institute, Sweden. I would like to thank Research Director Fantu Cheru for inviting me to attend the workshop. A different version was published as "BRICS: Dynamics, resilience and role of China", *BRICS–Africa: Partnership and interaction* (Moscow: Institute for African Studies, Russian Academy of Sciences, 2013).
2 "In 2020, the Bank approved 19 loans, adding USD 10.3 billion to our loan book, which totalled US$24.4 billion at the end of 2020, a 63.6% increase over the previous year's portfolio" (Troyjo 2021).
3 According to Kose & Prasad (2010), there are 23 EMEs.
4 This policy not only focuses on Brazil's international strategic layout, but also intends to change the national identity of race. At the same time, it lays down a foundation for improving and developing cooperation with Africa, such as funding the

editing UNESCO General History of Africa (Volume IX). I am honoured to be a member of the International Scientific Committee of UNESCO's General History of Africa, Volume IX–XI, and was elected Vice Chairman of the Committee at its first meeting in El Salvador, Brazil.

5   However, there is a tendency to criticise the "Brazilian development model" based on the increase of primary good production (Favareto 2021: 123–134).
6   GOI, Ministry of Commerce. Focus Africa Program: a Program for Enhancing India's Trade with the African Region. www.pdexcil.org/news/53N0204/focus1.htm
7   German Development Institute Briefing Paper, *India's development cooperation: Opportunities and challenges for international development cooperation* (2009).
8   "Russia proposes energy association within BRICS", Xinhua, 10 July 2014.
9   On 5 December 2020, the African Union declared in its 13th special summit of the free trade area of the African continent that the first transaction of the African continent free trade area would start on 1 January 2021. This event will be one of the most important milestones in the African continent integration project, which will greatly promote intra African trade, promote industrialisation and competitiveness, and help create employment opportunities.
10 German Development Institute Briefing Paper, *India's development cooperation: Opportunities and challenges for international development cooperation* (2009).
11 Hu Jintao's speech at the opening ceremony of the fifth Ministerial Conference of the Forum on China Africa Cooperation,19 July 2012. www.gov.cn/ldhd/2012-07/19/content_2187072.htm
12 In a speech on 14 March 2002, President Bush outlined a proposal for a major new US foreign aid initiative. The Millennium Challenge Account (MCA) is managed by the Millennium Challenge Corporation (MCC) and provides assistance, through a competitive selection process, to developing nations that are pursing political and economic reforms in three areas: ruling justly, investing in people and fostering economic freedom, with a startup capital of US$1 billion earmarked by the Congress.
13 Millennium Challenge Corporation, United States of America, *Guide to the MCC Indicators for Fiscal Year 2021*, 23 October 2020, www.mcc.gov/resources/doc/guide-to-the-indicators-fy-2021#introduction.
14 On the one hand, the US government subsidises domestic farmers in order to make their products cheap in international markets. Yet on the other, it forces the developing country to open its market. For instance, In Africa, a total of 20 million cotton growers in 33 countries depend on cotton production for their livelihood. However, owing to the US Government's subsidies to American cotton farmers, the prices of cotton in West Africa kept dropping after 2003. In the United States, cotton farmers can get US$230 from the government for growing an acre of cotton. Between 2004 and 2005, the US Government totally subsidised domestic cotton farmers to the tune of US$4.2 billion, but in the same period, cotton farmers in Burkina Faso suffered losses of more than US$81 million, even though they experienced a good harvest (Bannerman 2007).
15 How does us quantitative easing affect the global economy?, China Macroeconomy Forum, 26 July, http://ier.ruc.edu.cn; www.163.com/dy/article/GFRILQ9U0552A9XP.html
16 Leslie Maasdorp, vice president of the BRICS New Development Bank (NDB): The role and development potential of multilateral banks in the crisis, 23 July 2021. http://finance.sina.com.cn/jjxw/2021-07-23/doc-ikqciyzk7228122.shtml

References

African Development Bank. 2011. *African economic outlook Africa and the New Partnership (2011)*. Paris: OECD.
African Development Bank. 2012. *African economic outlook 2012: Promoting youth employment*. Paris: OECD.
African Development Bank. 2013. *African economic outlook 2013: Structural transformation and natural resources*. Paris: African Development Bank.
Akemu, Ona. 2013. Beyond China and Africa: Chinese and Western multinationals in Kenya. ERIM. www.erim.eur.nl/centres/china-business/featuring/detail/3158-beyond-china-and-africa-chinese-and-western-multinationals-in-kenya
Akomolafe, Femi. 2006. No one is laughing at the Asians any more. *New Africa*, June: 48–50.
Alves, Ana Cristina. 2013. Brazil in Africa: Achievements and challenges. In Nicholas Kitchen, ed., *Emerging Powers in Africa*. London: LSE, 37–44.
ANC. 2012. *Concept paper for the ANC's 3rd International Solidarity Conference*. Tshwane City Hall, South Africa, 26–28 October.
Bannerman, L. 2007. The farmers ruined by subsidy. *The Times*, 9 April.
Biswas, Aparajita. 1992. *Indio-Kenyan Political and Economic Relations*, New Delhi: Kanishka.
Biswas, Aparajita. 2012. Growing trade relations of BRICS with low income countries: Special reference to the role of India and China in Africa's development paradigm. *International Politics Quarterly* 3: 37–48.
Biswas, Aparajita. 2013. Changing dynamics of India–Africa relations in the 21st century. In Tatiana Deych & Evgeiy Korendyasov, eds, *BRICS–Africa: Partnership and interaction*. Moscow: Institute for African Studies, Russian Academy of Sciences, 110–122.
Brezhneva, A. & Ukhova, D. 2013. *Russia as a humanitarian aid donor*. London: Oxfam.
BRICS. 2013. *Fifth BRICS Summit Declaration and Action Plan*. BRICS document.
Burger, Delien, ed., 2005/2006. *South Africa yearbook, 2005/06*. Pretoria: South African Government.
Calderisi, R. 2006. *The trouble with Africa: Why foreign aid isn't working*. New York: Palgrave Macmillan.
Cao Shengsheng. 2013. Brazil Lula government's African policy: Dynamics, performance and limitations. *Asia & Africa Review* 3: 41–45.
Collier, P. 2006. Africa left behind – editorial: Rethinking assistance for Africa. *Economic Affairs* 26: 4.
Cooper, A.F. 2007. *The logic of the B(R)ICSAM model for G8 reform*. Waterloo, ON: Centre for International Governance Innovation.
Donaldson, R.H., ed. 1981. *The Soviet Union in the Third World: Successes and failures*. Boulder, CO: Westview Press.
Du Ying. 2011. Research on the relationship between India and East African countries (1964–2000). PhD dissertation, East China Normal University.
Dubey, Ajay K., ed. 1989. *Indo-African relations in the post-Nehru era (1965–1985)*. New Delhi: Kalinga.
Dubey, Ajay K., ed. 2009. *India and Francophone Africa under globalization*. New Delhi: Kalinga.
Dubey, Ajay K., ed. 2010. *Indian diaspora in Africa: A comparative perspective*. New Delhi: M.D. Publication.

The Economist. 2011. Angola and Portugal: Role reversal, 3 September.

Easterly, W. 2006. *White man's burden: Why the West's efforts to aid the rest have done so much ill and so little good.* New York: Penguin.

Favareto, Arilson. 2021. The 2030 agenda, the territorial dimension of Brazilian development and the drivers of sustainability transition. In Rahma Bourqia & Marcelo Sili, eds, *New paths of development: Perspective from the global south.* New York: Springer, 123–134.

Freemantle, Simon. 2015. Trade patterns underline Africa's shifting role, May 25. www.bdlive.co.za/opinion/2015/05/25/trade-patterns-underline-africas-shifting-role

Gabas, J. 2002. *Nord-Sud: l'impossible cooperation.* Paris: Presses de Sciences Po.

The Guardian. 2011. Angola pours oil money into debt-ridden Portugal. www.guardian.co.uk/world/2011/nov/18/angola-boom-debt-riddled-portugal

Gupta, U. 2011. MIST, the next tier of emerging economies. *Institutional Investor,* 7 July. www.institutionalinvestor.com/Article/2762464/Research/4213/Overview.html

IMF. 2012. *World economic outlook 2012: Growth resuming, dangers remain.* www.imf.org/en/Publications/WEO/Issues/2016/12/31/Growth-Resuming-Dangers-Remain

IMF. 2013. *World economic outlook 2013: Transitions and tensions.* www.imf.org/external/pubs/ft/weo/2013/02

Inikori, Joseph E. & Engerman, Stanley L., eds. 1992. *The Atlantic slave trade: Effects on economies, societies, and people in Africa, the Americas, and Europe.* Durham, NC: Duke University Press.

Iye, Ali Musa. 2017. Pan Africanism and African renaissance: Will the 21st century be the era of Africa? *West Asia and Africa* 1: 34–43.

Jiang Shixue. 2007. *Latin American and Caribbean development report 2006–2007.* Beijing: Social Sciences Academic Press.

Jiang Tianjiao. 2015. The development of informal international organizations among emerging market countries from the perspective of soft checks and balances theory: a case study of India, Brazil and South Africa Dialogue Forum (IBSA). *Journal of Latin American Studies* 3: 11–19.

Kose, M. Ayhan & Eswar S. Prasad, 2010. *Emerging markets: Resilience and growth amid global turmoil.* Washington, D.C.: The Brookings Institution Press.

Li Anshan, 2021. African Economic Autonomy and International Development Cooperation, in Rahma Bourqia & Marcelo Sili, eds, *New paths of development: Perspective from the global south.* New York: Springer, 43–53.

Li Xiaoyun, Xu Xiuli & Wang Yihuan, 2013. *International development assistance foreign aid of non-developed countries.* Beijing: World Affairs Press.

Liu Haifang, Wan Ru, Liu Jun & Ke Wenqing, eds. 2018. *Transformation and development of African agriculture and South–South cooperation.* Beijing: Social Sciences Academic Press.

Lin Yifu. 2013. *Structural transformation in Africa.* Presentation to the National School of Development, Peking University, 19 June.

Lin Yueqin ed. 2012. *Annual report on BRICS development (2012).* Beijing: Social Sciences Academic Press.

Lovejoy, Paul. 1983. *Transformations in slavery: A history of slavery in Africa.* Cambridge: Cambridge University Press.

Manning, Patrick. 1990. *Slavery and African life: Occidental, Oriental, and African slave trades.* Cambridge: Cambridge University Press.

Miers, Suzanne & Roberts, Richard, eds. 1988. *The end of slavery in Africa.* Madison, WI: University of Wisconsin Press.

Naidu, S. & Hayley, H. 2009. *Africa's development partners: China and India – challenging the status quo?* Stellenbosch: Stellenbosch University.

Ochieng, Chris Shimba & Musyoka, Philip. 2017. Enhancing Africa–India regional trade agreements: Issues and policy recommendations: Advances in African economic, social and political development. In Odularu Gbadebo & Adekunle Bamidele, eds, *Negotiating South–South regional trade agreements*. New York: Springer, 49–60.

O'Neill, J., Wilson, D., Purushothaman, R. & Stupnytska, A. 2005. *How solid are the BRICs?* New York: Goldman Sachs.

Qiang Xiaoyun. 2019. Russia's Africa policy from the perspective of hedging. *West Asia and Africa* 6: 3–21. www.xyfzqk.org/UploadFile/Issue/y3c4sz5g.pdf

Qiu Changqing & Liu Erwei. 2012. Analysis of India's economic diplomacy to Africa from the perspective of political powers. *South Asia Studies* 1: 30–44.

Rashidi, Runoko & van Sertima, Ivan, eds. 2007. *The African presence in early Asia*, New Brunswick, NJ: Transaction Books.

Ray, Julie. 2019. Image of U.S. leadership now poorer than China's. Gallup, 28 February.

Russian Satellite News Agency. 2019. Putin: Russia's cooperation with African countries is strategic and long-term, 25 October. www.sohu.com/a/349536788_626761

Sakarai, Lawrence J. 1980. Indian merchants in East Africa, Part I: The triangular trade and the slave economy. *Slavery and Abolition* 1(3): 292–338.

Sakarai, Lawrence J. 1981. Indian Merchants in East Africa, Part II. The triangular trade and the slave economy." *Slavery and Abolition*, 2(1): 2–30.

Shen Dechang. 2008. Analysis of India's foreign policy towards Africa after the Cold War. *South Asian Studies Quarterly* 3: 27–31.

Sheth, F.S., ed. 2008. *India–Africa relations: Emerging policy and development perspective*. New Delhi: Academic Excellence.

Shikwati, J. 2015. Aid and development: Why Africans must dream and go out. In Li Anshan & Pan Huaqiong, eds, *Annual review of African studies in China 2014*. Beijing: Social Sciences Academic Press, 237–250.

Stolte, Christina. 2015. *Brazil's Africa strategy role concept and the drive for international status*. New York: Palgrave Macmillan.

Sule, A. 2011. BRICS can build common currency. *China Daily*, 8 April.

Tang Lixia & Liu Xinmiao. 2016. India Africa Summit: India's interest demands and strategy for Africa. *South Asia Research Quarterly* 3: 33–41.

Tarabrin, E.A., ed. 1977. *USSR and countries of Africa*. Moscow: Progress Publishers.

Thurow, L.C. 1992. *Head to head: The coming economic battle among Japan, Europe and America*. New York: William Morrow and Company.

Troyjo, Marcos. 2021. Message from the President. *New Development Bank Annual Report 2020*. www.ndb.int/wp-content/uploads/2021/06/NDB-AR-2020_complete_v1.pdf

UNCTAD. 2010. *The economic development in Africa report 2010: South–South cooperation: Africa and the new forms of development partnership*. https://unctad.org/webflyer/economic-development-africa-report-2010#tab-3

UNCTAD. 2011. *The economic development in Africa report 2011: Fostering industrial development in Africa in the new global environment*. https://unctad.org/webflyer/economic-development-africa-report-2011#tab-2

UNECA. 2013. *Economic report on Africa 2013: Making the most of Africa's commodities – industrializing for growth, jobs and economic transformation*. Nairobi: United Nations Economic Commission for Africa.

University of Natal. 1952. *The Durban Housing Survey*. Durban: University of Natal.
Vahed, Goolam H. 1995. The making of Indiana identity in Durban, 1914–1949. PhD dissertation, Indiana University.
Van Agtmael, A. 2012. Think again: BRICS. *Foreign Policy*, 8 October. www.foreignpolicy.com/articles/2012/10/08/think_again_the_brics?page=0,0
Vidyarthee, Kaushal K. 2008. India's trade engagements with Africa: A comparison with China. *Indian Economic Review* 5: 192–198.
The Wall Street Journal. 2010. CIVITS replace BRICs as growth hotspots, 29 September.
Wang Tao & Yi Xianglong. 2010. On the development of contemporary Latin American and African relations. *Latin American Studies* 5: 20–25.
Weinstein, Warren & Henriksen, Thomas H., eds. 1980. *Soviet and Chinese aid to African nations*. New York: Praeger.
Wu Jing. 2013. The relationship between Brazil and Africa and Its revelation to China. *Latin American Studies* 35(3): 17–21.
Xu Guoqing. 2012. Evolution and characteristics of Brazil's relations with Africa. *West Asia and Africa* 6: 135–152.
Xu Guoqing. 2014. Analysis of agricultural cooperation between Brazil and Africa. *Journal of Southwest University of Science and Technology (Philosophy and Social Sciences Edition)* 31(4): 6–14.
Xu Guoqing. 2015. Energy cooperation between Russia and Africa. *Russian Central Asian & East European Market* 4: 92–110.
Xu Guoqing. 2017. The evolution of Russia's policy towards Africa and the cooperation between China and Russia in the field of relations with Africa. *Academic Journal of Russian Studies* 4: 57–65.
Xue Rongjiu. 2012. On goods trade's features and cooperation vision among the "BRICS" countries. *Intertrade* 367: 4–8.
Yu Zhongjian. 2009. The background, characteristics and trend of India's policy adjustment towards Africa. *Asia and Africa Review* 1: 49–53.
Zhang Laiyi. 2007. Difficulties and countermeasures of economic relation between Russia and Africa. *West Asia and Africa* 3: 34–38.
Zhao Yanrong & Chen Yingqun. 2012. Shoeing into Ethiopia. *China Daily*, 25 December.
Zhou Zhiwei. 2014. Brazil's African policy since the new century: Goals, means and effects. *West Asia and Africa* 1: 125–140
Zhu Mingzhong. 2005. India and Africa (1947–2004). *South Asian Studies* 1: 20–26.

Part III
Cooperation and dynamics

11 Bilateral cooperation and co-development

Introduction

Nigeria is a country with a great civilisation. Besides the Nok culture represented by the terracotta sculptures from as early as the middle of the first millennium BCE, there are the highly skilled wood and ivory works of Ife and the famous stone images of Esie (Stevens 1978).[1] The bronze sculptures of Benin are also a wonderful achievement. When German scholar Leo Frobenius found a bronze head in Nigeria in 1910–1912, he could not hide his admiration: "the setting of the lips, the shape of the ears, the contour of the face, all prove, if separately examined, the perfection of a work of true art which the whole of it obviously is … It is cast in what we call the 'cire perdue', or the hollow cast, and is very finely chased, indeed like the best Roman examples" (Frobenius1936, in Du Bois 1992: 152). In 1897, in order to control trade and avenge the death of eight British officials, the British force broke into Benin City, the capital of Benin Kingdom, and took 2500 pieces of precious bronze sculpture. The British force effectively demolished the longstanding kingdom.

China's great civilisation is characterised by a rich historical heritage of the invention of paper-making, printing technology, the compass, gunpowder and the Great Wall. Yet in 1860, 37 years before the damage in Benin, Britain and France launched the Second Opium War against China in order to force her to open her markets. They raided the prestigious royal Summer Palace, stole the treasures and destroyed the imperial court. A military officer who took part in the looting wrote to Victor Hugo, expecting his praise. The famous French writer criticised the destruction in his reply of 25 November 1861, later entitled *Lettre au capitaine Butler* (or *Expedition de Chine*). He condemned the British and French invaders as destroyers of civilisation, saying that two robbers broke into a museum, destroying, looting and burning, and left laughing hand in hand with their bags full of treasures; one of the robbers was called France and the other Britain (Hugo 1861; Cheng Zhenhou 2011).

The two incidents indicate similarities between Nigeria and China: both have a history of civilisation, both suffered from imperialist invasion and both shared the experience of humiliation by colonial powers. This chapter explores

DOI: 10.4324/9781003220152-14

why China and Africa can develop a strong foundation for their cooperation. It is divided into four parts: China's perspective on African development; China's principles of cooperation; China's experiences of development; and African initiative in development, which might be helpful to understand China's attitude towards Africa, China's development experiences, African initiatives in history and the present, and China's role in promoting African development.

China's perspective on African development

There have been many debates and arguments about China's engagement in Africa, yet very few have discussed the difference between China and the West in terms of the perspective and principles of their relations with Africa; Deborah Brautigam is an exception (Brautigam 2009). An analysis of the difference is definitely needed. What are the differences between China's view of Africa and China's principle in making policies on China–Africa cooperation?

First, how should we look at Africa? Is it a great continent or a backward continent? Raphael Armattoe, a Ghanaian doctor and philosopher nominated for the 1949 Nobel Peace Prize, once said, "Throughout the whole of Middle Ages, West Africa had a more solid politico-social organization, attained a greater degree of internal cohesion and was more conscious of the social function of science than Europe" (Armattoe 1946: 35). He was talking about West African achievements during the Middle Ages. What about Africa's achievements after independence? It is unnecessary to understand how the West sees Africa, since so many discouraging or even humiliating terms are used to describe the continent. If we take a historical perspective, we will find that Africa is not a backward continent – indeed, many countries have made great progress since independence in areas such as integration, human rights, border issues and nation-building, to name a few.

Africa is the only continent that speaks with one voice on big issues in the international arena, through the African Union (AU). Since independence, African leaders have tried every means to make up their weaknesses of "being too small for the big things" by setting up a number of cooperation organisations, an act described as "a doctrine of integration". The latest example of the practice is the implementation of the African Continental Free-Trade Zone (ZLECAf) in July 2019. "No other continent has ever been committed to establishing regional entities as much as Africa." (Sall 2021: 74) Another example is that the United States cannot find a location for the headquarters of USAFRICOM, which had to be settled in Stuttgart in Germany.

Human rights is another issue. African countries are usually picked up and blamed for violations of human rights, yet "human rights" is not a hollow slogan but contains concrete elements. We understand that European women fought for their rights for a hundred years in modern times and women in some countries such as France, Italy and Belgium only won suffrage after

World War II. If we look at women's rights in Africa, things are different. It is very impressive that Africa has produced its own female ministers, a UN Chair, Nobel Prize winners, two presidents and an African Union Chair in only about 50 years, which other continents can hardly match.

Compared with what occurred in Europe, with countless wars over border disputes in modern times, there is no such phenomenon in Africa except in a few countries. This is even more impressive considering that the border between African countries are mainly the result of imperial scramble and colonial occupation. According to the statistics regarding African border lines, 44 per cent are marked by longitude and latitude, 30 per cent by straight lines and only 26 per cent by natural markers (Boutros-Ghali 1972). The first generation of African leaders realised the difficult situation of border issue and emphasised the importance of respecting the current border regardless of its irrationality. The principle of respect for the current border is written in the Charter of the Organization of African Unity.

Nation-building is another achievement, although the process is still ongoing (Li Anshan 2004: 285–318). We understand that nation-building is not an easy job for other countries, without exception. Nation-building in the United States has faced a long struggle against secession and to achieve integration (Faust 2008). In Europe, the situation is no better (Blanning 2008). The difficulty in Africa is that the predecessor of the modern state is a colony whose territory and scale was arbitrarily defined by European powers during the imperialist scramble. Moreover, numerous socio-political problems were created after the application of divide-and-rule policies in the colonies.

China has never used the concept of "donor–recipient" to describe China–Africa relations; the term "partner" is preferred, which is more proper. China believes that assistance is not unilateral but mutual. The status between China and Africa is equal, not that of superior and inferior. Although the relationship is strategic, it is equal, candid and friendly; China and Africa appreciate one another and cooperate cordially. It is noticeable that the "donor–recipient" notion prevalent in the West reflects a philanthropic idea with the donor condescending and the recipient humble and obedient. With an "if-you-don't-I-will" attitude, donors are unable to see recipients as their equal partners. On the contrary, they want to "preach" and usually threaten to withdraw the aid if they are not satisfied with what happens in the recipient countries. Therefore, no matter what aid they offer, they are not appreciated by the recipients, owing to the donor's arrogance.

China takes Africa as a promising, not a "hopeless", continent. The cover of *The Economist* of 13 May 2000 has the title "Hopeless Africa", showing clearly how some Western media perceived Africa at the time. Yet in the same year the Forum on China–Africa Cooperation was set up, which began a new period of China–Africa relations and gave a big push to China–African cooperation.[2] This attitude is demonstrated by Chinese investment in Africa in recent years. According to Western media, Angola, a country that has close relations with China, started to make progress rapidly:

Luanda is changing fast. A few years after the end of a devastating civil war, cranes are crowding the skyline of Angola's capital ... Last year Angola's economy grew by an estimated 15.5%, the fastest on the continent ... the rest of Africa has also been doing well: a recent report by OECD estimates that Africa's economy grew by almost 5% last year, and is expected to do even better this year and next ... Is Africa, often dubbed the hopeless continent, finally taking off?

(*The Economist* 2006)

China has adopted an optimistic perspective on Africa, taken African countries as its strategic partner and increased its engagement in the continent, which has changed not only the image of Africa, but also the attitude of other countries towards Africa. A Tanzanian professor says, "Thanks to China's push into Africa, the continent's image in the global world has changed. The continent is now a strategic partner" (Mihanjo 2012: 133). With so many advantages such as human resources, natural resources and cultural heritage, why should Africa be poor and hopeless?

China's principles of cooperation

After the 12th Party Congress in 1982, the CPC started its new policy of development assistance. During his visit to Africa in 1982, Zhao Zhiyang put forward four principles regarding China–African economic cooperation: equal bilateralism, stress on effectiveness, variety of cooperative form and common development. In my view, the principles guiding China–Africa relations can be summarised as equality and mutual respect, bilateralism and co-development, no-[political]-strings-attached, non-interference in domestic affairs and stress on self-reliance (Li Anshan 2012).

Principle of equality

The relationship between countries is like a person-to-person relationship: only with equality and mutual respect can it endure any difficulties. Although the ideology of equality has been the major theme in human history and is written in the constitution of almost all nations, equality has never been mentioned in international relations, where the concept that "might is right" speaks louder. Equality is a unique principle underlying the relationship between China and Africa. As early as 1963–1964, Chinese Premier Zhou Enlai put forward Eight Principles of foreign aid (*People's Daily*, 18 January 1964).

If we carefully study these principles, it is obvious that they are a kind of self-discipline, an obligation on China's part – what China should do and what the Chinese should avoid. One example illustrates this. The building of the Tanzania–Zambia Railway (TAZARA) is one of the lasting monuments to be remembered by African people (Shen Xipeng 2018). China helped Tanzania and Zambia build the railway of 1860 kilometres for US$500 million during

1968–1986. From 30,000 to 50,000 Chinese were involved and 64 died. As Jamie Monson points out:

> the Chinese had articulated their own vision of development assistance in Africa through the Eight Principles of Development Assistance ... these principles reflected China's efforts to distinguish its approach to African development from those of the United States and the Soviet Union. Several of these principles had direct application to the TAZARA project.
> (Monson 2008: 148)

Principle of co-development

This is a principle that can guarantee the sustainability of cooperation. China–Sudan cooperation offers a good case for co-development. The Canadian oil firm Talisman decided to sell its interests in a Sudan consortium that also involved Chinese and Malaysian firms. The China National Petroleum Corporation wanted to purchase the interest, but Khartoum turned down the Chinese offer and awarded the shares to an Indian firm instead (Mohan 2002). The deal by no means disturbed the relationship between China and the Sudan. This indicates two things: first, China and Sudan are equal partners; and second, both side can make decisions according to their own willingness so as to guard their national interests independently. As Mkumbwa Ally, Deputy Managing Editor of *Tanzania Standard Newspapers*, stated clearly, the cooperation between China and Africa is based on mutual benefit, not the "power matters the most" policy adopted by some Western countries. China–Sudan cooperation is also an example of how co-development should also be based on equality. On the one hand, China has obtained oil for its rapid economic development from Sudan and other countries. On the other hand, after the cooperation with the Chinese company, the Sudanese people have benefited from the oil production and Sudan has changed from an oil-importing country to one with a system of oil exploration, drilling, refining and exporting.

Principle of non-interference

No-political-strings-attached and non-interference in domestic affairs is another important principle. China and African countries have similar experiences of being colonised, so they put great emphasis on national sovereignty. In anything regarding African affairs, China always follows the decision of the United Nations or African Union's stand in order to make a good decision. Moreover, international affairs show clearly that external interference seldom settles the problem, but instead often worsens the situation. As Deborah Brautigam observes:

> Where the West regularly changes its development advice, programs, and approach in Africa ... China does not claim it knows what Africa must

do to develop. China has argued that it was wrong to impose political and economic conditionality in exchange for aid, and that countries should be free to find their own pathway out of poverty. Mainstream economists in the West today are also questioning the value of many of the conditions imposed on aid over the past few decades.

(Brautigam 2009: 308)

Principle of self-reliance

China's policy also stresses self-reliance, which is based on China's own experience of development. With the help of China, Sudan has moved from being a net oil importer to an oil exporter. The collaboration between China and Nigeria to launch a communications satellite, NigSat I, is a good example. While Nigeria acquired satellite technology, China also gained from the collaboration by burnishing its credentials as a reliable player in the international commercial satellite market (Xinhua News Agency 2007). There are quite a few examples of this principle, such as brewing beer in Cameroon, making sugar in Mali, growing mushrooms in South Africa and shoe-making in Ethiopia.

Aid from the West does not work properly in Africa. Walt Rostow called for doubling foreign aid in 1960; World Bank President McNamara called for doubling aid in 1973; the World Bank again called for doubling aid with the end of Cold War in 1990; World Bank President Wolfensohn called for doubling aid at the beginning of terrorist wars in 2001; and the G8 Summit in July 2005 agreed to double aid to Africa. "Aid to Africa did indeed rise steadily throughout this period (tripling as a percent of African GDP from 1970s to 1990s), but African growth remained stuck at zero percent per capita" (Easterly 2005: 3). A similar view is expressed in other works by New York University Professor Easterly and ex-World Bank employee Robert Calderisi (Easterly 2006; Calderisi 2006). Zambian scholar Dambisa Moyo, who once worked for the World Bank, published a book entitled *Dead aid: Why aid is not working and how there is another way for Africa,* which severely criticises the aid regime. Moyo explains that the trillion dollars of aid poured into Africa over the last half-century had failed to have any positive outcome – in fact, had been damaging. She terms aid a "silent killer of growth" and maintains that:

> Africa's development impasse demands a new level of consciousness, a greater degree of innovation, and a generous dose of honesty about what works and what does not as far as development is concerned. And one thing is for sure, depending on aid has not worked.
>
> (Moyo 2009: 154)

Moyo calls for an end to aid, yet she has a chapter entitled "The Chinese are our friends" to praise China's way of cooperating with Africa (Moyo 2009: 108–113).

Why can China's cooperation with Africa effectively help Africa's development? The reason, in my opinion, can be attributed to China's view of African countries as equal partners and a belief that aid should be mutually beneficial and make Africans self-reliant. China and Africa have both been colonised or semi-colonised, and the experience has offered them similar norms by which they conduct international relations – for example, mutual respect and an equal footing.

China's experience: Learn but no copy

There is a tendency for the African countries to "look East", and some Nigerian scholars think positively of China's development model. There are debates within Chinese academia regarding the "China model" or the "Beijing consensus", yet the Chinese seem reluctant to accept these terms (Ramo 2002).[3] The reason could be that China has some negative experiences of copying others' models.

China's development is simply a process of learning from anybody who can provide a better way for development, and the process is still ongoing and open to change or adjustment. Learn but not copy. To apply others' experiences and lessons, their successes and failures, to your own conditions is the only applicable lesson that China can offer. From China's development experience, four fields – political leadership, social stability, agricultural production and reasonable use of foreign aid – may shed some light on African development.

Political leadership

In China, the political leadership is strongly emphasized. The CPC leadership is supposed to represent the people's will and serve the people's interests, with party school, party commission and party branch the organizational guarantee. The leadership comprises two elements: the paramount party leadership and political leadership. Party leadership over almost everything has existed for a long time and will continue for some time. I analyse political leadership and its succession below.

Chairman Mao once pointed out that, "When the political map is determined, cadres are the decisive factor" (Mao Zedong 1991: 526). After the Cultural Revolution, selecting a new generation of leaders was difficult. In 1980, Deng Xiaoping emphasised this issue and later put forward the standards for the young CPC leaders, which was termed the "four-way transformation" (*sihua*) of the cadre corps – younger leaders around the age of 40 who were "revolutionary, younger, more educated, and more technically specialized" (*geminghua, nianqinghua, zhishihua, zhuanyehua*) (Deng Xiaoping 1993: 90–193, 261–265, 384–388). Both Jiang Zemin and Hu Jintao also put great emphasis on the political leadership of the CPC.

Various methods are used to train good leaders and guarantee a healthy power transition, such as a strict process of selection, fieldwork, party school training and shiftwork experiences. Young carders are usually sent for field study or fieldwork at the local grassroots level. There is continuous and systematic theoretical training, which is usually held on different levels in party schools, of which the Central Party School is the pinnacle. Promising leaders are also shifted from one position to another to give them different work experiences.

Power succession

This is a key issue in the history of the CPC. It is true that the moment of power succession is sometimes accompanied by political crisis, interruption or disturbances. According to the theory of political science in the West, "authoritarian regimes" such as that of China are inherently fragile because of their weak legitimacy, over-reliance on coercion, over-centralisation of decision-making and the predominance of personal power over institutional norms (Chang 2001; Pei 2002, 2006). This presumption has been less convincing with China's experience of development. Andrew Nathan points out that China's leadership was stable and the regime resilient, which presents a new challenge to classical political science. Nathan lists several phenomena indicative of the institutionalisation of the succession process:

- Jiang Zemin finished his full term in office and did not stay past the time when the rules said he should leave. Jiang was the first leader in the history of the People's Republic of China (PRC) not to select his own successor.
- The retired elders did not attempt to intervene in the succession or, indeed, in any decision; the military exercised no influence over the succession.
- The selection of the new politburo was made by consensus within the old politburo. Meritocracy played a larger role, and factionalism a smaller role, in the rise of the fourth generation than was the case with earlier generations of Chinese leaders.
- Five of the nine members of the new Politburo Standing Committee had been alternate members of the Central Committee as long ago as 1982.
- Never before in the PRC's history had there been a succession whose arrangements were fixed this far in advance and where the results were so unambiguous in transferring power from one generation of leaders to another (Nathan 2003:17).

Nathan's observation is fairly good, but his presumptions are inaccurate or incorrect. His judgement of the CPC's "weak legitimacy" is definitely wrong. No party in the world could have enjoyed more legitimacy than the CPC by solving the problem of feeding more than one billion people. Again, "over-reliance on coercion" is not an accurate description. Nathan's judgement is more or less contradictory to the reform that is being carried out by the Chinese people right now. It is noticed that the process of going up and down has frequently been practised in political reform, economic development or social experiments. The criticism of the "over-centralisation of decision-making" is not accurate either. China has the largest population in the world and the political mechanism has a historical rationale. We cannot copy the political system of other country that has no roots in China. Ironically, centralisation has proven to be more workable and effective than the neoliberal way in the current financial crisis, in both its cause and its solution. The criticism of the "predominance of personal power over institutional norms" is true in some senses, but is not a reasonable generalisation. The Chinese are clever enough to adapt their own system to the different situation and reform right now is an adjustment. Along with the West, Chinese people have realised that, thanks to the staunch leadership of the CPC, China has kept a constant pace of development, although with some setbacks and failures along the way. China will continue its own way of development with great momentum.

Social stability

In a conference to celebrate the 30th anniversary of China's reform, President Hu Jintao talked about *bu zheteng*. When he finished the speech, every Chinese participant laughed, which indicated that they understood and agreed. The English translations such as "don't flip-flop", "don't get sidetracked", "don't sway back and forth" and "no dithering" can hardly express the real meaning of the phrase, which is grounded in Chinese politics. Every Chinese knows what *zheteng* means, but there is no equivalent in English. The essence of *bu zheteng* is simply "do not create a disturbance". Why did President Hu use this expression? Because the CPC and the Chinese people once had a very negative experience of *zheteng* and have wasted a lot of time. This is a hard lesson they have learned from their contemporary history. In other words, we should maintain a stable social order in order to achieve our goal of development.

With the opening up policy, the CPC realised that in order to maintain social stability, China should put more emphasis on economic construction. Deng Xiaoping made this very clear by saying, "Stability is more important than everything" (Deng Xiaoping 1993: 284–285). For a society to develop in a consistent way, a stable political order is extremely important, especially for a developing country. Samuel Huntington and many other political scientists also emphasised the importance of stability in the process of modernisation. What is a "stable social order", or simply "social stability"? It means that there is no destruction of or threat to the present social order or legislative system by any person, organisation or social group within the society, and the social life in the country runs in a normal and orderly way. Stability is sign of a peaceful and orderly society, but it does not indicate that there are no social contradictions or confrontations. If the contradictions and confrontations between different political forces and interest groups neither present a threat to the frame of present social order and the legislative system, nor cause open conflicts and chaos, the society should be considered stable.

There are three types of social stability: traditional order, coercive order and institutionalised order. Traditional society is characterised as having lower productivity and less social stratification and social mobility, and therefore the social order is rather stable. In Chinese academia, this kind of stability is termed "super-stability", which exists mostly in the pre-capitalist stage and is therefore out of our discussion here. Coercive stability means social stability achieved by force. When social contradictions and political conflicts cannot be solved within the existing political framework and legislative system, the government can decide to control or even suppress acute contradictions by force or violence to maintain or strengthen the present social order, and therefore to keep the socio-political situation in order. Institutionalised stability is a situation where all the social contradictions and political conflicts can be controlled or constrained within the framework of politics and the legal system, which can be adjusted or settled through the channels of democracy or social reform, and the reorganisation or improvement of the political system, so both politics and society can maintain stability (Weber 1958).

Generally speaking, none of the three types of stability purely exists. Coercive stability is not all negative; it may create a temporary situation suitable for adjustment and reform, which is sometimes necessary. Institutional stability does not mutate into coercive stability (although there are occasional exceptions). Coercive stability does not last long and it may transform in two different directions. In some cases, with the improvement of social and political conditions and the legal system, institutional stability is gradually established. In other cases, coercive stability may only last for a while before it turns into disaster. The transformation depends on the orientation of the government's interests and its choice of policy. Moreover, it is important to note that a democratic system does not just exist in the West, nor in the modern party system. For example in African countries there are various democratic channels to settle political crises and social contradictions, and various indigenous methods to solve different types of conflicts. In other words, there are other ways to reach public consensus except for party polity, such as reconciliation or compromise (Wiredu 2001).[4]

Emphasis on agriculture

China is a country with a long history of agriculture – as is Africa. In China, 90 per cent of the population used to be rural; now this figure has decreased to about 600 million, yet it is still an agricultural state. China has put great emphasis on rural development, with agricultural production at the pinnacle. There is a very common expression, *wu liang bu wen*, which means "without grain there is no stability". The stress on agricultural production in policy has been practised since the founding of the PRC.

With the opening up of 1978, although there was a shift in emphasis to economic development, agriculture remained a key issue on the agenda of the Chinese government. It was well understood that China, with such a big population, simply could not afford to depend on the international market for food – something that has been taken seriously as a strategic issue by every generation of Chinese leaders. Although there occasionally was neglect of peasants' interests, agricultural production has always been stressed and food provision is kept as the number one issue.

Since poverty is concentrated in the rural areas and the food issue is the key factor of poverty, the CPC keeps a sharp eye on three rural issues: agriculture, peasants and the countryside. As early as 1982, the first document issued by the Central Party Committee of the CPC and the State Council was about agriculture. Since then, the first document issued each year has mostly been on peasants or rural issues such as the agricultural economy, agricultural planning, peasants' income and the new socialist countryside. For example, the first document of 2009 was about improving the stable development of agriculture and achieving a continuous increase in peasants' income. Since great attention has been paid to the rural issue, China has sped up the reduction of its poverty. The impoverished section of the population decreased from 32 million at the end of 2000 to 23.65 million in 2005. A total of 8.35 million people were lifted out of poverty within five years, down by 5.87 per cent per year (Zhang Lei 2007: 337).

Reasonable use of foreign aid

Although China has gradually changed its position from aid beneficiary to aid provider, the country has a long history of receiving aid. Internally, providing financial support to poor individuals or areas has always been an important issue in poverty reduction in China, though the notion has changed constantly. At first, the measure called "blood transfusion" was adopted, with money provided to less developed areas. The result is not ideal; money is spent but the situation does not change, year after year, necessitating reflection. Then another notion, that of "blood-making", was introduced; it involved mobilising the initiative of the poor and making the best use of local conditions to achieve development. All financial aid – whether money, personnel or technology – was provided to support measures beneficial to the development of the locality.

The policy of "blood-making" seems to be much more successful than that of "blood transfusion". With the new idea of scientific development, in some areas the environment is targeted for particular protection. In those areas, blood-making certainly works for material development. Yet, from a longer-term perspective, what is workable for a particular locality may not be good for the whole region – or, worse still, it may not be sustainable and could bring disaster to the people. Moreover, the less-developed areas are usually ecological areas chosen for environmental protection. In other words, for areas that serve an ecological role and are thus not suitable for industrial development, the government should compensate by blood transfusion to support the strategy of sustainable and scientific development. In sum, blood policies should combine blood transfusion and blood-making (Zhang Lei et al. 2008; Li Xiaoyun et al. 2008). Whatever the notion, it is clear that only if the needy realise the importance of poverty reduction and get down to solid work can the goal be achieved, with or without support from outside.

For a long time, China has received financial support from outside, from either international organisations or individual countries. The 1950s witnessed financial support from the Soviet Union for 156 projects, which contributed a great deal to China's early infrastructure (Donaldson 1981; Liu Xiao & Shaburov 2006). In 1979, Deng Xiaoping pointed out that China also needs to borrow money for development. For more than 20 years, overseas development assistance (ODA) received from Japan was worth some 3225.4 billion yen, about 60 per cent of the total aid to China from 24 foreign countries. The Chinese government rewarded Japan with access to cheap natural resources (Zhu Fenglan 2004; Dai Yan 2008). China consistently adheres to the principle of "self-reliance first, foreign aid second". This principle is crucial because it guarantees that China can develop according to its own strategy and needs.

First, while China can compromise on some issues, it would never give up its sovereignty for aid. In 1958, the Soviet Union asked China to make a concession on the issues of a long-wave radio station and an allied fleet. In order to safeguard China's sovereignty, Chairman Mao Zedong refused resolutely (Wu Yuenong 2011).[5] Second, China will not let an aid provider interfere with its internal affairs and will decide its own development strategy, with foreign aid as a subsidiary measure. Third, China will put foreign money where it is most needed, thus making the best use of foreign aid. How to make the best use of money provided by external sources has always been a serious consideration of the Chinese government. Fourth, China will always try to keep foreign aid – especially aid in the form of debt – under control. If a country relies on foreign aid too much, it will gradually develop a mentality of aid dependency. When you depend on aid yet cannot get it, you may sacrifice your sovereignty for financial support.

What is the lesson of China's development? Indigenous solutions to indigenous problems might be the most important one. Nigerian historian Femi Akomolafe points out:

> Whilst the Chinese opted for an indigenous solution to their economic backwardness, African governments (against the advice of eminent African economists such as Professor Adedeji) chose to follow the prescriptions of the World Bank and the IMF. These Western-dominated organizations prescribed the vile Structural Adjustment Programs (SAPs) which later metamorphosed into the Enhanced Structural Adjustment Programs (ESAP) which, in turn, metamorphosed into the insulting Highly Indebted Poor Country (HIPC) programs.
>
> (Akomolafe 2006)

This observation is correct, but it is incomplete. To make matters worse, the prescription prepared by outsiders will eventually fail, simply because it is made by those who don't understand the African local situation (and have a "vile" intention?). When the prescription does not work, the prescription-makers do not take the responsibility and Africans become the scapegoat. It is the African leaders who are scolded for their lack of capability. Then a new development strategy is provided by the outsiders and inevitably fails again with more damage, creating a vicious circle. And it is always the Africans and their leaders who are blamed. It is not fair! With the frequent changes to the West's development strategy, advice, programs and approach, how can Africa find its own path and develop itself?

African initiative in development

The argument is clear: African initiative with African creativity is needed in African development.

Initiative is vital in the use of international aid as well as a very important issue for developing countries. The "initiative" and "aid" here have various aspects; while the former comprises individuals, the local level and the state, the latter encompasses the internal and external, including individuals, companies, states and international organisations. Obviously, only the needy require aid. What is more important, the primary goal of receiving aid for African development is to achieve economic autonomy, which is closely related to both the realisation of sustainable development and the establishment of an effective international order (Li Anshan 2021).

Human history has witnessed the decline of the indigenous American culture in North America and the annihilation of the indigenous culture in Australasia. Yet African culture stands firm and vigorous. Africa is still there after various disasters brought about by history, such as several centuries of slave trade, which resulted in the loss of their most capable labour force; several decades of colonialism, which brought about material and spiritual damage; and half a century of unequal international economic and political order, which has placed Africa in a disadvantageous position. Yet Africa not only continues to exist; its philosophy of optimism and harmony between humans and nature, its religion, art, music and dance have spread all over the world.

Africans displayed their initiative as early as in ancient times and they have created civilisations and wonders of human history – for example, the Egyptian pyramids and hierarchical system, Nubian construction and political structure, Ethiopian architecture and language; Greater Zimbabwe in the south, African empires (Ghana, Mali, Songhai and Hausa Emirs) in the Middle Ages in the west, the Congo kingdom in the forest, and Swahili coastal cities in the east. With trade, immigration and the enslavement process, African cultural achievements spread to other parts of the world. Their lively bronze figures and artistic sculptures brought new life to declining Western art, which entered a new period of growth.

Even during the colonial period, African chiefs (such as JaJa in Nigeria) competed with their counterparts in Britain and France in various enterprises. As the King of Opubu in Niger Delta, JaJa controlled the palm oil trade within his jurisdiction, which soon became the largest palm oil export centre in the area. In order to break JaJa's monopoly, the Europeans jointly lowered the price to buy his palm oil, trying to force him to submit by means of bargaining. JaJa even decided to open up a shipping route from Niger Delta to the United Kingdom, and directly transported a large amount of palm oil to the United Kingdom for sale. As an effort of African resistance to European penetration in the Niger River Basin, JaJa displayed his strategy and courage in the competition with European merchants (Dike 1956: 193–216; Cookey 1974). The British official Johnston hated JaJa very much and cursed him maliciously (Crowder 1978:160–161; Falola 1987: 48)). Finally, JaJa was lured by a British official to a warship and put into exile. JaJa showed his capability as a business leader and African nationalist, a reputation he still enjoys in Nigeria.

African intellectuals showed their talents in finance, such as Ghanaian businessman Tete-Ansa, who was highly praised during the colonial period and known as the "Napoleon" of West African commerce had set up his own company and bank (Hopkins 1966):

> Between 1925 and 1935, Tete-Ansa founded producers' cooperatives in Nigeria and the Gold Coast in an attempt to strengthen the bargaining position of farmers and lower their costs; he formed the Industrial and Commercial Bank in Nigeria, which was intended to finance African participation in external trade; he set up an agency in New York to sell produce and to buy imports for shipment to West Africa. The scheme was a radical one, but the aims behind it were moderate enough. Tete-Ansa and his backers were seeking a better place for Africans (especially educated Africans) within the colonial system, but they were not asking for total African control of the economy, still less for political independence. Tete-Ansa's plans were unsuccessful, but the Waterloo of this Napoleon had its significance.
>
> (Hopkins 2020: 310)[6]

By the same token, in the early 20th century South African peasants had the upper hand over the White farmers in the agricultural sector. At that time, the tenancy system prevailed in South Africa and the White farmers left their fields to agents or Africans for farming. Some industrious Africans gradually had their own land and farms. For Afrikaners, this became a sword of Damocles hanging over their heads (Ngubane 1973: 85). More important, the African peasants soon became strong competitors for the White farmers, who realised that if it went on like this, it would not only cause labour shortages, but would destroy the master–slave relationship. Once Africans can live on their own land, who is willing to work hard for White people? The situation should not continue any more. Under their demand, the South African government issued the Native Land Act, the supra-economic means adopted so that the White farmers finally defeated the African farmers (Bundy 1972, 1979). But the African initiative is still remembered.

Today, Africans need to fully use their capabilities in their dealings with outsiders, and to display initiative in regional cooperation and integration in order to catch up with others. Africa has tremendous human resources and natural resources. The issue is how to make the best use of them. Take land, for example. Africa's cultivable land represents about 26.41 per cent of the total area of the continent, yet there is a huge amount of uncultivated land and a large poor population. In fact, in many African countries food production could have been established in the first decade after independence. Yet later periods have witnessed the deterioration of the food situation, and food crises have occurred more frequently in recent years. Kenya and Zimbabwe are good examples. There are external problems and obstacles, such as the fluctuation of food prices in the international market and foreign interference, yet we should also ask this question: Do African governments pay enough attention to agricultural production and its rural population?

If a government cannot feed or clothe its people, it is in a very difficult situation. It must either obtain food aid or spend precious foreign currency to buy food. When Ghana needed both food and money, the World Bank agreed to a loan on the condition that Ghana must open its market for rice. The condition was accompanied by an unfair trade rule of the International Monetary Fund (IMF), which opened the market for cheap American rice subsidised by the US government. Although Ghanaian rice is better nutritionally, Ghanaians prefer the cheap rice from the United States (Oxfam Annual Report 2005–2006). In many other African countries, there is still suffering from shortages of food. These countries should reconsider their strategy again and put more emphasis on agricultural production.

Most African countries have received foreign aid for quite a long time. According to William Easterly's figures, for the past 40 years the West has spent more than US$568 billion on foreign aid to Africa. Easterly also observes that very little improvement has occurred in Africa (Easterly 2005: 3). For example, Tanzania has been heavily dependent on foreign aid, which makes up 40 per cent of its revenue, yet it has a high percentage of maternal deaths, with 24 mothers and 144 newborn babies dying every day. How to make the best use of foreign aid is a serious issue facing African countries. First, it is not proper to rely on foreign aid, yet most African countries still need it to promote their economic development. There should be a balance between the introduction of foreign aid and the mobilisation of initiatives at the local level. Second, foreign aid should be used in the most suitable place. In Africa, it is a common practice for the top leaders, whether presidents or ministers, to use the foreign aid or foreign-aided projects to benefit their own home villages. I am not sure that this is the best way to serve the whole country, or the best way to use foreign aid – probably not.

In the contemporary world, various great figures have appeared in Africa, such as Nkrumah, Cheikh Anta Diop, Nyerere and Mandela. Nigeria has produced figures such as Nnamdi Azikiwe the nationalist leader, Wole Soyinka the Nobel Prize winner and Philip Emeagwali the computer wizard. Can Africa bring new hope to the world in this difficult time? I am sure it can. With the united effort of a hardworking people and good leadership, its rich natural and human resources, the integration and unity of the continent and self-determination of its development, Africa will rise again.

Conclusion

It is time to clarify several points regarding "international aid". It seems that the West has been keen on the international aid system and on trying hard to keep it going with the argument that it is necessary and rational, although the system has been implemented for more than half a century while poverty in Africa has changed little (Easterly 2005, 2006; Calderisi 2006). Although Western countries have realised the outdated name of "international aid" and replaced it with "international development cooperation", the change is in name only, not reality. Some African leaders have made it clear that investment is better than aid, and for Africa investment and equal trade are much more effective. As early as 1993, during the first Tokyo International Conference on African Development (TICAD), African leaders realised that strategic investment would be much more important than aid. At the fourth TICAD, which ended in May 2008, former South African President Mbeki once again stressed that aid was a good thing, but investment was more important: "While aid is important, partnerships based on trade, investment, and joint ventures are much more important." (Butty 2012). African scholars have stated the absurdity of the international aid system and maintained that Africans should have their own initiatives (Prah 2006).[7] Shikwati made it straightforward:

> The global development aid architecture is premised on the erroneous view that some parts of the world are equipped with solutions while the other parts perennially seat idle and wait for the solutions. This view masks the fact that the aid industry dominated by the United States of America, Europe, Australia, Japan and their allies is designed to address donor country interests that range from access to markets; the fear of a deluge of political, economic and climate change induced migrants from Africa; broad security concerns that range from terrorism, and diseases; the quest to access and control the continent's vast natural resources and geopolitical power games.
>
> (Shikwati 2015)

For Africans, the image of China is favourable, investment welcomed and friendship cherished, although there are many challenges. China's reputation is enduring and has even surpassed that of the United States (Olander 2020).[8] African scholars acknowledged the value of cooperation with China: "What Africa needs is economic growth. Africa needs to create jobs and get out of dependency ... Africa will continue embracing China because China is contributing significantly to Africa's growth" (Mihanjo 2012: 131). However, some of them understand the opportunity and support that China has brought to Africa, although they are concerned about "a potential neocolonial relationship":

> In the first place, on the on hand is the opportunities the rise of China as a global economic power presents for development on the continent, including its financial support to deal with African development needs, for example, infrastructure needs, and increasing power for the continent to engage with the international community on changes in the system that disadvantage Africa. On the other hand, this has given rise to a potential neocolonial relationship developing between China and the continent, and in particular a majority of its countries, that could undermine African development.
>
> (Soudien & Houston 2021: 38)

Some of them even distinguish two blocs, e.g., the Western bloc and the Chinese bloc, and want to keep an independent position for Africa (Sall 2021).

What role can China play in African development? In my opinion, China can offer investment to Africa in various fields, especially in infrastructure such as roads, railways, bridges, power stations and so on, as well as in agriculture, manufacturing, renewable energy and green food agribusiness. As part of cooperation with African countries, technology transfer is very important in order to speed up African development. Experience-sharing is another important field where China can offer its help and gain from Africa. Chinese experience show that national sovereignty is very important in current international affairs, especially for African countries with a heartbreaking history of colonial suffering. A strategic plan is needed for a sustainable development. China can learn from Africa's philosophy of harmony between humans and nature, its optimism and its broad-mindedness (Li Anshan 2009).

Therefore, China–Africa cooperation is one of the examples in the world today, a "practical coevolution" (Tang Xiaoyang 2020: 266). It is not a perfect or ideal form, yet it is workable within the framework of contemporary international order. Judging from history, Africa will make its own leap forward if both its leaders and people work hard on their own. As the Nigerian historian Femi Akomolafe points out, "China's economic performance is nothing short of a miracle. It shows what a people with confidence, determination and vision can achieve" (Akomolafe 2006: 48). One Nigerian claims proudly, "Nigeria will rise again!" (Ahamefule 2011). Of course, Africa too will rise again, despite the suffering during the colonial period and the difficulties of today.

Notes

1 Nok culture or Nok civilisation flourished around Nok, a small village of Kaduna, Nigeria. Discovered in 1928, it is believed to have existed in central Nigeria as early as 1000 BC and the oldest society in the sub-Saharan Africa. The later Yoruba civilisation closely resembles the sociocultural organisation of the Nok civilisation.
2 There are various interpretations of the origin of FOCAC, yet it was the African side that initiated the scheme and the Minister of Foreign Affairs in Madagascar kicked it off. See Chapter 6 of this book.
3 Since Joshua Ramo's frequently quoted phase was published, there have been several discussions relevant to China's engagement in Africa and to China's soft power. See Thompson (2005: 4); Oxford Analytica Daily Brief (2006); Cooke (2009).
4 It is important to keep in mind that modern party system has created various problems in African countries after the drive towards democracy, either under the name of "majority rule" or multi-party election. "African dictators, civilian and military, were under sustained Western pressure to adopt the multi-party way of life … One of the most persistent causes of political instability in Africa derives from the fact that in ever so many contemporary African states certain ethnic groups have found themselves in the minority both numerically and politically. Under a system of majoritarian democracy this means that, even with all the safeguards, they will consistently find themselves outside the corridors of power. The frustrations and disaffections, with their disruptive consequences for the polity, should not have caught anybody by surprise" (Wiredu 1996: 189). In other words, by neglecting the interests of ethnic minorities, the practice of the party system resulted in most chaotic situations in Africa. That is why non-party polity comes up as a political-philosophical solution (Wiredu 1996: 182–190). This blind faith in party system, or the "myth of party polity" as I call it, is another topic that needs more detailed study, both in political science and sociology. For a different view, see Lagerkvist (2009).
5 There is a discussion of the nature of this event (Shen Zhihua 2002; Liu Minggang 2007)
6 After his business failed, he went to Canada as a kind of self-imposed exile, which "symbolised the failure of his brand of moderate leadership and reformist proposals" (Hopkins 2020: 310).
7 Dr Antoine Roger Lokongo in Congo-Kinshasa told me that Congo is endowed with plentiful natural resources and needs no aid, but rather fair trade and investment. Many African scholars expressed the same view.
8 This attitude is also indicated in Pew Research Center's annual Opinion of China poll since 2015 and Afrobarometer's annual survey (https://afrobarometer.org).

References

Ahamefule, U. 2011. Nigeria will rise again, Part 1, 9 November. www.modernghana.com/news/359893/1/nigeria-will-rise-again-part-1.html
Akomolafe, F. 2006. No one is laughing at the Asians anymore. *New African* 452: 8–49.
Armattoe R. 1946. *The golden age of Western African civilization*. Londonderry: Lomeshie Research Center.
Blanning, T. 2008. *The pursuit of glory: Europe 1648–1815*. Harmondsworth: Penguin.
Boutros-Ghali, B. 1972. *Les conflicts de frontieres en Afrique*. Paris: Editions techniques et économiques.

Brautigam, D. 2009. *Dragon's gift: The real story of China in Africa*. Oxford: Oxford University Press.
Bundy, Colin. 1972. The emergence and decline of a South African peasantry. *African Affairs* 71(285): 369–388.
Bundy, Colin. 1979. *The rise and fall of the South African Peasantry*. London: Heinemann.
Butty, James. 2012. Assessing Obama's Africa policy: Looking at 2012 and beyond. *Africa*, 11 January.
Calderisi, R. 2006. *The trouble with Africa: Why foreign aid isn't working*. Houndmills: Palgrave Macmillan.
Chang, Gordon. 2001. *The coming collapse of China*. New York: Random House.
Cheng Zhenhou. 2011. Qui est le Capitaine Butler? A propos d'une lettre de Victor Hugo sur le palais d'eté. *Revue d'Histoire Littéraire de la France* 111: 891–903.
Cooke, Jennifer. 2009. China's soft power in Africa. In Carola McGiffert, ed., *Chinese soft power and its implications for the United States: Competition and cooperation in the developing worlds*. Washington, DC: CSIS.
Cookey, S.J.S. 1974. *King Jaja of the Niger Delta: His life and times, 1821–1891*. New York: Nok.
Crowder, Michael. 1978. *The story of Nigeria*. London: Faber and Faber.
Dai Yan. 2008. Does China need foreign aid anymore? Half-monthly talk. China.com.cn. www.china.com.cn/international/txt/2008-02/07/content_9661029.htm
Deng Xiaoping. 1993. *Selected works of Deng Xiaoping, Vol. 2*. Beijing: People's Press.
Dike, K.O. 1956. *Trade and politics in the Niger Delta, 1830–1885*. Oxford: Oxford University Press.
Donaldson, R.H., ed., 1981. *The Soviet Union in the Third World: Successes and failures*. Boulder, CO: Westview Press.
Du Bois, W.E. Burghardt 1992 [1946]. *The world and Africa: An inquiry into the part Africa has played in world history*. New York: International Publishers.
Easterly, W. 2005. *Can foreign aid save Africa?* New York: Saint John's University.
Easterly, W. 2006. *White man's burden: Why the West's efforts to aid the rest have done so much ill and so little good*. New York: Penguin.
Falola, Toyin, ed. 1987. *Britain and Nigeria: Exploitation or development?* London: Zed Books.
Faust, Drew Gilpin. 2008. *This republic of suffering: Death and the American Civil War*. New York: Alfred A. Knopf.
Frobenius, L. 1936. *Histoire de la Civilisation Africaine*. Paris: Gallimard.
Hopkins, A.G. 1966. Economic aspects of political movements in Nigeria and in the Gold Coast, 1918–1939. *The Journal of African History* 7: 133–152.
Hopkins, A.G. 2020. *An economic history of West Africa*. London: Routledge.
Hugo, Victor. 1861. Lettre au capitaine Butler (sur le sac du palais d'Été à Pékin), 25 novembre (A. & P.II), *Victor Hugo Œuvres complètes*). Paris: Club français du livre.
Lagerkvist J. 2009. Chinese eyes on Africa: Authoritarian flexibility versus democratic governance. *Journal of Contemporary African Studies* 27(2): 19–134.
Li Anshan. 2004. *A study of African nationalism*. Beijing: China International Broadcasting Press.
Li Anshan. 2009. China's experiences in development: Implications for Africa, 18 June. www.pambazuka.org/en/category/africa_china/57079
Li Anshan. 2012. China and Africa: Cultural similarity and mutual learning. In James Shikwati, ed., *China–Africa partnership: The quest for a win–win relationship*. Nairobi: Inter Region Economic Network, 93–97.

Li Anshan. 2021. African economic autonomy and international development cooperation. In Rahma Bourqia & Marcelo Sili, eds, *New paths of development: Perspective from the Global South*. New York: Springer, 43–53.

Li Xiaoyun et al., eds. 2008. *Status of rural China (2006–2007)*. Beijing: Social Sciences Documentation.

Liu Minggang. 2007. Do not the long wave broadcasting station and the joint fleet relate to a state sovereignty? *Journal of Hubei University (Philosophy and Social Science)* 34(5): 69–71.

Liu Xiao & Shaburov. 2006. Protocol on amending and supplementing the agreement of the Soviet Union on technical assistance to the People's Republic of China in the construction and reconstruction of industrial enterprises and other projects, *CPC History Material* 2: 4–25.

Mao Zedong. 1991. *Selected works of Mao Zedong, Vol. 2*. Beijing: People's Publishing House.

Mihanjo, Reginald P. 2012. Understanding China's neo-colonialism in Africa: A historical study of China–Africa economic relations. In James Shikwati, ed., *China–Africa partnership–The quest for a win-win relationship*: 130–136.

Mohan, C. Raja, 2002. Sakhalin to Sudan: India's energy diplomacy, *The Hindu*, 24 June.

Monson, J. 2008. *African Freedom Railway: How a Chinese development project changed lives and livelihoods in Tanzania*. Bloomington IN: Indiana University Press.

Moyo, D. 2009. *Dead Aid: Why aid is not working and how there is another way for Africa*. London: Allen Lane.

Nathan, A. 2003. China's changing of the guard: Authoritarian resilience. *Journal of Democracy*, 14(1):17.

Ngubane, Jordan K. 1973. *An African Explains Apartheid*, New York.

Olander, Eric, 2020. China's surprisingly durable reputation in Africa, *The Africa Report*, September 11. www.theafricareport.com/41380/chinas-surprisingly-durable-reputation-in-africa/.

Oxfam Annual Reports. Oxfam. www.oxfamamerica.org/explore/research-publications/annual-report-2018

Oxford Analytica Daily Brief Service. 2006. China/Africa: Emerging Beijing Consensus shapes policy. 24 January.

Pei, Minxin. 2002. China's Governance Crisis, *Foreign Affairs*, 81(5): 96–104.

Pei, Minxin. 2006. *China's Trapped Transition*. Cambridge MA: Harvard University Press.

People's Daily. 1964. Premier Zhou answered the questions of the news reporter of the Ghana news agency, stating a new independent powerful Africa will appear in the world and China will support the newly rising countries in developing their independent national economy strictly according to the eight principles, 18 January.

Prah, Kwesi Kwaa. 2006. *The African nation: The state of the nation*. Cape Town: Centre for Advanced Studies of African Society (CASAS).

Ramo, J.C. 2002. *The Beijing Consensus*. London: Foreign Policy Centre.

Sall, Alioune. 2021. What can be the position of Africa in the contemporary globalisation? A few thoughts in the matter. In Rahma Bourqia & Marcelo Sili, eds, *New paths of development: Perspective from the Global South*. New York: Springer, 69–75.

Shen Xipeng, 2018. *A study on China aided construction of Tanzania–Zambia Railway*. Heifei: Huangshan Publishing House.

Shen Zhihua. 2002. Nikita Khrushchev, Mao Zedong and unconsummated military cooperation between China and the Soviet Union. *Journal of Communist Party of China History Studies* 5: 32–43.

Shikwati, J. 2015. Aid and development: Why Africans must dream and go out. In Li Anshan & Pan Huaqiong, eds., *Annual Review of African Studies in China 2014*. Beijing: Social Sciences Academic Press, 237–250.

Stevens, Phillip Jr. 1978. *The stone images of Esie, Nigeria*. Ibadan: Ibadan University Press and Nigerian Federal Department of Antiquities.

Soudien, Crain & Houston, Gregory. 2021. African perspectives on development in the context of a changing international system. In Rahma Bourqia & Marcelo Sili, eds, *New paths of development: Perspective from the Global South*. New York: Springer, 25–41.

Tang Xiaoyang. 2020. *Coevolutionary pragmatism: Approaches and impacts of China–Africa economic cooperation*. Cambridge: Cambridge University Press.

Thompson, D. 2005. China's soft power in Africa: From the "Beijing Consensus" to health diplomacy. *China Brief*, 5(21): 4.

Weber, M. 1958. *From Max Weber: Essays in sociology*. New York: Oxford University Press.

Wiredu, Kwasi. 1996. *Cultural universals and particulars: An African perspective*. Bloomington & Indianapolis: Indiana University Press.

Wiredu, Kwasi. 2001. Democracy by consensus: Some conceptual considerations. *Philosophical Papers* 30(3): 227–244.

Wu Yuenong. 2011. The time of the sudden change of China–Soviet Relations: Mao Zedong's rejection of Khrushchev's suggestion of co-run the long-wave radio station. *CPC History Wenhui* 2: 31–33.

Xinhua News Agency. 2007. China launched satellite for Nigeria, 14 May.

Zhang Lei, ed. 2007. *The course of poverty reduction and development in China (1949–2005)*. Beijing: China Financial and Economic Publishing House.

Zhang Lei et al., eds. 2008. *Poverty monitoring and evaluation*. Beijing: China Agriculture Press.

Zhu Fenglan. 2004. Japanese ODA to China: Positioning and evaluation. *Contemporary Asia-Pacific* 12: 8–12.

12 Chinese medical teams in Africa[1]

Introduction

On 26 January 1965, a pregnant Algerian woman was critically ill and rushed to the hospital where Chinese doctors were working. She was very weak from loss of blood and needed a blood transfusion. The Chinese Medical Team (CMT) director mobilised Chinese doctors to contribute their blood. Doctors Shen Hangzhi and Xu Zexian had the same blood type and willingly donated blood to the dying woman immediately (Jiangxi Health Department of Jiangsu Province 2004: 26). A Tanzanian woman was in shock from excessive loss of blood after the resection of a huge fibroid weighing 7.5 kilograms. Dr Liu Fangyi resolutely donated her blood to this unknown Tanzanian sister. Dr Liu went out to work in Africa three times and finally died on the operating table from a deadly illness. President Nyerere highly praised her as "a medical ambassador to spread friendship and love" (Liu Jirui 1998: 2–63).

A Chinese doctor in Tanzania recalled:

> In December 1971, ENT physician Yu Xiuying and I arrived in Lukuadi for a medical tour. This place is 300 kilometres away from the station of the CMT. We stayed there for three days, and treated more than 200 patients/time, did 10 small operations and a delivery. We were extremely busy and we had to cook ourselves. The most difficult is the stay at night. Our residence was a broken room in the church, with a hole in the roof, where we can see the moon and stars in the sky. The room was filthy, probably being long uninhabited. After a hard day at work, we felt very tired and would like to have a good sleep. Yet the rats were running around squeaking, and a few doves and sparrows flying, which made us impossible to sleep. The exotic alien environment added the fear, and we can only wait in light till dawn next morning.
>
> (Liu Jirui 1998: 12)

Sending Chinese medical teams (CMTs) abroad is an important form of South–South cooperation, which has a history going back to 1963. Based on

DOI: 10.4324/9781003220152-15

various data and personal interviews, this chapter looks at the history and scale of CTMs abroad, rectifies the incorrect data openly published and frequently used by media, and analyses the role of the teams in local affairs and in China's foreign affairs, and their impact on world peace. CMTs have not only treated African patients and served China's diplomacy in a special way, but have also contributed a great deal to spreading the ideology of equality, promoting humanitarianism and strengthening the understanding of traditional Chinese medication.[2]

Conventional experience indicates that the starting point of cooperation is understanding one another. What is the concept and principle of cooperation or aid? What is the history of cooperation or aid? What are the forms of cooperation and aid? Only by knowing each other – and by acknowledging the differences and similarities – can trilateral cooperation be carried out smoothly and achieve a better result. The argument is that only by settling the issue of "how could" are we able to get down to the business of "how should". This chapter provides some background to China–Africa medical cooperation. It is divided into five parts, focusing on a historical survey, a critique of the popular assumption of its scale, its contribution to African society, its achievements for China and its dedication to world peace.

As an important part of China's official assistance and South–South cooperation, Chinese medical cooperation with other countries (mainly African countries) generally involves providing CMT and their services, building hospitals and clinics, providing medicines and medical facilities, training medical personnel and staff, and setting up medical centres for campaigns against AIDS and malaria, and other tropical infectious diseases. According to the protocol signed with relevant countries, the Chinese government sends the medical team to do volunteer work, meets the cost of their medical training, their wages abroad and related costs, while the host country is responsible for providing medical facilities, medication, instruments, medical devices and housing for medical treatment and related medical activities, and for the security of the personal property of CMTs and their family members.

China sent the first CMT to Algeria in 1963. Since then, China has dispatched more than 20,000 CMT members to five continents with a focus in Africa and treated 240 million patients abroad. China has provided CMT to 45 countries or regions, signed 46 CMT protocols and currently has 47 CTMs operating in 122 medical-care points abroad (Chen Zhu 2010: 6). This type of assistance provides a good model for South–South cooperation, yet very little research has been done either at home or abroad.[3] In recent years, there has been increasing international concern about China–Africa relations and China's Africa policy.[4] This chapter explores the history, scale and impact of CMT, with an emphasis on CMT in Africa, in order to promote further research on the subject.

CMTs in Africa: History and present

After the Algerian people won their independence on 3 July 1962 after a long armed struggle against French colonialism, they faced a dire shortage of doctors and medication with the immediate withdrawal of French doctors and asked the world for help. China received the call via two channels: an emergency call to the international community for help from International Red Cross and a request for assistance from the Algerian government. In 1963, the Chinese government was the first in the world to provide a medical team to Algeria, initiating the history of CMTs. In that year, three CMTs arrived in Algeria, mainly under the governance of Hubei Province (*People's Daily* 1963; Health Department of Hubei Province 1993: 4–16). The CMT team included members from various provinces and cities. Up to 2006, Hubei Province had provided about 3 000 p/t (person/time) to Algeria and Botswana.[5]

During the 1960s, China sent CMT to Zanzibar (Jiangsu 1964),[6] Laos (Yunnan 1964), Somalia (Jilin 1965), the Republic of Yemen (Liaoning 1966), Congo (Brazzaville) (Tianjin 1967), Mali (Zhejiang 1968) Tanganyika (Shandong 1968), Mauritania (Heilongjiang 1968), Vietnam (Yunnan 1968) and Guinea (Beijing 1968). In December 1963, during their visit to Algeria, the Chinese premier Zhou Enlai and Vice-Premier Chen Yi met CMT staff. Premier Zhou Enlai told them, "You should work better, and treat the health of the Algerians as that of the Chinese. You should learn from and carry forward Doctor Norman Bethune's spirit" (Health Department of Hubei Province 1993: 2–23). Foreign assistance in the form of CMTs has provided a new dynamic for Chinese cooperation with other countries.

During the 1970s, there was a great increase in the number of CMTs in Africa. Three factors contributed to this. First, their reputation began to spread among African countries, many of which asked China to provide medical assistance. Second, China established diplomatic relations with 25 newly independent African countries and renewed relations with seven that had severed their relations with China in the 1960s (Zaire, today's Democratic Republic of the Congo, Burundi, Central Africa, Benin, Ghana, Kenya and Tunisia). Third, China resumed its legal seat in the United Nations with the support of developing countries. To express its gratitude and mutual support, China increased its foreign assistance. The period 1971–1978 is therefore termed the "rapid growth stage of Chinese foreign assistance" (Ministry of Foreign Trade and Economic Cooperation, PRC 1984).[7]

In 1970, Chinese sent CMTs to the Democratic Republic of the Yemen (from Anhui Province). In 1971, CMTs arrived in the Sudan (Shaanxi) and Equatorial Guinea (Guangdong). China sent CMT to Sierra Leone (Hunan), Tunisia (Jiangxi), Zaire (Hebei) and Albania (Liaoning) in 1973, Ethiopia (Henan) and Togo (Shanghai) in 1974. In 1975, five countries received CMTs: Cameroon (Shanghai), Cambodia (Shanxi), Senegal (Fujian), Madagascar (Gansu) and Morocco (Shanghai). In 1976, CMTs arrived in Niger (Guangxi), Mozambique (Sichuan), São Tomé and Principe (Heilongjiang),

Upper Volta (Beijing), Guinea Bissau (Guizhou) and Kuwait (Liaoning), and in 1977 CMTs came to Gabon (Tianjin) and Gambia (Guangdong). In 1978, China dispatched CMTs to six countries: Benin (Ningxia), Zambia (Henan), Central Africa (Zhejiang), Chad (Jiangxi), Syria (Chinese Medicine Research Institute of the Ministry of Health) and Iran (Jiangsu). During the 1970s, China stopped medical cooperation with several countries, including Vietnam (1971), Laos (1974), Albania (1974), Cameroon, Ethiopia, Chad and Iran (all in 1979).

From the late 1970s to the beginning of the 1980s, China began a transitional period to end the Cultural Revolution and begin reform. The new attitude to the international situation (peace and development as the two major themes to replace revolution and war) and the change of strategic thinking (the focus shifted to economic construction) caused a strategic transformation in China. During the period 1979–1982, China–African relations showed transient fluctuations, indicated by the reduction of Chinese assistance to Africa, the downfall of bilateral trade and a decrease in the number of medical teams (Kim 1989: 38; Ministry of Foreign Trade and Economic Cooperation, PRC 1984).

There were a few reasons for this change. The end of the Cultural Revolution resulted in a thousand things needing to be done, as well as an urgent need for money for domestic construction, easing the relationship between China and the West followed by China's strengthening relations with the West for the introduction of technology and capital. The deterioration of relations with both Albania and Vietnam made China reconsider its mode of foreign assistance. In the 1980s, however, China continued to despatch CMTs to Botswana (Fujian 1981), Djibouti (Shanxi 1981), the United Arab Emirates (Sichuan 1981), Rwanda (Inner Mongolia 1982), Zimbabwe (Hunan 1983), Uganda (Yunnan 1983), Libya (Beijing 1983), Cape Verde (Heilongjiang 1984), Liberia (Heilongjiang 1984), Malta (Jiangsu 1984) and Samoa (Anhui 1986) (Huang Shuze & Lin Shixiao 1986:1–62; Shi Lin 1989), as well as Burundi (Guangxi 1987) and the Seychelles (Guangxi 1987). In 1988–1995, China did not send any CMT to African countries owing to three factors: first, the Chinese government had basically met the requirements of the hope for medical assistance in Africa; second, the end of the Cold War affected the strategic position of Africa; and third, the marginalisation of Africa had led to a chaotic situation and strife in the continent.

In 1993, the CMT arrived in Guyana, this is the first time China sent its medical team to Latin America. The Chinese government also dispatched CMT to Namibia (Zhejiang, 1996), Comoros (Guangxi, 1996), Lesotho (Hubei, 1997), Eritrea (Henan, 1997) and Nepal (Hebei,1999). During the 21st century, more countries received CMTs, such as Papua New Guinea (Chongqing, 2005) and Malawi (Shaanxi, 2008). Since the 1990s, some changes have occurred regarding the CMTs in Africa. They had to withdraw for different reasons – for example, the expiration of the contract in Libya (1994) or chaotic situations caused by war, such as in Somalia (1991) and the Democratic

Republic of the Congo (1997). China evacuated the CMTs because of the recognition of Taiwan by Liberia, Central Africa and Niger in 1989, 1991 and 1992 respectively, and they later returned to the three countries in 2005, 1996 and 1998 after the resumption of diplomatic relations. China stopped medical cooperation with Burkina Faso (1994), Gambia (1995) and Sao Tome and Principe (1997) for their recognition of Taiwan. China sent CMTs to Senegal in 1975, but this was interrupted in 1996 by fluctuation in bilateral relations, and the CMTs returned there in 2007. The CMTs also resumed operation in the Democratic Republic of the Congo in 2006. Malawi established diplomatic relations with China in 2007, and the CMTs arrived in the country in June 2008. China also planned to send the CMTs to Angola and Ghana. In addition, China provided medical assistance to various countries in emergency situations, such as during the tsunami in Thailand, Indonesia and Sri Lanka, as well as earthquakes in Pakistan and Burma. China sent its peacekeeping medical teams to the Democratic Republic of the Congo (2003) and Lebanon (2007). The Inner Mongolia sent its medical team to Mongolia in 2007.

The history of Chinese medical cooperation abroad shows that China has had to withdraw the CMTs because of the local instability or a souring of diplomatic relations. Therefore, we can draw the conclusion that the dispatch of the CMTs is closely related to China's diplomacy, and the work of the CMTs is decided by the political stability of the host country.

CMT in Africa: Number and scale

In recent years, the Chinese government has unremittingly sent CMT to friendly countries and provided medical assistance. This is rare in the history of international relations, and resulted in attention from international academia (Thompson 2005: 4; Shinn 2006: 4–16). How many doctors has China sent to other countries? How many patients abroad have been served by CMTs? To how many African countries has China sent CMTs? There are public reports relating to the first and second questions.

In 2003, the Ministry of Health reported that, "For the past 40 years, CMT members have reached a total of 18 000, and they are in 65 countries/regions all over Asia, Africa, Latin America, Europe and Oceania" (Department of International Cooperation of Ministry of Health 2003: 15). A report of 2006 said, "From 1963, our country has successively sent 18,000 CMT members to countries/regions of Africa, Asia, Latin America, Europe and Oceania. They treated 240 million patients" (Pei Guangjiang 2007). An article by an official from the Ministry of Health indicated that "for the past 43 years, the Chinese government has sent 19,000 medical team members [who] served 240 million patients" (Wang Liji 2006: 308). Data from 2007 show that, "Currently there are 47 CMT spread in 45 countries, including 122 medical service points with 1235 members. During the past 44 years, China has dispatched 20,029 CMT members and treated 240 million patients abroad" (Peking University Health Science Center 2007: 1).

To how many African countries has China sent CMTs? This simple question does not have an appropriate answer. The official media and networks don't give the same answer and some versions are obviously wrong. For example, an article entitled "CMT in Africa" claimed that, "For the past 40 years, CMT grew from small to big, and China has sent about 15 000 CMT members to 47 countries/regions in Africa" (*China Daily* 2003). It indicated that origin of the 2003 data was a special issue of *China Today*.[8] The version that "China sent CMT to 47 countries/regions in Africa" was frequently quoted at home and abroad;[9] unfortunately, it is wrong.[10] In 2006, a report in *People's Daily* said "Since China sent its first CMT to Africa in 1963, we have sent 16,000 CMT members to 47 African countries/regions, serving 160 million African patients" (Li Xinfeng 2006: 3). The official FOCAC website also used this version.[11] To celebrate the anniversary of the China–Africa Summit, in 2007 *People's Daily* created a special column entitled "Implementing the FOCAC–Beijing Summit". It reported that, "The footprints of CMT are in 48 African countries/regions" (Pei Guangjiang 2007). These data are not accurate.

Reviewing the history of CMT in Africa, my research shows that China has sent CMTs to the following 45 African countries/regions: Algeria, Zanzibar (Tanzania), Somalia (evacuated in 1991 owing to the civil war), Congo (Brazzaville), Mali, Tanganyika (Tanzania), Mauritania, Guinea, the Sudan, Equatorial Guinea, Sierra Leone, Tunisia, Democratic Republic of the Congo, Ethiopia, Togo, Cameroon, Senegal, Madagascar, Morocco, Niger, Mozambique, São Tomé and Principe (evacuated due to the suspension of diplomatic relations), Burkina Faso (evacuated due to the suspension of diplomatic relations), Guinea–Bissau, Gabon, Gambia (evacuated due to the suspension of diplomatic relations), Benin, Zambia, Central Africa, Chad, Libya (the contract is about to expire), Botswana, Djibouti, Rwanda, Uganda, Zimbabwe, Cape Verde, Liberia, Seychelles, Comoros, Burundi, Namibia, Lesotho, Eritrea and Malawi (see Table 12.1). African countries that have never had CMTs are Egypt, South Africa, Nigeria, Ghana, Kenya, Ivory Coast, Swaziland, Mauritius and Angola. CMTs will arrive in Ghana and Angola soon.

To how many African countries/regions has China sent CMT? Up to 2008, these numbered 45 (excluding Angola and Ghana). In 2007, China began building anti-malaria centres in Africa to help fight this widespread tropical disease.

CMTs' contribution to African people

CMT members have withstood various difficulties of environments, diseases, disasters and war; some have even scarified their lives. Hu Yaobang, the former General Secretary of the CCP, once pointed out that, "The impact of those things related to the mass will not disappear easily, yet they need much less money. Among China's friendly activities with the Third World, CMT is a successful case" (International Cooperation Office of Health Department

Table 12.1 Chinese medical teams abroad, 1963–2008

Country	Province in charge	Dispatch date	Changes
Algeria	Hubei	April 1963	Withdrew in February 1995 due to war and re-dispatched in 1997
Zanzibar	Jiangsu	August 1964	
Laos	Yunnan	December 1964	Interrupted in 1974
Somalia	Jilin	June 1965	Withdrew in 1991 due to civil war
Rep. Yemen	Liaonin	July 1966	
Congo (Brazzaville)	Tianjin	February 1967	Withdrew in 1997 due to civil war, and returned in December 2000
Mali	Zhejiang	February 1968	
Tanganyika (Tanzania)	Shandong	March 1968	
Mauretania	Heilongjiang	April 1968	
Guinea	Beijing	June 1968	
DR Yemen	Anhui	January 1970	
Vietnam	Yunnan	December 1968	Interrupted in 1971
Sudan	Shanxi	April 1971	
Equatorial Guinea	Guangdong	October 1971	
Sierra Leone	Hunan	March 1973	Withdrew in 1993 due to war, and re-dispatched in December 2002 formally
Tunisia	Jiangxi	June 1973	Helped set up the first acupuncture center in 1994
DR Congo (Kinshasa)	Hebei	September 1973	Withdrew in 1997 due to war and returned in June 2006. Shenyang Military Region sent peacekeeping soldiers in 2003
Albania	Liaonin	September 1973	Interrupted in 1974
Ethiopia	Henan	November 1974	Interrupted in September 1979 and returned in December 1984
Togo	Shanghai	November 1974	
Cameroon	Shanghai	June 1975	Interrupted in January 1979 and dispatched by Shanxi in 1985
Cambodia	Shanxi	June 1975	Interrupted in March 1981
Senegal	Fujian	July 1975	Withdrew in 1996 and re-dispatched in September 2007
Madagascar	Gansu	August 1975	
Morocco	Shanghai	September 1975	Jiangxi Province joined in 2000

Table 12.1 Cont.

Country	Province in charge	Dispatch date	Changes
Niger	Guangxi	January 1976	Withdrew in July 1992 and re-dispatched in December 1996
Mozambique	Sichuan	April 1976	
São Tomé and Principe	Heilongjiang Sichuan	June 1976	Withdrew in 1997 after Sino-São Tomé and Principe diplomatic relationship suspended
Burkina Faso (Upper Volta)	Beijing	June 1976	Withdrew in 1994 after Sino-Burkina Faso diplomatic relationship suspended
Guinea-Bissau	Guizhou	July. 1976	Withdrew in 1990 and re-dispatched by Sichuan in 2002
Kuwait	Liaonin	November 1976	
Gabon	Tianjin	May. 1977	
Gambia	Tianjin	May 1977	Dispatched by Guangdong province instead in 1991, and withdrew in 1995
Benin	Ningxia	January 1978	
Zambia	Henan	January 1978	
Syria	Chinese Medicine Research Institute of the Ministry of Health	May 1978	Interrupted in June 1981
Central African Republic	Zhejiang	July 1978	Withdrew in July 1991, re-dispatched in August 1998
Iran	Jiangsu	August 1978	Interrupted in September 1979
Chad	Jiangxi	December 1978	Withdrew in 1979 and re-dispatched in 1989; withdrew in 1997 and re-dispatched in 2006; withdrew in February 2008 due to the war and re-dispatched in May
Botswana	Fujian	February 1981	
Djibouti	Shanxi	February 1981	
UAE	Sichuan	October 1981	
Rwanda	Inner Mongolia	June 1982	
Uganda	Yunnan	January 1983	
Libya	Jiangsu	December 1983	Contract expired in 1994 and not renewed
Malta	Jiangsu	April 1984	

(*continued*)

Table 12.1 Cont.

Country	Province in charge	Dispatch date	Changes
Cape Verde	Heilongjiang	July 1984	Dispatch province changed to Sichuan in February 1998, and later to Hunan
Liberia	Heilongjiang	July 1984	Withdrew in 1989 and returned in 2005
Zimbabwe	Hunan	May 1985	
Vanuatu	Shaanxi	1985	
Samoa	Anhui	1986	
Burundi	Guangxi	December 1986	The dispatch province was changed to Qinghai
Seychelles	Guangxi	May 1987	Guangdong recruited five CMT members as a Chinese volunteer project in 2007
Guyana	Jiangsu	July 1993	
Namibia	Zhejiang	April 1996	
Comoros	Guangxi	1994	
Lesotho	Hubei	June 1997	
Eritrea	Henan	September 1997	
Nepal	Hebei	1999	
Timor-Leste	Sichuan	January 2000	
Papua-New Guinea	Chongqing	October 2002	
Thailand*	Shanghai	December 2004	Medical assistance during the tsunami
Indonesia*	People's Military Army	January 2005	Medical assistance during the tsunami
Sri Lanka*	Beijing	January 2005	Medical assistance during the tsunami
Pakistan*	Hospital of People's Military Army	October 2005	Disaster relief
Lebanon*	Chengdu Military Region	January 2007	Peacekeeping force (medical team)
Mongolia**	Inner Mongolia	May 2007	
Myanmar*	China	2008	Disaster relief
Malawi	Shanxi	June 2008	
Angola	Sichuan	(Planned) 2007	Postponed because accommodation not provided by Angola
Ghana	Guangdong	(Planned) 2008	

* Special case, not dispatched by the Ministry of Health
** Dispatched by the local government in China

of Zhejiang Province 2003: 26). CMT members serve their African patients wholeheartedly.

Fighting against tropical diseases

CMTs have provided medical service across five continents, mainly concentrated in Africa. For a long time, tropical and infectious diseases have threatened lives. According to statistics, every year one million children die of malaria; of all deaths in Africa, 90 per cent are from malaria. In 2002, Africans accounted for 50 per cent of deaths from infectious and parasitic diseases in the world. In 2004, 99 per cent of those who died of cholera in the world were Africans.

There is a shortage of doctors in Africa, where the ratio of surgeon to population is 1:40,000. In about 30 African countries, there is only one doctor for every 30,000 people (Siringi 2003; Shinn 2006). Since 1963, CMTs in Africa have freely served the masses and brought about tremendous change to the lives of the local poor patients. Take Algeria as an example. In recent years, about 3000 CMTs have provided medical services to 21 provinces/cities, involving various specialties such as general surgery, aural surgery, plastic surgery, orthopedics, obstetrics and gynaecology, cardiology, ophthalmology, anesthesia and acupuncture, and set up 102 medical care clinics (Health Department of Hubei Province 1993: 7–21). Their advantage is traditional Chinese medicine and acupuncture therapy. When the Algerian Defence Minister was paralysed in a riding accident, he was treated by famous doctors in different countries without success. Chinese doctor Shi Xuemin treated him with acupuncture therapy and he could move his leg again (Anonymous 2006). The miracle of the silver needles surprised the Algerians and an acupuncture boom spread to Morocco and other Arab countries. The Algerian Minister of Health pointed out that, "The effect of Chinese medical teams has gone beyond Algeria's borders, and extended to the whole world" (Health Department of Hubei Province 1993).

Chinese acupuncture has an excellent reputation in all countries where CMTs work. When Cameroon President Paul Biya was informed of the effects of acupuncture therapy, he invited Doctor Wen Hong to provide healthcare services for him.[12] Doctor Wen realised the superiority of Chinese traditional medicine and that it could never be replaced by Western medicine: "There is really a close link between the popularity of acupuncture and CMT. Wherever [there is a] CMT, even if there is only one medical care point with two doctors, one of them must be a doctor of acupuncture."[13]

In Mali, the climate and living conditions result in the frequent occurrence of rheumatism, arthritis and lumbar muscle strain, and acupuncture has a good effect on these diseases (International Cooperation Office of Health Department of Zhejiang Province 2003: 50). Unbalanced eating habits, malaria and the abuse of quinine easily give rise to hemiplegia, which frequently attacks people between 20 and 70 years of age. Doctor Cai Weigen has used his silver needle to cure many patients.[14] CMT in Niger treated 57,330 patients in 2006; 5120 were cured by acupuncture therapy. Several government ministers have shown great interest in Chinese medicine and acupuncture.[15]

Serving the common people

The most impressive characteristic of CMT doctors is their service to the common people, who benefit personally from their superb medical skill and professionalism. The director of an Algerian hospital said, "Mascara Hospital became well known because of the arrival of CMT" (Health Department of Hubei Province 1993: 77). There are many touching stories about the services of CMTs. Doctor Dai Zhiben and his colleagues in Algeria successfully reattached a severed limb for an African youngster named Osman, the first such operation in Africa. "Chinese Mother" Song Yingjie served in Algeria for seven years and was awarded the Algerian National Medal. CMTs in Algeria not only had the honour of being invited to dinner with the president; they were also called the "most trusted people" by the local people (Health Department of Hubei Province 1993: 3–34). In Mali, Dr Li Shiji of Zhejiang CMT successfully resected a tumour and performed the subsequent repair; Dr Chen Yijun lengthened a femur for the first time and Dr Jiang Xiugao removed a huge cervical cancer. All these excellent operations caused a sensation (International Cooperation Office of Health Department of Zhejiang Province. 2003: 2–63, 119–128).

A CMT from Ningxia removed an ovarian tumor weighing 23 kilograms from a Benin woman and Dr Shang Yanjun and his colleagues performed a craniotomy to save a dying patient, which was a miracle in the medical history of Benin (Lu Shuqun & Wu Qiong 2003: 6–31). Using closed perfusion and drainage technology, Jiangxi doctor Qiu Xiaohong performed skilful surgery on an old man in Morocco who was suffering from an infection after a fracture operation (Ying Mingqin 2003: 8–79). Dr Xiong Renjie and other doctors from Jiangsu Province rescued a girl whose heart stopped beating for 30 minutes, which created a sensation (Health Department of Jiangsu Province 2004). With superb skill, Sichuan doctor Jiang Yongsheng cured 22 Mozambican patients suffering from hemiplegia within a short time (Wei Yixiong 2006). CMT from Hunan Province launched the Action of Brightness in Sierra Leone and performed cataract operations for 248 patients free of charge, which won praise (Dai A-Di 2006). All these have become significant cases in African medical history.

Improving local medical systems

Another achievement of CMTs is in helping to improve local medical and health systems. To do this, China has cooperated with African countries in various ways, such as building hospitals and medical facilities, providing free medication and teaching Chinese medical techniques. In the Congo, the

Brazzaville Hospital for Gynaecology and Obstetrics was small in the 1960s. With the help of China in the 1970s, it is now the third biggest comprehensive hospital in Brazzaville. It has 23 Chinese doctors on its staff who play a significant role.

Chinese doctors also helped establish medical specialties and technical facilities. The specialty of acupuncture has become evident in Tunisia, Cameroon, Lesotho, Namibia and Madagascar. The acupuncture department in the Hospital for Women and Children in Cameroon has a very good reputation, and there is a long queue of patients awaiting treatment every morning.[16] CMT in Lesotho set up a Department of Acupuncture to serve both the King and his subjects, who for the first time have the opportunity to experience the magical effects of the small silver needle (Liang Tao 2006). In Namibia, after establishing a Department of Acupuncture, CMT very quickly stimulated the people's interest in acupuncture and related treatment and the First Lady invited Chinese doctors to practise in the president's house (International Cooperation Office of Health Department of Zhejiang Province 2003: 204).

CMTs also promoted innovations in the medial systems of African countries, such as the establishment of a Center of Acupuncture in Tunisia. China set up the Marsa Center of Acupuncture in the capital in 1994, the first in Africa, at the behest of the Tunisian government. The staff comprises four or five Chinese doctors and several Tunisian assistants who work together harmoniously. Besides medical treatment, the centre is responsible for teaching and providing training materials to students, who are working doctors from other medical institutions and hospitals. After theoretical studies, operating studies, examinations and the defence of their theses, students can obtain a special diploma in acupuncture. The centre treated 20,530 patients between 1996 and 1998 and the Tunisian Minister of Health has proudly pointed to it as a symbol of friendship between the two countries. In his words, the centre is number one in the Arab world, in African countries and in developing countries (Ying Mingqin 2003: 65, 110, 163). In order to meet the needs of the people, the state health insurance company in Tunisia decided to set up a department of acupuncture at Bizerta Hospital. Since the graduates of the Marsa Centre had already undertaken important work in the hospital, this was not difficult (Ying Mingqin 2003: 31, 65, 110, 163). Tunisian and Chinese doctors jointly ran a "Chinese Medicine and Acupuncture Day" in 2007 and demonstrated various procedures and techniques, as well as answering questions. The day generated a great amount of excitement and local interest, along with reports by TV stations (Tu Zixian 2007).

CMT in Guyana overcame various difficulties and set up a pathology department in Georgetown, which was highly praised by the local people (Health Department of Jiangsu Province 2004: 71–76, 311–19). The Mediterranean Centre of Chinese Medicine created by the joint efforts of China and Marta provides an opportunity for the local people to receive Chinese medical treatment, thus setting up a platform for bilateral medical cooperation and creating conditions for the spread of Chinese medicine.

There are courses on acupuncture at universities in various African countries. A Guinean student named Segu Kamala began to study medical science and Chinese medicine as early as 1973, and spent eight years in China. After his return to Guinea, he insisted on performing an operation using acupuncture, which finally brought acupuncture to public attention. Conakry University has listed acupuncture as a required course since 2000, the first in Africa (Yan Ye & Chen Yao 2006). Chinese doctor Jiang Yongshen has treated 140,000 patients in Mozambique, trained a group of local medical specialists in acupuncture and initiated a course in traditional Chinese medical techniques at the Universidade Eduardo Mondlane Medical School (Wei Yixiong 2006). Under the auspices of a CMT, Madagascar's State School of Public Health set up a special class in acupuncture.[17]

Raising local medical standards

Chinese doctors have also tried to transfer medical techniques and knowledge to local doctors. When Premier Zhou Enlai visited Zanzibar in 1965, he pointed out to CMT members there that they would sooner or later return home. It was therefore necessary to train Zanzibar's doctors and help them to work independently. In this way, China would "leave a medical team which would never go away" and thus "support the liberation cause of African people" (Health Department of Jiangsu Province 2004: 3). When Mao Zedong met President Nyerere, he pointed out that the work of CMTs in Tanzania should be "helping" and "teaching". Premier Zhou Enlai added:

> Now we have several dozens of CMT abroad, yet it is not enough. CMT should not only cure the disease, but also help training work. They should bring medicine and facilities, train African doctors, who can be self-reliant and would work even if CMT went away … We would provide sincere help to any independent country. Our assistance is to make the country able to stand up. Just like building a bridge, so you can cross the river without a staff. That would be good.
>
> (Liu Jirui 1998: 74)

CMTs usually help local doctors by offering free lectures, training courses and instruction in operating procedures. In Tanzania, in order to train local medical staff in acupuncture, CMT members allowed local doctors to practise on their own bodies. In this way, they were able to train a large number of medical specialists. CMT also made the best use of local media to publicise their medical knowledge (Liu Jirui 1998: 4–78). In Algeria, CMTs ran training courses on acupuncture for anyone who was interested. They tried by every means to raise local medical standards, such as giving small lectures on reattaching severed limbs, acupuncture and anesthesia observation, which was welcomed by local medical staff. Until 2008, CMT in Algeria had offered more than 20 training courses and more than 30 lectures, and trained more than 300 medical personnel, who have become the backbone of local medical institutions (Health Department of Hubei Province 1993: 7–21).

Liberia suffered from war and chaos for a long time, with a huge number of people requiring medical attention. CMT doctors have provided medical services and taught new techniques to local medical personnel. Their activities caught the eye of David Shinn, the former US ambassador to Ethiopia and Burkina Faso, who said:

> China received praise in Liberia for its medical teams because they prioritize the transfer of knowledge and technology. They sent specialists and general practitioners, who upgraded and built the professional skills of local health workers. In the case of war-torn Liberia, this is a critical medical need.
>
> (Shinn 2006: 15)

The CMT in Zanzibar started to train local doctors in 1971. The Zanzibar government sent four students to study internal medicine, surgery, gynaecology and obstetrics, and stomatology. Four Chinese doctors created the syllabus, class structure and content of examinations. Vice-President Aboud Jumbe's eldest son studied surgery under the supervision of Dr Xu Wuyin and published academic papers under the guidance of Dr Zhang Zuxun, which generated great respect. Vice-President Jumbe said, "I just gave him the physical body, Chinese doctors made him a useful talent." Two young people, Nassur and Moyo, used to be doctors' assistants. Thanks to guidance from Chinese doctors, they entered the Mombasa Medical College. Another assistant has become a famous ophthalmologist in the locality. Vice-President Jumbe said with deep feeling:

> CMT's training method is very good, with theory and practice combined. It only takes two to three years then you can do a lot of operations. In other countries, it takes six to seven years for study, and you can only do some small operations.
>
> (Health Department of Jiangsu Province 2004: 9, 63–65)

In 1975, CMTs in Algeria opened the first full-time Chinese medicine and acupuncture training class. The Chinese doctors devised the curriculum, compiled teaching materials and translated them into French. In just two years, they trained 25 acupuncture technicians. In Benin, CMTs from Ningxia provided training for local medical personnel. They gave lectures on epidural anesthesia in children, toxic dysentery, normal delivery process, anemia diagnosis and treatment, liver function tests, chest perspective and aseptic operations. As a reference for Benin doctors they wrote *One hundred cases of experience of African children with cerebral malaria control*, thus leaving a "forever staying medical team" (Health Department of Hubei Province 1993: 81–186).

In 1985, CMTs in Cameroon held four training classes on acupuncture, gynaecology and obstetrics, pediatric water and electrolyte balance, and ECG.

They prepared lessons late into the night, made teaching aids such as charts and translated the lectures into French. Owing to the shortage of brush ink, they used a cotton swab dipped in gentian violet solution instead. They even presented the students with a certificate to encourage them (Lu Shuqun & Wu Qiong 2003: 29). The hospital director Ali said at the summing-up meeting, "CMT doctors have improved our medical staff at the theoretical level of medical science and clinical diagnosis technology. They have left a medical team here forever. We are very grateful to all the Chinese doctors working in our hospital in Jeddah city" (Liu Wan 2007). In Gabon, Namibia, Madagascar and Liberia, CMTs did the same and used a variety of training methods to improve the skills of African doctors.

A number of African leaders have highly praised the fruitful cooperation between China and Africa and the CMTs' great achievements. Tanzanian President Nyerere once said, "I trust Chinese doctors. They have not only got expertise, but also a very strong sense of responsibility." Gabon President Bongo commented that, "CMTs have achieved great success", while Mauritanian President Hairare praised CMTs thus: "Chinese experts are good at working hard with high efficiency. They are not afraid of hardship and work in our areas short of doctors and medicines and are most welcomed by the masses." The vice-president of Zimbabwe said, "The CMT has promoted the cause of medicine and health in Zimbabwe." The wholehearted service has brought awards and honours for CMT; African governments have awarded various medals to more than 600 CMT members in recognition of their great contribution to the improvement of public health in Africa (Department of International Cooperation of Ministry of Health 2003: 16).

Carrying out anti-malaria campaigns

To fight against malaria in Africa, the Chinese government adopted several measures simultaneously, namely CMT, training programs, anti-malaria projects, free facilities and drugs, and anti-malaria centres.

Fighting malaria has been one of the major tasks for CMTs, and their staff have had to contend with malaria themselves. They usually distribute free medication to patients. Côtecxin, the most effective anti-malaria drug produced in China, has won a great reputation in Africa. In certain areas, lifestyle and abuse of medication can result in very serious illness. In Mali, for example, malaria is very common and people have to take quinine for treatment – yet many suffer from limb hemiplegia caused by over-use of this drug. Chinese acupuncture expert Cai Weigeng has cured many patients and a CMT from Ninxia provides services in Benin. In the 1990s, the Zanzibari minister of culture suffered from the sequelae of malaria and was treated by CMT doctor Zhang Zidian.

China continually holds training programmes either in Africa or China to provide adequate knowledge of anti-malaria measures to African medical specialists and government officials. In 2002 the Jiangsu Centre for

Verminosis Control and Prevention was designated by the PRC Ministry of Commerce as the base for international assistance in human resource development. Since then, the centre has run six programs offering training courses to 169 officials and special technicians from 43 countries in Africa. In July and August 2003, two anti-malaria training programs ran in Madagascar, Kenya and Cameroon. Six Chinese experts and 28 African participants from 14 countries attended the one-week program in Nairobi, which was greatly praised by the African participants as well as the Kenyan Minister of Health and the Chinese ambassador. The distinguished malaria expert Gao Qi went to Madagascar, Kenya and Cameroon in 2003 to give courses on the control and prevention of malaria to medical practitioners from 35 African countries.

In Uganda, malaria kills over 80,000 people per year, mostly pregnant women and children. China has fulfilled its pledge of donating anti-malaria medicine and carrying out anti-malaria training programs in Uganda. In November 2006, soon after the China–Africa summit, a three-day anti-malaria program was held in Kampala as part of China's efforts to join forces with Uganda to fight malaria. Stephen Malinga, Ugandan Minister of Health, hailed the Chinese government for financing the course, saying it was an indication of the growing cordial relations between the two countries.[18] The Jiangsu Center of Verminosis Control and Prevention in east China sent experts to Senegal and Uganda to give anti-malaria training to more than 180 local health officials and medical specialists.

Carrying out the project of control and prevention effectively is the third arm of anti-malaria cooperation. For example, in Moheli island in the Comoros, villages are severely affected by malaria. The highest rate is 94.4 per cent and malaria is the most common cause of death for children under the age of five years. In 2007, a joint project between Moheli Island and the Tropical Medicine Institute at Guangzhou University of Chinese Medicine in southern China was initiated, with the purpose of eradicating the parasite from the human body. According to Li Guoqiao (sometimes misspelled as Li Guoqiang), the project leader and a professor at the Institute at the university, the real source of malaria is the human body. He believes that when it is driven out of humans, mosquitoes will not carry it since mosquitoes get it from humans. And once the parasite is not around, malaria will be exterminated (Liu Dun, 2015). Under the plan, the islanders were prescribed a single dose of artemisinin-based combination therapy (ACT) and primaquine, which they would all consume at the same time to clear the parasite from their bodies.[19] As part of growing Chinese aid and investment in Africa, Beijing would fund the estimated $320,000 for the drugs used in the Moheli treatments and would also meet the cost of additional drugs used to clear up remaining infections over a five-year period (Lague 2007).

On 22 December 2008, a meeting of the China Aid Project of Eradication of Malaria, run by GUTCM, was held at Moheli, Comoros. President Ahmed Abdalla Mohamed Sambi and the UN representative attended the meeting with the Chinese ambassador and experts from GUTCM. According to a survey in September 2007, affected residents made up 23 per cent, and in some villages as much as 94.4 per cent, of the population. Average infections are 200–300 per month and 10–20 people die of malaria every year. With the implementation of the measures invented by Professor Li, the rate of infection decreased by 98.7 per cent to below 1 per cent, and the number of infections decreased by 89.9 per cent. What is more, there were no deaths from malaria during the first year of implementation. At the meeting the President of Comoros concluded that the Moheli case indicated that the eradication measures were the most effective in the world and should be introduced not only in the whole of Comoros but also in all affected areas (Chinnock 2009).[20]

Drugs are vital to combat malaria. When a delegation of 13 senior African government officials visited a Shanghai-based pharmaceutical company in 2005, they called for further cooperation with China in producing anti-malaria drugs. Among the delegation were Comoros Vice-President Caabi El-Yachroutu Mohamed and Commissioner for Social Affairs of the African Union Bience Gawanas. They also called on Chinese pharmaceutical companies to set up branches in African countries for medicine production.[21]

Facilities and anti-malaria drugs are provided to African countries free of charge. One of the most important drugs is Côtecxin. As early as 1993, Beijing Holley-Côtec developed a new medicine called DihydroArtemisinin, or Côtecxin, which was approved by the World Health Organization (WHO) as an effective anti-malaria drug (Lu Chunming 2006). In 1996, the Chinese Ministry of Health designated Côtecxin as the required medicine for CMT to use and it began to spread to all countries where CMTs serve. It is also frequently chosen for official development aid. The pharmaceutical companies also donate artemisinin to African countries – for example, Yunnan Kunming Pharmaceutical Company offered the anti-malaria drug (worth 42 million African francs) to Côte d'Ivoire for control and prevention of the disease in 2007; President Gbagbo expressed sincere thanks to the company.[22]

Côtecxin has been chosen many times as a state gift when Chinese leaders visit Africa. When President Jiang Zemin visited Africa in 2002, he presented the drug to Nigeria for a project on the control and prevention of malaria in children. In 2004, Chinese National Congress Chair Wu Bangguo went to Africa with a donation of Côtecxin to the countries he visited. In April 2006, the gift of President Hu Jintao when he visited Africa was again the anti-malaria drug. In 2006, the artesinate injection developed by the Guilin Pharmaceutical Company was found to be the most effective and listed by WHO as the first choice in emergency treatment for malaria. The company has met the good manufacturing practices (GMP) requirements of WHO, and it has developed holograms as a security device to fight against counterfeits. ACTs are recognised by WHO as the best and safest treatment for malaria. The organisation has stepped up cultivation of *Artemisia annua* in east Africa in a bid to ensure a reliable supply and reduce costs.

The last and most important measure is the setting up of anti-malaria centres in Africa, a direct result of the 2006 summit. Preparations started

Table 12.2 China-supported anti-malaria centres in Africa

Country	Date opened	Location
Liberia	1 February 2007	Monrovia
Chad	28 December 2007	Ndjamena (Ndjamena Freedom Hospital)
Burundi	27 March 2008	Bujumbura
Uganda	15 May 2008	Kampala (Mulago Hospital)
Congo (Brazzaville)	13 August 2008	Brazzaville
Gabon	28 September 2008	Libreville (China–Gabon Cooperation Hospital)
Guinea-Bissau	10 December 2008	Bissau
Togo	7 January 2009	Lomé
Mali	13 February 2009	Bamako (Kadi Hospital)
Cameroon	26 March 2009	Yaoundé (Women and Children Hospital)

Source: *People's Daily,* February 2007 to April 2009.

right after the summit: several teams went to Liberia, Tanzania, Zambia, South Africa, Kenya and Madagascar to prepare the centres. In addition, the first group of 60 medical experts who would work in the anti-malaria centres in Africa attended a ten-day professional training course at Jiangsu Center of Verminosis Control and Prevention in October 2007. The trainees were selected from hospitals, medical labs and academies across the country, and once trained they went to Africa to treat malaria-affected patients and pass on their knowledge to African colleagues. Deputy Minister Wei Jianguo oversaw medical cooperation with Africa. At a meeting on anti-malaria centres held on 16 January 2008, he called for the sustainable development of the centres and discussed this issue with leaders from different departments of the ministry, as well as CEOs of the companies producing anti-malaria drugs.[23]

After an anti-malaria centre was built, Chinese experts would set up and test the facilities, exchange ideas with local specialists and give technological training to the medical staff. The Chinese government would provide free facilities and drugs to the centre for three years. It is important that the centre should serve as a national base. It should be not just a laboratory and clinical department, but should serve as a centre for research on anti-malaria strategies and measures of malaria prevention, as well as the exchange of advanced technology and training of medical staff.

CMTs' devotion to China

Former Vice-Premier Wan Li once pointed out:

> Sending CMT as a form of foreign assistance is an important channel in the friendship and cooperation between China and the Third World

320 *Cooperation and dynamics*

> ... This is a political task, which will go on for a long time. We should strengthen the work and carry out CMT better and better.
> (International Cooperation Office of Health Department of Zhejiang Province 2003: 36)

History shows that CMTs are a form of assistance that has cost less money, achieved better results and exerted greater influence than many others. This kind of assistance has changed the lives of many people, especially patients in African countries, and has thus become an important part of China's public diplomacy. CMTs have received praise for their achievements several times from national leaders at China's conferences on foreign assistance. Their efforts are also confirmed by the mutual support between China and developing countries in the international arena. CMT members' spirit of devotion, medical ethics and superb skills have strengthened China's influence and even affected high-level government policy.

Presenting a friendly image of China by serving the masses

In the more than half a century since its founding, the PRC has gradually become an influential power in the international arena, which would have been impossible without the support of developing countries including those in Africa. This support originates in an attitude of mutual respect and trust. The successful work of CMTs is an important way to realise this mutual trust. By carrying out this service, CMTs have helped the people of many developing countries further understand China; they have thus been a unique way of expressing China's influence.

During the early 1960s, some countries demanded the restoration of China's legal seat in the United Nations. In the 26th session of the UN Assembly, 23 countries headed by Algeria and Albania introduced a proposal for the PRC to resume its legitimate rights in the United Nations (the "Double A Proposal"). Of the 23 countries, 17 had CMTs in service.[24] Most of the countries that voted "yes" to the proposal were developing countries. When the result of the vote was declared, the permanent representatives of 17 African countries stood up and cheered; the representative of Tanzania left his seat and started to dance in the hall to express his joy (Wu Miaofa 2006).[25] This great achievement in China's diplomacy clearly indicates the success of CMTs' hard work.

CMTs have established a profound friendship with local people. There are several foreign medical teams in Algeria, but the CMT is "the most popular team" (Health Department of Hubei Province 1993: 7). When CMT doctor Zhang Zongzhen died in Zanzibar in 1965, more than 300 people from all walks of life came to say goodbye to him despite the pouring rain (Health Department of Jiangsu Province 2004: 26). At the beginning of the 1980s, when the Zambian government decided to transfer CMTs to another city, the media of the host city reported, "We need Chinese doctors"; "CMTs can't be transferred". Local crowds held spontaneous demonstrations and shouted, "Chinese doctors can't go!" The media commented that "the Chinese doctors have won the hearts of Zambian people with their excellent work" (Wang Liji 2006: 310). After a doctor saved his great-grandchild's life, to show his sincere gratitude an elder of Benin knelt on one knee holding the CMT leader's arm – a local gesture to show the highest esteem, expressing that he had nothing with which to reward the doctor except in the afterlife.

In the late 1980s, a CMT in Guinea received an invitation from the government to sit on the reviewing stand to watch the parade for the country's National Day. Owing to misinformation about the time, the CMT only arrived when the parade had almost finished. When the district and provincial leaders learned of this, they ordered the participants to conduct the parade again. The CMT members were deeply moved by this gesture (Lu Shuqun & Wu Qiong 2003: 55).

A CMT from Ningxia established a good relationship with the people of Benin. When the Belgian doctors withdrew, a Benin doctor wrote a letter saying, "Many patients go to the hospital where CMT are working and like to cooperate with Chinese. What's more, everybody wants to see you again. You have cured and saved many patients here. People don't want CMT to leave Nadidanji. Belgians can go, Chinese can't go!" The prime minister of Madagascar said "building a good relationship and deep friendship" was one of the reasons for the CMT's success (Wang Liji 2006: 311–312).

CMT doctors have left a good impression in other ways. Dr Qi Jipeng in Brazzaville once found a wallet containing 800,000 francs in the hospital. He inquired at each unit one by one and finally found the owner: the money was for her medical care. This story was reported by the local newspaper *The Star*, and the honesty of the Chinese doctor was widely praised. Friendly feelings have become the foundation of African countries' China policy. In the words of a CMT, "The brand of CMT is the brand of China" (Lu Shuqun & Wu Qiong 2003: 321).

Serving top leaders and building mutual respect and trust

Many leaders of African countries either benefited from the Chinese doctors' superb medical skill or simply placed their own healthcare in the hands of CMT, as did many senior government officials.[26] They trusted Chinese medical professionalism, and CMT doctors have also shown the Chinese spirit and spread awareness of the principles and position of the Chinese government. As expressed in one of the memoirs:

> They give medical treatment to presidents, prime ministers, ministers. In the course of time, they have gradually developed close relations with them, thus have played a role that diplomats such as ambassadors are unable to play.
>
> (Health Department of Tianjin 2007: 71)

Zanzibar's President Jumbe once asked the interpreter Zhang Meilan to tell the Chinese doctor about his coming visit abroad. He gave Zhang details of his schedule and showed her the document he was reading. The president's trust in Chinese doctors greatly moved Zhang: "Why did President Jumbe take no precaution against me by showing the documents that he was reading? As can be seen, how the leader of Zanzibar trusts our Chinese!" (Health Department of Jiangsu Province 2004: 46). The Chinese doctors can go freely to the presidential palace or any government offices, and the president is open with the Chinese doctors about government affairs. After the assassination of President Sheikh Abeid Amani Karume, martial law was imposed on citizens – with the exception of Chinese doctors (Health Department of Jiangsu Province 2004: 60). All this shows how much the Zanzibari government and people trust CMT.

Tanzanian President Nyerere sent his plane to transport CMT doctor Zheng Sufang to the capital for treatment as soon as he learned that Dr Zheng was ill. When the Chinese ambassador heard of this incident, he said, "You doctors' work of foreign affairs is doing so well that you are invited to be guests to the President's home, and can take the special plane of the President. Even I as ambassador haven't enjoyed this treatment" (International Cooperation Office of Health Department of Zhejiang Province 2003: 44). The Tunisia–China Friendship Association was set up thanks to the efforts of Tunisian President Ben Ali, his senior advisor and former prime minister, who had all benefited from CMT's services. The senior advisor had suffered from a serious illness, which was cured by a CMT (Liu Jirui 1998: 8).

African heads of state have shown their gratitude to CMT in various ways.

- Tanzanian President Nyerere sent sheep to CMT doctors in recognition of their contribution.
- Algerian President and Defence Minister Houari Boumediène invited Chinese doctors for dinner.
- Central African President André-Dieudonné Kolingba had a long talk with Chinese doctors and awarded them the Renaissance Medal.
- Benin President Mathieu Kérékou and his wife attended the funeral of Dr Wang Shula, who died of overwork, and awarded the leader of CMT in Benin the National Knight Medal.
- Mali President Alpha Oumar Konaré sent ten large sheep to a CMT with good wishes on New Year's Eve, and also on Aid El Kebir (International Cooperation Office of Health Department of Zhejiang Province 2003: 53).
- At the end of July 1997, President Konaré of Mali wished to say farewell to the old CMT and welcome the new, yet the protocol office considered it improper for a president to do such a thing. Using the excuse of consulting his doctor, President Konaré went to the hospital to meet the old and new CMT members and gave everyone a gift to express his gratitude (International Cooperation Office of Health Department of Zhejiang Province 2003: 53).

The development of state relations is the result of the participation of various individuals, while the state leaders' role is crucial. The West is fond of making carping comments on China's assistance to Africa, yet the mutual trust between CMTs and Africa leaders is the best refutation of this slander (Li Anshan 2008 2008a).

Serving foreign policy goals through medical service

The high quality of CMT service has made a great impact and the dispatch of CMT is one of the conditions under which some countries establish or resume diplomatic relations with China. The president of Namibia, Sam Nujoma, is an old friend of China. He has visited the country 10 times and learned of the magical effects of Chinese medicine and acupuncture long ago. The Namibian Minister of Health, who accompanied the president on his first visit to China in September 1992, was the dean of the medical clinic of the Namibian People's Liberation Army during the national liberation period and had high praise for the safe and simple style of Chinese medicine, acupuncture and moxibustion therapy. At that time, the Namibian delegation put forward a formal demand "requesting China to provide civilized medical assistance with Chinese characteristics" – that is, to dispatch Chinese doctors of acupuncture (International Cooperation Office of Health Department of Zhejiang Province 2003: 187).

After four years' suspension, Niger resumed diplomatic relations with China in 1996. During the negotiations, the Foreign Minister made an important request: China should resend its CMT within in 15 days of the resumption of relations. When the team arrived at the international airport in Niamey, government officials from the President's Office of Protocol, the Ministry of Foreign Affairs, the Ministry of Health, Niamey City Hall, Capital Hospital and the students who had studied in China were all lined up to welcome them. The team members were greatly moved. The official of the Protocol Office told the delegation,

> When the president learned of the news of the coming visit of Chinese delegation of health and advance members of CMT to Niamey, he personally arranged the routine of the Chinese survey delegation. He ordered the opening of the VIP guest room of the airport and give permission to reporters to do live interviews.
>
> Wang Liji 2006: 311)

The Niger Minister of Health said, "The people of Niger have waited for CMTs for four years. Niger people warmly welcome CMTs" (Wang Liji 2006: 311). This indicates that the work of CMTs in Niger had won the local people's recognition and praise.

In addition, Chinese doctors made contributions to the issue of Taiwan. When Dr Jiang Yongsheng was treating the President of Mozambique, Joaquim Alberto Chissano, he constantly illustrated the achievements of

China's reform and opening up, as well as the principle of peaceful reunification and "one country and two systems". President Chissano said, "Even my old mother knows what 'one country and two systems' is" (Wei Yixiong 2006). When the Mozambique Association for Peaceful Reunification of China was founded in 2002, Dr Jiang was elected as chair. He invited President Chissano to serve as honorary chairman and Chissano happily agreed, thus becoming the first head of state to fill this post. To express their respect for the CMTs, President Guebuza and Prime Minister Diogo accepted Jiang Yongsheng's invitation in 2005 to serve as Honorary Chairman and Honorary Advisor of the Association for Peaceful Reunification of China in Mozambique respectively.[27]

With strong support from Chinese embassies and consulates, CMTs have also played a role in promoting foreign trade and economic cooperation between China and Africa. CMTs from Ningxia have made the best use of their irreplaceable advantage and actively explored new ways of combining medical cooperation and trade activities. They have tried their best to introduce Chinese entrepreneurs to the Benin Minister of Commerce; to assist Chinese companies to win contracts to build the infrastructure of the Ministry of Health in Benin; to help settle a long-standing dispute over a traffic accident caused by a CMT; and to solve the difficulty of providing encephalitis medicine and cholera vaccines to Chinese living in Benin, thus becoming "the window and promotion ambassador of China in the country where they are working" (Lu Shuqun & Wu Qiong 2003: 9–20). CMT members said that, "In a foreign country, in the eyes of foreigners, our every move represents China; therefore, no matter our work or words, we should not discredit China" (Lu Shuqun & Wu Qiong 2003: 406). This sense of national pride is the motivation for the work of the CMTs.

CMT's dedication to world peace

A report about Chinese foreign assistance to Algeria had "The world is small and we are a family" as its sub-title. On a higher level, as practitioners of internationalism that embodies the spirit of humanitarianism, CMTs have made a contribution to world peace. This contribution takes three forms: spreading the idea of equality; promoting humanitarianism; and deepening understanding of traditional Chinese medicine.

Spreading the idea of equality

Owing to the long period of colonial rule, racism and hierarchical ideas became an essential part of the ideology in many developing countries. CMTs have brought a totally new concept of equality: racial equality, equality between different hierarchies, equality between doctor and nurse, and equality between doctor and patient. CMT members treat African patients as their family members, and in return they are welcomed and respected by African people. During the colonial period, doctors and nurses were in a different position; doctors were superior while nurses were at a lower level. This norm changed with the arrival of CMTs.

The concept of equality between doctor and patient is particularly pertinent. Usually, people from the countryside come to the city to see the doctor. CMTs broke the rule by better serving local communities, thus revolutionising the concept. It is conventional practice for the patient to go to the doctor, yet the Chinese doctors regularly go to the countryside to provide free medical services. Doctors from other countries are unable to do this.

When the first CMT arrived in Algeria, the first question they heard was, "What do you come here for?" Their answer was, "To provide medical service for peasants and herders." In 1968, after an advance group from the Chinese Ministry of Health did an investigation in Tanzania, they reported the shortage of doctors and poor medical conditions there to Premier Zhou Enlai (Liu Jirui 1998: 11). Dr Jiang Yedu recorded the difficulties experienced by CMT doctors' mobile service in the rural regions; they worked in really hard conditions with a heavy workload. Mr Mkupa, the First Secretary of the Tanzanian Ministry of Health, said, "The Chinese doctors mainly work in the countryside, while our work in rural regions just has a lot of problems, and needs help most. Doctors from other countries can hardly adjust to the life conditions there, yet Chinese doctors are working there with enthusiasm" (Liu Jirui 1998: 32). The Prime Minister of Madagascar considered that the Chinese doctors saw the treatment of patients as the most important thing; they worked wholeheartedly and set a good example for the local medical staff, which also shows the spirit of solidarity and mutual help among developing countries (Wang Liji 2006: 311). These comments are not only an evaluation, but also a kind of praise.

Spread of humanitarianism

The humanitarian spirit is capable of evoking praise and tears. It is common practice for Chinese doctors to donate blood to patients in Africa.

CMT doctors are dedicated to the improvement of African people's health conditions; they contribute their blood for transfusion to save African patients. Some of them have died on the operating table in Africa (Health Department of Jiangsu Province 2004: 26; Liu Jirui 1998: 2–63). CMT doctor Wang Dunmei, who worked in Gabon, died of lung cancer, and in her will she requested that her ashes be scattered there (Health Department of Tianjin 2007: 69).

Every time CMT doctors are given an AIDS test, it is torture to wait for the result, and their nervousness cannot be expressed in words.[28] Yet when they are retrieving the dying and rescuing the wounded, they have no time to consider their own safety. Chen Shuming's experience illustrates this point:

> I had [to perform] a C-section caesarean operation and the newborn baby's heart stopped beating. I had no time to consider infection with

the AIDS virus, what I was thinking was how to seize every minute to rescue the baby. Therefore I [started] mouth-to-mouth breathing immediately. The effect was very good and the patient's heart started to beat and breath was restored.[29]

Two CMT doctors have died of AIDS and altogether 45 CMT members have sacrificed their lives to give medical assistance in Africa (CCTV 2006). They have really shown great love in their service to local people. As one Chinese doctor said,

> Now I can only spend my little efforts every day to help patients with pain, to feel the different people's desire for life. When they praise me by saying 'medico chino bien' (Chinese doctor, great!), I always have a kind of pride and joy.[30]

This great love for humankind cannot be measured by either diplomatic needs or material standards.

The service of CMTs is not confined to the host countries. CMT in Algeria are famous both locally and in diplomatic circles in the country. Diplomats and people from many countries living in Algeria, including the United States, United Kingdom, Germany and Japan, are willing to go to the CMTs for treatment. The American ambassador to Algeria consulted a CMT about his lumbago the day after diplomatic relations between China and the United States were established. The American ambassador said humorously, "This is a practical action to celebrate the establishment of diplomatic relations between two countries" (Health Department of Hubei Province 1993: 337). Heads of state and top officials of the Democratic Republic of the Congo, Mali, Saudi Arabia, Morocco and Palestine all came to CMTs for treatment when they visited Algeria (Health Department of Hubei Province 1993: 12).

CMTs in Mali have also established a good reputation. Besides Malians, patients from 22 countries and regions come to CMT stations (International Cooperation Office of Health Department of Zhejiang Province 2003: 5–26). The CMT in Tunisia, which is from Jiangxi Province, has served diplomats from Indonesia, Romania, Germany, Côte d'Ivoire and Cuba, and the Chinese doctors' excellent service is highly praised (Ying Mingqin 2003: 65). CMT doctors therefore work for the welfare and happiness of humankind.

Deepening the understanding of traditional medicine

Because of the dissemination of modern Western medicine and Eurocentrism, traditional medicine is often neglected. CMT have changed this tendency. Chinese medical science pays great attention to the whole, emphasising a breakthrough via a combination of traditional and modern medicine. During operations, CMT doctors often use Chinese traditional therapy. This, particularly easy and effective acupuncture, makes other countries recognise the magic role of Chinese medicine. The Prime Minister of Madagascar, Jacques Sylla, thinks that one of CMT's successes is expressed in the new vision of medical service in Madagascar and the positive thinking about traditional medicine.

Traditional medicine and Western medicine are equally important, forming two complementary components of the medical system. For example, in Benin an old man was suffering from cataract blindness accompanied by hypertension and *paralysis agitans*. Whenever he was put on an operation table, his blood pressure would elevate, accompanied by paroxysmal head tremors. Western medicine could do nothing about this; Dr Li Qingtian used the ancient Chinese medical treatment called "gold needle couching" for this problem (Ma Yuzhang 1998: 57–258). With the growing influence of CMT, there is an increasing understanding of traditional medicine. More and more countries have expressed willingness to cooperate with China in the application of traditional medicine and the research, development and production of medicinal plants.

Conclusion

Over the past half-century, China has dispatched CMT to countries which need medical assistance and provided free services to the local people. This magnanimous action is unique in contemporary international relations. CMT is also the project arising from China–Africa cooperation which has lasted the longest and covered the most countries with great achievement and influence. It is difficult to realize that this is a demonstration of great love for mankind. The Chinese doctors carry the cause of internationalism forward and spread the spirit of humanitarianism. They have not only made a great contribution to other countries and to China; they have also contributed a great deal to human well-being and world peace.

Notes

1 This chapter is a revised version of several papers published in Chinese and English. The research was funded by the Centre for International Strategic Studies (CISS) at Peking University, and is also part of a project of the Sustainable Development of Africa–China Cooperation funded by China's National Philosophy and Social Sciences Fund. Another result of the project was published as *Chinese medical cooperation in Africa: With special emphasis on the medical teams and anti-malaria campaign (Discussion Paper 52,* 2011). During the research and fieldwork, doctors and officials in different provinces helped me in one way or another. More than 20 students, including my graduate students Imen Belhadj (Tunisia), Erfiki Hicham (Morocco), Zeng Aiping, Xu Liang and Yang Tingzhi, helped me by collecting materials in their home towns.

2 In the workshop co-organised by the CSIS-CIIS conference, "China's Emerging Global Health and Foreign Aid Engagement", I was assigned to write on the topic "How should the US and China launch the pilot project in Africa?" The presumption is that US–China cooperation in providing assistance to Africa is possible; however, turning that possibility into reality needs a lot of work. The reason is simple: how can two parties discuss an important issue concerning a third party without the third party's knowledge? How can the two parties carry out this kind of cooperation without the third party's participation from the very beginning? How can we start the cooperation without much understanding of, let alone agreement with, each other – especially on the concept of the issue? This is the original idea of the work. At the invitation of Dr Chen Luxin of the Global Health Institute of Peking University, I took a field trip in 2008 to the Sudan, Tanzania and Botswana to make a survey of Chinese Medical Teams (CMTs) there, where we were well received by the Chinese embassies, CMT members and local people. I would like to thank all who helped me in the research.
 3 For general studies, see Huang Shuze & Lin Shixiao (1986: 59–62); Department of International Cooperation of Ministry of Health (2003); Wang Liji (2006). For studies abroad, see Yu (1975: 10–14); Thompson (2005: 4); Shinn (2006: 4–16); Hsu (2007: 22) Hsu (2008: 21–35).
 4 Regarding the author's research on the characteristics and evolution of China's Africa policy, see Li Anshan (2006, 2007).
 5 Evening Daily connecting Director Duan Weiyu of Algerian CMT from Hubei. www.sina.com.cn. Retrieved on 5 November 2006.
 6 The content of the brackets indicates the provinces and municipalities which are responsible for sending CMT and the year of dispatch.
 7 From 1971 to 1978, the Chinese government provided assistance to 30 countries. It also provided economic and technological assistance to additional 36 countries including 27 in Africa (Shi Lin 1989: 6–57).
 8 "The CMT in Africa". 2005. *China Daily* (Special issue on China–Africa), www.china.com.cn/zhuanti2005/txt/2003-10/22/content_5426974.htm
 9 For example, see Pei Guangjian (2006); Wang Zhe (2008); Thompson (2005); Shinn (2006: 14).
10 In that year, CMTs were working in 34 African countries (Department of International Cooperation of Ministry of Health 2003).
11 Records of CMTs (group pictures), 15 October 2006. Xinhua, quoted from FOCAC Network. www.focac.org/chn/tptb/tptb/t400292.htm
12 "CMT in Cameron: Using acupuncture and traditional medical therapy to serve patients", Xinhua News Network, 6 July 2008. http://news.sohu.com/20070822/n251723582.shtml
13 "Cameroon – African princess cured by acupuncture", 29 November 2007. www.acucn.com/sub/zhongfei/zhenjiu/200611/1956.html
14 "Using Chinese medicine and acupuncture benefits Mali people", 9 July 2007. www.acucn.com/sub/zhongfei/zhenjiu/200709/3428.html
15 "CMT in Niger enthusiastically serve the local people". www.acucn.com/sub/zhongfei/zhenjiu/200611/1961.html
16 "Cameroon – African princess cured by acupuncture", 3 November 2006. www.acucn.com/sub/zhongfei/zhenjiu/200611/1956.html
17 "Chinese Ambassador Li Shuli attending the opening ceremony of an acupuncture class at the National Public Health Institute". www.fmprc.gov.cn/chn/wjb/zwjg/zwbd/t296059.htm

18 "China joins forces with Uganda in fighting malaria", 27 November 2006. http://en.people.cn/200611/27/eng20061127_325691.html
19 The WHO recommends ACT as the drug of choice against malaria. Artemisinin is a compound extracted from a herb mostly grown in China, and primaquine is another anti-malaria drug that blocks transmission of the infection after 24 hours. See also Tan (2007).
20 "Chinese Ambassador Tao Weiguang attended the summary meeting of the project of eradication of malaria in Comoros". http://new.fmprc.gov.cn/chn/wjb/zwjg/zwbd/t474089.htm.
21 "Africa seeks co-op with China in anti-malaria drugs". Xinhua News Agency, 3 November 2005. www.china.org.cn/english/scitech/147429.htm
22 "Chinese company sent anti-malaria drugs to Côte d'Ivoire", china.com.cn, 27 October 2007. www.china.com.cn/international/txt/2007-10/27/content_9132442.htm
23 "Vice-Minister Wei held a meeting to discuss the issue of sustainability of anti-malaria centers in Africa". Ministry of Commerce. http://yws.mofcom.gov.cn/aarticle/ztxx/v/200801/20080105342493.html
24 The 23 countries are Albania, Algeria, Myanmar, Sri Lanka, Cuba, Equatorial Guinea, Guinea, Iraq, Mali, Mauritania, Nepal, Pakistan, Democratic People's Republic of Yemen, People's Republic of Congo, Romania, Sierra Leone, Somalia, Sudan, Syria, Tanzania, Yemen Arab Republic, Yugoslavia and Zambia.
25 The 17 countries are Algeria, Botswana, Burundi, Cameroon, Egypt, Equatorial Guinea, Guinea, Kenya, Mali, Ghana, Mauritania, Morocco, Nigeria, Rwanda, Togo, Uganda, and Tanzania.
26 For a detailed record, see Li Anshan (2009).
27 "Chinese doctors treated Mozambican President's illness by acupuncture and developed a friendship". www.acucn.com/sub/zhongfei/zhenjiu/200611/1960.html
28 "CMT under the threat of AIDS". www.39.net/aids/channel/world/77809.html
29 "CMT who spread health and friendship". www.crionline.cn
30 "Visitor Bata APOCC's words". http://nilixiang.blshe.com/post/754/48732.

References

Anonymous. 2006. Phoenix's dance in the needle point: Dr Shi Xuemin of the Chinese Academy of Engineering Acupuncture Network. www.acucn.com/sub/zhongfei/zhenjiu/200611/2027.html

Assistance to Sierra Leone Brightness II and Opening ceremony of female health care action held in Freedom. 2007. 12 December http://sl.mofcom.gov.cn/aarticle/todayheader/200712/20071205291533.html

Cameroon – African princess cured by acupuncture. www.acucn.com/sub/zhongfei/zhenjiu/200611/1956.htm

CCTV. 2006. Hubei doctors' life of foreign assistance. 28 August. http://news.cctv.com/society/20060828/101023.shtml

Chen Zhu. 2010. Speech at the national meeting regarding international cooperation in medical heath. 10 January.

China Daily. 22 October 2003. CMTs in Africa. Special issue on China–Africa. www.china.com.cn/zhuanti2005/txt/2003-10/22/content_5426974.htm

China joins forces with Uganda in fighting malaria. 27 November 2006. http://enBeijing.people.cn/200611/27/eng20061127_325691.html

China plans to build 10 anti-malaria centers in Africa this year. 2007. Xinhua News Agency. 15 November.
Chinese Ambassador Li Shuli attending the opening ceremony of an acupuncture class at the National Public Health Institute. www.fmprc.gov.cn/chn/wjb/zwjg/zwbd/t296059.htm
Chinese Ambassador Tao Weiguang attended the summary meeting of the project of eradication of malaria in Comoros. 1963. http://new.fmprc.gov.cn/chn/wjb/zwjg/zwbd/t474089.htm
Chinese CMT members set off to Algeria. 1963. *People's Daily*, 7 April.
Chinese company sent anti-malaria drugs to Côte d'Ivoire. 2007. china.com.cn, 27 October. www.china.com.cn/international/txt/2007-10/27/content_9132442.htm
Chinese doctors treated Mozambican president's illness by acupuncture and developed a friendship. 2007. 28 November. www.acucn.com/sub/zhongfei/zhenjiu/200611/1960.html
Chinnock, P. 2009. Malaria drug passes major milestone. Worldwide Antimalarial Resistance Network, 28 October. www.wwarn.org/fr/node/2760
CMT in Cameroon: Using acupuncture and traditional medical therapy to serve patients. 2008. Xinhua News Network, 6 July. http://news.sohu.com/20070822/n251723582.shtml
CMT under the threat of AIDS. 2007. www.39.net/aids/channel/world/77809.html
CMT who spread health and friendship. 2006. www.crionline.cn
CMT's spread in Africa. 2003. *West Asia and Africa* 5: 67.
CMTs in Niger enthusiastically serve the local people. 2006. www.acucn.com/sub/zhongfei/zhenjiu/200611/1961.html
Dai A-Di. 2006. Brightness action benefits cataract patients in Sierra Leone. 19 October. http://news.qq.com/a/20061019/001729.htm
Department of International Cooperation of Ministry of Health. 2003. To reform the medical assistance to Africa from a perspective of a new strategy. *West Asia and Africa* 5: 15–18.
Evening Daily connecting Director Duan Weiyu of Algerian CMT from Hubei. 2006. *Wuhan Evening Daily*, 5 November. http://news.sina.com.cn/c/2006-11-05/092110423857s.shtml
Health Department of Hubei Province, ed. 1993. *Famous doctors in North Africa*. Beijing: Xinhua Press.
Health Department of Jiangsu Province. 2004. *Glorious footprints: Memorial collection of the 40th anniversary of the Jiangsu Medical Team*. Nanjing: Jiangsu Science and Technology Press.
Health Department of Tianjin. 2007. Footprint: In memory of 35th anniversary of the dispatch of Tianjin CMT. Health Department of Tianjin. Not formally published.
Hsu, E. 2007. Chinese medicine in East Africa and its effectiveness. *IIAS Newsletter* 45: 22.
Huang Shuze & Lin Shixiao, eds. 1986. *Medical health in contemporary China, Vol. 2*. Beijing: Chinese Social Sciences Press.
International Cooperation Office of Health Department of Zhejiang Province. 2003. Zhejiang CMT in Africa – 35th anniversary of dispatch of CMT by Zhejiang Province. Not formally published.
Kim, S. 1989. *The Third World in Chinese world policy*. Princeton, NJ: Princeton University Press.

Lague, D. 2007. On island off Africa, China tries to wipe out malaria. *The New York Times*, 5 June. https://www.nytimes.com/2007/06/05/world/europe/05iht-malaria.2.6006557.html
Li Anshan. 2006. China's Africa policy: Adjustment and change. *West Asia and Africa* 8: 1–20.
Li Anshan. 2007. China and Africa: Policy and challenges. *China Security* 3(3): 9–93.
Li Anshan. 2008. China's new policy towards Africa. In R. Rotberg, ed., *China into Africa: Trade, aid, and influence*, Washington, DC: Brookings Institution Press, 21–49.
Li Anshan. 2008a. In defense of China – China's Africa strategy and state image. *World Economics and Politics* 4: 6–15.
Li Anshan. 2009. Chinese medical teams abroad: History, scale and impact. *Foreign Affairs Review* 1: 9–40.
Li Xinfeng. 2006. A bosom friend afar brings a distant land near-Premier Wen Jiabao visited CMT in Republic of Congo and Brazzaville Middle School. *People's Daily*, 21 June, 3.
Liang Tao. 2006. Chinese doctors support ancient African country Lesotho and are highly respected for their superb medical skill. 21 August. www.acucn.com/sub/zhongfei/zhenjiu/200608/1375.html
Liu Dun 2015. Li Guoqiao: 48 years in pursuit of malaria. 9 October. Guangzhou University of Chinese Medicine. www.gzucm.edu.cn/info/1173/9971.htm
Liu Jirui. ed. 1998. Chinese Medical Teams in Tanzania. Health Department of Shandong Province. Not formally published.
Liu Wan. 2007. Life in Cameroon 22 years ago. 2 May. http://ju.qihoo.com/topframe/dingzhen.php?ju=2056840&ml=2056884&u=5dcfd8e21374467b2a596795108fb7ab&r=2056848&d=2056853&surl=http%3A%2F%2Fwww.daynews.com.cn%2Fsxwb%2Faban%2F21%2F194613.html
Lu Shuqun & Wu Qiong. 2003. *Into Benin*. Yinchuan: Ninxia People's Press.
Ma Yuzhan. 1998. Days and nights in Benin: In memory of twenty years of the dispatch of Ninxia CMT. Health Department of Ninxia. Not formally published.
Ministry of Foreign Trade and Economic Cooperation, PRC. 1984. *Almanac of China's Foreign Economic Relations and Trade: 1984*. Beijing: Chinese Financial & Economic Publishing House.
Ministry of Foreign Trade and Economic Cooperation, PRC. 1990. *Almanac of China's Foreign Economic Relations and Trade: 1990*. Beijing: Chinese Financial & Economic Publishing House.
Pei Guangjiang. 2007. White angels – CMT in Africa. *People's Daily*, 5 November, 7.
Peking University Health Science Center. 2007. To strengthen China's African health diplomacy: Suggestions and recommendations. Not formally published.
People's Daily. 2007. China plans to build 10 anti-malaria centers in Africa this year. 15 October. http://english.peopledaily.com.cn/90001/90776/90883/6282747.html.
Researchers claim malaria success. 2009. SBS, 30 March www.sbs.com.au/news/article/2009/03/30/researchers-claim-malaria-success
Shi Lin, ed. 1989. *Foreign economic cooperation in contemporary China*. Beijing: Chinese Social Sciences Press.
Shinn, D.H. 2006. Africa, China and health care. *Inside AISA* 3&4: 4–16.
Siringi, S. 2003. Africa and China join forces to combat malaria. *The Lancet* 362: 45.
Tan, Ee Lyn. 2007. Chinese scientists take malaria fight to Africa. Reuters. www.alertnet.org/thenews/newsdesk/B155919.htm

Thompson, D. 2005. China's soft power in Africa: From the "Beijing Consensus" to health diplomacy. *China Brief* 5(21): 1–4.

Tu Zixian. 2007. Summing-up of the work of the 17th batch of CMT in Tunisia (2006/10–2007/6). *Jiangxi CMT Bulletin* 1: 64.

Using Chinese medicine and acupuncture benefits Mali people. 2007. www.acucn.com/sub/zhongfei/zhenjiu/200709/3428.html

Vice-Minister Wei held a meeting to discuss the issue of sustainability of anti-malaria centers in Africa. Ministry of Commerce. 2008. http://yws.mofcom.gov.cn/aarticle/ztxx/v/200801/20080105342493.html

Visitor Bata APOCC's words. n.d. http://nilixiang.blshe.com/post/754/48732.

Wang Liji. 2006. Great achievement in China–Africa medical cooperation. In Lu Miaogeng, Huang Shejiao & Lin Yi, eds, *United as gold – glorious path of China–Africa friendly relations*. Beijing: World Affairs Press.

Wang Zhe. 2008. Man on a mission. *Chinafrica* 3(3): 7.

Wei Yixiong. 2006. Jiang Yongsheng: Let Chinese traditional medicine yield unusually brilliant results in Mozambique. 3 November. www.acucn.com/sub/zhongfei/zhenjiu/200611/1959.html

Wu Miaofa. 2006. The story of African support to China in the resumption of its legitimate rights in the United Nations. *Party History Aspects* 10: 2–25.

Yan Ye & Chen Yao. 2006. Chinese acupuncture has qualified successor in Africa – Guinean acupuncture expert Segu Kamala. 27 October. www.acucn.com/sub/zhongfei/zhenjiu/200610/1895.htm

Ying Mingqin, ed. 2003. *The White emissary: 30 Years of Jiangxi medical teams abroad, 1973–2003*. Nanchang: International Office of Health Department of Jiangxi Province.

Yu, G.T. 1975. *China's African policy: A study of Tanzania*. New York: Praeger.

13 China's technology transfer in Africa[1]

Introduction

Andrew Udeh (Nigerian official) told me that Nigeria had been using technical experts from China for more than six years: "The Chinese transfer their technology. They will monitor it. They will supervise it. If you wish, they will manage it for some years before transferring it over. Their presence in Nigeria is empowering Nigerians, particularly the Ibos, who believe in manufacturing" (Brautigam 2009: 160).

> Technical cooperation means that China dispatches experts to give technical guidance on production, operation or maintenance of projects after they are completed and train local people as managerial and technical personnel; to help developing countries grow crops, raise animals and process products on a trial basis, and teach local people China's agricultural technologies and traditional handicraft skills; and to help developing countries in inspection, survey, planning, research and consultation work of some industries. [Human resource development cooperation means] China, through multilateral or bilateral channels, runs different kinds of research and training programs for government officials, education programs, technical training programs, and other personnel exchange programs for developing countries.
> (Information Office of the State Council, 2011)

Technology is one of the serious bottlenecks in African industrialisation. In the discourse on China–Africa relations, technology transfer (TT) is one of the less-studied subjects. There are two contradictory views on the issue. One holds that for sub-Saharan African manufacturing firms, increasing trade openness with China does not generally appear to result in the transfer of technology, or China has seldom or never offered technology transfer to African countries (Elu 2010).[2] The other argues that capital goods from China are an important technology transfer channel that enhances economic growth in Africa, or that Chinese companies have transferred technology in various ways and China's TT has a positive impact (Munemo 2013: 6–116).[3] One scholar even used the

DOI: 10.4324/9781003220152-16

notion in an analysis of Ethiopia copying the so-called "China model" (Fourie 2015). Zimbabwe thanked China for its technological transfer and President Robert Mugabe once hailed as "a great success China's technology transfer to Zimbabwe and Africa", hoping China would further speed up the process in the future (*China Daily* 2012). Is this only rhetoric or truth? What are the facts? The topic really needs detailed study and elaboration.

It is necessary to first define "technology transfer". TT occurs when the holder of the technology of production, management and sale passes it, with its rights, to others in various ways (Huang Jingbo 2005: 5–16). In China, the phrase "technical cooperation" (TC) is usually used, since China wishes to promote African self-development in fields such as industry, agriculture, management, education and the social sector. This chapter looks at TT in the history of China–Africa relations. It has existed since the issue of the Eight Principles in 1964 in different forms or different terms – such as technical assistance (TA), knowledge transfer (KT) or knowledge sharing (KS). Yet Chinese companies still have much room for improvement, both in scale and depth, if common development is to be achieved.

Why China and Africa? Two challenges

Since the 21st century, there has been an increasing stress on China–Africa relations in the international community, especially in the West. This phenomenon has a direct links with China's rise, which is assumed to be a threat to the West. Why is the West so afraid of China–Africa cooperation? This can only be explained by the current international political and economic transformation (Li Anshan 2008: 15). The West owes its present position in colonial history and the unequal international order that came into being afterwards. The hegemony of the West did not disappear with African independence and its dominance has remained in the political, economic, cultural and social dimensions. For example, Niger has a glorious history and rich natural resources. But since independence, its mining industry – especially uranium – has been tightly controlled by Areva, the French energy group, and the country is still among the least developed countries (LDC). After more than half a century of independence, Côte d'Ivoire still has to pay rent to the French for its own parliament building and presidential palace![4] These cases are only a small reflection of the relationship between Africa and the West. It is strategically vital for the West to maintain the unequal relationships, but they are being challenged by two forces.

Since independence, several courageous African leaders have been murdered, removed in coups or pushed aside, such as Lumumba, Nkrumah, Thomas Sankara, Gaddafi and Salim Ahmed Salim.[5] All these figures showed a determination to get away from the control of the West, voiced opposition to Western dominance and fought for their own sovereignty or independence. The plots against them were directly carried out either by the West or by its agents. Various difficult situations have occurred in Africa, such as the separation of Sudan,[6] the chaotic situation in Libya and the resource wars in the Democratic Republic of the Congo, which were directly instigated by the West or where the West was behind the scenes (Campbell 2013; Lokongo 2015).

Economic measures such as sanctions and aid are more frequently used; the threat is "If you don't listen to the West, there will be sanctions." Zimbabwe is a good example (Hanlon et al 2013: 2–93).[7] Economic aid becomes a frequently used means of control. James Shikwati, a Kenyan economist and the founder and director of the Inter-Region Economic Network (IREN), points out that:

> The aid industry dominated by the United States of America, Europe, Australia, Japan and their allies is designed to address donor country interests that range from access to markets; the fear of a deluge of political, economic and climate change-induced migrants from Africa; broad security concerns that range from terrorism and diseases; the quest to access and control the continent's vast natural resources; and geopolitical power games.
>
> (Shikwati 2015)

Africans started to ask questions. Why can our ancestors create wonders and not us? Why do we have such rich resources but they are not developed? How can we develop ourselves without the outsiders' interference? They started to find other options. "Looking East"[8] has become an alternative for Africa, and the development model designed by the West since the 1960s is facing a great challenge. This is an expression of African self-consciousness.

Another push to reform the current international political and economic order comes from BRICS and other emerging countries. For Africa, those countries not only indicate an alternative to the development model; they also provide different types of development cooperation. China takes a leading role among these countries. An African scholar, criticising the view of China's "neo-colonialism", illustrated China's role thus: "China's model of development gives African countries an alternative model of development that is both workable and without strings attached. All these reasons make African countries to warm up to China as opposed to the USA and Western Europe" (Mihanfo 2012: 142). The former President of Senegal, Mr Wade, pointed out that the China model, which had promoted rapid economic development, could teach many things to Africa (Wade 2008).

Therefore, in order to safeguard its advantageous position in its traditional "backyard", the West's concern over China–Africa relations is by no means surprising.

Debate and comparison

There are many debates on the issue of China–Africa relations (Large 2008: 45–61; Li Anshan 2014). American professor Deborah Brautigam is an influential scholar who has been engaged in the study for several decades and once made some comparisons between the West and China regarding their respective action in Africa. She illustrates the long relationship between China and Africa in agricultural cooperation (Brautigam 1998), compares China's large investment with that of the World Bank (Brautigam 2009: 91) and points to the "PD 20" regulation imposed by the US Congress, which prohibits any foreign aid that may lead to American workers losing their jobs. "China has no such restriction" (Brautigam 2009: 93). She makes a different judgement by analysing some characteristics of China's activities in Africa, which are different from those undertaken by Western countries, such as focusing on infrastructure, providing a combination of aid and economic activities and showing respect for African ownership, no-strings-attached aid and capacity-building (Brautigam 2009: 148–161).

Africans' accounts are much more convincing. For example, while comparing China with other donors, Sierra Leone's former Minister of Foreign Affairs Alhaji Momodu Koromahe said: "There is a difference, and it is huge. What they want to help you with, is what you have identified as your need. With Britain, America, *they* identify your needs." According to Brautigam, "In his eyes, there was still some way to go before the traditional donors really trusted Sierra Leone's country ownership (Brautigam 2009: 139–40).[9] When it comes to international development aid, the terms "donor" and "donee" crop up frequently without much questioning. However, in China's foreign aid documentation, such terms are never used. This tiny difference shows the distinction between China's aid philosophies and those of the Western countries. As the term "donor–donee" is a reflection of a state-to-state relationship, it defines the standing of the two parties on an unequal footing, leading to a series of consequences that would hinder the development of recipients.[10]

Even among the comments in networks, there are interesting comparisons. In an article by Alfred Wong, there are two interesting comments. One reads:

> Just like the West, the Chinese exploit Africa for resources and regional influence using loans that will never be repaid. It is hard to see a sustainable mobile revolution when the end consumer is unable to repay said loans. The Chinese in the end will forgive the loans as they profit from extracting resources from these nations. While I have not spent considerable time like this student researching these Chinese lead phenomena, I only need to raise how French and Euro influence (Total, Shell) have not changed the region to illustrate my argument.
>
> (Wong 2015)

The other reads:

> Before China, what have the WEST done in Africa? Demand democracy system regardless the difference of education level and culture; Induce Wars in Africa, Sell Weapons and Suck wealth from that continent. Of

course, Chinese also exploit Africa for resources and regional influence. But unlike the WEST, China invest infrastructure, which is the fundamental base for Africa's economic growth, without any prerequisite for the political system in any country. That's the difference between China and West in Africa. Chinese took resources and left Africa with schools, railways, highways, and hospitals. In contrast, West took resources and left that continent with WARS.

(Wong 2015)

The African economy has developed rather smoothly, with an average 4–5 per cent growth annually over the past 20 years. Did China–Africa relations contribute to this? According to Martyn Davies, a South African scholar, China and Africa's growth trajectories intertwined as a "new coupling". Therefore, "A shift in Africa's economic relations is occurring – away from traditional economies, toward the East and China" (Davies 2011: 204). Following the assessment of the World Bank and the IMF, a new report by the US Council on Foreign Relations acknowledges that "Chinese investment in Africa has helped spur consistently high economic growth" (Alessi & Beina Xu 2015).

Regarding various interpretations of China–Africa relations, one should ask a basic question: "What is the general opinion of African people about China?" In the Pew Global Attitudes survey *Opinion of China* for 2015, African respondents expressed a favourable view. Ghanaians are most favourable (80 per cent), followed by Ethiopia and Burkina Faso (75 per cent), Tanzania (74 per cent), then Senegal, Nigeria and Kenya (70 per cent), and finally South Africa (52 per cent) (Opinion of China 2015).

As for TT in China–Africa relations, opinions differ. An article in Chinese reviews both criticism of China's TT in Africa and Chinese state-owned enterprises' (SOEs) TT in different areas and diverse modes in Africa. It argues that Chinese enterprises have been actively engaged in TT in various ways, such as personnel training, technological cooperation, middle-range technical training and technological spillover. What are the driving forces behind this? According to the author, three factors have contributed to TT: market constraints, the motives of enterprises and the Chinese government's encouragement. It contends that TT by Chinese SOEs has contributed in four ways to African development: it has improved the technological environment and supported industry in African countries; it has helped African employees increase their income, thus raising their living standards; it has brought self-employment and promoted the growth of entrepreneurs; and it has helped Africa develop new industries, thus speeding up industrialisation (Project Team of "Teaching how to fish" 2015).

What is the truth? Does China's engagement play any positive role in Africa's development? To better understand China's TA and TT in Africa, let's look at two cases, the Tanzania–Zambia Railway (TAZARA) and the Huawei Company, and related fields.

TAZARA: Technical assistance

The Tanzania–Zambia Railway (TAZARA) has become a modern legend in China–Africa relations. While other Western countries and international organisations declined a request for help with this project from Tanzania and Zambia, China took up the challenge. Together with the two countries, China finished the monumental project after overcoming various difficulties and with the sacrifice of 65 Chinese lives. It is the best case of China–Africa cooperation, exemplifying various types of TA and cooperation (Shen Xipeng 2018).

Railway transportation is a complicated enterprise using high levels of technology. In China, to produce a qualified engine driver requires more than six years' technical training covering technology theory for three years and practical experience as an assistant driver for another three years. A high-level railway technician needs more than 10 years. Chinese workers, technicians and engineers had "a sense of a technical mission" to train African technicians, as George Yu puts it.[11] President Nyerere praised Chinese engineers and workers at the opening of the Friendship Textile Mill in 1969, saying that, "These Chinese workers have helped in the establishment of the factory, and are actively training Tanzanians to take over from them. I should add that they have set an example to us all by their hard work and their dedication" (Yu 1975: 109).[12] There are three TA training modes: training technical students in China; training classes in Tanzania and Zambia; and on-the-job training (Shen Xipeng 2018).

In June 1972, a total of 200 students from Tanzania and Zambia came to North Jiaotong University in Beijing for training courses and 179 graduated in 1975. Among them, 41 majored in transportation, 45 in locomotives, 21 in vehicles, nine in communication, nine in signal specialty, 31 in railway engineering and 23 in financial and professional skills. They played an important role in the railways of their own countries and economic construction after their return home (Zhang Tieshan 1999).

A second mode is to train Africans in Tanzania and Zambia, where training classes/schools were set up. According to the bilateral agreement signed on 5 September 1967, the Chinese government was responsible for training the necessary number of technicians for building, administering and repairing TAZARA. Classes in communication signals and line-bridges were set up in Mang'ula in Tanzania in July 1971, and in transportation in Mgulani in February 1972. Special training classes started in Dar es Salaam and Mbeya and the TAZARA Training School in Mpika in Zambia opened in December 1975 (Monson 2009: 44). In 1978, two other special classes in internal combustion engines and railway communication began. Chinese experts trained 1257 special talents over ten years, comprising one-sixth of the technicians in TAZARA. The team finished the job by the end of 1981 (Zhang Tieshan 1999: 379; Shen Xipeng 2018).[13]

The third way is on-the-job training, providing more direct and practical experiences to African workers and technicians. It is the most popular practice in TA in TAZARA since it does not need any special facilities and costs almost nothing. African workers learnt drilling, assembly and dismantling on the spot and their work efficiency improved greatly. The Chinese "preferred to teach without words" owing to the language barrier. "A technician would assemble and dismantle a piece of machinery and encourage his African apprentices to follow suit until they got the procedure right" (Snow 1988: 163).[14] This process involves passing on knowledge, demonstrating skills, conducting short lectures, demonstrating models and sharing experiences.

From 1976 to 1986 there were four periods of technological cooperation. During 1976–1978, Chinese experts played an important role. Chinese technicians either provided guidance to African technicians or did the job independently. The general rules of TAZARA's operation were established. During the second period of 1978–1980, two incidents occurred. A severe flood in Tanzania damaged the railway and two bridges in Zambia were bombed by South African racists. Some 750 Chinese experts helped in the restoration. During the third period of 1980–1982, 150 Chinese experts helped to maintain the operation and provided guidance in fields such as engineering and electricity. The contract was extended for one year. The fourth period ran from 1983 to 1986. The Chinese government sent 250 experts to help in nine units and engaged in planning, transportation, finance and other technological aspects of TAZARA's operation (Liu Haifang & Monson 2011).

George Yu describes 19 types of Chinese TA to Tanzania in seven areas in 1964–1971: agriculture, culture and social, education and training, health, industry, natural resources, transport and communications. In the field of industry, China provided TA to train personnel in technology and management in 1966, farm implement personnel in 1970 and shoe-manufacturing personnel from 1968. In the field of transport and communication covering radio stations and railways, China helped Tanzania train construction personnel, radio technical personnel and marine personnel.[15] In the Friendship Textile Mill, various types of training were provided, including the operation of the printing and dyeing mill, design preparation, engraving and use of screen machines (Yu 1975: 115). There were other Chinese TA activities in Africa, such as sugar planting in Mali and tobacco planting in Somalia, all once claimed to be impossible, according to the Europeans.[16]

Knowledge sharing: From political solidarity to economic cooperation

As the first systematic study of African students in China, Gillespie's work is one of the few that focuses on African experiences in the context of South–South relations, emphasising the knowledge transfer of China's educational exchange programs for Africa (Gillespie 2001). From the very beginning of China–Africa cooperation, TA and KS were emphasised. When Premier Zhou Enlai visited Ghana in 1964, he put forward the Eight Principles in a press conference in Accra.[17]

Carefully analysing the principles, we found that they are obligations and self-discipline on China's side – for example, what China should do and what it should avoid. The principles indicate that the purpose of China's assistance is helping recipient countries to gradually achieve self-reliance and independent development (item 4); providing the best-quality equipment and materials of its own manufacture (item 6). In providing TA, China would see to it that the personnel of the recipient country fully mastered such techniques (item 7). Obviously, this is a process providing technology, equipment and training for personnel.

Why did the Chinese government greatly emphasise KS at the time? The most important reason is closely linked to China's position in the international system and its future perspective on world order. All the developing countries are more or less oppressed by the contemporary political and economic order dominated by the West. The CCP believes that uniting developing countries and fighting against the unequal world system is the only way to liberate humankind, including the Chinese people. Promoting the economic growth of developing countries is the best way to help each other and consolidate unity, which is not only an economic endeavour but also a political cause.

Be it TA, TT, TC, KS or KT, China–Africa cooperation contains the element of KS. Brautigam studied China's efforts in agricultural aid programs with Liberia, Sierra Leone and the Gambia, including knowledge transfer (Brautigam 1998). Although there were various failures, China also helped African countries to develop agricultural projects, which had a very positive impact. Burkina Faso is a good example. During the late 1980s, three rice-planting areas became well known in the country, one growing from a small village to a town of more than 8000 people. In 1987, the net income of each peasant family in the region reached 400–800,000 African francs (US$1300–2600). Peasants from other places and neighbouring countries migrated to the rice-planting areas. The achievement is closely linked to the hard work of Chinese experts, who gave the local people experience, management skills and organisational capacity. To thank the Chinese agricultural experts, the Burkina Faso government awarded them each a National Medal in 1988 (Jiang Xiang 2007).[18]

KS is not one-way traffic – that is, from China to Africa. It is always a two-way process. In fact, during the years when China was blocked by the West, African countries helped China in KS in various ways. Zhou Boping, the former Chinese Ambassador to Algeria and Zaire, tells vivid stories of how the two countries helped China to solve technological problems. During the mid-1970s, China planned to build a pipeline from the gas-rich province of Sichuan to Shanghai. The project required stud-welding technology, which was not familiar to Chinese engineers. There was a stud-welding pipe factory in Algeria and Ambassador Zhou discussed the possibility of Chinese engineers making a study tour of the factory with the CEO of the national petroleum-gas company in 1975. The CEO was very enthusiastic, arranged the whole trip and put up the Chinese delegation in the best hotel. The Chinese learned much from Algerian colleagues and were moved by their friendly reception. During Zhou's Ambassadorship to Zaire (Democratic Republic of Congo) in 1978–1982, two Chinese delegations visited a diamond mining company there. Both delegations were received by the Zaire Ministry of Mining and Société Minière de Bakwanga (MIBA), the largest diamond company in the world. The experienced experts introduced the Chinese to metallogenic theory, diamond prospecting and their advanced experience of mining. The delegations also visited different diamond mines. With their enthusiastic help, Chinese delegations realised their own weakness in theory and practice, and benefited a great deal from their Zairean colleagues (Zhou Boping 2004: 233–238, 298–30).

Since reform and opening up in 1978, China's strategic consideration has shifted from "war and revolution" to "peace and development". Economic cooperation with developing countries has thus witnessed a dramatic change, from economic aid to multiform and mutually beneficial cooperation. China has shifted its emphasis from ideology to economic construction. As a result, it has adjusted the scale, procedure, structure and sectors of its foreign aid in accordance with its economic situation. During his trip to Africa in 1982, Premier Zhao Ziyang put forward the four principles of China's economic cooperation and foreign assistance: equality and mutual benefit, effectiveness, various forms and common development. Foreign assistance was provided in more diversified and flexible ways (Li Anshan 2006). In 1995, China's national banks, such as the Export–Import Bank of China, started to be engaged in foreign aid by providing medium- and long-term low-interest loans to developing countries. Since the availability of qualified human resources is essential for any successful TT, both China and African countries have put great emphasis on training courses aimed at capacity-building in various fields. Most were initiated in relation to foreign aid projects, and companies started to link TT with their business in Africa (Zhou Hong & Xiong Hou 2013).

Brautigam describes China's training program in her book: "In my travels across Africa between 2007 and 2009, I frequently ran into people who volunteered to me that they had been on training courses in China." (Brautigam 2009: 119). Rhoda Toronka, CEO of an African Chamber of Commerce, Industry and Agriculture, talked about her own experience in Beijing, where she spent three weeks on a training course for African chambers of commerce. She found "the course was pretty in-depth" and acknowledged the importance of learning from China (Brautigam 2009: 119–120).[19]

Human resource development cooperation, or personnel training, has been a significant channel for TT in China–Africa cooperation. From 1953 to 1979, China ran different programmes of human resources development cooperation and trained a large number of personnel from developing countries, including African countries. The programmes covered 20 sectors, including agriculture and forestry, water conservancy, light industry, textiles, transportation and healthcare. In order to expand its efforts to help developing countries, China has worked with the United Nations Development Program (UNDP) since 1981 and held various training courses in different fields. During the 1990s, China ran 167 training programs including 2667 participants from developing countries (Zhou Hong & Xiong Hou 2013: 158).

It is understood that the successful TT relies on the human resources of both the host country and the home country (Kim 2014; Li Anshan & April 2013). FOCAC set up the African Human Resource Development Fund (AHRDF) "for the training of professionals of different disciplines for African countries".[20] During 2000–2003, China organised training courses or programs of diverse forms for Africa under the special fund. At the second FOCAC, China increased its financial contribution to AHRDF for training up to 10,000 African personnel in different fields. In 2004 and 2005, China trained 2446 and 3868 African professionals respectively, covering trade and investment, economic management, telecommunication networks and new agricultural technology (Li Anshan 2006: 19; Li Anshan 2015). During his visit to Egypt in 2006, Premier Wen stressed that technological aid was combined with economic assistance and cooperation in order to strengthen Africa's self-development capability, and promised that China would help Africa to train technicians and administrators.[21] In addition, China sent over 2000 experts in 2010–2012 to more than 50 countries to "conduct technical cooperation, transfer applicable techniques, and help improve these countries' technical management capacity in agriculture, handcrafts, radio and television, clean energy, and culture and sports".[22]

KS has also occurred in the medical field. In the work of CMT in Africa, Chinese doctors passed on their expertise to local medical staff and helped African countries to improve their health services. In Tanzania, to help African trainees better understand acupuncture, CMT members allowed them to practise on their own bodies, thereby providing direct tuition in the technique. In this way, they trained a large number of medical specialists. CMT made the best use of local media to publicise their medical knowledge (Liu Jirui 1998). Chinese doctors also helped to establish medical specialties and technical facilities. The specialty of acupuncture is now evident in Tunisia, Cameroon, Lesotho, Namibia and Madagascar.

China holds training programs either in Africa or China to provide knowledge of anti-malaria measures to African medical specialists and government officials. CMT doctors from Ninxia Province provide medical services in Benin. Besides their daily work, they run various medical training courses. To help local medical workers, they compiled a book entitled *One hundred cases of prevention and treatment of African children's brain malaria* as a reference work for Benin doctors. In Algeria, by 2008 the CMT had presented more than 20 training courses, given more than 30 lectures and trained more than 300 medical personnel who have become the backbone of local medical institutions. With their hard work and contribution, CMT doctors have won respect and praise from the governments and peoples of these countries (Li Anshan 2011).

Huawei: Technology transfer

In the 21st century, telecommunication in Africa developing rapidly. *AfricaFocus Bulletin* stated that Tanzania had witnessed an unprecedented increase in mobile financial services in five years. In 2008, less than 1 per cent of the adult population had access to mobile financial services, yet the figure reached 90 per cent by September 2013. Likewise, active use has shown a similar improvement, with 43 per cent of the adult population actively using this service in September 2013. Statistics show that approximately 298 million people were using the internet in Africa as of 30 June 2014, equivalent to 16.5 per cent of the population. The countries with the highest level of penetration were Madagascar (74.7 per cent), Morocco (61.3 per cent), the Seychelles (54 8 per cent), Egypt (53.2 per cent), South Africa (51.5 per cent) and Kenya (47.3 per cent). The countries with the largest numbers of internet users were Nigeria (23.6 per cent of the total in the continent), Egypt (15.5 per cent), South Africa (8.4 per cent), Kenya (7.1 per cent) and Madagascar (5.8 per cent).[23] The fast growth of internet users in Africa has a close connection with the role of China's telecom companies. It indicates great potential for increased ICT in Africa in the future.[24]

China–Africa relations have expanded to various fields. The most typical example involved in TT is Huawei, a telecommunication company. With the rapidly increasing internet use in Africa, Huawei and ZTE, two ICT firms in China became very active on the continent. Huawei entered Africa in 1998 as a new comer, yet its sales in Africa had topped $2 billion across 40 countries by 2006 and it established regional office in Southern, East and West Africa respectively in 2007.[25] One of the factors of Huawei's success in Africa highly relies to its adaptation of local situation, including TT in recent years. In other words, Huawei's TT is closely linked to its operational strategy. Huawei has adopted several measures for TT in Africa, closely linked to its global corporate social responsibility program. Various programs are now implemented in the continent. The most welcomed is the "Seeds for the Future" program. As a project to help young talents of telecommunication, it has been implemented in more than 40 countries and benefited over 10,000 students from over 100 universities.

The program was launched in 2011 through a partnership with Moi University, Jomo Kenyatta University of Agriculture and Technology, the University of Nairobi, Safaricom Ltd, the Ministry of Information and Communication (through the Kenya ICT Board), and the Ministry of Higher Education of Kenya. It includes reviews of the university curriculum, training and the organization of an Android Application Challenge to enhance localized innovation. In its first stage, it provided scholarships, training and internship opportunities.[26]

In 2014, Huawei updated "Seeds for the Future" in Kenya to a program that is aimed at up skilling top engineering students drawn from various local universities with the requisite ICT skills and providing them with the opportunity to learn and apply the latest technologies. The chosen students will travel to China for training on Chinese culture, language and innovative ICT technologies, and interaction with top IT specialists at the Huawei University.[27] In October 2015, more students were chosen and sent to Huawei Headquarters for training. Forty students were expected to complete the two-month internship program and 100 students in three-year period. The program aims to enrol top engineering students from Kenyan universities in their third, fourth and fifth year of study and equip them with necessary industry skills. The ICT Authority signed a Memorandum of Understanding with Huawei in June 2014 to develop local ICT talent, enhance knowledge transfer, promote a greater understanding of and interest in the ICT sector, and improve and encourage regional building and participation in the digital community. So far, 28 Kenyan engineering students have benefited from the program. Of the 28 past beneficiaries, four have already been employed at Huawei Kenya, with two others at Kenya Education Network and McKinsey Consulting Limited. The rest have gone back to complete their university studies.[28]

It is the same case with Uganda and Ghana. Huawei signed a partnership agreement with Makerere University in 2012 to offer scholarships and ICT training to top students as well as sponsorships for research projects. An Android Application Challenge was also launched to develop technological innovations. The program has provided internships to 11 students and ICT training to 10 students. Hundreds of local students are expected to benefit from the program in the future. On 2 April 2015, the new phase of the program began in Uganda and 10 young students were chosen for the "Seeds for the Future"; they had the opportunity to go to Huawei Headquarters for high-level training. In addition, Huawei will donate 40 desktop computers to students in the Karamoja district of Uganda. This was highly praised by the Ugandan government. President Yoweri Museveni said:

> Huawei is a leading global ICT company, and we appreciate Huawei's contributions to improving ICT development and bridging the digital divide in Uganda. Looking forward, I hope that Huawei will continue investing in cultivating more local ICT talent, especially with the launch of the "Seeds for the Future" program, to contribute to the long-term development and construction of the ICT industry in Uganda.[29]

The program also started in Ghana with 15 students chosen for "Seeds for the Future". There are now 3700 Ghanaian students studying in China and nearly 500 Ghanaian trainees sponsored by the Chinese government.[30]

Huawei always puts a great emphasis on better conditions for education. In Ethiopia, it delivered a project that aims to promote resources sharing and educational exchanges among schools in Addis Ababa in October 2015. The Addis Ababa School Net Project will create connectivity among 65 education institutions, including 64 secondary schools and one university college through ICT infrastructure. The Addis Ababa City Education Bureau has implemented the project, which amounted to an investment of more than 240 million Ethiopian Birr ($11.5 million). Huawei has contributed to educational system in Ethiopia by successfully carrying out the project. With long-term ICT capacity-building cooperation, Huawei will help Ethiopia in its future capacity-building in education.[31]

There is training for clients and customers as well. In Kenya, Huawei set up a fully-fledged regional training centre in Nairobi's industrial area, which provides training to the clients who purchase their systems (Huawei going strong in Africa 2011). The majority of the training is done by Kenyan engineers to other Africans in the client firms, with only some occasional training being provided by a specialist from China. Equally, there is some training provided on site, some in China and some in the region. There are other different projects as well, such as the "She Leads Africa (SLA)" Project, the first program to provide African female technology entrepreneurs the opportunity to visit China and connect with industry leaders,[32] and the "SchoolNet Project", which aims to connect schools through ICT-specific training projects.[33]

CRBC's technology transfer and other ways

China also co-runs vocational schools with African partners to train specific technicians.

The Mombasa–Nairobi Railway Project started in December 2014. In order to train local railway workers and technicians, and develop a whole educational system of railway specialty, China Road and Bridge Corporation (CRBC), the company in charge, set up a comprehensive three-level training system including technology training in the building of railway, railway operation/management and railway engineering educational system. The whole training program is designed to cooperate with local institutions.

The first level comprises three measures: general training of various technologies; co-run training base with local training institution such as Rene Descartes Training Institute (RDTI); and an advanced training program in China. Now about 18,000 Kenyans have received the first level training. The first measure includes training for personnel in different fields with different technics. The second measure set up a training base with master-apprentice relation. A Chinese technician is master and a Kenyan the worker apprentice. The Chinese master is responsible for teaching practical skill and technology while RDTI in charge of theoretical teaching. The training takes in worksites at nights and weekend. The excellent trainees have been selected for further study in China, an opportunity provided by the Ministry of Commerce of China. From July to December 2015, 13 Kenyans were sent to attend a Seminar on Railway Project Management and Construction for Developing Countries of 2015 held in Southwest Jiaotong University, and they all successfully finished the courses and received their diplomas issued by the university. The second batch of about 20 for 2016 had been already selected at the time of writing.

The second level is designed for the training of railway operation and administration, which also includes two phases. Mombasa–Nairobi Railway planned to start operation in 2017 and a many engineers and technicians are needed. Yet there is neither vocational technical teaching nor undergraduate education for railway specialty in Kenya. Therefore, the second level training is very important and the first phase of training class started in April 2016. Ten Kenyan teachers from the Railway Training Institute (RTI) were sent to Southwest Jiaotong University in China for training of railway technology specialty and ten Chinese professors arrived in Kenya to teach. The first program was scheduled for four months with 105 local students in three majors: transportation major, locomotive major and communication major. CRBC is planning to spend $10 million to build a railway technology training centre and it will train 3000 Kenyan railway technicians in seven years. Now CRBC is preparing the second phase training for railway administration, which includes key position training, vocational education training of teachers and training of adaptability for on-the-job railway workers. Key positions involve train operation, train maintenance, management and technicians. Local teachers' training for railway vocational education will finish a number of times within five years in China, which means the Kenyan teachers can take up the responsibility for training in the future. The on-the-job adaptability training involves security and safety training, standardisation operation training, seasonal training and training of new technology, facilities, rules, process and capacity of emergency management.

The third level is at the phase of planning in order to help Kenya set up a specialty of railway engineering. At present, there is no such specialty in Kenya. CRBC hopes that China can help Kenya to set up such railway specialty with its perfect educational system of railway engineering. Now the planning has received a positive response from both Nairobi University and the Chinese embassy, and Southwest Jiaotong University has promised to take an active part in the training of high-level talents in railway management with Nairobi University.[34]

In another field, TT is offered by Chinese SOEs. The Sudan, once an oil-importing country, has now a whole system of exploration-production-refinery-exporting with its own efforts plus the help of CNPC and others. At the very beginning, CNPC has set up the goal to help build the Sudanese oil industry by starting a project on training local talents. From 1998, CNPC selected 35 Sudanese teachers and experts from Khartoum University and sent them to China to learn oil specialty, all received PhD or other degrees in oil related major and became the backbone of the oil industry of their country. Since 2006, CNPC signed several agreements with Sudan Ministry of Energy and Mining to train oil specialists and donated money for the purpose. The Sudanese government acknowledged that to help train a batch of oil talents is the CNPC's most important contribution to the Sudanese people. For CNPC's investment projects, localization has reached 95 per cent, for petroleum engineering construction and technology service, localisation reached

75 per cent (Zhang Anping, Li Wen & Yu Qiubo 2011). During my visit to Khartoum Refinery Company Limited in north of Khartoum, I learned that when the new employees enter the company, half go to work and half engage in training courses. After more than a decade, Sudan has now its own engineers and technicians specialised in oil refinery, thus finished the transformation from an oil-importing country to an oil exporting country with technology of oil exploration, extraction and refining. Sudanese engineers are now not only playing a key role in Khartoum Refinery Company or CNPC projects in the Sudan, but they have also become the backbone of the national oil industry. There are other TT related projects as well, such as the Belet Uen–Burao Highway in Somalia, the Lagdo Hydropower Station in Cameroon, Nouakchott's Friendship Port in Mauritania, railway improvement in Nigeria and Botswana and the Gotera Interchange in Addis Ababa, Ethiopia.

China also co-runs vocational schools with African partners to train specific technicians. For example, the China–Ethiopia Joint School has been offering courses including engineering, electrics, electronics, automobile, computer, textiles and apparel.[35] The parallel in China is the Tianjin University of Technology and Education, which has trained many young African technicians and engineers in various fields. Similar training centres or schools are also operating in Uganda and Angola. There are more than 6000 African students with Chinese scholarship and more are coming at their own cost. Most are engaged in the subjects of science and technology.[36]

Helping African countries in high education and university facilities is another means of cooperation. For example, the University of Dar es Salaam (UDSM) of Tanzania is undergoing infrastructural transformations including construction of a modern library designed as both a public library and resource centre, with a conference room for up to 2100 and a Confucius Institute center accommodating up to 500. The library will accommodate more than 800,000 books and host up to 6000 people. The project is being financed by China with a grant (Domasa 2016).

Conclusion

In summary, the element of TT or KS can be found in China–Africa cooperation. Be it TA, technological cooperation, knowledge transfer or knowledge sharing, it has existed in China–Africa relations for a long time, thus helping African countries in their development in one way or another. However, with the increasing number of imports, Africans are facing the danger of "deindustrialization". What China should do is help African industry to raise its productivity and avoid "deindustrialization". Nig-Sat I and the Sudanese oil industry are good examples of cooperation with technology transfer. During the fourth FOCAC, China has promised it will "enhance cooperation on satellite weather monitoring, development and utilization of new energy sources, prevention and control of desertification and urban environmental protection", build clean energy projects for Africa covering solar power, bio-gas and small hydro-power projects and "combine economic cooperation and trade with technology transfer". All these high-tech projects require technology transfer, and it is hoped that this Action Plan of the FOCAC Fourth Ministerial Conference will bring this into practice (Li Anshan 2009).

In a recent publication, Tang Xiaoyang noticed that TT is combined with the transfer of experiences. Fast development indicates various experiences resulted from practice, which is worthwhile for mutual learning. Therefore, the long-lasting and comprehensive growth of China–Africa bilateral relations since the 1980s should be attributed to the adoption of pragmatism in the collaboration, which he terms "coevolutionary pragmatism" (Tang Xiaoyang 2020).

TA during the period of TAZARA was part of strategical planning of the Chinese government. Because of the character of being leadership-centred, the TA is cooperative work involving various ministries in China, coordinated and led directly by the top leaders. On African side, this project was designed by the Tanzania and Zambia governments and promoted by the frontier countries, and the issue was raised to the Chinese government by the top leaders and negotiated among them as well. Although it was an economic project from its original planning, breaking through the South African and other White regimes had very important political implications. The trilateral relation between Tanzania, Zambia and China in TAZARA, together with other forms of TT, not only showed solidarity, but also strengthened South–South cooperation.

The key feature of TT during this period is threefold: first, the organizer and coordinator of TT is the Chinese government, no matter how big or small the action; second, TT is always linked with some projects financed by China's official assistance, be it in industry, agriculture, infrastructure or the medical field; and third, although the transmission of knowledge is carried out by individual enterprise or institution, TT itself is regarded as a political task.

With the opening up policy, China's strategic emphasis was switched to economic construction, which also brought related changes in the dimension, scale and depth of TT. China continues to train African youth since the availability of qualified personnel is the key to the success of TT. In other aspect, unlike the TA during the early period, TT during the 21st century is generally carried out by SOEs, with few examples of private companies as Huawei. Since the Chinese government has more direct links with the SOE than the private ones, there are more obligations for SOEs to carry out TT as a duty, such as CNPC, ZTE. Moreover, TT is a good strategy for the company to open African markets. TT is carried out shoulder to shoulder with corporate social responsibility (CSR) and is usually reflected in its localisation. The company is concerned with expanding its market and winning more customers. TT is therefore regarded as a strategic move to attract more local people, both African consumers and agents. Yet by doing so the company offers much better conditions for the development of the local community, therefore making its own contribution to industrialisation in Africa. It is therefore an economic measure with political obligations.

However, for the present situation of TT, there is much room for improvement in order to achieve mutual benefits. Now Huawei, ZTE and a few SOEs have realised the importance of TT in the development of both the local economy and their own business, more Chinese enterprises should join the trend. In addition to agriculture and industrialisation, TT or KS should cover more fields and higher technology should be transferred with African industrialisation on the way.

In the FOCAC Johannesburg Action Plan (2016–2018), issued at the China–Africa Summit, "technology transfer" is greatly emphasised. The expression appears 12 times in the text, covering fields such as agriculture, industry, civil aviation, energy and resources, tax and logistics. In addition, similar expression such as "knowledge sharing" appear twice and "share experience" four times. For example, "share development experience" is mentioned in the field of space sciences (4.5.3), as is "experience sharing on security" (6.1.4.). Moreover, the Action Plan states that, "The two sides attach importance to knowledge sharing and technology transfer, and will carry out exchanges in technological innovation policies and the building of science and technology parks and encourage research institutions and enterprises to have intensive cooperation" (4.5.2).[37] This is a promising sign, with knowledge sharing and technology transfer emphasised.

Notes

1 This is a revised version of an article entitled "Technology transfer in China–Africa relation: Myth or reality", originally published in *Transnational Corporations Review*, 8(3), 2016. I would like to thank the journal for permission to publish it here.
2 For a critical assessment, see also Patroba (2012); Youngman (2013).
3 For a positive view, see Project Team of "Teaching how to fish: the investigation of the status quo of Chinese enterprises' technology transfer to Africa" (2015).
4 Mr Antoine Roger Lokongo, PhD student at Peking University, informed me of this. I could not believe it and he provided me with the source. On 16 October 2013, when I delivered a talk on the history of China–Africa relations at a seminar for young diplomats of African French-speaking countries held by Peking University, the information was confirmed by two young diplomats from Côte d'Ivoire.
5 Salim Ahmed Salim is a former Prime Minister of Tanzania. When he campaigned for the post of UN General Secretary in 1981, he was opposed by the US delegation 16 times, simply because he took the lead in the event of the vote on China's return to the United Nations on 25 October 1971 and showed great excitement at China's win. At the same time, China opposed the candidate supported by the United States 16 times (Cilliers 2016).
6 Interview with Mr Baak Valentino A. Wol, Director of Regional Cooperation in Juba, August 2008.
7 A total of 118 Zimbabwean citizens and 11 Zimbabwean companies are on the list of sanctions.

350 *Cooperation and dynamics*

8 African Centre for Economic Transformation (ACET), *Looking East: A guide to engaging China for Africa's policy-makers* (Accra: ACET, 2009). Other African leaders have also voiced their favourable opinion of the option.
9 Braudigam used a lot of Africans' accounts to explain the contrast between China's approach and the "detailed and intrusive conditions often considered necessary by international donors". The former Sierra Leone government minister Dr Sesay told her that the Chinese will simply build a school, a hospital, and then supply a team of doctors to run it. "The World Bank will say: 'You must not have so many teachers on your payroll. You must employ some expatriate staff. You must cut down on your wages.' The Chinese will not do this. They will not say 'You must do this, do that, do this!'"(Brautigam 2009: 149).
10 Once a Chinese official from the Ministry of Commerce told me about his conversation with an official of the World Bank. The World Bank official asked, "Do you know why Chinese aid is more successful?" The Chinese official said no. The World Bank official went on to explain, "The World Bank thinks it knows what Africa needs, while China does not. Because you do not know, you ask the Africans, and they tell you what they need. This is the reason for your success."
11 TAZARA is 1860.5 kilometres long. The construction started in October 1970 and finished in July 1976.
12 Two volumes of selected speeches by President Nyerere were translated into Chinese and published by East China Normal University in 2015.
13 For a good study of TT in TAZARA, see Liu & Monson (2011: 226–251).
14 As a visiting scholar at the University of Hong Kong at the time, Professor Philip Snow sent me this book as a gift in 2006 when I was invited by Professor Kenneth King to give a speech on China–Africa relations there.
15 Table 5.1, "Chinese Technical Assistance to Tanzania, 1964–71" (Yu 1975: 111).
16 Philip Snow gave a general survey of Chinese assistance to Africa in a chapter entitled "The Poor Help the Poor" in his book *The Star Raft*. He sent me this book as a gift in Hong Kong when I was invited by Professor Kenneth King to give a speech at Hong Kong University.
17 *People's Daily*, 18 January 1964. See also Huang Zhen (1987). For the English version, see Information Office of the State Council, *China's Foreign Aid*, April 2011, Appendix I "China's Eight Principles for Economic Aid and Technical Assistance to Other Countries (January 1964)" http://news.xinhuanet.com/english2010/china/2011-04/21/c_13839683_8.htm
18 Jiang Xiang is a diplomat who served in several African countries and as Ambassador in Burkina Faso.
19 She sent me her book in Bamako when China–DAC Project invited her to a conference on "China–Africa Experience Sharing in Agriculture" in 2011 in Mali.
20 "Programme for China-Africa Cooperation in Economic and Social Development", First FOCAC. www.focac.org/eng/ltda/dyjbzjhy/DOC12009/t606797.htm
21 "Wen Jiabao held press conference in Egypt", *Bulletin of PRC State Council Bulletin*. 2006. www.gov.cn/gongbao/content/2006/content_346289.htm
22 Information Office of the State Council, *China's Foreign Aid (2014)*, July 2014. Beijing. http://news.xinhuanet.com/english/china/2014-07/10/c_133474011.htm. For a general study of African students, see Li Anshan & Liu Haifang, "Evolution of the Chinese policy of funding African Students & an evaluation of its effectiveness", Draft of UNDP Project, 2013. For a case study, see King (2010).

23 "Africa: Internet Usage Rising Rapidly", *AfricaFocus*, www.africafocus.org/docs15/ict1509.php
24 "The African internet effect: Everything it touches turns different", www.balancingact-africa.com/news/en/issue-no-795#sthash.RvtY3yy0.dpuf.
25 "Huawei Technologies: A Chinese Trail Blazer in Africa", http://knowledge.wharton.upenn.edu/article/huawei-technologies-a-chinese-trail-blazer-in-africa, "Huawei going strong in Africa"; www.oafrica.com/mobile/huawei-going-strong-in-africa; Alfred Wong, "China's Telecommunications Boom in Africa: Causes and Consequences".
26 "Telecom Seeds for the Future" Program, http://pr.huawei.com/en/social-contribution/charitable-activities/hw-u_202448.htm#.Vkr9tMLotes.
27 "Kenya: Nine Kenyan Students to Benefit From Huawei's 'Seeds for the Future' Program", http://allafrica.com/stories/201412090706.html; "Huawei Technologies: A Chinese Trail Blazer in Africa", http://knowledge.wharton.upenn.edu/article/huawei-technologies-a-chinese-trail-blazer-in-africa
28 "Chinese firm trains Kenyan students on ICT", www.focac.org/eng/zfgx/t1305735.htm; "China tour an eye opener for Kenyan engineering students", www.icta.go.ke/china-tour-an-eye-opener-for-kenyan-engineering-students
29 "Uganda: Huawei's 'Seeds for the Future' Program Launched in Uganda", http://allafrica.com/stories/201504030275.html
30 "China's Huawei to offer more training opportunities for African students", http://news.xinhuanet.com/english/2015-06/28/c_134362929.htm. See also "China's Huawei to offer Botswana's youth technical training", http://news.xinhuanet.com/english/2015-06/05/c_134301459.htm
31 "China's Huawei boosts schools' connectivity via project in Ethiopia", www.focac.org/eng/zfgx/t1305384.htm
32 "5 tech-entrepreneurs chosen for exclusive Huawei She Leads Africa Innovation Visit to China", http://africanbrains.net/2015/07/14/5-tech-entrepreneurs-chosen-for-exclusive-huawei-she-leads-africa-innovation-visit-to-china
33 "Ethiopia SchoolNet Project Builds Desktop Cloud with Huawei", www.huawei.com/en/EBG/Home/videos/global/2015/201512111618
34 China Road and Bridge Corporation. 2016. "CSR Report of Mombasa–Nairobi Railway Project".
35 "Largest China–foreign joint school to founded in Ethiopia", www.china.org.cn/international/news/2008-12/24/content_17003029.htm
36 As for African students, please refer to Chapter 20 of this book. See also Li Anshan (2014).
37 Section 4.5.2. of "The Forum on China–Africa Cooperation Johannesburg Action Plan (2016–2018)", 25 December 2015. www.focac.org/eng/ltda/dwjbzjjhys_1/hywj/t1327961.htm

References

Africa: Internet usage rising rapidly, Africa Focus. www.africafocus.org/docs15/ict1509.php
African Center for Economic Transformation (ACET). 2009. *Looking East: A guide to engaging China for Africa's policy-makers*. Accra: ACET.
The African internet effect – everything it touches turns different. www.balancingact-africa.com/news/en/issue-no-795#sthash.RvtY3yy0.dpuf

Alessi, C. & Beina Xu. 2015. China in Africa. Council on Foreign Relations, 27 April. www.cfr.org/china/china-africa/p9557

Brautigam, D. 1998. *Chinese aid and African development: Exporting green revolution.* London: Macmillan.

Brautigam, D. 2009. *The dragon's gift: The real story of China in Africa.* Oxford: Oxford University Press.

Bulletin of PRC State Council. 2006. Wen Jiabao held press conference in Egypt. www.gov.cn/gongbao/content/2006/content_346289.htm

Campbell, H. 2013. *Global NATO and the catastrophic failure in Libya.* New York: Monthly Review Press.

China Daily. 2012. Zimbabwe praises China's technology transfer, 10 May.

China Road and Bridge Corporation. 2016. CSR Report of Mombasa–Nairobi Railway Project. Not formally published.

China tour an eye-opener for Kenyan engineering students. n.d. www.icta.go.ke/china-tour-an-eye-opener-for-kenyan-engineering-students

China's Huawei boosts schools' connectivity via project in Ethiopia. n.d. www.focac.org/eng/zfgx/t1305384.htm

China's Huawei to offer Botswana's youth technical training. 2015. http://news.xinhuanet.com/english/2015-06/05/c_134301459.htm

China's Huawei to offer more training opportunities for African students. 2015. http://news.xinhuanet.com/english/2015-06/28/c_134362929.htm

Chinese firm trains Kenyan students on ICT. 2015. www.focac.org/eng/zfgx/t1305735.htm

Cilliers, J. ed. 2016. *Salim Ahmed Salim: Son of Africa.* Nairobi: African Union.

Council of European Union. 2011. Council decision 2011/101, CFSP of 15 February 2011 concerning restrictive measures against Zimbabwe. *Official Journal of the European Union*, 16 August.

Council Decision 2011/101, CFSP of 15 February 2011 Concerning Restrictive Measures Against Zimbabwe. 2011. *Official Journal of European Union*, 16 August.

Davies, M. 2011. How China is influencing Africa's development? in Jing Men & Benjamin Barton, eds, *China and the European Union in Africa: Partners or competitors?* Aldershot: Ashgate, 187–207.

Domasa, S. 2016. Tanzania: UDSM launches 90 billion state-of-the-art multi-storage library. *Daily News* (Tanzania), 3 June. http://allafrica.com/stories/201606030383.html

Elu, J.A. 2010. Does China transfer productivity enhancing technology to Sub-Saharan Africa? Evidence from manufacturing firms. *African Development Review* 22(S1): 87–98.

Ethiopia SchoolNet project builds desktop cloud with Huawei. www.huawei.com/en/EBG/Home/videos/global/2015/201512111618

5 tech-entrepreneurs chosen for exclusive Huawei: She Leads Africa innovation visit to China. http://africanbrains.net/2015/07/14/5-tech-entrepreneurs-chosen-for-exclusive-huawei-she-leads-africa-innovation-visit-to-china

Forum on China–Africa Cooperation Johannesburg Action Plan (2016–2018). 2015. 25 December. www.focac.org/eng/ltda/dwjbzjjhys_1/hywj/t1327961.htm

Fourie, F. 2015. China's example for Meles' Ethiopia: When development "models" land. *The Journal of Modern African Studies* 53(3): 289–316.

Gillespie, Sandra. 2001. *South–South transfer: A study of Sino-African exchange.* New York: Routledge.

Hanlon, J., Manjengwa, J. & Smart, T. 2013. *Zimbabwe takes back its land*. Cape Town: Jacana.
Huang Jingbo. 2005. *International technology transfer*. Beijing: Tsinghua University Press.
Huang Zhen. 1987. Paving the road of friendship to the awakening Africa. In *Endless Remembrance*. Beijing: CPC Literature Press.
Huawei going strong in Africa. 2011. www.oafrica.com/mobile/huawei-going-strong-in-africa
Huawei Technologies: A Chinese trail blazer in Africa. 2015. http://knowledge.wharton.upenn.edu/article/huawei-technologies-a-chinese-trail-blazer-in-africa
Information Office of the State Council. 2011. *China's Foreign Aid*, April. Appendix I.
Information Office of the State Council. 2011. *China's Foreign Aid*, April.
Information Office of the State Council. 2014. *China's Foreign Aid*, July.
Jiang Xiang. 2007. *My seventeen years in Africa*. Shanghai: Lexicographical Publishing House.
Kenya: Nine Kenyan students to benefit from Huawei's "Seeds for the Future" Program. http://allafrica.com/stories/201412090706.html
Kim, Yejoo. 2014. China–Africa technology transfer: A matter of technology readiness, 17 February. www.ccs.org.za/wp-content/uploads/2014/02/CCS_Commentary_China_Africa_Tech_2014_YK1.pdf
King, K. 2010. China's cooperation in education and training with Kenya: A different model? *International Journal of Educational Development* 30: 88–96.
Large, D. 2008. Beyond "dragon in the bush": The study of China–Africa relations. *African Affairs* 107(426): 45–61.
Largest China–foreign joint school to founded in Ethiopia. 2008. www.china.org.cn/international/news/2008-12/24/content_17003029.htm
Li Anshan. 2006. On the adjustment and transformation of China's African policy. *West Asia and Africa* 8: 191–220.
Li Anshan. 2008. In defense of China: China's African strategy and state image. *World Economics and Politics* 4: 6–15.
Li Anshan. 2009. What's to be done after the Fourth FOCAC? *China Monitor*, November: 7–9.
Li Anshan. 2011. *Chinese medical cooperation in Africa: With special emphasis on the medical teams and anti-malaria campaign*. Uppsala: Nordic African Institute. http://nai.diva-portal.org/smash/get/diva2:399727/FULLTEXT02.pdf
Li Anshan. 2014. China–Africa relations in the changing international discourse. *World Economics and Politics* 2: 19–47.
Li Anshan. 2015. The history and reality of international aid. In Li Anshan & Pan Huaqiong, eds, *Annual Review of African Studies in China 2014*. Beijing: Social Sciences Academic Press, 121–141.
Li Anshan & Liu Haifang. 2013. Evolution of the Chinese policy of funding African students & an evaluation of its effectiveness. Draft of UNDP Project. Not formally published.
Li Anshan & Funeka Yazini April, eds. 2013. *Forum on China–Africa Cooperation: The politics of Human Resource Development*, Pretoria: Africa Institute of South Africa.
Liu Haifang & Monson, Jamie. 2011. Railway time: Technology transfer and the role of Chinese experts in the history of TAZARA. In Tom Dietz, Kjell Havnervik, Mayke Kaag & Terje Oestigaard, eds, *African engagements: Africa negotiation an emerging multipolar world*. Leiden: Brill, 26–51.

Liu Jirui ed. 1998. *Chinese medical teams in Tanzania*. Health Department of Shandong Province, 1998. Not formally published.

Lokongo, A.R. 2015. US policy and resource wars in Democratic Republic of Congo, (1982–2013). PhD dissertation, Peking University.

Men Jing & Barton, Benjamin, eds. 2011. *China and the European Union in Africa: Partners or competitors?* Aldershot: Ashgate.

Mihanfo, E.P. 2012. Understanding China's neo-colonialism in Africa: A historical study of the China–Africa economic relations. In James Shikwati, ed., *China–Africa partnership: The quest for a win–win relationship*. Nairobi: IREN, 130–136.

Monson, J. 2009. *Africa's freedom railway: How a Chinese development project changed lives and livelihoods in Tanzania*. Bloomington, IN: Indiana University Press.

Munemo, J. 2013. Examining imports of capital goods from China as a channel for technology transfer and growth in sub-Saharan Africa. *Journal of African Business* 14(2): 6–16.

Opinion of China. 2015. www.pewglobal.org/database/indicator/24.

Patroba, H. 2012. *China in Kenya: Addressing counterfeit goods and construction sector imbalance*. Beijing: SAIIA.

People's Daily. 1964. 18 January.

Programme for China-Africa Cooperation in Economic and Social Development, First FOCAC. 2009. www.focac.org/eng/ltda/dyjbzjhy/DOC12009/t606797.htm

Project Team of "Teaching how to fish: the investigation of the status quo of Chinese enterprises' technology transfer to Africa". 2015. Status quo and prospects of Chinese enterprises' technology transfer to Africa. *West Asia and Africa* 1: 129–142.

Shen Xipeng 2018. *A study on China aided construction of Tanzania–Zambia Railway*. Heifei: Huangshan Publishing House.

Shikwati, J. 2015. Aid, development: Why Africans must dream and go out. In Li Anshan & Pan Huaqiong, eds, *Annual review of African Studies in China 2014*. Beijing: Social Sciences Academic Press, 237–250.

Snow, P. 1988. *Star Raft: China's encounter with Africa*. London: Weidenfeld & Nicolson.

Tang Xiaoyang. 2020. *Coevolutionary pragmatism: Approaches and impacts of China–Africa economic cooperation*. Cambridge: Cambridge University Press.

Telecom Seeds for the Future Program. http://pr.huawei.com/en/social-contribution/charitable-activities/hw-u_202448.htm#.Vkr9tMLotes

Uganda: Huawei's 'Seeds for the Future' Program Launched in Uganda. http://allafrica.com/stories/210504030275.html

Wade, A. 2008. Time for the West to practise what it preaches. *Financial Times*, 29 February.

Wong, A. 2015. China's telecommunications boom in Africa: Causes and consequences. *E-International Relations*, 21 September. www.e-ir.info/2015/09/21/chinas-telecommunications-boom-in-africa-causes-and-consequences

Youngman, F. 2013. *Strengthening Africa–China relations: A perspective from Botswana*. Stellenbosch: Centre for Chinese Studies, Stellenbosch University.

Yu, George T. 1975. *China's African policy: A study of Tanzania*. New York: Praeger.

Zhang Anping, Li Wen & Yu Qiubo. 2011. Analysis of China's oil cooperation model: Evidence from Sudan. *West Asia and Africa* 3: 3–11.

Zhang Tieshan. 1999. *The road of friendship: The memoirs of the development assistance of Tanzania–Zambia Railroad*. Beijing: China International Business and Economics Press.
Zhou Boping. 2004. *Diplomatic life during the unusual period*. Beijing: World Affairs Press.
Zhou Hong & Xiong Hou, eds. 2013. *China's foreign aid: 60 years in retrospect*. Beijing: Social Sciences Academic Press.

14 People-to-people contact in China–Africa relations

Introduction

In the early morning of 8 August 2000, an old Shanghai woman named Madame Zhu Shuibao picked up an abandoned Black baby on the way back from the grocery store (*Global Times* 2016). She took him home and started to wash him, but found she could not clean his skin. She was very anxious and rushed him to the hospital. The doctor, after the check-up, told her, "He is fine. His skin is Black – that's why you can't wash it off." Madame Zhu gave the Black baby a Chinese name, Zhu Junlong, and brought him up through kindergarten, primary school and middle school with various difficulties. Last year, Zhu Junlong received a Shanghai *Hukou* (registration identity) and Madame Zhu went through the procedure of adoption. In 2018, Zhu Junlong became a university student (*Global Times* 2016).

A Chinese news reporter Gui Tao told us a story. His Kenyan friend once asked him a question, "Do you know why your Chinese football team always failed in international games?" "I don't know. Why?" Hui Tao asked. The Kenyan man answered, "Because your Chinese football players all look alike and they change the player frequently in the games. The international referee gets very angry, so lets them fail" (Gui Tao 2012).

These two stories tell us how ignorant both the Chinese woman and the Kenyan man are of other people's images. One does not know the Black skin is unwashable, the other thinks every Chinese man has the same appearance. The stories also tell us how important people-to-people (P2P) contact is in global communication.

For any bilateral relations in the international arena, indirect contact always goes before direct contact, informal contact before formal contact, non-official contact before official contact. China and Africa have brilliant civilisations in common and there is a long tradition of bilateral cultural contact (Shen Fuwei 1990; Li Anshan 2019). In modern times, both China and Africa have had the same experience of being colonised and humiliated by the European powers, and both have witnessed the struggle for liberation, independence, development and national dignity.

DOI: 10.4324/9781003220152-17

Starting from the late 19th century, when European colonialism spread all over the world, China and African countries either totally or partially lost their independent status. There were almost no official links between China and Africa. Even the few that did exist were distorted, since the Chinese government signed treaties with European powers regarding Africa, or set up consulates in European colonies in Africa. A treaty was reached between the Chinese government and Congo Free State as early as 1898, so the latter could recruit labourers from China (Wang Tieya 1982: 76–77). Except for a few Chinese consulates in South Africa, Egypt, Madagascar and Mozambique during that period, most contact was non-official (Li Anshan 2000). After independence, China and Africa resumed direct contact.

In China, the commonly used expression *min-jian jiao-wang* (民间交往), meaning contacts between communities or societies in an international context, is equivalent to people-to-people (hereafter P2P) contact. P2P contact and exchange are usually carried out by Chinese *min-jian zhu-zhi* (民间组织), or Chinese civil organizations (CCOs). In this chapter, the term "CCO" replaces "NGO" in the case of China for four reasons. First, in China CCO has been used for much longer than NGO. Second, African governments and many intellectuals have a negative impression of NGOs, mainly because the funding is usually from the West and African NGOs face the dilemma of serving two masters (the fund provider and their own nation). Third, "civil organization" is a much wider term than NGO. Fourth, a CCO must be registered in China, with records kept: the *Annual Report on Chinese Civil Organizations* has been published since 2008.

Generally speaking, diplomatic relations have three elements: official contact, semi-official contact and P2P contact. Obviously, P2P contact forms an important part of bilateral relations in foreign affairs. However, diplomacy is not the sole element of bilateral relations. One of the important aspects of P2P contact is cultural offering and cultural learning. "Culture" is a very colourful yet ambiguous term, with countless interpretations. I prefer Richard A. Shweder's definition, which considers culture as "community-specific ideas about what is true, good, beautiful and efficient" (Shweder 2000: 163). In the world community of different peoples and cultures, people need to know one another, understand other cultures and learn from one another. Cultural offering represents a concept of equality and a sense of sharing – an important element in P2P contact that lays down the foundation of better bilateral relations and makes a greater contribution to a more harmonious world.

CCOs have mushroomed in China in recent years.[1] However, there are very few academic studies on China–Africa P2P contact (Deng Guosheng 2013). Wei Hong's research is concentrated on the pressure of African NGO on China–Africa relations (Wei Hong 2009: 37–141). Wang Xuejun analysed the links between African NGOs and China–Africa relations (Wang Xuejun 2009). Zhao Minghao studied the challenge of the CCO and its future perspective (Zhao Minghao 2010). Feng Zuoku considered that the China–Africa P2P contact was characterised by officials leading people, friendship promoting economy and culture improving friendship (Feng Zuoko 2012). Taking the China Foundation for Poverty Alleviation (CFPA) as an example, Lai Yulin probed Chinese NGO's contribution to international development cooperation (Lai Yulin 2013). Long and Chen dealt with the possible roles of Chinese NGOs (Long Xiaonong & Chen Yue 2013). The features of media interaction between China and Africa were illustrated (Li Anshan 2012a; Ran Jijun 2015). David Brenner's study probed the general trend of Chinese NGOs' role in China's "going out" strategy and engagement in China–Africa relations (Brenner 2012). Yazini April analysed the civil society's role in China–Africa relations (April 2015). China–African daily encounters are illustrated to indicate their potential for African development (Mohan et al. 2014). Almost all these works concentrate on politics, such as the "soft power" connotation of China's strategy, a very narrow understanding of P2P contact.

This chapter discusses the history and achievement of China–Africa P2P contact in order to deepen our understanding of the issue. It is divided into three parts. The first is a historical survey from the late 19th century to the present. The second illustrates P2P with a focus on the period after 2000, the year of the establishment of FOCAC, based on three levels: FOCAC-sponsored P2P contact, individual contact and organisational P2P contact. The third part presents a conclusion and suggestions, with an analysis of the characteristics of the three types of P2P contact, the weakness of present P2P contact and suggestions for future cooperation.

People-to-people contact: History and level

During the first half of the 20th century, the African continent (with the exception of Ethiopia) was colonised by European powers. Chinese free immigrants and indentured labourers went to Africa, and the indentured labourers were employed by the British, French, Germans, Spanish, Portuguese and Belgians. They worked as farmers on St Helena Island; mine workers in the goldmines of South Africa and Ghana; and as builders of railways in Tanganyika, Mozambique and the French colonies of Equatorial Africa. They constructed various projects such as buildings, ports and roads/railways in South Africa and Madagascar, and they served as indentured labourers in Mauritius and Reunion (Li Anshan 2019: 299–309).

The indentured labourers stayed for several years in a totally strange environment, working hard and living a life very different from that at home. Except for those who died of hard labour, serious injuries, cruel torture and deadly disease, most returned home. The information provided by the indentured labourers, together with the Chinese already there, became the source of information about the continent, and modern Chinese people learned that there was a place called "Africa".

During the mid-1930s, Ethiopia was fighting the Italian army and China was threatened by the Japanese invasion. China's Nationalist Party and Communist Party united during the Anti-Japanese War. The Chinese government joined the League of Nations in imposing sanctions against Italy, and the Communist Party issued a communiqué calling the Chinese to learn from the Ethiopians. It was reported that the St John Red Cross of Hong Kong would send medical volunteers to Ethiopia and cinemas showed a documentary about Ethiopia's resistance.[2] Chinese newspapers and magazines published news reports, commentaries and articles showing the strongest support for the Ethiopian struggle for independence. With the impending invasion by Japan, the Chinese people showed sympathy and admiration for Ethiopia. They compared Italy with Japan and shared the same feeling of a people being invaded. Most of the important Chinese media voiced a desire for peace, condemned the imperialist militancy and expressed strong support for Ethiopia, especially when the Ethiopians waged a guerrilla war against the Italian army. Both Chinese leaders and ordinary people learned great deal from the Ethiopian Anti-Italian War (Zhang Zhongxiang 1993).

During the period of African liberation movements, China gave African countries both moral and political support. From 1949 to1960, more than 1000 Africans from 41 countries were invited to China through P2P channels, including leaders of national liberation movements, delegates of trade unions and organisations of youth, students and women. Quite a few prominent nationalist figures, such as Samuel Daniel Shafiishuna Nujoma, former

Table 14.1 Chinese major articles related to the Ethiopian anti-Italian war

Year/m/d (issue)	Name of media	Title of article
1935/8/1 (102)	*National Communications*	Brave Ethiopia
1935/12/9	*Saving the Nation Times*	Chinese medical team go to Ethiopia
1935/12/28	*Saving the Nation Times*	Celebrating the Ethiopians' victory
1936/1/4	*Saving the Nation Times*	Lessons of national revolutionary war
1936/1/9	*Red China*	National revolutionary war in Ethiopia
1936/1/29	*Saving the Nation Times*	The key to the national survival
1936/4/20	*Saving the Nation Times*	Ethiopia swears to die refusing to yield
1936/5/1 (4:4)	*World Affairs*	Best example of national defense
1936/5/16 (4:5)	*World Affairs*	Causes and lessons of the Ethiopian army
1936/6/24	*Shun Pao*	Ethiopian army continues to fight
1936/8/9	*Red China*	Ethiopian people continue to fight against Italy
1937/2/1 (5:10)	*World Affairs*	The Blacks are still fighting
1937/3/1 (5:12)	*World Affairs*	The bombs of Ethiopia
1938/1/5	*Saving the Nation Times*	Ethiopian people continue guerrilla war against fascist Italy
1941/11/30	*Xinhua Daily*	British army of East Africa occupies Gondar

President of Namibia, and Robert Gabriel Mugabe, President of Zimbabwe, were invited to China while they were leading their people in the anti-colonial struggle. In April 1960, the China–Africa People's Friendship Association was formed in Beijing, comprising 20 Chinese national organizations (Feng Zuoko 2012).

In the early 1950s, the South African government passed the Group Areas Act and a series of other discriminatory Acts that aroused strong protests from non-White people. Chairman Mao Zedong strongly denounced the apartheid policy and expressed support for the South African people. China condemned the South African government, stating that the Group Areas Act would affect South African merchants and entrepreneurs and that it was a violation of the righteous daily life of African people, including Chinese living in South Africa (*People's Daily*, 29 May 1950; *People's Daily*, 20 September 1950).

The Chinese also supported the struggle against colonial rule in Egypt, Ethiopia and Tanzania. In 1951, a vigorous and vital anti-British movement arose in Egypt, which received an enthusiastic response from the Chinese people. Newspapers published letters from ordinary people showing support to the Egyptian people. Professor Ma Jian of Peking University, who had studied in Egypt, expressed his belief that "we two countries will win our final victory in the fight against imperialist robbers" and wrote an article on the Egyptian anti-British struggle (Ma Jian 1951). In January 1952, while the Egyptian people fought bravely against the British invasion, the Chinese Democratic Youth League sent a telegram to Egyptian students to show its support for them and to tell them that Chinese young people would unite with them in the fight against imperialism and defence of world peace.[3]

In 1953, a Chinese youth delegation had extensive contact with delegates from Egypt, Algeria, Tunisia, Morocco, Madagascar and French West Africa during the International Conference on the Defence of Youth Rights held in Geneva. According to the statistics, in the early 1950s more than 540 letters, telegrams, reports and articles appeared in major Chinese newspapers supporting the African struggle against colonialism and imperialism. The statistics come from 22 newspapers, journals and magazines (Lu Ting-en 1997). Ethiopia had no diplomatic relations with China in the 1950s, yet China sent a cultural delegation to Ethiopia in 1956 and Ethiopia returned the gesture; however, the establishment of official relations had to wait until 1970 (Daddi & Zhang Yongpeng 2009: 9–32).

After many African countries won their independence in the 1960s, China sent various cultural delegations to Africa and learned different types of African dance. The African countries sent young people to China for further study and students from 14 countries regularly came to China until the end of 1966, when the Cultural Revolution started and all universities were closed until 1970. One of the young students was a Ghanaian named Emmanuel Hevi, who complained about racism and other unpleasant experiences in China (Hevi 1963; Liu Zhirong 2013). Hevi's complaint was understandable for various reasons. Although the African students, like all foreign students in

China, enjoyed some privileges and lived a better life than ordinary Chinese citizens, China could not provide any better conditions for anyone because the early 1960s witnessed the worst economic situation in China after the founding of the People's Republic. What is more, dogmatism, social taboos and regulations created a kind of "segregation" between African students and ordinary Chinese, especially African men and Chinese women. To make things worse, the pervasive politics of the 1960s and 1970s suppressed social interaction and thus made life less interesting for foreign students. However, this was a period in which young African students saw China with their own eyes and had their first contact with Chinese people (Li Anshan & Liu Haifang 2013).

During the 1960s and 1970s, two important events greatly improved P2P contact between China and Africa: the building of the Tanzania–Zambian Railway (TAZARA) and the dispatch of Chinese medical teams (CMTs) to Africa. Would-be engineers from Tanzania and Zambia who were trained to work on the railway and were the biggest group of students had various experiences during their training. TAZARA not only made a great contribution to the frontier countries at the time; building the railway also improved African understanding of China. More than 60,000 Chinese workers went to Africa, creating a good opportunity for mutual contact (Monson 2009; Shen Xipeng 2018). After China sent its first people team to Algeria in 1963, CMTs were dispatched to 47 African countries. More than 16,000 Chinese doctors have worked in Africa and more than 240 million Africans have received medical treatment, greatly improving bilateral contact (Li Anshan 2011). China will always remember the efforts of those African countries who helped China to resume its position in the United Nations in 1971.

If people's contact with Africa in the 1960s and 1970s was more or less under the auspices of the Chinese government, the 1980s and 1990s experienced opening up and reform, and P2P contact entered a new period. A great number of state enterprises brought many engineers and workers to Africa and gave them the opportunity to experience the continent. Chinese tourists visited Africa and had direct contact with African people. Ordinary Chinese people such as Hu Jieguo, Wang Jianxu and Li Songshan began private businesses in Africa in the 1980s. During this time, various channels of cultural contact were opened, such as the first sister-city connection established between Changsha in Hunan Province of China and Brazzaville in the Republic of Congo in 1982. A Chinese delegation attended the Expo International held in Zimbabwe in 1983 and the first Chinese Cultural Centre was set up in Mauritius in 1988 (Li Anshan 2006: 318–407).

There were problems as well, especially among African students in China. The problems had various causes, such as economic dissatisfaction, living conditions, political divergence of the United States and the Middle East, and different social values. Complaints and grievances resulted in conflict and even demonstrations. Clashes between African and Chinese students occurred in Tianjin, Nanjing and other cities at the end of the 1980s, a natural phenomenon for people with different values (Li Anshan & Liu Haifang 2013). The trigger was the Chinese attitude to the behaviour of African male students and young Chinese women. Some scholars even described the incidents as "national racism" (Sulliven 1994: 438–457).

After Premier Zhou Enlai's visit in the 1960s, few Chinese top leaders visited Africa until 1982, when Premier Zhao Ziyang visited 11 African countries. He raised Four Principles regarding China–Africa cooperation (equality and mutual benefit, emphasis on effectiveness, variety of forms and common development). Other Chinese top leaders left their footprints in African countries too – Chairman Li Xianlian in 1986, Chairman Yang Shangkun in 1989 and 1992, Chairman Jiang Zemin in 1996 and Premier Li Peng in 1997. Mao Zedong and Zhou Enlai treated African people as "brothers". Deng Xiaoping called young African leaders "young friends". In a speech at the OAU headquarters, Jiang Zemin described China and Africa as "all-weather friends", a term coined in 1967 by Kenneth Kaunda, former President of Zambia, which Jiang has frequently used to describe African people. Visits to Africa by top Chinese leaders became a normal pattern.

Another interesting practice is also worth noting. In January 1991, Minister of Foreign Affairs Qian Qichen visited Africa and since then it has been a convention for the Chinese Minister of Foreign Affairs to visit Africa at the beginning of every year. Those are obviously official contacts, but they have paved the way for broader and deeper P2P contact.

In the 21st century, there are more opportunities for cultural contact between Chinese and Africans. After the founding of FOCAC, China–Africa relations have developed rapidly in various fields such as politics, economy, the social and cultural arena, education and medical health and environmental protection. P2P contact has gradually caught the attention of the policy-makers. There are three types: cultural contact organized by the government, especially under the aegis of FOCAC; contact by various individuals; and social exchanges sponsored by CCOs. The three types overlap but we will concentrate on the first.

FOCAC and people-to-people exchange

At the first FOCAC, in which I had the fortune to participate, the agenda did not pay much attention to P2P contact and the emphasis was on economic cooperation. With more involvement in Africa, accompanied by criticism from both the West and Africa, both Chinese and African governments gradually realised the importance of grassroots exchanges. They began to include various cultural activities on the agenda, such as training Africans including young students, and promoting cultural contact and grassroots exchanges. Comparing the agendas of the first FOCAC in 2000 with the fifth in 2012, the increase in measures of P2P exchange is impressive. In the program of cooperation of the first FOCAC, only one sentence deals with cultural contact: "increasing cultural exchanges, particularly the exchange of visits by high-level cultural delegations and sports and art groups, setting up more art exhibitions in each other's territory, and making a greater effort to study and promote each other's culture". In the second FOCAC in 2013, there were already four items of "cultural exchange and cooperation" (5.3.1, 5.3.2) and "people to people exchange" (5.4.1, 5.4.2) included in the action plan. Second, a trend of increasing emphasis on cultural activities and P2P contact is observable. After the second FOCAC, more and more attention was paid to the field. The fifth FOCAC in 2012 featured a separate category, "Cultural and people-to-people exchange and cooperation", with six sections (6.1–6.6) including 24 concrete measures (6.1.1–6.5.7) for follow-up action. Third, the areas of cultural contact and P2P exchange expanded. When P2P exchanges were first raised, only cultural festivals and exchanges between Chinese and African youth were listed. In the fifth FOCAC, extensive areas of P2P exchange were brought in (6.5.1–6.5.7), including contact and exchange between youth, women, NGOs, young leaders and volunteers.

Another characteristic is the change of perspective. In the early FOCAC meetings, although the word "exchange" was used, concrete measures were more about introducing Chinese culture to Africa, and the exchange was conducted more by the Chinese. Gradually, a real exchange of both sides developed thanks to several factors. African initiatives gathered momentum and more efforts were made by African countries. More P2P contacts raised the problem of a lop-sided process of contact, which also attracted criticism from ordinary people and academics in Africa, China and the West. Through contact, both African and Chinese realized that African culture could offer much more than expected. Chinese scholars began to study what China could learn from Africa (Li Anshan 2012: 93–97).

P2P exchange through FOCAC takes many forms, including various fora such as the China–Africa People's Forum, the Agricultural Cooperation Forum, the Young Leaders Forum, the Cultural Ministers' Forum, the Educational Cooperation Forum, the FOCAC Women's Forum, the FOCAC Legal Cooperation Forum, the FOCAC Think Tanks Forum and the Radio and Television Cooperation Forum. To promote cultural exchange, FOCAC has set up cultural centres on both sides and designed programs including the China–Africa Cultural Cooperation Partnership Program, the 20+20 Cooperation Plan for Chinese and African Institutions of Higher Education, the China–Africa Joint Research and Exchange Program and the China–Africa Think Tank 10+10 Partnership Plan. There are cultural activities such as Meet in Beijing and African Culture in Focus (held in even-numbered years in China) and Chinese Culture in Focus (held in odd-numbered years in Africa), and exhibitions are held frequently in both countries. Up to September 2009, a total of 281 volunteers had served in African countries.

An important measure of P2P contact under FOCAC is the training of African youth. The number of training programmes is increasing rapidly, from 7000 in the first FOCAC to 10,000 in the second, 15,000 in the third, 20,000 in the fourth and 30,000 in the fifth.[4] Young Africans who have had the opportunity to study in China relate their experiences back home, and more African youngsters come to China for further study, sponsored either by their own government or their families. Training African personnel is both a way to promote the African economy and a measure of cultural exchange. Africans have brought their values, skills, painting, sculpture, dances, musical instruments and films, thus contributing a great deal to the understanding of African culture.

Cultural contact through individual efforts

There are many cultural exchanges at the grassroots level. There are various clubs of African culture in many Chinese cities, such as African dance, African music and African drumming. My former student Wang Hanjie (王涵洁) wrote her BA dissertation on "The history and spread of the Djembe drum in China". When I asked her why she chose this topic, she told me proudly that she was a member of the Djembe Club at Peking University! There is an annual International Cultural Festival at Peking University where African students set up their stands to introduce their culture. The Centre for African Studies at Peking University and the popular magazine *Half-Monthly Talks* (半月谈) co-run a special column entitled "Entry into African culture" and so far 15 articles on different aspects of African culture have appeared, covering African world heritage, African languages, African films, the role of African chiefs, Léopold Sédar Senghor, Nobel Prize winner Wole Soyinka, Ibn Battuta, Ibn Khaldun, the civilisation of Ethiopia and more.

Chinese artists or ordinary people who love African culture and African art also express their feeling and passion in different ways. Li Songshan (李松山) and Han Rong (韩蓉), a Chinese couple who worked in Tanzania for more than 10 years, built up the Songshan-Hanrong African Art Collection Museum in Changchun, Jilin Province. It has a special feature on the Makonde style and Tinga-Tinga art of Tanzania, with letters of congratulation from two Tanzanian presidents. The Chinese couple love African art so much that they spent all their savings to build another African Art Village in Beijing.[5]

There are quite a few African art museums or collections in China, such as Museum of African Art at Zhejiang Normal University, African art exhibitions organised by Guo Dong （郭栋） in Beijing, Hainan and Chengdu, an African art collection by Wang Shaobo (王少波) in Lianyungang in Jiangsu Province and an African Cultural Museum in Shenzhen by Liao Xuhui (廖旭辉). Artist Li Bin (李斌) created a big oil painting 38 metres long and 3.8 metres high entitled *Mandela*, containing three themes (prisoner, president and peacemaker), as a tribute to the great leader of South Africa (Liu Jian 2015). Zhang Xiang (张象), a professor of history, is an expert on African history. At the age of 80, he published *Selected Songs for Chinese–African Friendship* with titles full of his love of Africa, such as "China–Africa, loving brothers"; "Angels in White who sow seeds of love – to the Chinese medical teams in Africa"; and "TAZARA friendship forever in Africa". Many friends helped him translate them into English, French, Arabic, Kiswahili and Hausa. He said, "I am eager to express my affection for Africa with music as a way of combining academic pursuit and music aspiration ... I sincerely wish my dedication to African music will contribute to the amicable relationship between China and Africa" (Zhang Xiang 2014: 13). All these ordinary Chinese tried to introduce African art to Chinese people and devoted their love to Africa.

Several African singers have become the hottest pop stars in China and frequently perform on TV. The most famous are a Nigerian, Uwechue Emmanuel who has a Chinese name, Hao Ge (郝哥), and Steven, born in Liberia with the Chinese name Hao Di (郝弟). Their songs are in Chinese and their pronunciation is idiomatic.[6] A charity sale for Ebola in Africa was organised by Ada Yang, an artist in Chinese calligraphy from Sierra Leone. As chair of the Duyi Queennak Foundation, she and her husband initiated the donations with the help of CAPFA. More than ten calligraphers and painters showed their work in the hall of the Chinese People's Association for Friendship with Foreign Countries (Chen Yingqun 2014). There are African reporters on CCTV and in the media, African dance groups, African drum clubs and African arts clubs in China. Chinese athletes are learning long-distance running in African countries, and young Africans are learning acrobatics in China. There are 38 Confucius Institutes and ten Confucius Classrooms in 32 African countries.

Besides promoting bilateral business, African businesspeople also contribute their knowledge, language skill and values to China. Gizelle, a Cameroonian businesswoman, has her shop in Yiwu selling handmade African decor and furniture to Chinese customers, and is happy with her business expansion.[7] Many African merchants are like Gizelle in China. The market in Yiwu set up a Foreign Dispute Mediation Office in 2013 in order to settle up disagreements in business. The office comprises volunteer mediators from 12 different nations. Senegalese Tirera Sourakhata and his Guinean colleague acted as mediator for help (Anonymous 2018). The African diaspora in China also has problems, such as language communication difficulties, pressure from Chinese immigration system, the dilemma of cultural adjustment and misunderstanding of the surrounding Chinese people and society (Bodomo 2012; Li Anshan 2015).

Mutual understanding is a key in bilateral relations. Increasingly, young Africans are coming to China for advanced study in various subjects. I still remember a student from the Republic of Congo who saw telecommunications products "Made in China" and decided to come to China. He is now a graduate student of telecommunications at the Beijing University of Posts and Telecommunications. African students are doing master's programs, such as Serge Mundele at Beijing University of Science and Technology; PhD studies, such as Erfiki Hicham (李杉), a Moroccan doing international politics at Peking University; post-doctoral studies, such as Imen Belhadj (伊美娜), a Tunisian at Peking University, and Oodo Stephen Ogidi, a Nigerian working as a post-doctoral fellow in electrical engineering at Dalian University of Technology. As a Ghanaian government official and later a student in China for five years, Lloyd G. Adu Amoah used his experience to demonstrate that "Africa remakes China challenging the conventional view that Africans act passively in China–Africa relations" (Amoah 2012). They bring their culture to China and learn Chinese culture, thus acting as a cultural bridge. Their cultural offering enriches multiculturalism in China.[8]

Talking about her experience of studying in China, Ghanaian student Zahra Baitie discussed Chinese attitudes towards Africans in *The Atlantic*. Although there are good relations between China and Africa on a governmental level,

> on a person-to-person basis, ignorance, misunderstanding, and intolerance still persist … I never felt discriminated against or antagonized, but rather treated with warmth and friendliness. Because I spoke Mandarin, I could often understand what people said about me, and they were rarely disparaging or maligning.
>
> (Baitie 2013)

This attitude towards Africans is verified in a website, *Guancha* (Observer), where the report of an African-speaking French, English, Arabic and Chinese serving as volunteer-mediator in Yiwu market attracted 135 responses, 127 being joyful, five feeling novel, three being moved and almost all comments positive.[9] Ignorance and curiosity obviously exist, but not discrimination.

In Africa, there is a Chinese diaspora, which gradually plays a role of cultural offering, exchange and mixing, and works as a cultural centre to introduce Chinese customs and cuisine, Chinese calligraphy and dance, Chinese acupuncture and medicine, Chinese films and pop operas to attract African audiences. Chinese language has also become a popular subject in universities. At the University of Nairobi, Chinese language is a welcomed subject. When I was giving a speech at the Confucius Institute at Cairo University last year, students asked me questions in fluent Mandarin. The students in Zimbabwe University can sing lovely songs in Chinese. There are football friendship matches here and there, even carried out with Chinese and Africans in the same team to challenge another mixed team of Chinese and Africans (Liu Chang 2015).

With more and more migrants moving from China to Africa or Africa to China, there are more opportunities for contact at the grassroots level, and both sides can work and play together and directly exchange ideas. This would expand a once-existing channel for a broader and deeper P2P contact.

Contact and exchange by civil organisations

In 2003, former foreign minister Tang Jiaxuan said that China should seriously consider the role of NGOs in international affairs and strengthen China's voice in the field of NGOs. CCOs' involvement in African development cooperation embodies significant implications. CCOs have gradually become involved in China–Africa development cooperation with their own advantages. In 2006, there were 354,000 CCOs of various kinds, such as poverty reduction, educational support, society (community), agriculture, environmental protection, medical-health and different associations of walks of life. There were 435,000 CCOs in 2010, which increased to 462,000 in 2011. In 2012, the number of CCOs reached 499,000, an increase of 8.1 per cent, and CCOs became both a base and focus for further reform in China. At the end of 2013, 547,000 CCOs are registered (Huang Xiaoyong 2014).[10] Obviously, as in other parts of the world, there are some GNGOs as well.

As a major player, CCOs have taken an active part in various activities and played an important role in P2P contact, thus promoting mutual understanding between China and Africa. The first civil society dialogue between China and Africa was organized in 2008 by the Heinrich Böll Foundation (Harneit-Sievers et al. 2010). Four examples will be used to illustrate what CCOs have done to promote cultural contact and exchanges between China and Africa. They are the Chinese–African People's Friendship Association (CAPFA), China's Network of NGO International Exchanges, the International Poverty Reduction Center in China and CFPA.

CAPFA was established in 1960 and affiliated with the Chinese People's Association for Friendship with Foreign Countries (CPAFFC). It has carried out various contacts with different peoples in African, most with its African counterpart, but also senior people of the society and local government. There are organisations friendly toward China in 33 African countries, including Burkina Faso which had no diplomatic relations with China. Those friendly organisations cover various fields, including politics, economy, education, culture and charity; all remain on good terms with CAPFA. In 1979–2011, CAPFA invited more than 100 delegations from 52 African countries. The most impressive activity was the visit by traditional leaders, which greatly improved their understanding of Chinese culture and China's political system, and strengthened the bilateral relations.

King Goodwill Zwelithini of the Kingdom of KwaZulu-Natal in South Africa was invited by CAPFA to visit China in 2005. He established good relations with Fujian Agriculture and Forestry University then, and would like to learn agricultural skill and Chinese language.[11]

King Otumfuo Osei Tutu II of Ashanti in Ghana visited China in 2006 with a delegation of chiefs, officials of royal family and merchants. As the Chancellor of Kwame Nkrumah University of Science and Technology, he signed a friendly cooperation agreement with Beijing Institute of Technology.

A delegation of Zambian chiefs was invited to China in 2009, exchanging ideas of ethnic policy and the new rural construction with CAPFA and other Chinese leaders.

In 2010, Ibrahim Mbombo Njoya, Sultan of the Bamoun Kingdom of Cameroon, visited Beijing, Chengdu and Guangzhou with a six-person delegation. During their stay in China, the group exchanged ideas with the State Ethnic Affairs Commission of China and other places.

On behalf of HIM Oba Okunade Sijuwade, Ooni of Ife of Nigeria, the Crown Prince Adetokunbo Sijuwade and three princes of Ile-Ife paid a friendly visit to China in 2011. The visit was aimed at strengthening the cooperation with the CAPFA and relevant Chinese enterprises, such as SINOMA, CNADC and CCECC. A six-person delegation led by Chief Kachallah Mahamat Kasser of the N'Djamena region of Chad was also invited to China by CAPFA in 2012 and visited Beijing and other cities.

Besides organising bilateral visits between China and Africa, CAPFA is also involved in coordinating various organisations in activities related to friendly relations with Africa and holding different conferences. One of its major missions is to hold a China–Africa Local Government Cooperation Forum. The first Forum on China–Africa Local Government Cooperation was held in 2012 and delegations from 40 African countries and 29 provinces of China attended. Now it is preparing the second forum, which will be held in August this year. By April 2013, 113 sister-cities had been formed between China and African countries; the number is now 120.[12] The *South Africa in Beijing* photo exhibition, organised by CAPFA under the leadership of CPAFFC and the South African Embassy in Beijing, was opened in Wangfujing Pedestrian Street on 12 August 2014. CPAFFC Vice-President Feng Zuoku and South African Ambassador Dr Bheki Langa attended and addressed the opening ceremony.[13]

The China NGO Network for International Exchanges (CNIE) caught the eyes at home and abroad for recent years. CNIE was established in 2005 and emerged as a major player in China–African P2P contact. Among various activities, the most important is the holding of China–Africa People's Forum in 2011, 2012 and 2014 respectively.

In 2011, the first forum with the theme of *Develop partnerships, promote China–Africa friendship* was co-run by CNIE and the NGO Coordination Board of Kenya in Nairobi. More than 200 participants from China and 19 African countries approved the Nairobi Declaration.

In 2012, 300 delegates from China and 35 African countries attended the second forum in Suzhou, China, with the theme of "People's Voice, People's Friendship and Cooperation for the People". Erfiki Hicham, a Moroccan PhD student at the School of International Studies at Peking University suggested that NGOs from China and Africa should create a new cooperative model that conformed to the actual conditions of China and Africa.

"Joint Efforts Towards Poverty Reduction" was the theme of the third forum, jointly held in Khartoum by CNIE and Sudan NGO Network. Some 200 delegates from China and 27 African countries discussed three topics: experience-sharing on poverty alleviation; promoting the implementation of China–Africa people-to-people friendship and partnership program; and promoting business cooperation for common prosperity. They reached a consensus, published as the *Report on China: Africa People-to-People Friendship and Partnership Program*.

CNIE also organised various activities with African NGOs and invited traditional leaders to visit China. In December 2009, CNIE, the China Family Planning Association, the Beijing NGO Association for International Exchanges and the Beijing Charity Association jointly carried out a training program on the prevention of HIV/AIDS in Harare, Zimbabwe, together with Zimbabwe New Hope Foundation and Africa Medical-Volunteer Association. CNIE also coordinated the China National Committee of Blindness Prevention, China Association for Promoting Democracy, Beijing Tongren Hospital, Anhui Foreign Economic Construction (Group) Co. Ltd. and Hainan Air Group, and carried out a "China–Africa Brightness Action" in Malawi and Zimbabwe in November 2010. Chinese doctors performed operations on more than 600 cataract patients and treated many patients free of charge.[14] The action started in 2011 and is still ongoing.[15]

CNIE has direct contact with African NGOs and it has invited African NGOs to visit China and attend the China–Africa NGO Seminar. In October 2009, 16 representatives from NGOs in Ethiopia, Zimbabwe, South Africa, Uganda, Kenya, Sudan, Tanzania and Botswana were invited to visit China under the theme of "Development of China–Africa Cooperation and Role of the Civil Society in the New Century"; they attended the China–Africa NGO Seminar entitled "Increasing Mutual Understanding, Promoting Exchanges and Cooperation". In 2010, CNIE invited 34 representatives from NGOs in Sudan, Kenya, South Africa, Zimbabwe, Zambia, Nigeria, Mauritius, Namibia, Malawi, Botswana and Ghana to visit China. During their stay in Beijing, the delegates attended the China–Africa NGO Seminar and discussed how to promote the UN MDGs, They also visited the Disabled Persons' Rehabilitation Center in Beijing and other cities to exchange ideas with Chinese partners of capacity-building, rural poverty relief, protection of disadvantaged groups, the trade union in the township enterprise, the development of minority nationalities and NGO activities in China. In April 2011, an NGO delegation headed by Pauline Musyoka, President of Kalonzo Musyoka Foundation of Kenya, was invited to China. The representatives were from Kenya, Uganda, Tanzania, Liberia, Zambia and Sierra Leone under the theme of "Promote People-to-People Exchanges, Deepen Friendly Cooperation" and they attended the China–Africa NGO Seminar. The delegation also visited local cities to learn about efforts of local governments and NGOs in poverty relief and protection of vulnerable groups.

The International Poverty Reduction Center in China (IPRCC) is another important actor engaged in development cooperation with African countries. On 14 September 2005 at the UN 60th Anniversary Summit on Development Funding, Chinese President Hu Jintao declared that "IPRCC was established in Beijing with a mission to make contributions to the Global Poverty Reduction". Launched in 2005, IPRCC is an international organization jointly initiated by the Chinese Government, the UNDP and other international organizations. With its efforts and strategic planning, IPRCC has

370 *Cooperation and dynamics*

become one of the flagship organisations in China for South–South cooperation. Its core activities are organizing international exchange on poverty reduction through sharing of knowledge, information and experiences; providing training and consultancy services to professionals involved in poverty reduction worldwide; organizing theoretical and applied research for knowledge building; policy analysis; and advocacy.

Since its establishment in 2006, IPRCC has carried various activities of development cooperation with African countries. Cooperating with international organizations to design and implement poverty reduction has held various seminars of experience sharing in development issues with officials from African countries. Through its cooperation with OECD-DAC, IPRCC has been trying to introduce Chinese experience of development and poverty reduction to Africa. It also held various conferences in Africa, exchanging experiences and lessons in agricultural development and cooperation, and the amelioration of the investment environment. IPRCC also set up two development centres in Africa: Tanzania-IPRICC and Mozambique-IPRCC.

Table 14.2 illustrates IPRCC's work in the period 2006–2013. It is impressive that, over seven years, 108 activities related to Africa were carried out, with the number of training classes of African officials (47) at the top. The most important activities include China–Africa Experience Sharing Program of different topics such as special economic zones (SPZ) and infrastructure development, agricultural development, investment environment and the China–Africa Poverty Reduction and Development Forum, which has been running continuously.

The China Foundation for Poverty Alleviation (CFPA) was founded in 1989. After making a great contribution to China's poverty alleviation, CFPA started its activities in Africa. Poverty reduction is an important area for P2P contact. In 2007, CFAP initiated "Safe Mother–Child 120 Action"

Table 14.2 IPRCC international cooperation with Africa, October 2006–October 2013

Year	IPRCC activities				
	Research	Training	Exchange	Cooperation	Total
2013		5		7	12
2012		9	1	19	29
2011	2	13	1	5	21
2010	3	6	4	3	16
2009	2	3	5	5	16
2008	2	3	1		6
2007		3			3
2006		5			5
Total	9	47	12	39	108

Source: IPRCC website (www.iprcc.org.cn/publish/page) and various reports.

in Guinea-Bissau. In 2011, CFPA established the Sudan–China El Gezira Friendship Hospital, in cooperation with the Sudan NGO partner and the Sudanese government to make an agreement in order to standardise the management. China Red Cross has also carried out its own medical assistance in Africa. In 2014, CFPA and Chinese Lingshan Public Charity Promotion Association jointly launched the "Smiling Children Africa Project". Africa Philanthropy Fund was set up in CFPA and the project is oriented specifically to donations; Ethiopia was chosen as the first country for assistance. Lingshan Public Charity Promotion Association, as the first support agency, donated RMB3 million and was committed to the donation of RMB10 million in the coming five years, specifically for free nutritious meals for children in Ethiopia. It was decided that a new country would be chosen for assistance whenever donations reached $500,000 (Zhang Mulan 2014). In 2014, it held a meeting with Chinese experts, former ambassadors to Africa and African diplomats from African embassies to discuss further action in Africa.

Other CCOs are also involved in cooperation with Africa. For educational cooperation, the China Youth Development Foundation (CYDF) set up its African department in 2011 in charge of assistance for building Hope Primary School in Africa. "Project Hope into Africa" was co-sponsored by the organisation and WECBA at the end of 2010. The project set up Hope Primary School in Tanzania and other African countries, thus providing help for the African countries that need improvements to their basic education. In order to conduct technical training to African youth, the China International Trust and Investment Corporation (CICIT) set up its business school, the BN Vocational School (BNVS).[16] The school provides free training for local talent and brings hope to young people. Another CCO, Zhongnan House, founded and headed by Huang Hongxiang, has been actively engaged in various P2P activities and has become rather popular among those involved in China–Africa relations.

CCOs are also engaged in environment protection in Africa. In 2013, the Mara Conservation Fund and East African Wildlife Society signed a cooperation agreement in Nairobi, the capital of Kenya. As the first civil organisation established by Chinese in Africa, the Mara Conservation Fund is committed to habitat protection to save endangered animals such as lions and elephant. The two sides will establish a strategic cooperative partnership, and work together to push through the international coordination and cooperation to promote the ecological environment and wildlife protection. The East African Wildlife Society will provide a co-working office for Mara Conservation Fund and the two sides will co-publish a magazine in Chinese to promote the idea of wildlife protection in China.[17]

Conclusion

In November 2006, a poll of Chinese people's knowledge about Africa was carried out by *Chinese Youth Daily*. Although 91.6 per cent of the respondents

Table 14.3 CFPA foreign aid projects, 2007–2011

No.	Date	Program	Cooperation Partner	Value in RMB 10,000	Remarks
1	December 2007	Africa maternal and child assistance in Guinea	Care Action Macao; The First Lady Foundation	400.00	Equipment
2	March 2010	Medical equipment assistance to Sudan	BTO	38.80	Medical equipment
3	April 2010	Training program of poverty alleviation capacity building for Sudan	China International Poverty Reduction Centre; BTO	56.00	Training
4	June 2010	Office equipment assistance to Sudan	BTO	6.22	Office equipment
5	June 2011	Africa poor maternal and child assistance	Care Action of Macao; The First Lady Foundation	350.00	Medical equipment
6	July 2011	Aid for Sudan Abu Oushe hospital	China National Petroleum Corporation; BTO	463.50	House, equipment, furniture
7	August 2011	Rescue in the Horn of Africa	World Food Programme; Sina	31.60	Fund
8	May 2014		Chinese Lingshan Public Charity Promotion Association	300.00	Fund

Source: CFPA website (www.cfpa.org.cn) and various reports.

said they would "follow FOCAC with interest", their knowledge about Africa is rather limited, only 18.4 per cent "very familiar with Africa" while 71.7 per cent were "a bit familiar". Regarding their impression of the continent, the first categories were "poor and backward" and "AIDS", followed by "various wildlife", "talent of sports, music and dance", "one of the origins of human civilization" and "rich products". Responding to the questionnaire of "your understanding of Africa", "hunger", "primitive" and "chaos caused by war" came first, followed by "friendly", "enthusiastic" and "full of vigor". Obviously, their impression and understanding (or misunderstanding) of Africa did not come from their own experiences, so it was most probably from the media, since the overwhelming majority of the interviewees know very little[18] about Africa. They have no idea of the history of the continent, its ancient civilization, its suffering during the slave trade, its encounters with the West and the experience of humiliation from colonialism, Almost the same can be said about Africans' impression of Chinese. A Chinese lived and worked in Africa for a long time and had contact with Africans at various levels. He wrote about Africans' understanding of the Chinese and listed ten impressions: the Chinese are hard-working; they have very limited desires and simple pleasures; Chinese goods are cheap; the Chinese have little legal consciousness; they don't pay attention to image; they disrupt markets; they don't hang together; they don't have religious beliefs; they eat everything; and they grab Africans' jobs (Liu Zhirong 2013). Although this was a summary by a Chinese, it resulted from his own experience of contact with Africans. The impressions about the Chinese are true in some sense, but the generalisation is obvious. When the Africans saw the Chinese construction workers dressed in shabby clothes, the impression of "don't pay attention to image" came out.

What do the two examples indicate? It is clear that Chinese and Africans know very little about each other and they really need P2P contact and mutual understanding to break down this barrier. It is imperative to promote P2P activities and get more people involved in China–Africa cooperation, to form a partnership within a triple coordinate system of government–enterprise–CCO (NGO in Africa). In this way, ordinary people and CCOs can fulfil the development task, which is the most important one for the time being.

As mentioned, China and Africa have rather similar historical experiences and there is a long history of P2P contact. Since FOCAC was set up, three types of cultural contact and exchange have played their role, and each has its own characteristics. P2P contact sponsored by FOCAC has several advantages, particularly large-scale, guaranteed funding and big influence. Using the organisational network, the activities cover various aspects. Since the activities are financed with the government budget, there are no worries about the funding. The government can mobilise various media to report on the activities and the news is accessible to the public. Yet there are disadvantages as well. Most obviously, the contact is connected to the organised level and so it is difficult to get to the grassroots. If the government is a good one, the result is positive; if the governance is bad, the effect might be negative. Moreover, the credibility is reduced with an element of propaganda from both sides.

As for the cultural contacts through individual efforts, they are presented or performed by everybody every day and everywhere where there are mixed Chinese and Africans. This type of contact is cultural offering and exchange, characterised by its natural features, spreading slowly and smoothly without intentional design, premeditated intervention or a governmental plan. People come and go, exchange their language, greetings and laughter, mix in an ordinary way. They do things out of their own need and willingness. There is not much immediate effect, so no counter-effect. Penetrating the daily lives of ordinary people, the cultural influence is usually mutual and lasts for a long time.

The cultural exchange organised by CCOs is the most popular type in China–Africa interaction. It can be more effective than individual exchange in a rather short time. It can also avoid the government image, so it is better perceived by ordinary people. The way of doing things can be continuous and the involvement can be very active. However, the sustainability needs both a rather highly mobilised civil society and a better source of funding to make the actors more active. Since there is a process of choice of partners and participants, it has to depend on either the government or individuals.

However different their characteristics are, P2P contacts between China and Africa are very promising, and are involved in a wide range of activities, such as cultural offering and exchange, development cooperation, experience sharing, medical assistance, poverty reduction, educational cooperation and environment protection.

Most Chinese scholars have argued that P2P contact between China and Africa should be emphasised in order to strengthen China's "soft power" – that is, the promotion of Chinese culture, or the amelioration of China's image in Africa. This approach is problematic. It is essential to get a clear idea of the nature and purpose of P2P contact, which is neither propaganda nor what Joseph Nye termed "soft power" (Nye 2004) but cultural interaction, cultural offering and cultural mixing. It is a means of mutual learning and mutual understanding, not a kind of "soft power" (Cooke 2009). It is understandable that the strategy of public diplomacy becomes an important tool in the creation of a positive image of China abroad. I do not agree with the use of the expression since the connotations are harmful.

First, the word "power" itself used in the context of international relations is usually linked with the meaning of coercion, threat, force or military control. This does not quite fit China's traditional philosophy of peace under the heaven or peaceful coexistence. Second, Joseph Nye coined this concept at a time when the hard power of the United States is declining. It is an imperative for the United States, a superpower, to find another kind of power to exert its influence, and thus to develop the ability to attract and co-opt rather than coerce, using force or money, as a means of persuasion. It is natural for a big power that is used to controlling the world with force. Yet China is pursuing a policy of peaceful rise and calls for the building of a harmonious world. To use the concept of "soft power" would be contradictory to its principle. Moreover, to encourage or seek "soft power" may scare away the old friends of developing countries, especially those small and weak nations (Li Anshan 2017: 178–179).

If we return to the process of P2P contact, which is the equal exchange of ideas without superiority and inferiority to promote cultural contact and P2P exchange, the following suggestions are offered.

1. Set up a joint cultural committee. The task of the committee is threefold:
    - Introduce basic textbooks for both sides – concise histories of China by Chinese historians and of African history by African historians.

In addition, it should also prepare and authorise the introduction of Chinese culture and African culture, and the world cultural heritage of China and African countries.
- Give long-term cultural thinking regarding the impact of the development strategy or big investment projects on local culture or ethnic communities.
- Be in charge of appointing cultural consultants for both sides, thus reducing the risk of offending a partner's cultural taboos or violating their customs.
2. Promote CCSs' (NGOs in Africa) involvement in China–Africa cooperation. The governments of both sides can act in three aspects:
    - Carry out public diplomacy in order to educate the masses about the importance of international cooperation.
    - Include the CCO (NGO in Africa) in the FOCAC framework and increase the opportunity for their engagement in trilateral cooperation (government–enterprise–CCO or NGO) for various activities such as teaching work and medical service in primary schools and hospitals built by an aid project, professional training or vocational education.
    - Make laws related to international cooperation to regulate their actions in the locality.
3. Encourage enterprises' engagement in P2P contact and cultural exchange, both in China and Africa:
    - Promote mutual understanding of both sides in general sense.
    - Improve companies' public relations with local communities.
    - Strengthen companies' sense of corporate social responsibility.[19]
4. Provide favourable conditions for migrants in both sides since they are a natural bridge for communicating both sides.
    - Mobilise their initiative to play a positive role for cultural interaction and mutual understanding.
    - Lengthen their visa so that they would work and live decently, thus having more time to contribute to the building of better relationships.
    - Use their talent of language and their knowledge (such as knowledge of law or customs) of the settled country to develop a closer relationship and promote mutual understanding.
5. Strengthen religious contact between China and Africa.
6. P2P involvement in development cooperation should adhere the following:
    - Start from local reality. It should avoid making its own choices or decisions without taking local communities' views into consideration.
    - Contacting and coordinating with the locality is a golden rule in order to achieve the best results from development cooperation.
    - Learn from the local community or NGO.

It is claimed that the "China–Africa honeymoon" is over (Lewis 2009), yet the cooperation between China and Africa is developing rapidly. As part of

China–Africa relations, P2P has a dual purpose: to understand the other culture, thus laying a basis for better relations between China and Africa; and to make yourself understood by your partners or friends. If propaganda replaces P2P contact, the result is not only less effective or even negative, but the friendship may be damaged.

Notes

1 During the 1950s, there were 44 national civil organizations; in the 1960s, there were fewer than a hundred. The year 1989 witnessed 1600 CCOs and 200,000 local ones. In 2006 there were 354,000 CCOs of various kinds, such as poverty reduction, support for education, society (community), agriculture, environmental protection, medical health and associations from different walks of life. There were 435,000 CCOs in 2010, which increased to 462,000 in 2011. In 2012, the number of CCOs reached 499,000, an increase of 8.1 per cent, and the CCO became both base and focus for further reform in China. At the end of 2013, 547,000 CCOs were registered. An annual survey of CCOs has been published in China since 2008.
2 An accident occurred in a cinema in Shanghai on 20 February 1937. When the film *Ethiopia*, a documentary about the Ethiopian people's armed struggle against Italy, was shown, a group of Italian marines attacked the audience and destroyed the film projector, which caused great anger among the people in Shanghai.
3 *People's Daily*, 22 May 1952.
4 Except for those otherwise indicated, all data are taken from the FOCAC website: www.focac.org/eng/ltda
5 "A lifelong African dream: A Chinese couple devotes themselves to promoting African culture". http://news.sogou.com/ntcweb?level=2&show=all&from=newsretry&g_ut=3&url=http%3A%2F%2Fwww.bjreview.com.cn%2Fspecial%2F2014-04%2F29%2Fcontent_616753.htm.
6 "Hao Ge & Hao Di: popular African brothers in China". https://v.youku.com/v_show/id_XMzU2NTE5NTQxNg==.html
7 "African merchants thrive in China". http://english.cntv.cn/program/newshour/20120720/110441.shtml
8 China Africa Project, "Leading China scholar Li Anshan recalls his experiences teaching African students". www.chinaafricaproject.com/leading-china-scholar-li-anshan-recalls-his-experiences-teaching-african-students-translation
9 "Senegalese merchant turned out to be a foreign mediator for the dispute mediation commission in Yiwu". www.guancha.cn/video/2015_02_04_308534.shtml
10 The Ministry of Civil Affairs is in charge of registration of CCO, while the China Network for International Exchanges (CNIE), established in 2005, is responsible for various exchange activities with international NGOs.
11 "Zulu King 'embracing enthusiastically' Chinese elements: Plant mushroom, raise rice and leaning Chinese is important". www.nanfei8.com/news/nanfei/2013-03-28/3107.html
12 www.cifca.org.cn/Web/SearchByZhou.aspx?zhouID=3&zhouName=%b7%c7%d6%de%E3%80%82
13 "*South Africa in Beijing* exhibition launches". www.capfa.org.cn/en/news_js.asp?id=840&fatherid=238

14 "2010 China-Africa Brightness Action". www.cnie.org.cn/english/NewsInfo.asp? NewsId=1178
15 "Chinese doctors to perform free eye operations". www.herald.co.zw/chinese-doctors-to-perform-free-eye-operations. In December 2014, Shanxi Province in China received the task of helping Togo and Cameroon in terms of the Brightness Action Project.
16 Established in China in 2005, the BNVS is China's first tuition-free, non-profit charitable vocational school at the senior secondary level. CITIC BNVS was established in Angola 2014 (Li Xiaoyu 2019).
17 "Chinese NGO cooperated with East African NGO to protect wildlife". http://gongyi.sina.com.cn/gyzx/2013-07-03/111543912.html
18 "Africa will be like China in 30 years". http://zqb.cyol.com/content/2006-11/06/content_1563126.htm
19 In 2009, we visited the headquarters of China Road and Bridge Corporation in Nairobi and had an interview with the manager. He listed a lot of things the company had donated to the local society, such as facilities for primary schools and money to charities for local people after disasters. Yet there was a high wall around the headquarters and there was no communication with the outside world except for the work, nor was there any information available about the company. Few local people knew what the China Road and Bridge Corporation did in Kenya.

References

2010 China–Africa Brightness Action. 2010. www.cnie.org.cn/english/NewsInfo.asp?NewsId=1178

Africa will be like China in 30 years. 2006. http://zqb.cyol.com/content/2006-11/06/content_1563126.htm

African merchants thrive in China. http://english.cntv.cn/program/newshour/20120720/110441.shtml

Anonymous. 2018. A Senegalese businessman's road to success from Yiwu. *China Daily*, 22 September. www.chinadaily.com.cn/kindle/2018-09/22/content_36964136.htm

Amoah, Lloyd G. Adu. 2012. Africa in China: Affirming African agency in Africa–China relations at the people to people level. In James Shikwati, ed., *China–African partnership: The quest for a win–win relationship*. Nairobi: Inter Region Economic Network, 104–115.

April, Yazini. 2015. Civil society participation and China–Africa cooperation. *Pambazuka News*. http://pambazuka.org/en/category/features/60701

Baitie, Zahra. 2013. On Being African in China. *The Atlantic*, 28 August. www.theatlantic.com/china/archive/2013/08/on-being-african-in-china/279136

Bodomo, A. 2012. *Africans in China: A sociocultural study and its implications for Africa–China relations*. New York: Cambria Press.

Brenner, D. 2012. Are Chinese NGOs going out? The role of Chinese NGOs and GONGOs in Sino-African relations. *Journal of Public & International Affairs* 22: 31–152.

Chen Yingqun. 2014. Chinese, African artists donate to defeat Ebola. www.chinadaily.com.cn/china/2014-08/25/content_18483941.htm

China Africa Project. 2015. Leading China scholar Li Anshan recalls his experiences teaching African students. www.chinaafricaproject.com/leading-china-scholar-li-anshan-recalls-his-experiences-teaching-african-students-translation.

Chinese doctors to perform free eye operations. 2013. www.herald.co.zw/chinese-doctors-to-perform-free-eye-operations

Chinese NGO cooperated with East African NGO to protect wildlife. 2013. http://gongyi.sina.com.cn/gyzx/2013-07-03/111543912.html.

Cooke, Jennifer. 2009. China's soft power in Africa. In Carola McGiffert, ed., *Chinese soft power and its implications for the United States: Competition and cooperation in the developing worlds*. Washington, DC:CSIS Report.

Daddi, K.M. & Zhang Yongpeng. 1997. The establishment of diplomatic relations between China and Ethiopia and the evolution of the relations, 1949–1970. *West Asia and Africa* 5: 9–32.

Deng Guosheng. 2013. *Strategy and means of internationalization of Chinese civil organizations*. Beijing: China Social Sciences Press.

Feng Zuoko. 2012. A survey of people's diplomacy of the Chinese–African People's Friendship Association. *Public Diplomacy Quarterly* 11: 5–11.

Global Times. 2016. Shanghai old woman raised an abandoned Black boy for 15 years with love beyond family bond, 1 June. http://world.huanqiu.com/photo/2014-06/2736818.html

Gui Tao. 2012. *This is Africa*, Beijing: Encyclopedia of China Publishing House.

Harneit-Sievers, Axel et al., eds. 2010. *Chinese and African perspectives on China in Africa*. Nairobi: Pambazuka Press.

Hao Ge & Hao Di. Popular African brothers in China. https://v.youku.com/v_show/id_XMzU2NTE5NTQxNg==.html.

Hevi, E. 1963. *An African student in China*. London: Pall Mall.

Huang Xiaoyong, ed., 2014. *Annual report on Chinese civil organizations (2014)*. Beijing: Social Sciences Academic Press.

Lai Yulin. 2013. Civil organization's engagement in foreign aid: China Foundation for Poverty Alleviation's aid to Africa. *International Forum* 15(1): 36–42.

Lewis, Ian. 2009. China in Africa: The honeymoon is over. *Petroleum Economist*, 18 November.

Li Anshan & Liu Haifang. 2013. The evolution of the Chinese policy of funding African students and an evaluation of the effectiveness. Draft report for UNDP. Not formally published.

Li Anshan. 2000. *A history of Chinese overseas in Africa*. Beijing: Chinese Overseas Publishing House.

Li Anshan. 2006. *Social history of Chinese overseas in Africa: Selected documents (1800–2005)*. Hong Kong: Hong Kong Press for Social Sciences.

Li Anshan. 2011 *Chinese medical cooperation in Africa: With special emphasis on the medical teams and anti-malaria campaign*. Uppsala: Norkiska Afrikainstitutet.

Li Anshan. 2012. China and Africa: Cultural similarity and mutual learning. In J. Shikwati, ed., *China–African partnership – The quest for a win-win relationship*. Nairobi: Inter Region Economic Network, pp.93–97.

Li Anshan.2012a. Neither devil nor angel-The role of the media in Sino-African relations, 17 May, Opinion Pambazuka News (later appeared in allAfrica website. http://allafrica.com/stories/201205180551.html.

Li Anshan. 2015. 10 questions about migration between China and Africa. http://blogs.nottingham.ac.uk/chinapolicyinstitute/2015/03/04/10-questions-about-migration-between-china-and-africa

Li Anshan 2017. Probe on the sustainability of China Africa political cooperation. In Su Ge, ed., *Theory and practice of diplomacy with great powers with Chinese characteristics*. Beijing: World Knowledge Press.

Li Anshan. 2019. *The social and economic history of the Chinese overseas in Africa* (3 vols). Nanjing: Jiangshu People's Press.

Li Zhigang et al. 2009. An African enclave in China: The making of a new transnational urban space. *Eurasian Geography and Economics* 50(6): 699–719.

A lifelong African dream: A Chinese couple devotes themselves to promoting African culture. 2014. http://news.sogou.com/ntcweb?level=2&show=all&from=newsretry&g_ut=3&url=http%3A%2F%2Fwww.bjreview.com.cn%2Fspecial%2F2014-04%2F29%2Fcontent_616753.htm

Liu Chang. 2015. China–Zimbabwe football friendship match. http://gb.cri.cn/42071/2015/02/23/7211s488 0002.htm.

Liu Jian. 2015. Remembering Nelson Mandela. *Chinafrica* 7: 6–27.

Liu Zhirong. 2013. Ten impressions about the Chinese by Africans. www.aisixiang.com/data/62701.html.

Long Xiaonong & Chen Yue. 2013. NGO and China's international influence and construction of discourse in Africa. *Modern Communications* 7: 7–61.

Lu Ting-en. 1997. China–African relations during the early 1950s. *West Asia and Africa* 1: 8–44.

Ma Jian. 1951. The imperialist invasion to Egypt and the Egyptians' struggle. *People's Daily*, 19 November.

Mohan, G., Lampert, B., Tan-Mullins, M. & Chang, D. 2014. *Chinese migrants and Africa's development*. London: Zed Books.

Monson, J. 2009. *Africa's freedom railway: How a Chinese development project changed lives and livelihoods in Tanzania*. Bloomington, IN: Indiana University Press.

Nye, Joseph. 2004. *Soft power: The means to success in world politics*. New York: PublicAffairs.

People's Daily. 1950. Mao Zedong' telegraph to South African Indian National Congress, 29 May.

People's Daily. 1950. He Xiangning's talk opposed to the Group Areas Act issued by the South African government, 20 September.

Ran Jijun. 2015. Media interactions between China and Africa: Concepts, paradigms and features. *West Asia and Africa* 1: 43–160.

Senegalese merchant turned out to be a foreign mediator for the dispute mediation commission in Yiwu. 2015. www.guancha.cn/video/2015_02_04_308534.shtml

Shen Fuwei. 1990. *China and Africa: Relations of 2000 Years*. Beijing: Zhonghua Book Company.

Shen Xipeng, 2018. *A study on China aided construction of Tanzania–Zambia Railway*. Heifei: Huangshan Publishing House.

Shweder, R.A. 2000. Moral maps, "First World" conceits, and the new evangelists. In L.E. Harrison & S.P. Huntington, eds. 2000. *Culture matters: How values shape human progress*. New York: Basic Books.

South Africa in Beijing exhibition launches. www.capfa.org.cn/en/news_js.asp?id=840&fatherid=238

Sulliven, M.J. 1994. The 1988–89 Nanjing anti-African protests: Racial nationalism or national racism? *The China Quarterly* 138: 438–457.

Wang Tieya, ed. 1982. *A compilation of old foreign treaties, vol. 1*. Beijing: SDX Joint Publishing Company.

Wang Xuejun. 2009. African NGO and China–Africa relations. *West Asia and Africa* 8: 6–61.

Wei Hong. 2009. The pressure of African NGO on China–Africa relations and the counter measure. *Socialism Studies* 4: 37–141.

Zhang Mulan. 2014. A try in Africa for China's philanthropy: From government to people. *China Philanthropy Times*, 20 May. www.gongyishibao.com/html/yaowen/6478.html

Zhang Xiang. 2014. *Selected songs for Chinese–African friendship*. Beijing: World Affairs Press.

Zhang Zhongxiang. 1993. A glorious page in modern history of China–African relations: The Chinese people's support for the Ethiopian anti-Italian war. *West Asia and Africa* 2: 6–70.

Zhao Minghao. 2010. China–Africa people-to-people contact: Development and challenge. *International Perspective* 6: 9–62.

Zulu King 'embracing enthusiastically' Chinese elements: Plant mushroom, raise rice and leaning Chinese is important. 2013. www.nanfei8.com/news/nanfei/2013-03-28/3107.html

15 Cultural similarities and mutual learning

Introduction

Africa is a continent of human origins with a long history, and African culture has made a tremendous contribution to the world in various aspects (Diop 1987).[1] It has become fashionable to cite Hegel's statement in *Philosophy of History* as a typical biased view that Africa "is not a historical continent; it shows neither change nor development", and that its peoples were "capable of neither development nor education". If Hegel's statement is understood in terms of the lack of archaeological discovery at the time, which had little influence on the study of history, another contemporary statement of the Regius Professor of Modern History at Oxford University is particularly irrational and insulting. In his opening remarks of the first lecture of a series on 28 November 1963, Professor Hugh Trevor-Roper stated: "Perhaps, in the future, there will be some African history to teach. But at present there is none: there is only the history of the Europeans in Africa. The rest is darkness … and darkness is not a subject of history" (Trevor-Roper 1963). Even more intolerable was French President Nicolas Sarkozy's speech in Senegal on 26 July 2007, which claimed that the tragedy of Africa is that Africans have not completely entered history and now live too much in the paradise of missing Africa's childhood and they never rush to the future (*Le Monde* 2007).[2] This assertion not only shows his ignorance, but also his contempt for and arrogance towards the African people. In 2008, more than 20 African experts and scholars published a book entitled *L'Afrique réspond à Sarkozy – Contre le discours de Dakar*, which refutes Sarkozy's insulting remarks to the African people. There is a call from historians that a textbook of African history should be compiled for Western countries to help them improve their knowledge of Africa to a proper level (Rey 2008).

Human beings live in different natural surroundings and have gradually developed different cultures. The African and Chinese have historical-cultural similarities and differences as well. Therefore, they can share the commonalities, learn from each other, yet retain the differences. The 21st century has shown paradoxical signs, with promises and failures evident. During this ambiguous time, could China and Africa learn from each other? This chapter

DOI: 10.4324/9781003220152-18

addresses this question. First, I analyse the similarities in history and culture between China and Africa. "History" is easy to understand; however, "culture" is a rich but ambiguous term with countless possible interpretations. I would like to narrow it down to a more concrete meaning. Samuel Huntington considers that language and religion are two major factors of any culture or civilisation (Huntington 1996). I do not discuss these two major elements here; instead, in this chapter "culture" specifically means "values". This relates to culture as "community-specific ideas about what is true, good, beautiful and efficient" (Shweder 2000: 163; Li Anshan 2018). Then the subject of mutual learning between Chinese and Africans is studied, with an exploration of the challenges that both China and Africa are facing.

Historical similarities between China and Africa

There are several similarities in the history of China and African countries. It is now acknowledged by the world that Africa and China both have a long history and splendid civilisation, enjoyed a glorious time and were admired by early visitors. Both later experienced the plunder of the great powers, resisted the invasions bravely and were crushed brutally by the aggressors and colonialists. It is time for China and Africa to finally stand up and try to develop their own goals.

Africa is regarded as among the birthplaces of human beings and the origin of language expansion (Armitage et al. 2011; Atkinson 2011, 2012; Cysouw et al. 2012). The African continent contributed various civilisations to human development, such as the Egyptian and Nubian civilisations nurtured in the Nile Valley, Carthaginian and Arabic civilisations in the north, Ethiopian civilisation and Swahili civilisations in the east, the Ghana, Mali and Songhai empires, and the Nok, Ife and Asante cultures in the west. There are other cultural regions in central Africa – for example, Kanem-Bornu Kingom in the Chadian Basin and Kongo Kingdom in the Congo Basin – while the southern Great Zimbabwe enjoyed a long-time reputation of gold trade spread to the eastern coast in early times, which attracted the Portuguese to enter the kingdom in later years (Sellassie 1972; Davidson 1978; Adams 1978; Stevens 1978; Connah 1987; Du Bois 1992; Yamauchi 2001; Holl 2015). The Chinese culture contains various branches besides two major civilisations along two rivers, the Yellow River and the Yangtze River (Gernet 1996).

The Europeans who visited African continent acknowledged or even praised the splendid scenery. In the 17th century, Dutch explorer Dapper (1635–1689) mentioned the civilised people with their own law and well-organized policemen in Benin Kingdom (located in today's Nigeria), and their fair and friendly attitude towards the Dutch traders in their land (Fage 1969). British explorer Mungo Park (1771–1806) was very excited when he saw a unbelievable civilised scenery in Segu, an inland town in present-day Mali, with so many people and boats (Davidson 1978). Compared with the inhumane machinery in Europe in the mid-19th century, German geographer Heinrich Barth highly praised Kano's textile industry and thought Kano should be one of the happiest countries in the world (Davidson 1960). French head of the exploration team Hourst was very much moved when he visited the ruins of the capital of Songhai Empire in 1895–1896, claiming that the empire was the most powerful country not only in Africa but also in the world (De Rivières 1965). H.R. Palmer even claimed that some of the early chiefs of Bornu Kingdom in the 12th century were more civilised than some European kings at the same period (Du Bois 1992). The Dutch ambassadors visited Kongo Kingdom and called on the King of Kongo in 1642. They were careful to pay him the respect they would give to a king in Europe – for example, dropping to their knees. About one and half centuries later, British envoys led by George Macartney (1737–1806) visited China in 1793 and called on the Qianlong emperor. He knelt on one knee without kowtowing as a compromise between two sides. The "China cult" or cult of "Chinoiserie" and "sinophilism" in Europe during the Enlightenment period indicates the influence of Chinese culture on the continent. Although the rise and decline of Sinomania marked a natural course, even in 1769 Pierre Poivre could proclaim that "China offers an enchanting picture of what the whole world might become, if the laws of that empire were to become the laws of all nations. Go to Peking! Gaze upon the mightiest of mortals [Confucius]; he is the true and perfect image of Heaven" (Clarke 1997: 42). It is generally recognised that the spread of Chinese culture in Europe during the Enlightenment became a historical event (Dawson 1967; Clarke 1997; Hobson 2004; Zhang Xiping 2014).

In the forced migration of labour, Africa and China share a common fate. During the Atlantic slave trade, the African continent suffered a great deal and Africans were forced to move to Americas to work as plantation slaves. The global labour migration has brought a lot of wealth to Europe and North America, which constitutes one of the main sources of primitive accumulation (Williams 1944). About 22 million Black Africans were exported to the rest of the world from 1500 to 1890 (Ogot 1992: 83). Most were sent to the Americas, thus laying the foundation for the development of Europe and making a direct contribution to the British Industrial Revolution. The total annual average value of Atlantic commerce grew from £3.241 in 1501–1550 to £57.696 million in 17611–80, and £231.046 million in 1848–1850 (Inikori 2002: 479). Even during the slave trade, a lot of Chinese indentured labourers were illegally sent to various places in the world without the Chinese government's permission. After the abolition of slave trade, the indentured labour system formally came to the stage, and many Chinese indentured labourers spread across Asia, the Americas, Europe and Africa (Chen Hansheng 1980s; Wu Fengbin 1988).[3]

China and Africa underwent similar misery during the imperialist partition. Africa suffered a great deal and was scrambled by European powers during the Berlin Conference while China had almost the same experience.

Because China was too big to be swallowed by one country, the imperialist powers could only divide the Chinese territory among themselves as "spheres of influence". During the second Opium War in 1860, Britain and France destroyed the Summer Palace in China and plundered its treasures. French writer Victor Hugo condemned the crime, calling Britain and France two "deux bandits", and hoped that one day France would feel guilty and return what it had plundered from China (Hugo 1861; Cheng Zhenhou 2011).[4] The same thing occurred in African countries, such as Egypt, Benin Kingdom in Nigeria, the Sudan and later Ethiopia, where the treasure house was crushed and wealth was taken away. During and after the partition, both Africans and Chinese fought bravely against the foreign invasion, yet were crushed by the aggressors (Crowder 1971; Hu Sheng 1952; Department of History of Peking University 1973). Both suffered different results – either losing their sovereignty and becoming a colony or paying a huge price (Li Yumin 2010; Hou Zhongjun 2012).[5]

Being development partners, China and African countries are now on their way towards striving for a better society for their people. Of course, there will be many difficulties and more obstacles in the days to come. "It was the best of times, it was the worst of times" was how Charles Dickens described the period of the French Revolution. We are now living in a similar situation. In China, on one hand, we have achieved a great deal in the economic field and people's lives are getting better. We have various ways to express ourselves and enjoy more freedom than ever before. Yet we are gradually losing many good things, such as virtue, friendship, generosity and endurance. There are also concerns about the security of our food and the environment, and the basic requirements for social stability. That is why former Premier Wen Jiabao remarked after the National People's Congress on 15 March 2007 that although China had experienced rapid growth, she could not remain complacent and China's growth was "unsteady, unbalanced, uncoordinated and unsustainable" (Wen Jiabao 2011).

Africa is also facing a similar situation. We have seen many good signs of Africa rising, such as GDP continuing to grow at 4–5 per cent for more than a decade at the beginning of the 21st century; many countries have established a stable political structure; several countries have made great progress in their economies, either winning praise from the international community such as Rwanda, Ethiopia and Angola, or paying off their foreign debt – Nigeria and the Sudan are examples. "Africa's economic growth accelerated after 2000, making it the world's third-fastest growing region ... Many countries enacted microeconomic reforms, and this was correlated with more rapid growth." In 2008, Africa's collective GDP was US$1.6 trillion and African consumers' spending was worth US$860 billion; the number of African mobile phone subscribers reached 316 million and 20 companies had revenue of more than $3 billion. Moreover, Africa's share of the world's uncultivated and arable land is 60 per cent (McKinsey Global Institute 2010). *The Economist* even published a special issue entitled "The Hopeful Africa – Africa Rising" (*The*

Economist 2011). At the same time, Africa faces very serious problems. The majority of people have not enjoyed the results of economic development and many still live in poverty; the "resource curse" has gradually fermented in several countries with rich natural resources, which has either resulted in political disasters or created serious social problems. Additionally, Western forces have interfered shamelessly in African affairs, bringing about the breakdown of the Khadafi regime which created great disorder in the Sahelian belt.

Cultural similarities between China and Africa

There are many cultural similarities between China and Africa. Four elements are stressed here: collectivism, respect for the elderly, a sense of equality, and tolerance or forbearance.

Collectivism and a sense of community

Chinese and African values emphasise collectivism more than individualism. Collectivism can be described in different ways, such as communalism (*Ujama*), nationalism and socialism, or expressed in different ways, such as Blyden's Black consciousness (Blyden 1967), Lembede's philosophy of Africanism (Gerhart 1978), Nkrumah's Pan-Africanism (Nkrumah 1963), Senghor's negritude (Senghor 1964), Nyerere's *Ujama* (Nyerere 1968) and Mazrui's "Pax Africana" (Mazrui 1980:113–138). In China, collectivism as a basic concept and survival skill has existed for thousands of years. Additionally, China has embraced socialism as her leading ideology in her contact with the West in modern times, which reflects how the concept fits with Chinese society. In Africa, there are four levels of agreed-upon shared values: individual, national, regional and continental. Although the first level is individual – that is, "the values include those inherent in universal and inalienable human rights" – many values reflect collectivism, such as "tolerance", "participation in governance and development processes", "reciprocal solidarity in times of need and sharing", "dignity and respect", "justice", "sense of fairness", "equality of persons", "respect for the elderly", "integrity" and "community cohesion and inclusive societies" (African Union Commission 2009: 31).

South African scholar Metz has studied the relationship between African philosophy and Chinese Confucianism (Metz 2007, 2014, 2015). In his analysis, both Confucian and African traditions treasure human sociability or social nature. A person can be a person only because they exist in relationship with others. This kind of personality is not that of Robinson Crusoe in Daniel Defoe's work *The Life and Strange Surprising Adventures of Robinson Crusoe*, who cannot exist when he is drifting away from society, but exists at a higher level that is only expressed in a person's relationship with other members of society. Therefore, being generous, calm and humble, polite and respectful to others is regarded as good character (Mokgoro 1998). In this sense, "harmonious" and "filial" are expressions emphasising a relationship with others.

The stress on mutual or community relationships is quite different from Western thinking, which places great emphasis on independence, freedom, control, self-confidence, particularity and self-expression. Metz notices that Confucius thought highly of *Ren* (仁) or the principle of virtue, benevolence or humanity. He links this with the same character that the Akan cherish: one who thinks that possessing virtue is better than possessing gold. If only there is virtue, the town will prosper. There are only two themes in the African philosophy of harmony: human beings' interdependence and sympathy/help for others. There is no sense of hierarchy (Metz 2007, 2014, 2015).

A common essence is embodied in Confucianism and Ubuntu, and both pay much attention to the community – that is, the relationship between individual and community and the key interests of the community. Ubuntu has another characteristic: the value of partiality of an individual towards all the persons who have social relations with them, especially their responsibilities towards their family. The individual also has the duty to take care of any strangers, since they are members of human society – that is, to show hospitality. This kind of hospitality is different from the hospitality of the West, which is based on respect towards individuals and helps the other to realise their individual purpose, but does not take the other as a member of one's own family. The third is respect towards the elderly, which will be discussed later. This view contains two important points. First, there are quite a few commonalities between Confucian tradition and Ubundu tradition, especially in the social relationship between individual and community. Second, the same concepts and ideologies of Africa and China form the different system of ideology and principles of practice that constitute the important basis of South–South cooperation (Bell & Metz 1998: 88–95).

Respect for the elderly

China and Africa share the value of respect for the elderly. In China, "to respect the elderly and cherish the young" (尊老爱幼) is one of the leading principles of virtue. No matter whether you are a good person or not, you must respect the elderly. In Africa, there are many proverbs to describe the same principle. For example, "An elder is a library" (Tanzania and other countries), "If you want to learn proverbs, go to ask the elders" (Nigeria), "Bald head and white-haired should be respected because they are the symbol of excellence" (Liberia), "When a person gets old, the wisdom comes" (Congo), "The elderly can tell the best stories" (the Swahili), "An old hunter won't fall in the trap" (Southern Africa), "The advice is the salt of dishes" (Ghana) (Li Baoping 2011: 39). Both Chinese and Africans realise from their tradition that time creates experience, and the elderly's knowledge can serve others and the whole community, thus providing the best lessons. That is why "respect for the elderly" is a central Chinese and African shared value.

A sense of equality

The Chinese and African cultures both emphasise equality and a sense of sharing. Although equality is a modern concept, and one of the most important concerns in social movement and human history, both Chinese and African people have a long history of cherishing equality. The concept was embodied in ancient Chinese philosophy and expressed in various ways. Zi Xia (子夏, 507–400 BCE), one of Confucius's students, once said, "All men under the Heaven are brothers", and there is a strong sense of equality in Confucianism. Confucius (孔子, 551–479 BCE) himself claimed this principle as his educational philosophy: "Education for all", or "To teach everybody without prejudice". In another case, he even treated teacher and student as equal by saying "teaching and learning improve each other". As another Confucian thinker and a typical equalitarian, Mencius (孟子, 372–289 BCE) was famous for his ideology of *min beng* (people-oriented) community. He once described his ideal society by saying, "Treat your elders as elders, and extend it to the elders of others; treat your young ones as young ones, and extend it to the young ones of others" (Liang Hui Wang to Mencius, in Mencius 1960). It is noticeable that here every elder is equal, and so is every youngster. The principle of equality has been understood as that of socialism, and also claimed as the guiding principle of the Communist Party of China. In African shared values, "reciprocal solidarity in times of need and sharing", "dignity and respect", "justice", a "sense of fairness" and "equality of persons" all indicate the importance of equality. Human beings should care for each other and treat others as equal, as their own family – that is the ideal world for both China and Africa. In world history, to realise the principle of equality was not only one of the major aims of revolutions in Britain, France and America, but was also highly praised in the West. However, in international politics the concept that "might is right" reigns everywhere and equality is never mentioned. Chairman Mao Zedong always emphasised the same status of Chinese and Africans. When talking with African friends, he mentioned that China and African countries were equal: "The mutual relations between us are that of brotherhood, not father–son relations" (Mao Zedong 1994: 538). This has also been the view of other Chinese leaders.[6]

Tolerance and forbearance

China and Africa both stress the value of tolerance or forbearance. When his student Zigong (子贡, 520–456 BCE) asked him about the most important doctrine in life, Confucius answered, "That should be 'forbearance'" – in other words, what you do not want done to yourself, do not do to others ("Zhigong asked" in *Confucius* 1980). In the contemporary world, the concepts of "tolerance" and "forbearance" have become more important since some countries like to use their own value standards to judge other cultures. In Africa, "tolerance" is a tradition and a philosophy as well as a way of life. Only by practising this principle can African people maintain their "community cohesion and inclusive societies". For example, the former Senegal's President Senghor is a Roman Catholic, yet he governed a Muslim country without any trouble. As a pious Catholic, Tanzanian President Julius Kambarage Nyerere skilfully managed a nation with both Muslims and Christians. Family members with different religious views live in harmony.[7] As an important principle of social relations in the daily life of the Chinese people, this doctrine has also left some imprint on China's foreign policy. The most criticised policy in China's relationship with African countries is the principle of no-strings-attached or non-conditionality. China follows its own principle of non-interference, thus attaching no political conditions to its assistance to Africa. However, certain countries like to criticise others for their own interests, be they economic, political or cultural. And the criticism is usually carried out under the cover of "universal values" or "international standards", taking Western doctrines or principles as universal. That practice has worked for some time in modern history, but it is no longer effective.

Second, both China and Africa are facing similar challenges in terms of the dynamic relationship between tradition and modernity. In Africa:

> Whereas in traditional communities there had always been a sense of belonging and sharing, these communities are also experiencing deprivation, powerlessness, violation of human dignity, social isolation, gender inequity, corruption and ineffective service delivery systems; thus leading people to increasingly turn to State institutions, development partners and CSOs for their survival.
>
> (African Union Commission 2009: 30)

This is the same challenge faced by Chinese society. On the one hand, the traditional communities still play an important role in social life. On the other, every tradition is experiencing erosion from the process of development. In addition to this dilemma in terms of tradition and modernity, there are other contradictions embodied in development itself, such as between collectivism and individualism, economic growth and environmental protection, state control and free market. How to make these contradictions harmonious is a tremendous challenge to both China and Africa.

What China can learn from Africa

After the analysis of the historical and cultural similarities between China and Africa, we can ask the question: Could China and Africa learn from each other? The answer is undoubtedly positive. There are two situations in mutual learning among different cultures or civilisations. One is the interlinking of different civilisations: the other is the complementarity of different civilisations (Li Anshan 2018).

The conventional thinking is that China is developing very fast and Africa should learn from China. Yet this is a lopsided view. In fact, both China and Africa should learn from each other. Let me first deal with how China can benefit from Africa (Li Anshan 2014). There are several points about which China should learn from Africa.

Harmonious relations between human and nature

First, Africa has a very strong belief in the balance between nature and human beings. People are part of nature and the two are linked in various ways. In traditional belief, land belongs to the community – it is passed down through the generations. Land and people belong to one unseparated world. African women working in the fields does not necessarily indicate male chauvinism, as the outside world usually believes; rather, it is because women, as the mothers of children, are believed to have closer links with the land – of which all the people are children. There are various rituals in relation to land or nature.

In China, although people stressed the links between human beings and nature (天人合一) in ancient times, their sense was much weaker, probably because the harsher natural conditions and the tense population forced them to get more food or necessities from the nature. In addition, after the founding of People's Republic of China, the philosophy of "human will conquer the nature" (人定胜天) was practiced, which left some unmeasurable consequences. To make things worse, the economic development since the reform of the early 1980s has put great pressure on nature, owing to the increasing demands for energy and resources, which obviously threatens the balance between human beings and nature. It is only in recent years that the concept of scientific development has gradually taken the lead. Respecting nature is the first thing the Chinese should learn from Africans.

Strong sense of family

African people have a very strong sense of family, a sense that the urban Chinese are now losing. No matter how rich a man is, or how high a position he holds, he has to take responsibility for his family and kin. We heard that some government minister has to take care of the whole extended family and feed various relatives who come to his house, and my African friends would send money to their families as soon as they received their scholarship salary. Doubtless, the Chinese in the countryside are now still tied to the family, which occupies a very important position in their mind. Yet individualism is gradually eroding the sense of family, especially with the rapid urbanisation and strengthening of materialism. As the basic element of social structure, family defines the balance of social structure in terms of development. To stress and maintain the role of family is the second thing that China could learn from Africa.

Women's rights in civil life

China should also learn from Africa that women generally enjoy more rights in some African countries. This may sound strange to some Chinese, who have heard of many stories about the prejudice suffered by African women. Yet fact speaks the truth. Like Chinese women, African women have played a key role in sustaining their family and kingdoms in history. In a lecture given to a community, the new Chairperson Nkosazana Dlamini-Zuma mentioned two historical facts. In North Africa in 690 CE, Dahia Al-Kahina of Mauritania, an African woman freedom fighter, resisted the invasion of the Arabs. She commanded her forces in battle, was a ferocious and courageous fighter who eventually took her own life rather than admitting defeat to the Arabs. The great African city of learning, Timbuktu of Mali, is named after a woman called Buktu, and in this city of scholarship is the medieval mosque Sankore, also founded by a woman (Dlamini-Zuma 2012). During the anti-colonial period, African women contributed a great deal to their motherland. After independence, African women surely enjoyed the political rights much earlier than their European partners.[8]

Although women in some countries are still looked down upon, as early as 1969 Liberian Angie E. Brooks was selected as chair of the UN Assembly, and she claimed that she was proud of her continent, her nation and her gender (Mazrui 1995: 915).[9] African Princess Toro Elizabeth Bagnya Nyabongo is a Ugandan lawyer, politician, diplomat, model and actress, active since the 1960s. As the first female lawyer in Uganda, she was appointed foreign minister in 1974 (Elizabeth of Toro 1983). During the 1970s and 1980s, African female ambassadors in Paris caught the eye of other countries (Mazrui 1995: 20). Now increasing numbers of African women are involved in social and political activities and have become known worldwide as Nobel Prize winners and ministers of their own countries. Two excellent women, Ellen Johnson Sirleaf and Bingu wa Mutharika, became the presidents of Liberia and Malawi respectively, and Dr Nkosazana Dlamini-Zuma is the chairperson of the AU, a unique phenomenon in world politics. In addition, in the AU and several African countries, more women are now serving the interests of Africa in general and their country and gender in particular. There is even a quota of positions reserved specifically for women. For example, in South Africa many more women have become civil servants. In 2011 there were 2382 people in the foreign ministry, 1300 women and 1082 men (Zhang Weijie 2012: 44).

While progress has been made in Africa, the situation in China has regressed somewhat. In China, there is a long tradition of prejudice against women. After the founding of the PRC, there was a great change in the concept of "superior male and inferior female" (男尊女卑), yet the prejudice against women still exists – especially in employment (Liu Xiao-nan 2005; Guo Yi-ling 2009). In the political field, some positions are reserved for women, but there are very few women in top positions. The situation has changed somewhat but is still very unbalanced. China ranks 106th in the Global Gender Gap Index 2020 issued by World Economic Forum. Since 2006, China has narrowed the gap only marginally (a gain of just two points). Owing to the fact that

> many countries have moved closer to parity, causing China to slip from 63rd position in 2006 to today's rank. The Chinese political landscape remains dominated by men. The country ranks 95th, with a score of 15.4%, on the related subindex. Women hold only two ministerial positions and make up only one-quarter of the National People's Congress membership (as of 2018).

Although China has virtually closed the educational gender gap, with both sexes achieving universal literacy, "the very skewed sex ratio at birth (885 girls per 1000 boys) weighs heavily on China's performance on the Health and Survival subindex, where it ranks 153rd and last with a score of 92.6%".[10] It is undeniable that China, with a huge population of more than 1.3 billion people, has made a great progress in the field, according to the White Paper entitled *Equality, Development and Sharing: Progress of Women's Cause in 70 Years Since New China's Founding* (State Council of PRC 2019). Yet there is still a long way to go for China to narrow the gap between men and women.[11]

Border control disputes

Borders in Africa are a very unfortunate legacy of colonialism. According to statistics, about 44 per cent of African borders are drawn by longitude and latitude, 30 per cent by straight lines and only 26 per cent by natural markers such as rivers or mountains (Boutros-Ghali 1972). This left enormous problems for Africa after independence, such as the separation of ethnic groups in different countries and problems with natural resources including mining, water and grassland, which have caused many conflicts and wars. Just think about the various border wars in Europe in modern times! Yet the first generation of African leaders used every means to prevent disaster. In the OAU Charter, it was made clear that, although they are not always rational, there would be no changes to borders and every country should respect existing borders. It is clear that African leaders have saved many lives with their wisdom and tolerance. China has borders with 14 countries and there are some conflicts with neighbouring countries, both on land and sea. In this aspect, China can learn from the African attitude or skill.

Indeed, there are many strong points in Africa from which the Chinese can learn, such as their friendliness towards outsiders, a great sense of optimism and their positive attitude towards life.

What Africa can learn from China

What can African countries learn from China? It is necessary to point out that different countries have different historical backgrounds, cultural heritage, international surroundings and economic capability (Li Anshan 2011). Therefore, no country can just copy other countries' models. Answering a question at a press conference at the fourth FOCAC, Premier Wen Jiabao said

> Many people are trying to offer prescriptions for Africa's development, such as the "Washington Consensus" or the "Beijing Model". Yet it seems to me that Africa's development should be based on its own conditions and should follow its own path. All countries have to learn from other countries' experience in development. At the same time, they have to follow a path suited to their own national conditions and based on the reality of their own countries. In the final analysis, the development of a country depends on the efforts of its own people.[12]

This shows a clear vision. China or others can offer help, but the work should be done by Africans themselves.

China has various negative lessons from copying other's models in modern times, yet sharing each other's experience and learning from the other's strong points will definitely benefit their development. China's economic success testifies that political leadership is the key to success; social stability set up the conditions for economic growth, and self-reliance with rational use of foreign aid is also important for developing countries. An emphasis on agriculture could provide a strong base for development, since if a country depends too much on the international market for basic food, it will be impacted either by the fluctuations of the international market or other countries' pressure on certain occasions (Li Anshan 2009; An Chunying 2016; He Wenping 2017; Luo Jianbo 2019). Autonomy is another experience for China's success. Autonomy means that a sovereign government has the right to govern its own affairs in various fields, and to self-reliance and self-determination in its international relations (Li Anshan 2021: 43–53).

The United States seems to be very worried that China is disseminating the China model to Africa: "While foreign observers are debating whether China is exporting its model overseas, Beijing is evidently striving to encourage African countries to adopt its governance practices in an effort to make them better client states … Spreading the China model to African countries is an integral part of China's strategy toward the continent" (Rolland 2021: 2, 24). It is true that some Chinese scholars presume that the Chinese experience of success may be suggestive for African countries and try to show how China has overcome various difficulties and developed itself. An Chunying lists several economic policies, such as alleviating poverty by developing agriculture, improving low-level industrial structure to enlarge industrial capacity and employment structure, solving under-capitalised problems, promoting the ability of the labour force to participate in economic activities by enhancing their physical health and scientific and technical knowledge, and fostering the domestic consumer market. Africa countries need concentration on their local conditions and to be aware of the strengths and weaknesses of Chinese experience in order to explore their own road of economic development (An Chunying 2016). Luo Jianbo explored the road of independent development, which may be suggestive to developing countries in three aspects: first, the technical level – that is, the specific experience and professional skill such as poverty reduction and economic development; second, the institutional level – that is, the improvement of national institutional construction and governance capacity; and third, the theoretical level – that is, China's independent spirit and the independent choice of development path (Luo Jianbo 2019: 16–18). He Wenping holds that two experiences in China could provide examples for African countries. One is to carry out gradual reform, thus situating balanced relationship of triple courses – for example, reform, development and stability, based on the concept of development with the times. Another is to have a strong government committed to development, visionary leaders and correct policies. "For developing countries in transition, it is necessary to gather the unity and will of all the people and concentrate national efforts to promote orderly economic, social and even political reforms" (He Wenping 2017: 71–74).

However, there is no reason for the United States to be so sensitive. The Republic of Liberia, the first African country established in 1847 by copying the American model, has existed for more than one and half centuries, yet it is still "the Least Developed Country".[13] There appears criticism about the "Black imperialism" (Akpan 1973) in Liberia. The United States, Great Britain and France have strongly promoted their own model in the continent since the 1960s, when most African countries won their independence. What has happened in Africa since then is now a plain fact. It is natural for African countries to choose their own way to develop themselves. The Chinese people just want to exchange experiences of development with other countries. Moreover, the Chinese government stressed that China should strictly follow three "no's" in conducting exchanges of experiences in governance: no "importing" foreign models, no "exporting" the China model and no requiring other countries to "copy" China's practices (Xi Jinping 2017). Not only the Chinese leader but also scholars have shown this attitude clearly by emphasising that different countries have their own characteristics and should not copy the models of others. They either stressed that China should learn from the African culture or other cultures (Li Anshan 2014, 2018), or emphasised that the achievement of China's development resulted from China's unique historical and cultural conditions and not from depending on "policies and rules introduced from outside", warning of the danger of copying other country's model (An Chunying 2016: 115). Sharing experience has always been a two-way process and equality, two-way exchange and adaptability are the keys to promoting the integration of Chinese experience and African development (He Wenping 2017). China should adhere to the principles of mutual equality, mutual learning and seeking common ground on major questions while reserving differences and being modest and prudent in the exchange of governing experiences (Luo Jianbo 2019: 20–22). This attitude or policy is very different from the West's way of setting up conditions to force other countries to adopt its political system.

Conclusion

In the 20th century, China and Africa shared a common destiny; the 21st century will be a century when China and Africa will develop together and make a great contribution to humankind. The similarity between China and Africa in the 20th century is mainly characterised by the partition by the imperial powers, drastic changes in society, and a revival of nationhood and state-building. However, in the 21st century, both China and African countries will face the similar destiny and common tasks – for example, building a peaceful international political order, promoting world economic development and shaping an inclusive and sustainable human community. Only in this way can China and Africa make greater contributions to humankind.

Most recently, the international community has suffered greatly from the impact of COVID-19. According to WHO data on 7 July 2021, more than four million people had died from COVID-19. More than 600,000 thousand people died in the United States alone (600,457 cases), followed by Brazil (525,112 cases) and India (404,211 cases). Africa has to go through a more grievous experience. Although the situation in China is less serious (5554 cases of death), the threat of crisis is no less than in other places.[14] The Chinese word for "crisis" (危机) is made up of two characters, meaning "danger" and "opportunity". The time of danger usually provides opportunities to those who are ready and able to use it to their advantage. Both China and Africa have made a tremendous contribution to the world throughout history. Other parts of the world have borrowed a great deal from African culture; China has just started to appreciate this treasure house but still has much to learn. As for what Africa could learn from China, the most important thing is China's efforts to uphold its sovereignty while developing its economy and combining the positive elements of the state strategy, a market economy and social stability. Regarding international aid, China's experience is to adhere to the principle of "self-reliance first, foreign aid second", so China can develop according to its own strategy. Furthermore, if a country relies too heavily on aid, it will gradually develop a "mentality of dependency". Reform is necessary, yet reform is an ongoing process of learning from your partners but not copying. Africa can look to a bright future with its rich human and natural resources if its leaders can just combine its capability and responsibility with its hardworking people.

Notes

1 The direct evidence shows that the human origin is in Africa. The earliest human skull fossils found in Africa are the most complete – from a 22 million-year-old ape to a two million-year-old human species. Research in molecular genetics in

1. recent years provided new evidence for the origin of human beings in Africa (Holl 2015). Some anthropological studies presume that world languages originated in Africa (Atkinson 2011, 2012), yet there are different opinions about this conclusion (Armitage et al. 2011).
2. "Le drame de l'Afrique, c'est que l'homme africain n'est pas assez entré dans l'histoire ... Le problème de l'Afrique, c'est qu'elle vit trop le présent dans la nostalgie du paradis perdu de l'enfance ... Le problème de l'Afrique, ce n'est pas de s'inventer un passé plus ou moins mythique pour s'aider à supporter le présent mais de s'inventer un avenir avec des moyens qui lui soient propres." President Sarkozy's speech was published by *Le Monde* on 9 November 2007, later issued formally by Elysée Presidence de la République, see "Discour á l'Université du Dakar, M le Président de la République Française, 27.05.2010".
3. Chinese indentured labourers were sent to different places from the 18th century to the early 20th century. In the period 1700–1910, there were 172,000 Chinese indentured labourers in various colonies in Africa (Li Anshan 2019: 293–359).
4. "Un jour, deux bandits sont entrés dans le palais d'Été. L'un a pillé, l'autre a incendié. La victoire peut être unevoleuse, à ce qu'il paraît. Une dévastation en grand du palais d'Été s'est faite de compte à demi entre les deux vainqueurs. On voit mêlé à tout cela le nom d'Elgin, qui a la propriété fatale de rappeler le Parthénon. Ce qu'on avait fait au Parthénon, on l'a fait au palais d'Été, plus complètement et mieux, demanière à ne rien laisser. Tous les trésors de toutes nos cathédrales réunies n'égaleraient pas ce formidable et splendide musée de l'Orient. Il n'y avait pas seulement là des chefs-d'œuvre d'art, il y avait des entassements d'orfèvrerie. Grand exploit, bonne aubaine. L'un des deux vainqueurs a empli ses poches, ce que voyant, l'autre a empli ses coffres; et l'on est revenu en Europe, bras dessus, bras dessous, en riant. Telle est l'histoire des deux bandits ... J'espère qu'un jour viendra où la France, délivrée et nettoyée, renverra ce butin à la Chine spoliée." (Victor Hugo 1861; Cheng Zhenhou 2011).
5. China was forced to sign many unequal treaties with foreign powers after 1840, and the biggest indemnity was concluded in the treaty of 1900. According to the "Austria-Hungary, Belgium, France, Germany, Great Britain, Italy, Japan, Netherland, Russia, Spain, United States and China – Final Protocol for the Settlement of the Disturbances of 1900", the indemnity is 450 million taels of silver, with a total principal and interest of 980 million taels.
6. For more details on the issue, see Li Anshan (2011).
7. Alisa is a Nigerian student and received her PhD degree from Peking University. She is a Christian while her husband is a Muslim. She told me that this kind of family is not rare in her country.
8. We understand that the European women only enjoyed universal suffrage after a long struggle after the modern state was set up: Russia in 1918, Germany in 1919, Britain in 1928, France in 1945, Italy in 1946 and Belgium in 1948 (Mowat 1980: 23).
9. The first Chinese female ambassador was Ding Xuesong, who became Ambassador to the Netherlands in 1979.
10. World Economic Forum, The Global Gender Gap Index 2020."Selected Country Performances". http://reports.weforum.org/global-gender-gap-report-2020/the-global-gender-gap-index-2020/selected-country-performances
11. The English version of the White Paper on the women issue in China can be found at http://english.www.gov.cn/archive/whitepaper/201909/20/content_WS5d8433 44c6d0bcf8c4c13ba7.html

12 "Wen Jiabao held a press conference during the Ministerial Conference of the FOCAC", 10 November 2009. www.gov.cn/ldhd/2009-11/10/content_1460418.htm
13 United Nations, Department of Economic and Social Affairs Economic Analysis, "Least Developed Country category: Liberia profile". www.un.org/development/desa/dpad/least-developed-country-category-liberia.html
14 WHO Coronavirus (COVID-19) Dashboard. World Health Organization, 7 July 2021. https://covid19.who.int/table

References

Adams, W.Y. 1978. Nubia: Corridor to Africa. Princeton, NJ: Princeton University Press.
African Union Commission. 2009. *Strategic Plan 2009–2012*. Nairobi: African Union Commission.
Akpan, M.B. 1973. Black imperialism: Americo-Liberian rule over the African peoples of Liberia, 1841–1964. *Canadian Journal of African Studies*, 7(2): 217–236.
An Chunying. 2016. China's experience and lessons for African countries' economic development. *Journal of Shanghai Normal University (Philosophy and Social Science Edition)* 2: 108–117.
Armitage, Simon J., Jasim, Sabah A., Marks, Anthony E., Parker, Adrian G., Usik, Vitaly I. & Uerpmann, Hans-Peter. 2011. The southern route "out of Africa": Evidence for an early expansion of modern humans into Arabia. *Science* 331(6016): 453–456.
Atkinson, Q.D. 2011. Phonemic diversity supports a serial founder effect model of language expansion from Africa. *Science* 332(6027): 346–349.
Atkinson, Q.D. 2012. Response to comment on "phonemic diversity supports a serial founder effect model of language expansion from Africa". *Science* 335(6072): 1142.
Bell, D. & Metz T. 1998. Confucianism and Ubuntu: Reflections on a dialogue between Chinese and African tradition. *Journal of Chinese Philosophy* 38: 8–95.
Blyden, E.D. 1967. *Christianity, Islam and the negro race*. Edinburgh: Edinburgh University Press.
Boutros-Ghali, B. 1972. *Les Conflits de frontieres en Afrique*. Paris: Editions techniques et économiques.
Chen Hangsheng. 1980s, *Compilation of the selected historical data of Chinese laborers going abroad (Books I–X)*. Beijing: Zhonghua Book Company.
Cheng Zhenhou. 2011. Qui est le Capitaine Butler? A propos d'une lettre de Victor Hugo sur le palais d'eté. *Revue d'Histoire Littéraire de la France* 111: 891–903.
Clarke, J.J. 1997. *Oriental enlightenment: The encounter between Asian and Western thought*. London: Routledge.
Confucius. 1980. "Zhigong asked." *Analects*. Annotated by Yang Bojun. Beijing: Zhonghua Book Company.
Connah, G. 1987. *African civilizations: Precolonial cities and states in tropical Africa: An archaeological perspective*. Cambridge: Cambridge University Press.
Crowder, Michael. 1971. *West African resistance: The military response to colonial occupation*. London: Hutchinson.
Cysouw, Michael, Dediu, Dan & Moran, Steven. 2012. Comment on "Phonemic diversity supports a serial founder effect model of language expansion from Africa". *Science* 335(6069): 657.

Davidson, Basil. 1960. *Old Africa rediscovered*. London: Victor Gollancz.
Davidson, Basil. 1978. *Discovering Africa's past*. London: Longman.
Dawson, R. 1967. *The Chinese chameleon: An analysis of European conceptions of Chinese civilization*. Oxford: Oxford University Press.
De Rivières, Edmond Sévé. 1965. *Histoire du Niger*. Paris: Editions Berger-Levrault.
Department of History of Peking University. 1973. *History of Chinese people's anti-imperialist struggle* . Beijing: Beijing People's Publishing House.
Diop, Cheikh A. 1987. *The African origin of civilization: Myth or reality?* New York: Lawrence Hill.
Dlamini-Zuma, N. 2012. Lecture to the ANC Women's League, 29 July. www.safpi.org/news/article/2012/nkosazana-dlamini-zuma-auc-lecture
Du Bois, W.E. Burghardt. 1992. *The World and Africa: An inquiry into the part which Africa has played in world history*, New York: International Publishers.
The Economist. 2011. The hopeful continent – Africa rising. December.
Elizabeth of Toro. 1983. *African princess: The story of Princess Elizabeth of Toro*. London: Hamish Hamilton.
Fage, J.D. 1969. *A history of West Africa: An introductory survey*. Cambridge: Cambridge University Press.
Gerhart, G.M. 1978. *Black power in South Africa: The evolution of an ideology*. Berkeley, CA: University of California Press.
Gernet, Jacques. 1996. *A history of Chinese civilization*. Cambridge: Cambridge University Press.
Guo Yi-ling. 2009. Analysis on the reasons for present women's employment discrimination in China. *Journal of Women's Academy at Shandong* 2: 17–21.
He Wenping. 2017. China's experiences and African development: Reference, integration and innovation. *West Asia and Africa* 4: 68–87.
Hobson, John M. 2004. *The Eastern origins of Western civilization*. Cambridge: Cambridge University Press.
Holl, Augustin F.C. 2015. *Africa: The archaeological background*. Dakar: Editions du CERDOTOLA.
Hou Zhongjun. 2012. *Unequal treaties in modern China*. Shanghai: Shanghai Bookstore Publishing House.
Hu Sheng. 1952. *Imperialism and Chinese politics*. Beijing: People's Publishing House.
Hugo, Victor. 1861. Lettre au capitaine Butler (sur le sac du palais d'Été à Pékin), 25 novembre (A. & P.II). *Victor Hugo Œuvres complètes)*. Paris: Club français du livre.
Huntington S. 1996. *The clash of civilizations and the remaking of world order*. New York: Simon and Schuster.
Inikori, Joseph E. 2002. *Africans and the Industrial Revolution in England*. Cambridge: Cambridge University Press.
Li Anshan. 2009. China's experiences in development: Implications for Africa, 18 June. www.pambazuka.org/en/category/africa_china/57079
Li Anshan. 2011. Cultural heritage and China's African policy. In Jing Men and Barton, Benjamin, eds, *China and the European Union in Africa: Partners or competitors?* Farnham: Ashgate, 41–59.
Li Anshan. 2014. Similarities between Chinese culture and African culture: With reference to what China can learn from Africa. *West Asia and Africa* 1: 49–63.
Li Anshan. 2018. Studies on mutual learning among civilizations. *Journal of Northwestern Polytechnical University (Social Sciences)* 4: 42–50.

Li Anshan. 2019. *The social and economic history of the Chinese overseas in Africa* (3 vols). Nanjing: Jiangshu People's Press.
Li Anshan. 2021. African economic autonomy and international development cooperation. In Rahma Bourqia & Marcelo Sili, eds, *New paths of development: Perspective from the Global South*. New York: Springer, 43–53.
Li Baoping. 2011. *Tradition and modernity: African culture and political transformation*. Beijing: Peking University Press.
Li Yumin. 2010. *Treaty system in modern China*. Hefei: Hunan People's Publishing House.
Liu Xiao-nan. 2005. Feminist legal theory in U.S.: From center to margin. *Hebei Law Science* 8: 139–144.
Luo Jianbo. 2019. Exchanges of governance experiences between China and developing countries: History, theory and world significance. *West Asia and Africa* 4: 3–23.
Mao Zedong. 1994. *Mao Zedong on diplomacy*. Beijing: Documentation Office of Communist Party of China Central Committee Publisher & World Affairs Publisher.
Mazrui, A. 1980. *The African condition: A political diagnosis*. London: Cambridge University Press.
Mazrui, A.A., ed. 1995. *General history of Africa since 1935, Vol. 8*. Paris: UNESCO.
McKinsey Global Institute. 2010. *Lions on the move: The progress and potential of African economies*. New York: McKinsey.
Men Jing & Barton, Benjamin, eds. 2011. *China and the European Union in Africa: Partners or competitors?* Farnham: Ashgate.
Mencius. 1960. Liang Hui Wang to Mencius. In *Mencius*. Annotated by Yang Bojun. Beijing: Zhonghua Book Company.
Metz, E.T. 2007. Toward an African moral theory. *Journal of Political Philosophy* 15: 21–34.
Metz, T. 2014. Harmonizing global ethics in the future: A proposal to add South and East to West. *Journal of Global Ethics* 10: 46–155.
Metz, T. 2015. Values in China as compared to Africa: Two conceptions of harmony. In H. Du Plessis, ed., *The rise and decline and rise of China: Searching for an organising philosophy*. Johannesburg: Real African Publishers.
Mhando, L. 2011. Pax Africana: Reflections on paradoxes of violence and African cultural and moral values. In S. Adem, ed., *Public intellectuals and the politics of global Africa: Essays in honour of Ali A. Mazrui*. London: Adonis & Alley.
Mokgoro, Y. 1998. Ubuntu and the law in South Africa. *Potchefstroom Electronic Law Journal* 1: 5–26.
Le Monde. 2007. Le discours de Dakar de Nicolas Sarkozy, *L'intégralité du discours du président de la République, prononcé le 26 juillet 2007*, 9 novembre.
Mowat, C.L., ed. 1980. *The new Cambridge modern history, Vol. 12*. Cambridge: Cambridge University Press.
Nkrumah, K. 1963. 1963. *Africa must unite*. London: Heinemann.
Nyerere, J. 1968. *Ujamaa essays on socialism*. London: Oxford University Press.
Ogot, B.A. 1992. *General history of Africa·V: Africa from the sixteenth to the eighteenth century*. Paris: UNESCO.
Rey, Philipp, ed., 2008. *L'Afrique réspond à Sarkozy – Contre le discours de Dakar*. Paris: Dirigé par Makhily Grassman.
Rolland, Nadège. 2021. *A new great game? Situating Africa in China's strategic thinking*. Washington, DC: National Bureau of Asian Research.

Sellassie, Sergew Hable. 1972. *Ancient and Medieval Ethiopian history to 1270*. London: United Printer.

Senghor, L.S. 1964. *Negritude or humanism*. Paris: Editions du Seuil.

Shweder, R.A. 2000. Moral maps, "First World"' conceits, and the new evangelists. In L.E. Harrison & S. Huntington, eds, *Culture matters: How values shape human progress*. New York: Basic Books.

State Council of the PRC. 2019. *Equality, development and sharing: Progress of women's cause in 70 years since New China's founding*. Beijing: The State Council Information Office of the People's Republic of China.

Stevens, Phillips Jr.1978. *The stone images of Esie, Nigeria*. Ibadan: Ibadan University Press and The Nigerian Federal Department of Antiquities.

Trevor-Roper, Hugh. 1963. The rise of Christian Europe. *The Listener*, 28 November, 871.

Wen Jiabao. 2011. The problem of being unsteady, unbalanced, uncoordinated and unsustainable in development is still serious, 5 March. http://news.cntv.cn/20110 305/105099.shtml.

Williams, Eric. 1944. *Capitalism and slavery*. Durham, NC: University of North Carolina Press.

Wu Fengbin. 1988. *A history of Chinese indentured labor*. Nanchang: Jiangxi People's Publishing House.

Xi Jinping. 2017. Join hands to build a better world. *People's Daily*, 2 December.

Yamauchi, Edwin M. 2001. *Africa and Africans in Antiquity*. Ann Arbor, MI: Michigan State University Press.

Zhang Weijie. 2012. African agenda of South Africa's diplomatic strategy, with a focus on the relation between South Africa and the African Union. PhD dissertation, Peking University.

Zhang Xiping. 2014. Enlightenment thought and Chinese culture: A restudy of the influence of Chinese cultural classics on Europe in the 16th–18th century. *Modern Philosophy* 6(137): 57–66.

Part IV
Migration and diaspora

16 Chinese indentured labour in South Africa

Introduction

On 20 October 1904, a Cantonese man named Chen Ziqing was tricked into going to the Witwatersrand as a mine labourer. He had been an official under the Qing Dynasty and had been awarded a prestigious position for his military accomplishments. When he arrived in South Africa and realised the actual position in which he found himself, he could not bear the shame. Thinking of the favours bestowed on him by the Qing Dynasty (1636–1912), he made up his mind to commit suicide. Before dying, he wrote a poem:

> I was born in China and have lived there for forty-three years,
> and unfortunately came to this barbarian country today;
> Even a hero would be at the end of his resources in this situation;
> it is almost impossible to return to China, so far away.
> Today I have decided to give up my life and leave this world forever,
> and I feel sorry to have caused trouble for my countrymen here.
> My fellow villagers, after you finished [sic] the contract in three years.
> Please bring back to China your brother's spirit.
> (Chen Hansheng 1984: 285)

With the rapid increase of the international diaspora, academia's attention has started to switch to the migration groups, their origins and trends, the integration and role in their country of residence, and the contribution to and linkage with their country of birth. In terms of Africa, there is a sensitive feeling, or even some fear, about the Chinese there. There appeared worries, speculation, accusation or even rumours about the Chinese presence in Africa.[1] There are a few studies on Chinese immigrants in South Africa (Yap & Leong Man 1996; Harris 2007; Accone 2007; Park 2009, 2009a; Huynh, Park & Chen 2010; Harrison, Moyo & Yang 2012). If we ask what country has the most immigrants in the African continent, the answer might be extremely surprising. The statistics show that the former colonial powers have many more immigrants in the respective African countries. Take South Africa, for example. According to the census of the South African government, there

DOI: 10.4324/9781003220152-20

were 1.6 million British people in South Africa in 2011.[2] Therefore it is necessary to draw a clear picture about Chinese presence in Africa, especially their history.

Soon after the abolition of slavery in the British Empire, followed by other colonial powers, a new source of labour had to be sought. China and India, two nations with the largest populations, which have great civilisations since ancient times but were then experiencing a bitter period in their history, became the target of the labour-seekers. Treaties and contracts were signed and the labour problem was gradually solved in the colonies of the European powers, especially the Great Britain (Craton 1982; Saunders 1984; Carter 1996; Lai 2006; Li Anshan 2000, 2006a; Allen 2017).

Chen Hansheng collected different types of materials from various sources – for example, bilateral treaties, official documents, statistics of customs, local records, foreign works – and compiled ten books with many volumes (Chen Hansheng 1980s).

Indentured labour formed an important part of the early overseas Chinese presence in Africa.[3] About 64,000 Chinese indentured labourers were employed in the South African gold mines between 1904 and 1910 (Richardson 1982; Yen Ching-Hwang 1985).[4] This development not only became an important factor in China–British relations, but also led to the collapse of the British Conservative government.[5] Scholars who have studied the subject have concentrated on issues such as the shortage of labour in South Africa (Gluckstein 1904; Denoon 1967); the conflict between South Africa and Britain caused by the importation of Chinese labour (Weeks 1968); the recruitment, employment, and repatriation of Chinese labour (Richardson 1977, 1982); and the contribution of Chinese labour to South African history (Song Xi 1974). However, the control of Chinese labourers by their employers and their resistance to this exploitation have received little attention (Zhang Zhilian 1956; Ai Zhouchang 1981).

There have been four trends in the study of overseas Chinese in the 20th century. At the beginning of the century, interest in the issue of Chinese indentured labour in South Africa led to a close examination of the recruitment system and of their treatment. This contributed to the collapse of the British government in the early 20th century (Naylor 1904; Coolidge 1909). During the 1920s, the shortage of labourers in Europe following World War I resulted in a flow of Chinese indentured labour to the continent. Their status, their links with the world economy and the policy of the Chinese government towards them became matters of interest to contemporary scholars (e.g. Chen Da 1923; Campbell 1923).[6] With the rise of nationalism after World War II, there was a growth in the number of studies of minorities in international politics. The worldwide presence of overseas Chinese and anti-Chinese movements in Southeast Asian countries attracted international attention (Purcell 1951; Skinner 1958; Willmott 1960, 1967; Newell 1962).[7] After the Chinese government adopted an open-door policy in 1978 and the Chinese economic "miracle" occurred, the important role of overseas

Chinese gradually became a popular subject of academic study. In 1992, an international conference, Luo Di Sheng Gen (Taking Roots, 落地生根), was held in Berkeley, California. The founding of the International Society for the Study of Chinese Overseas (ISSCO) after the conference has greatly promoted this academic field. Numerous international and regional conferences and symposia on this topic have been held in various places, including Shantou (1993), Hong Kong (1994), Xiamen (1995), Taiwan (1996), Paris (1997), Manila (1998), Taibei (2001), Hong Kong (2003) and Copenhagen (2004). These developments reflect the growing interest in this field – a fourth boom in the study of overseas Chinese (Wang & Reid 1981; Reid et al 1996; Wang 1991; Skeldon 1995; Wang & Wang 1998; Sinn 1998; Zhuang Guotu, Huang You & Fang Yongpu 1998; Laczko 2003). This chapter offers both a detailed case study of this "fourth wave" of research on overseas Chinese and some new theoretical perspectives.

Based on source materials in both English and Chinese, this chapter discusses the measures adopted by South African mine owners to control Chinese labour and examines the corresponding resistance by Chinese workers. It argues that the experience of the Chinese indentured labourers in the gold mines of South Africa was akin to "modern slavery"; their resistance was a natural response to the mistreatment meted out to them by the mine owners and capitalists. Making a contribution to the growing literature on the study of the global lives of overseas Chinese in the 19th and 20th centuries, the chapter also shows that the presence of the Chinese indentured labourers marked the beginning of a process of globalisation and cross-cultural fertilisation between Asia and Africa, the effects of which are still felt today.

Life and working conditions

Generally speaking, the contract signed by the indentured labourers with the Transvaal mines stipulated several conditions. The contract that was used between 1904 and 1910 had articles covering almost all aspects of the treatment and living conditions of the labourers, including the period of service, accommodation, medical care, and payment. The following were the general terms of the contract (Chen Da 1923; Richardson 1982; Ly-Tio-Fane-Pineo 1981):

1. Chinese labourers were to work in the mines of the Transvaal for a period of three years.
2. Chinese labourers would engage mainly in hard physical jobs in the gold mines.
3. The employer would provide free board and accommodation.
4. Chinese labourers would work ten hours a day, with a payment of 25 shillings a month. They could enjoy holidays according to Chinese custom.

5. If Chinese labourers were sick, they would receive free medical treatment from the mining company.
6. If a Chinese labourer were injured at work or became disabled, the employer would give him 50 shillings in compensation. If any Chinese labourer died at work, the employer would give his family five pounds as a pension.[8]

However, none of the men understood English and some even thought that they were going to the gold mines in California. Yet every Chinese labourer believed that a bright future awaited him. However, the fate that befell them was entirely unexpected. Although the British capitalists considered Chinese indentured labour a solution to the shortage of labour, the local Boers regarded them as a new problem in an already ethnically complicated society. And British workers (and even African labourers) regarded the Chinese labour as potential competitors (Davenport 1991). Since their contract was for three years, the mine owners tried every means to exploit them in order to maximise their profit. The Chinese indentured labourers did the most dangerous work, received the lowest pay and were kept in a compound under tight control.

On the South African side, there were strict regulations regarding the occupation and movement of Chinese labour. The Labour Importation Ordinance of 1904 mandated that contracted Chinese workers had to be repatriated after their stipulated contract period, and they were to be employed only in the mines as unskilled labourers (Li Anshan 2006: 36–40; Harris 1998; Richardson 1982).[9] As soon as the Chinese labourers arrived in South Africa, they were sent to different mines after a medical check-up (Richardson 1982; Yap & Leong Man 1996).

The conditions of their compounds varied. According to Xie Zixiu,[10] a Chinese who was working for the East Rand Proprietary Mines Ltd at the time, the new compounds were fairly good; each room held 32 to 36 people. The old compounds, which were used by African labourers, were in a worse condition. The roofs were low and made of white iron, and ventilation was rather poor. Each room could hold 16 people. On hot days, people living there complained that it was like being "in a steamed cage" (Chen Hansheng 1984: 279).

When the Chinese labourers first arrived, their food was fairly good. A British observer who visited Glen Deep mine in South Africa found that rice, meat and vegetables were provided and that the Chinese workers in the dining hall seemed to be satisfied (Phillips 1905: 110–111). The reason for this was simple. The mine owners wanted to send a positive message back to China about the good conditions in South Africa, which would bring in more labourers. However, this situation soon changed. Xie Zixiu wrote that, "When I arrived, I saw the food the workers got becoming worse and worse. I could not bear it and asked the mine owner for better food and to let the workers have enough to eat." But the mine owner replied that there was no improvement in the mine's productivity and claimed that the workers were lazy: "I do this in order to save some money, it is none of your business." According to the contract agreement, the workers were to receive three meals a day, but this requirement was often ignored. Since eating lunch at a central place required time and hence cost money, the manager changed the rule. Every worker was given a piece of bread made of coarse rice, which was difficult to eat, along with some meat and vegetables, to take with him into the pit, and this would suffice for lunch. Since the quality was bad and the quantity insufficient, the Chinese workers had to buy extra food to keep up their strength (Chen Hansheng 1984).

Wages of the Chinese labour

According to the contract, Chinese labourers had to work ten hours a day. Their payment was very little, only one shilling a day, less than the wage of a local African worker. Zhang Deyi, the Chinese Ambassador to London, noted this difference even before the Anglo-Chinese Convention of Labour was formally signed in May 1904.[11] Some mine owners lowered the payment to workers in order to extract as much profit as possible (Song Xi 1974; Richardson 1976; Li Anshan 2019: 414–419).

In addition to receiving unfair payment, workers were also subjected to harsh supervision. In a letter to the *Morning Leader*, one Frank C. Boland wrote: "At the Nourse Deep, severe punishment was meted out. Every boy who did not drill his thirty-six inches per shift was liable to be, and actually was, whipped, unless he were ill, and could show that it was a physical impossibility for him to do a day's work" (An English Eyewitness 1905: 64–65).

The Annual Report of the Transvaal Government Mining Engineering shows that the Chinese labourers received the lowest wages of all the miners in South Africa until 1908. In addition, workers had to buy necessities, which were expensive and could be purchased only from the mine's company store. In a letter back home, a Chinese labourer wrote:

> The goods inside the compound was [sic] ten times the price outside, no matter how poor the quality is. Therefore, one pound and five shillings earned a month are far from enough. When Chinese labourers finished the three years according to their contract, they had nothing except an empty hand. Then they had to continue to do these hard jobs. Some worked to death without a penny left.
>
> (Zhang Zhilian 1956: 92)[12]

British government statistics from the year 1904–1905 show that the percentage of Chinese labourers working in the Rand gold mines was the highest, at 79.18 per cent, while the local African workers and White workers accounted for 67.18 per cent and 42.15 per cent respectively (Peng Jiali 1983: 187). In the gold mines, the most difficult and dangerous job was working in the pit, which was done mostly by Chinese labourers. The

Table 16.1 Mine workers' wages, 1901–1910

	Average number of employees				Average monthly wages				
	White	Black	Chinese	Total	White	Black		Chinese	
					s.	s.	d.	s.	d.
1901–02	4 090	18 887	1 004	22 977	409	26	8	33	6
1902–03	10 285	48 653	22 890	58 938	444	38	6	39	9
1903–04	12 665	74 139	47 639	87 808	491	48	10	41	6
1904–05	15 371	89 846	53 062	128 107	485	52	0	44	3
1905–06	18 089	95 599	36 044	161 327	505	51	11	47	3
1906–07	17 513	102 420	12 206	172 995	515	52	3	55	2
1907–08	17 655	131 931	2 245	185 630	469	49	1		
1908–09	19 891	166 845		198 942	465	46	4		
1909–10	23 341	180 283		205 869	456	48	7		

Sources: Annual Report of the Transvaal Government Mining Engineering for 1909–1910, Tables 2, 10 and 11.

depth of the pits varied widely, from 100 to 200 feet, or from 500 to 600 feet. Workers went up and down on machines. If one slipped and fell, he would be killed. In the pit, Chinese labourers used an iron stick to drill holes or used dynamite to blow up rock. When pieces of rock fell, it was very dangerous – it was not unusual for Chinese workers to be killed in these explosions. About 3192 Chinese labourers died in the Rand gold mines from 1904 to 1910, and 986 died needlessly in mine accidents because of unsatisfactory working conditions (Richardson 1982).

In addition, many Chinese labourers suffered from beri-beri, dysentery, phthisis, pneumonia, tuberculosis and other respiratory diseases after working for a time in the pit. These diseases also resulted in death (Chen Da 1923; Yap & Leong Man 1996). According to statistics cited by Chen Zexian, a Chinese scholar who specialises in the study of indentured labour, from 1 May 1904 to 31 December 1906, the number of dead Chinese labourers reached 2485, while 3787 became disabled (Chen Zexian 1984: 252).

Measures to control the Chinese labour

The contract for Transvaal made it clear that the Chinese labourers should be employed only for hard labour. In every mine, a general supervisor was in charge of Chinese labourers. Another overseer was in charge in the pit. Supervisors were usually employed from China – that is, they had some experience of having lived in China. Most of them had lived in China for a considerable period and were familiar with Chinese customs and habits. Hence, they were fond of making their own rules and judgements. The overseers in the pit generally knew very little of the Chinese language. Whenever they found Chinese labourers talking, they suspected them of planning some trick or of evil intentions. The overseers got angry easily and Chinese workers usually suffered owing to the difficulties with language and communication.[13] A letter to *The Times* by one Douglas Blackburn describes how a White manager punished two Chinese labourers because of a misunderstanding resulting from cultural and language differences:

> A compound manager was examining the passes of a number of coolies. When we left the compound we were followed by two Chinamen who shouted and gesticulated violently, and clutched at the arm of the manager. I could see that he failed to understand them, for he shouted wildly in return, exhibited signs of great alarm, and eventually knocked them both down, called the guard, had the pair locked up, and later in the day he confided to me that he was in fault. He had inadvertently put the passes into his pocket and misinterpreted the clamoring request for their return into threats against himself.
> (An English Eyewitness 1905: 74)

The Chinese indentured labourers were confined to their compounds, surrounded by iron railings, even before they boarded ship (Hamill 1931).[14] After they arrived in the mines, the labourers were not allowed to leave their compounds, which were also surrounded by iron railings. Friends were not allowed to visit each other and visits by relatives were strictly forbidden. Anyone who kept or hid others (because there were many runaways) was severely punished. The penalty could be a fine of as much as £500 or imprisonment for several years with hard labour. Labourers were given iron coins made especially for workers to use in the mine only. Only after their contract was over would the mine owner pay them in real money in exchange for the company coins. Besides exploiting the workers to the utmost, the owners used this currency as a measure to control them. Since these coins were useless outside the mines, it would be very difficult for the Chinese workers to escape or even to move around. The Chinese indentured labourers "were tied up like cows and horses".[15]

In his brilliant work about the social history of South African mine workers, Van Onselen (1982) analyses the vicious practice of the Rand capitalists of using alcohol as a means of controlling the mine workers. Another method of social control was the use of drugs. In order to control Chinese workers, the Transvaal government legalised the consumption of opium, which was offered to Chinese labourers regularly. The acting Consul, Liu Yi,[16] wrote a letter to the Cape Colony authorities and to the Transvaal government suggesting that both these entities should cooperate in stopping opium consumption among the Chinese. His suggestion received a positive response from the Cape Colony authorities, but the Transvaal government showed no interest in his idea.[17] The reason was obvious: opium could be used as a tool of control.

The supervisors kept a close watch on Chinese workers who were sick and hospitalised. In order to prevent what they considered malingering, they repeatedly checked on workers in the hospital. At one mine, a prison cell located just beside the hospital was used to lock up those who were regarded as malingerers by the mine doctor. So-called malingers were punished with starvation. Those who were thought to be pretending to be sick were put in the cell and denied meals (they were given only coarse porridge). Anyone who sent food to them faced the same penalty – that is, being locked up. Sometimes a cell would hold more than 30 individuals. Of course, the diagnoses of the doctors were not always correct. Xie Zixiu once saw two men regarded as malingerers who were unable to move by themselves and had to be carried out by others. This was only one example of the doctors' carelessness in treating Chinese workers (Chen Hansheng 1984: 283–284; Richardson 1982).

If any worker was found to be rebellious, he received severe punishment, including lynching, flogging, being put in fetters and handcuffs, imprisonment, starvation and hanging. Seldom did a manager or supervisor send a Chinese labourer through the standard judicial system.

Flogging

In July 1904, the Transvaal government adopted an amendment that permitted Chinese labourers to be flogged if they were found to violate the mine regulations. "In short, the law was so ingeniously amended that the Chinaman can be flogged for anything" (An English Eyewitness 1905: 63). All the mines followed this stipulation. Flogging could be on the back or the buttocks. Some mines even made their own rules. For example, in the Nourse Deep mine, the punishment was very cruel. Those who did not finish the quota of work during the shift would be flogged. A Chinese policeman carried out the torture. As a letter to the *Morning Leader* said, "Even the sight of blood did not matter. The policeman would go right on to the last stroke" (An English Eyewitness 1905: 65). The instrument of torture was the *sjambok* (a whip made of rhino skin). Later, the *sjambok* was replayed by the rubber whip, since the use of the latter inflicted more pain yet did not cause bleeding, thus leaving no trace of the lashing. Bamboo sticks or clubs were also used for the same purpose.

Handcuffs

Flogging was officially discontinued in June 1905, but other forms of torture were adopted instead. Handcuffing was one such measure. This was by no means ordinary handcuffing; it was designed to cause unbearable suffering. The hands were handcuffed to a crossbeam placed at a height that ensured that the man was unable to stand up straight or sit. He could do nothing except bend his back and half squat. He was forced to maintain this posture in order not to hurt his wrists, but could only do so for a while. When he could no longer walk or even stand, he was released.

Hanging

Here again, hanging was not done in the usual way, but was designed to inflict maximum pain and humiliation. The first method was hanging by the wrist. One end of a rope was tied to the left wrist of the labourer, while the other end was tied to an iron hoop attached to a crossbeam, which was placed 9 feet above the ground. When the rope was tightened, the labourer's left arm was raised perpendicular to the ground so he could just touch the ground standing on his tiptoes. He was hung in this manner for several hours. If he did not want his body swaying in the air, he had to try everything possible to touch the ground with his tiptoes, which was very difficult and tiring (An English Eyewitness 1905: 66). The second method was hanging by the pigtail. During the reign of the Qing Dynasty, Chinese males were required to wear a pigtail. One of the punishments involved stripping erring workers naked and leaving them tied by their pigtails to a stake in the compound for two or three hours. The manager ordered other Chinese labourers to stand by, watching their poor countryman suffer (Peng Jiali 1983: 65–66, 191).

Sometimes the compound manager punished the Chinese mine workers by himself. A manager named Bless tortured a Chinese labourer. He first gave the labourer a cold-water bath, then a hot-water bath. He had the labourer stripped naked and then strapped by his wrists to two large nails hammered into the door of his dining room, tied his pigtail up to his hands and then tied his feet. Bless kept the Chinese labourer tied up from 7.00 pm. to 11.15 am. At mealtimes, Bless brought food and put it on a chair in front of the coolie, where he could smell it but was unable to reach out for it. The torture was continued until the coolie could no longer stand and had to be admitted to the hospital (Campbell 1923).

It is worth mentioning that punishment with a club was permitted by the British government. According to *The Times* of London, Mr Lyttelton, the Colonial Secretary, while answering a question by a member of the Lower House regarding the treatment of Chinese labourers, admitted that in South Africa, "although the rattan was no longer used in punishment, the club was preferred, no more than twenty-four strokes at one time. We can imagine that when a labourer with poor health had less rest, long-time work and poor food, how could he endure 24 strokes of the club?" (Anonymous 1905).

A Chinese doctor in a French gold mine on the Rand once told Xie Zixiu that mine workers there who did something wrong were whipped 50 times with a rhino skin. Three workers who had received this punishment had been treated by him for two weeks and they had still not recovered. He was very angry at the cruel torture of his countrymen and defended the interests of Chinese labour. He was dismissed by the manager because of this bold move (Chen Hansheng 1984).

Forms of resistance

Faced with difficult living conditions and ill-treatment, the Chinese labourers tried to fight back. They adopted two forms of resistance: passive and active.

The active forms of resistance can be classified as violent and non-violent. Violent resistance took two forms: uprisings and acts of revenge against either the overseer or the manager. Non-violent resistance took different forms: strikes, refusal to pay fines, organising and sabotage. Passive resistance included slowdowns, malingering, spreading rumours, escape and suicide.[18]

The Rand mine owners and managers tried every means to cover up the bad living and working conditions of the Chinese labourers, yet news of the labourers' ill-treatment and their rebellions leaked out once in a while in the newspapers, especially in the British press. From July 1904, the third month after the arrival of Chinese labourers, acts of violent resistance occurred continuously (An English Eyewitness 1905; Zhang Zhilian 1956; Richardson 1982; Peng Jiali 1983). A young South African policeman wrote to his parents in England, describing one of his experiences dealing with rebellious Chinese labourers – "a nice old job":

> They are giving a lot of trouble – 5000 of them started rioting last week, and 100 foot police and 200 South African Constabulary had to go to stop them, and a nice job we had. They threw broken bottles and stones when we charged them. Some of our fellows were very badly cut. The Chinamen also made dynamite bombs and threw them at us, and we had to shoot into the crowd to drive them back. We aimed low and wounded a good many of them. They are nasty devils to tackle, and always show fight when there are a lot of them together.
>
> (An English Eyewitness 1905: 84)

According to British government statistics, during the period from June 1904 to June 1905, there were 28 riots and 232 coolies were convicted for leading the disturbances (Campbell 1923).

It was not uncommon for Chinese labourers to take revenge on an overseer or a manager. Owing to the lack of mutual understanding caused by language differences, Chinese labourers could hardly understand the orders of their overseers. Thus, they were often scolded or punished physically. In response, the Chinese labourers often returned with any "stones and clubs" they could get their hands on.

Mr Joubert, a manager at the Bronkhorstspruit Mine, was murdered by four Chinese workers. The reason for the act was simple. The Chinese labourers were not allowed to eat so, enraged by ill-treatment, overwork and starvation, they committed the murder. The four men were caught and executed in a Pretoria jail. The author tells the story with sympathy: "Perhaps the most tragic part of the whole business is that one cannot completely blame them for such an awful act. They have grown to hate the White man" (An English Eyewitness 1905: 95–96). Although this was an extreme example, it shows how miserable and angry the punished Chinese labourers felt, and reveals their determination to control their own destiny.

Strikes were the most common form of active resistance, occasionally accompanied by violence (Richardson 1976). The chairman of the Chamber of Mines confessed that the innumerable riots that had occurred in the mines were not the result of "the White men's machinations" (An English Eyewitness 1905: 59). In July 1904, the Chinese labourers in the New Coma Mine refused to do their night shift and broke windows. In October 1904, in a gold mine run by the French in the Rand, 1400 Chinese labourers drove away the supervisor and occupied the mine. On the night of 24 October 1904, the mine owner of the Jumpers Deep Mine arrested two Chinese labourers for infringing mining regulations. This resulted in a strike by all the Chinese labourers. The manager tried every means to convince them to return to work, but failed. At last he sought the intervention of the local official in charge of Chinese labour affairs, and he arrested 40 Chinese labourers.

On 1 April 1905, Chinese labourers in the Brunfontein Gold mine went on strike because they were dissatisfied with a mistake in their pay after six months' hard work. On 6 and 7 January 1908, about 40,000 Chinese labourers in different mines in the Rand struck in support of other Chinese and Indians in South Africa in their struggle against the adoption of the 1907 racial prejudice law (Zhang Zhilian 1956; Peng Jiali 1983; Richardson 1982). "By the end of June the contentious legislation was formally proclaimed and made effective from 1 July 1907. All Asiatics were to be registered and fingerprinted within four months, at stipulated times and places throughout the Transvaal" (Yap & Leong Man 1996: 142).

The most popular forms of passive resistance were slowdowns and escapes. For example, in many mines drilling in the pit was the most tiring job. When a group of Chinese workers were tired and hungry, they stopped working, squatted and began to eat the food they had brought with them. The overseer shouted at them or beat them. But no matter how much he scolded or tried to persuade them to resume work, he failed. They took no notice of his orders and continued to enjoy their food. After finishing the bread, they slowly took out cigarettes and began to smoke. They were not worried at all, since they knew that if the work was not finished it was not only their fault; the overseer had to take responsibility as well. Their answer was quite reasonable: "Me get one little shilling. Me do plenttee work for me pay" (An English Eyewitness 1905: 55).

In order to "break the chains" – to use the title of Martin Klein's 1993 book on slavery (Klein 1993) – it was common for Chinese labourers to try every means to escape from the gold mines. From June 1904 to July 1905, 259 Chinese labourers were convicted for refusal to work, 570 were convicted for going out without permits and 1165 were convicted for desertion. During the same period, there were 21,205 cases of Chinese labourers being unlawfully absent from work. From June 1905 to June 1906, the average number of Chinese labourers employed was 47,600. However, 13,532 were convicted for various offences; the number of deliberate "desertions" was 1700 (Campbell 1923: 194, 197, 209).

A young policeman wrote of his experience of capturing escaping Chinese labourers:

> Last night, I captured six Chinamen who had run away from the mines. The six I captured were trekking across the veld. I chased them on horseback and they ran on top of a kopje and commenced to roll rocks down. I managed to get a shot at one with my revolver: the bullet struck him on the wrist. Then they all put up their hands and surrendered.
> (An English Eyewitness 1905: 84–85)

Since the Chinese labourers at large did not have any money and faced a hostile community, stealing or robbery became their only means of survival. In the daytime, they hid themselves in the mountains or valleys and came out at night in search of food. Hence they were feared and hated by the local Boers, and conflicts broke out between them. On 17 August 1905, a Boer was killed by escaped Chinese labourers. How this happened is unclear, but the incident caused great panic in the area. On 22 September 1905, the government issued the Amendment to the Importation of the Labour Act. The tenth clause stipulated that anyone could arrest Chinese labourers outside the Rand region with no warrant required. This amendment added fuel to the fire, and the conflict between Chinese labourers and local Boers became all the more serious. Between 1905 and 1906, 210 Chinese labourers were charged with house-breaking (Chen Da 1923; Campbell 1923: 209).

Chinese labourers set up secret societies such as the Hong Men. This organisation, which originally was established during the struggle against the Qing Dynasty, imposed very strict discipline on its members, which served to unify them. They enjoyed their mutual fellowship and helped each other overcome difficulties. When it was decided to take revenge against a White overseer, the man assigned this task carried it out bravely, even though he knew that the result would be certain death. Nevertheless, he was resolute in carrying out his duty because he knew that everything had been settled by the organisation. His family would be taken care of, so he did not have to worry (An English Eyewitness 1905: 57, 82–83).

It is even more striking that some Chinese labourers committed suicide in protest against their ill-treatment. For example, Cheng Yincai from Yi Ning in Guangdong Province could no longer bear his suffering under the intolerable working conditions. He tried to hang himself in the washroom of the dormitory but was found and saved by his fellow workers. The manager was afraid that he would try to commit suicide again, so he let him do odd jobs on the grounds and never sent him down into the mine (Chen Hansheng 1984: 285).

Workers in the mines committed suicide for various reasons. Some could not bear the fate of being enslaved by others; these were usually those who had been lured to South Africa under false pretenses, without knowing the full facts. Some could not endure the hard work conditions or the severe punishment meted out to them. No matter what the real reason, this drastic action was no doubt a means of resistance to the mistreatment of workers in the gold mines. According to statistics published by the British Government, up to 30 June 1906, a total of 49 Chinese labourers committed suicide (Chen Da 1923).

Although the Chinese lived in very difficult circumstances, they exhibited outstanding adaptability and tried to make the best of their hard lives. For example, those who were fond of drama bought costumes and stage property, and played different characters. After long rehearsals, they presented plays on public holidays. Some Chinese labourers made stilts and walked on them at various gatherings. Some who enjoyed natural beauty cultivated flowers around their compound, and some raised birds and taught them to talk. Occasionally, they participated in sports and held competitions with African workers. All these after-work activities showed their longing for their homeland and hometowns, and helped ease the psychological pressures brought on by their harsh working and living conditions. But it should be pointed out that a few Chinese labourers could not stand the loneliness and developed bad habits such as opium smoking and gambling (Yap & Leong Man 1996; Shen 1980).

Conclusion

During the period from 1904 to 1910, Chinese indentured labourers in the South African mines used various means to express their grievances. From late 1904 to early 1905, their protests became more frequent and violent. There are two reasons for this. First, the earlier Chinese labourers knew nothing about South Africa, and believed the alluring accounts narrated to them by the recruiting agents, which turned out to be lies. When they came to the Rand and experienced life as miners, they were bitterly disappointed because the harsh reality was vastly different from what they had been led to believe. They were enraged by a sense of betrayal and angered by their mistreatment. Second, the first Chinese Consul-General, Liu Yulin, arrived in Johannesburg only in May 1905. During the year between the arrival of the first Chinese labourers and Liu Yulin's assumption of his post, the workers had no channel through which to voice their grievances. They could only adopt radical measures in an attempt to change their situation or to seek revenge against the mine owners.

It is not difficult to see that "Eyewitness", the author of *John Chinaman on the Rand* (An English Eyewitness 1905), was a racist. He attacked the Chinese indentured labourers, but he made an honest confession: "Of course the immediate cause which leads to the Chinese committing the above-recorded acts of violence is the result of bad treatment" (An English Eyewitness 1905: 95). He was absolutely right about this.

The Chinese indentured labourers certainly did more than resist. Most of them returned to China after the completion of their contracts. They had come as poor peasants but left as miners, after contributing a great deal to the recovery of South Africa's gold-mining industry. These men had come to know a totally different people, and vice versa, which created a cross-cultural exchange. This facilitated the settlement of the overseas Chinese in South Africa. Their arrival unfortunately reinforced anti-Chinese feeling among some South Africans and led the government to increase its control over Chinese settlers. A few Chinese mine labourers stayed behind, and together with the free Chinese in South Africa provided services for the local Chinese population. Thus, they were instrumental in forming the first real Chinese community in South Africa. Those who returned took back knowledge about South Africa to China, and this information in turn brought more poverty-stricken Chinese peasants to Africa. The coming and going of Chinese indentured labourers facilitated a process of globalisation of people, knowledge and culture.

Notes

1 For worries, see French (2014), for speculation, see Games (2005); Ovadia (2010); for accusation, see Labin (1965); Lorenz (2007); Jones (2011; Bauer (2012); for rumours, see Cohen (1991); Redvers (2012). Deborah Brautigam clarifies rumours about the proportion of loans in an Angolan project used to buy Chinese products, and false reports about the amount of Chinese aid and the rumour of the so-called "Baoding Villages" (Brautigam 2009: 152–153, 177–179, 266–268).
2 In 2014, the population of China was 1.368 billion, that of India was 1.267 billion and that of Britain was 64.51 million. "Census 2011, Census Brief".
3 There is a misconception that the present-day South African Chinese are descendants of the indentured Chinese labourers who arrived on the Rand in the early 20th century. Melanie Yap and Leong Man have criticised this viewpoint in their work (Yap & Leong Man 1996).
4 Statistics for indentured Chinese labour in South Africa during the period 1904–1910 vary widely, especially those cited by Chinese scholars. For a new synthesis, see Li Anshan (2019: 340–346).
5 More accurately, it was a Unionist government (1895–1905), a coalition of the Conservative and Liberal Unionist parties. The Union government decided to import contracted workers from China, which led to many protests among the British people. On 26 March 1904, a demonstration against Chinese immigration to South Africa was held in Hyde Park, attended by 80,000 people. With this and other difficulties, Prime Minister Arthur Balfour resigned in December 1905, leading to the appointment of a Liberal government under Sir Henry Campbell-Bannerman. The party also lost in the following election.
6 Many Chinese scholars wrote books on the subject in this period, including Li Changfu, He Hanwen and Qiu Hanping and many other writers.
7 It is understandable that the early attention was focused on the overseas Chinese in Southeast Asia, yet some scholars began to study overseas Chinese in Africa as well (see Labin 1965; Slawecki 1971).
8 For Chinese versions, see *Nanfeizhou Ying Su Telanshiwaer Zhaomu Hua Gong Kai Kuang Hetong* (Contract of the employment of Chinese labourers for gold mining

by the Transvaal of the British South Africa), *Wai Jiao Bao* (Bulletin of Foreign Affairs), 8 June 1904, No. 79; *Nanfeizhou Ying Zhaomu Yue Gong Kaikuang Hetong* (Contract of the employment of Chinese labourers from Guangdong Province for gold mining by the Transvaal of the British South Africa), *Wai Jiao Bao* (Bulletin of Foreign Affairs) 8 July 1904, No. 82; *Huagong Yu Guzhu Qian Ding de Hetong* (Contract between Chinese labour and Employer), *Bei Guo Chun Qiu* (Spring and Autumn of the Northern Country) 1960 No. 2. The contract also appeared in *Da Gong Bao* (Tianjin) on 17 and 18 September 1904.

9   As early as the end of the 19th century, the free Chinese who came to the mines did so as traders and small businessmen since they were prevented by law from engaging in mining. Karen Harris cites the *Statute Law of the Transvaal 1839–1910*, Law no. 15 of 1898: "no coloured person may be a license holder or be in any way connected with the working of the digging, unless they were employed as workmen in the service of whites" (Harris 1998: 560).

10 Xie Zixiu, born into a Chinese family in Australia, was the younger brother of Xie Tsantai, a famous revolutionary in the fight against the Qing Dynasty. Xie Zixiu took part in some activities in Hong Kong and Canton along with his elder brother. After the death of their father, he went to South Africa. Owing to his capability, impressive personality and fluent English, he was soon selected as the Secretary-General of the Chinese Association in Johannesburg. In May 1904, when the indentured Chinese were to arrive, he resigned from the association and joined the British Royal service, working for the British government in South Africa as a civil servant "not for the high payment, but to probe the conditions [of] workers". Later, he was employed as a council member of the East Rand Proprietary Mine in charge of Chinese labourers.

11 Archives of the Ministry of Foreign Affairs; Chinese Ambassador to London Zhang Deyi's letter to the Ministry of Foreign Affairs suggesting that a convention be signed before the government allows South Africa to employ Chinese labour. Guangxu, 29 October 1916 (Chen Hansheng 1985: 1650).

12 I found at least four letters in contemporary journals and newspapers that described the miserable life of the Chinese indentured labourers in South Africa. For example, *Nan Feizhou Huaqiao Canzhuang Ji* (Record of the miserable situation of overseas Chinese in South Africa) in *Xin Min Cong Bao* Third Year, No. 1, 28 June 1904, pp. 105–108; and *Xin Min Cong Bao* Third Year, No. 2, 13 July 1904, 89–92.

13 General Consul in South Africa Liu Yulin's letter to the Ministry of Foreign Affairs regarding his inspection of Chinese labour. Guangxu 31/6/5 (Chen Hansheng 1985: 1746–1747).

14 The 31st president of the United States, Herbert Clark Hoover (1874–1964), was one of the important figures actively involved in this "modern slave trade". This book disclosed his role in the importation of indentured Chinese labour to South Africa in this period, especially during the time when he was in charge of the Chinese Engineering and Mining Company.

15 *A letter from the Transvaal*, in Zhou Peizi, *Warning to Nationals*, 1906 (Zhang Zhilian, 1956: 92–93); An open letter from South Africa, *Journal of Spring and Autumn of the Northern Country*, 2 (1960): 82–83.

16 Also spelled as Liu Ngai (Yap & Leong Man 1996: 68).

17 Liu Yi's letter was sent out on 1 July 1908. The Cape government replied positively on 10 July, while the Transvaal government sent a negative response on

17 July. See Chinese General Consul Liu Yi's memo to the Ministry of Foreign Affairs regarding the prohibition of opium (Guangxu 34/7/1) (Chen Hansheng 1985: 1785–1787).

18 It is helpful to compare their resistance with that of slaves. For the forms of resistance of West Indian slaves, see Craton (1982: 241–253).

References

Accone, Darryl. 2007. Chinese communities in South Africa. *China Monitor* 19.
Ai Zhouchang. 1981. Modern Chinese labour in South Africa. *Historical Research* 6: 171–180.
Allen, Richard B. 2017. Asian indentured labour in the 19th and early 20th century colonial plantation world. *Oxford Research Encyclopedias: Asian History*. https://oxfordre.com/asianhistory/view/10.1093/acrefore/9780190277727.001.0001/acrefore-9780190277727-e-33
Anonymous. 1905. Note by the British colonial minister on the management of Chinese workers in South Africa. *Bulletin of Foreign Affairs* 106, 15 April.
Bauer, William. 2012. China: Africa's new colonial power. www.policymic.com/articles/1657/china-africa-s-new-colonial-power
Brautigam, D. 2009. *The dragon's gift: The real story of China in Africa*. Oxford: Oxford University Press.
Campbell, P.C. 1923. *Chinese coolie emigration to countries within the British Empire*. London: P.S. King & Son.
Carter, Marina. 1996. *Voices from indenture: Experiences of Indian migrants in the British Empire*. London: Leicester University Press.
Chen Da. 1923. *Chinese migrations, with special reference to labour conditions*. Washington, DC: Government Printing Office.
Chen Hangsheng. 1980s. *Compilation of the selected historical data of Chinese labourers going abroad, Book I-X*. Beijing: Zhonghua Book Company.
Chen Hansheng, ed. 1984. *Compilation of the selected historical data of Chinese labourers going abroad, Book IX*. Beijing: Zhonghua Book Company.
Chen Hansheng, ed. 1985. *Compilation of the selected historical data of Chinese labourers going abroad, Book I(4)*. Beijing: Zhonghua Book Company.
Chen Zexian. 1984. Collection of historical data on the Chinese labour employed by the British for the gold mines in South Africa. In Chen Hansheng, ed., *Compilation of the selected historical data of Chinese labourers going abroad, Book IX*. Beijing: Zhonghua Book Company, 178–253.
Cohen, Roberta. 1991. China has used prison labour in Africa. *The New York Times*, 11 May.
Coolidge, M. 1909. *Chinese immigration*. New York: Henry Holt.
Craton, Michael. 1982. *Testing the chains: Resistance to slavery in the British West Indies*. Ithaca, NY: Cornell University Press.
Davenport, T.R.H. 1991. *South Africa: A modern history*. Toronto: University of Toronto Press.
Denoon, D.J.N. 1967. The Transvaal labour crisis 1901–1906. *The Journal of African History* 8(3): 481–494.
An English Eyewitness. 1905. *John Chinaman on the Rand*. London: R.A. Everett.
French, Howard W. 2014. *China's second continent: How a million migrants are building a new empire in Africa*. New York: Knopf.

Games, Dianna. 2005. Chinese the new economic imperialists in Africa. *Business Day*, 21 February.
Gluckstein, S. 1904. *Black, White or yellow? The South African labour problem: The case for and against the introduction of Chinese Coolies.* London: Forgotten Books.
Hamill, John. 1931. *The strange career of Mr Hoover under two flags.* New York: William Faro.
Harris, Karen L. 1998. "The formidable unwelcome competitor": Overseas Chinese merchants in South Africa. In Zhuang Guotu, ed., *Ethnic Chinese at the turn of the centuries, Vol. 2.* Fuzhou: Fujian People's Publisher, 542–563.
Harris, Karen L. 2007. Waves of migration: A brief outline of the history of Chinese in South Africa. *China Monitor* 21.
Harrison, Philip, Moyo, Khangelani & Yang, Yan. 2012. Strategy and tactics: Chinese immigrants and diasporic spaces in Johannesburg, South Africa. *Journal of Southern African Studies* 38(4): 899–925.
Huynh, Tu, Park, Yoon Jung & Ying Chen, Anna. 2010. Faces of China: New Chinese migrants in South Africa, 1980s to present. *African and Asian Studies* 9(3): 286–306.
Jones, Mark T. 2011. China and Africa: Colonialism without responsibility. *Somalilandpress*, 20 March. http://somalilandpress.com/china-and-africa-colonialism-without-responsibility-21113
Klein, M.A., ed. 1993. *Breaking the chains: Slavery, bondage and emancipation in modern Africa and Asia.* Madison, WI: University of Wisconsin Press.
Labin, Suzanne. 1965. *Les Colonialistes Chinois en Afrique.* Paris: Éditions de la Ligue de la Liberté.
Laczko, Frank, ed. 2003. Introduction: Understanding migration between China and Europe. *International Migration* 41(3): 5–19.
Lai, W.L., ed. 2006. *Essays on the Chinese diaspora in the Caribbean.* Trinidad: Public Library.
Li Anshan. 2000. *A history of Chinese Overseas in Africa.* Beijing: Overseas Chinese Publishing House.
Li Anshan. 2006. *Social history of Chinese overseas in Africa: Selected documents 1800–2005.* Hong Kong: Hong Kong Press for Social Science.
Li Anshan. 2006a. A historiographical survey of the study of Chinese immigrants in Latin America and the Caribbean. In W.L. Lai, ed., *Essays on the Chinese diaspora in the Caribbean.* Trinidad: Public Library, 192–222.
Li Anshan. 2019. *The social and economic history of the Chinese overseas in Africa* (3 vols). Nanjing: Jiangshu People's Press.
Lorenz, Andreas. 2007. The age of the dragon: China's conquest of Africa. *Spiegel Online International*, 30 May. www.spiegel.de/international/world/the-age-of-the-dragon-china-s-conquest-of-africa-a-484603.html
Ly-Tio-Fane-Pineo, Huguette. 1981. *La Diaspora Chinoise dans L'Ocean Indien Occidental.* Aix-en-Provence: Association des Chercheurs de l'Ocean d'Indien, Institut d'Histoire des pays d'Outre-mer, Greco Ocean Indien.
Naylor, T. 1904. *Yellow labour: The truth about the Chinese in the Transvaal: Being a study of its moral, economic and imperial aspects.* London: n.p.
Ovadia, Jesse. 2010. China in Africa: A "both/and" approach to development and underdevelopment with reference to Angola. *China Monitor*, August: 11–17.
Park, Yoon Jung. 2009. *A matter of honour: Being Chinese in South Africa.* Lanham, MD: Lexington Books.

Park, Yoon Jung. 2009a. *Chinese migration in Africa.* Johannesburg: South African Institute of International Affairs.
Peng Jiali. 1983. The event of the employment of the Chinese labour by the British for the gold mines of South Africa at the end of [the] Qing Dynasty. *Historical Research* 3: 177–192.
Phillips, Lionel. 1905. *Transvaal problems: Some notes on current politics.* London: n.p.
Purcell, V. 1951. *The Chinese in Southeast Asia.* New York: Oxford University Press.
Redvers, Louise. 2012. Angola's Chinese-Built ghost town. *BBC News*, 2 July. www.bbc.com/news/world-africa-18646243
Reid, Anthony, Alilunas-Rodgers, Kristine & Wayne Cushman, Jennifer. 1996. *Sojourners and settlers: Histories of Southeast Asia and the Chinese.* Sydney: Allen & Unwin.
Richardson, Peter. 1976. Coolies and Randlords: The North Randfontein Chinese miners' strike of 1905. *Journal of Southern African Studies* 2(2): 151–177.
Richardson, Peter. 1977. The recruiting of Chinese indentured labour for the South African Gold-Mines, 1903–1908. *The Journal of African History* 18(1): 85–108.
Richardson, Peter. 1982. *Chinese mine labour in the Transvaal.* London: Macmillan.
Saunders, K., ed. 1984. *Indentured labour in the British Empire 1834–1920.* London: Croom Helm.
Shen, I-yao. 1980. *A century of Chinese exclusion abroad.* Beijing: Chinese Social Sciences Publishing House.
Sinn, Elizabeth, ed. 1998; *The last half century of Chinese overseas.* Hong Kong: Hong Kong University Press.
Skeldon, Ronald. 1995. Conference report: The Last Half Century of Chinese Overseas (1945–1994): Comparative perspective, *The International Migration Review* 29(2): 576–579.
Skinner, George William. 1957. *Chinese society in Thailand: An analytical history.* Ithaca, NY: Cornell University Press.
Slawecki, Leon M.S. 1971. *French policy towards the Chinese in Madagascar.* New Haven, CT: The Shoe String Press.
Song Xi. 1974. *The Chinese labourer's contributions to the Transvaal gold mines in South Africa at the end of Qing Dynasty.* Taipei: Huagang.
Van Onselen, Charles. 1982. *Studies in the social and economic history of the Witwatersrand – Volume 2: New Nineveh.* New York: Longman.
Wang Gungwu. 1991. *China and the Chinese overseas.* Singapore: Times Academic Press.
Wang Gungwu & Reid, Anthony, eds. 1981. *Community and nation: Essays on Southeast Asia and the Chinese.* Singapore: Heinemann Educational.
Wang Ling-chi & Gungwu Wang, eds. 1998. *The Chinese diaspora: Selected essays* (2 vols). Singapore: Times Academic Press.
Weeks, J.A. 1968. The controversy over Chinese labour in the Transvaal. PhD thesis, Ohio State University.
Willmot, Donald Earl. 1960. *The Chinese of Semarang: A changing minority community of Indonesia.* Ithaca, NY: Cornell University Press.
Yap, Melanie & Leong Man, Dianne. 1996. *Colour, confusion and concessions: The history of the Chinese in South Africa.* Hong Kong: Hong Kong University Press.
Yen Ching-Hwang. 1985. *Coolies and Mandarins: China's protection of overseas Chinese during the Late Ch'ing period 1851–1911).* Singapore: Singapore University Press.

Zhang Zhilian. 1956. The truth about the employment of Chinese indentured labour in the Transvaal in British South Africa, 1904–1910. *Journal of Peking University* 3: 78–96.

Zhuang Guotu, Huang You & Fang Xiongpu. 1998. *Ethnic Chinese at the turn of the centuries*, *Vol. 1*. Fuzhou: Fujian People's Publisher.

17 Early Chinese and Indians in South Africa

Introduction

> Since the Chinese have no facilities for lodging, they have started a Cantonese Club which serves as a meeting place, a lodge and also as a library. They have acquired for the Club land on a long lease and have built on it a pucca one-storey building. There they all live in great cleanliness and do not stint themselves in the matter of living space; and seen within and from outside, it would look like some good European Club. They have in it separate rooms marked drawing, dining, meeting, committee room and the Secretary's room and the library, and do not use any room except for the purpose for which it is intended. Other rooms adjoining these are let out as bedrooms. It is such a fine and clean place that any Chinese gentleman visiting the town can be put up there. The entrance fee is £5 and the annual subscription varies according to the members' profession. The club has about 150 members who meet every Sunday and amuse themselves with games. The members can avail themselves of Club facilities on weekdays also.
>
> (Gandhi 1961: 65)

This is the description by the Indian nationalist leader Mahatma Gandhi after he visited the Cantonese Club, or *Wei Yi She* (维益社), in South Africa. What is the origin and what is the life of the Indian and Chinese in South Africa? This chapter will deal with the subject.

Although the former colonial powers had the most numerous immigrants on the African continent, the world's interest still focuses on China or India, two developing countries with the largest populations. As South Africa and India belonged to the British Empire in history, the conditions for Indians to migrate to South Africa were relatively relaxed, and the number of Indians has always been far greater than the number of Chinese. According to the official survey of India, the number of Indian immigrants in South Africa reached at least one million at the end of the 20th century.[1] According to the website of the Ministry of Overseas Indian Affairs, as of the beginning of 2015 there were 28,455,026 Indian expatriates, of whom about 10 per cent were

DOI: 10.4324/9781003220152-21

from Africa, accounting for 2,760,438 people. Among them, South Africa has the largest number of Indian immigrants in Africa, reaching 1.55 million, followed by Mauritius with 891,894.[2] The number of Chinese immigrants in Africa is far less than that of India: the number of Chinese in South Africa was about 30,0000 in 2008 (Naidu 2008: 185); it was estimated to be 350,000 in 2008–2009 (Park 2009) and reached 500,000 in 2011(Statistical Release 2011; Lin 2014: 182).[3]

We can trace their origin in history. After the abolition of the slave trade and slavery, the Chinese and Indians – either indentured labour or free immigrants – quickly spread to the West Indies, the Asia-Pacific region and Africa, including countries such as Trinidad, Jamaica or British Guiana, Mauritius, Madagascar, Reunion, Fiji and Malaya, Uganda, Nigeria and South Africa (Richardson 1982; Saunders 1984; Bhana 1991; Lai 1993, 2006; Tinker 1993; Northrup 1995; Carter 1996; Wilson 2004; Li Anshan 2004, 2006; Allen 2017).[4] This chapter endeavours to compare the two groups in South Africa at the turn of the century and throws some light on the relations between different immigrant communities in a new place.

First Chinese and Indian arrivals

The first contact between China and Africa was as early as the Han Dynasty (206 BCE–220 CE) (Sun Yutang 1995: 424–427; Xu Yongzhang 2019; Li Anshan 2015, 2019). India is directly linked with the Indian Ocean and its trade to Africa by sea road is natural and has existed for a long time, while China traded with the African continent via the overland "Silk Road". In 1993, archaeologists discovered silk fibre in the hair of a female corpse of the 21st dynasty (1070–945 BCE) in Egypt. Only China had the technology to produce silk at the time (Lubec, et al., 1993).[5] Therefore, the product was probably made in China and taken to Egypt – either directly or indirectly. Another trade route to Africa is through the Indian Ocean by way of South India. Since the Mamluk Dynasty destroyed the Sudanese port Aihdab around 1428 CE, Port Swakin began to show its important position and strengthened its trade with various places, including India and the Far East. The Sudanese scholar pointed out that after the rise of Ottoman Empire in 1453, Swakin was still trading with India and China. In addition, Sudan's relations with China are not limited to Aihdab and Swakin's two ports.

> At that time, the influence of Egypt gradually weakened, and the trade in the Red Sea also slowly declined. Only Swakin and Jeddah still welcomed merchant ships from India and China. Although the commercial influence of the Red Sea weakened during the Ottoman Turkish period, and Swakin and Massawa were also controlled by the Turks, the contact between Swakin and/or Massawa and China was not interrupted. Indian merchants still transported the goods from these two places, such as gold

sand, ivory, rhinoceros horn, gum, pearl and hawksbill shell, to China, and sell them there in equal weight gold.

(Ahmed 1999, 1999a, 2014: 37–38)

Although Chinese people appeared in South Africa in earlier centuries (Armstrong 1996), a large group of indentured labourers arrived there at the beginning of the 20th century to work in the gold mines as indentured labour (An English Eyewitness 1905). Yap suggests that the origin of the South African Chinese was not this group, but rather free immigrants (Yap & Leong Man 1996: 4, 103–104, 135). I would argue that the origins of the South African Chinese are threefold: the free immigrants from China and Southeast Asia, including the anti-Qing activists who escaped from the persecution of the Chinese government (Li Anshan 2000: 211–232);[6] the exiles from Dutch colonies in Southeast Asia or Chinese ex-convicts (Elphick & Giliomee 1989: 217, 219–220);[7] and the indentured labourers who successfully escaped from the repatriation process and stayed behind in South Africa (Yap & Leong Man 1996: 133).[8]

When Jan van Riebeeck, the leader of the first Dutch settlers in South Africa, arrived with three ships to settle in Table Bay on 6 April 1652, he intended to import some industrious Chinese to the Cape of Good Hope for the "dirtiest and heaviest" work. In a journal entry dated 22 April 1652, van Riebeeck mentions the industrious Chinese he met in Asia, and he repeatedly urged the Council of the Dutch East India Company to import slaves as well as free Chinese labourers – but in vain (Elphick & Giliomee 1989: 5–66, 193). The early Chinese settlers formed a small part of the group of convicts of different ethnic origin (Indonesians, Javanese, Singhalese, Chinese and Indians) who were sent to the Cape by the Dutch to serve their sentences. The number of Chinese convicts greatly increased after 1740, the year Chinese settlers in Batavia were cruelly suppressed by the colonial government.

A Chinese convict named Wancho who was sent to the Cape on the *Arnhem* in 1660 was probably the first Chinese person to settle in Africa. He was later sent to Robben Island to serve out his term for the crime of attacking a woman. James Armstrong's work gives us a vivid description of the life of early Chinese convicts: some served their term peacefully and became rich after several years, some were trapped in South Africa for years by red tape after finishing their term, and some served as basket-makers, fishermen and masons. Mortality among them was high; "of the 17 Chinese convicts listed on a roll in February 1727, four of them died within two years, as did one other Chinese" (Armstrong 1996: 5–66, 193; Ly-Tyo-Fane Pineo 1985: 210).

In the early 18th century, some Chinese, called "free Blacks" at the time and "coloured" later, organised as local militia together with some Black Africans (Elphick & Giliomee 1989: 184, 219, 220; Yap & Leong Man 1996: 6–9). The Chinese also began businesses and expanded quickly. Among the early prosperous Chinese was a man from Guangdong Province named Horloko, who left traces in Cape records as a goldsmith and interpreter. In his will of 1724, he asked that his property be transmitted to the leader of the Chinese community in Batavia, and then to his son and daughter in China (Armstrong 1996: 13). Several Chinese even became slave owners (Elphick & Giliomee 1989: 209). However, their success caused concern to the Whites in the Cape colony, who sent four delegates to Amsterdam with a petition listing the unfair deeds of the Chinese. The petition asked the colonial government to restrict the Chinese competitors' business activities (Walker 1964: 1–2).

Like the early Chinese, the first Indians were brought to South Africa as convicts and slaves (Elphick & Giliomee 1989: 116). In the 19th century, the development of Natal needed a great deal of labour and two groups of Indians arrived. The first group came in 1860 as indentured labour to work on the sugar plantations.[9] Between 1860 and 1866, 6445 Indians arrived in Natal from different parts of India, mainly low-caste Hindus from Madras and south India. When the first indentured labourers completed their contracts they returned to India on the ship *Red Riding Hood*, taking with them complaints that caught the attention of the Indian authorities. The Government of India forbade further recruitment and immigration was stopped. A commission of inquiry was set up under the chairmanship of the Attorney-General, M.H. Gallwey, who handed in the commission's recommendations. In order to put right the abuses disclosed by the Indian indentured labourers and to keep the supply steady, the Natal legislature appointed a Protector of Indian Immigrants in 1872. Immigration resumed and thereafter a steady stream of Indians arrived each year until the Natal scheme was finally terminated by the Indian authorities in 1911 (Brain 1983: 23–25; Thompson 1990: 65; Davenport 1991: 5).

Early settlement and occupation

Between 1814 and 1882, more than 300 Chinese arrived in Port Elizabeth in the Cape colony and Pietermaritzburg in Natal (Yap & Leong Man 1996: 15–24; Li Anshan 2019: 270–275). Most of them were artisans and labourers employed by the colonial government. As for the settled Chinese, they gradually established their own businesses. The Boer War had ended with no winner and the reconstruction and sudden rise of the gold-mining industry needed a large number of labourers. Within a year, 299 new companies were set up in the mining industry (Campbell 1923: 167). The mining capitalists suggested that Chinese labour should be introduced. The proposal was quickly adopted and an agreement was reached between the British and Chinese governments. During the period 1904–1910, about 64,000 Chinese indentured labourers arrived in the Transvaal. The indentured labour was soon followed by free Chinese immigrants who formed an important part of the Chinese community in South Africa. Unlike the Indian indentured labourers, who chose to stay in South Africa, most of the Chinese workers returned home after they finished their contracts.[10] At the beginning of the 20th century, fewer than 2500 Chinese had settled in South Africa (Yap & Leong Man 1996: 177).

Table 17.1 Indians and Africans in the canefields

Year	Indians		Africans	
	Number	%	Number	%
1860–61	436			
1875–76	5 292	42	7 457	58
1887–88	6 043	72	2 387	28
1895–96	6 632	77	1 989	23
1907–08	10 924	82	2 484	18
1910	18 270	88	2 380	12
1925	11 440	29	27 873	71
1933	8 020	17	40 263	83
1945	4 500	7	55 778	93

Source: Compiled from Vahed (1995: 35, 71).

Indian indentured labourers came on five-year contracts at agreed minimum wages. Table 17.1 indicates an increase in the number of Indians in the canefields during 1860–1910 and a decline afterwards. Before 1910, there was a stable increase in both the number and percentage of Indian labourers in the fields; the majority were indentured immigrants. Two factors may have contributed to this.

Indian indentured labourers came to South Africa to address the shortage of labour. During the 1870s and afterwards, the African peasant economy expanded in South Africa for a number of reasons: increased marketing of commodities such as wool, hides, timber and crops; the purchase or hiring of farmland and its cultivation with the plough; participation in agricultural shows; and the conclusion of business deals with White merchant houses interested in supplying a growing variety and volume of trade goods. However, the demand for Black African workers mounted in the mining industry and so did the need for African labourers on farms or in the canefields, as the urban economy stimulated the expansion of agriculture. The Natives Land Act of 1913 was enacted to meet the demand and to eliminate once and for all the possibility that large numbers of rural Africans would be able to maintain a self-sufficient peasant existence (Bundy 1972: 69–78; Bundy 1979). The Act deprived many African peasants of their land, with the result that they either had to join the mining industry as workers or move to the White farms and canefields as labourers.

In addition, the Indians gradually adapted to the local conditions and those who stayed preferred to work on their own with their family members who were newly arrived from India rather than signing a contract. This desire was supported by two other factors: the arrival of Gujerati traders and the favourable policy of the local authorities. In the late 1870s, another group of Indians arrived in South Africa, obviously as a result of both encouragement from South Africa and the demands of service to the Indians who stayed there. Most of them were Gujerati traders who established a long tradition of trade and business. They were generally involved in three kinds of economic activity and began to emerge as a sizeable separate Indian community at the beginning of the 20th century; eventually they outnumbered the Whites in Natal. First, they were good at retail business, which set up competition with Whites in Natal, the Transvaal and the Orange Free State. Second, many quickly adapted to local life and became involved in a wide range of economic activities, as shoemakers, cigarette makers, clerks, cooks, domestics, firemen, laundry workers, jewelry makers, mineral water manufacturers, plumbers, fishermen and tailors. Third, some acquired a small piece of land and grew fruit and vegetables for sale in Durban or Pietermaritzburg (Vahed 1995: 7–47). In 1875, there were 10,000 Indians in the colony; by the end of the 19th century, the figure had increased to 100,000 (Bhana 1991: 20; Davenport 1991: 105).[11] Between 1860 and 1911, 152,184 Indian immigrants arrived in Natal; some were from North India but most were from South India (Brain 1983: 202, 247).[12]

The local policy encouraged the Indians to settle. Indians who wanted to remain could get land allocated by the local authorities, and those who were willing to stay for another five-year contract could get a free passage home. As the Indians completed their contracts, some stayed in South Africa, either working in the canefields or as servants. According to the statistics, an increasing percentage chose to stay (Vahed 1995: 47).

Similarities

Both China and Indian are great nations. They have a long history of civilisation, and have suffered under colonialism in modern times. In terms of the history of migration, the obvious similarity is that both Chinese and Indians were in a strange land with a policy of racial segregation, facing the same problem of discrimination. Moreover, they were both caught between the Whites and the Africans.

The Asiatic issue

Grouped together as "Asiatic", both Chinese and Indians were susceptible to racial discrimination from the very beginning of their settlement. Like the Indians who mainly lived in Natal, the Chinese concentrated in Cape Colony and Transvaal (Yap & Leong Man 1996: 177).[13] However, the two groups were also spread and mixed in other cities. In early times, the place where both Chinese and Indians (also Malays) lived was called "Malay Camp", a motley collection of "squalid, tightly packed", makeshift hovels and shacks that served as home for the coloureds, Indians and Chinese (Yap & Leong Man 1996: 7–48). For example, in the diamond city of Kimberley, some Chinese shopkeepers and laundrymen lived in the Malay Camp on the outskirts of the town. Even in this difficult situation, their adaptability and competence in business quickly caused alarm in the White business sector, which constantly urged the local government to take more stringent measures to limit Asiatic immigration and trade.

During the early days before the establishment of the Union of South Africa, different colonies issued various anti-Asiatic measures. In Natal, the Immigration Restriction Act 1 of 1897 and the Dealers Licensing Act 18 of 1897 gave the local authorities great power to decide whether or not Chinese and Indians were to be granted entry, or any Asiatic trading licence to be granted. The introduction of the Transit Immigrants Act 7 of 1904 "allowed for all Chinese contracted as labourers in the territories adjoining Natal to be confined to compounds during their stay in Natal and prohibited anyone in the colony from harbouring or employing such Chinese" (Yap & Leong Man 1996: 4–45). The Act had an impact on Chinese settlers in Natal, since they were required to furnish their fingerprints for a special domicile certificate proving their status as residents there and to carry the certificate with them wherever they went.

In Transvaal, the fear of "an invasion of Indian traders" facilitated the introduction of Law 3 of 1885, which stipulated that any of the native races of Asia, including the "coolies", Arabs, Malays and "Mohammedan subjects of the Turkish Dominion" were prohibited from acquiring citizenship rights in the Zuid-Afrikaansche Republiek (ZAR), and restricted Asiatic rights in the territory. At the end of the 19th century, several laws or regulations were issued to restrict Asiatic immigration or work in the Transvaal – for example, a resolution of 5 July 1888 to institute an inquiry into and prohibit the residence of Asiatics on business premises not in locations; and a resolution of 5 August 1892 to take stringent measures to prevent coolies, Chinese or Asiatics from trading in towns and to move all coolie shops opened after 1889. A resolution of 8 September 1893 applied Law 3 of 1885 strictly to confine Asiatics to trading and living in locations. Every "Chinaman" who applied for a special and annually renewable pass had to pay £25. The authorities could arrest, fine or imprison any Chinese who did not produce the pass on demand to an official, and banish any repeat offenders from the ZAR. A resolution of 20 March 1894 allowed only licence holders or their heirs to reside on stands in Braamfontein. A resolution of November 1898 moved all Asiatics to locations before 1 January 1899, and the state president's proclamation of 26 June 1899 set aside certain streets, areas and locations for occupation and trade by coolies and Asiatics in terms of Law 3 of 1885 (Yap & Leong Man 1996: 76). The Asiatics were not permitted to walk on footpaths and pavements, or to drive in public carriages; they were only permitted to travel in third-class train compartments, and were not allowed to buy or possess liquor. Cape Town, the Transvaal and Natal issued more than 11 laws from 1902–1908 to restrict Asiatic rights of immigration, residence and trade activities (Li Anshan 2000: 151–152).

Hostile situation

With more free immigrants and indentured labourers entering South Africa, the Whites began to get more nervous. The "White League Association" was established in 1902 with the clear purpose of obtaining repatriation of Asiatics or restricting the activities of Asiatic traders to bazaars. According to *Indian Opinion*, the leading Indian newspaper for the merchants in South Africa:

> By the Transvaal law, Chinamen and Indians were precluded from holding licences, but this law had been suspended by the present government for Chinamen and Indians who were engaged in business illegally previous to the war ... The question might be asked whether we should not ask for repatriation of the whole of these people now here, who as traders, simply act as a drag on the real advancement of this country.
>
> (*Indian Opinion* 1903)

The stand of the White League Association was strongly supported by the White business sector. Making no difference between coolies and free traders, the President of the Chamber of Commerce of Potchefstroom claimed that "the coolie question has engaged the serious attention of the Chamber", and urged the members to leave "no stone unturned to restrict the importation of coolies as they will undoubtedly prove a source of serious danger to the European trader", reported by Indian immigrants' newspaper *Indian Opinion* on 8 October 1903 (Ly-Tyo-Fane Pineo 1985: 226).

As immigrants, both Chinese and Indians were facing a paradoxical situation. If they did not work hard or failed to develop, they could hardly survive, since the environment was generally unfriendly; if they tried to develop or expand, it would cause alarm and antagonism from the Whites, resulting in new laws or restrictions from the local government. In a hostile environment, the response from both Chinese and Indians was the same. In order to survive, they fought White superiority with various strategies, using evasion, petitions and organised protest in the struggle. In the Transvaal, Indians discovered that it was possible to establish businesses under the Transvaal Companies Act of 1909, thus evading the Gold Law and Townships Act of 1908 which restricted the right of Asiatics to open businesses. They also found that they could evade Law 3 of 1885 respecting the ownership of property by registering it in the names of companies, which was declared lawful by the courts in 1916 and confirmed on appeal in 1920. The number of Indian private companies in the Transvaal grew from three in 1914 to 103 in 1916 (Davenport 1991: 241). It was difficult to get a licence for normal trade activities as the authorities delivered only around 70 licences weekly to Asiatic traders. New Asiatic immigrants found a way to obtain a trade licence via the Whites, who gave them the cover of their names (Ly-Tyo-Fane Pineo 1985: 226).[14] Petitioning was another strategy. Both the Chinese and Indians frequently filed petitions to the South African government and to London to voice their grievances and protest.

United struggle

By June 1905, a total of 10,237 Indians and 1115 Chinese were legally entitled to be in the Transvaal. The Whites worried that the actual number was much higher and asked the government to interfere. In August 1906, the authorities issued a measure requiring Asiatics over the age of eight to surrender their permits in order to obtain new registration certificates, to provide their fingerprints and to produce the certificate on demand. Only those with certificates would be granted trading licences, and failure to comply was punishable by a fine, imprisonment or deportation. On 6 December 1906, the Transvaal and the Orange River Colonies were granted self-government. The Transvaal parliament passed the Asiatic Law Amendment Bill, which was an exact copy of the 1906 ordinance. On 21 March 1907, it was rushed through all its stages and received royal assent in May of the same year (Tendulkar 1951: 100).[15]

The Act was to take effect from 1 July and the Asiatics were required to register under it by 31 July. However, the policy met strong opposition from both Chinese and Indians. In the course of the struggle, which united the Chinese and Indians, Gandhi's idea of *Satyagraha*, meaning "the force which is born of truth and love or non-violence", emerged.[16] At first, the Indians who claimed British citizenship held mass meetings to protest against this measure, while the Chinese tried to use the diplomatic channel by handing a petition to the Imperial Chinese Consul-General for South Africa in Johannesburg (Ly-Tyo-Fane Pineo 1985: 50–52).[17] They both wanted fair treatment in immigration and trade activities. The Transvaal Chinese Association called a meeting and the Chairman of the Cantonese Club, Leung Quinn (梁佐钧), invited the Indian leader Gandhi to make a speech. Gandhi pointed out the new law put the Asiatics in a humiliating position, which "no self-respecting subject of a civilized country could possibly accept". He called on the Chinese to ignore the compulsory clause to re-register and submit themselves to imprisonment (Yap & Leong Man 1996: 141) as a passive protest being carried out by the majority of the Indians.[18]

In challenging the Transvaal government's action, Gandhi said, "We must congratulate the Transvaal Government for the courage of their convictions. If we are conscious of the mark of slavery the Act will put on us, we will meet it and refuse to submit to it. The brave rulers, who know the value of action rather than of any speech, can only respond to bravery and practical action" (Tendulkar 1951: 100). On 31 July, the last day for registration, a mass meeting of Indians was convened at Pretoria. Delegates from all over the Transvaal were present, representing 13,000 Indians. The government sent its delegate to make the final threat. It did not make any difference. The Indians and Chinese stood firm against the Act, with mass meetings, processions and picket lines. A Johannesburg firm of wholesale provision merchants, having a large Chinese clientele, informed the Chinese that unless they registered all further credit would be stopped. The Chinese replied by asking the total amount of the debit entries against their names, promised immediate payment and threatened a complete boycott. This brought the firm round, and it immediately apologised. An Indian firm in Pietersburg, pressed by a European wholesale house in Durban to comply with the provisions of the Act, indignantly cancelled its order (Tendulkar 1951: 102).

The boycott was very successful. In Pretoria, only about 100 people out of a population of 1500 registered. Although the government extended the time-limit until 30 November, only 511 out of a population of over 13,000 submitted to registration. Leaders and ordinary people in both the Chinese and Indian communities took part in the struggle. Moreover, they shared the experience of prison. On 27 December, 25 Asiatics were arrested; among them were Gandhi and Leong Quinn, the Chinese leader, accused of defying the law. At the conclusion of the court proceedings, Gandhi told the large crowd of Indians, Chinese and Europeans in Government Square, "It is better to leave the colony than lose our self-respect and honor. This is a religious struggle and we shall fight to the bitter end" (Tendulkar 1951: 5–6). On 10 January 1908, Gandhi and others who attended court for sentencing pleaded guilty to the charge of disobeying the order to leave the colony within the time limit, and he was joined by Leung Quinn on 14 January. By 29 January, 155 passive resisters had been imprisoned.[19] Gandhi remembered their common experience in prison and thought highly of his Chinese comrade: "Truly Mr Quinn is a pillar of Satyagraha. I feel proud when I come across a man of his type during my experience of our struggle. I am not disheartened by those who drop off. Be sure victory is ours" (Ly-Tyo-Fane Pineo 1985: 236).

On 10 November, a Chinese named Zhou Guihe (Chow Kwai) signed the registration form under pressure from his European employer. After he heard about the boycott by the Chinese community, he committed suicide, leaving a farewell letter:

> My employer advised me to re-register. At first, I refused to do so, but I was informed that I would be dismissed from my employment. I thought that I should have to lose my situation. Therefore, I was obliged to re-register, but I did not know the degradation that would follow until my friend talked to me about the registration matter and showed me the translation of the law. I found that I would be treated as a slave, which

Table 17.2 Average numbers of Indians and Chinese in Transvaal prisons, 1902–1908

Period	Indian men	Chinese men
1902–03	19. 3	—
1903–04	Not available	Not available
1904–05	40.2	202.3
1905–06	41.1	1089.0
1906–07	54.3	1206.5
1907–08	64.9	885.5

Sources: Cd. 4564. Further correspondence relating to legislation affecting Asiatics in the Transvaal. Enclosure in no. 19; Yap & Leong Man (1996: 160). This government figure did not differentiate between passive resisters and other prisoners, and the high numbers of the Chinese indicate that they included the Chinese indentured labourers working on the Reef gold mines from 1904.

would be a disgrace to myself and my nation. I was not aware of all this before. Now it is too late for me to repent. I cannot look my countrymen in the face. I hope all my countrymen will take warning from my error.

(Ly-Tyo-Fane Pineo 1985: 353)[20]

In the memorial meeting, Leung Quinn condemned the Transvaal government: "I do deliberately charge the Transvaal government of the murder of an innocent man, and this because he is an Asiatic" (Ly-Tyo-Fane Pineo 1985: 231).[21] Mr Zhou Guihe's farewell letter was published in *Indian Opinion* and circulated among all the passive resisters; his deed encouraged all the Asiatics.[22]

Dissimilarities

Race was at the core of the segregation system in South Africa. The idea strongly held was that the population comprised four "racial groups" – White, coloured, Indian and African. It is clear that Indians were regarded as one of the racial groups, but the Chinese were not.[23] This certainly has something to do with the figures (Table 17.3).

Demography

In South Africa, there are many more Indians than Chinese. In 2001, of a total population of 44.6 million, 2.6 per cent were Asian (about 1.09 million). More than 90 per cent were Indian and the rest were Chinese. Another figure may be also helpful in understanding the differences. People of the Hindu faith numbered 581,000, about 1.35 per cent of the total population, while about 598,000 believed in Islam. The first group and the majority of the second were Indian. Some Indians were Christians (Republic of South Africa 2001: 5).

Besides "push" and "pull" factors, which are common in migration history, two other factors may have contributed to the migration of such a large number of Indians to South Africa, compared with Chinese immigrants.

Table 17.3 Chinese in South Africa, 1904–1995

Year	Number	Year	Number	Year	Number
1904	2 457	1946	4 340	1972	8 700
1910	2 399	1954	7 000	1981	8 500
1921	1 828	1955	5 163	1986	9 710
1930	2 907	1959	5 105	1990	23 000
1936	2 944	1966	8 000	1995	27 515

Source: Li Anshan (2000: 562–563).

Table 17.4 Racial composition of Durban's population, 1904–1989

Year	Whites	Coloureds	Indians	Africans	Total
1904	31 302	1 980	15 631	18 929	67 842
1911	31 903	2 497	17 015	17 750	69 165
1921	46 113	4 000	16 400	29 011	93 515
1931	59 250	4 240	17 860	43 750	125 100
1936	88 065	7 336	80 384	63 762	239 547
1949	129 683	11 280	123 165	109 543	373 771
1989	381 000	69 000	624 000	2 301 000	3 775 000

Sources: University of Natal (1952); Vahed (1995).

First, India used to be a colony within the British Empire, later a member of the Commonwealth. Indians were regarded as British subjects during that time, so immigration to another British colony presented fewer obstacles for them than for the Chinese, who were deemed "aliens".

The Indian government could also put pressure on South African government for any unfair treatment of Indians. In 1872, the government of India forbade further recruitment as a protest against the ill-treatment of Indian immigrants. At the 1917 Commonwealth Conference, the Indian government again warned that it intended to "press for fair treatment for Indians in Commonwealth countries". This stand was clearly shown in 1921 and 1923, and most Dominion prime ministers agreed that South African policies on Asians were capable of improvement. At the 1923 conference, Sir Tej Bahadur Sapru of India stated clearly, "I tell him frankly that if the Indian problem in South Africa is allowed to fester much longer it will pass ... beyond the bounds of a domestic issue and will become a question of foreign policy of such gravity that upon it the unity of the Empire may founder irretrievably" (Davenport 1991: 242).

However, at that time China was weak and thus fell victim to European powers. It was not in a position to bargain with other nations regarding the treatment of its migrants in a remote country. Families also played a role. From the very beginning, some Indian women came to South Africa with their husbands while the Chinese workers came alone. According to Wu Jingchao, a Chinese sociologist, women play a very important role in stabilising migrant societies. In other words, the more women who migrated with the group, the more stable the settler community would be. The statistics show that more than half the early male Indian immigrants came with their wives, much more than the ratio of the Chinese in South Africa.[24] Of course, the majority of indentured Indians were men, but of the first Indians who arrived in Natal, more than a third were women (Davenport 1991: 105). According to Bhana's study, the Indian indentured labourers who arrived between 1860 and 1911 were mainly men, and the actual proportion of men to women was 64:28 (Vahed 1995: 171). What about the Chinese? First, the indentured labourers

Table 17.5 South African Chinese population, 1904–1911

Place	1904			1911		
	Men	Women	Total	Men	Women	Total
Cape	1 366	14	1 380	804	19	823
Natal	161	4	165	161	11	172
Transvaal	907	5	912	905	5	910
Total	2 434	23	2 457	1 870	35	1 905

Source: Yap & Leong Man 1996:177.

were all men. Second, among the free immigrants, women were very rare. In the early 20th century, the ratio of men to women among the Chinese was more than 100:1 (Table 17.5).

Organizations

Another interesting phenomenon is worth noticing. The Indians in South Africa had more religious and social places to congregate than the Chinese. From the end of the 19th century, the Chinese gradually organised themselves into different clubs, even secret societies, as a means of benefitting and defending themselves. Gandhi once visited a Cantonese Club, or *Wei Yi She* (维益社), which made a deep impression (Ghandi 1961: 65) We can tell from the entrance fee that it was more or less an elite organisation, since ordinary Chinese could not afford it. Yet the Chinese Association (*Zhonghua Hui Guan*, 中华会馆) was generally an organisation for all Chinese. Early in the 20th century, there were about 13 organizations among the Chinese community in South Africa (Li Anshan 2019: 393–396).

In 1890, the Durban Indian Committee was formed to represent the merchants "who focused largely on problems specific to them although they did occasionally take up the grievances of indentured Indians" (Vahed 1995: 47). Gandhi was the founder of the first Indian political organisation, the Natal Indian Congress (NIC). Mainly representing the interests of the Indian merchants, he set up the NIC in 1894, the year the Natal Indian population of 46,000 first exceeded the White population of 45,000. This political organisation was the "most prominent elite organization" in South Africa.[25] The annual membership fee was £3 and 75 per cent of NIC members were merchants (Vahed 1995: 47). Although politically oriented, it paid much more attention to issues such as protection of the trade, franchise and residence rights of merchants. No wonder it attracted less interest from the ordinary people, who were more concerned about taxes and everyday problems. One article in *Indian Opinion* complained: "It is hopeless to expect the NIC to move in any matter … Will it ever be more than a name? It can if it would only interest itself in the people whom it presumes to represent, and by allowing all Indians to participate in its deliberations ... I hope the Congress will shake off its lethargy and make itself a power among and for the Indians" (Vahed 1995: 48).

Some social organisations appeared at the beginning of the 20th century. The Hindu Young Men's Society was set up in 1906 by Professor Bhai Parmanand, who arrived in Durban in 1905. His purpose was to encourage Indians to study Tamil, engage in missionary work and visit India in order to understand their culture and heritage. P.S. Aiyar, a political activist in Natal, formed the Natal Indian Patriotic Union, which took the poll tax as its main target. The Indian Farmer's Association was organised by Swami Shankeranand, who helped to establish Hindu societies as soon as he arrived in 1908. Those Indians born in South Africa also formed their own organisation, the Colonial Born Indian Association, in 1911 to protest against restrictions on inter-provincial migration. With a wider intellectual life in the community, more scholars from India visited South Africa. At a result, 12 Hindu organizations emerged between 1905 and 1915. During the 1920s, some welfare organizations also appeared (Vahed 1995: 118–31, 183–85).

This difference may also be explained from a religious-cultural perspective. In Durban, for example, the majority of Indians were Hindu. The first group who arrived in Natal in 1860 were overwhelmingly Hindu; only 12 per cent were Muslim and 5 per cent were Christian (Thompson 1990: 100). In 1936, there were 79.64 per cent Hindus and 14.74 per cent Muslims, with only a small percentage of Christians (Vahed 1995: 81). All the temples and mosques became the centers of community life. Early temples were built in Umbilo (1869), Mount Edgecombe (1875), Newlands (1896), Cato Manor (1882), Isipingo Rail (1870) and Sea View (1910), and early mosques and madrasahs included those in Grey Street (1881), West Street (1885), Riverside (1896), Springfield (1904), Westville (1904), Overport (1905), Sherwood (1905) and Sea Cow Lake (1906). We can see the progress of temples and mosques following the communities. They not only gathered people together to worship, preserve their religion and culture, and help to build and cherish community life; these places became the symbols of a community as well as its major achievement, thus providing a sense of belonging and security for those far from home. They also became places for the exchange of ideas and information, and the locations where cultural events were held. Religious education was carried out, various social activities, rituals and festivals were practised and languages were taught to retain the vernacular (Vahed 1995).

As for the Chinese, they came from different regions and spoke different local dialects. The Fujianese who spoke the Min Nan dialect could hardly understand Cantonese, while another group, the Hakka, who settled in the coastal region spoke a totally different dialect. Unable to understand one another's languages, they grouped according to their home villages. Although they believed in Confucianism, it was less a formal religion than a way of life, or a value system. They worshipped *Tian Gong* (Heaven, 天公), *Tian Hou* or *Ma Zu* (Sea God, 天后, 妈祖), *Guan Sheng Di Jun* (关圣帝君), Guan Shi Ying

436 *Migration and diaspora*

(Bodhisattva, 观世音) and *Tu Di Shen* （土地神), or *Da Bai Gong* (Earth God, 大伯公). But those figures belonged to Chinese local religion, which is less formalised, and the worship was not systematic except for some common features such as annual rituals.

Leadership

Another reason for the extent of organisation is the leadership. Unlike the Chinese immigrants, who were mainly poor peasants, the Indians were merchants, lawyers, missionaries and professors alongside the large number of indentured labourers. Indian intellectuals such as Gandhi, P.S. Aiyar, M.C. Anglia and Fatima Meer provided leadership and the community was organised through various channels such as newspapers, schools, performances, congregations and conferences. Take the newspaper, for example. The first Indian newspaper, *Indian Opinion*, was started by Gandhi in 1903, followed by *African Chronicle* in English and Tamil published by Gandhi's political rival P.S. Aiyar in 1908. The third was *Indian Views*, written in English and Gujarati, founded by M.C. Anglia in 1914. However, the first Chinese newspaper in South Africa did not appear until 1931. The *Chinese Consular Gazette*, or *Chiao Sheng Pao* (侨声报), was started by the Chinese Consulate in South Africa as a semi-official newspaper.

Conclusion

South African Chinese and Indians have similarities as well as differences. On one hand, they encountered the same obstacles in a strange land in terms of ethnic identity, economic hardship, social status and political rights. As the "Asiatic menace", they were seen by Africans as intruders who came to lower local wages and were treated by Whites as poor uncivilised coolies. Not uncommonly, both groups united to fight against the hostile situation and segregation policy. On the other hand, owing to their different history, culture and political situation, there were dissimilarities between the two groups. There were many more Indians than Chinese and they had a more definite position in the country. Thanks to their religious-cultural traditions and the efforts of early intellectuals, the Indians were better organised, which helped them in the struggle for the rights and benefits of the community as a whole.

Notes

1 "High Level Committee on the Indian Diaspora and India Council of World Affairs", Report of High Level Committee on the Indian Diaspora, 7.29.2001, p. 84. http://indiandiaspora.nic.in/diasporapdf/chapter7.pdf
2 "Population of overseas Indians". http://moia.gov.in/writereaddata/pdf/Population_Overseas_Indian.pdf
3 *Mid-year population estimates*, statistical release (Pretoria: Statistics South Africa, 2011).

4 Scholars have published various works on individual colonies. For the Chinese indentured labour, see Chen Hangsheng (1980s), *Collection of historical documents concerning emigration of Chinese labourers (Books I–X* (Beijing: Zhonghua Book Company). See Richardson (1982); Bhana (1991); Lai (1993).
5 It is said the famous Egyptian Queen Cleopatra (69–30 BCE) loved Chinese silk clothes (Charlesworth 1970).
6 The anti-Qing revolutionary Yang Chuyun went to South Africa in 1896 after a rebellion failed, tried to mobilise the mass there and organised a branch of Xing Zhong Hui (Revive China Society). Chen Jingman, another activist in Transvaal, once wrote a letter to *Xin Min Cong Bao*, a newspaper published by Chinese reformer-exiles in Japan, describing the horrible conditions of the Chinese in South Africa. Xie Zixiu, also an anti-Qing activist, went to South Africa and served as secretary of Transvaal Chinese Association. This force later strongly supported the 1911 Revolution led by Dr Sun Yat-sen.
7 It is clear that almost all of the Chinese in the free Black community were ex-convicts. For the early life of Chinese in Africa, see Li Anshan (2012).
8 They might be few but they did exist. A book by a contemporary author also mentions some Chinese who had escaped from the mines (Anonymous 1905). The resistance of Chinese indentured labour is another subject that needs specific exploration (Li Anshan 2010: 41–61).
9 Indians were imported to various parts of the British Empire soon after the abolition of slavery: Mauritius 1834, British Guiana and Trinidad 1844, St Lucia 1856, and Grenada 1858. The French colonies of Reunion, Martinique, Guadeloupe and Guiana, Danish St Crois and Dutch Surinam followed the practice after the 1860s.
10 Their time in South Africa was short, but two results were undeniable. First, the introduction of Chinese indentured labour contributed to the gold-mining industry of South Africa. Second, their treatment caused repercussions in British politics, for example the failure of the Conservative Party in the 1906 election (Yap & Leong Man 1996: 129).
11 According to Bhana's study based on ships' lists, the first indentured Indian emigrants to Natal between 1860 and 1902 numbered 95,382.
12 Among them, 2150 were Christians, including members of the Roman Catholic, Syrian and Protestant churches.
13 In 1904, among 2457 Chinese in South Africa, 1380 lived in Cape Town and 912 in the Transvaal; in 1911, there were 923 in Cape Town and 910 in the Transvaal.
14 This quickly caused alarm in the white community. In December 1903, the executive of the Johannesburg Chamber of Commerce passed a resolution to recommend to government that "no Asiatic should be allowed to trade in a White man's names, or have any interest on the profits of any business in which the license is taken out in the name of a White name" (*Indian Opinion*, 28 January 1904).
15 There are various reports of the Act in Chinese newspapers at the time, such as *Foreign Affairs Newspaper* (*Waijiao Bao*) and *The Eastern Miscellany* (*Dongfang Zazhi*). See for example, "News of overseas Chinese No.1, The new bad act towards Chinese in Transvaal in South Africa", *Foreign Affairs Newspaper*, No. 166, 9 January 1907 (Guangxu 32nd Year, 11th Month, 25th Day); News of overseas Chinese No. 2; The new bad act towards Chinese in Transvaal in South Africa. *Foreign Affairs Newspaper*, No. 208, 14 May 1908 (Guangxu 34th Year, 4th Month, 15th Day) (Li Anshan 2006).

16 "As the struggle advanced, Gandhi found the name 'passive resistance' inadequate to express its real meaning. It also appeared to him 'shameful' that the Indian struggle should be known only by an English name. A small prize was, therefore, announced in *Indian Opinion* to be awarded to the reader who invented the best designation for the new struggle. Maganlal Gandhi suggested the word '*sadagraha*', meaning 'firmness in a good cause'. Gandhi liked the word but as it did not fully represent the whole idea, he changed it to '*satyagraha*'" (Tendulkar 1951: 103).
17 Document XIII. Petition of Leung Quinn to explain the decision taken by the Chinese of Transvaal not to submit to the Asiatic Act.
18 *Indian Opinion*, 1 June 1907.
19 Leung Quinn was unlawfully deported to Ceylon, returned and immediately proceeded to the Transvaal to participate in the struggle. On 19 January, he was sentenced to three months' rigorous imprisonment for not possessing the registration certificate (Tendulkar 1951: 152).
20 Document XIV. Farewell letter of Chow Kwai (Zhou Guihe). For the original Chinese version (Li Anshan 2006: 122).
21 *Indian Opinion*, 16 November 1907. The English version of Zhou Guihe's letter was published in the same issue of *Indian Opinion*. As a memorial, the Chinese society of the Transvaal set up a monument (Li Anshan 2006: 124).
22 The struggle was finally ended with a compromise between the Asian immigrants and the government. For details, see Vahed (1995: 47–52); Tendulkar (1951: 108–185).
23 The Official Yearbook of the Union used to list four groups: White, Indian, Coloured and African. The position of the Chinese in South Africa is ambiguous in history. They have been labelled "free Blacks", "coloured" and "Asiatic". During the 1972–1990 reclassifications, only 11 Indians and 67 Chinese were reclassified as white (Yap & Leong Man 1996: 319).
24 For Indian women's role in the family, see Vahed (1995: 70–81).
25 For Gandhi's activities in the founding of the organisation, see Johnson (1973: 31–45).

References

Ahmed, G.K. 1999. China–Arab relations during the Tang Dynasty 618–907 CE. *Tang Studies* 5: 323–366.
Ahmed, G.K. 1999a. Sudan–China relations during the Tang Dynasty to the end of Yuan Dynasty. In Qiu Shuseng, ed., *Collected essays on Yuan History 7*. Nanchang: Jiangxi Educational Press, 197–206.
Ahmed, G.K. 2014. *Explore the history of Sudan–China relations over the past 2000 years*. Beijing: Current Affairs Press.
Allen, Richard B. 2017. Asian indentured labour in the 19th and early 20th century colonial plantation world. *Oxford Research Encyclopedias: Asian History*. https://oxfordre.com/asianhistory/view/10.1093/acrefore/9780190277727.001.0001/acrefore-9780190277727-e-33
Armstrong, J.C. 1996. *The Chinese at the Cape in the Dutch East Company period, 1652–1795*. Johannesburg: SA–Chinese History Project.
Bhana, S. 1991. *Indentured Indian emigrants to Natal, 1860–1902: A study based on ships' lists*. New Delhi: Promilla.

Brain, J.B. 1983. *Christian Indians in Natal, 1860–1911: An historical and statistical study*. Cape Town: Oxford University Press.
Bundy, C. 1972. The emergence and decline of a South African peasantry. *African Affairs* 71(285): 69–88.
Bundy, C. 1979. *The rise and fall of the South African peasantry*. London: Heinemann.
Campbell, P.C. 1923. *Chinese coolie emigration to countries within the British Empire*. London: P.S. King & Son.
Carter, Marina. 1996. *Voices from indenture: Experiences of Indian migrants in the British Empire*. London: Leicester University Press.
Davenport, T.R.H. 1991. *South Africa: A modern history*. Toronto: University of Toronto Press.
Elphick, R. & Giliomee H., eds. 1989. *The shaping of South African society, 1652–1840*. Middletown, CT: Wesleyan University Press.
An English Eyewitness. 1905. *John Chinaman on the Rand*. London: R.A. Everett & Son.
Ghandi, M.K. 1961. *Collected works of Mahatma Gandhi, Vol. 5 (1905–1906)*. Delhi: Ministry of Information and Broadcasting.
Johnson, R.E. 1973. Indians and Apartheid in South Africa. PhD thesis, University of Massachusetts.
Lai, W.L. 1993. *Indentured labour, Caribbean sugar: Chinese and Indian migration to the British West Indies, 1838–1918*. Baltimore, MD: Johns Hopkins University Press.
Lai, W.L., ed. 2006. *Essays on the Chinese diaspora in the Caribbean*. Trinidad: Public Library.
Li Anshan. 2000. *A history of Chinese overseas in Africa*. Beijing: Chinese Overseas Publishing House.
Li Anshan. 2004. Survival, adaptation, and integration: Origins and development of the Chinese community in Jamaica. In Andrew R. Wilson, ed., *The Chinese in the Caribbean*. Princeton, NJ: Markus Wiener, 41–68.
Li Anshan. 2006. A historiographical survey of the study of Chinese immigrants in Latin America and the Caribbean. In W.L. Lai, ed., *Essays on the Chinese diaspora in the Caribbean*. Trinidad: Public Library, 192–222.
Li Anshan. 2006a. Early Chinese and Indian immigrants in South Africa: Similarities and dissimilarities. *Overseas Chinese History Studies* 3: 21–34.
Li Anshan, ed. 2006b. *Social history of Chinese overseas in Africa: Selected documents (1800–2005)*. Hong Kong: Hong Kong Press for Social Sciences.
Li Anshan. 2015. Contact between China and Africa before Vasco da Gama: Archeology, document and historiography. *World History Studies* 2(1): 34–59.
Li Anshan. 2019. *The social and economic history of the Chinese overseas in Africa* (3 vols). Nanjing: Jiangshu People's Press.
Lin, Edwin 2014. "Big fish in a small pond": Chinese migrant shop keepers in South Africa. *International Migration Review* 48(1): 181–215.
Lubec, G., et al. 1993. Use of silk in ancient Egypt. *Nature*, 362 (March 4 1993): 6415, p.25.
Ly-Tyo-Fane, Pineo H. 1985. *Chinese diaspora in the western Indian Ocean*. Port Louis: Editions de l'Ocean Indien – Chinese Catholic Mission.
Naidu, Sanusha 2008. Balancing a strategic partnership? South Africa–China relations. In Kweku Ampiam & Sanusha Naidu, eds, *Crouching tiger, hidden dragon? Africa and China*. Pietermaritzburg: University of KwaZulu Natal Press.

Northrup, David. 1995. *Indentured labour in the age of imperialism, 1834–1922*. Cambridge: Cambridge University Press.

Park, Yoon. 2009. Recent Chinese migrations to South Africa: New intersections of race, class and ethnicity. In Tina Rehima, ed., *Representation, expression and identity: Interdisciplinary perspectives*. Oxford: Inter Disciplinary Press.

Republic of South Africa. 2001. Government communication and Information. *South Africa Yearbook, 2000–2001*. Pretoria: Government Printer.

Richardson, P. 1982. *Chinese mine labour in the Transvaal*. London: Macmillan.

Saunders, K. ed. 1984. *Indentured labour in the British Empire 1834–1920*. London: Croom Helm.

Statistical Release. 2011. *Mid-year population estimates*, Pretoria: Statistics South Africa.

Sun Yutang, 1995. *Collection of Sun Yutang's academic papers*. Beijing: Zhonghua Book Company

Tendulkar, D.G. 1951. *Mahatma, life of Mohandas Karamchand Gandhi, Vol. 1*. Bombay: Vithalbhai K. Jhaveri & D.G. Tendulkar.

Thompson, L. 1990. *A history of South Africa*. New Haven, CT: Yale University Press.

University of Natal. 1952. *The Durban Housing Survey*. Durban: University of Natal.

Tinker, Hugh. 1993. *A new system of slavery: The export of Indian labour overseas, 1830–1920*, 2nd ed. London: Hansib.

Vahed, G.H. 1995. The making of Indian identity in Durban, 1914–1949. PhD thesis, Indiana University.

Walker, E.A. 1964. *A history of Southern Africa*. London: Longman.

Wilson, Andrew R., ed. 2004. *The Chinese in the Caribbean*. Princeton, NJ: Markus Wiener.

Xu Yongzhang. 2019. *Historical manuscripts of ancient China–Africa relations*. Shanghai: Shanghai Lexicographical Publishing House.

Yap, M. & Leong Man, D. 1996. *Colour, confusion and concessions: The history of the Chinese in South Africa*. Hong Kong: Hong Kong University Press.

18 Chinese migration and China's African policy

Introduction

On 24 April 2008, Heinrich Böll Foundation held a public lecture on China–Africa relations at the Safari Club Hotel in Nairobi as part of the "China Africa Civil Society Dialogue" sponsored by the foundation, and more than 100 people attended, including NGOs, business circles, ordinary people, media reporters and diplomatic missions in Kenya.[1] After I spoke about the history of China–Africa relations, a participant raised a question, "Are all the Chinese labourers in Kenya prison labourers?" I was quite surprised and answered, "Definitely not!", for it is unthinkable for the Chinese government or companies to use prison labour in Africa. Yet there are news reports about this fabrication. After the study of the pattern of Chinese labour in African countries, it is understandable that the wrong image is portrayed.

The first reason is the appearance of Chinese labourers, who are mostly peasants going abroad for the first time to make money, dressed in their working clothes. The second concerns segregation. The peasants know very little about Africa – neither local language nor the surroundings – and have little interest in communicating with the local people. In addition, the factory is usually in a compound surrounded by fences or other obstacles and the workers seldom go out. The third reason is the workload. Usually the Chinese company works to a very tight schedule because the contract takes a longer period to issue than expected and there is not enough time to complete the work.[2] Therefore, labourers have to work three shifts a day, each eight hours. Yet the local people only hear the machines running and see Chinese labourers working. This increases their suspicion. Who are they? They work hard, dressed in shabby clothes and "locked" in a compound. They must be prisoners.

Yet another explanation can be found in a vicious rumour spread by a US high-ranking official in *The New York Times* on 11 May 1991 with the shocking headline "China Has Used Prison Labour in Africa". The author described her ideas obtained in Africa where she sometimes worked: "The Chinese not only export goods made by prison labour, but they export prison workers too … The company was able to underbid all its competitors by

DOI: 10.4324/9781003220152-22

a wide margin because its labour costs were so cheap" (Cohen 1991).[3] The author is the Deputy Assistant Secretary of State for Human Rights in the Carter Administration. Where did she get the information? Does she have any evidence? If so, she would definitely have indicated as much. However, this malicious slander spread all over the world, which might hinder the development of China–Africa economic cooperation (Sautman & Yan 2009). In addition, the term "prisoner" severely damaged the image of Chinese in Africa.

China-Africa bilateral migration has become a concern and even a political debate among international academics. Many diaspora-related questions are interesting to both the public and academia (Alpers 1997, 2000). In terms of the Chinese in Africa, how many Chinese are there in Africa? Who are the Chinese in Africa? Are the Chinese in Africa part of a "grand strategy"? Are the Chinese in Africa taking Africans' jobs? What brings the Chinese to Africa? Regarding Africans in China, people ask: Why do Africans choose to go to China? Is there discrimination towards Africans in China? Why do Africans come to China to study? What role do Africans play in China? Is there a wave of intermarriage between Africans and Chinese in China? (Li Anshan 2015) Of course, these questions cannot be answered in just a few words. This chapter will study Chinese migration to Africa and its linkages with China's African policy.

A link always exists between migration and policy (Li Anshan 2000, 2016; Mohan & Kale 2007; Mohan & Tan-Mullins 2009; Röschenthaler & Jedlowski 2017). Generally speaking, there have been three major periods in China–Africa relations since the founding of the People's Republic of China in 1949. In 1950–78, China's African strategy focused primarily on winning allies in Africa by breaking the blockade imposed by the West and later the Soviet Union. China's aid to Africa during the period mainly consisted of supporting anti-colonial movements, the struggle against hegemonism and Africa's economic construction. From 1978 to 1995, the strategy on Africa emphasised two features: coordinating China's reform and opening up with its African strategy, indicated by the improvement of the relations between the Communist Party of China (CPC) and African parties, and competing with Taiwan to win over African countries. Since 1995, China's policy on Africa has been characterised by new strategic decisions, from an emphasis on ideology to neutral diplomacy; from economic support to exchanges in various fields; and from mere financial aid to emphasising mutual benefits. The new type of strategic partnership features mutual political trust, mutual benefits of economy, common development and mutual cultural learning. The policy has become more vigorous through summit diplomacy and standardised mechanisms (Li Anshan 2006a).

Since its reform and opening up, China has developed rapidly and has strengthened cooperative relations with Africa. The release of China's African Policy in 2000 symbolizes the gradual formulation of China's policy on Africa in the 21st century. The contemporary migration of the Chinese to Africa is closely related to China's development strategy and foreign policy.

This chapter deals with three aspects: an overview of Chinese immigration in Africa; new Chinese immigrants in Africa; and China's policy concerning its immigrants in Africa.

The history of Chinese migration to Africa

The history of China–Africa contact is long. Evidence suggests that different trade goods might have been taken from Africa to China and vice versa, and Africans travelled to China through the Middle East or India a long time ago (Sun Yutang 1979; Shen Fuwei 1990; Li Anshan 2015a, 2015b; Xu Yongzhang 2019). As previously mentioned, in the Sudan National Museum located in Khartoum, a Chinese-type *ding* (鼎), a three-legged cooking vessel made of bronze or ceramic, is exhibited. A royal symbol of political power in ancient China, the *ding* was discovered in the ruins of Meroe, the ancient capital of the Kush Kingdom (1070 BCE–350 CE) (Zhang Junyan 1986: 10).

Chinese migration to Africa has a long history, yet it only began to involve larger numbers of people about three centuries ago (Levathes 1996: 200–201; Li Anshan 2000: 82–125). The reasons were diverse: most came to work as indentured labourers in construction and infrastructure projects, while others came as merchants and business people or hoped to continue their journey to Europe or North America (Ma Mung 2008).

The emigration of Chinese to Africa began in the 1770s and underwent different phases. The first phase took place in the late Qing Dynasty (1644–1911) as a result of three key factors. First, during the late Qing period it became increasingly difficult for peasants to survive and they were compelled to go abroad to make a living. At the turn of the 20th century, China was undergoing an internal crisis and the government experienced its most vulnerable period. China had to face several invasions from imperialist powers, which resulted in two Anglo-Chinese Opium Wars (1840–1842 and 1856–1860), the China–Japanese War (1885–1886) and the Eight-Power Allied Forces War of Aggression against China (1900). Many cities were damaged, villages were destroyed and a huge indemnity was imposed by the victors, placing a heavy burden on the people. At the same time, massive infrastructure projects initiated by European colonial powers in Africa provoked a significant demand for cheap labour for the construction of railways and highways. The discovery of gold after the Anglo-Boer War (1899–1902) also led to a great demand for labour in South Africa (Bright 2013). Similarly, the Belgian Congo, British and French West Africa, the German colony Tanganyika, the Portuguese colony Mozambique, and the French colony Madagascar all employed Chinese indentured labourers to build roads and railways and work in the mining industry. There were approximately 142,000 Chinese indentured labourers in Africa between 1700 and 1910 (Li Anshan 2012: 55–93; Li Anshan 2019: 293–359). Most arrived in the late 19th and early 20th centuries.

The second factor is the political persecution of some opponents of the Qing Dynasty, who had to leave their homes in order to avoid incarceration.

Some of them, such as Yang Quyun, a close friend of Sun Yat Sen (1866–1925), came to South Africa to organize the *Xing Zhong Hui* (兴中会, Society for the Revival of China) in 1897 (Li Anshan 2019: 480–514). The third factor is related to a treaty between China and Great Britain, which was signed on 14 May 1904; it agreed to provide Chinese indentured labour for the gold mines in South Africa. This resulted in approximately 64,000 labourers arriving between 1904 and 1910. They were controlled by mine owners and suffered particularly bad working conditions (An English Eyewitness 1905; Li Anshan 2012: 132–147). At the end of their contract, while most returned to China, a few stayed on. They joined other Chinese migrants who planned to begin a new life in Africa (Bright 2013; Richardson 1982; Song Xi 1974; Yap & Leong Man 1996).[4]

Some Chinese arrived to take advantage of the economic opportunities of post-war reconstruction. Roads had to be rebuilt, cities reconstructed, agriculture redeveloped and industrialisation restarted. Most of these migrants went to Europe and the United States; only a small percentage went to Africa – mostly to Mauritius, Reunion, South Africa and Madagascar, as most parts of Africa were still colonized by Western powers (Ly-Tio-Fane-Pineo 1981; Wong-Hee-Kan 1996; Yap & Leong Man 1996; Slawecki 1971). Chinese immigrants who had already settled in Africa readily helped their newly arrived relatives and they often established business ventures together. When the CPC came to power in 1949, some fled China to escape the regime.

The second phase of Chinese migration to Africa occurred during the 1960s and 1970s. Migrants to Africa during this period were primarily from Taiwan and Hong Kong, with degrees from the United States or other developed countries; they therefore differed in an important way from previous immigrants. They had experienced living or studying in a developed country and had acquired considerable expertise in various professional fields. They were therefore able to invest in economic sectors that differed from those occupied by their predecessors, including department stores, retail and wholesale businesses, import and export firms, the garment trade, agriculture and fruit planting.

Although Taiwan had not yet lifted the ban on travelling abroad at the time, there were already numerous interactions with Africa. During the period, a few Chinese students from Taiwan with expertise in modern technology – especially agriculture and engineering – came to Africa to start businesses after they finished their studies overseas, mainly in the United States. Taiwan also sent different development aid teams to African countries. Some members of the Taiwan Agriculture Aid Team settled in Africa after completing their service (Program of African Studies 1974).[5] Due to their initiative, various Chinese-led enterprises were created in different African countries, such as those dealing with flour, textiles, garments, leather, plastics and chemical products (Wang Shengwan 1969). The owners invested their own technology, money and even machinery. An article in Chinese describes the thriving and lively atmosphere in a Chinese community from Taiwan in Madagascar in the 1960s:

> Once you arrive in Madagascar, it seems as if you arrived in your own country, no feeling that you are in Africa, since you can see various shop brands with Chinese characters here and there on the streets. When we shop in these stores, we feel cordial and warm. The overseas Chinese here are mostly in commercial business, such as import and export, daily goods, photo shops, or wine and tobacco factories. All these show that the overseas Chinese have a solid economic foundation. The main reason for them to have such an important status in economy is that they are both industrial and thrifty, and they are running the business with painstaking efforts.
>
> (Zheng Xiangheng 1966: 25)[6]

From the late 1970s, China's reform offered a good opportunity for Chinese to emigrate as the government realised that the overseas Chinese could provide a bridge between China and the world, thereby making a great contribution to China's development. As the Chinese overseas policy from then on permitted the relatives of overseas Chinese to go abroad to inherit their family's property, some went to Africa (especially to South Africa, Madagascar and Mauritius) to continue their family businesses. This coincided with the United Nations Security Council Resolution 418 (1977), creating sanctions against South Africa in reaction to the government's suppression of local anti-apartheid movements (Xia Jisheng 1996: 200–205). These mainly concentrated on the oil and arms sectors. To meet this challenge, the South African government welcomed immigrants. This happened at the same time as the opening up of China's and Taiwan's tourism sectors, and accordingly some new migrants from Taiwan, mainland China, Hong Kong and Southeast Asia went to South Africa to start a new business.

There have been Chinese medical teams in various African countries since 1964. After completing their term, some doctors chose to stay and run their own Chinese medicine clinics in African countries. Similarly, some Chinese construction workers decided to stay in Africa after finishing their projects because they felt there were lots of commercial opportunities (Hsu 2007, 2008).

From the mid-1990s, more Chinese arrived in Africa. The implementation of the "two resources and two markets" strategy, whereby the Chinese economy required resources from both China and other countries while Chinese products needed both internal and external markets, stimulated Chinese enterprises to invest in Africa. At that time, most African countries had immigration policies that encouraged Chinese migrants. Chinese from Taiwan also actively migrated to Africa at the time. In 1994, of the 869 Chinese new immigrants in South Africa, 596 were from Taiwan, 252 from mainland China and 21 from Hong Kong. Between January and October

1995, there were 350 new Chinese immigrants: 232 from Taiwan, 102 from mainland China, and 16 from Hong Kong (Yap & Leong Man 1996 419).

Some of the Chinese immigrants who had gone to Europe found it far too complicated to settle there and during the 1990s, so they re-migrated to Africa. For example, migrants from Qingtian, a county of Zhejiang Province in Eastern China with a long history of international migration, usually chose Europe as their destination. In 1995, there were 231 Qingtian Chinese in Africa; by the end of 1996, the figure had reached 1231, an increase of 400 per cent. In addition, the target countries in Africa increased from six to nine: Libya, Algeria, Cape Verde, Congo–Brazzaville, Uganda and Gabon, with new additions Togo, Equatorial Guinea and Cameroon (Zhang Xiuming 1998). It is important to note that these Chinese overseas nurtured strong relationships with their home villages and towns. They regularly travelled back home to visit their relatives, make donations, engage in philanthropic activities and invest in the Chinese economy.

Chinese new immigrants: Speculation and figures

A History of Chinese overseas in Africa (Li Anshan 2000) predicted that the number of Chinese overseas in Africa would increase significantly in the 21st century. The argument is based on four considerations. First, the development of the Chinese economy needs new markets, which would speed up the investment of Chinese enterprises in Africa and Chinese immigration as well. Second, Africa has a long history of contact with the West, with little success in its development. With its desire for development, Africa is willing to learn from China's experience, therefore providing huge potential for cooperation with China. Moreover, the continent has rich natural resources that would benefit both sides. Third, the East Asian developmental experience offers an example to Africa, which also witnesses the achievements of Chinese immigrants in the process. Moreover, the old generation of Chinese in Africa have built up a solid base and Chinese immigrants in the 1970s and 1980s set a good example for the newcomers. Finally, African countries' emigration policies are generally different from those of the West; flexible and even favourable, they welcome Chinese immigrants: "Hence the number of Chinese immigration toward Africa will greatly increase" (Li Anshan 2000: 513–514). Judging by the current situation, the above prediction has been realised. Those Chinese who went abroad after the reform and opening-up of the mid-1990s are called "new emigrants" in China. They make up the majority of Chinese in Africa and their numbers have increased significantly in the 21st century (Li Anshan 2016). However, estimates of the number of Chinese in Africa vary to a great extent.

Estimates of the number of Chinese in Africa vary and to date there are no accurate statistics.[7] *Jeune Afrique*, a French magazine, estimates the number at 500,000; a German weekly's statistic is about 750,000. Some scholars hold that the number of Chinese-Africans has reached 800,000. Based on the data of individual African countries, there has been a great increase in Chinese emigration to Africa. The Chinese in Nigeria numbered about 5100 in 1996 and the number was 60,000 in 2006.[8] In Ghana, the Chinese community numbered about 700 in 1996; it is currently about 4000. In Zambia, the number of Chinese grew from 3000 to 30,000 in ten years (Lyman 2006: 132). The Chinese community in South Africa has grown rapidly in the 21st century, and its population is currently estimated at 250,000 (*Asian Week* 2008). There is a claimed official Chinese government figure of 750,000 (Alden 2012: 19–20), I have to admit that I have never heard a figure of Chinese immigrants in Africa issued by the Chinese government. Li Xinfeng estimated that there were 1.1 million Chinese in Africa in 2012 (Li Xinfeng 2012). If the number of the new Chinese immigrants to Africa is added to the first generation of Chinese immigrants, my estimation of the number of the Chinese community in Africa was about 1 million in 2017 (Li Anshan 2019: 79–81, 1297–1307).[9]

Chinese new immigrants: Characteristics

The new Chinese immigrants to Africa mainly manifest the following characteristics. Unlike the old generation, their professions or occupations vary a great deal, including students, entrepreneurs, merchants, peasants, workers and tourists. They very quickly established themselves in some sectors of the host country's economy, such as wholesale, retail and restaurants, and the population is growing rapidly (Brautigam 2003; Anonymous 2008a; Cissé 2013, 2016).

Their reasons for emigrating to Africa vary significantly. As in other countries, the Chinese in Africa choose either to settle there permanently, or become naturalised, or just remain immigrants. Regarding their original province, some are from Taiwan, some from Hong Kong or Southeast Asia, but most are from the Chinese mainland. Compared with past generations of Chinese immigrants, who mainly came from Chinese coastal provinces such as Guangdong and Fujian, the new Chinese immigrants to Africa are from almost all parts of China, such as Zhejiang, Jiangsu, Jiangxi, Sichuan, Shanghai, Beijing and the northeast region. Some have invested directly in Africa based on their sense of commercial opportunities on the continent. Some just came to visit but, attracted by the continent's richness, they decided to settle. Some students choose to stay after obtaining their degrees from African universities (especially in South Africa), and some others just consider Africa as their springboard to emigrate to other countries.

In the 1980s and 1890s, Chinese immigrants came to Africa to invest or inherit their family property. Successful in business, they became entrepreneurs and leaders of the Chinese community in Africa, such as Sherry Chen (Chen Qianhui), Eugenia Chang, Chris Wang, Shiaan-Bin Huang, Wang Jianxu, Li Xinzhu and Hu Jieguo. Take Sherry Chen, for example. In 1981, she came to South Africa from Taiwan with the dream of starting a new life. Starting as an English-speaking secretary in a company, she acquired seven companies in the real estate, farm products and import-export sectors after years of struggle. In 1994 she joined the New National Party, one of the major political parties in South Africa. She reasoned that many Chinese people would come to do business or settle in South Africa with the development of China–African relations. Although the Chinese overseas have made a contribution to South Africa's economy, they are generally excluded from the mainstream. If Chinese immigrants are not involved in politics in South Africa, there will be no one to uphold their interests.

Mrs Chen decided to become a spokesperson for the Chinese community in South Africa. Starting as an ordinary party member, she gradually proved herself and was accepted by others through perseverance and hard work. She once said, "I try my best to do everything. If I didn't do it well, people would not just say 'Sherry Chen is not good', they would say 'the Chinese are not capable'." As a businesswoman, Chen enthusiastically explains South Africa's policies and laws to Chinese investors. As a prominent member of the Chinese community, she has tried to promote relations between South Africa and China. In 1995, she led a dance troop to the Qingdao Beer Festival and greatly promoted cultural exchanges by both sides. She considers it her obligation to speak for the local Chinese immigrants. When she became a city councillor in Johannesburg, she advocated that the Chinese community could light fireworks on the new year of the Chinese lunar calendar as is their traditional custom. In a by-election Chen was elected as a member of the National Council of Provinces in 2004 and became the first Chinese person in South Africa's National Assembly (Li Anshan 2006: 355–356, 368–371).

If Sherry Chen is a representative of successful Chinese originating from Taiwan, He Liehui is one from mainland China. Majoring in law, He Liehui graduated from Shanghai Maritime University. His father, a Chinese businessman in Botswana, is one of the first-generation private entrepreneurs after China's reform and opening up. In 1998, He Liehui went to Botswana on a business trip and saw the many commercial opportunities available in Africa. On his father's advice, He decided to start businesses in Africa. After he failed to get a visa to enter Botswana, he went to Ghana instead. Although both Botswana and Ghana are African countries, their economic development is quite different. The per capita GDP of Botswana is about $5000 while that of Ghana only about $100. However, He Liehui set up his successful Touchroad Company in Ghana. He later went to Nigeria and succeeded again, being awarded the title of chieftain there. To promote China–African economic trade, Mr He spent about RMB 1 million to hold the first Touchroad China–Africa Investment Forum in Shanghai in March 2008. The forum attracted many African government delegations and enterprises, and had a very positive impact. Then he accompanied the African delegates to the 18th East China Faire in Shanghai. He founded Touchroad International Company in 2002 and hopes that Touchroad group will become one of the top 500 enterprises in the world in 20 years. Currently, he is planning to lay a solid foundation for the Touchroad company and transform it from a family firm to a public enterprise.[10]

Few Chinese overseas are as lucky as Mrs Chen and Mr He. More of them are still struggling to establish their businesses in Africa. Take Botswana, for example. In December 2008, I met a young man from Jiangxi province who has done business for four years in Botswana and rents a booth in the marketplace. His wife has now joined him and they are doing quite well. There are also more than 10 Chinese restaurants in Botswana, one of which, Xinyue, is doing well. Xinyue specialises in Shaanxi cuisine. Its Chinese dishes, such as tofu, steamed cold noodles and handmade noodles, are delicious. Liu Long and Yang Hongqing, both young and from Shaanxi Province, are the restaurant's chefs. Their salary is about 6000–7000 pula per month (one US dollar equals about eight pula). Qiao Liang, the restaurant's boss, is a local Chinese celebrity; with one hand he runs his business, with the other he helps to organise the Chinese community in Botswana.

Some Chinese immigrants choose to stay after they have finished their aid projects in Africa, such as the aforementioned members of the Taiwan Agriculture Aid Team or a Chinese medical team. One can see Chinese doctors in Tanzania, Zambia and Botswana and other African countries.

Although most Chinese are law-abiding, some are unfamiliar with or unaware of local laws; some even disregard local laws and morality. They sell poor-quality goods, violate regulations and evade tax, which has provoked local people in one way or another. Cheap Chinese commodities and Chinese businessmen have put pressure on or even threatened the local markets and textile industry, thus causing dissatisfaction and conflict. Although African consumers are generally satisfied with cheap Chinese goods, the textile industries and local businessmen are not happy with those cheap Chinese goods and businessmen. For example, in Dakar, Senegal, two completely opposite demonstrations were held in 2005, one supporting Chinese goods and businessmen, the other opposing them (Scheld 2010).[11] This phenomenon is both paradoxical and reasonable, which indicates that the Chinese presence in Africa has a different economic impact on different social groups there.

Regarding the different groups among the Chinese immigrants, scholars have usually overlooked Chinese intellectuals in Africa. In addition to professionals and technicians, some Chinese intellectuals have made great contributions to Africa. Dr Sun Bohua is a good example. He completed his studies in China, culminating in a doctorate at Lanzhou University and post-doctoral research at Tsinghua University. From 1991 to 1992, Sun Bohua worked as research fellow at Delft University of Technology, focusing on buckling theory of structures and sandwich conical shells. Before that he was an Alexander von Humboldt fellow at Ruhr Universität Bochum from 1992 to 1993, researching infinite deformation of shells and continuum mechanics. He has been based in South Africa since 1993, and was elected to both the Academy of Science of South Africa (ASSA) and the Royal Society of South Africa (RSSA) in 2010.[12] Other prominent Chinese academics in South Africa include Xia Xiaohua, a professor at the University of Pretoria, a member of ASSA and fellow of the South African Academy of Engineering (SAAE);[13] Xu Hongkun, professor at KwaZulu-Natal University, member of ASSA (2005) and the Third World Academy of Sciences (TWAS 2012);[14] and Zhao Baojin, a professor of geology at the University of Fort Hare.[15]

China's policy towards Chinese immigrants in Africa

The current growth of the Chinese community in Africa is closely related to the Chinese strategy for Africa. This has different interest at different times, but its obvious continuity is characterised by four points. First, in its international strategy, China sees African countries as important allies that are ignored by other great powers. Second, China sees the African continent as a single unit, which is different from the traditional diplomatic strategy based on the country-by-country model; this is also in agreement with African Union's strategy in international arena, although there is a specific policy related to each country. Third, China considers African countries as equal strategic partners, whether they are small or big, strong or weak. Fourth, China seeks a mutually beneficial co-development strategy when developing its cooperation with Africa. The essence of China's policy on Africa is to establish a strategic partnership with the continent to realise China's strategic goals on one hand and promote development in Africa on the other.

China's strategy on Africa has had a great impact in the international order, which has long been dominated by Western powers but is now gradually being eroded by other rising powers. For example, FOCAC and various events between China and Africa have manifested China's political strength (Li Anshan 2014; Li Anshan et al. 2012). China's economic power is illustrated by its being Africa's largest trading partner for 12 consecutive years in 2021, with China Africa trade volume reaching US$204.2 billion, up 20 per cent yearly in 2019.[16] With China's support, African countries such as the Sudan and Zimbabwe turned a deaf ear to the Western powers' warnings. Despite the Great Britain's admonition, Nigeria is still very keen to cooperate with China. With China's entry into the market, the French companies could no longer monopolise the African franc zone. Even the newly established US African Command cannot find a base in the continent. In an article published in the *Financial Times* in January 2008, Mr Wade, the Senegalese President, called on the West to learn from China as far as African affairs are concerned (Wade 2008).

Based on a survey of the development of Chinese people in Africa, we can argue that China's policy on Chinese overseas is highly correlated with its development strategy. In the early period of China's reform and opening up, the Chinese government encouraged the offspring of Chinese abroad to inherit their parents' patrimonies. Since the mid-1990s, certain large-scale Chinese enterprises have invested in Africa, and this is largely related to China's strategic decision to use "two resources and two markets". The

Chinese government also plays a guiding role in China's investment in Africa. As the China–Africa relationship deepens, protecting Chinese overseas becomes one of the main tasks of Chinese embassies and consulates in Africa.

After the Cultural Revolution, China changed its view on the current situation in international politics, as well as the relationship between the economy and diplomacy. China realised that the theme of international relations should no longer be "war and revolution" but rather should become "peace and development". In relation to this transformation, the idea of "economy serving diplomacy" changed to that of "diplomacy serving economy". With this strategic decision, the Chinese government began to vigorously encourage the descendants of Chinese overseas to go abroad to inherit their families' property; some successful overseas Chinese entrepreneurs did go to Africa for this reason. For example, Hu Jieguo's father is a Chinese living in Nigeria. Hu was educated in Shanghai, then recommended as a university student during the Cultural Revolution. In 1976, he was encouraged to emigrate to Nigeria and went on from there to Canada to learn hotel management. After his first job in a hotel in Canada, he invested in many industries such as restaurants, engineering, forestry and machinery. In the mid-1990s, he invested US$8 million to build the Jingmen Grand Hotel in Lagos, the former Nigerian capital. The hotel became a landmark because of its fine decoration and exquisite craftsmanship, and its restaurant is famous. It has hosted many high officials and celebrities from China and other countries, and many high-ranking Nigerian officials hold their banquets and parties there. Hu enjoys a high reputation in the country, and in 2001 he was awarded the title of chief by Nigerian traditional leaders. Hu has offered assistance to Chinese institutions and companies in Nigeria and helped the China Civil Engineering Construction Corporation with the winning bid for a railway construction project. When the China National Petroleum Corporation (CNPC) began to enter the Nigerian market, Hu helped it to make contacts with his recommendation to the Nigerian Minister of Petroleum. When a staff member of the Chinese embassy in Nigeria was kidnapped, Hu led the police to successfully rescue the victims. He also undertook to renovate the embassy. Being one of the leading Chinese entrepreneurs in Africa, he holds many posts, such as the Deputy Director of the China Council for the Promotion of International Trade, the Premier Vice-president of the Nigeria–China Friendship Association, the honorary President of the China–Nigeria Federation of Industry & Commerce and special consultant to the Nigerian president (Li Anshan 2006: 470–474; Li Anshan 2019: 1019–1020).

At the start of the 1990s, Chinese companies started to increase their investment in Africa and the number of Chinese in Africa increased rapidly. Chinese construction workers are prevalent in Angola, Zambia, Mozambique, Nigeria, Tanzania and the Republic of Seychelles, Although most Chinese companies normally hire local labourers, they do employ Chinese construction workers in certain circumstances (CCS 2006) for the following reasons. The first is the tight time constraints of the construction projects, since the

Chinese workers are able to work beyond the working hours stipulated by local labour law. Second, the Chinese labourers are more manageable, staying together and sharing a similar language, culture and customs. Third, they are more skilled than local workers, and most of them have experience in construction work. Frequently, after a few years on a Chinese project, construction workers realise that the local conditions are good and the host country is open to foreigners, and they are willing to work in Africa.

The Chinese government provides timely assistance to Chinese settling or investing in Africa. With growing China–Africa engagement, some ministries in the Chinese central government also play an important role in guiding Chinese firms to invest in the continent. They offer all kinds of commodity information, such as the products needed in the African markets to encourage investment. The Chinese government once set up more than ten China–Africa trade centers to promote the sale of Chinese products in Africa; unfortunately these were unsuccessful.

The Comoros is an example of an African country with a very favourable policy on foreign investment. Except for certain regulations on the import and production of pork and alcohol products, Comoros law sets no limits on the economic and commercial activities of foreign firms and individuals. On 31 August 2007, the Comoros parliament passed a new law to regulate investment in such sectors as agriculture, fishery, husbandry, fish breeding and poultry raising, tourism and information technology, all of which would be exempt from tax for a term extended from five to 10 years. The Comoros government also provides preferential policies and encouraging measures for enterprises with investment in industries which need to buy land. The government has also set up the investment promotion bureau, which helps foreign firms and individuals to invest and provides them with consultancies and other services in the country. The business service of the Chinese embassy in Comoros soon noticed this and suggested that Chinese companies take advantage of the preferential policy to engage in the development of its agriculture, fishery, farming, tourism, mineral resources, offshore oil, volcanic and terrestrial heat, and solar energy, and the privatisation of its state-owned enterprises (Anonymous 2008b).

The Chinese government also makes available the laws and regulations of relevant African countries to help Chinese people emigrate to or invest in Africa. These laws and regulations are listed on the website of the Ministry of Commerce or its annual report. After collecting articles on laws on commerce, taxation and environment protection, the Chinese embassies and consulates in Africa send them back to the Ministry of Commerce. The media of Côte d'Ivoire are relatively tolerant of the commercial activities of foreign enterprises in their country; there are few negative reports and they are mainly about trade disputes. But in 2008, there were two negative reports on Chinese products. One was about shoes and the other was about milk. In March, the Shoes Merchants Association of Côte d'Ivoire held a strike against the dumping of cheap Chinese shoes, which was reported by the local media and had a negative impact. After negotiations between the Chinese embassy and the Federation of Industry and Commerce of Côte d'Ivoire, this issue was resolved satisfactorily and the Côte d'Ivoire press publicly corrected its former misleading reports. In September and October, due to a scandal surrounding Sanlu milk powder in China, the Ministry of Livestock, Husbandry and Water Resources of Côte d'Ivoire sealed up stores of milk powder imported from China and sent samples to the European Union for testing. The results were satisfactory, and the press of Côte d'Ivoire reported this issue objectively.[17]

The Chinese government has started to strengthen its management of the corporate social responsibility (CSR) of Chinese companies and state-owned enterprises in Africa. In August 2008, China's Ministry of Commerce and other related ministries held a conference on strengthening the CSR of Chinese in Africa. The conference pointed out clearly that, in the long run, if Chinese companies wanted to invest in Africa they had to pay more attention to their CSR. Sixty-seven enterprises published a declaration to strengthen their CSR in Africa.[18]

In fact, the protection of the Chinese in Africa has become one of the main missions of Chinese diplomacy. With the growing population of Chinese in Africa, some abuse of the Chinese community has occurred in certain African countries such as South Africa, Madagascar, Nigeria and Sudan. In response to the serious safety concerns faced by Chinese immigrants in South Africa, in September 2004 Luo Tianguang, the former Director-General of the Department of Consular Affairs of the Chinese Ministry of Foreign Affairs, was dispatched to Johannesburg to negotiate with the Ministry of Foreign Affairs and the South African police on the issue of the security of Chinese citizens and Chinese living in South Africa. Later, the Chinese government signed a series of agreements on police cooperation with its South African counterpart. In 2005, the Chinese government dispatched a liaison official for police affairs to its embassy in South Africa (Li Anshan 2006: 478–481).

A report issued by Afrobarometer, a think-tank in Africa, indicates that China enjoys a favourable attitude among Africans. Thirty-six African countries were surveyed and 63 per cent think China's economic and political influence is positive, with Mali showing the highest appreciation (92 per cent).[19] This report is echoed by the 2015 Pew survey *Opinion of China*; nine African countries interviewed indicated favourable attitudes to China.[20] The Africans' impression of China mostly comes from their contact with Chinese in their countries, and thus is strongly related to the behavior of overseas Chinese and their contribution to African society.[21]

Conclusion

Tracing the movement of Chinese people to different parts of Africa, beginning with southern Africa and expanding to other countries, this chapter has summarised the various paths of Chinese migrants to Africa. It has also highlighted their close connection to state policies related to overseas Chinese, which reflect China's interest in furthering the country's foreign presence in order to support Chinese activities and projects while encouraging African development at the same time. The chapter illustrated these developments through the trajectories of individual Chinese entrepreneurs.

Contact between China and Africa has a long history, and people-to-people (P2P) contact took place long before the official relationship. Interaction between the two regions is exemplified by trade and migration, and bilateral migration has opened various channels for cultural exchange and provided a very important form of P2P contact. Through contact, an equal exchange of ideas is achieved without superiority and inferiority. Frankly speaking, the Chinese workers and immigrants have made their contribution to the mutual understand between Chinese and Africans. Still, there is some misunderstanding.

Four conclusions can be drawn from this chapter. First, the history of the Chinese in Africa shows that their emigration is highly correlated with both China's domestic affairs and the policy of the target country. Second, since the reform and opening up of China, the new trend of Chinese emigration to Africa and its development are closely related to China's African policy (Li Anshan 2013). Third, the issue of Chinese overseas will become more important in China's African diplomacy, since they can be at the same time a factor in China's economic growth, a political influence and a source of cultural interaction. Fourth, the purpose of contact between individuals is twofold: to understand the culture of others as a means of establishing better relations, and to make your own culture better understood. Individual migrants must appreciate this contact, introduce their culture and absorb that of their hosts.

Notes

1 Chinese Ambassador Zhang Ming made an opening remark and Chinese scholars Xu Weizhong, He Wenping and Li Anshan gave a lecture on specific topics of the history, current situation and future of China–Africa relations respectively.
2 Interview in a meeting with Chinese state-owned companies, Nairobi, Kenya, 23 May 2009.
3 I would like to thank Barry Sautman and Yan Hairong for providing me with the information and the specific article about the fabrication that was to be published in *The China Quarterly*.
4 There are different calculations of the numbers of Chinese indentured labourers in South Africa; for a synthesis, see Li Anshan (2019: 340–346).
5 The book lists cooperation projects between Taiwan and 25 countries.
6 For the Taiwanese in Africa, see also Wang Shengwan (1969); Tang Xiyiong (n.d.).
7 My estimate of Chinese overseas in 1996 is 136,000 (Li Anshan 2000: 568–569).
8 The statistics were given by the Nigerian general consul in Hong Kong at the China–Africa Links Workshop held in in Hong Kong University of Science and Technology, 11–12 November 2006.

9 According to my calculation in "(5) Statistics of Overseas Chinese in African Countries or Regions (1968–2017)", even based on the largest figure if there are different figures, the total population of the Chinese community in Africa is 989,900 (Li Anshan 2019: 1303–1307).
10 *Liberation Daily* (Shanghai), 8 March 2008.
11 The correspondence between the author and D.Z. Osborn, an American scholar. The author also had the chance to discuss the manifestations with Adama Gaye, a Togolese journalist, at an international conference, "China in Africa: Geopolitical and Geoeconomic Considerations", held at the Kennedy School of Government, Harvard University from 31 May to 2 June 2007.
12 See Professor Bohua Sun's website at http://cn.linkedin.com/pub/bohua-sun/71/13b/487
13 See Professor Xia Xiaohua's website at www.up.ac.za/eece/article/1952621/postgraduate-students
14 See Xu Hongkun's website at http://newspaper.hdu.edu.cn/Article_Show.asp?ArticleID=8341
15 See Zhao Baojin's website at https://za.linkedin.com/pub/baojin-zhao/12/947/617
16 "Ministry of Commerce: China has become Africa's largest trading partner for ten consecutive years", 19–06–05, 13:01, Official account number of CCTV financial channel. https://baijiahao.baidu.com/s?id=1635475987756048341&wfr=spider&for=pc
17 On 22 October 2008, *Le Journal International* of Côte d'Ivoire published the whole text of the public response of the Business Service of the Chinese Embassy to the reports of the media of Côte d'Ivoire on the issue of Sanlu milk powder. For a later research, see Aurégan (2012).
18 "Proposal by 67 enterprises to build a sense of responsibility and create harmonious win-win economic relations between China and Africa". http//:xyf.mofcom.gov.cn/aarticle/ghlt/cksm/200709/20070905111119.html.
19 "Here's what Africans think about China's influence in their countries". www.afrobarometer.org/blogs/heres-what-africans-think-about-chinas-influence-their-countries
20 "Opinion of China". www.pewglobal.org/database/indicator/24/survey/17
21 For a recent poll, see "Friend or foe: China's surprisingly durable reputation in Africa", 11 September 2020. www.theafricareport.com/41380/chinas-surprisingly-durable-reputation-in-africa

References

Alden, Chris. 2012. China and Africa: From engagement to partnership. In Marcus Power & Ana Cristina Alves, eds, *China and Angola: A marriage of convenience?* Nairobi: Pambazuka Press.
Alpers, Edward A. 1997. The African diaspora in the northwestern Indian Ocean: Reconsideration of an old problem, new directions for research," *Comparative Studies of South Asia, Africa & the Middle East* 17(2): 62–81.
Alpers, Edward A. 2000. Recollecting Africa: Diasporic memory in the Indian Ocean world. *African Studies Review* 43(1): 83–99.
Anonymous. 2008a. Chinese are new immigrants in South Africa. *Asian Week*, 4 February.

Anonymous. 2008b. Comoros government encourages foreign firms and individuals to engage in economic and commercial activities. http://fec.mofcom.gov.cn/aarticle/duzpb/cf/ap/200812/20081205955276.html

Aurégan, Xavier. 2012. *Les "communautés" chinoises en Côte d'Ivoire: analyse comparative de l'hétérogénéité des acteurs, de leur intégration et des territoires en Afrique de l'Ouest.* Paris: Institut Français de Géopolitique. https://geopolitique.hypotheses.org/122

Brautigam, Deborah. 2003. Close encounters: Chinese business networks as industrial catalysts in sub-Saharan Africa. *African Affairs* 102: 447–467.

Bright, Rachel. 2013. *Chinese labour in South Africa, 1902–10: Race, violence, and global spectacle.* London: Palgrave Macmillan.

Centre for Chinese Studies (CCS). 2006. *China's interest and activity in Africa's construction and infrastructure sectors.* www.icafrica.org/fileadmin/documents/Knowledge/DFID/China's%20Interest%20and%20Activity%20in%20Africa's%20Infrastructure%20and%20Construction%20Sectors.pdf

Cissé, Daouda. 2013. A portrait of Chinese traders in Dakar, Senegal. *Migration Information Source*, 18 July. www.migrationpolicy.org/article/portrait-chinese-traders-dakar-senegal

Cissé, Daouda. 2016. Chinese traders in Windhoek. *Pambazuka News*, 3 February.

Cohen, Roberta. 1991. China has used prison labour in Africa. *The New York Times*, 11 May.

An English Eyewitness. 1905. *John Chinaman on the Rand*. London: R.A. Everett & Son.

Hsu, Elisabeth. 2007. Chinese medicine in East Africa and its effectiveness. *IIAS Newsletter* 45 (Autumn): 22.

Hsu, Elisabeth. 2008. Medicine as business: Chinese Medicine in Tanzania. In Chris Alden, Daniel Large & Richardo Soares de Oliveira, eds, *China returns to Africa: A rising power and a continent embrace.* London: Hurst & Company, 221–235.

King, Kenneth. 2013. *China's aid and soft power in Africa: The case of education and training.* Oxford: James Currey.

Levathes, L. 1996. *When China ruled the seas: The treasure fleet of the dragon throne, 1405–1433.* New York: Oxford University Press.

Li Anshan. 2000. *A history of Chinese overseas in Africa.* Beijing: Chinese Overseas Publishing House.

Li Anshan. 2006. *Social history of Chinese overseas in Africa: Selected documents 1800–2005.* Hong Kong: Hong Kong Press for Social Science Ltd.

Li Anshan. 2006a. On the adjustment and transformation of China's African policy. *West Asia and Africa* 8: 1–20.

Li Anshan. 2012. *A history of overseas Chinese in Africa to 1911.* New York: Diasporic Africa Press.

Li Anshan. 2013. China's Africa policy and the Chinese immigrants in Africa. In Chee-Beng Tan, ed., *Routledge handbook of the Chinese diaspora.* London: Routledge, 59–70.

Li Anshan. 2014. Origin of the Forum on China–Africa Cooperation. In Jinjun Zhao & Zirui Chen, eds, *China and the International Society.* Beijing: World Century, 259–294.

Li Anshan. 2015. 10 questions about migration between China and Africa. China Policy Institute. http://blogs.nottingham.ac.uk/chinapolicyinstitute/2015/03/04/10-questions-about-migration-between-china-and-africa

Li Anshan. 2015a. African Diaspora in China: Reality, research and reflection, *The Journal of Pan African Studies* 7: 10–43.
Li Anshan. 2015b. Contact between China and Africa before Vasco da Gama: Archaeology, document and historiography'. *World History Studies* 2(1): 34–59.
Li Anshan. 2016. Chinese immigrants in international political discourse: A case study of Africa. *West Asia and Africa* 1: 76–97.
Li Anshan. 2019. *The social and economic history of the Chinese overseas in Africa* (3 vols). Nanjing: Jiangshu People's Press.
Li Anshan et al. 2012. *FOCAC twelve years later: Achievements, challenges and the way forward.* Uppsala: Nordic Africa Institute.
Li Xinfeng. 2012. On the number of the overseas Chinese in Africa. *Huaqiao yu Huaren* 1–2: 7–12. http://iwaas.cass.cn/xslt/fzlt/201508/t20150831_2609329.shtml
Ly-Tio-Fane-Pineo, Huguette. 1981. *La Diaspora Chinoise dans L'OceanIndien Occidental.* Aix-en-Provence: Association des Chercheurs de l'Occan d'Indien, Institut d'Histoire des pays d'Outre-mer, Greco Ocean Indien.
Lyman, P. 2006. China's involvement in Africa: A view from the US. *South African Journal of International Affairs* 13(1): 129–138.
Ma Mung, Emmanuel. 2008. Chinese migration and China's foreign policy in Africa. *Journal of Chinese Overseas* 4(1): 91–109.
Mohan, Giles & Kale, Dinar. 2007. *The invisible hand of South–South globalisation: Chinese migrants in Africa.* New York: Rockefeller Foundation.
Mohan, Giles & Tan-Mullins, May. 2009. Chinese migrants in Africa as new agents of development? An analytical framework. *European Journal of Development Research* 21: 588–605.
Program of African Studies. 1974. *Agreements on technical cooperation between the Republic of China and African states.* Taipei: National Chengchi University.
Richardson, P. 1982. *Chinese mine labour in the Transvaal.* London: Macmillan.
Röschenthaler, U. & A. Jedlowski, eds. 2017. *Mobility between Africa, Asia and Latin America: Economic networks and cultural interactions.* London: Zed Books.
Sautman, Barry & Yan Hairong. 2009. African perspectives on China–Africa links. *The China Quarterly* 199: 729–760.
Scheld, Suzanne. 2010. "The China challenge": The global dimensions of activism and the global economy in Dakar. In Ilda Lyndell, ed., *Africa's informal workers: Collective agency, alliances and transnational organizing in urban Africa.* London: Zed Books, 153–168.
Shen Fuwei. 1990. *China and Africa: Relations of 2000 years.* Beijing: Zhonghua Book Company.
Slawecki, Leon M.S. 1971. *French Policy Towards the Chinese in Madagascar.* Connecticut: The Shoe String Press.
Song Xi. 1974. *The Chinese labourer's contributions to the Transvaal gold mines in South Africa at the end of the Qing Dynasty.* Taipei: Huagang.
Sun Yutang. 1979. China and Egypt in the Han Dynasty. *Journal of Chinese Historical Studies* 2: 142–154.
Tang Xiyiong. n.d. Taiwanese in Lesotho: A case study of Taiwanese in Africa, 1970–80. Unpublished paper.
Wade, Abdoulaye. 2008 Time for the West to practice what it preaches. *Financial Times*, 23 January. www.ftchinese.com/story/001017597/en?page=2

Wang Shengwan. 1969. Gather-together of Chinese in Ghana. *Overseas Affairs Monthly* (Taipei) 199: 30.

Wong-Hee-Kan, Edith. 1996. *La Diaspora Chinoise au Marscareignes: Le cas de la Reunion*. Paris: Editions L'Harmattan.

Xia Jisheng, ed. 1996. *A study of racial relations in South Africa*. Shanghai: East China Normal University Press.

Xu Yongzhang. 2019. *Historical manuscripts of ancient China–African relations*. Shanghai: Shanghai Dictionary Press.

Yap, Melanie & Leong Man, Dianne. 1996. *Colour, confusion and concessions: The history of the Chinese in South Africa*. Hong Kong: Hong Kong University Press.

Zhang Junyan. 1986. *Contact at sea between China and West Asia and Africa during the ancient times*. Beijing: China Ocean Press.

Zhang Xiuming. 1998. A study of Qingtianese abroad: Past and present. *Overseas Chinese History Studies* 3: 49–59.

Zheng Xiangheng. 1966. The overseas Chinese in Madagascar. *Overseas Affairs Monthly* (Taipei) 166: 25.

19 African diaspora in China
History and present[1]

Introduction

In the world-famous Small Commodity Circulation Center located in Yiwu City, Zhejiang Province, nearly 500,000 foreign businesspeople enter and leave the country every year. In 2014, Yiwu's total import and export of small commodities reached US$24.19 billion, including export of US$23.71 billion, an increase of 30 per cent and 30.2 per cent respectively. With the growth of foreign trade, a large number of foreign-related disputes there have emerged, arising from contract conclusion, language communication, product quality and other issues in commodity sales. In 2013, Yiwu City pioneered the establishment of the Foreign Dispute Mediation Office for foreigner-related disputes and a "United Nations" foreigner-related dispute-mediation team. These appointed voluntary foreign mediators are honest and trustworthy businessmen from 12 countries and regions in the world. Tirera Sourakhata from Senegal served as a mediator for Muhammad. It has been eight years since Tirera Sourakhata was in Yiwu and he is an "old Yiwu". Proficient in French, English, Arabic and Chinese, Tirera Sourakhata is a "main player" of the United Nations mediation team (Duan Jingjing, Ying Yuanliang & Pu Guofu 2015).

The history of human beings is a history of migration. From ancient times, African people have moved from Africa to other parts of the world to find a better environment for survival or development. In the modern international system with borders being a necessity of the nation-state, immigration has become an issue, be it one of national policy or international concerns. With the strengthening of China–Africa relations, a wave of bilateral migration has occurred, which has created enthusiasm for the study of migration between China and Africa. The previous chapter studied Chinese immigration to Africa; this chapter examines the African diaspora in China.

There are studies of Chinese either on the African continent (Li Anshan 2000, 2012, 2019), in particular regions (Ly Tio Fane-Pines 1981, 1985) or in specific countries (Human 1984; Yap & Leong 1996; Wong-Heekan 1996; Smidt, 2001; Ly-Tio-Fane Pines & Lim 2008; Park 2008), yet the African diaspora in China is much less frequently studied. Bodomo

DOI: 10.4324/9781003220152-23

correctly points out that Africans coming to China has a long history and it should be placed in the context of the wider African presence in Asia, a subject that needs a sustained research (Bodomo 2012; Cissé 2021). There are quite a few studies of the definition of African diaspora as a whole (Harris 1993; Shepperson 1993; Alpers 1997, 2000; Davies, 2008, African Union, 2005; Zeleza, 2005, 2008). The term "diaspora" is used here in the sense that Africans in China (or in any other part of the world) are not only a migration group but also a community with its own social network, cultural pattern and value system, which does not need assimilation (Bodomo 2012). In addition, the African Union recognises the African diaspora as the sixth group of African people alongside five groups in the continent (African Union 2005).

This chapter constitutes a history of the African presence in China that is aimed at a clearer understanding of the connections between reality and research, and if possible providing some areas for future study. It is divided into four parts: Blacks/Africans in early China; the issue of *Kunlun*; the origin and jobs of Blacks/Africans in ancient China; and the study of Africans in contemporary China. The terms "Blacks" or "Black people" are used in the chapter to indicate various Black peoples in Chinese history, including those from Southeast Asia, Africa and other places.[2]

Were there Africans in China in early times?

There is a long history of China–Africa contact, illustrated by Chinese classics such as dynastic histories and classics by Du Huan, Duan Chengshi, Zhou Qufei, Zhao Rukuo, Wang Dayuan, Fei Xin and Ma Huan, as well as contemporary studies. Yet whether Africans existed in early China is another question. Chinese historians generally agree that Blacks/Africans came to China during the Tang Dynasty (618–907 CE). Yet archaeological discoveries seem to challenge this view; they indicate the possibility of contact between China and Africa in an earlier time. A report on excavations in the Shang Dynasty (17th–11th centuries BCE) sites at Anyang, the capital of Shang, shows similarities between the skull discovered there and that of Black people. Many images of Black people in stone, metal and jade were also found in Anyang (Yang Ximei 1966; Chang Kwang Chih 1968).

During the Han Dynasty, *kilin*, or *qilin*, an imaginary lucky animal in ancient China, appears in a stone sculpture and looks like a giraffe (Xuzhou Museum 1980). Ferand discussed the link between giraffe and *qilin* (or *kilin*) in *Journal Asiatique* in 1918. Ethiopia and Alexandria were mentioned in *Shi Ji* (Records of the Grand Historian, 104–91 BCE), *Han Shu* (*History of the Han*, 80 CE) and *Wei Lue* (Brief accounts of the Wei Kingdom). The astronomer-geographer Claudius Ptolemaeus of Alexandria (90–168 CE) described China and the Silk Road in his *Geography* in the second century. The earliest indication of Black people (*hei-se-ren*) in China seems to be in *Juyan Han Jian*.[3] Sixty *Juyan Han Jian* documents record the personal details of individuals, including their residential locations, such as *jun* (prefecture, a unit above a county), *xian* (county) and *li* (grassroots unit), and their rank, age, height and skin colour. With height and skin colour identified it is possible to understand the physical features of individuals at the time. Two studies are particularly interesting. According to Zhang's study, 55 cases giving skin colour are identified among 60 individual cases, and 53 are recorded as "Black". In addition, one was labelled "brown Black" and another "yellow Black". This is very impressive, even considering that Han China was a multi-ethnic empire. Were the Black-skinned people from a specific area? Or did they belong to an ethnic group different from the Han Chinese? The significance of the study lies in the analysis of height and colour. The author argues that since the 53 Black-skinned individuals were from different parts of the empire, they were ordinary Han Chinese (Zhang Chunshu,[4] 1977).

Yang came to a different conclusion after the study of *Juyan Han Jian* and related literature such as *Yilin*, published at almost the same time. First, there were hundreds of thousands of foreigners living in the Hexi area and the surrounding area of Chang-an, the capital at the time and an international metropolis. Second, most of the Black-skinned people lived in the Hexi area, a fact that Zhang fails to explain. Among 25 cases of Black-skinned people in the records of *Ji-guan* (birthplace or origin), 17 were from the Hexi area. Third, the Black-skinned people were generally 165.6–177.1 centimetres, which is taller than ordinary Chinese (161.2–167.6 centimetres) but similar to the Black people in Northeast Africa or the Pamiri. Fourth, married Black-skinned men working as border officials who lived with their families could have settled in the region much earlier, possibly at the beginning of Emperor Zhaodi's rule (94–74 BCE). Fifth, two Black women with sunken eyes mentioned in *Yilin* lived a different life and were not married to Han Chinese. This should be regarded as a different cultural pattern. Yang believes that the Black-skinned people may have been foreigners who probably came from the vast area west of China. The conclusion is that there were Black people in early China, possibly of foreign or even African origin (Yang Ximei 1995).

After a long period of war and instability, China entered an era of prosperity in the Tang Dynasty (618–907 CE). Foreigners came to China as diplomats, officials, visitors, traders and workers, and some settled in China. Two terms, *Sengzhi* (sometimes spelt as *Sengchi*) and *Kunlun,* appear in the literature referring to Black people. The record shows that in the year 724 CE two *Sengzhi* (Zandj) girls from the Kingdom of Palembang were offered to the Chinese emperor, and four *Sengzhi* slaves – five *Sengzhi* boys and two *Sengzhi* girls – were sent to Emperor Xian Zhong (805–820 CE) as tribute in 813, 815 and 818 CE respectively, all from islands of present-day Indonesia. *Kunlun,* used as a name for a mountain, water or place (Goodrich 1931), an official position and a state in ancient times, turned out to be a name for an ethnic group with a specific meaning: Black-skinned (Zhang Xinglang 1930; Ge Chengyong 2001; Xu Yongzhang 2019).

Kunlun or Black people: Different views and ethnocentrism

There was an increase in the number of Black people in China during the Tang and Song dynasties (960–1279 CE) and *Kunlun* became a fashionable topic (more than *Sengzhi*)[5] in the literature. Who were the *Kunlun* people? Where did they come from? What did they do in ancient China? There are three kinds of evidence supporting the presence of *Kunlun* during that period: paintings, pottery figures and literature.

Dunhuang (敦煌) is located in northwest China, where hundreds of Buddhist caves with the paintings of the Tang Dynasty are preserved. Among the famous Dunhuang cave-paintings, quite a few depict Black-skinned figures, such as Dunhuang Yulin Cave No. 23, Dunhuang Caves No. 103, 194, 220, 332, 335 and 431. Black people also appeared in silk paintings. Since the 1940s, many Black pottery figures have been discovered in the Xi-an (formerly Chang-an) area, the former capital of the ancient dynasties. These pottery figures aroused excitement among archaeologists. One, in Madam Pei's tomb (850 CE) in Xi-an, is obviously a Black person; it is 15 centimetres tall with curly hair, red lips, white eyes, a high and wide nose, impressive muscles and short in body, a typical African figure (Du Baoren 1979). Third, *Kunlun* became a popular subject in various writings during the Tang Dynasty and later, either in official works or in literature, such as *Jiu Tang Shu, Xin Tang Shu, Zizhi Tongjian, Tang Hui Yao, Cefu Yuangui, Youyang Zazu, Taiping Guangji, Zhu Fan Zhi,* and *Pingzhou Ketan*. There are several studies on the topic, either during the Tang period or after, or by contemporary scholars as discussed in Chapter 1.

As mentioned previously, regarding the identity of *Kunlun*, there are generally two views: they are either seen as Black people from Africa (Zhang Xinglang 1930, 1977) or they are from Southeast Asia (Ge Chengyong 2001). There are few studies on Black people in pre-modern China in international academia, and the mastery of classical Chinese is apparently a necessary condition. I would like to comment on the works by Julie Wilensky and Don Wyatt. Wilensky made a detailed study of the concept of *Kunlun* and the shifts in Chinese perceptions of people with dark skin and knowledge of Africa in ancient China (Wilensky 2002). Although the author borrows heavily from Zhang's work in the first two chapters, her mastery of Chinese is impressive. The work uses various Chinese sources: dynastic histories, fictional literature, and geographical and travel notes. The writings of officials are important sources in the article, such as customs official Zhao Rukuo, or Fei Xin and Ma Huan, who both worked in Zheng He's fleet as a navy official and interpreter respectively. Owing to the length of the period and the enormous amount of material on the subject, her conclusion is somewhat ambiguous. On one hand, the author acknowledges that, "It is difficult to assess the complex legacy of pre-modern Chinese perceptions of Africa and dark-skinned people." On the other hand, she draws a contradictory conclusion that the Chinese have had specific "negative attitudes towards Africans and other people with dark skin"

(Wilensky 2002: 43), However, this is a rather common view (Dikotter 1992; Wyatt 2010).

Wyatt's book (Wyatt 2010) is also an important work in the field, although less promising than the ambitious title *The Blacks of Premodern China* suggests. As a professor of history, Wyatt is skilful enough to make maximum use of two pieces of information. One is a paragraph recorded in the dynastic history of the Tang about the murder of Lu Yuanrui, a rapacious governor who wanted to cheat foreign merchants in the sale of their goods. As it happened, the murderer was a courageous *Kunlun*, who not only killed the governor in front of his guards but also other officials, and successfully escaped. The author puts the case in a broad historical context and elaborates on the implications of murder by a *Kunlun*. Another is Zhu Yu's *Pingzhou Ketan* (*Tales of Pingzhou*) (1119 CE), a collection of anecdotal trifles and notes that describe the social life of Guangzhou, especially that of foreign residents. It contains several references to *Kunlun* as domestic slaves and labourers employed on board a ship to caulk leaky seams below the waterline from the outside, as they were expert swimmers.

> However, for any modern Western observer who, more than a millennium after the fact, seeks to penetrate and decipher this most unexpected of references in a premodern Chinese text, understandably and justifiably, endeavors to reconstitute the context of Zhu Yu's striking commentary depend most of all on the question of origins. In short, where *were* these slaves?
>
> (Wyatt 2010: 55)

Did he find the answer to their origin? Yes: it was "nowhere else than Africa" – they were "Africans" (Wyatt 2010: 10, 78), a conclusion drawn by Zhang Xinglang 80 years earlier.

Taiping Guangji (*Comprehensive collections of the Taiping era,* 978 CE) is a work containing various stories of *Kunlun* as positive figures.[6] It is interesting that Wyatt does not quote anything from this book except in a footnote. One reason might be that the book is fiction, so not deemed worthwhile as evidence. Yet fiction is a meaningful form that reflects reality and social or ideological change, and a historian should use any material possible to explain what happened. Intentional or unintentional bias might be another reason., since the cases in the book are contrary to Wyatt's view. For example Mo *Kunlun*, a Black boy, was born in an unusual way after his mother's dream of a visitation by an alien monk (similar to Jesus Christ's conception), yet grew up to be a brave guard and lived a happy life bestowed by the emperor. Another case is a hero in *Kunlun Nu,* a fictional story with a strong, smart and brave *Kunlun* hero named Mole who helps and is trusted by his master in a unique way. Do the positive figures reflect something of the period? Another case of Wyatt's bias is the interpretation of *huan chang* (or *huan changwei,* change in bowels or stomach) as "cultural imperialism". In Zhu Yu's passage about the slaves, he says, "They eat raw food. But once they are acquired as slaves, they are fed cooked food. They thereupon endure days of diarrhoea, which is referred to as 'converting the bowels' (*huan chang*)." This has in fact been a long-time experience in China, a vast land with different climatic regions and food styles. It takes time for newcomers to adjust to local food. For example, diarrhoea may occur in the first few days after a Hunanese moves to Guangdong. Yet Wyatt translates it as "converting the bowels", and the word "convert" somewhat implies "being forced to change", which better fits the author's description of *huan chang* as "cultural imperialism" (Wyatt 2010: 60).[7] It is noticeable that Dikotter translates *huanchang* as "changing the bowels" (Dikotter 1992: 9).

Since *Kunlun* or *Kunlun nu* was frequently used during the period to refer to Black people and has the connotation of "race" and colour, I would like to make two points here. First, ethnocentrism is a universal phenomenon. Second, Chinese prejudice was against all foreigners, not just Africans and other people with dark skin. Ethnocentrism is an attitude or action of a group of people who regard themselves as normal, beautiful and clever while looking down upon other human groups as abnormal, ugly and foolish, or using various derogatory terms. Ethnocentrism is universal among any groups of people without communication and mutual understanding with others, especially in ancient times. As Wyatt correctly points out, "during this period in global history, so much before the time when frequent transcontinental contact would begin to become commonplace, people were willing to believe or at least entertain even the most prejudicial and outlandish things about people foreign to themselves" (Wyatt 2010: 65). The Romans looked upon all non-Romans as barbarians and the Greeks regarded themselves as the most civilised people in the world. The Indians thought they were living in the centre of the world as the Chinese did. Africans had prejudices against Whites. Ibn Battuta tells us that Malian cannibals did not eat Whites, since "eating a White man is harmful because he is not ripe" (Hamdun & King 1975: 51; Ibn Battuta 1929).

The Chinese were "by no means immune to such willfully misanthropic misconceptions" (Wyatt 2010: 65). Being self-centred, the Chinese in early time looked down upon others, using derogatory names to describe their neighbours in all four directions: *dong yi* (east barbarian), *nan man* (south barbarian), *xi rong* (west barbarian) and *bei di* (north barbarian). In extreme cases, foreigners were called *gui* (devil) – that is, not human. They termed the foreigners *fan nu* (barbarian slaves) Black people *hei gui* (Black devils) or *Kunlunnu* (*Kunlun* slaves) and Whites *yang guizi* (foreign devils), *hong mao gui* (red-haired devils), *fan gou* (barbarian dogs) or *gui lao* (devil males) and *gui po* (devil females) (Dikotter 1992).[8] Keeping this in mind, we can understand that Chinese prejudice was against not only Black people but also Whites – or any "others", for that matter.[9] However, when ethnocentrism changes to racism, which is mobilised to justify the military suppression, economic exploitation and political domination of other human groups as modern colonialism did, that is another story – one that is beyond the scope of this chapter.

Kunlun or Black people: Origins and jobs in China

As mentioned above, foreigners were present in China during the Han Dynasty, and during the Tang and Song dynasties China was an empire with many metropolitan cities hosting foreign residents. The cities enjoyed international fame, such as Chang-an, Guangzhou and Quanzhou. As the capital of the Han, Chang-an attracted many foreigners during the Tang Dynasty, including prosperous Arabs, Indians and other Asians. Guangzhou in the south, with a reputation for hosting foreign traders, had close relations with the outside world even during the Han period. Another southern port, Quanzhou, was named *Shijing Shizhou Ren* (市井十洲人, city with people from ten continents) or "foreigner's port" at the time, and was reputed to be "the most important port in the world" in the Song and Yuan dynasties (1206–1368 CE).

However, Arabs carried on trade on the East African coast for a long time; African slaves were just one of many commodities (Beachey 1976; Segal 2001). Many Arab merchants brought Black Africans with them to China as attendants, porters and slaves, who they presented to the Chinese authorities as gifts. During the Tang and Song dynasties, an increasing number of Black-skinned people appear in the literature as *Kunlun*, and are usually described as honest, brave, strong, willing to help others, or having some special skills, reflecting the reality at the time.

Black-skinned people are a large group who settled in various places in the world. There is no reason to assume that the Black people in China had only one origin. When Arabia sent a delegation headed by its ambassador to China in 977 CE, "their attendants had sunken eyes and Black skin and they were called *Kunlun nu*", according to the *History of the Song Dynasty*. They could have been from Africa. As for those of Indian origin, there were two groups. One is known as the "untouchables", who as the indigenous inhabitants contributed a great deal to the civilisation of the Indus River Valley.[10] The other group comprises those who migrated to India or were brought by Arabs or Indians from East Africa as slaves (Rashidi & Sertima 2007: 65–120). The third origin is Southeast Asia, which many works have mentioned, Ge Chengyong being representative of this view (Ge Chengyong 2001).

As mentioned previously, regarding the origin of the Black people in the Tang period, Zhang Xinglang points to Africa and Ge Chengyong suggests Southeast Asia, a kind of "singular origin". After examining both arguments, although based on rich material and sound logic, it is clear that each emphasises the positive evidence while neglecting materials contrary to their view. Historical research should be more careful and open the door for alternative explanations. In sum, multiple origins might be a more reasonable and convincing answer to the question.

Were the Black people all slaves in ancient China? This is a very sensitive or even provocative question, which is raised here for three reasons. First, a common impression among Chinese – that the Black people were mainly slaves (especially during the Tang period) – is held for several reasons, including the influence of Zhang's work. Second, several published works in English suggest the same view, with titles such as *Magical Kunlun and 'devil slaves'* (Wilensky 2002) or "The slaves of Guangzhou", the title of a major chapter in *The Blacks in Premodern China* (Wyatt 2010), a book that "bolsters a conceptualization of African history and of Africa's historical connections with the rest of the world as a history of slavery", which is always "defined by master–slave relations" (Bodomo 2013: 245–246).[11] Third, as Runoko Rashidi correctly points out, "The story of the African presence in early Asia would be incomplete without the exposé of the Black role as servant or slave" (Rashidi & Sertima 2007: 144; Chandler 2007). An objective answer to the question can provide a more comprehensive picture of their life and work at the time, which is one purpose of the study. It finds that the Black people held many jobs, such as soldiers or military leaders, royal guards, government officials, traders, artists, animal trainers and labourers in ancient China.

Since various writings of the Tang Dynasty and beyond illustrate that some of the Black people were *nubi* (slave-servants), there is no doubt that being domestic servants was one of their major roles (Liang Jingwen 2004). Wyatt does make a comparison at one point:

> The perceptible cultural shortcomings that all *Kunlun*, regardless of breed, exhibited had the effect only of encouraging Chinese designs on their enslavement and reinforcing the moral legitimacy of the practice as beneficial to the enslaved, much in the same way that the "White man's burden" premise justified the most egregious imperialist actions whereby Victorian Britons subjugated millions of people of colour around the globe in the 19th century.
>
> (Wyatt 2010: 41)

However, this comparison is inadequate, since there was a world of difference between the two in system, pattern, scale, treatment and volume. It is beyond the scope of this chapter to examine the issue, yet it is notable that Joseph Needham argues that the Chinese and other Asian nations had been using Black slaves for many centuries, yet their slavery was basically domestic thus it kept the practice within bounds, which is different from the massive imports for plantation labour that dominated the Trans-Atlantic Trade (Needham 1971). Bodomo points out that although Africans and Chinese met a long time ago, they were "on equal footing for the most part, and Africans and Chinese never owned each other as slaves on any large scale or in any systematic manner" (Bodomo 2013: 245). Moreover, as early as the Tang Dynasty, several emperors issued orders prohibiting trade in slaves (Schafer 1963: 45). The Chinese government prohibited the trade in Chinese women by foreigners in 1614 because of serious problems caused by European slave traders in the coastal regions of China.

Juyan Han Jian indicates that quite a few Black-skinned people in the army became officials, nobles or border officers. Among 53 Blacks, 16 had the rank of nobility, including four officials, the highest rank being the first class (Zhang Chunshu 1977). It is worth keeping in mind that the time is the Han Dynasty. Black people also became members of the retinue of royal families or even of the emperor. *Song Shu* records that Emperor Xiaowu (454–465 CE) trusted a *Kunlun* named Baizhu, who was often ordered to cane the officials. The Asian Art Museum in San Francisco possesses a 14th century Chinese painting of a Black-skinned official, who is of a high rank judging by his costume and bearing (Rashidi 1985; Rashidi & Sertima 2007: 141). A famous artist, Liu Guangdao, painted *Yuan Shizhu's hunting* (1280 CE), which portrays Emperor Kublai Khan on a hunting expedition. The picture shows the emperor and empress with two attendants and a Black person on horseback on the emperor's left. He must have been an important military officer or a personal guard.[12] Some Black Africans also served in the army: when the Dutch invaded Taiwan, there were Africans in both the Dutch and Chinese armies.

Some Africans were merchants in China. When Ibn Battuta visited China, he met a fellow-countryman doing business in China who "had about fifty White slaves and as many slave girls, and presented me with two of each" (Ibn Battuta 1929). Ahamed, a post-doctoral student at Peking University, researched the contact between the Sudan and China and found a long history of business between the two countries. In an interview with Ahmed Salih Sabit, he discovered that Salih's grandma was a Chinese woman who went to the Sudan with her husband Mohamed al Haj, who did business in China for several years (Ahmed 1999, 1999a, 2014).

Black people in China worked as actors, musicians, acrobats, wild animal trainers, businessmen, royal guards, porters and peasants. European encounters with China also brought African slaves to the coastal regions. An increasing number of Africans served as porters, guards, soldiers and domestic attendants in foreigners' residences or in the coastal areas in China (Ai Zhouchang 1989). Zhu Wan, an official of the Ming Dynasty (1368–1644 CE), indicates in his work *Pi Yu Zaji* that Africans were used in the Portuguese army in the colonial occupation of Macao; the Chinese army once captured more than 60 soldiers in a battle, three of them from Morocco, Ethiopia and the Sudan respectively. In a fight against the Dutch army in Taiwan, African soldiers were in the Chinese army led by Zheng Chenggong (郑成功) during the Ming period.

African diaspora in contemporary China

With the expansion of China–Africa relations, the African diaspora in China became an interesting subject for international academia. As a survey of Africans in China has been published (Bodomo 2014), I discuss the topic very briefly and focus more on issues that the survey does not cover, such as special contributions by Africans in China. I also examine the works of Chinese scholars with which international academia is less familiar.

Various African social groups exist in China, such as traders, diplomats, artists, students and professionals. Traders are by far the largest group, which has aroused great interest among the international community. Studies generally concentrated on African trading communities in China (Bertoncello & Bredeloup 2006, 2009; Bodomo 2007, 2009c; Bertoncello, Bredeloup & Pliez 2009; Cissé 2013) or their economic activities in Guangzhou, the city hosting the largest group of Africans (Bertoncello & Bredeloup 2007a, 2007b; Bodomo 2010; Lyons et al. 2008, 2012, 2013; Osnos 2009; Li Zhigang & Du Feng 2012a, 2012b; Bodomo & Ma 2010; Diederich 2010; Bork et al. 2011; Müller 2011; Haugen 2012; Bredeloup 2012; Yang 2013) and Yiwu, the biggest commodities centre in China (Le Bail 2009; Bertoncello, Bredeloup & Pliez 2009; Pliez 2010; Bodomo & Ma 2010, 2012; Ma 2012), and their business negotiations and deals in Hong Kong (Bodomo 2007, 2012; Mathews 2000; Mathews & Yang 2012) and Macau (Morais 2009; Bodomo 2012; Bodomo & Silva 2012).

Other studies include the living conditions, social practices or religious activities of the African diaspora (Li Zhigang 2009a, 2009b; Li Zhigang & Du Feng 2012a, 2012b; Bertoncello & Bredeloup 2009; Bodomo 2009a, 2010; Xu Tao 2009a, 2009b; Yang Yang 2011; Müller 2011; Haugen 2013); difficulties between Africans and Chinese; management of the African diaspora by the Chinese authorities; and the reactions of Chinese citizens (Li Zhigang & Du Feng 2012b; Xu Tao 2009a; Osnos 2009; Morais 2009; Bodomo 2010; Haugen 2012). The African entrepreneurs' role in transmitting their concept of China to their own countries explains the impact of Chinese development in a global context (Marfaing & Thiel 2014; Cissé 2013). A cyber-network, The African Diaspora in Asia (TADIA) was established to bring together scholars of different disciplines, and it is recognised as a project associated with UNESCO (Jayasuriya & Pierre-Angenot 2006).

Among scholars of the African diaspora in China, two are prominent: Adams Bodomo and Li Zhigang. Bodomo made the best use of his experience of living in Hong Kong for more than ten years and studied the African diaspora in China, covering various aspects. His training as linguist offered him sensitivity about language, food and the lifestyles of diasporic groups. Being an African made it easy for him to contact Africans in different cities in China; he published extensively on the subject. Bodomo's important contribution lies in his "immigrant community as bridge" theory. Since the push/pull theory was first applied in 1959, it has been well received in academia. Yet this is a "double-ended" approach, which neglects the process itself and the immigrants' role after their arrival.[13] Using a three-dimensional approach that recognizes the target community, its source community and its host community, Bodomo devised his theory, suggesting that given the right conditions, the target community can serve as a bridge, connecting its place of origin (its source community) with its new place of domicile (its host community) (Bodomo 2010, 2012).

Li Zhigang has studied on the African community in Guangzhou. As an expert on urban and human geography, Li puts the African diaspora in the context of economic globalization and transnational migration. Using the theoretical framework of "enclaves" in migration studies, Li analyzes the development of "ethnic economic enclaves" with a double character, high mobility and diversity on one hand and high possibility of residential segregation on the other (Li Zhigang et al. 2008). The enclave includes three circles of social ties: the core of African traders, encircled by their communities, and the third, so-called China–Africa circle of interactions between Africans and local Chinese, which forms a part of the process of globalisation. The social space and networks under transnational entrepreneurialism mark the coming of a new era of globalisation in urban China, providing opportunities and challenges for local government (Li Zhigang et al. 2009; Li Zhigang & Du Feng 2012a). The most impressive feature of Li's study is his approach of taking the "ethnic economic enclave" as a historical process that forms and transforms constantly and is not just a pattern.

Sociologist Xu Tao's works emphasise the social adaptation of African merchants in Guangzhou and finds them to have multiple features of social relations. Concentrated or spread, their adaptation takes three forms: individual, resocialization, and networks with various means of support. The characteristics of the African diaspora are coexistence and heterogeneity, and an emerging international community (Xu Tao 2009a, 2011, 2012, 2013). Ma Enyu has studied the African community in Yiwu, analysing its change from a small town to an internationally well-known commercial hub and its role in China–Africa relations (Ma Enyu 2010, 2012; Bodomo & Ma 2010, 2012). A comparison between the international community in Yiwu and the African community in Guangzhou indicates various differences, especially of social capital (Chen Xiaoying 2012). The theory of social support is applied to analyse the extent, role and impact of social support on or the social capital of the African diaspora in Guangzhou (Xu Tao 2009b; Chen Xiaoying 2012). It is notable that the media played an important role in formulating the image of Africans in Guangzhou and creating more contact, leading to more positive view of Africans (Li Zhigang et al. 2009). British media coverage of immigrants and its strategy are discussed to provide a lesson for Chinese media on the coverage of the African diaspora in China (Dang Fangli 2013).

In the above-mentioned works, several features are common. They are the fruits of fieldwork and data collected in Guangzhou, Hong Kong or Yiwu. Second, most of the works are project-based, research combined with reality, either as a result of or explanation for the strengthening of China–Africa relations. Third, the influential works usually involve team-based research, which includes African, Chinese or European partners. The African diaspora is characterised by its full engagement in the economy of its host cities and by poor social integration, caused by a lack of communication, misunderstanding, strict immigration policies, cultural differences and an absence of religion in Chinese society. There seem to be different views on whether there is racism in China (Baitie 2013).

Although most Africans are not classified as immigrants, Bodomo correctly points out that the process of trade between Africa and China began with Africans who studied in China and were involved there in business (Bodomo 2012). After African countries won their independence, they started to send African students or technicians to China for advanced studies. Students from 14 African countries regularly came to China until the end of 1966, when China closed all universities because of the Cultural Revolution. Among them a Ghanaian student, Emmanuel Hevi, complained about racism and other unpleasant phenomena in China (Hevi 1963; Liu 2013). From a country whose President Nkrumah was strongly pro-socialist, Hevi's negative story about China behind the iron curtain brought applause from Western analysts, who were looking for ammunition against China.

China resumed educational cooperation with Africa in 1972 and trainees in railway technology came first from Tanzania and Zambia, then regular students followed in 1973. African students in China in 1973–1976 numbered 355. With the increasing numbers, problems occurred, and racial tension broke out at the end of the 1980s when African and Chinese students both held demonstrations and accused each other of various wrongs (Sautman 1994). Analysing this from today's perspective, cultural differences seem to have been a major cause, since the trigger was usually close contact between African male students and Chinese girls (Li Anshan & Liu Haifang 2013). With the setting up of FOCAC, the number of African students greatly increased.[14] The first studies on the issue in China were by scholars at the Centre for African Studies at Peking University, based on the archives of the Ministry of Education with the focus on African students in China (Li Baoping 2006, Li Baoping & Luo Jianbo 2013).[15]

Conclusion

Since the title covers a wide range, the limitations of this chapter are obvious. It should be taken as an "opening remark" rather than a "conclusion". It indicates that there are various issues in China–Africa relations, be they historical, contemporary or in different disciplines. Bilateral migration provides both opportunity and challenge. There are cultural similarities and differences between China and Africa and mutual learning is always beneficial to both (Li Anshan 2012a).

There is still a lack of solid study on the topic (Bodomo 2020; Cissé 2021). How do we carry out research on the historical links between Africans and Chinese? What is the best way to build a link between the two cultures, thus facilitating the process to mutate from "enclave" to "bridge"? How do we promote the efficiency of talented African people as they study in China with the hope of promoting African development? Why is there a gap between the African diaspora and local communities in China, and how do we narrow this gap? How can we manage intermarriage and the existence of an increasingly mixed group of children? And who should be in charge of the African community – the Chinese authorities or African community leaders, or a combined team? Is it necessary to give up one's own culture and adapt to another, or is there a better way for diasporic communities to keep their own culture and fit into the host society? All these questions are also relevant for Chinese communities in Africa.

Notes

1 This subject has been presented on various occasions in Beijing, Shanghai, Hong Kong, South Africa, Kenya and so on, and was originally published topically in different Chinese versions. Entitled "African diaspora in China: Reality, research and reflection", the English version is published in *The Journal of Pan African Studies* 7, a journal open to the public that can be accessed free at www.jpanafrican.org/docs/vol7no10/Bodomo-3-Anshan.pdf. This chapter is a revised version of the article and I would like to thank the journal and also Adams Bodomo, Li Zhigang, Xu Liang, Shen Xiaolei, You Guolong and Tian Xin for their help in my writing of this chapter.
2 These terms are used as in forensic and physical anthropology.
3 *Juyan Han Jian* literally means government records of Juyan, located in the northwest part of China. "*Han*" indicates the Han Dynasty, "*Jian*" means records carved in wood or bamboo. About 10,000 *Juyan Han Jian*, ranging from 102 BCE to 30 CE, were discovered in the 1930s by Chinese archaeologists and Folke Bergman, a Swedish scholar. As official archives, *Juyan Han Jian* covers various subjects both collectively and individually, such as the political system, economic activities, military organisations, and the fields of science and culture. For a study of the subject, see Yang Ximei (1995); Li Anshan (2019).
4 Zhang Chunshu is spelt as Chang Chun-shu in Taiwan and North America.
5 Wilensky argues that, "The scarcity of references to *sengchi* and *zengqi* (here meaning *Sengzhi*) in nonfiction sources suggests that the Chinese did not necessarily link the word *Kunlun* to the Arabs' *sengchi* slaves during the Tang" (Wilensky 2002: 8).
6 There are different translations of the title, such as *Records of the Taiping Era, Extensive gleanings of the Reign of Great Tranquillity* and *Extensive gleanings from the Reign of Great Peace*. Yet the book comprises various aspects of literature from the Han Dynasty to the beginning of the Song Dynasty. A monumental work of 500 volumes ordered by Emperor Taizhong (939–997 CE), it cannot be considered as mere "gleanings". It was compiled in the Taiping Kaiyuan period (978 CE) so I translate it as such.
7 Wyatt claims that *Kunlun Nu* is an "anonymous tale" (Wyatt 2010: 146). It is not. The story was written by the famous novelist Pei Xing in the Tang Dynasty, published in his work titled *Chuanqi* (*Legend*) and later included in *Taiping Guangji*.

8 Master Cui told his servant Mole the most salient secret in his mind (his love for a singing girl) and Mole helped him to overcome various difficulties to fulfil his wish. This is scarcely credible considering the master–servant relationship. Because of the interesting figure of the Tang legend, Mole became a popular hero in fiction and drama.
9 Zhou Zikui, a *Jinshi* (a successful candidate in the highest imperial examinations) in the late Ming dynasty even thought that the Europeans (*xiyang ren*) could not be called barbarians (*yi*), but only *qin* (birds and beasts), because barbarians were still human beings, and Europeans were not human beings (Zhu Chunting 2004).
10 It is believed that "India would experience many magnificent 'Transformations', spurned and perpetuated by the race that gave India her first civilisation and culture – the Black race" (Rashidi & Sertima 2007: 105, 233–249).
11 This worry is by no means groundless. In a special issue of *African and Asian Studies,* although the editors seem to emphasise various aspects of the African diaspora in Asia, most articles describe Asia–Africa historical relations as "master–slave relations" (Jayasuriya & Pierre-Angenot 2006).
12 For the picture, see Li Anshan 2019: 182. It can also be found by the title in website.
13 Push factors are conditions in the country of origin and motives for migration (instability, poor economy), while pull factors are what attracts migrants (education, better social conditions) (Bogue 1959).
14 In 1996, the number of Chinese scholarships for Africans jumped from 256 the previous year to 922, while the self-funded African students reached 118, over 100 for the first time. Between 1996 and 2011, there were 84,361 African students in China; 36,918 enjoyed Chinese scholarships while 47,443 were self-funded. In 2005, for the first time self-funded Africans (1390) surpassed the scholarship students (1 367). In 2011, the self-funded African students reached 14,428, more than double those Africans on scholarships (6316) (Li Anshan & Liu Haifang 2013).
15 Reports and memoirs also provide information on the experiences of African students in China (Li Jiangtao & Li Xiang 2006; Lokongo 2012; Li Anshan 2013; China Africa Project 2013).

References

African Union. 2005. Report of the meeting of experts from the members of the States on the Definition of African Diaspora, April 11–12, Addis Ababa.

Ahmed, Gaafar Karrar. 1999. China–Arab relations during Tang Dynasty 618 AD. *Tang Studies* 5: 323–366.

Ahmed, Gaafar Karrar. 1999a. Sudan–China relations during the Tang Dynasty to the end of Yuan Dynasty. *Yuan Historical Studies* 7: 197–206.

Ai Zhouchang, ed. 1989. *Selection of materials on China–African relations (1500–1918)*. Shanghai: East Normal University Press.

Alpers, Edward A. 1997. The African diaspora in the northwestern Indian Ocean: Reconsideration of an old problem, new directions for research. *Comparative Studies of South Asia, Africa & the Middle East* 17(2): 62–81.

Alpers, Edward A. 2000. Recollecting Africa: Diasporic memory in the Indian Ocean world. *African Studies Review* 43(1): 83–99.

Baitie, Zahra. 2013. On Being African in China, *The Atlantic*, 28 August. www.theatlantic.com/china/archive/2013/08/on-being-african-in-china/279136

Beachey, R.W. 1976. *The slave trade of Eastern Africa*. New York: Harper and Row.
Bertoncello, B. & Bredeloup, S. 2006. La migration chinoise en Afrique: accélérateur du développement ou "sanglot de l'homme noir". *Afrique Contemporaine* 218: 199–224.
Bertoncello, B. & Bredeloup, S. 2007a. De Hong Kong à Guangzhou, de nouveaux "comptoirs" africains s'organisent. *Perspectives Chinoises* 98(1): 98–110.
Bertoncello, B. & Bredeloup, S. 2007b. The emergence of new African "trading posts" in Hong Kong and Guangzhou. *China Perspectives* 1: 94–105.
Bertoncello, B. & Bredeloup, S. 2009. Chine-Afrique ou la valse des entrepreneurs-migrants. *Revue européenne des migrations internationales*. 25(1): 45–70.
Bertoncello, B., Bredeloup, S. & Pliez, O. 2009. Hong Kong, Guangzhou, Yiwu: de nouveaux comptoirs africains en Chine. *Critique International* 44: 105–121.
Bodomo, Adams. 2007. An emerging African-Chinese community in Hong Kong: The case of TsimShaTsui's Chungking Mansions. In Kwesi Kwaa Prah, ed., *Afro-Chinese relations: Past, present and future*. Cape Town: Centre for Advanced Studies in African Societies, 367–389.
Bodomo, Adams. 2009a. Africa–China relations in an era of globalization: The role of African trading communities in China. *West Asia and Africa* 8: 62–67.
Bodomo, Adams. 2009b. Africa–China relations: Symmetry, soft power, and South Africa. *The China Review: An Interdisciplinary Journal on Greater China*, 9(2): 169–178.
Bodomo, Adams. 2009c. The African presence in contemporary China. *China Monitor*, January.
Bodomo, Adams. 2010. The African trading community in Guangzhou: An emerging bridge for Africa–China relations, *The China Quarterly* 203: 693–707.
Bodomo, Adams. 2011. *African students in China: A case study of newly arrived students on FOCAC funds at Chongqing University*. Hong Kong: University of Hong Kong.
Bodomo, Adams. 2012. *Africans in China: A sociocultural study and its implications on Africa–China relations*. New York: Cambria Press.
Bodomo, Adams. 2013. Book review: *The Blacks of Premodern China* by Don Wyatt, *African Studies Review* 56(3): 244–246.
Bodomo, Adams. 2013. African diaspora remittances are better than foreign aid funds. *World Economics* 14(4): 21–28.
Bodomo, Adams. 2014. Africans in China: A bibliographical survey. In Li Anshan & Lin Fengmin, eds, *Annual Review of African Studies in China 2013*. Beijing: Social Sciences Academic Press (China), 109–121.
Bodomo, Adams. 2016. *Africans in China: Guangdong and beyond*. New York: Diasporic Africa Press.
Bodomo, Adams. 2020. Historical and contemporary perspectives on inequalities and well-being of Africans in China. *Asian Ethnicity* 21(4): 526–41.
Bodomo, Adams & Ma, Grace. 2010. From Guangzhou to Yiwu: Emerging facets of the African diaspora in China. *International Journal of African Renaissance Studies* 5(2): 283–289.
Bodomo, Adams & Ma, Grace. 2012. We are what we eat: Food in the process of community formation and identity shaping among African traders in Guangzhou and Yiwu. *African Diaspora* 5(1): 1–26.
Bodomo, Adams & Silva, Roberval. 2012. Language matters: The role of linguistic identity in the establishment of the lusophone African community in Macau. *African Studies* 71(1): 71–90.

Bogue, D.J. 1959. International migration. In P. Hauser & O.D. Duncan, eds, *The study of population*. Chicago: University of Chicago Press.

Bork, T. et al. 2011. Global change, national development goals, urbanization and international migration in China: African migrants in Guangzhou and Foshan. In F. Kraas, S. Aggarwal, M. Coy & G. Mertins, eds, *Megacities: Our global urban future*. London: Springer.

Bredeloup, S. 2012. African trading posts in Guangzhou: Emergent or recurrent commercial form? *African Diaspora* 5(1): 27–50.

Bredeloup, S. 2014. West-African Students Turned Entrepreneurs in Asian Trading Posts: A new facet of Globalization. *Urban Anthropology* 43(1/2/3): 17–56.

Chandler W.B. 2007. The jewel in the lotus: The Ethiopian presence in the Indus Valley civilization. In R. Rashidi & I. van Sertima, eds, *The African presence in early Asia*. New Brunswick, NJ: Transaction Press, 233–249.

Chang Kwang Chih. 1968 [1963]. *The archaeology of Ancient China*. New Haven, CT: Yale University Press.

Chen Xiaoying. 2012. Chinese new immigrants' dilemma and causes in South Africa. *Huaqiao Huaren Historical Studies* 2: 28–35.

China Africa Project. 2013. Leading China scholar Li Anshan recalls his experiences teaching African students. www.chinaafricaproject.com/leading-china-scholar-li-anshan- recalls-his-experiences-teaching-african-students-translation

Cissé, Daouda. 2013. South–South migration and trade: African traders in China. *Policy Briefing* 4.

Cissé, Daouda. 2021. As migration and trade increase between China and Africa, traders at both ends often face precarity. *Migration Information Source*, 21 July. www.migrationpolicy.org/article/migration-trade-china-africa-traders-face-precarity

Dang Fangli. 2013. British media's coverage of immigrants and its enlightenment to Chinese media: Basing on the event of Africans' protest in Guangzhou *Tangdu Journal* 29(5): 82–86.

Davies, Carole Elizabeth Boyce. 2008. *Encyclopedia of the African diaspora: Origins, experiences and culture*. New York: ABC-CLIO.

Diederich, Manon. 2010. Manoeuvring through the spaces of everyday life. Transnational experiences of African women in Guangzhou, China. PhD dissertation, University of Cologne.

Dikotter, Frank. 1992. *The discourse of race in modern China*. London: C. Hurst and Co.

Du Baoren. 1979. Black African pottery figure in Tang tomb of Xi-an. *Cultural Relic* 6: 88–90.

Duan Jingjing, Ying Yuanliang & Pu Guofu. 2015. "Foreigners are not foreign": Yiwu City hires foreigners to be the mediator for foreign-related disputes. Xinhuanet, 8 February. https://world.huanqiu.com/article/9CaKrnJHB24

Ge Chengyong 2001. On the origin of Blacks in the Tang Dynasty. *Zhonghua Studies of Culture and History* 65: 1–27.

Goodrich, L.C. 1931. Negroes in China. B*ulletin of the Catholic University of Peking* 8: 37–39.

Hamdun, Said & King, Noel. 1975. *Ibn Battuta in Black Africa*. London: Collings.

Harris, Joseph E., ed., *Global dimensions of the African diaspora*. Washington, DC: Howard University Press.

Haugen, H.Ø. 2012. Nigerians in China: A second state of immobility. *International Migration* 50(2): 65–80.

Haugen, H.Ø. 2013. African Pentecostal migrants in China: Marginalization and the alternative geography of a mission theology. *African Studies Review* 56(1): 81–102.
Hevi, Emmanuel. 1963. *An African student in China*. London: Pall Mall.
Human, Linda. 1984. *The Chinese people in South Africa: Freewheeling on the fringe*. Pretoria: University of South Africa.
Ibn Battuta. 1929. *Ibn Battuta travels in Asia and Africa 1325–1354*. Translated and selected by H.A.R. Gibb. London: George Routledge & Sons.
Le Bail, Hélène. 2009. Les grandes villes chinoises comme espace d'immigration internationale: le cas des entrepreneurs africains. *Asie Visions* 19.
Li Anshan. 2019. *The social and economic history of the Chinese overseas in Africa* (3 vols). Nanjing: Jiangshu People's Press.
Li Anshan. 2000. *A history of Chinese overseas in Africa*. Beijing: Overseas Chinese Publishing House.
Li Anshan. 2006. *Social history of Chinese overseas in Africa: Selected documents 1800–2005*. Hong Kong: Hong Kong Press for Social Science.
Li Anshan. 2012. *A history of overseas Chinese in Africa till 1911*. New York: Diasporic Africa Press.
Li Anshan. 2012a. China and Africa: Cultural similarity and mutual learning. In James Shikwati, ed., *China–Africa partnership: The quest for a win–win relationship*. Nairobi: Inter Region Economic Network (IREN), 93–97.
Li Anshan. 2013. My African students. In Cheng Tao & Lu Miaogeng, eds, *Chinese ambassadors telling African stories*. Beijing: World Affairs Press, 156–168.
Li Anshan. 2019. *The social and economic history of the Chinese overseas in Africa* (3 vols). Nanjing: Jiangshu People's Press.
Li Anshan & April, Funeka Yazini, eds. 2013. *Forum on China–Africa Cooperation: The politics of human resource development*. Pretoria: Africa Institute of South Africa.
Li Anshan & Liu Haifang. 2013. The evolution of the Chinese policy of funding African students and an evaluation of the effectiveness. Draft report for UNDP.
Li Baoping. 2006. China–Africa educational cooperation and intellectual assistance to Africa. www.cpaffc.org.cn/c06/yw20020904.html.
Li Baoping & Luo Jianbo. 2013. Dissecting soft power and Sino-Africa relations in education and exchanges cooperation. In Li Anshan & Funeka Yazini April, eds, *Forum on China–Africa Cooperation*. Beijing: AIAS, 28–42.
Li Jiangtao & Li Xiang. 2006. China is my second hometown: African students' life in Beijing. http://news.xinhuanet.com/world/2006-10/21/content_5232813.htm
Li Zhigang et al. 2008. The African enclave of Guangzhou: A case study of Xiaobeilu. *ACTA Geographica Sinica* 63(2): 207–218.
Li Zhigang et al. 2009. An African enclave in China: The making of a new transnational urban space. *Eurasian Geography and Economics* 50(6): 699–719.
Li Zhigang et al. 2009a. The local response of transnational social space under globalization in urban China: A case study of African enclave in Guangzhou. *Geographical Research* 28(4): 920–932.
Li Zhigang et al. 2012. China's "chocolate city": An ethnic enclave in a changing landscape. *African Diaspora* 5(1): 51–72.
Li Zhigang & Du Feng. 2012a. Production of China's new social space in city under "transnational entrepreneurialism": A case study on African economic zone in Guangzhou. *Urban Space Studies* 36(8): 25–31.
Li Zhigang & Du Feng. 2012b. The transnational making of "chocolate city" in Guangzhou. *Renwen Dili* 27(6): 1–6.

Liang Jingwen. 2004. A study on *Kunlun nu* in the Tang Dynasty. *Maritime History Studies* 2: 58–62.
Liu, P.H. 2013. Petty annoyances? Revisiting John Emmanuel Hevi's *An African Student in China* after 50 years. *China: An International Journal* 11(1): 131–145.
Lokongo, Antoine Roger. 2012. My Chinese connection. Chinafrica, July: 50.
Ly-Tio-Fane-Pineo, Huguette. 1981. *La Diaspora Chinoise dans L'OceanIndien Occidental*. Aix-en-Provence: Association des Chercheurs de l'Ocean d'Indien, Institut d'Histoire des pays d'Outre-mer, Greco Ocean Indien.
Ly-Tio-Fane, Pineo Huguette. 1985. *Chinese Diaspora in Western Indian Ocean*. Port Louis: Editions de L'océan Indien and Chinese Catholic Mission.
Ly-Tio-Fane Pineo, Huguette & Edouard Lim Fat. 2008. *From alien to citizen: The integration of the Chinese in Mauritius*. Port Louis: Éditions de l'océan Indien.
Lyons, M., Brown, A. & Li Zhigang. 2008. The "third tier" of globalization: African traders in Guangzhou. *City* 12(2): 196–206.
Lyons, M., Brown, A. & Li Zhigang. 2012. In the dragon's den: African traders in Guangzhou. *Journal of Ethnic and Migration Studies* 38(5): 869–888.
Lyons, M., Brown, A. & Li Zhigang. 2013.The China–Africa value chain: Can Africa's small-scale entrepreneurs engage successfully in global trade? *African Studies Review* 56(3): 77–100.
Ma Enyu. 2010. Walking into the Yiwu Muslim community. *China Religion* 6: 56–57.
Ma Enyu. 2012. Yiwu mode and Sino-African relations. *Journal of Cambridge Studies* 7(3): 93–108.
Marfaing, Laurence & Thiel, Alena. 2014. *"Agents of translation": West African entrepreneurs in China as vectors of social change*. Working Paper no. 4, DFG Priority Program 1448. www.spp1448.de/fileadmin/media/galleries/SPP_Administration/Working_Paper_Series/SPP1448_WP4_Marfaing-Thiel_final.pdf
Mathews, G. 2000. Les traders africains a Kong Hong (Hong Kong) et en Chine. *Les Temps Modernes* 657: 110–124.
Mathews, G. & Yang, Y. 2012. How Africans pursue low-end globalization in Hong Kong and mainland China. *Journal of Current Chinese Affairs* 41(2): 95–120.
Morais, I. 2009. "China wahala": The tribulations of Nigerian "Bushfallers" in a Chinese Territory. *Transtext(e)s Transcultures. Journal of Global Cultural Studies* 5: 1–22.
Müller, Angelo 2011. New migration processes in contemporary China: The constitution of African trader networks in Guangzhou. *Geographische Zeitschrif* 99(2):104–122.
Needham, Joseph. 1971. *Science and Civilization in China, Vol. 4*. New York: Cambridge University Press.
Osnos, Evan. 2009. The Promised Land – Guangzhou's Canaan market and the rise of an African merchant class. *The New Yorker*, 9 February, 50–56.
Park, Y. Jung 2008. *A matter of honour: Being Chinese in South Africa*. Johannesburg: Jacana Media.
Pliez, O. 2010. Toutes les routes de la soie mènent in Yiwu (Chine). Entrepreneurs et migrants musulmans dans un comptoir économique chinois. *Espace Géographique* 2: 132–145.
Rashidi, Runoko. 1985. Commentaries, *Journal of African Civilizations* 1: 147–148.
Rashidi, Runoko & Sertima, Ivan Van, eds. 1995. *The African presence in early Asia*. New Brunswick, NJ: Transaction Press.

Sautman, Barry. 1994. Anti-Black racism in post-Mao China. *The China Quarterly* 138: 413–437.
Schafer, Edward. 1963. *The golden peaches of Samarkand: A study of Tang exotics*. Los Angeles, CA: The Regents of the University of California.
Segal, Ronald 2001. *Islam's Black slaves, the other Black*. New York: Farrar, Straus and Giroux.
Shepperson, George. 1993. African diaspora: Concept and context. In Joseph E. Harris, ed., *Global dimensions of the African diaspora*. Washington, DC: Howard University Press.
Smidt, Wolbert. 2001. A Chinese in the Nubian and Abyssinian kingdoms (8th century): The visit of Du Huan to Molin-guo and Laobosa. *Chroniques Yemenites* 9. http://cy.revues.org/document33.html.
Wilensky, Julie. 2002. The magical *Kunlun* and "devil slaves": Chinese perceptions of dark-skinned people and Africa before 1500. *Sino-Platonic Papers*, 22 July. Philadelphia, PA: University of Pennsylvania. http://sino-platonic.org/complete/spp122_chinese_africa.pdf
Wong-Hee-Kan, Edith. 1996. *La Diaspora Chinoise au Marscareignes: Le cas de la Reunion*. Paris: Editions L'Harmattan.
Wyatt, Don J. 2010. *The Blacks of premodern China*. Philadelphia, PA: University. of Pennsylvania Press.
Xu Yongzhang, 2019. *Historical manuscripts of ancient China–Africa relations*. Shanghai: Shanghai Lexicographical Publishing House.
Xu Tao. 2009a. An analysis on Africans social relations and interaction logics in Guangzhou. *Youth Research* 5: 71–86.
Xu Tao. 2009b. African's social support in Guangzhou: Weakening, fracture and reconstruction. *South China Population* 24(4): 34–44.
Xu Tao. 2011. Re-analysis of the relations of social contact of African merchants in Guangzhou. *Journal of Zhejiang Normal University* 4: 10–15.
Xu Tao. 2012. Analysis of characteristics of the behavior of African merchants in Guangzhou. *Journal of Zhejiang Normal University* 4: 55–63.
Xu Tao. 2013. *The social adaptions of African merchants in China*. Hangzhou: Zhejiang People's Press.
Xuzhou Museum. 1980. On Xuzhou stone carvings in the Han Dynasty. *Cultural Relics* 2: n.p.
Yang Ximei. 1966. A preliminary report of human crania excavated from Hou-chia-chuang and other Shang Dynasty sites at An-yang Honan, North China. *Annual Bulletin of the China Council for East Asian Studies* 5: 1–13.
Yang Ximei. 1995. *Collection on cultural history in pre-Qin period*. Beijing: China Social Sciences Press.
Yang, Y. 2013. African traders in Guangzhou, In G. Mathews, G.L. Ribero & C.A. Vega, eds, *Globalization from below: The world's other economy*. London: Routledge.
Yang Yang 2011. New silk roads: African and Chinese traders in South China and South Africa. *China Monitor* 61: 4–8.
Yap, Melanie & Leong Man, Dianne. 1996. *Colour, confusion and Concessions: The History of the Chinese in South Africa*. Hong Kong: Hong Kong University Press.
Zeleza, Paul Tiyambe. 2005. Rewriting the African diaspora: Beyond the Black Atlantic. *African Affairs* 104: 414: 35–68.
Zeleza, Paul Tiyambe. 2008. The challenges of studying African diasporas. *African Sociological Review* 12(2): 4–21.

Zhang Chunshu. 1977. *Collected essays of history of frontier of the Han dynasty*. Taibei: Shihuo Press.

Zhang Xinglang [Chang Hsinglang]. 1928. The importation of Black African slaves to China during the Tang. *Furen Xuezhi* 1: 101–119.

Zhang Xinglang [Chang Hsinglang]. 1930. The importation of Black slaves to China in Tang Dynasty (618–907). *Bulletin of Catholic University of Peking* 7: 37–59.

Zhang Xinglang (Chang Hsinglang), ed. 1977 [1930]. *A compilation of historical materials of Chinese and Western communications, vol. 2*. Annotated and revised by Zhu Jieqing. Beijing: Zhonghua Book Company.

Zhu Chunting. 2004. The Western image in the eyes of Chinese during Ming and Qing Dynasty. *Journal of Jiangxi Institute of Education* 5: 98–103.

20 African students in China
Trend, policy and roles[1]

Introduction

On 20 March 1962, a clash between Africans and Chinese occurred at the Peace Hotel in Beijing, followed by an exodus of African students from China – among 118 African students, 96 left their schools in China and returned to their home countries.[2] From June 1972, 200 students from Tanzania and Zambia were trained in China for the future Tanzania–Zambia Railway (TAZARA) project. They took different courses in public transportation, then trained in different specialist fields. Of this group, 179 finally graduated in September 1975.[3] Through 1979 to 1989, several incidents concerning African students occurred in China, either Chinese students' demonstration about African students or African students' protest against the prejudice in and outside campus in Shanghai, Tianjin and Beijing, etc.[4] On 4 November 2006, Benin student Guilluaume Moumouni was selected as one of the hosts of the FOCAC Beijing Summit Gala. He skilfully used Chinese, English and French to host the event in front of 48 African heads of state and Chinese top leaders and won praise from the guests. A Ghanaian student talked about her experience in China. Since she knows Chinese language, Baitie can understand what people say about her: "Many of the experiences I had were borne of ignorance, not racism. Despite always being identified as 'Black' and 'African', I never felt discriminated against or antagonized, but rather treated with warmth and friendliness" (Baitie 2013). In 2021, an African student stated that:

> Studying in China is a once-in-a-lifetime chance. You'll never get these years back, so make the most of them while you still have the chance. The experience will remain something you value and remember fondly for the rest of your life. Finally, I am grateful to the Chinese Government for giving the opportunity to acquire knowledge in this prestigious country and also thanks to the UESTC for such a great opportunity.
>
> (Owusu-Ansah 2021)

DOI: 10.4324/9781003220152-24

African communities in China have become an impressive phenomenon. Various African diasporic groups exist in China, such as traders, students, artists and professionals, yet students form the second-largest group in the African community. In 2017, a report was published in *The Conversation* stating that:

> The surge in the number of African students in China is remarkable. In less than 15 years the number of African student has grown 26-fold, from just under 2000 in 2003 to almost 50,000 in 2015. According to the UNESCO Institute of Statistics, the US and UK host around 40,000 African students a year, China surpassed this number in 2014 … This dramatic increase in students from African can be explained in part by the Chinese government's targeted focus on African human resources and education development.
>
> (Breeze & Moore 2017)

Studying African students in the context of China–Africa relations, this chapter is divided into five parts: a review of literature; the history; an analysis of China's policy on African students; the favourable conditions that attract African students and their motivations; and their contribution to both Africa and China. I argue that African students in China and their interaction with the Chinese have brought various new things to China and made a great contribution to Africa as a whole.[5]

Research, discussion and views

The world is currently absorbed with the issue of China–Africa relations. Different issues and contradictory views are presented (Li Anshan 2014). The African diaspora has also become a fashionable topic among academics. It is generally presumed that an African community only appeared in China in recent years, yet there is a long history of migration and contact between China and Africa (Li Anshan 2015, 2019). Owing to the fast growth of bilateral trade, with the total volume increasing from US$10.8 billion in 2000 to more than US$208 billion in 2019, it is undeniable that the African community has boomed in China during the period.

Since China–Africa trade is a very important component of bilateral relations, traders are by far the largest group among the African community in China. Studies include the living conditions, social practices and religious activities of the African diaspora, barriers between Africans and Chinese, and the management of the African diaspora by the Chinese authorities, as indicated in the previous chapter. African entrepreneurs also describe how they transmitted their concept of China to their own countries, thus explaining the impact of Chinese development in a global context. Now studies have gradually moved beyond Guangdong (Bodomo 2016).

African students form the second-largest group of the African diaspora in China, yet far fewer scholars have been involved in the study of this topic. The earliest work was done by a Ghanaian student who had personal experience of studying in China in the early 1960s. After independence, 14 African countries sent their students to China up to the end of 1966, when China closed all universities during the Cultural Revolution. Emmanuel Hevi was among them. He wrote the first book about African students in China, complaining about racism and other unpleasant phenomena there. He lists six causes of African student dissatisfaction: undesirable political indoctrination, language difficulties, poor educational standards, an inadequate social life, outright hostility and racial discrimination (Hevi 1963). He claimed that many African students returned home in 1961–1962, yet there is disagreement about this statement (Larkin 1971). The book attracted attention from the West, yet the study of the topic almost stopped since all the African students returned to their countries when the Cultural Revolution started. It has only been in recent years that scholars have reviewed the historical context or explained the social background of China at the time (Liu 2013; Cheng Yinghong 2014; Jiang Huajie 2016).

China resumed educational cooperation with Africa in 1973 and trainees in railway technology arrived in China from Tanzania and Zambia, followed by formal student enrolment. There are several works on the Tanzania–Zambia Railway (TAZARA) with the study of documents and records, and the African trainees are mentioned occasionally (Zhang Tieshan 1999; Monson 2009; Liu & Monson 2011; Shen Xipeng 2018). Gillespie studied African students' experiences in China in the context of China–Africa relations and touched the issue of technology transfer (Gillespie 2001). There are several studies on the conflicts between African students and Chinese students in the 1980s, with a criticism of Chinese racism (Seidelman 1989; Sautman 1994; Sulliven 1994). From today's perspective, cultural difference seems to be a major cause of this since the trigger was usually close contact between African male students and Chinese girls (Li Anshan & Liu Haifang 2013).

With the setting up of FOCAC, African students in China greatly increased. As for studies of African students currently in China, there is a greater interest among Chinese scholars (or African scholars in China) than those outside China. The first study on the issue in China was by the Centre for African Studies at Peking University. It is a general survey with data based on the archives of the Ministry of Education (China Africa Education Cooperation Group 2005, hereafter CAECG). Current research on African students generally focuses on four subjects: cultural adaptation, China–Africa educational cooperation, educational management and professional teaching,, such as language, mathematics and engineering. Using the key words "African overseas students" flags 47 articles in the Chinese Journals Network (2003–2014) containing journal articles and MA dissertations. Among them, five are on cultural adaptation, six on educational management, 14 on teaching Chinese language and the rest on China–Africa relations. Reports and memoirs provide various information on African experiences in China (Li Jiangtao & Li Xiang 2006; Li Anshan 2013a; China–Africa Project 2013).

Psychology is often applied in cross-cultural studies, and two works are worth mentioning. One is an article based on a SASS (Study Abroad Stress Survey) of Africans and Western students in China in 2003 to evaluate gender differences and cultural differences (Africa vs West) in the perception of stress. The survey sent out 200 forms to foreign students at colleges in three cities in China. The 30 questions were divided into four categories: interpersonal, individual, academic and environment. Returned valid forms numbered 156: 82 from Africans (46 men, 36 women) and 74 Westerners (32 men, 42 women). There is no group difference in the respondents' perceptions of the four stressors. Group variations existed only in the subdivision of stress. Cross-cultural orientation is suggested for foreign students, as there are indications that academic and interpersonal sources of stress are the most common, as are daily hassles defined as high pressure and challenges among both men and women (Hashim et al. 2003; Hashim & Yang 2003). Another psychological study is an MA dissertation by an African student based on an investigation of 181 responses out of 210 forms sent out – a rather high ratio for such a survey. The aim of the study was to get a real picture of the cultural shock and adaptation experienced by African students in China. The study found that cultural shock is common for all African students in China and the best way to overcome it is to increase social contact with local people. It also found that although all African students experienced cultural shock, the extent varied according to the grade and gender; it was more serious for undergraduates than graduates and for women than men (Disima 2004). Other studies are either on cultural adaptation (Yi Pei & Xiong Lijun 2013; Gong Sujuan 2014), cultural difference and its impact (Long Xia & Xiong Lijun 2014) or different concepts of time and family (Ye Shuai 2011).

As for China–Africa educational cooperation, Ketema et al. suggest that Chinese universities play an important role in bilateral cooperation (Ketema et al. 2009). King uses African students in China as indicator of China's soft power (King 2013). Haugen analyses China's policy of enrolment of African students and its effect and outcome (Haugen 2013). Others argue that China's educational assistance forms an essential part of China–Africa cooperation and offers substantial support to Africa (Li Baoping 2006; Xu Hui 2007; He Wenping 2007; Lou Shizhou & Xu Hui 2012). Studies have also discussed the management of African students or graduates in China, either in universities or society (Zheng Jianghua 2012, 2013; Zheng Jianghua et al. 2013; An Ran et al. 2007). The fourth subject involves language teachers who are probing better ways to teach Chinese language to Africans (Lin Lunlun & Ren Mengya 2010). African students themselves write about their experiences in China and emphasise African agency in their behaviour in Chinese society (Amoa 2012; (Lokongo 2012; Baitie 2013).

There are criticisms of the teaching methods and suggestions for improvement. Different views are held about the effect of China's educational policy on African students. One view is that African scholarship holders are generally satisfied with their experiences in China, which promotes a positive view of the potential for strengthening friendship with African countries through educational programs (Dong & Chapman 2008). Although there are shortcomings and room for improvement, China's policy is rather successful in promoting China–Africa relations, helping African capacity-building and bettering China's image (Li Anshan & April 2013; Li Anshan & Liu Haifang 2013; Niu Changsong 2016). Haugen asserts that China fails to reach its policy objectives because of African students' disappointment with the quality of the education they receive, and because their disappointment obstructs the promotion of Chinese values and China–African educational exchanges (Haugen 2013).

The above-mentioned studies are all characterised by similar features: they are based on cross-cultural theory, using questionnaires as methodology plus the collection of direct data of life experiences and providing concrete suggestions. Researchers are sometimes African students themselves. Since the research is usually based on a case study of African students in a particular place (or university), or from a particular country, the limitation is inevitable. How to apply theory in case studies is another issue. Bilateral migration provides both opportunity and challenge. With similarity between Chinese culture and African culture, mutual learning is always beneficial to both, especially through people-to-people contact. Solid study on the topic is still lacking.

History, reality and trend

The history of African students in China began in 1956 with the arrival of four Egyptian students in China. If we compare this figure with the 61,594 African students in China in 2016, the upward trend is dramatic. The history of African students in China can be divided into four periods: the first runs from 1956 to 1966, when the Cultural Revolution closed all the universities; the second mainly concerns the trainees for TAZARA; the third runs from the 1970s to 2000; and the fourth began in 2000, the year of China–Africa Cooperation (FOCAC) and extends to the present day (Li Baoping 2006; He Wenping 2007).

The first contact of African students with China is in the period 1956–1966. In 1953, a Chinese youth delegation had broad contact with delegates from Egypt, Algeria, Tunisia, Morocco, Madagascar and French West Africa during the International Conference of the Defense of Youth Rights held in Geneva, when students on both sides established links. Even before the establishment of China–Egypt diplomatic relations on 30 May 1956, the two countries signed the agreement on cultural cooperation on 15 April 1956 (Jiang Chun & Guo Yingde 2001: 524), which began the exchange of scholars and students from both countries. Four Egyptian students came to China in 1956, three under the academic supervision of the famous artist Professor Li Keran to learn the skill of Chinese painting. They became well-known artists in Egypt after their studies at the China Central Academy of Fine Arts (Li Baoping 2006; Jiang Chun & Guo Yingde 2001: 530).

In 1957, 11 African students came to study in China from Cameroon, Kenya, Uganda and Malawi (countries that were not yet independent). During the 1950s, 24 African students came to China on scholarships of the Chinese government. When many African countries won their independence in the 1960s, China started educational cooperation with those countries. African students or technicians came to Chinese universities for advanced study under various agreements or programs. China sent various cultural delegations to Africa, learning different types of African dance, while African countries sent young people to China for further study. In 1960, the number of African students in China increased to 95. When the Cultural Revolution occurred in 1966, there were 164 students from 14 African countries who had to go back home since all the universities were closed (CAECG 2005: 14–17).

Among young students from African countries, a Ghanaian student, Emmanuel Hevi, complained about racism and other unpleasant experiences in China (Hevi 1963). He served as General Secretary of the African Student Union in China at the time, and his negative statements about China behind the Iron Curtain became immediately popular in the West. Moreover, Hevi was from Ghana, where President Nkrumah was strongly pro-socialist. As suggested in Chapter 14, it might be simplify the incident by racism, since Hevi's complaint is understandable for several reasons (Cheng Yinghong 2014; Jiang Huajie 2016).

The 1970s was characterised by brotherly friendship because many of the African students were connected with the Tanzania-Zambia Railway (TAZARA). During the 1960s and 1970s, two important events greatly improved China–Africa contact: the dispatch of Chinese medical teams to Africa and the building of TAZARA. After China sent its first medical team to Algeria in 1963, Chinese medical teams were eventually dispatched to 47 African countries (Li Anshan 2011). Supported by the Chinese government, TAZARA was built specifically to break the blockade of the White racial regimes in southern Africa. TAZARA not only made a great contribution to the transportation of minerals from Zambia to the Port of Dar es Salaam, thus helping the frontier countries, but also improved the lives of the local people. Furthermore, the process of building TAZARA provided an opportunity for mutual contact, since more than 60,000 Chinese engineers, technicians and workers joined the workforce in Africa, which helped the Africans to better understand China and the Chinese people. In order to help Tanzania and Zambia run TAZARA, China agreed to train engineers of the two countries from June 1972. Thus trainees in railway technology came to China, followed by formal African students enrolled in Chinese universities in 1973 (Monson 2009; Shen Xipeng 2018).

This large group was trained for the future TAZARA project in various specialties. They started training courses in Beifang Jiaotong University, the North University of Transportation. The 200 would-be engineers from Tanzania and Zambia enjoyed various experiences. They took different basic courses in public transportation, then trained in different specialist fields such as transportation, locomotives, vehicles, communication, signals, railway engineering and finance. Of this group, 179 finally graduated in September 1975. In 1973, China resumed the enrolment of international students. There were 37 African students, followed by 61 in 1974. In 1975 the numbers increased to 113 and in 1976 to 144. At the end of 1976, China had 355 students from 21 African countries and the number with Chinese scholarship increased as well (CAECG 2005). After their return, they played a very important role in transportation and other fields in their own countries (Liu Haifang & Monson 2011; Shen Xipeng 2018).

The period 1978–2000 forms the third period, which saw increasing contacts. Since the opening up, China has resumed normal educational cooperation with African countries. However, the economic situation in China was rather poor and international students were few. In 1978, China enrolled 1236 new international students, with 95 per cent enjoying Chinese Government Scholarships (hereafter CGS); among them, 121 were African students – about 10 per cent of the total (Chen & Xie 2010). Together with nearly 300 African students enrolled during 1976–1977, they amounted to more than 400 African students in China, accounting for one-quarter of all foreign students. However, only 30 African students received CGS in 1979, 43 in 1980 and 80 in 1981 (CAECG 2005) (see Table 20.1).

The statistics indicate that numbers of African students went on increasing in the 1980s, except for 1989, when the number dropped to 249 from 325 the previous year. The number kept fluctuating between 200 and 300 in the following years, never surpassing 300. This might be explained by the clashes between African and Chinese students in the 1980s, especially the incident at Hehai University in Nanjing in 1988.

For many Chinese people, it was the first time they had seen foreigners and they could not help pointing fingers at foreign students, especially Africans. This became a very complicated issue affected by various factors, such as African students' complaints about economic or living conditions, political divergence between the United States and the Middle East, different social values and Chinese prejudice towards Africans (Li Anshan & Liu Haifang 2013). Complaints and grievances resulted in conflict and even demonstrations. Clashes between African and Chinese students occurred in Tianjin, Nanjing, Beijing, Shanghai and other cities during the 1980s. African students voiced their grievances in different ways, such as demonstration inside or outside campus, boycotting class, hunger strike and petition. Occasionally, Chinese students also took part in the demonstrations, resulting in clashes. The incidents were described as "national racism" by some scholars (Sautman 1994; Sulliven 1994).

Table 20.1 African students in China, 1976–1995

Year	Scholarship	Self-financed	Total
1976	144	0	144
1977	142	0	142
1978	121	0	121
1979	30	0	30
1980	43	0	43
1981	80	0	80
1982	154	0	154
1983	230	0	230
1984	247	0	247
1985	314	0	314
1986	297	0	297
1987	306	0	306
1988	325	0	325
1989	249	2	251
1990	252	6	258
1991	272	15	287
1992	267	20	287
1993	225	58	283
1994	220	246	466
1995	256	721	977
Total	4 174	1 068	5 242

Analysing the situation from today's perspective, difference in social systems, values and culture could be the major cause. With a rather traditional character, the Chinese were not used to close relationships between men and woman in public, while African students had a more open attitude. Therefore, the trigger for conflicts was usually close contact between African male students and Chinese girls. which ordinary Chinese disliked. Of course, China was undergoing a dramatic social transformation at the time. With six Chinese students in a dormitory room, they were not happy with just two foreign students living in a room. In addition, the foreign students enjoyed stipends and better conditions in other aspects of campus life. Therefore it was natural for both Chinese students and ordinary citizens to use this opportunity to give vent to other social grievances and dissatisfaction, which led to conflicts. But there were also promising signs. One phenomenon was that numbers of self-financed students from Africa increased during the first half of the 1990s. In 1990 there were six, jumping to 15 in 1991. The number increased to 246 in 1994 and 721 in 1995. More and more African youths wanted to come to China for further study; the low fees and easy acquisition of visas were among the reasons for this.

After 1996, the history of African students in China entered a period of fast growth. Why 1996? What is the significance of that year? On 22 May 1996, the people of Harare, the capital of Zimbabwe, were dancing and singing to see

Table 20.2 African students in China, 1996–2015

Year	Scholarship	Self-funded	Total
1996	922	118	1 040
1997	991	224	1 215
1998	1 128	267	1 395
1999	1 136	248	1 384
2000	1 154	234	1 388
2001	1 224	302	1 526
2002	1 256	390	1 646
2003	1 244	549	1 793
2004	1 317	869	2 186
2005	1 367	1 390	2 757
2006	1 861	1 876	3 737
2007	2 733	3 182	5 915
2008	3 735	5 064	8 799
2009	4 824	7 609	12 433
2010	5 710	10 693	16 403
2011	6 316	14 428	20 744
2012	6 717	20 335	27 052
2013	7 305	26 054	33 359
2014	7 821	33 856	41 677
2015	8 470	41 322	49 792
Total	67 231	169 010	236 241

Sources: *China Education Yearbook, 2003–2015*, Beijing: People's Education Press.

off Chinese President Jiang Zemin, who was on his way home after a visit to six African countries: Kenya, Ethiopia, Egypt, Mali, Namibia and Zimbabwe. During the visit, he put forward five proposals for China and Africa to build up long-time stable and all-round cooperation for the 21st century: sincere friendship, equality, solidarity and cooperation, and common development for the future. The visit and policy might have brought about a great increase of CGS to African students, with numbers increasing from 256 in 1995 to 922 in 1996. With 118 self-financed students that year, for the first time African students in China numbered more than 1000 (CAECG 2005: 16).

After FOCAC was set up in 2000, promoting China–Africa educational cooperation became an important issue. At the end of 2002, of 85,800 foreign students, 1600 were Africans (CEY 2003: 343). In 2009, foreign students in China surpassed 230,000, with 12,436 African students (CEY 2010: 400). The figures indicate that the increase in the number of African students is closely linked to the number of international students in China. During 1996–2011, there were 84,361 African students in China: 36,918 enjoyed CGS while 47,443 were self-funded.

The year 2005 was a turning point. For the first time, self-funded students (1390) from Africa outnumbered scholarship students (1367). This may be due to the success of the scholarship programs and the Chinese Education

488 *Migration and diaspora*

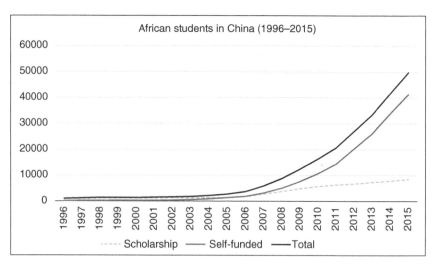

Figure 20.1 African students in China (1996–2015)

Exhibition held in Egypt and South Africa since 2003. However, this trend conforms with the situation of international students in China as a whole. In 2005, there were 133,869 self-funded students from 175 countries studying in China, about 94.88 per cent of international students, and the growth rate was 28.56 per cent greater than 2004. In 2009, of the 238,184 foreign students in 610 Chinese universities and scientific research institutions, 219,939 were self-funded (CEY 2009: 440). The dramatic increase may be explained by the Beijing Olympic Games in 2008. In 2011, self-funded African students reached 14,428, more than double the number of African CGS holders (6316). In 2014, 84 per cent of African students in China had a degree as their goal and only 16 per cent chose non-degree courses. In 2015 there were 8470 African CGS holders and the number of self-financed students reached 41,322, nearly five times as many as the CGS holders. Most African students in China, whether CGS holders or self-financed, are pursuing a degree and this category increased rapidly.

The trend of the African students is impressive, with three characteristics. First, the increase was rapid, together with the increase of international students. Second, self-financed African students increased even faster than CGS holders. Third, the overwhelming majority of African students are pursuing degrees.

Policy, implementation and effect

As a newcomer in the international arena of educational cooperation, the Chinese government has devised a policy on international students and carried it out step by step. There is no specific law regarding any group of international students, such as US students or African students, yet the policy is the product of international relations. No doubt the policy is closely linked to or even decided by China's strategy. In the decades from the 1950s to the 1970s, the major decisive factor in China's policy was ideology, a desire to unite African countries in the struggle against first the capitalist camp headed by the United States, then the two hegemonies, the United States and the Soviet Union. Since China's international education policy took shape only after the opening up, the emphasis here is on the policy since the 1980s.

As early as 1978, the State Council of the Chinese government endorsed a document requesting the Chinese to treat foreign students in a friendly way, for foreign students were allowed to go shopping on the streets and marry Chinese. The 1980s witnessed the setting up of primary rules, regulations and policy in the field of the management of foreign students. In 1985, the State Council approved the "Measures of Administration of Foreign Students" issued by the State Education Commission and the Ministries of Foreign Affairs, Culture, Public Security and Finance. The government realised that "the enrolment and training of foreign students is a strategic work in our diplomacy" and required ministries and different levels of government to carry out the instruction. The document has eight chapters with 43 clauses, covering general principles, enrolment and status management, teaching, professional practice/fieldwork, various types of management such as ideological work and political activities, livelihood and socializing, and organisation leadership.[6]

It seems that the Chinese government regarded foreign students as an element of the Chinese society and the regulations were dogmatic and strict. They covered a broad range, even the course, Chinese language teaching, teaching materials and physical training. This important document governed the management of international students for many years. On 21 July 1999, the Ministry of Education issued regulations on the enrolment of foreign students in primary and secondary schools.[7] In 2000, the document "Provisions on the Administration of Foreign Students in Universities" was issued, with eight chapters and 50 clauses. The provisions contain two added chapters, "Scholarship" and "Entry–Exit and Residence Procedures", which make the implementation more applicable and are more systematic than the previous version.[8] In March 2017, a new document was issued by three ministries regarding the enrolment and training of international students; it came into practice on 1 July 2017.[9]

Although the rules and regulations relate to all foreign students, there are specific measures regarding African students, especially when special events or unusual things occur. For example, during the troublesome days in the early 1980s, racial discrimination occurred in Shanghai. Some Chinese called the African students names and there were occasional clashes. In one case, in February 1983 the Chinese Minister of Education had a meeting with the leader of the African Diplomatic Corps and 15 African ambassadors to discuss the problems between Shanghai residents and African students.

The African ambassadors warned that the Chinese government should restrain the police as well as residents since the African students were often harassed by the police. If the situation continued, friendly relations would be damaged. Different local governmental departments also promulgated various documents regarding specific issues with African students (Li Anshan & Liu Haifang 2013).

During the mid-1990s, after their graduation in China, some African students took jobs in a third country instead of going back to their home countries. This phenomenon did not tally with the original intention of the Chinese government to help build capacity in African countries. In 1996, the Chinese Ministry of Education issued a document requesting that the African graduates' return tickets be handed directly to the Beijing embassy of the students' country at the end of the academic year so the students would go directly back home. This is now routine. A report commented on this policy:

> Due to Chinese visa rules, most international students cannot stay in China after their education is complete. This prevents brain-drain and means that China is educating a generation of African students who – unlike their counterparts in France, the US or UK – are more likely to return home and bring their new education and skills with them.
> (Breeze & Moore 2017)

In 2005 when Chinese President Hu Jintao participated in the high-level meeting on financing for development at the 60th Session of the United Nations, he promised that in the next three years China would increase its assistance to developing countries, African countries in particular. "China will train 30,000 personnel of various professions from the developing countries within the next three years so as to help them speed up their human resources development" (Hu Jintao 2005). Since the CGS is closely related to China's international strategy, it is also a reflection of the focus of China's policy. The statistics shows that before 2005 the number of African students who received CGS was always smaller than that of European students. The situation started to change in 2006, a year after Hu Jintao's declaration. The actual number of African CGS holders (1861) surpassed that of Europeans (1858) for the first time. From 2007 onwards, the number of African students with CGS began to increase substantially.

There are continual policy changes. During the Third FOCAC also China-Africa Summit in 2006 in Beijing, CGS for African students was raised from 2000 to 4000 annually. At the Fourth FOCAC in 2009, the CGS again increased to 5,500 and it reached 5,710 in 2010 (Li Anshan et al. 2012:58–60). In 2012, the Fifth FOCAC announced the scholarships would be 20,000 for the next three years. In 2011, the number of African CGS holders was 6,316, it was 6,717 in 2012, 7,305 in 2013 and 7,821 in 2014. In 2015, African CGS holders reached 8,470 (CEY 2010–2016).

In order to implement the policy, different strategies were planned by agents, universities, municipalities, various departments, and even individuals (Li Anshan & Liu Haifang 2013). Generally speaking, the situation is improved immensely. Regarding the CGS, there was no evaluation system until 1997 when the "Provisional Measures of Annual Review of Scholarship of Foreign Students" were issued by the State Education Commission. The measures made it clear for the first time that students had to be reviewed and meet certain standards to obtain a "pass" or "no pass".[10] Within three years, 7118 CGS holders took the review: 7 008 passed and 110 did not, accounting for 1.55 per cent. In 2000, two documents were issued by the Ministry of Education regarding the CGS annual review system and method.[11]

With more specific standards, the method gave greater autonomy to the institutions entitled to enrol foreign students, thus making it easier for universities to carry out the review independently. In the same year, 2342 CGS holders in 81 universities went through the review; 2314 (98.8 per cent) passed and 28 did not. Among the unqualified students, 17 were Asian, seven European, two African and two American (CEY 2002). As for the universities with the authority to offer CGS, there are strict qualifications. Usually only those universities that have a high standard of education, qualified professors who can offer courses in foreign languages and adequate educational facilities can take the responsibility to enrol international students. In 2015, only the 279 designated Chinese universities under the CGS-Chinese University Program were entitled to accept individual scholarship applications.[12]

The Chinese government wanted to become actively engaged in international educational cooperation (Wang Luxin 2000). Therefore, different ministries, provinces, municipalities and companies started to offer various types of scholarships. Owing to the complicated scholarship system and shortage of space, one example is described here: the Shanghai Government Scholarship (see Table 20.3).

At the end of the 1990s, a general framework for international student education, which was compatible with Chinese culture and educational system, was in place in China. Since then, China has continued to improve its international educational cooperation in an effort to make itself one of the most popular destinations for foreign students. In the meantime, as economic globalization accelerates, international demand is increasing for young, talented people who can speak Chinese or have a solid knowledge of China. As a result, the number of China's international students continues to grow rapidly. In 2016, international students in China increased to 442,773, which was 45,138 more than in 2015 – a growth rate of 11.35 per cent. African students increased by 11,802 to 61,594, a growth rate of 23.7 per cent.[13] This fact demonstrates that education in China is more popular than before.

The theory and practice of African development have long been dominated by Western countries. In recent years, the world economy has been volatile and major changes have taken place in the international balance of power. On one hand, the US financial crisis and the debt crisis in Europe have landed the

Table 20.3 Annual cost of a Shanghai Government scholarship – Class A[1]

Supporting categories	Field of study	Tuition (RMB)	Accommodation (RMB)	Stipend (RMB)	Medical insurance (RMB)	Total (RMB)
Undergraduate students	I	20 000	8 400	30 000	800	59 200
	II	23 000	8 400	30 000	800	62 200
	III	27 000	8 400	30 000	800	66 200
Master's students	I	25 000	8 400	36 000	800	70 200
	II	29 000	8 400	36 000	800	74 200
	III	34 000	8 400	36 000	800	79 200
Doctoral students	I	33 000	12 000	42 000	800	87 800
	II	38 000	12 000	42 000	800	92 800
	III	45 000	12 000	42 000	800	99 800

Note:
1. Full scholarship covers tuition waiver, accommodation, stipend, and comprehensive medical insurance. Field of Study I includes Philosophy, Economics, Legal Studies, Education, Literature, History, and Management; Field of Study II includes Science, Engineering, and Agriculture; Field of Study III includes Fine Arts and Medicine.

Source: "Shanghai Government Scholarship – Class A", China Scholarship Council Date: 28 March 2016. www.csc.edu.cn/Laihua/scholarshipdetailen.aspx?cid=105&id=1293

Western economy in trouble; on the other, emerging economies have become the driving force of the world economy. This contrast and the reality of their own countries' development led a lot of African leaders and intellectuals to realise that the development model advocated by the West did not seem to be working. The African road to development should be determined by Africans themselves.

The Chinese experience is that, in order to pursue the development of its own economy, a country can only rely on its own concerted efforts and determination. Never in history has a nation based its own economy entirely on foreigners (Li Anshan 2013). Therefore, some African governments send their young people to China for further study. In 2005, the government of Rwanda signed an agreement with the Chinese Ministry of Education to train its undergraduates, who were given scholarships by the Rwandan government. In the same year, the government of Tanzania signed an agreement with the China Scholarship Council and agreed to send Tanzanian students to train in China's universities under Tanzanian scholarships (CEY 2006). The two cases demonstrate not only the friendship between China and African countries, but also the high quality of education in China, which has won the trust of African governments. These are indicators of the positive effect of China's policy of international educational cooperation.

Reason, motivation and purpose

Why do more and more Africans come to China for further study? There are various reasons: the favourable conditions provided by China, various personal motivations and the pragmatic purpose of personal development. Learning more about China and gaining advanced technological skills are the main reasons why young Africans come to China for further studies.

China's economic development and strong economy are true attractions for young Africans. The Beijing Olympic Games in 2008 showcased China as never before and Africans were surprised at the impressive place they saw on TV. Africans used to know very little about China and most of them want to come to China to see it with their own eyes.[14] The African media has been dominated by the West and there are various untrue stories and descriptions of China (Yan & Sautman 2017). In 1991, Roberta Cohen, former Deputy Assistant Secretary of State for Human Rights in the Carter administration even spread rumor of China using prison labour in Africa in *The New York Times* (Cohen 1991; Yan & Sautman 2012). BBC irresponsibly reported the "ghost town in Angola" (Redvers 2012). Yet this new residential area soon sold out after it opened to the public.

More and more African youths want to know more about China's rapid growth and its experience of development with modern technologies. They want to understand why China was Africa's largest trading partner for consecutive years and is now the second largest economy in the world. It is China's growing presence in Africa, the commodities, television shows, Confucius Institutes and Chinese people working in Africa that have aroused the growing interest among African students. Maxwell Zeken is a 16-year-old Liberian who lives in rural Nimba County. Asked where he dreams of studying, he says, "I want to study engineering in China and come back to Liberia to build our roads and our cities. They say you must visit the Great Wall of China. I regret that my country didn't build something like that" (Pilling 2017).

China's readiness for educational cooperation has undoubtedly promoted the boom of African students coming to China.[15] The Chinese government has adopted several measures to encourage African students to become familiar with China, such as the Confucius Institutes for young Africans to learn Chinese, and scholarships to attract African students (Liu Haifang 2008). In 2017 there were 48 Confucius Institutes and 27 Confucius Classrooms located in 33 African countries, which provide various grades of Chinese language learning.

Many African students learned Chinese before they applied for a scholarship or to enrol at a Chinese university (Niu Changsong 2016). For example, Dr Belhadj Imen won the Chinese Bridge Competition in Tunisia and the Chinese government offered her a scholarship to study in the Department of Chinese Language and Literature at Peking University. Since Peking University is the top university in China, many international students must learn the language before applying for enrolment or scholarships. It is the same with other Chinese universities entitled to enrol international students. At the Shanghai Institute of Technology, about 130 African students are majoring in civil engineering and architecture. In their first year, they master Chinese and take a language proficiency test. This is normal for international students including Africans pursuing their degrees in China. Christian King, a student in philosophy and international trade at Renmin University, told Panview, "I started studying Chinese back home in Zimbabwe and it was very difficult at first. The tones and characters were challenging, but after several years in China I am almost fluent. I love and enjoy Chinese now."[16]

The scholarships also encourage African students to come to China. As for CGS holders, Asian students are always at the top. Europe, although now receiving far fewer CGS than Africa, was for a long time in second place. Yet the situation has changed since 2006, when Africa took over the second place in terms of CGS.

As Table 20.4 shows, the percentage of CGS for Africa and Europe was the same in 2006, but the African students are a bit more. The number reached 2733 in 2007, outnumbering Europeans by 626. Now, students from 51 African countries are eligible for CGS (for Europeans the number is 39). In 2010, CGS was extended to 22,390 beneficiaries – 4145 more than in 2009 (22.72 per cent). A total of 11,197 were offered to Asia (50.01 per cent), 5710 to Africa (25.5 per cent), 3283 to Europe (14.66 per cent), 1761 to America (7.87 per cent) and 439 to Oceania (1.96 per cent) (CEY 2011).

Besides the CGS, different types of scholarships are offered to international students, such as provincial scholarships, ministerial scholarships, university scholarships and various scholarships with specific purposes provided by companies and charity organisations. The CGS covers various expenses on campus, including tuition, teaching materials, research and survey fees, dissertation guidance fees, a one-off resettlement fee, on-campus accommodation, medical insurance, one round-trip international airfare each year for home visits and one round-trip international airfare for all students. In addition, international students get a monthly stipend. With economic development, the scholarship has been raised many times over the past years.[17]

However, self-funded African students have greatly surpassed holders of CGS since 2005. In 2015, among 49,792 African students in China, only 8470 were CGS holders while 41,322 were self-funded. I once met a Zambian

Table 20.4 Comparison of CGS holders between Africa and Europe, 2003–2010

Year	Total scholarship	Africa	%	Europe	%
2003	6 153	1244	20.20	1 442	23.40
2004	6 715	1317	19.60	1 880	23.50
2005	7 218	1367	18.80	1 761	24.40
2006	8 484	1861	21.90	1 858	21.90
2007	10 151	2733	26.90	2 107	20.80
2008	13 516	3735	27.60	2 628	19.40
2009	18 245	4824	26.44	3 022	16.56
2010	22 390	5710	25.50	3 283	14.66

Source: CEY (2011).

student in the Shangdi region of north Beijing where I live. He told me that he came to learn Chinese in a small language school in Wudaocao, an area well known among foreign students. That surprised me, since he looked very young, came to China alone and lived in an area rather far from the city centre and was determined to study Chinese.

Why do the African students come to China? There are different motivations: some like the reputation of Chinese universities; some want to pursue specific fields (King 2010, 2013; Tsui 2016). China's experience of development with advanced technologies has inspired young Africans. Roads, bridges, hospitals, schools, dams, oil refineries and modern railways in Africa were built by Chinese companies. Moreover, Huawei has been successful in the African IT industry and China is cooperating with Nigeria in the field of satellites. The presence of Chinese companies has attracted talented youngsters in different countries. Young African students see it as an honour to work in Chinese companies such as Huawei. I have met various African students who are doing their master's programs, such as Serge Mundele at Beijing University of Science and Technology and Oodo Stephen Ogidi, a Nigerian student who worked as a post-doctoral fellow in electrical engineering at Dalian University of Technology. African students are also engaged in the study of social sciences, such as Erfiki Hicham, a Moroccan student who completed his study in the School of International Studies, Imen Belhadj, a Tunisian student who finished her MA in Chinese language and literature, and her PhD in international politics and post-doctoral work in Arab studies, and Antoine Lokongo, a student of the Democratic Republic of Congo. They all finished their PhDs under my supervision.

All these phenomena make China an ideal country for young students to pursue further studies. More African students are engaged in professional studies (Bodomo 2011: 29). According to a survey of 2000 samples in 2014, 84 per cent of African students had getting a degree as their goal. Among them, 41.61 per cent applied for medical science as their major, 21.56 per cent chose an engineering-related subject as their major while 13.94 per cent went for business and management. The applications for the top five Chinese universities are 98.33 per cent.[18] A student from the Republic of Congo who came to China in 2007 told me that after he saw several telecommunication products marked "Made in China", he decided that he would go there. With the dream of becoming the minister of telecommunications in his country, he is now a graduate student of the specialty at the Beijing University of Posts and Telecommunications.

Obviously there are other practical reasons. In China, tuition fees are lower and it is easier to get a visa than in Western countries. Moreover, if you have grasped the Chinese language and have some understanding of Chinese culture, it is more convenient for you to find a good job in Chinese companies such as Huawei and ZTE in your own country. It is true that Chinese people know very little about Africa and there is undoubtedly ignorance among the Chinese people regarding the Black skins of African students. However, the friendliness and warm feeling of Chinese people may also encourage young Africans to study in China.

Role, contribution and agency

African students are a big group in China. What role do they play? What contributions do they make to both China and Africa, or to bilateral relations?

Although international students are sometimes not classified as immigrants or diaspora, their similarity to a diaspora is obvious. The most important is their role as a bridge. As the second-largest group in the African community in China, they constantly function as a bridge between African culture and Chinese culture. As soon as they enter China and begin their social life on campus, they start an exchange of culture through conversation with their fellow students, contact with authorities and ordinary Chinese, courses and debates, social interaction and so forth.

In their new situation, young Africans face new challenges and experience cultural shock – worse for undergraduates than graduates and for women than men (Disima 2004). Adaptation thus becomes important and occurs in daily life, learning processes and social contacts, leading to better relations with the host community (Hashim et al. 2003). Cultural adaptation becomes an active response to new conditions, a process of mutual learning. I personally supervised many African graduates, including three PhD students from Tunisia, Morocco and the Democratic Republic of the Congo respectively, and they told me various stories about their experiences. They found ignorance, bias and friendliness – all with warm feeling.

Moses is a Nigerian student majoring in Chinese language teaching. He came to China in 2013 and has a typical Chinese name, Wu Wengzhong. Having learned Chinese in Nigeria from childhood, he became addicted to Chinese culture during his stay. He learned various Chinese arts, including some superior arts such as *Xiangsheng* (Chinese crosstalk or comic dialogue) and the lion dance, and attended various performances and art shows. With his profound interest in Chinese language and culture, Moses participated in the Hebei Provincial Foreign Scholars' Chinese Talent Show in November 2014. He showed his *Kung Fu*, recited Chinese classic poems and performed self-composed Chinese crosstalk with his foreign partner. Thanks to his excellent perform and skill, he won Best Creative Award, Best Eloquence Award and a Silver Award for Recitation of a Classic Poem. He also received the Best All-Around King award for his talents in Chinese cultural activities. Because he spoke Mandarin and understood Chinese culture, Chinese friends called him "China-hand" (Yang Mengjie et al. 2016).

Besides their school fees contributing to China's economy, learning about Africa has brought about multiculturalism in China. Cultural exchanges are happening all the time between African and Chinese students. They are learning the Chinese language, culture and work ethic (King 2013), and at the same time they are transmitting African culture, values and skills (Amoah 2012).

There are various clubs in Chinese cities, such as African dance, African music and African drumming, thanks to the African students' contribution. Francis Tchiégué is a Cameroonian student who came to China for his PhD many years ago, although he eventually received his PhD in Cameroon. During his time in China, he was attracted by the similarity between Cameroonian and Chinese culture and began to learn Chinese arts and skills and Chinese crosstalk. Through his activities, he introduced African culture, and even made a traditional Chinese costume using Cameroonian cloth. Francis was named "Envoy of Art Exchange between China and Africa" and now he is trying his best to introduce African films to China.

The Chinese students in London serve as a bridge between Chinese and British culture, and between the Chinese diaspora in Britain and British society (Wu Bing 2015, 2016). African students play the same role in China. They not only serve as a bridge between African and Chinese culture, but also as a bridge between the African community in China and Chinese people who are interested in Africa (Bredeloup 2014). Thanks to their efforts, Chinese people are becoming familiar with African values, ideas, dances, drums, pictures and sculpture. A good example is my former student Wang Hanjie, who wrote her BA paper on the history and spread of Djembe drums in China. When asked why she choose this topic, she told me with a smile: "Because I am a member of the Djembe Club at Peking University!" (Wang Hanjie 2013).

There is an annual International Cultural Festival at Peking University and African students set up their stands to proudly introduce their own culture to Chinese audiences.[19] In Wuhan, an important metropolitan city in middle China where advertisements projecting foreign brands and tastes are rather popular, some local ladies were interviewed about their taste for African cultural products in China. The young ladies found them *hen ku* (very cool):

> Their choice showed that they were avant-garde, cosmopolitan and even modern in their fashion tastes and preferences. This African cultural influence in Wuhan has been facilitated in no small measure by the annual Wuhan University Autumn International Cultural Festival.
> (Amoah 2012)

In other universities in Beijing, such as Minzu University of China, there is even a special African Culture Day.

Although some African students choose to move to a third country after they finish university in China, many decide to return home after graduation and make an important contribution to their own country (Bodomo 2011; Li Anshan & Liu Haifang 2013). In addition to working in different fields, some attain important positions and assume high posts in government. As of 2005, eight former recipients of CGS held posts at ministerial level or above in their home countries; eight served as ambassadors or consuls to China; six were secretaries to their countries' presidents or prime ministers; and three were secretary-generals of the Association for Friendship with China, not to mention many experts in other fields (CAECG 2005: 20–21). Taking Peking University as an example, its former student Mulatu Teshome Wirtu became Speaker of Parliament in Ethiopia and was later the President of Ethiopia. After studies, Lucy Njeri Manegene worked for the Ministry of Foreign Affairs in Kenya. Rakotoarivony R.J. Manitra went back to Madagascar after her MA studies and now serves in the Madagascar Embassy in China. Mapulumo Lisebo Mosisili returned to Lesotho after being awarded an MA and is now Principal Secretary of the Labour Department in Lesotho (Li Anshan 2013a).[20]

Another important experience for African students in China is making pan-African connections on campus. Answering the BBC's question about why he came to China, Mikka Kabugo, a Ugandan student of the African Students Association of Peking University, said he started to know China through a doctor of traditional Chinese medicine in Uganda. When he came to China he found Beijing was a global village and he could exchange ideas about African affairs with fellow African students from other countries. This makes the students broad-minded and gives them a global view. They look at African issues from a Pan-African perspective and think about how they can help the continent.[21] Moreover, through classes, debates and various seminars held jointly by the African Students Association and the Center for African Studies at Peking University, they have learned a great deal about world affairs and African problems and solutions.

Following their fellow students at Peking University, the African students of Tsinghua University formed an African Students Association on Africa Day, 25 May 2017. Students from 27 African countries joined the organisation. At the inauguration, African students had discussions about various issues, such as the thoughts of President Julius Kambarage Nyerere and President Kwame Nkrumah, and watched a presentation of the continent's contribution to knowledge development by Dr Chabalala, a student from the School of Public Health at Tsinghua University. Professor Tang Xiaoyang from the School of International Relations and the Carnegie–Tsinghua Center talked about structural changes in China–Africa relations, and Professor John Akokpari from the Center for African Studies at Peking University gave a talk on opportunities for African students in the diaspora to be change makers for the development of their countries. There are other African student associations, such as the General Union of African Students in China (GUASC) and the General Union of African Students in Tianjin (GUAST) (King 2013).

Regarding whether international students should be classified as immigrants, Bodomo correctly points out that the process of trade between Africa and China began with Africans who studied in China and remained there to do business (Bodomo 2013), and some African students in China who ended up trading with China (Haugen 2013). Therefore, Africa–China trading began with the African students who remained in China and started their businesses after graduation. Although they had little capital to begin with, they had the advantage of a solid social and linguistic background.

Gradually they became major intermediaries of the trade between Africa and China, thus contributing to economic activities of both sides. Dr Abdul is a good example. Working as a veterinary official for the Niger Government, he received a Niger–China Friendship Scholarship from the Chinese government. After he finished his degree, he decided to change his profession and take up a new occupation unfamiliar to him but more profitable. In 2000, Dr Abdul established himself in Guangzhou to export medicine and related products for veterinary use to Africa and Europe. He obtains the products directly from factories in north China. With his success, he resumed his connections with the Niger government. Now speaking fluent Mandarin, Dr Abdul serves as honorary consul for Niger, responsible for conveying the demands of Nigerien students with scholarships at Chinese universities to any Nigerien minister who visits Guangzhou. He describes his role as turning "brain drain" to "brain gain". According to Bredeloup, a situation like this resulted from two things: the opportunities created by China's rapid economic development and the change or even devaluation of the position of civil servants in Africa. There are quite a few examples like Abdul, including Patrick from Democratic Republic of the Congo and Aziz from Mali (Bredeloup 2014).

It is generally assumed that China makes every move in China–Africa relations while the African side is either paralysed or inactive in shaping and influencing her deepening relations with China. It is interesting that some African students have started to research African's agency in the making of Africa–China relations. Adu Amoah, a former Ghanaian government official, later became a student in China and married a Chinese girl. As the president of the African Students' Representative Committee of Wuhan University, he used his own observations and experiences to indicate that African students can be masters of their own life in China. He described a lively African migrant community emerging in Wuhan, "which may potentially add to the makings of an African diaspora in contemporary China … this migrant African population is constituted fundamentally by students … comprising a dynamic fashion of those pursuing their course of study and those who stay on after graduation" (Amoah 2012: 108). Amoah describes how the African presence in China influenced the reality of Chinese society in the form of fashion, intermarriage and the exchange of language learning (Marsh 2014). Africans can explain their own worldview and experience in Mandarin while teaching English to Chinese students, and SMEs such as nightclubs are run by Africans: "This is necessary to dispel the interpretation of Africa 'under the sign of crisis' in popular and academic discourses in general and specifically, the patronizing idea of Africa as a clueless, pliant and suppliant partner in Africa–China relations" (Amoah 2012).

Conclusion

In terms of improvement of the situation of African students in China, three parties all need more consideration.

On the Chinese side, it must be kept in mind that Africa is not a single entity but a continent of 54 countries, which all have different cultures, religions, political conditions and realistic needs (Apithy 2013). African students are not a uniform group – they are different individuals. Besides scholarships, does the Chinese government provide adequate living conditions for African students with different religions, lifestyles and cuisine, in a society that is unfamiliar to them? Are Chinese teachers qualified in transmitting their knowledge to African students? Are there good ways for African students to introduce their own culture to Chinese society? Is there enough room for African students to exchange ideas and experience with their Chinese partners?

For the African countries, it is essential to remember that the returned African students are those who love their own country and want to contribute the knowledge learned in China to their motherland. Do African governments offer a good opportunity for African students to work at home after graduating in China? Does the government show enough concern and care for their study and life in China and create good conditions to facilitate their study and daily requirements? Does the embassy provide a suitable channel for communication with the African students in China and look after their interests and reasonable demands?

For African students in China, they should always keep in mind and be reminded that they carry a great dream for themselves, great hopes of their families, and great expectation of their country. Do you make good use of the scholarship and study hard to meet the challenges ahead, thus preparing yourself for future work? Do you take every opportunity to introduce African culture or the culture of your own country to ordinary Chinese or to fellow students from other countries? Do you learn good lessons about the development of other countries and take the opportunity to use them to realize your dream after your return?

It is a fact that more and more African students have come to China in recent decades and the number is constantly increasing. They serve as the carriers of African culture, transmitters of social organisation and way of life, mediators of bilateral trade and business, and bridges between Africa and China. African students in China have not only immensely improved cooperation between Africa and China and contributed a great deal to cultural exchange, but have also promoted the internationalisation of China's universities (Li Anshan 2018). "It's still too early to tell how these new dynamics might be shaping geopolitics on the continent" (Breeze & Moore 2017). Yet the African students are definitely creating a new world. To integrate into a host society or adapt to another culture does not mean giving up one's own culture. To build links between two cultures and transform from an enclave to a bridge remains a difficult task. It is worth trying, and it is workable.

Notes

1 This chapter is a revised version of an article entitled "African Students in China: Research, Reality and Reflection", published in *African Studies Quarterly* 17(4) (2018). I would like to thank the journal for providing me the copyright and Professor Lin Fengmin, Xu Liang, Liu Qinglong, Li Zhen for their help with writing.
2 As a leader of the African students group, Emmanuel John Hevi was a Ghanaian student among the African exodus in 1962. He said, "In my view there were two causes of the student exodus: First, China failed us miserably by not offering a standard and quality of education acceptable to us. Second, *we were disenchanted with socialism when we discovered that the Chinese brand of socialism was not the material of our dreams*-nor the nostrum by which we dreamed to cure all the ills of Africa" (Hevi 1964: 71). Jiang Huajie also analysed the cause of the African exodus in the 1960s. His conclusion is that there are contradictions between African students and the Chinese side in terms of living conditions, political education and the man–woman relationship. The obstacle of political identity is the main reason that makes it difficult for African students to adapt to Chinese higher education and social life. China's education department always insisted on reforming African students through revolutionary education. Instead of eliminating obstacles, it led to various misunderstandings (Jiang Huajie 2016).
3 The railway helped Tanzania and Zambia to overcome the obstacles of the white regimes of southern Africa. The trainees had various experiences in China and played an important role in the running of the railway in the early period (Shen Xipeng 2018).
4 There are different opinions about the phenomenon, mainly of racism, which is less convincing. Cheng Yinghong tries to explain it by combining nationalism with racism: "The development from campus racism to cyber racism shows how nationalism and racism have justified and reinforced each other in the perception of the Sino-African connections against a more general background of racial discourse since the 1980s" (Cheng Yinghong 2011: 578).
5 There are debates about whether international students can be classified as immigrants, yet the prevailing opinion is that they can (Wu Bin 2015, 2016).
6 State Council Document No. 121 1985. Circular of State Council's endorsement of "Methods of Management of Foreign Students" issued by the State Education Commission, Ministry of Foreign Affairs, Ministry of Culture, Ministry of Public Security and Ministry of Finance, 14 October 1985. www.chinalawedu.com/news/1200/22598/22615/22822/2006/3/he9995243111118360023570-0.htm
7 Decree No. 4 1999. Provisional measures of the Ministry of Education for the administration on enrolment of foreign students by primary and secondary schools. 21 July 1999. www.pkulaw.cn/fulltext_form.aspx?Gid=23504.
8 Decree No. 9 2000. Provisions on the administration of foreign students in universities, issued by the Ministry of Education, Ministry of Foreign Affairs and Ministry of Public Security, 31 January 2000. www.moe.edu.cn/s78/A20/gjs_left/moe_861/tnull_8647.html
9 Decree No. 42 2017. Measures of the administration of enrolment and training of international students by the educational institution, issued by Ministry of Education, Ministry of Foreign Affairs and Ministry of Public Security, 20 March 2017. www.gov.cn/xinwen/2017-06/02/content_5199249.htm

10 Provisional measures of annual review of scholarship of foreign students, issued by the State Commission of Education, 28 March 1997. www.bjfao.gov.cn/affair/oversea/wglxsfg/23801.htm
11 Education No. 29 2000. Notice of the Ministry of Education on the implementation of the annual review system of the Chinese Government Scholarship. 26 April 2000. www.moe.edu.cn/s78/A20/gjs_left/moe_850/tnull_1183.html
12 Chinese Government Scholarship Application. 12 August 2015, China Scholarship Council. http://en.csc.edu.cn/laihua/newsdetailen.aspx?cid=66&id=3074.
13 Statistics of foreign students in China in 2016. 1 March 2017, Ministry of Education. www.moe.edu.cn/jyb_xwfb/xw_fbh/moe_2069/xwfbh_2017n/xwfb_170301/170301_sjtj/201703/t20170301_297677.html.
14 I can never forget my own experiences as student in Toronto during the early 1990s. A Zambian friend of mine once asked me, "Can China produce cars?" "Yes, of course, China can also produce trains," I answered coolly, and could not help thinking, "How could he be so ignorant about China?"
15 I personally supervised dozens of graduate students from various African countries in Peking University and the International College of Defence Studies of China People's Liberation Army National Defence University. They are now working in different fields in their own countries (Li Anshan 2013a, 2013b).
16 "Africans learning Chinese can boost cooperation channels", 23 March 2015. http://english.cntv.cn/2016/03/23/ARTIvEEYI0kItdGxV6F2JBK0160323.shtml
17 "China's government scholarship for international students raised", 22 January 2015. http://old.moe.gov.cn//publicfiles/business/htmlfiles/moe/s5147/201501/183255.html
18 "EOL & CUCAS jointly published 2014 Report of International Students in China". www.eol.cn/html/lhlx/content.html
19 "African student's speech at International Festival in Peking University", 29 October 2013. www.fmprc.gov.cn/zflt/chn/zxxx/t1094003.htm
20 Lisebo Kikine to Li Anshan, 12 February 2013.
21 "Why are African students flocking to Chinese universities?" BBC World Service Newsday, 29 June 2017. www.bbc.co.uk/programmes/p0577s49?ocid=socialflow_facebook

References

African communities in China hail Xi's visit. 2013. *China Daily*, 24 March.
African community needs more attention. 2009. *China Daily*, 2 November.
Africans create community in Guangzhou. 2013. *China Daily*, 14 October.
African Union. 2005. *Report of the meeting of experts from the members of the States on the definition of African diaspora April 11–12*. Addis Ababa: African Union.
Amoah, Lloyd G. Adu. 2012. Africa in China: Affirming African agency in Africa–China relations at the people to people level. In James Shikwati, ed., *China–Africa partnership: The quest for a win–win relationship*. Nairobi: Inter Region Economic Network, 104–115.
An Ran et al. 2007. African students' educational needs and the recruitment style. *High Education Exploration* 5: 110–113.
Apithy, Sedozan. 2013. The policy of Sino-African educational cooperation: What does Africa expect for Sino-African educational cooperation? In Li Anshan & Liu Haifang, eds., *Annual review of African studies in China 2012*. Beijing: Social Sciences Academic Press, 326–329.

Baitie, Zahra. 2013. On being African in China. *The Atlantic*, 28 August.
Bodomo, A. 2011. African students in China: A case study of newly arrived students on FOCAC funds at Chongqing University. PPT Outline, University of Hong Kong.
Bodomo, A. 2012. *Africans in China: A sociocultural study and its implications on Africa-China relations.* New York: Cambria Press.
Bodomo, A. 2013. African diaspora remittances are better than foreign aid funds. *World Economics* 14(4): 21–28.
Bodomo, A. 2014. Africans in China: A bibliographical survey. In Li Anshan & Lin Fengmin, eds, *Annual review of African studies in China 2013*. Beijing: Social Sciences Academic Press (China), 109–121.
Bodomo, A. 2016. *Africans in China: Guangdong and beyond*. New York: Diasporic Africa Press.
Bredeloup, Sylvie. 2014. West-African students turned entrepreneurs in Asian trading posts: A new facet of globalization. *Urban Anthropology* 43(1/2/3): 17–56.
Breeze, Victoria & Moore, Nathan. 2017. China tops the US and UK as destination for Anglophone African students. *The Conversation*, 28 July. http://theconversation.com/china-tops-us-and-uk-as-destination-for-anglophone-african-students-78967
Brief Statistics of Foreign Students Studying in China, 2012–2015. Department of International Cooperation and Exchanges, Ministry of Education of China.
Chen, Changgui & Xie Liangao. 2010. *Approaching nationalization: Research on international exchange and cooperation of education in China.* Guangzhou: Guangdong Educational Press.
Cheng Yinghong. 2011. From campus racism to cyber racism: Discourse of race and Chinese nationalism. *The China Quarterly* 207: 561–579.
Cheng, Yinghong. 2014. An African student's impression of China of the 1960s. *Phoenix Weekly* 14. www.ifengweekly.com/detil.php?id=490l
CAECG [China Africa Education Cooperation Group]. 2005. *China Africa education cooperation.* Beijing: Peking University Press.
China Africa Project. 2013. Leading China scholar Li Anshan recalls his experiences teaching African students. www.chinaafricaproject.com/leading-china-scholar-li-anshan-recalls-his-experiences-teaching-african-students-translation
China Education Yearbook (CEY). 2003–2015. Beijing: People's Education Press.
Cissé, Daouda. 2013. South–South migration and trade: African traders in China. *Policy Briefing*. Beijing: Center for Chinese Studies.
Cohen, Roberta. 1991. China has used prison labour in Africa. *The New York Times*, 11 May.
Department of International Cooperation and Exchanges, Ministry of Education of China. 2015. *Brief statistics of foreign students studying in China, 2012–*2015.
Disima. 2004. Cultural adaptation of foreign students in China. M.A. thesis of psychology, Nanjing Normal University.
Dong, L. & Chapman, D.W. 2010. China's scholarship program as a form of foreign assistance. In D.W. Chapman, W.K. Cummings & G.A. Postiglione, eds, *Crossing borders in East Asian higher education.* Hong Kong: Comparative Education, 145–166.
Gillespie, Sandra. 2001. *South–South transfer: A study of Sino-African exchange.* New York: Routledge.
Gong Sujuan. 2014. A study on African students in China and their cross-cultural adaptation. *Journal of Kaifeng Institute of Education* 34(2): 127–130.

Han, H. 2013. Individual grassroots multilingualism in Africa Town in Guangzhou: The role of states in globalization. *International Multilingual Research Journal.* 7(1): 83–97.

Hashim, Ismail Hussein et al. 2003. Cultural and gender differences in perceiving Stressors: A cross-cultural investigation of African and Western students at Chinese colleges. *Psychological Science* 26(5): 795–799.

Hashim, I.H. & Yang, Z.L. 2003. Cultural and gender differences in perceiving stressors: A cross-cultural investigation of African and Western students in Chinese colleges. *Stress and Health* 19(4): 217–225.

Haugen, H.Ø. 2013. China's recruitment of African university students: Policy efficacy and unintended outcomes. *Globalisation, Societies and Education* 11(3): 315–344.

He Wenping. 2007. A summary analysis of China–Africa educational exchanges and cooperation: Development phases and challenges. *West Asia and Africa* 3: 13–18.

Hevi, Emmanuel John. 1963. *An African student in China.* London: Praeger.

Hevi, Emmanuel John. 1964. An African student in Red China. *Harper's Magazine,* January: 63–71.

Hu Jintao. 2005. Written statement by President Hu Jintao of China at the High-Level Meeting on Financing for Development at the 60th Session of the United Nations. 15 September. http://politics.people.com.cn/GB/1024/3696504.html

Jiang Chun & Guo Yingde. 2001. *History of China–Arab relations.* Beijing: Economic Daily Press.

Jiang Huajie. 2016. An analysis of the drop out phenomenon of African students in China in the 1960s. *CPC History Research and Teaching* 2: 52–62.

Ketema, M., Xu, J.L., & Li, Q. 2009. The research on educational cooperation between China and Africa: An African perspective. *Studies in Foreign Education* 36(1), 50–53.

King, K. 2010. China's cooperation in education and training with Kenya: A different model? *International Journal of Educational Development* 30(5): 488–496.

King, K. 2013. *China's aid and soft power in Africa: The case of education and training.* Melton: James Currey.

Larkin, Bruce D. 1971. *China and Africa 1949–1970: The foreign policy of the People's Republic of China.* Berkeley, CA: University of California Press.

Li Anshan. 2005. African studies in China in the twentieth century: A historiographical survey. *African Studies Review* 48(1): 59–87.

Li Anshan. 2011. *Chinese medical cooperation in Africa: With special emphasis on the medical teams and Anti-Malaria Campaign.* Uppsala: Norkiska Afrikainstitutet.

Li Anshan. 2012. China and Africa: Cultural similarity and mutual learning. In James Shikwati, ed., *China–African Partnership: The quest for a win–win relationship.* Nairobi: Inter Region Economic Network, 93–97.

Li Anshan. 2013. African countries encouraged to "Look East". *Guangming Daily,* 28 March.

Li Anshan. 2013a. My African students. In Cheng Tao & Lu Miaogeng (eds), *Chinese ambassadors telling African stories.* Beijing: World Affairs Press, 156–168.

Li Anshan. 2013b. Leading China scholar Li Anshan recalls his experiences teaching African students. The Chinafrica Project, 12 March. www.chinaafricaproject.com/leading-china-scholar-li-anshan-recalls-his-experiences-teaching-african-students-translation

Li Anshan. 2014. Changing discourse on China–Africa relations since the 1990s. *World Economy and Politics* 2: 19–47.

Li Anshan. 2015. African diaspora in China: Reality, research and reflection. *The Journal of Pan African Studies* 7(10): 10–43.
Li Anshan. 2018. African students in China: Research, reality and reflection. *African Studies Quarterly* 17(4): 5–44.
Li Anshan. 2019. *The social and economic history of the Chinese overseas in Africa* (3 vols). Nanjing: Jiangshu People's Press.
Li Anshan et al. 2012. *FOCAC twelve years later: Achievements, challenges & the way forward*. Uppsala: Nordic Africa Institute.
Li Anshan & April, Funeka Yazini, eds. 2013. *Forum on China–Africa Cooperation: The politics of human resource development*. Pretoria: Africa Institute of South Africa.
Li Anshan & Liu Haifang. 2013. *The evolution of the Chinese policy of funding African students and an evaluation of the effectiveness*. Draft report for UNDP.
Li Anshan & Liu Haifang, eds. 2012. *Annual review of African studies in China 2012*. Beijing: Social Sciences Academic Press (China).
Li Baoping. 2006. On the issues of China–Africa educational cooperation. www.docin.com/p-747065460.html
Li Jiangtao & Li Xiang. 2006. China is my second hometown: African students' life in Beijing. http://news.xinhuanet.com/world/2006-10/21/content_5232813.htm
Liu Haifang. 2008. China–Africa relations through the prism of culture: The dynamics of China's cultural diplomacy with Africa. *Journal of Current Chinese Affairs* 3: 9–44.
Liu Haifang & Jamie Monson. 2011. Railway time: Technology transfer and the role of Chinese experts in the history of TAZARA. In Ton Dietz et al., eds, *African engagements: Africa negotiating an emerging multipolar world*. Leiden: Brill, 226–251.
Lin Lunlun & Ren Mengya. 2010. A sociolinguistic study upon Chinese language learning concept of African overseas students. *Journal of Hanshan Normal University* 31(5): 32–37.
Liu, P.H. 2013. Petty annoyances? Revisiting John Emmanuel Hevi's *An African Student in China* after 50 years. *China: An International Journal* 11(1): 131–145.
Lokongo, Antoine Roger. 2012. My Chinese connection. *Chinafrica*, July, 50.
Long Xia & Xiong Lijun. 2014. The influence of China–African cultural difference on the education of African students in China: Taking Angola students as the example. *Journal of Chongqing University of Education* 27(1): 133–136.
Lou Shizhou & Xu Hui. 2012. The development and transition of China–Africa educational cooperation in the new period. *Educational Research* 10: 28–33.
Marsh, Jenni. 2014. Afro-Chinese marriages boom in Guangzhou: but will it be "til death do us part"? www.scmp.com/magazines/post-magazine/article/1521076/afro-chinese-marriages-boom-guangzhou-will-it-be-til-death
Monson, J. 2009. *Africa's freedom railway: How a Chinese development project changed lives and livelihoods in Tanzania*. Bloomington & Indianapolis: Indiana University Press.
Niu Changsong. 2016. A survey of African students' satisfaction of Chinese government scholarship. www.docin.com/p-1445264169.html
Owusu-Ansah, Priscilla. 2021. China in my eyes: China's development in a hundred years' glory series. Second "China in My Eyes – Development of China" Essay Contest, University of Electronic Science and Technology, Chengdu.
Pilling, David. 2017. Ports and roads mean China is "winning in Africa". *Construction Review*, 6 May. https://constructionreviewonline.com/2017/05/ ports-and-roads-mean-china-is-winning-in-africa

Pinto, Jeanette. 2006. The African native in diaspora. *African and Asian Studies* 5(3–4): 383–397.
Redvers, Louise. 2012. Angola's Chinese-built ghost town. BBC, 2 July. www.bbc.com/news/world-africa-18646243
Sautman, Barry. 1994. Anti-Black racism in post-Mao China. *The China Quarterly* 138: 413–437.
Seidelman, Raymond. 1989. The anti-African protests: More than just Chinese racism. *The Nation*, 13 February.
Shen Xipeng. 2018. *A study on China aided construction of Tanzania–Zambia Railway*. Heifei: Huangshan Publishing House.
Sulliven, M.J. 1994. The 1988–89 Nanjing anti-African protests: Racial nationalism or national racism? *The China Quarterly* 138: 438–457.
Tsui, Chak-Pong Gordon. 2016. African university students in China's Hong Kong: Motivations, aspirations, and further exchanges. In Adams Bodomo, ed., *Africans in China: Guangdong and beyond*. New York: Diasporic Africa Press, 119–137.
Wang Hanjie. 2013. The spread and distribution of African drums in China, In Li Anshan & Liu Haifang, eds, *Annual review of African studies in China 2012*. Beijing: Social Sciences Academic Press (China), 442–458.
Wang Luxin. 2000. Educational exchange and cooperation between China and African countries. In Lu Ting-en & Ma Ruimin, eds, *China and Africa*. Beijing: Peking University Press.
Wu Bin. 2015. Links between Chinese international students and overseas Chinese communities: An empirical study in Nottingham, UK. *Overseas Chinese History Studies* 2: 1–11.
Wu Bin. 2016. Local engagement of Chinese international students in host societies: A perspective of diasporic Chinese community building. *The International Journal of Diasporic Chinese Studies* 8(2): 13–30.
Xu Hui. 2007. China–Africa educational cooperation under the FOCAC framework. *Educational Development Research* 9: 1–7.
Yan Hairong & Sautman, Barry. 2012. Chasing ghosts: Rumours and representations of the export of Chinese convict labour to developing countries. *The China Quarterly* 210: 398–418.
Yan Hairong & Sautman, Barry. 2017. *China in Africa: Discourses and reality*. Beijing: Social Sciences Academic Press (China).
Yang Mengjie et al. 2016. China-hand's dream of Mandarin. *Chinanews*, 28 November. www.chinanews.com/sh/2016/11-28/8076600.shtml
Ye Shuai. 2011. A comparative analysis of the cross-cultural communication based on the Somali students and the Chinese students on time and family concepts. *Kexue Wenhui* 11: 30–31.
Yi Pei & Xiong Lijun. 2013. An empirical study of intercultural adaptation of African students in China. *Journal of Shenyang University (Social Science)* 15(3): 364–368.
Zhang Tieshan. 1999. *Friendship road: A report on the construction of Tanzania–Zambia Railway*. Beijing: China Economic and Foreign Trade Press.
Zheng Jianghua. 2012. Research on safety management of African students on university campus. *Journal of Tianjin University of Technology and Education* 22(4): 72–74.

Zheng Jianghua. 2013. Exploration of compound applied talents training mode on African students. *Journal of Tianjin University of Technology and Education* 23(4): 64–70.

Zheng Jianghua et al. 2013. Construction of community management system for foreign students in universities. *Vocational and Technical Education* 34(23): 66–68.

Postscript
China–Africa relations in globalisation

There are five basic facts about China–Africa relations, which are acknowledged by all. The relations have developed very fast; China has provided a choice for Africans which they can choose or decline; China's infrastructure building in Africa benefits everyone – Africans, visitors and investors from around the world; Africans' perspective on China is generally favourable according to the poll; and the Chinese have little knowledge about Africa, and vice versa.

International affairs have experienced great change. Brexit brings a new situation in Europe and the United Kingdom may or may not enjoy its independence, while Germany and France are trying to adjust to the new context. A racial crisis is spreading all over the United States, which just withdrew from Afghanistan where it created many troubles during its stay. The Middle East faces tremendous obstacles in bringing peace to the region. African leaders have reached an agreement on an African Continental Free Trade Area, which is designed to unite 1.3 billion people under one market. The Communist Party of China has just passed its 100th anniversary and continues the struggle for the people's benefit. Most tragically, the globe is suffering from the COVID-19 pandemic, which is killing people and destroying economies in every corner of the world.

By all accounts, globalisation is now sweeping across Africa. Farmers in Ghana are in a precarious position because of the inflow of subsidised cheap rice from the United States; American drivers refuel their cars with oil imported from Nigeria; Senegalese are buying clothes made in China and Vietnam; Beijingers drink South African beer while checking newspapers for the stock values of Naspers there; Africans have regular business deals in the Yiwu market; Ethiopian Mursi's pictures spread to Japan via the internet; the African diaspora forms the sixth part of Africa. Globalisation penetrates everywhere.

As for the future of China–Africa relations, China will face great challenges – both internal and international. With the updating of bilateral cooperation, there are a lot of question to answer. How can the goal of sustainable green development be achieved in the African continent, which is endowed with an abundance of natural resources? How can dialogue mechanisms for China–Africa cooperation be made more effective? How can FOCAC be used more effectively as platform to promote mutual understanding between China and Africa, and how can countries and peoples of the rest of the world be made to better understand this forum? More important, how is it possible to encourage Chinese (companies) to understand African culture and people? The key issue is to do the right thing. If you do the right thing and take responsible action, you do not have to worry about what others say about you.

Africa should define its development goals more clearly and ensure that it is not unduly affected or obstructed by external influence. Different countries have different needs, yet regional or continental integration is taking place and the strategic plan should take this into consideration. For example, infrastructure projects such as railways or hydro-power stations can be shared by the continent, especially among the countries that do not possess the required domestic capacity. Independent industry in the continent with a division of labour in different regions should be considered accordingly. Besides foreign investment, internal and African diasporic investment and trade should be encouraged as the internal investment will create an opportunity to build capacity among African enterprises while trade would pave the way for the development of internal markets – both very important for the growth of African entrepreneurship.

For both China and African countries, sovereignty is extremely important, and unity and mutual help on the international stage is vital, especially during critical times such as the fight against COVID-19. It is necessary to develop a strategic plan based on the regional, continental and global context, and adopt comprehensive thinking about bilateral relations. Joint-venture projects may be a win–win strategy for African and Chinese companies, as risks and resources are shared, resulting in favourable profit-sharing. Moreover, both sides should address their respective needs – for example, technological transfer, managerial training, agricultural production, industry construction, natural resource and human resource administration.

Regarding China–Africa relations in the future, certainly there will be more problems ahead. Yet my view is unique: the more problems, the better. Why? If there is no contact, there will be no problem. When relations get wider and deeper, more problems would definitely occur. However, with equal relationships and mutual respect, China and Africa can sit down, exchange ideas freely and find a solution. Once the problem is solved, relations become more solid. A view that the "China–Africa honeymoon is over" has been lingering for more than a decade (Lewis 2009), yet China–Africa cooperation keeps going and gets stronger. As an Arabic proverb goes, "Dogs are barking, yet the camels are heading forward."

Reference

Lewis, Ian. 2009. China in Africa: The honeymoon is over. *Petroleum Economist*, 18 November.

Appendix A
Overseas Chinese in Africa (1968–2017)

Country (region)	1968	1975	1984	1990	1996	2001	2003	2009–17
Algeria					200	2000		20000
Angola	500	550	250	250	300	500		20000–40000
Benin	32				100			4000
Botswana			25	45	25	300	40	3000–10000
Burkina Faso							20	1000
Burundi								150
Central Africa R.								300
Djibouti								?
Equatorial Guinea					388			300
Cameroon	18	10	10	10	407	50		1000–7000
Cabo Verde					50			2000
Chad	20						14	300–500
Comoros								200[1]
Republic of Congo	1	1			142			7000
D.R. of Congo	25	160	200	200	200	200		500–10000
Cote d'Ivoire	146	80	180	200	1300	200	35	10000
Egypt	20	30	110	110	100	110	2000	6000–10000
Eritrea								1000[2]
Ethiopia	55	60	50	55	55	100		3000–5000
Gambia	15				150		11	?
Ghana	100	320	320	320	700	500	40余	6000
Gabon	16				30			6000
Guinea					10			5000–8000
Guinea-Bissau					60			100[3]
Kenya	150	160	145	150	150	190		7000+
Lesotho		30	200	500	450	1000	6600	5000
Liberia	20	150	120	120	120	120		600
Libya	260	2000	356	356	400	500		3000
Rwanda	15							1700[4]
Madagascar	8489	11500	13600	14500	27000	30000	20000+	60000

Country (region)	1968	1975	1984	1990	1996	2001	2003	2009–17
Malawi	38	50	33	50	40	40	70+	2000
Mali								3000–4000
Mauritania								?
Mauritius	23300	27400	30716	30700	40000	40000	30000	30000+
Morocco	15	15	20	20	20			2000[5]
Mozambique	3500	5000	650	200	600	700		1500
Namibia								5000(40000)
Niger	15	15	15	15	22			1000
Nigeria	1	500	1500	1500	5100	2000		100000
Senegal					10		500	2000
Seychelles		300	650	650	2000			1000
Sierra Leone	10	20	25	20	20	20		400–500
South Africa	8000	9000	8850	20000	28000	30000	45000	200000–400000
South Sudan								?
San Tome & Principle					100		8	100+
Somali								?
Sudan						45	45	20000–74000
Swaziland			80	90	200	90	1700	300
Tanzania	350	450	500	510	510	600		3000–20000
Togo					112	50		3000
Tunisia								2000
Uganda	75	80	80	80	80	100		5000–10000
Zambia	70			30	40	150		4000–6000 (40000)
Zimbabwe	300	660	250		500	300		5300–10000
Reunion	3000	12000	13400	13400	25000	20000	20000+	25000
Canary Islands					300			10000
Est. total	50000				136000	129605		600000–850000

Source: Li Anshan, *The Social and Economic History of the Chinese Overseas in Africa*, Nanjing: Jiangsu People's Press, 2018, Appendix 1, 1297–1307. The estimated total is changed.

* Most of the figures are estimated. The added data are indicated by footnotes.
1 Yu Jiahai, Zhu Xianlong, "Research on the overseas Chinese in the Indian Ocean island countries from the perspective of the community of human destiny", 12 August 2020. www2.scut.edu.cn/sfl/2020/1230/c22503a418180/page.htm.
2 "Are there many Chinese in Eritrea? How's the security situation", 12 June 2017. www.quvisa.com/news/3145.html
3 "Overseas Chinese in Guinea Bissau are not hurt. The embassy reminds them not to go out" 3 March 2009. www.chinaqw.com/hqhr/hrdt/200903/03/153275.shtml.
4 Dr. Zhao Jun (赵俊), a Chinese expert on Rwanda, did a field survey in 2015 and calculated about 1700 Chinese there. President of Rwanda Chinese Association Yin Qingri (尹晴日) estimated 3000 Chinese in 2019 yet about 1000 in 2021 according to the figure of vaccine inoculation. I would like to thank them both for the help.
5 "Overseas Chinese in Morocco", 6 January 2015. www.360doc.com/content/15/0106/11/11567645_438578424.shtml.

Appendix B
Confucius Institutes and Confucius Classrooms in Africa

Country	Confucius Institutes	Confucius Classrooms
Angola	Agostinho Neto University	
Benin	University of Abomey-Calavi	1
Botswana	University of Botswana	
Burundi	University of Burundi	
Cameroon	University of Yaounde II	1
Cape Verde	University of Cape Verde	
Comoros		University of Comoros
The Republic of Congo	Marien Ngouabi University	
Côte d'Ivoire	University of Felix Houphouette Boigny	
Egypt	Cairo University, Suez Canal University	3 at the Nile Television of Egypt
Equatorial Guinea	National University of Equatorial Guinea	
Eritrea	National Board for Higher Education of Eritrea	
Ethiopia	Confucius Institute at TVET Institute of Ethiopia, Addis Ababa University	Mekelle University Hawassa University (in total 5)
Ghana	University of Ghana, University of Cape Coast	
Kenya	University of Nairobi, Kenyatta University, Moi University	2 at CRI in Nairobi
Lesotho		Machabeng College International School
Liberia	University of Liberia	
Madagascar	Antananarivo University, University of Toamasina	1
Malawi	University of Malawi	
Mali		Lycee Askia Mohamed
Mauritius	University of Mauritius	
Morocco	University of Mohammed of V-Agdal, University Hassan II	
Mozambique	Eduardo Mondlane University	
Namibia	University of Namibia	

Country	Confucius Institutes	Confucius Classrooms
Nigeria	University of Lagos, Nnambi Azikiwe University	1
Rwanda	College of Education, University of Rwanda	1
Senegal	Cheikh Anta Diop University, Dakar	
Seychelles	University of Seychelles	
Sierra Leone	University of Sierra Leone	
South Africa	University of Stellenbosch, University of Cape Town, Rhodes University, Durban University of Technology, University of Johannesburg	The Cape Academy of Mathematics, Science and Technology, Westerford High School, Chinese Culture and International Exchange Center (in total 5)
Sudan	University of Khartoum	
Tanzania	University of Dodoma, University of Dar es Salaam	Zanzibar Journalism and Mass Media College of Tanzania
Togo	University of Lome	
Tunisia		CRI in Sfax
Uganda	Makerere University	
Zambia	University of Zambia	2
Zimbabwe	University of Zimbabwe	
Total	48 Confucius Institutes	27 Confucius Classrooms

Index

Abirewa 49, 92–9, 101–3, 105–9, 111
Abosom 100, 103
Accone, Darryl 418
Accra 39, 44, 51, 97, 104, 108–9, 111–12, 124–5, 129, 133–4, 136, 139, 198, 233, 339, 350–1
ACET 192
acupuncture 308, 311–16, 323, 327–30, 332, 342, 366
Adam Mahamat 192
Adams, W. Y. 396
Addo-Fening, R. 138
Adejumobi, Saheed A. 74
Ademola, Oyejide Titiloye 192
Aden 9, 14, 19
Afghanistan 165, 186, 235, 253, 508
Africa 3–27, 29–91, 99, 109, 111–12, 138–40, 143–79, 181–226, 228–32, 234, 236–44, 246–51, 253–67, 269–77, 282–7, 290, 293–307, 309, 311–21, 323–37, 339–43, 345, 347–99, 403–7, 409, 411, 413–63, 465–6, 469–77, 480–4, 486–8, 490, 493–506, 508–13
African civilization 37, 40–1, 74, 90, 298
African culture(s) 37, 62, 293, 363, 364, 375, 382, 387, 393, 483, 496, 497, 500, 509
African development 61, 70, 150, 151, 153, 180, 181, 183, 187, 190, 203, 225, 248, 256, 262, 263, 282, 285, 287, 293, 296, 297, 337, 358, 393, 454, 471, 491
African Development Bank 150–1, 181, 190, 199, 256, 262, 274
African Development Report 70
African diaspora 25, 75, 78, 81, 195, 365, 455, 457, 459–61, 463, 465, 467–9, 471–5, 477, 480–1, 499, 502–3, 505, 508
African Economic Development Report 70

African Economic Review 70
African Growth and Opportunity Act 150
African nationalism 62, 80, 168, 221, 299
African renaissance 40, 67, 75, 275, 473
African socialism 39, 52, 222
African Studies Association (ASA) 69
African Studies Review 48, 56, 77, 80, 84, 140, 197, 200, 472, 475–6, 504
African studies 21, 24–6, 29, 31–49, 51, 53, 56–9, 61, 63–77, 79–87, 89–91, 133, 139–40, 155–6, 159, 168–9, 178, 190, 193, 197, 200–2, 218, 220–3, 240, 243–4, 272, 274, 276, 299, 301, 352–4, 364, 396, 419–20, 444, 457, 470–3, 475–6, 481, 498, 502–6
Africanization 61
African Union 55, 61, 63, 66, 84, 89, 148, 151, 160, 165, 185, 192, 195, 203, 209, 257, 260, 265–266, 273, 282–283, 285, 318, 352, 385, 388, 396, 399, 450, 460, 472, 502
African Union Commission 385, 388, 396
Agbodeka, F. 138
Agence France-Press 185, 192
Agency for International Development 150
agriculture 41, 47, 49–50, 56–7, 59, 64, 80, 84, 86, 163, 177–8, 217–18, 228, 257–8, 262, 265, 267, 275, 290–1, 297, 301, 334, 339, 341–3, 348–50, 367, 376, 392, 426, 444, 449, 452, 492
Agyeman-Duah J. 138
Ahmed, G. K. 22
Aidoo, Richard 192
AIDS 59, 75, 188, 218, 260, 303, 316, 325–6, 329–30, 369, 372
Aihdab 13, 16, 20, 423

Ai Ping 220
Ai Zhouchang 4, 7, 9–10, 19, 22, 30, 37, 40–1, 44, 46, 60, 64, 74, 205, 404, 418, 467, 472
Ajakaiye, Olu 192
Akaki, Sam 192
Akan 92, 94, 100, 102–3, 108–9, 111–13, 115–16, 119–20, 126–8, 133–4, 138–40, 386
Akemu, Ona 274
Akim 96, 111–12, 137, 139–40
Akomolafe, F. 192
Akpan, M. B. 396
Aksum 6, 8, 37, 40
Akuapem 96–7, 103–4
Akyem Abuakwa 107, 114–15, 117–19, 123–4, 129, 133–8
Akyempo, K. 138
Alden, C. 144, 183, 192, 447
Algeria 45, 47, 50, 67, 79, 174, 176, 216, 231, 244, 258, 263, 303–4, 307–8, 311–12, 314–15, 320, 324–6, 329–30, 340, 342, 360–1, 446, 483–4, 510
Al Idrisi 14, 24
Allen, Richard B. 418
Allman, J. 138
Almanac of China's Foreign Economic Relations and Trade Editorial Board 167
Al Nasser, Jamal Abd 33
Alpers, Edward A. 472
Alves, Ana Cristina 274
America–Africa 21st Century Partnership Ministerial Conference 150
Ameyaw, Bismark 74
Amoah, Lloyd G. Adu. 502
Ampiah, K. 241
An Chunying 65, 67, 70, 82, 89, 392–3, 396
Anglo-Boer War 31
Angola 35, 61, 86, 151, 176, 194, 198–9, 216, 221, 252, 258, 260, 262, 275, 283–4, 306–7, 310, 347, 377, 384, 419–20, 451, 455, 493, 505–6, 510, 512
Ankomah, Baffour 193
Annan, Kofi 73
Annual Review of African Studies in China 26, 76, 276, 301, 473, 505–6
An Ran 482
Ansah, J. K. 110
apartheid 50, 62–3, 88, 145, 269, 300, 360, 439, 445

Apithy, Sedozan 502
Appiah-Kubi, K. 110
Appiah-Otoo, Isaac 74
Apps, P. 241
April, Funeka Yazini 81–2, 86, 88–9, 353, 358, 380, 475, 505
Arab (Arabic) 8–15, 17–19, 21, 67, 69, 165, 181, 206, 256, 260, 305, 311, 313, 326, 365, 366, 382, 390, 428, 459, 465, 495, 509
Arab League 165
archaeological 3–4, 7, 24, 30, 43, 68, 76, 79, 111, 381, 396–7, 460
archaeologist 11, 20, 30, 68
archaeology 6, 23–4, 60, 66–7, 79, 457, 474
Arhin, K. 138
Armitage, Simon J. 396
Armstrong, J. C. 438
Asafo 113–31, 133–7, 139–40
Asafoakye 114
Asante 75, 86, 92, 95–9, 102–9, 111–12, 114–15, 117–18, 121–3, 126, 128, 132–6, 138–40, 382
Asare, Andy Ohemeng 75
Asare-Kyire, L. 75
Asche, H. 168
Ashanti Confederacy 138
Asia 3, 6–7, 9–10, 16–17, 21–4, 26–7, 33, 42–4, 46–9, 51–4, 57–8, 64, 69, 75–8, 80–2, 88, 168–9, 189, 197, 201–2, 222, 241–4, 251, 258–9, 267, 271, 274–7, 301, 306, 330–1, 353–4, 378–80, 383, 397–8, 405, 416, 419–20, 423–4, 428, 445, 447, 455–8, 460, 462, 465–6, 468, 472–6, 494, 504
Asian and African Studies 36, 40, 44–6, 49, 70, 84, 86
Association of Southeast Asian Nations (ASEAN) 165
Atkinson, Q. D. 396
Atlantic Ocean 18, 20, 259
AU Commission 190, 209
Aurégan, Xavier 456
Austin, D. 138
Australia 149, 158, 165, 230, 296, 335, 417
Autesserre, S. 193
Ayandele, E. 138

Bagby, Philip 242
Baitie, Zahra 366, 370, 479, 482
Bannerman, L. 274

Barnouin, B. 193
Barton, B. 198
Basel missionary 97
Bauer, William 418
BBC 24, 224, 420, 493, 498, 502, 506
Beachey, R. W. 473
Beecham, J. 110
Beijing 14, 18, 23–8, 41, 43–54, 57, 63, 68, 70, 73–80, 82–91, 143, 146–7, 153, 159–60, 167–70, 173, 176–7, 180, 189–90, 192–203, 205, 211, 219–23, 240, 242–5, 275–6, 287, 299–301, 304–5, 307–8, 310, 317–18, 330–2, 338, 341, 350, 353–5, 360, 363–5, 367–9, 376, 378–80, 392, 396–9, 418, 420, 437–40, 447, 456–8, 471, 473, 475, 477–9, 485, 487–8, 490, 493, 495, 497–8, 502–6
Beijing Foreign Language University 70
Belhadj, Imen 365, 493, 495
Bell, D. 396
Ben Bella, Ahmed 33
Benin 58, 143, 153–4, 174, 241, 281, 304–5, 307, 312, 315–16, 321–2, 324, 327, 331, 342, 382, 384, 479, 512
Benin Kingdom 281, 382, 384
Berger, B. 184, 188, 193, 215, 242
Berhe, Mulugeta Gebrehiwot 75
Bertoncello, B. 473
Best Doctoral Thesis Award of the Lagos Studies Association 69
Bhana, S. 438
Bi Jianhai 190, 202
Bi Jiankang 66
bilateralism 179, 181, 238, 284
Biswas, Aparajita 254, 261, 262, 270, 274
Blair, D. 193
blood-making 291, 292
Blyden, E. D. 396
Boadi, Evans Asante 75
Bobali 8, 12
Bodomo, A. 56, 75, 365, 377, 459, 460, 466–70, 480, 495, 497, 498, 503
Bogue, D. J. 474
Borgya 108
Bork, T. 474
Bosman, W. A. 110
Bossard, P. 220
Botswana 34, 58, 71, 87–9, 150, 174, 176, 200, 266, 304–5, 307, 309, 328–9, 347, 351–2, 354, 369, 448–9, 510, 512
Boutros-Ghali 38, 46, 150, 283, 298, 391
Bowdich, T. E. 111, 138

Bo, Z. 242
Brain, J. B. 439
Braudel, Fernand 242
Brautigam, D. 176, 183, 184, 193, 204, 205, 225, 239, 282
Bredeloup, S. 473, 503
Breeze, Victoria 503
Brenner, D. 377
BRICs (Brazil, Russia, India, China) 81, 250, 251, 258
BRICS (Brazil, Russia, India, China, South Africa) 81, 165, 246–73, 335
Bright, Rachel 456
British Museum 12
British policy 111–12, 138, 140
Brokensha, D. 111
Brookes, P. 221
Brose, M. C. 46, 75
Brown, E. J. P. 138
Brunson, J. 23
Brzezinski, Z. 193
Bulawa (Brava) 17, 19
Bundy, Colin 299
Burger, Delien 274
Burkina Faso 79, 273, 306–7, 309, 315, 337, 340, 350, 367, 510
Burns, A. Sir 46
Burundi 35, 58, 304–5, 307, 310, 329, 512
Busia, K. A. 106, 107, 111, 114, 117, 121, 129, 132
Butty, James 299

Cabo Verde 172, 258
Cai Gaojiang 75
Cairo 10, 15, 50, 366, 512
Calderisi, R. 247, 274, 286, 296
Cameron 162, 328
Campbell, H. 334
Campbell, P. C. 404, 411–14, 418, 425
Canada 108, 149, 158, 243, 250, 298, 451
Canadian Journal of African Studies 46, 139–40, 396
Cantonese Club 422, 430, 434
Cao Shengsheng 274
Cape of Hope 3
Cape Town 18, 61, 82, 150, 199, 241, 300, 353, 428, 437, 439, 473, 513
Carbone, M. 168
Carter, Marina 418
Cengtan State 12, 24

Center for African Studies (Peking University, PKU) 36, 75, 168, 221, 223, 498
Central Africa 32, 34–5, 48, 174, 304–7, 382
Centre for South African Studies 36
Cen Zhongmian 4, 31, 44
Chad 44, 201, 261, 305, 307, 309, 319, 368, 510
Chairman Mao Zedong 32, 45, 145, 233–4, 237, 292, 360, 387
Chandler, W. B. 474
Chang, Gordon 170, 193, 288
Chang Jiang 72, 75
Chang Kwang Chih 5, 23, 460, 474
Changsha 11, 13, 49–50, 361
Chao Feng 38, 48
Chaponnière, Jean-Raphal 193
Charlesworth, M. P. 23
Chazan, N. 194
Chen Changgui 503
Chen Da 404, 414
Chen Fenglan 66, 75
Chengdu 47, 76–7, 177–8, 194, 310, 364, 367, 505
Cheng Guofu 10, 23
Chen Gongyuan 7, 23, 36–7, 46–7, 52, 70, 75, 145, 160, 168, 192, 220
Cheng Siwei 216, 221
Cheng Tao 71, 76, 475, 504
Cheng Ying 69, 76, 481
Cheng Yinghong 481, 501
Cheng Zhenhou 395
Chen Hansheng 42, 47, 383, 404, 417–18
Chen Hong 56, 58, 75
Chen Jianwen 7, 23
Chen Lemin 23
Chen Li 47
Chen Mo 47, 70
Chen Tiandu 63, 76
Chen Tianhua 31
Chen Xiaochen 72, 76
Chen Xiaohong 62, 76
Chen Xiaoying 66, 76, 469
Chen Xinxiong 23
Chen Yifei 40, 47
Chen Yingqun 267, 277, 377
Chen Yue 358, 379
Chen Yulong 11, 27
Chen Zexian 408, 418
Chen Zhili 194
Chen Zhongdan 47
Chen Zhongde 37, 41, 47, 56

Cheru, Fantu 194
Chiluba, Frederick Jacob Titus 160
China 3–7, 9–61, 63–91, 143–227, 229–46, 248–56, 258, 262, 267–74, 276–7, 281–92, 296–301, 303–7, 310, 312–24, 326–95, 397–9, 403–4, 406, 408, 415–16, 418–20, 422–5, 427, 433, 437–509
China African Peoples' Friendship Association (CFPA) 145
China Africa Project 376, 472
China–Africa relations 23, 25, 27, 33, 41, 56, 61, 66, 70, 75, 78, 82–3, 85–9, 147–8, 157, 168, 171, 173–4, 187, 190–1, 196–7, 199, 201, 205–6, 208, 211, 214, 216, 222, 225, 237, 243, 283–4, 333–5, 337, 343, 350, 353, 357–8, 362, 371, 376, 379, 441, 454, 459, 469, 480, 482–3, 498–9, 504–5, 508–9
China–Africa Think Tanks Forum (CATTF) 65, 70
China Daily 192, 194, 208, 210, 221–2, 242, 276–7, 307, 329, 502
China Foundation for Poverty Alleviation (CFPA) 358, 370
China Institute of Contemporary International Relations 69
China Institute of international Studies 69
China International Strategy Review 69
China Network for International Exchanges (CNIE) 376
China Petroleum Daily 221
China Road and Bridge Corporation (CRBC) 345
China's African Policy 51, 78, 81, 168, 204, 208, 224–6, 243, 332, 353, 397, 441–3, 445, 447, 449, 451, 453–7
Chinese Academy of Social Sciences (CASS) 6, 33, 36, 40, 43, 43, 58, 69, 70
Chinese–African People's Friendship Association (CAPFA) 365
Chinese Association of African Studies 36, 43, 47, 53, 159, 168
Chinese civil organizations (CCOs) 357
Chinese culture 186, 226, 239, 244, 344, 363, 366–7, 374–5, 382–3, 397, 399, 483, 491, 495–7, 513
Chinese Embassy in Rwanda 76
Chinese Government Scholarships (CGS) 485

518 *Index*

Chinese medical team (CMT) 58, 174, 230, 302–32, 359, 361, 364, 445, 449, 484
Chinese People's Association for Friendship with Foreign Countries (CPAFFC) 367
Chinese Society of African Historical Studies 36–8, 43, 46–7, 53, 58, 67, 74–5, 82, 156, 167
Chirac, Jacques 151
Chisan 6–7
Chissano, Joaquim Alberto 323
Chong Xiuquan 64, 76
Chou Yi Liang 6, 13, 23
Christensen, B. 139
Christian (Christianity) 95
Chukwukere, I. 139
Chutian Metropolis Daily 185, 194, 221, 242
Cissé, Daouda 456, 474, 503
civil society 65, 240, 263, 267, 358, 367, 369, 374, 380, 441
Clarke, J. J. 396
Clinton, Bill 150
Clinton, Hillary 184
CNTextile.com 212
co-development 283, 285, 287, 289, 291, 293, 295, 297, 299, 301
coevolutionary pragmatism 57, 87, 216, 301, 348, 354
Cohen, Roberta 418, 442, 493
coins, of the Song Dynasty 12–13
Cold War 147, 168–9, 179, 198, 200, 212, 215, 223, 234, 264, 276, 286, 305
collectivism 42, 227, 385, 388
Collender, G. 194
Collier, P. 274
colonial policy 39, 130
Colonial Secretary 97–8, 109–10, 130, 136–7, 411
Colton, J. A. 25
Common Market for Eastern and Southern Africa 151
Community of Portuguese Speaking Countries (CPLP) 260
Comoros 305, 307, 310, 317–18, 329–30, 452, 510, 512
Confucius Institute 176, 189, 347, 366, 512
Congo 33–5, 45, 47, 49, 52, 71, 85, 162, 174, 176, 188, 191, 193, 211, 241–2, 258, 263, 266, 293, 298, 304, 306–8, 312, 326, 329, 331, 335, 341, 354, 357, 361, 365, 382, 386, 443, 446, 495–6, 499, 510, 512
Connah, G. 396
Contemporary International Relations 69, 168–9, 327
Cooke, Jennifer 378
Coolidge, M. 418
Coolies 409, 412, 419–20, 428–9, 436
Cooper, A. F. 274
Copenhagen 197, 405
Corkin, L. 194
Cornelissen, S. 221
Cornevin, R. 47
Corporate social responsibility (CSR) 348, 453
COVID-19 188, 396, 509
CPC (Communist Party of China) 32, 236, 387, 442, 508
Craton, Michael 418
Crowder, Michael 299, 396
Cruikshank, B. 111
CSIS Prospectus 194
Cui Jianmin 76
Cui Qinglian 47
Cultural Revolution 34–6, 38, 45, 171–2, 174–6, 193, 206, 220, 233, 239, 249, 287, 305, 360, 451, 470, 481, 483–4
culture 31, 37, 39–40, 49–51, 56, 59–60, 62, 64, 69, 72, 77, 79–80, 82–3, 89, 94, 133, 149, 156, 172, 179, 181, 186, 197, 216, 225–8, 230, 239–44, 248, 257, 261, 268, 281, 293, 298, 316, 336, 339, 342, 344, 357–8, 363–4, 366–7, 374–6, 379, 381–3, 393–4, 397–9, 416, 435–6, 452, 454, 471–2, 474, 483, 486, 489, 491, 495–7, 500–1, 505, 509, 513
Cysouw, Michael 396

Daddi, K. M. 378
Da Gama, Vasco 1, 3, 18, 20, 21
Dai A-Di 330
Dai Yan 292, 299
Da Ming Hun Yi Tu 18, 25
Dang Fangli 469
Danquah, J. B. 111, 139
Dao Yi Zhilue 11
Daqing 6
Darfur 63, 66, 78, 80, 185–6, 191–2, 194–5, 198, 201, 209–10, 219, 221, 232, 235, 241–4
Dart, R. 23
Dashi 56, 85
Datta, A. 139

Davenport, T. R. H. 418
Davidson, B. 47, 33, 35, 38, 382, 383, 397
Davies, Carole Elizabeth Boyce 474
Davies, M. 194, 221–2
Davies, P. 194
Dawson, R. 397
De Bary, W. T. 47
Debrunner, H. 111, 139
De Graft Johnson, J. D. 139
De Lacouperie, T. 23
De Marees, P. 111
Democratic Republic of the Congo, Congo (Kinshasa) 71, 191, 263, 266, 304, 306, 307, 308, 326, 335, 341, 495
democratization 39, 62–3, 78, 87, 152
Deng Guosheng 378
Deng Xiaoping 237, 242, 287, 289, 292, 299, 362
Denkyira 103
Denoon, D. J. N. 418
Department of African Affairs, MFA 154, 155, 159
Department of Aid to Foreign Countries 165–6
Department of Health of Hubei Province 179
De Rivières 397
destoolment 49, 113, 115–37, 139
De Tocqueville, A 242
development cooperation 57–8, 62, 78–9, 82–3, 90, 167, 175, 257–8, 260, 263, 265, 269–70, 273, 275, 296, 300, 333, 335, 341, 358, 366–7, 369–70, 374–5, 398
Diaspora 25, 75, 78–9, 81, 85, 195, 261, 267, 274, 365–6, 401, 403–4, 406, 408, 410, 412, 414, 416, 418–20, 424, 426, 428, 430, 432, 434, 436, 438–40, 442, 444, 446, 448, 450, 452, 454–78, 480–82, 484, 486, 488, 490, 492, 494, 496–500, 502–6, 508
Dickerson, Claire Moore 76
Diederich, Manon 474
Dike, K. O. 294, 299
Dikotter, F. 23
Ding Bangying 36, 47
Ding Yu 66
Diop, Cheikh A. 296, 381, 397, 513
Diop, Majhemout 33, 47
Director General of the WHO 145
Disima 503
Dlamini-Zuma, N. 397

Documentation Office of CPC Central Committee 180, 219, 221
Donaldson, R. H. 299
Dong, L. 503
Downs, E. S. 194
Dreher, A. 194
Duan Chengshi 3, 7–8, 44, 47, 460
Duan Jingjing 474
Du Baoren 462
Dubey, Ajay K. 274
Du Bois, W. E. 33, 36, 47, 229, 240–2, 281, 382, 383, 397
Du Huan 3, 7–8, 26, 29–30, 44, 47, 460, 477
Dumor, K. 76
Dupuis, J. 111
Durban 168, 246, 265, 267, 277, 427, 430, 433–5, 440, 513
Dutch 44, 104, 105, 115, 382–3, 424, 437–8, 467
Du Xiaolin 151, 168
Du Ying 90, 263
Duyvendak, J. J. L. 23

East Africa 9, 12, 14, 16, 19–21, 23–4, 26–7, 30–1, 44, 46, 60, 69–70, 260, 266, 276, 318, 330, 359, 456, 465
East Asia 26, 241
East China Normal University 23, 38, 46, 50–2, 70, 85, 220, 243, 274, 350
Easterly, W. 247, 275, 286, 295, 296, 299
The Eastern Miscellany 31
Economic Community of West African States 151
Economic Daily 219, 221, 504
economy 31, 37, 41, 50–1, 53–4, 56, 58–61, 63–4, 66–7, 72, 75, 78–9, 86, 88, 90–1, 140, 146–8, 150–1, 156–60, 162, 164, 166, 171–3, 175, 179, 193, 197–8, 207, 217, 221, 233–4, 244, 246, 248–53, 255–6, 264–5, 267–70, 272–3, 276, 284, 291, 294, 300, 337, 349, 358, 362, 364, 367, 394, 404, 426, 442, 445–8, 451, 457, 470, 472, 477, 491–3, 496, 504
Edinger, H. 194
Editorial Board of China Commerce Yearbook 178–9, 182
education 34, 36, 58–9, 62, 68, 80, 82–4, 87, 130, 146, 149–50, 156, 169, 173, 177–9, 189, 194, 197, 201, 229, 236, 257, 261, 264–5, 269, 333–4, 336, 339, 343–7, 353, 362–3, 367, 371, 375–6,

381, 387, 435, 456, 470, 472, 475, 478, 480–1, 483, 487, 489–92, 501–7, 512–13
Effutu 115, 140
Egypt 4–7, 9–11, 13–14, 16, 18–20, 22, 25–6, 29–31, 33, 37, 41, 44, 49–53, 58–60, 62–3, 67, 71–2, 75–7, 87–8, 145, 176, 205, 250–1, 263, 307, 329, 342–3, 350, 352, 357, 360, 379, 384, 423, 440, 457, 483–4, 487–8, 510, 512
"Eight Principles" 46, 175, 206, 233, 236, 238, 244, 284–5, 300, 334, 339, 350
Eisenman, J. 195
El Fasi, M. 23
Elizabeth of Toro 390, 397
Ellis, A. B. 111, 139
Elphick, R. 439
Elton, G. R. 23
Encyclopedia of Overseas Chinese 72
enterprises 56, 83, 86–7, 90, 147–9, 152, 159–60, 163, 178, 180, 183, 185, 187–8, 191, 196, 212–14, 216–17, 220–1, 258, 260–1, 264–5, 267–8, 294, 300, 337, 349, 354, 361, 368, 375, 444–6, 448, 450, 452–3, 455, 509
Equatorial Guinea 174, 195, 260–1, 304, 307, 329, 446, 512
Eritrea 6, 8, 41, 154, 305, 307, 510–12
Esteban, M. 195
Ethiopia 4, 6, 8, 13, 31, 34, 41, 52, 58–61, 63, 65, 72, 74, 88–90, 143, 153, 181, 203, 216, 263, 265, 267, 277, 286, 304–5, 307, 315, 334, 337, 344–5, 347, 351–3, 358–60, 364, 369, 371, 378, 384, 460, 467, 487, 498, 510, 512
Ethiopian Anti-Italian War 50, 359
ethnicity 23, 39, 60, 72, 88, 173, 440, 473
Europe 3, 18, 30, 39, 149, 152, 159, 200, 220, 228, 240, 246, 248–9, 252, 267, 269, 271, 275–6, 282–3, 296, 298, 306, 331, 335, 383, 391, 395, 399, 404, 419, 443–4, 446, 491, 494, 499, 508
European Union 80–1, 90, 158, 165, 168, 183, 185, 198, 218, 239–40, 254, 352, 354, 397–8, 453
Export–Import Bank 150, 158, 159, 262, 341
Eyadema, Gnassingbe 36
Ezeanya, C. 195

Fage, J. D. 47
Fang Jigen 38, 42, 48
Fante 104, 110–11, 114–17, 134, 139

Fang Wei 63, 77
Fan Wenxue 90
Fan Yong 47
Fan Zhishu 47
Farooki, M. 195
Fatima Dynasty 16
Favareto, Arilson 275
Fei Xiaotong 38, 46
Fei Xin. 4, 17, 18, 19, 20, 24, 48, 460, 462
Fei Yan 150, 158
Fei Zhi 37
Feng Jianwei 41, 48
Feng Yi 68, 89
Feng Zuoku 70, 357, 358, 360, 368
festival 103, 138, 364, 448, 497, 502
fetish 92, 94–7, 100–1, 103–5, 108–11, 114, 127, 240
Ffoulkes, A. 139
Fiamingo, C. 195
Field, M. 111, 139
Filesi, T. 48, 195
Financial Times 179, 204, 450, 457
Fink, H. 111
First, Ruth 48
Fitzgerald, Walter 48
FOCAC 55–7, 62, 81, 83, 86, 88–9, 143–4, 152–3, 155–6, 159–62, 166–7, 170, 176, 180, 187, 195, 203–4, 211–12, 216, 232, 234, 241–2, 298, 307, 328, 342, 347–54, 358, 362–3, 372–3, 375–6, 392, 396, 450, 457, 470, 473, 479, 481, 483, 487, 490, 503, 505–6, 508
Ford Foundation 40, 43
foreign aid 81, 84, 91, 146, 155, 169, 174–5, 180, 184, 189, 196, 199, 201, 220, 233–4, 236, 238–9, 242, 269, 273–5, 284, 286–7, 291–2, 295, 299, 328, 336, 341, 350, 353, 355, 372, 378, 392, 394, 473, 503
forms of resistance 411–12, 418
Fortescue, D. 139
Forum on China–Africa Cooperation (FOCAC) 41, 55, 143–67, 177, 203, 211, 262, 267, 283
Foster, V. 195
"Four Principles" (Zhao Ziyang) 147, 175, 207, 237–8, 284, 341, 362
France 33, 44–5, 150–1, 154–5, 158, 164, 169, 185, 192, 215, 230, 236, 263, 281–2, 294, 299, 384, 387, 393, 395–6, 490, 508
free Blacks 424, 438
Freeman-Greenville, G. S. P. 24

Freeman, S. T. 195
French, Howard W. 203, 221, 418
French policy 40
Friedman, E. 195
Friendship Textile Mill 338–9
Frobenius, Leo 281
Fuller, F. 111
Fyfe, Christopher 48
Fynn, J. K. 111

Ga 100, 102–3, 105, 110–11, 113–14, 117, 119, 125, 127, 135, 137, 139
Gabas, J. 247, 275
Gabon 159, 174, 196–7, 258, 305, 307, 309, 316, 319, 325, 446
Gambia 34, 58, 90, 174, 193, 305–7, 309, 340, 510
Games, Dianna 419
Gao Changrong 48
Gao Fei 157, 168
Gao, James 48
Gao Jinyuan 39, 48, 61, 77
Gardiner, R. K. A. 139
Gaye, A. 195
Ge Chengyong 9–10, 465
Ge Gongshang 39, 48
Ge Jie 37, 40, 43, 48
General Union of African Students in China (GUASC) 498
Gerhart, G. M. 397
Germany 32, 45, 185, 230, 249, 257, 260, 282, 326, 395, 508
Gernet, Jacques 397
Gertz, B. 195
Ghana 23, 34, 38–9, 49, 51, 58–9, 61, 68, 71–2, 75, 77, 80, 85–7, 89–90, 108–13, 115, 117, 119, 121, 123, 125, 127, 129, 131, 133, 135–40, 150, 154, 191, 201, 216, 232–3, 243–4, 258, 261, 263, 293, 295, 300, 304, 306–7, 310, 329, 339, 344, 358, 367, 369, 382, 386, 447–8, 458, 484, 508, 510, 512
Ghanaian National Archives 39
Ghandi, M. K. 439
Gill, B. 195
Gillespie, S. 195
Gilley, B. 195
Giovannetti, G. 195
giraffe 5, 22, 30, 460
Giry, S. 195
Glennie, J. 195
Global Review 69
Global Times 356, 379

Gluckman, M. 111
Gluckstein, S. 419
Gocking, R. 77
Gold Coast 49, 92–5, 97, 99–105, 107–12, 115, 118–19, 125, 130, 133–40, 294, 299
The Golden Stool 123, 126
Gong Sujuan 503
Goodrich, L. C. 24, 474
Goody, J. 111
Gordon, A. A. 168
Gordon, D. 168
Governor 97, 99, 102, 106, 110, 119, 122–30, 134–8, 463
Graduate Student Paper Prize 69, 74
Grauwe, P. 195
Greek 4, 15, 67
Grimm, S. 195
Group Area Act 145
Groves, C. P. 111
Guangyu Tu 18
The Guardian 195, 198, 221, 253
Guerrero, Dorothy-Grace 196, 242
Guggisberg, G. Sir 139
Guinea 45, 110–11, 154, 160, 174, 176, 195, 258, 260–1, 304–5, 307–8, 310, 314, 319, 321, 329, 371–2, 446, 510–12
Gu, Jing 196
Gu Mingyuan 72, 77
Gu Zhangyi 37, 77
Gui Tao 72, 356, 378
Gunther, John 48
Guo Chaoren 72, 77
Guo Dantong 69, 77
Guo Jing-an 77
Guo Xiaorui 77
Guo Yi-ling 397
Gupta, U. 275

Haggad, Ahmed 143
Hamdun, S. 24, 474
Hamill, John 419
Hammond, D. 242
Han, H. 504
Han Dynasty 5–7, 23, 26–7, 29, 33, 41, 51, 241, 423, 457, 460, 465, 467, 471, 477–8
Han Zhibin 77
Hao Di 365, 376, 378
Hao Ge 365, 376, 378
Hao Rui 67, 91
Hao, Y. 242
Harare 85, 185, 209, 369, 486

Harbeson, J. W. 168
Harneit-Sievers, Axel 78
Harris, Joseph E. 474
Harris, Karen L. 419
Harris, L. C. 196
Harrison, Philip 419
Hart, H. H. 24
Hashim, I. H. 504
Haugen, H. Ø. 474, 504
Hausa 40, 66, 86, 293, 365
Hayford, C. 95, 102, 111, 116
headquarters 55, 148, 191, 195, 197, 203, 282, 344, 362, 377
He Fangchuan 12, 37
Heinrich Böll Foundation 65, 260, 367, 441
He Liehui 57, 448
He Li-er 48
Herrmann, A. 24
He Qinhua 63
Hevi, Emmanuel 360, 378, 475, 470, 504
He Wenping 63, 65, 70, 77–9, 88, 157, 168, 183, 190, 196, 393, 454, 482, 504
He Xiaowei 180, 196
He Xiurong 56
Hicham, Erfiki 365
Hilsum, L. 196
Hirth, F. 24
HIV/AIDS 369
Hobson, John M. 397
Hodgson, Lady 111
Holl, A. F. C. (高畅) 68, 79, 382, 395, 397
Hong Kong 53, 74, 80, 88, 143, 153, 189, 191, 213, 350, 359, 378, 405, 417, 419–20, 439–40, 444–7, 454, 456, 458, 468–9, 471, 473, 475–7, 503, 506
Hong Yonghong 49, 63, 65, 77, 79
Hountondji, Paulin J. 228, 229, 242
Hou Renzhi 24
Hou Zhongjun 397
Hsu, Elisabeth 445, 456
Huajian Group 267
Huang, C. 221
Huang Hua 71, 79, 233, 242
Huang Hui 67, 79
Huang Shengzhang 18
Huang Shuze 328
Huang Sujian 216
Huang Wendeng 189, 196
Huang Xianjin 79
Huang Xiaoyong 367, 378
Huang Zengyue 31, 49

Huang Zequan 149, 167, 206, 221
Huang Zhen 221, 233
Huawei 337, 343–5, 348–9, 351–4, 495
Hugo, Victor 281, 299, 384, 397
Hu Jintao 148, 162, 171, 173, 211, 237, 287, 289, 318, 369, 490, 504
Human, Linda 475
human resource 82, 317, 333, 342, 353, 475, 505, 509
Human Rights Watch 185, 191, 196
human rights 79, 145, 185, 191, 196, 209–11, 214–15, 253, 282, 385, 442, 493
Huntington, S. P. 242, 397
Hu Sheng 384
Hutchinson, T. J. 111
Hutchison, A. 49, 196
Hutton, W. A. 111
Huynh, Tu 419
Hu You-e 49
Hu Zhaochun 24
Hwede, B. 196

Ibn Battuta 13–15, 22, 24–5, 30, 44, 49, 364, 464, 467, 474–5
Ibn Madjid 21–2, 24
Income Tax Ordinance 123
indentured labor 81, 399, 383, 403–9, 411, 413, 415, 417–21, 423–5, 437–8, 444
India 3–4, 13–14, 19–21, 45, 57, 76, 78, 188, 191, 193, 196, 198, 218, 243, 248–51, 253–6, 258–63, 267, 269–77, 300, 394, 404, 416, 422–7, 433, 435–6, 443, 465, 472
India–Africa Summit 263
Indian Ocean 3, 16, 19, 30, 44, 423, 439, 455, 472, 476, 511
indirect rule 62, 113, 132, 140
industry 15, 59, 67, 74, 87, 91, 163, 186, 198, 208, 212, 214, 232, 261–2, 296, 334–5, 337, 339, 341, 344–9, 383, 416, 425–6, 437, 443, 449, 451, 453, 495, 509
infrastructural construction 188
Inikori, Joseph E. 275
Institute for International and Area Studies 69
Institute of African Studies 35, 65, 70, 75, 85, 87
Institute of Afro-Asian Studies 32, 36, 53

Institute of Archaeology of Chinese Academy of Social Sciences 24
Institute of International and Strategical Studies 69
Institute of West Asian and African Studies (CASS) 36, 40, 44, 79
integration 42, 56–8, 60–2, 66, 84, 86, 88–9, 152, 162–3, 185, 235, 248, 257, 261, 265–7, 273, 282–3, 295–6, 393, 397, 403, 439, 470, 476, 509
International Monetary Fund 153, 295
International Poverty Reduction Center in China (IPRCC) 367, 369, 370
International Prize of the Arabic Language Sharjah (UNESCO) 67
investment 41, 54, 56–7, 67, 79, 87, 91, 146, 148, 150–1, 158, 162–3, 167, 178–80, 183, 187–8, 190–1, 196, 198–9, 202, 208, 213, 217, 219, 222, 236, 239, 247, 250–2, 254–8, 261–4, 266–9, 283, 296–8, 317, 336–7, 342, 345–6, 370–1, 375, 446, 448, 451–2, 509
Iraq 165, 186, 235, 253, 329
Irwin, G. W. 24
Islam 24, 40, 66, 121, 396, 432
Italy 11, 44–5, 282, 359, 376, 395
Iye, Ali Musa 275

Jaff, A. M. 196
Jansson, H. 184, 196
Jansson, J. 184, 196
Japan 11, 43–5, 67, 88, 150, 152, 154–5, 158, 165, 168–9, 179, 221, 234, 241, 246, 248–50, 276, 292, 296, 326, 335, 359, 395, 437, 508
Jayne, K. G. 24
Jenkins, R. 115, 134, 139, 196
Jiang Chun 483–4, 504
Jiang Dong 64, 79
Jiang Guanghua 172–3, 196, 205, 207, 221
Jiang Hengkun 66, 80
Jiang Huajie 481, 501
Jiang Hui 65, 67, 80
Jiang Shixue 275
Jiang Wenran 196
Jiang Xiang 71, 80, 340, 353
Jiang Xuecheng 36, 49
Jiang Zemin 40, 46, 71, 73, 90, 148–9, 152, 155–6, 160, 167, 171, 203, 237, 287, 318, 362, 487
Jiang Zhongjin 59, 64, 80
Jian Hong 72, 79

The *Jihad* movement 66
Jing Men 80–1, 90, 240, 352, 397
Jing Xing Ji 7, 8
Jing Zhaoxi 7, 10, 24
Jin Shoufu 67
Jin Xide 168
Johannesburg 87–8, 189, 349, 351–2, 398, 415, 417, 419–20, 430, 437–8, 448, 453, 476, 513
Johannes, E. M. 196
Johnson, R. E. 439
Johnson, T. 139
Jones, M. T. 196, 419
Journal of Ancient Civilizations 69, 77
Journal of China–Africa Studies 70
Joye, Pierre 49
Juyan Han Jian 22, 460–1, 467, 471

Kaplinsky, R. 183, 197
Kea, R. 139
Keating, J. 197
Keita, Mohamed 197
Kemp, D. 111
Kenya 8–9, 11, 13, 16, 20, 22, 26, 36–7, 45, 60, 63, 76, 143, 146, 153, 160, 176, 179, 189, 199, 216, 224, 263, 271, 274, 295, 304, 307, 317, 319, 329, 337, 343–6, 351, 353–4, 368–9, 371, 377, 441, 454, 471, 484, 487, 498, 504, 510, 512
Ketema, M. 504
Khartoum 4, 186, 285, 346–7, 368, 443, 513
Kilwa 11, 13–14, 19
Kimambo, I. N. 49
Kimble, D. 139
Kim, S. 330
King, K. 197
King, N. 24
Kiriama, Herman O. 24
Klein, M. A. 419
knowledge sharing (KS) 334
Kolingba, André-Dieudonné 322
Konaré, Alpha Oumar 322
Kose, M. Ayhan 275
Koyama Fujio 20
Kragelund, P. 197
Kroeber, A. 243
Kumasi 106, 121, 123, 134
Kunlun 7, 9, 11–12, 26, 460–7, 476
Kunlun Cengqi 11
Kunlun nu 7, 9, 463, 465, 476
Kuper, Adam 243

Kush 4, 443
Kwahu 96–7, 106, 118–20, 123, 125–6, 129, 133–7, 140

Labin, Suzanne 419
Laczko, Frank 419
Lai Yulin 358, 378
Lai, W. L. 419, 439
Lampert, B. 379
Lamu 8, 11, 266
Laobosa 26–7, 477
Large, D. 197
Larkin, B. D. 197, 504
Lartey, Victor Curtis 80
Latin America 149, 259, 305–6, 419, 439, 457
Laverty, William Henry 243
law 36, 49, 56–7, 59–60, 62–4, 66, 72, 74, 76–7, 79, 88, 92, 94–7, 104, 106, 120, 122–3, 128, 137, 140, 200, 246, 269, 322, 375, 382, 398, 410, 413, 417, 428–31, 448–9, 452, 489
Lawrence, P. 197
Le Bail, Hélène 475
legal seat in the United Nations 144, 304, 320
Leiden 21, 240, 353, 505
Leithead, A. 24
Le Monde 395, 398
Lesotho 34, 58, 176, 200, 262, 266, 305, 307, 313, 331, 342, 457, 498, 510, 512
Levathes, L. 25, 456
Lewis, Ian 378, 509
Lewin, Posine 49
Lewin, T. 139
Lian Chaoqun 83
Liang Gencheng 40, 50
Liang Jingwen 466, 476
Liang Qichao 31, 45
Liang Shanggang 202
Liang Yijian 57, 65, 67, 83, 90
Liang Yu 83
Li Baoping 40, 49, 62, 65, 82, 398, 470, 475, 482, 484, 505
Liberia 34, 71, 191, 209, 231, 305–7, 310, 315–16, 319, 340, 369, 386, 390, 393, 396, 493, 510, 512
Libya 8, 35, 45, 58, 63, 72, 85, 162, 164–5, 174, 253, 263, 305, 307, 309, 335, 352, 446, 510
Li Chi 25
Li Guangyi 82
Li Hongwei 25

Li Jiangtao 472, 475, 482, 505
Li Jianming 228, 243
Li Jiasong 206, 211, 222
Li Jidong 41, 49
Li Lanqing 148, 153, 158
Li Liqing 222
Li Miao 49
Lin, Edwin 439
Ling Shun-heng 25
Lingwai Daida 11, 12, 15
Lin, Justin Yifu (Lin Yifu) 59, 65, 83, 275, 267
Lin Lunlun 482, 505
Lin Mei 207, 222
Lin Zexu 30
Li Peng 152, 362
Li Qingyu 50
Li Tongcheng 82, 169, 201, 223
Liu Chang 379
Liu Guijin 153–5, 159
Liu Haifang 26, 65, 68, 76, 83, 183, 197, 350, 353, 361–2, 378, 470, 472, 475, 481, 483, 485, 490–1, 497, 505–6
Liu Hongwu 40, 46, 50, 57–8, 64–5, 75, 83–5, 87, 156
Liu Jian 379
Liu Jirui 231, 322, 325, 331, 342, 354
Liu Lan 42
Liu Naiya 42
Liu, P. H. 505
Liu Shaonan 56, 69, 84
Liu Yan 59
Liu Yueming 169
Liu Zhirong 360, 373
Li Weijian 57, 66, 82
Li Xiangyun 82
Li Xiannian 147
Li Xiaoyun 82, 260, 262, 275, 292, 300
Li Ximi 13
Li Xinfeng 17, 19, 22, 25, 56, 83, 331, 447
Li Yifu 38, 48
Li Yongcai 64, 83
Li Yumin 398
Li Zemin 18
Li Zhibiao 56, 83
Li Zhigang 468–9, 471, 475–6
Lokongo, Antoine Roger 197, 335, 472, 482, 495, 505
Long Xia 482
Long Xiangyang 172, 197, 239, 243
Long Xiaonong 379
look(ing) East 164, 191, 247, 287, 335

Looy, J. van de 197
Lorenz, Andreas 419
Lou Shizhou 59, 84, 482, 505
Lovejoy, Paul 275
Lu Chunming 232, 243, 318
Lu Miaogeng 71, 76, 332, 475, 504
Luo Gaoyuan 84
Luo Hongxian 18
Luo Hongzhang 36
Luo Jianbo 57, 63, 65–6, 83–4, 169, 393, 398, 470, 475
Luo Ke 50
Lu Ting-en 36–8, 50, 56, 61, 84
Lyman, P. 222
Lyons, M. 476
Ly-Tio-Fane-Pineo, Huguette 457

Macmillan, W. M. 139
Madagascar 13–14, 16, 58, 69, 143, 153–4, 174, 181, 203, 298, 304, 307–8, 313–14, 316–17, 319, 321, 325, 327, 342–3, 357–8, 360, 420, 423, 443–5, 453, 457–8, 483, 498, 512
Madame Pei 11, 30
Ma Enyu 56, 469, 476
Maghreb 8, 11, 263
Ma, Grace 75
Mahamat, A. 222
Mahatma Gandhi 422, 439
The Mahdi movement 36
Ma Huan 17–18, 44, 50, 460, 462
Maier, D. J. E. 111
Ma Jian 145, 360, 379
Maji Maji Uprising 36, 47
malaria, anti-malaria 58, 81, 188, 218, 231, 232, 303, 307, 311, 315, 316–19, 342
Malawi 34, 305–7, 310, 369, 390, 484, 511–12
Maldives 14, 19
Mali 35, 59, 90, 174, 176, 180, 202, 218, 231, 261, 286, 293, 304, 307, 311–12, 316, 322, 326, 328–9, 332, 339, 350, 382, 390, 453, 487, 499, 511–12
Malindi (Malin, Mande) 8, 16, 17
Mamluk 14, 16, 423
Ma Mung, Emmanuel 457
Mancuso 63–4, 84
Mandela, Nelson 40, 71, 296, 364
Mandela, Winnie 40
Manguro 93
Manila 405
Manji, F. 243

Manning, Patrick 275
Manoukian, M. 111, 139
Mao Tianyou 36, 50
Mao Zedong 32, 45, 50, 145, 197, 205, 222, 233–4, 237, 243, 292, 300–1, 314, 360, 362, 379, 387, 398
Marco Polo 14, 16, 22
Marfaing, Laurence 476
Marks, T. 198
Marsh, Jenni 505
Ma Shengli 169
Mathews, G. 476
Ma Tong 50
Mauritania 8, 34, 58, 82, 174, 209, 304, 307, 329, 347, 390, 511
Mauritius 34, 58, 153, 307, 358, 361, 369, 423, 437, 444–5, 476, 511–12
Ma Wenkuan 4, 11, 13, 20, 25, 44, 50, 205, 222
Mazrui, Ali A. 84
Mbachu, D. 198
Mbayem, S. 198
McCaskie, T. C. 111
McCormick, D. 196, 198
McKay, Vernon 50
McKinsey Global Institute 384, 398
McLeod, M. 111
McNeill, W. E. 25
Mearsheimer, J. J. 193, 198
measures to control 408
Mencius 236, 387, 398
Meng Fanren 4, 11, 13, 20, 25, 30, 44, 205, 222
Men, Jing 240, 354
Menzies, G. 25
Merle, Robert 50
Meroe 4, 8, 44, 443
Merowe Dam 162
Metcalfe, G. E. 111
Metz, E. T. 385, 386, 398
Meyerowitz, E. 140
Mhando, L. 398
Middle East 42, 53–4, 63, 70, 75, 83, 88, 149, 361, 443, 455, 472, 485, 508
Miers, Suzanne 275
migration, immigration 40, 56, 166, 185, 235, 271, 293, 365, 358, 383, 401, 403–507
Mikell, G. 140
military 17, 57–8, 60, 66, 105, 114, 116–17, 129, 138, 156–7, 164–5, 172–3, 179, 205, 208, 264, 266, 281,

526 *Index*

288, 298, 301, 308, 310, 374, 396, 403, 464, 466–7, 471
Millennium Challenge Account (MCA) 269, 273
Millennium Challenge Corporation (MCC) 269, 273
Millennium Development Goals 166, 265, 268
Ming Dynasty 3, 18–22, 24, 30, 33, 467, 472
mining 56–7, 59, 74, 86, 91, 121, 163, 185, 191, 199, 201, 259, 334, 341, 346, 391, 406–8, 413, 416–17, 425–6, 437, 443
Ministry of Commerce (MOC) 161
Ministry of Foreign Affairs (MFA) 323
Ministry of Foreign Trade and Economic Cooperation 149, 159, 199, 201, 304–5, 331
missionaries 30, 95, 97–9, 104, 107–8, 240, 436
Mogadishu 11, 13, 16–17, 19
Mohammed, A. 198, 243
Mohan, G. 198
Mohan, R. 198
Mokgoro, Y. 398
Molanpi 11
Molin 7–8, 26, 44, 477
Mombasa 14, 315, 345–6, 351–2
Monga, Célestin 84
Monson, J. 169, 198
Montinari, L. 198
Morais, I. 476
Morais, R. M. de. 198
Morocco 8, 11, 13–14, 22, 31, 34, 45, 47, 58, 174, 176, 258, 304, 307–8, 311–12, 326–7, 329, 343, 360, 467, 483, 496, 511–12
Morris, M. 196
Mowat, C. L. 398
Mo Xiang 59, 84
Mtshali, B. Vulindlela 50
Mudimbe, V. Y. 243
Muekalia, J. D. 198
Mugu Dushu 17
Mukanga, C. 198
Müller, Angelo 476
multiple cooperation 187
Munyoro, F. 199
Muslims 12, 88, 388, 395, 435, 476
Mu Tao 4, 9, 19, 23, 38, 41, 44, 46, 63–4, 85, 205, 220

Mutiiri, Onesmus Mbaabu 85
Mwanawina, I. 199

Naidu, S. 164, 168, 187, 199, 217, 225, 263, 423
Namibia 54, 58, 79, 151, 199, 265–7, 305, 307, 310, 313, 316, 323, 342, 360, 369, 487, 511–12
Nam, Moiss 199
Nan Hai 10
Nanjing University 36–7, 50, 64, 79–80
Nanshan Si Bei 17
Nasser, Gamal Abdul 33, 50
Natal 168, 241, 267, 277, 367, 425, 427–8, 433–5, 437–40
national independence 34, 39, 49, 52, 145, 173, 205, 261
Native Administration Ordinance 119–20, 122–3, 136–7
Native Authorities Ordinance 124
NATO 164, 352
Naylor, T. 419
Na Zhong 33, 50, 67
Needham, Joseph 50
Newbury, C. W. 111
New Development Bank (NDB) 270, 273
New Dwaben 96–7, 135
The New York Times 197, 331, 418, 456, 503
NGO 357–8, 367–9, 371, 373, 375, 377–9
Niger 34, 37, 44, 48, 53, 58, 85, 174, 201, 253, 294, 299, 304, 306–7, 309, 312, 323, 328, 330, 334, 397, 499, 511
Nigeria 34, 38, 46, 58–61, 63, 66, 68, 72–3, 83–8, 149, 176, 181–2, 184–5, 187, 192, 199, 201, 211, 215, 217, 219–20, 223, 250–1, 257–9, 262–3, 266, 281, 286, 294, 296–9, 301, 307, 318, 329, 333, 337, 343, 347, 368–9, 382, 384, 386, 399, 423, 447–8, 450–1, 453, 495–6, 508, 511, 513
Nin Sao 37, 39, 48, 51
Niu Changsong 483, 493, 505
Niu Dong 69, 85
Nketia, Kwabena 51
North Africa 11, 14, 20, 32–3, 42, 54, 72, 194, 242, 330, 390
Northeastern Normal University 177
Northrup, David 439
Nubia 5, 40, 293, 382, 396
Nujoma, Sam 323
Nye, Joseph 379

Nyerere, Julius Kambarage 62, 63, 70, 85, 231, 233, 296, 302, 312, 314, 322, 338, 385, 388, 398, 498
Nzongola-Ntalaja, G 85

oath 93, 103, 105, 113, 125, 129
Obwona, M. 199
Ochieng, Chris Shimba 276
Odada, John E. 199
OECD 247, 256, 274, 284, 370
Ofori Atta 118–19, 123, 129, 134, 136
Ogot, B. A. 85
Ogunkola, E. Olawale 199
Ogunsanwo, Alaba 199
Oh Il-kwan 51
Ohin 122
Olander, Eric 243
Oliveira, Ricardo Soares de 199
Oliver, R. 25
Olympic Games 67, 145, 488, 493
Onjala, Joseph 191, 199
Opinion of China 298, 337, 354, 453, 455
Opium War 30, 281, 384
Opoku, D. K. 85
Organization of African Unity (OAU) 61, 148, 160, 283
Osnos, Evan 476
Ottaway, M. 222
Ovadia, Jesse 419
Overseas 25, 32, 42, 45–6, 48–9, 56, 69, 72–3, 75, 77, 80–3, 86–7, 90–1, 150, 169, 184, 201, 203, 216, 222–3, 254, 267, 292, 378, 392, 398, 404–5, 416–17, 419–20, 422, 436–7, 439–40, 444–6, 448–51, 453–8, 475, 481, 505–6, 510–11
Owusu-Ansah, Priscilla 505
Owusu, Francis 199
Owusu, M. 140

Palmer, R. R. 25
Pan-Africanism 52, 60–2, 86, 385
Pan-African movement 36
Pan, Esther 222
Pan Guang 51
Pang Zhongying 65, 85
Pan Peiying 85
Paramount Chief 106, 118–19, 122–4, 127, 129, 136
Park, Y. Jung 403, 419, 423, 440, 459, 476
Parrinder, E. G. 51

Peh, Kelvin H. S. 199
Pei, Minxin 199, 300
Peking University 13–14, 21–2, 24–6, 32, 36–7, 41, 44, 46–7, 49–54, 56, 58–9, 61–2, 68–70, 73, 75–6, 90, 145, 168, 178, 181, 190, 193–4, 197, 202, 218, 221–4, 243–4, 275, 306, 327–8, 331, 349, 354, 360, 364–5, 368, 384, 395, 397–9, 421, 467, 470, 481, 493, 497–8, 502–3, 506
Peng Bangjiong 25
Peng Jiali 411, 413
Peng Kunyuan 39, 50, 58, 85
Penrose, B. 25
People's Daily 4, 25, 90–1, 145, 149, 167, 172, 175, 199, 202, 209, 219, 222–3, 233, 237, 244, 304, 307, 319, 330–1, 350, 354, 360, 376, 379, 399, 440
People-to-People (P2P) 356–81, 454, 483
Phillips, Lionel 420
philosophy 23, 49–50, 62, 168, 228, 236, 238–40, 242–3, 277, 293, 297, 300, 327, 374, 381, 385–9, 396, 398–9, 492, 494
Pietermaritzburg 425, 427, 439
Pilling, David 505
pingdeng (平等, equality) 230, 236–9, 256, 261, 272, 284, 285, 303, 324, 325, 341, 357, 362, 385, 387, 391, 393, 487
Pinto, Jeanette 506
PKU African Tele-Info 71
Pliez, O. 476
politics 29, 31, 37, 44, 46, 50, 56, 58–63, 69, 72, 82–3, 85–6, 112–14, 117, 123–7, 129–30, 133, 136, 138, 140, 156–8, 161–2, 164–5, 168, 171–3, 183, 186, 189, 193–4, 197, 200, 205, 210, 221–4, 234, 236–7, 253, 255, 264, 271–2, 274, 289–90, 299, 331, 353, 358, 361–2, 365, 367, 379, 387, 390, 397–8, 404, 420, 437, 448, 451, 475, 495, 504–5
porcelain 10–13, 16, 19–20, 25, 30
poverty reduction 57, 67, 82, 259, 291–2, 301, 367–70, 374, 376, 393
Power, Marcus 199
power succession 288
Prah, Kwesi Kwaa 85, 199, 300
Pretoria 82, 88–9, 353, 412, 430–1, 436, 440, 450, 475, 505
priest 93, 95–6, 99–105
prior solidarity regions 151

Public Records Office 39
Purcell, V. 420

Qiang Xiaoyun 276
Qian Mu 227–8, 244
Qian Qichen 45, 71–2, 85, 144–5, 148, 154, 176, 223, 234, 244, 362
Qi Jianhua 57, 85
qilin (kilin) 22
Qin Dashu 13, 20, 26, 56, 76, 85
Qin Dynasty 4, 6
Qing Dynasty 10, 30–1, 403, 411, 414, 417, 420, 443, 457, 478
Qin Hui 85
Qin Jie 6
Qin Xiaoying 36–7, 51
Qiu Deya 199
Qiu Yu 69, 85
Qu Xing 171, 199, 205, 223

Raftopoulos, Brian 85
Ramo, J. C. 300
Ran Jijun 358, 379
Rashidi, Runoko 26, 476
Rathbone, R. 140
Ratsifandrihama, Lila 143
Rattray, R. S. 112
Ravenstein, E. G. 26
Ray, Julie 244
Red Sea 8, 423
Redvers, Louise 420
Reid, Anthony 420
Reindorf, C. C. 140
religious leader 94
Renard, Mary-Françoise 199
Ren Baoluo 30, 51
Renjian 9
Ren Mei'e 31, 51
ren (仁, virtue, benevolence or humanity) 230, 384, 386
Ren Weidong 157
Republic of Congo, Congo (Brazzaville) 176, 188, 258, 361, 304, 307, 308, 329, 365, 495, 510, 512
Republic of South Africa 432, 440
Reuters 210, 219, 223, 331
Rey, Philipp 398
Richardson, P. 420, 440
Rocha, John 200
Rockhill, W. W. 24
Rolland, Nadège 200, 398
Ross, R. 200, 223
Rotberg, R. 200

Rothschild, R. 168
Rouzhi (月氏, Yuezhi, Yueshi) 7, 23
Rwanda 35, 63, 71, 76, 79, 150, 154, 174, 191, 305, 307, 309, 329, 384, 492, 510–11, 513

SADC 60, 151, 263, 265–6
Sakarai, Lawrence, J. 276
Sall, Alioune 244
San Lan 27
Santos, V. Silva 85
Sao Tome and Principe 258, 306
Sarbah, J. M. 140
Sarpong, P. 112
Satyagraha (non–violence) 430
Saunders, K. 420, 440
Sautman, Barry 183, 185, 186, 210, 442, 457, 470, 477, 481, 485, 491, 493, 506
Say, Joy 86
Schafer, E. 26
Scheld, Suzanne 457
School of Asian and African Studies 70
Secretary for Native Affairs 108–9, 122, 129–30, 133, 135–7
"Seeds for the Future" program 343–4, 351, 353–4
Segal, Gerald 170, 200
Segal, Ronald 465, 477
Seidelman, Raymond 506
Seligman, C. G. 51
Sellassie, Sergew Hable 26, 398
Senegal 45, 58, 68, 84, 150, 159, 174, 258, 261–3, 304, 306–8, 317, 335, 337, 381, 388, 449, 456, 459
Senghor, L. S. 36, 364, 385, 388, 399
Sengzhi (僧祇, Sengchi, Zengqi,Sengzhi) 7, 10, 461, 462
sense of community 385
sense of family 389
Seychelles 106, 305, 307, 310, 343, 451, 513
Shaloff, S. 140
Shang Dynasty 5, 27, 460, 477
Shanghai 23, 27–8, 43, 45–8, 50–3, 69–70, 74, 80, 82–3, 85, 87–9, 165, 168, 189, 200, 219–20, 223, 243, 304, 308, 310, 318, 340, 353, 356, 376, 379, 396–7, 440, 447–8, 451, 455, 458, 471–2, 477, 479, 485, 489, 491–3
Shanghai Cooperation Organization (SCO) 165
Shanghai Government Scholarship 491–2

Shanghai Institutes of International Studies 69
Shanghai Normal University 70, 168, 396
Shao Yunfei 75
Shelton, Garth 81, 88
Shen Dechang 276
Shen Fuwei 6–7, 16–17, 19, 41, 44, 205, 223, 356, 379, 457
Shengjiao Guangbei Tu 18
Shen, I-yao 420
Shen Xiaolei 66, 86, 471
Shen Zhihua 298, 301
Shepperson, George 477
Sheth, F. S. 276
Shibeika, Mekki 51
Shichor, Y. 200
Shikwati, James 65, 86, 256, 296, 335
Shi Lin 65, 328, 331
Shinn, D. H. 244, 331
Shi Yongjie 86
shu (恕, forbearance) 230, 234, 235, 385, 387
Shuyuan Zaji 17
Shu Yunguo 38, 61, 64, 86
Shu Zhan 154–5, 169
Shweder, Richard A. 244, 379, 399
Sierra Leone 34–5, 48, 58, 174, 193, 209, 304, 307–8, 312, 329, 330, 336, 340, 350, 365, 369, 511, 513
Sik, Endre 51
silk 4, 6–7, 18, 20, 25, 41, 44, 56, 85, 193, 423, 437, 440, 460, 462, 477
Simensen, J. 112, 140
Singapore 85, 241, 420
Sinn, Elizabeth 420
sin (信 trust, good faith) 33, 185, 209, 212, 215, 218, 230, 232–5, 237, 247, 255, 261, 268, 272, 312, 316, 320–3, 336, 442, 459, 463, 467, 492
Siringi, S. 244
Sirleaf, Ellen Johnson 340
Si Zhou Zhi 30
Skeldon, Ronald 420
Skinner, George William 420
slave 9, 24, 37–8, 47, 50, 52–3, 61, 115, 134, 257, 260, 275–6, 293, 373, 383, 417, 423, 425, 431, 466–7, 472–3
slave trade 37–8, 47, 50, 52–3, 61, 115, 257, 260, 275, 293, 373, 383, 417, 423, 473
Slawecki, Leon M. S. 457
Smidt, W. A. 26, 477

Smith, B. 200
Snow, Philip 4, 21, 51, 183, 200, 205, 339
social stability 161, 287, 289–90, 384, 392, 394
Somali 5, 12, 58, 174, 176, 506, 511
Song Dynasty 3, 11–16, 27, 465, 471
Songhai 293, 382–3
Song Limei 38, 48
Song Xi 404, 420, 444, 457
Sorbara, Mark 200
Soudien, Crain 301
Sourakhata, Tirera 459
South Africa 18, 23, 37–40, 42, 44–53, 58–63, 65, 67–9, 71–2, 74, 76–7, 80–3, 85–91, 145, 150–1, 160, 172, 176, 181, 196, 213–14, 246, 248, 250–1, 253–5, 257–9, 261–3, 265–7, 269, 271–2, 274–5, 286, 294, 307, 319, 337, 343, 353, 357–8, 360, 364, 367–9, 376, 379, 390, 397–9, 403–7, 409, 411, 413–40, 443–5, 447–9, 453–8, 471, 473–7, 488, 505, 511, 513
South African Chinese 416, 424, 434, 436
South America–Arab Summit 260
Southeast Asia 7, 9–10, 17, 44, 416, 420, 424, 445, 447, 460, 462, 465
Southern Africa 5, 18, 30, 37, 48, 60, 67, 74, 148, 151, 155, 191, 200, 261, 266, 386, 440, 453, 484, 501
South Korea 43, 165, 241, 250–1
South–South cooperation 143, 152, 190, 272, 275–6, 302–3
South Sudan 63, 511
Soviet Union 35, 45, 171–2, 174, 179, 200, 205, 219, 223, 233–4, 238, 264, 274, 285, 292, 299–301, 442, 489
Spring and Autumn Period 5
State Council, PRC 159, 399
State-owned enterprises (SOEs) 214, 216, 337, 346, 348, 349
Stevens, Phillips Jr. 399
Stith, C. 223
Stolte, Christina 276
Stone, R. 140
Strauss, J. C. 244
strike 98, 413, 420, 452, 485
student 14, 36, 38, 45, 67, 69, 74, 219, 224, 232, 234, 236, 271, 314, 336, 349, 356, 364–6, 368, 378, 387, 395, 451, 467, 470, 475–6, 479–82, 484, 491, 494–9, 501–5

Sudan 4, 8–9, 11, 13–14, 16, 20, 22, 34–6, 51, 58, 63, 66, 72, 148–9, 154, 162, 174, 182, 184–7, 191, 193, 195, 197–8, 201, 208, 210–11, 214–17, 219, 222–3, 232, 235–6, 241–4, 258, 262, 285–6, 300, 304, 307–8, 328–9, 335, 346–7, 354, 368–9, 371–2, 384, 423, 438, 443, 450, 453, 467, 511, 513
Suez Canal 31, 51, 512
Sule, A. 276
Sulliven, M. J. 506
Sun Hongqi 42, 62–3, 86
Sun Xiaomeng 65–6, 86
Sun Yat-sen 31, 437, 344
Sun Yutang 4, 6–7, 26, 44, 423, 440, 457
Suret-Canale, Jean 51
Su Shirong 37
Swahili (kiswahili) 40, 46, 293, 365, 382, 386
Swaine, M. D. 200
Swaziland 34, 200, 267, 307, 511
Sweden 11, 272
Symanski, L. C. P. 85

Taiwan 71, 74, 145, 159, 173, 183, 193, 211, 306, 323, 405, 442, 444–9, 454, 467, 471
Tan, Ee Lyn 331
Tanganyika 24, 36, 304, 307–8, 358, 443
Tang Dadun 36–7, 52
Tang Dynasty 3, 7, 9–11, 13, 22–4, 27, 29–31, 46, 438, 460–2, 465–6, 471–2, 474, 476, 478
Tang Jiaxuan 71, 143, 154–5, 169, 366
Tang Lixia 263, 276
Tang Tongming 36, 52
Tang Xiao 65
Tang Xiaoyang 57, 69, 86–7, 205, 216–17, 223, 301, 348, 498
Tan Shizhong 39–41, 51, 53
Tanzania 9, 13, 20, 34–5, 49, 58–9, 61–2, 69, 71–2, 86, 146, 169, 174, 176, 198, 201, 231, 233, 243, 245, 258, 261, 263, 284, 295, 300, 302, 307–8, 314, 319–20, 325, 328–9, 331–2, 337–9, 342–3, 347–50, 352, 354–5, 360–1, 364, 369–71, 379, 386, 449, 451, 456, 470, 479, 481, 484–5, 492, 501, 505–6, 511, 513
Tanzania–Zambia Railway (TAZARA) 58, 71, 72, 146, 233, 284, 285, 337–9, 348, 364, 479, 481, 483, 484, 485
Tarabrin, E. A. 276

Taylor, Ian 200, 221, 244
TAZARA training course 348
technology 4, 6, 40–1, 57, 67–8, 75, 80, 82, 86, 90, 146, 163, 166–7, 175, 177–8, 182, 184, 189, 191, 201, 207, 211, 213, 227, 236, 238–9, 261, 263, 268, 272, 277, 281, 286, 291, 297, 305, 312, 315–16, 319, 330, 333–5, 337–43, 345–9, 351–5, 365, 367, 423, 444, 449, 452, 454, 470, 481, 484, 493, 495, 505–7, 513
technology transfer (TT) 67, 184, 263, 297, 333–55, 481
Temu, A. J. 49
Tendulkar, D. G. 440
Terreblanche, S. J. S. 87
Tevoedjre, Albert 143
Third World 196, 205, 274, 299, 307, 319, 330, 450
Thoburn, John 201
Thompson, D. 301, 332
Thompson, L. 440
Thurow, L. C. 276
Tianjin 177, 201, 241–2, 304–5, 309, 321, 325, 330, 347, 361, 417, 479, 485, 498, 506–7
Tian Shumao 13, 26
Tinker, Hugh 440
Togo 34–5, 47, 154, 174, 176, 180, 209, 219, 304, 307–8, 319, 329, 377, 446, 511, 513
Tokyo International Conference on African Development (TICAD) 152–5, 296
Tong Dian 8, 47
Tordoff, W. 140
Toynbee, Arnold 244
trade 4, 6, 9, 12, 14, 19–20, 23, 27, 37–8, 47, 49–50, 52–5, 57, 61, 76–7, 81, 83, 85–7, 89–91, 98, 115, 118, 147–9, 151–3, 155, 159–60, 163, 166–7, 173–4, 178–85, 187–90, 192–6, 198–204, 206–8, 211–12, 214, 217, 219–21, 239, 243, 245, 247–8, 254–71, 273–7, 281–2, 293–6, 298, 304–5, 324, 331, 333, 342, 348, 359, 369, 373, 382–3, 417, 423, 426–30, 434, 437, 443–4, 448, 450–2, 454, 459, 465–6, 470, 473–4, 476, 480, 494, 498–500, 503, 506, 508–9
traditional medicine 311, 326–7, 332
transparency 195–6, 238
Trevor-Roper, Hugh 399

tribe/tribalism 39
Troyjo, Marcos 276
Tsikata, Dela 201
Tsinghua University 69, 353, 449, 498
Tufuhene 114–15, 117
Tull, Denis, M. 201
Tunisia 9, 34, 45, 47, 72, 89, 174–6, 231, 258, 304, 307–8, 313, 322, 326–7, 332, 342, 360, 483, 493, 496, 513

Uganda 34, 45, 58, 63, 67, 85, 87, 150, 173–4, 181, 199, 219, 261, 263, 305, 307, 309, 317, 329, 344, 347, 351, 354, 369, 390, 423, 446, 484, 498, 511, 513
UNESCO 23, 38, 52, 67–8, 72–4, 84–5, 273, 398, 468, 480
UNESCO General History of Africa 72, 74, 273
United States 43, 45, 50, 63, 145, 147, 149–51, 154–5, 158–9, 165, 168, 171, 183, 185–6, 190–1, 200, 204, 209, 218–21, 223, 225, 230, 235–6, 241, 243, 246, 248–9, 254, 263–4, 267, 273, 282–3, 285, 295–7, 299, 326, 335, 349, 361, 374, 378, 392–5, 417, 444, 485, 489, 508
UN Millennium Development Goals 268
UN's Economic Commission of Africa 151
UN Secretary-General 211
UN Security Council (UNSC) 146

Vahed, G. H. 277, 440
Van Agtmael, A. 277
Van Onselen, Charles 420
Van Sertima, I. 26
Vicente, Ruben Gonzalez 201
Vidyarthee, Kaushal K. 277
Villoria, Nelson 201
Vines, A. 201
Vliet, Geert van 201

Wade, Abdoulaye 225, 244, 335, 450, 457
Walker, E. A. 440
Wang, Jian-Ye 201
Wang Cunliang 52
Wang Dayuan 3, 14, 26, 460
Wang Dongmei 87
Wang Feng 154–5
Wang Gungwu 420
Wang Haili 69
Wang Hanjie 364, 497
Wang Junyi 52

Wang Ling-chi 420
Wang Luxin 506
Wang Qinmei 169, 239, 244
Wang Shaokui 52
Wang Shengwan 444, 454, 458
Wang Shu 71, 87
Wang Suolao 52
Wang Tai 59
Wang Taiping 175
Wang Tao 67, 87, 90
Wang Tieya 357
Wang Ting 8, 26
Wang Xuejun 65, 87, 357
Wang Yuhua 177, 201
Wang Zhen 52
Wan Siulan 59
Ward, B. 112
Ward, W. E. 140
Wartemberg, J. S. 140
Weber, M. 244, 301
Weeks, J. A. 420
Weidenreich, F. 26
Wei Hong 357
Wei Jianguo 71, 87, 181, 319
Weinstein, W. 201
Wei Xiaohui 67, 87
Wei Yuan 7, 30
Wenchi 107
Weng Ming 169
Wen Jiabao 162, 190, 331, 350, 384, 392, 396
Wen Shuang 69, 88
Wen Xian 40
Wen Yunchao 52, 56
West Africa 8, 26, 34–5, 37, 40, 47–8, 60, 66, 88, 90, 99, 111, 138–9, 158, 273, 282, 294, 299, 343, 360, 397, 443, 483
westernization 61, 228
West Sahara 58
West Zhou Dynasty 5
Wight, M. 140
Wilensky, Julie 477
Wilks, I. 140
Williams, Eric 383, 399
Williamson, S. G. 112
Willmot, Donald Earl 420
Wilson, Andrew R. 440
Winneba 68, 97, 116, 133
Wiredu, Kwasi 228, 244, 290
witchcraft, anti-witchcraft 90–112
Woddis, Jack 52
women's right 390
Wong-Hee-Kan, Edith 444, 458, 459

World Bank 61, 147, 151, 153, 180, 193, 195, 202, 240, 286, 292, 295, 336–7, 350
World History Studies 51, 77, 82, 87, 439
world order 143, 242, 253, 268, 340, 397
World War I 36, 241, 404
World War II 32–3, 40, 49, 124, 230, 241, 246–7, 249, 283, 404
Wu Bin 501, 506
Wu Bingzhen 37, 52
Wu Changchun 4, 26
Wuchisan 6–7
Wu Fengbin 399
Wu Jing 257
Wu Jun 71
Wu Qingzhou 26
Wusili 11
Wu Yuenong 292, 301
Wu Zengtian 39, 52
Wu Zhaoji 37, 47
Wu Zuncun 52
Wyatt, Don J. 4, 26, 462, 463, 464, 466, 477
Wyllie, R. W. 140

Xia Jisheng 38, 52–3, 62, 88, 150–1, 169, 458
Xiamen University 68
Xia Nai 4, 11, 13
Xiang Da 18, 22, 27
Xiangtan University 36, 74, 84, 91
Xiao Hongyu 88
Xiaoyi 9
Xiao Yuhua 63, 88
Xia Xinhua 64, 79, 88
Xida 9
Xie Zixiu 406, 410–11, 417, 437
Xi Jinping 73, 393, 399
Xingcha Shenglan 17, 20
Xinhua News Agency 46, 72, 185, 190, 201, 210–11, 219, 223, 235, 241, 301, 329
Xinhua Newsnet 201
Xin Tang Shu 9, 462
Xiya Feizhou 46
Xu Chunfu 179
Xue Rongjiu 277
Xu Guoqing 258, 265, 277
Xu Hui 482, 506
Xu Jiming 37, 39–40, 52–3, 65
Xu Liang 56, 65, 69, 88, 327, 471, 501
Xun Xingqiang 37, 53

Xu Tao 56, 88, 468–9, 477
Xu Wei 66, 88
Xu Yongzhang 7, 12, 14, 27, 61, 88, 423, 440, 458, 461, 477
Xuzhou 5, 460, 477
Xuzhou Museum 460

Yafei Yicong 33
Yafei Ziliao 33
Yamauchi, Edwin M. 399
Yang, Y. 476
Yang Bojun 232, 236, 245, 396, 398
Yang Dezhen 41, 53
Yang Guang 70, 75, 88, 240
Yang Guangsheng 63, 90
Yang Haocheng 37, 53
Yang Lihua 40, 57, 58, 65, 67, 89, 183, 201
Yang Mengjie 496, 506
Yang Renpian 7, 27, 37, 53
Yang Tingzhi 66, 89, 327
Yang Ximei 5, 27, 460–1, 471, 477
Yang Xuelun 64, 89
Yan Hairong 186, 190–1, 200–1, 210, 223, 454, 506
Yan Jin 53
Yan Qinshang 31, 51
Yan Wenru 27
Yan Yiwu 180, 189
Yao Guimei 41, 47, 56, 70, 89, 151, 153, 169
Yap, Melanie 420, 440, 458, 477
Yeboah, Nyamah Edmond 89
Yellow book of Africa 89
Yen Ching-Hwang 404
Ye Shuai 482
Yichengbu State 6, 23
Ying Mingqin 312–13, 332
Yingya Shenglan 17
Yi Pei 506
Young men (youngmen) 113–40
Youyang Zazu 7, 462
Yuan Dynasty 3, 14, 16, 22, 30, 44, 438, 472
Yuan Nansheng 71
Yuan Xihu 53
Yuan Ye 202
Yu, George T. 29, 169, 201
Yu Jing 214, 216, 221
Yuluhedi State 16
Yunnan University 36, 84, 178, 202
Yu Zhongjian 263, 277

Zafar, Ali 202
Zambia 34, 58, 61, 71, 86, 146, 165, 169, 174, 176, 181, 184–5, 191, 196–7, 199, 201, 216, 222, 233, 258, 261–3, 284, 300, 305, 307, 319, 329, 337–9, 348, 355, 361–2, 369, 379, 447, 449, 451, 470, 479, 481, 484–5, 501, 506, 511, 513
Zanj (Zinj, Zenj, Zandj, Zanghi, Sengzhi) 10, 11, 461, 462, 471
Zanzibar 9–14, 16, 56, 304, 307, 314–15, 320, 322
Zebra 17, 20, 30
Zeleza, Paul Tiyambe 43, 202, 460, 477
Zeng Jianhui 202
Zeng Qiang 65, 89
Zeng Zungu 37, 53
Zha Daojiong 214, 223
Zhai Fengjie 89
Zhang Chun 63, 65, 89
Zhang Chunshu 7, 27, 461, 467, 471, 478
Zhang Haibing 89
Zhang Hongming 44, 53, 57, 61–2, 65, 70, 89, 192, 202
Zhang Jin 60, 89
Zhang Junyan 6, 11–12, 18, 27, 44, 53, 443, 458
Zhang Laiyi 277
Zhang Lei 291, 301
Zhang Mulan 380
Zhang Qian 6, 22
Zhang Qiaowen 69, 89
Zhang Qiwei 30
Zhang Rongsheng 53
Zhang Tieshan 233, 245, 338, 355, 481
Zhang Tiesheng 12–13, 19, 27, 32–3, 53
Zhang Weichi 10, 24
Zhang Weijie 63, 89, 390, 399
Zhang Xiang 4, 7, 27, 43, 53, 58, 364–5, 380
Zhang Xiangdong 63, 90
Zhang Xinghui 65
Zhang Xinglang 4, 6–12, 44, 53, 461, 463, 465, 478
Zhang Xiping 383, 399
Zhang Xiuming 446, 458
Zhang Xiuqin 177, 202
Zhang Yichun 8
Zhang Yong 57, 90
Zhang Yonghong 57, 66, 90
Zhang Yongpeng 58, 90, 360, 378
Zhang Yun 72, 90
Zhang Yuxi 35, 38, 45, 53

Zhang Zhe 57, 90
Zhang Zhenke 64, 90
Zhang Zhilian 407, 412–13, 421
Zhang Zhongxiang 90, 180, 202, 359, 380
Zhan Shiming 179, 202
Zhao Changhui 158, 189
Zhao Guozhong 54
Zhao Huijie 155
Zhao Jianping 54
Zhao Jun 56, 72, 90, 511
Zhao Minghao 357, 380
Zhao Ping 56, 58–9, 75
Zhao Rukuo 3, 12, 14, 27, 460, 462
Zhao Shuhui 37, 54
Zhao Shurong 68, 90
Zhao Yanrong 277
Zhao Ziyang 147, 175, 341, 362
Zhao Zuojun 202
Zhejiang Normal University 36, 65, 70, 75, 85, 87, 177, 197, 364, 477
Zhen Feng 90
Zheng Bijian 170, 202
Zheng Daochuan 54
Zheng He 16–20, 22, 25–8, 30, 44, 56, 83, 462
Zheng He Hang Hai Tu 18
Zheng Jianghua 482, 507
Zheng Jiaxing 37–9, 46, 61, 64, 90
Zheng Xiangheng 445
Zheng Xizhen 64, 89
Zheng Yijun 20
Zhenla 10
Zhi Yingbiao 65, 90
Zhongli State 12
Zhong Weiyun 172, 202, 207
Zhong Zhicheng 90
Zhou Boping 71, 91, 340, 355
Zhou Enlai 33, 146, 172, 175, 206, 219, 222, 232, 237–8, 284, 304, 314, 325, 339, 362
Zhou Hong 58, 91, 169, 341–2
Zhou Jianqing 178–9
Zhou Nanjing 91
Zhou Zhiwei 277
Zhuang Guotu 419, 421
Zhubu 17–18
Zhu Chonggui 40, 54, 150
Zhu Chunting 472
Zhu Fan Zhi 462
Zhu Fenglan 292
Zhu Gang 54
Zhu Huayou 59

Zhu Mingzhong 261
Zhu Rongji 148, 152–3, 155, 173
Zhu Siben 18, 44
Zhu Weidong 64, 66–7, 74, 91
Zhu Weilie 38, 51
Zhu Yunming 18, 28
Zhu Zudi 245
Zimbabwe 13, 25, 35, 41, 48, 58, 72, 85–6, 154, 159, 176, 185, 195, 199, 221, 267, 293, 295, 305, 307, 310, 316, 334–5, 352–3, 360–1, 366, 369, 379, 382, 450, 486–7, 494, 511, 513
Zong He 179, 202
Zou Daijun 12, 28
Zou Hengfu 67, 91
Zweig, David 189, 190, 202

А б рамова, С. Ю. 46
Ольдерогге, Д. А. 51
Потехин, И. И. 51